Lecture Notes of the Institute for Computer Sciences, Social Informatics and Telecommunications Engineering 335

More information about this series at http://www.springer.com/series/8197

Noseong Park · Kun Sun ·
Sara Foresti · Kevin Butler ·
Nitesh Saxena (Eds.)

Security and Privacy in Communication Networks

16th EAI International Conference, SecureComm 2020
Washington, DC, USA, October 21–23, 2020
Proceedings, Part I

 Springer

Editors
Noseong Park
Yonsei University
Seoul, Korea (Republic of)

Kun Sun
George Mason University
Fairfax, VA, USA

Sara Foresti
Dipartimento di Informatica
Universita degli Studi
Milan, Milano, Italy

Kevin Butler
University of Florida
Gainesville, FL, USA

Nitesh Saxena
Division of Nephrology
University of Alabama
Birmingham, AL, USA

ISSN 1867-8211   ISSN 1867-822X (electronic)
Lecture Notes of the Institute for Computer Sciences, Social Informatics
and Telecommunications Engineering
ISBN 978-3-030-63085-0   ISBN 978-3-030-63086-7 (eBook)
https://doi.org/10.1007/978-3-030-63086-7

This Springer imprint is published by the registered company Springer Nature Switzerland AG
The registered company address is: Gewerbestrasse 11, 6330 Cham, Switzerland

Preface

We are delighted to introduce the proceedings of the 16th EAI International Conference on Security and Privacy in Communication Networks (SecureComm 2020). This conference has brought together researchers, developers, and practitioners from around the world who are leveraging and developing security and privacy technology for a safe and robust system or network.

These proceedings contain 60 papers, which were selected from 120 submissions (an acceptance rate of 50%) from universities, national laboratories, and the private sector from across the USA as well as other countries in Europe and Asia. All the submissions went through an extensive review process by internationally-recognized experts in cybersecurity.

Any successful conference requires the contributions of different stakeholder groups and individuals, who have selflessly volunteered their time and energy in disseminating the call for papers, submitting their research findings, participating in the peer reviews and discussions, etc. First and foremost, we would like to offer our gratitude to the entire Organizing Committee for guiding the entire process of the conference. We are also deeply grateful to all the Technical Program Committee members for their time and effort in reading, commenting, debating, and finally selecting the papers. We also thank all the external reviewers for assisting the Technical Program Committee in their particular areas of expertise as well as all the authors, participants, and session chairs for their valuable contributions. Support from the Steering Committee and EAI staff members was also crucial in ensuring the success of the conference. It was a great privilege to work with such a large group of dedicated and talented individuals.

We hope that you found the discussions and interactions at SecureComm 2020, which was held online, enjoyable and that the proceedings will simulate further research.

October 2020

Kun Sun
Sara Foresti
Kevin Butler
Nitesh Saxena

Organization

Steering Committee

Imrich Chlamtac	University of Trento, Italy
Guofei Gu	Texas A&M University, USA
Peng Liu	Penn State University, USA
Sencun Zhu	Penn State University, USA

Organizing Committee

General Co-chairs

Kun Sun	George Mason University, USA
Sara Foresti	Università degli Studi di Milano, Italy

TPC Chair and Co-chair

Kevin Butler	University of Florida, USA
Nitesh Saxena	University of Alabama at Birmingham, USA

Sponsorship and Exhibit Chair

Liang Zhao	George Mason University, USA

Local Chair

Hemant Purohit	George Mason University, USA

Workshops Chair

Qi Li	Tsinghua University, China

Publicity and Social Media Chairs

Emanuela Marasco	George Mason University, USA
Carol Fung	Virginia Commonwealth University, USA

Publications Chair

Noseong Park	Yonsei University, South Korea

Web Chair

Pengbin Feng	George Mason University, USA

Panels Chair

Massimiliano Albanese	George Mason University, USA

Tutorials Chair

Fabio Scotti   Università degli Studi di Milano, Italy

Technical Program Committee

Adwait Nadkarni	William & Mary, USA
Amro Awad	Sandia National Laboratories, USA
An Wang	Case Western Reserve University, USA
Aziz Mohaisen	University of Central Florida, USA
Birhanu Eshete	University of Michigan - Dearborn, USA
Byron Williams	University of Florida, USA
Cliff Zou	University of Central Florida, USA
Cong Wang	City University of Hong Kong, Hong Kong
Daniel Takabi	Georgia State University, USA
Dave (Jing) Tian	Purdue University, USA
David Barrera	Carleton University, Canada
Debin Gao	Singapore Management University, Singapore
Dinghao Wu	Penn State University, USA
Eric Chan-Tin	Loyola University Chicago, USA
Eugene Vasserman	Kansas State University, USA
Fatima M. Anwar	University of Massachusetts Amherst, USA
Fengyuan Xu	Nanjing University, China
Girish Revadigar	University of New South Wales, Australia
Gokhan Kul	University of Massachusetts Dartmouth, USA
Huacheng Zeng	University of Louisville, USA
Hyoungshick Kim	Sungkyunkwan University, South Korea
Jeffrey Spaulding	Canisius College, USA
Jian Liu	The University of Tennessee at Knoxville, USA
Jiawei Yuan	University of Massachusetts Dartmouth, USA
Jun Dai	California State University, Sacramento, USA
Kai Bu	Zhejiang University, China
Kai Chen	Institute of Information Engineering, Chinese Academy of Sciences, China
Karim Elish	Florida Polytechnic University, USA
Kuan Zhang	University of Nebraska-Lincoln, USA
Le Guan	University of Georgia, USA
Maliheh Shirvanian	Visa Research, USA
Martin Strohmeier	University of Oxford, UK
Mengjun Xie	The University of Tennessee at Chattanooga, USA
Mohamed Shehab	University of North Carolina at Charlotte, USA
Mohammad Mannan	Concordia University, Canada
Murtuza Jadliwala	The University of Texas at San Antonio, USA
Neil Gong	Duke University, USA
Patrick McDaniel	Penn State University, USA
Pierangela Samarati	Università degli Studi di Milano, Italy

Qiang Tang   New Jersey Institute of Technology, USA
Rongxing Lu   University of New Brunswick, Canada
Sankardas Roy   Bowling Green State University, USA
Selcuk Uluagac   Florida International University, USA
Seungwon Shin   KAIST, South Korea
Shouhuai Xu   The University of Texas at San Antonio, USA
Simon Woo   SUNY Korea, South Korea
Suzanne Wetzel   Stevens Institute of Technology, USA
Taegyu Kim   Purdue University, USA
Thomas Moyer   University of North Carolina at Charlotte, USA
Tzipora Halevi   Brooklyn College, USA
Vinnie Monaco   Naval Postgraduate School, USA
Wenhai Sun   Purdue University, USA
Wenjing Lou   Virginia Polytechnic Institute and State University,
                         USA
Wensheng Zhang   Iowa State University, USA
Xiao Zhang   Palo Alto Networks, USA
Xingliang Yuan   Monash University, Australia
Yanchao Zhang   Arizona State University, USA
Yingying Chen   Rutgers University, USA
Yinzhi Cao   Johns Hopkins University, USA
Yong Guan   Iowa State University, USA
Yuan (Alex) Zhang   Nanjing University, China
Yuan Zhang   Fudan University, China
Z. Berkay Celik   Purdue University, USA
Zhiqiang Lin   Ohio State University, USA

Contents – Part I

Contents – Part II

Email Address Mutation for Proactive Deterrence Against Lateral Spear-Phishing Attacks

Md Mazharul Islam[1]([📧]), Ehab Al-Shaer[2],
and Muhammad Abdul Basit Ur Rahim[1]

[1] University of North Carolina at Charlotte, Charlotte, NC 28223, USA
{mislam7,mabdulb1}@uncc.edu
[2] INI/CyLab, Carnegie Mellon University, Pittsburgh, PA 15213, USA
ehab@cmu.edu

Abstract. Email spear-phishing attack is one of the most devastating cyber threat against individual and business victims. Using spear-phishing emails, adversaries can manage to impersonate authoritative identities in order to incite victims to perform actions that help adversaries to gain financial and/hacking goals. Many of these targeted spear-phishing can be undetectable based on analyzing emails because, for example, they can be sent from compromised benign accounts (called lateral spear-phishing attack).

In this paper, we developed a novel proactive defense technique using sender email address mutation to protect a group of related users against lateral spear-phishing. In our approach, we frequently change the sender email address randomly that can only be verified by trusted peers, without imposing any overhead or restriction on email communication with external users. Our Email mutation technique is transparent, secure, and effective because it allows users to use their email as usual, while they are fully protected from such stealthy spear-phishing.

We present the Email mutation technique (algorithm and protocol) and develop a formal model to verify its correctness. The processing overhead due to mutation is a few milliseconds, which is negligible with the prospective of end-to-end email transmission delay. We also describe a real-world implementation of the Email mutation technique that works with any email service providers such as Gmail, Apple iCloud, Yahoo Mail, and seamlessly integrates with standard email clients such as Gmail web clients (mail.google.com), Microsoft Outlook, and Thunderbird.

Keywords: Lateral spear-phishing attack · Spoofing attack · Email phishing · Targeted attack · Moving target defense

1 Introduction

In recent years, email spear-phishing becomes the most effective cyber threat against individual and business victims. It has been reported that 90% of data

N. Park et al. (Eds.): SecureComm 2020, LNICST 335, pp. 1–22, 2020.
https://doi.org/10.1007/978-3-030-63086-7_1

breaches in 2017–2018 included a phishing element, 74% of public sector cyber-espionage, and 64% of organizations' attacks involve spear-phishing attacks, where 30% of these attacks are targeted [4]. Over \$26B has been lost to spear-phishing and account takeover in 2019 [1]. Only in the US, 71.4% of phishing attacks and data breaches associated with nation-state or state-affiliated actors used spear-phishing [29].

Unlike phishing, where adversaries send generic emails with malicious attachments or links to a massive number of users indiscriminately hoping that someone will take the bait, spear-phishing is more targeted. In spear-phishing attacks, adversaries impersonate key personnel or authoritative identities in order to incite victims to perform such actions that help them to gain certain goals. Adversaries carefully select their targets and send them well-crafted phishing emails that closely resemble what they usually receive. Mostly, these attack emails mimic a familiar style and signature of a known person to the victims, where both the email headers and body merely deviate from benign emails. Yet, the email contains a 'lure' that is convincing enough to engage the victim into an 'exploit' [13].

A common technique for spear-phishing attack is to spoof the name or email address of the sender, known as *source spoofing*, to convince the victim that the email is sent from a trusted source [13]. Solutions like SPF [19], DKIM [8], and DMARC [21] that verifies the sender authenticity may prevent email source spoofing [14]. However, adversaries are continuously evolving and adapting their attack strategies. As a result, a more stealthy variation of spear-phishing attack has been encountered recently, known as *lateral spear-phishing* attack, where adversary uses compromised email accounts of someone either socially or professionally connected with the victim to initiate the phishing email [12]. These phishing emails are very hard to detect because of the cleverly crafted content created by deep analyzing the prior conversation with the victim from that compromised account. Therefore, adversaries inherently win the cyber game against defenders in the lateral spear-phishing attack by evading any existing security regarding sender email authentication as the phishing email coming directly from a legitimate account and defeating behavioral anomaly detectors by accessing human anchoring as the email seemingly composed by a trusted entity [12]. These facts motivate our research to develop a proactive mechanism for protecting the number one targeted attack vector, email.

The current state of the art for detecting lateral spear-phishing emails mainly depends on email headers and body [5, 10–13, 15, 18, 27]. These defense techniques require users' historical data to model a behavioral profile for the sender or receiver in order to detect the anomalous behavior of the phishing email. They also depend on analyzing the content of phishing emails searching for malicious URLs or attachments, domains with low reputation, etc. However, spear-phishers can easily evade detection by mimicking users' behavior (from previous emails) and avoiding the use of bad features [12].

To address these limitations, we developed a novel moving target defense technique called sender Email address Mutation (EM) to proactively protect a group of users against lateral spear-phishing and spoofing attacks. EM is developed as a cloud-based service that can be easily integrated with existing email infrastructure for any organization to offer scalable email protection against spear-phishing with minimal management overhead. It deploys a secure gateway in the cloud that works transparently between end-users and email service providers. EM defends a group of socially or professionally connected members, called the VIP users. It creates a number of random *shadow* email addresses (accounts) associated with each VIP user besides their actual email address. These shadow email addresses are used as the sender for email delivery but are hidden to both end-users.

While two VIP members communicate with each other through EM, the email first goes to the secure email mutation gateway (EMG) in the cloud, where EMG translates the sender email address to a shadow email address corresponding to the sender before forwarding it. Similarly, when the receiver VIP user fetches that email, the EMG verifies the shadow email address and delivers the email to the recipient, if the verification is successful. Therefore, knowing the public email address will not be sufficient to attack the VIP users. Spear-phisher adversaries must correctly guess the current shadow email being used by each individual user in order to successfully impersonate a VIP user in an email sent to another VIP user. While EM achieves this protection between VIP users, it also maintains the email open communication model by allowing VIP users to receive and send emails to any external users without any restriction. Thus, EM can protect a group of socially or organizationally connected (VIP) users from any phishing emails that impersonate a VIP user even if the email is coming from a compromised VIP email account, without impacting users' usability or interaction with external users.

PGP[6], S/MIME [24], Two-factor authentication (2FA)[3] can be used to authenticate email senders and prevent email account hijacking. However, these techniques are not widely used in practice due to many users' transparency, usability, and management challenges [25, 26, 28]. For instance, PGP signature and encryption obfuscate the plaintext emails into cyphertext, immediately losing the content's visibility. Therefore, existing IDS and content-based behavioral analysis tools can not work with PGP encryption. Furthermore, PGP requires user training on Public key infrastructure (PKI) and maintains complex key management systems. Moreover, PGP signatures in email can be spoofed [23]. EM provides an alternative proactive mechanism for the majority of email users who are not using PGP and/or 2FA to protect against spear-phishing without compromising transparency, usability, or manageability. Therefore, although EM does not use a cryptographic approach like PGP or 2FA, it can provide comparable protection while maintaining high usability and deployability.

Our key contribution is three-fold:

- First, we introduced a novel protocol called EM, as a proactive defense against highly stealthy lateral spear-phishing attacks.
- Second, we verified that the EM protocol is valid and can be integrated with any existing email service provider.

– Third, we implemented the EM system (code available on GitHub) and
  deployed it in a real-world environment without imposing any usability or
  performance overhead on users or service providers.

2 Related Work

A vast amount of research has been done to detect phishing and spear-
phishing attacks [9–15,18,27]. The majority of these works depend on email
content or headers. For instance, Ho et al. presented a learning-based classifier
to detect lateral spear-phishing by seeking malicious URLs embedded in the
phishing email [12,13]. However, these solutions will not work against motivated
adversaries trying to evade detection simply just by not adding any malicious
ULR or no URL at all in the phishing email.

Spear-phishing detectors like EmailProfiler [10] and IdentityMailer [27] also
depend on email headers and body to build behavioral profiles for each sender
based on stylometric features in the content, senders writing habits, common
recipients, usual email forwarding time, etc. New emails get compared with the
profile to measure the deviation determining whether they are spear-phishing
email or not. These solutions can not detect lateral spear-phishing emails when
the contents are carefully crafted to avoid deviation from the norm. Moreover,
they show a high false-positive rate (10%), which becomes unacceptable when it
comes to the large volume of emails in a real-world enterprise network.

Gascon et al. [11] proposed a context agnostic spear-phishing email detector
by building behavioral profiles for all senders in a given user mailbox. They
create such profiles from the common traits a sender follows while composing an
email, like attachments types, different header fields, etc. However, in the lateral
spear-phishing attack, email headers do not deviate from the usual structure as
it is coming from a legitimate account. In addition, building profiles for each
sender can induce massive overhead in large scale deployment.

Existing sender authentication protocols such as SPF [19], DKIM [8], and
DMARC [21] can not detect lateral spear-phishing emails because they are not
spoofed and composed from valid email accounts. Other solutions, such as signing
emails with PGP [6], S/MIME [24], or 2FA [3] can prevent the lateral spear-
phishing attack. Unfortunately, these techniques are not widely used because of
usability, manageability, and transparency issues [25,26,28]. Moreover, a recent
study showed that PGP signatures in the email could be spoofed as well [23].

3   Threat Model

3.1   Attack Taxonomy

```
From: Alice <alice@org.com>
To: Bob <bob@org.com>
Subject: February, 2020 Meeting Budget (Event venue booking)
Hi Bob,
Process wire transfer of $100,543 to Trudy (account no. 5648132796, routing no. 026001234) to
finalize upcoming  event venue bookings. Send me an invoice of that transaction ASAP, thanks.
Alice
CEO, org.com
```

Listing 1: A carefully crafted lateral spear-phishing email sends to Bob from a compromised account Alice, without any malicious attachments or URLs.

In the lateral spear-phishing attack, adversaries send phishing emails to victims from a compromised account. To make such attacks trustworthy and effective, adversaries carefully choose those compromised accounts that are closely related to the victims, such as employees from the same organization [12]. Therefore, the attacker easily bypasses traditional email security systems like sender authentication, as the email is come from a legitimate account and make the victim fall for the attack, as it is seemingly composed by a person they already trust.

Listing 1 depicts an example of lateral spear-phishing email. Adversary Trudy compromises the email account of Alice, CEO of an organization (`org.com`). By examining her inbox, Trudy obtains that Alice directed Bob, finance department head of `org.com`, to make some wire transactions for arranging an upcoming business meeting. Exploiting this analysis, Trudy composes a phishing email from Alice's email account to Bob, directing him to make a wire transaction in Trudy's bank account. These types of lateral phishing are crafted carefully by observing previous emails and may not contain any malicious attachments or URLs that make it very hard to detect.

3.2   Attack Model

The EM protocol detects lateral spear-phishing and spoofing attacks where adversaries send phishing emails to the victim from a compromised benign email account or impersonate a benign person that the victim already trusts. Compromising an email account means adversary gain access only to that email account, not the physical machine such as laptop, desktop, or cell phone itself of the user. Moreover, any compromised account who never communicated with the victim before can hardly be successful in exploiting the victim. Therefore, EM solely focuses on compromised accounts and impersonated entities that are connected with the victim, e.g., employees from the same organization or different organization, but communicates frequently. The people who use EM to protect themselves against spear-phishing attacks are denoted as VIP users. To launch a lateral spear-phishing attack, an adversary needs to send the phishing email from a compromised account, Alice, for instance, whom Bob already connected with. EM can protect Bob against such an attack if both Bob and Alice are agreed prior to use EM; therefore, they are in the VIP user list. EM also protects VIP users from spoofing if the adversary impersonates any of the VIP users in the phishing email.

4   Email Mutation System

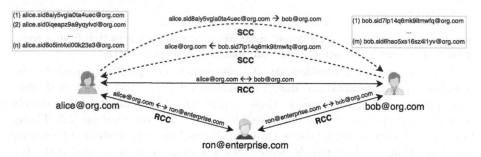

Fig. 1. Email Mutation overview. Alice and Bob send emails using their shadow email addresses (dashed line, single arrow).

4.1   Overview

Figure 1 depicts an overview of sender email address mutation, where two VIP users Alice and Bob from an organization (`org.com`), agreed to use EM to protect themselves against lateral spear-phishing attacks. Previously, they communicate with each other using their real email address (double arrow solid line), called Real channel communication (RCC). However, after EM starts, each VIP user gets a list of shadow email accounts. For instance, Alice and Bob get n and m number of shadow email accounts (addresses), respectively. Thus, each new email Alice composes for Bob now uses a different shadow email address as a sender instead of her real email address, and the modified (mutated) email is forwarded to Bob (dashed line single arrow). This is called Shadow channel communication (SCC). Sending an email in SCC by mutating the sender email address is known as *mutation*. When Bob receives such an email, the shadow email address gets verified for lateral spear-phishing detection. This is called *verification*. Similarly, when Bob composes a new email for Alice, the email is forwarded through SCC by mutating Bob's real email address to one of his shadow email addresses. Although Alice and Bob use shadow email addresses as the sender to communicate with each other through SCC, they use their real email address to communicate with external users (non-VIP), e.g., Ron from `enterprise.com`. VIP users group can comprise people from different organizations having different domains. For instance, John (not shown in the figure) from `gov.com` can be a VIP member with Alice and Bob from `org.com`.

Shadow Email Accounts. The shadow emails are a list of pre-created email accounts assigned to all VIP users but being kept hidden from them. These accounts are only used in email transmission as a sender address. Only EMG conducts with these email accounts. Depending on the impacts, the number of shadow email addresses assigned to a VIP user varies. EM is flexible to the creation of shadow email accounts as long as the shadow email domain is the same as the real email domain. However, in our experiment, we used a prefix "sid" (shadow ID) in the shadow email address to make a clear difference with the real email address. A possible shadow email address may look like: *real.email.address.x@domain*, where x is at least 16 byte long random alphanumeric sequence. For instance, *alice.sid8aiy5vgia0ta4uec@org.com* can be one of the shadow email addresses for Alice's real email address *alice@org.com*, where $x = sid8aiy5vgia0ta4uec$.

4.2 Architecture

The *mutation* and *verification* happens in the cloud by mutation gateways (EMG). Figure 2 illustrates the architecture of EM. Clients can use multiple devices such as laptops, desktop, or cell phones for accessing emails; therefore, EM provides an EM agent (EMA) for each of the devices. While sending an email, the

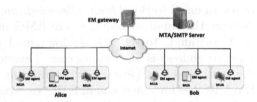

Fig. 2. Email mutation architecture.

agent delivers the email to the EMG for mutation. After mutation, the EMG forwards the mutated email to corresponding mail servers (SMTP/MTA). Similarly, while fetching a new email, the agent receives it from the EMG. The EMG first gets the email from the mail server and then verifies it to detect a lateral spear-phishing attack before responding to the agent. In large enterprise networks, multiple EMGs can be used for load balancing.

4.3 Algorithm

The VIP users supposedly send emails to each other, which use as ground truth G next time they send any new emails. For instance, when a VIP user i sends an email to another VIP user j, the last l emails between them will be used as ground truth $G_{i,j}$ to generate a mutation ID, *mID*. By indexing the *mID*, a shadow email address gets selected from a secret arrangement of shadow email addresses S_i assigned for the sender i. The shadow email address then used to forward the email. Similarly, as the receiver j has the identical ground truth, j can generate the exact *mID* to find the same shadow email address from S_i for verification.

Algorithm 1 shows the pseudocode of shadow email address selection. A hash function SHA-512 is used to get the digest of $G_{i,j}$, which then modulo with the size of S_i to select the current shadow email index, mID. Although from a compromised VIP user account,

---
Algorithm 1. Shadow Selection

1: **procedure** SELECTSHADOW($G_{i,j}$, S_i)
2:     $h \leftarrow$ SHA-512($G_{i,j}$)
3:     $mID \leftarrow h \ mod \ len(S_i)$
4:     $shadow \leftarrow S_i[mID]$
5:     **return** $shadow$
---

the adversary can achieve the ground truth $G_{i,j}$ to calculate mID, yet can not get the correct shadow email address because of not having the secret arrangement of S_i. Therefore, the adversary can not send an email with the right shadow email address, which immediately gets detected by the EMG.

4.4 Protocol

Communication Between VIP Users. Figure 3 explains the EM protocol through email communication between VIP users Alice and Bob. (1) Alice composes an email to Bob {*from: alice@org.com, to: bob@org.com*}. (2) Alice's EMA delivers the email to EMG, where EMG uses the ground truth between them in Algorithm 1, to select a shadow email address for Alice. Assume that the selected address is *alice.x@org.com*. Therefore, the EMG forwards the email to the mail server as {*from: alice.x@org.com, to: bob@org.com*}. (3) When Bob's EMA fetches for a new email, EMG receives the email from the mail server and deduce that the sender address is one of Alice's shadow email addresses. Therefore, EMG uses the ground truth between Bob and Alice in Algorithm 1 to select the current shadow email address for Alice. If the retrieved address matches *alice.x@org.com*, the email is benign. Otherwise, it is phishing. EMG delivers the benign email to Bob's EMA as {*from: alice@org.com, to: bob@org.com*}. Bob receives the email as how Alice composed it, making the whole EM mechanisms transparent to end-users. The replies from Bob to Alice is similar to the above three steps. The only secret in the protocol is the arrangement of the sender shadow emails.

Communication with External Users. EM only protects VIP users. Therefore, the EMG bypasses the following emails with external (non-VIP) users to decrease the overall email traffic processing:
No Mutation. A VIP user sends an email to a non-VIP user. Formally:

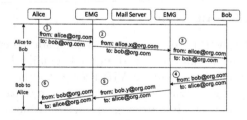

Fig. 3. EM protocol, demonstrating email communication between VIP users.

$$\{sender : x, \ recipient : y; \ where, \ x \in R \ and \ y \notin R\}$$

where R is the list of real email addresses of all VIP users.

No Verification. A VIP user receives an email from a non-VIP user. Formally:

$$\{sender : x, \; recipient : y; \; where, \; x \notin R \; and \; y \in R\}$$

4.5 Identifying Lateral Spear-Phishing Attack

In EM, the legitimate email communication between VIP users happens through SCC, where the sender address is always a valid shadow email address. Therefore, EMG detects an incoming email as phishing while fetching new emails that have a real email address of a VIP member as the sender's address. However, the adversary may send phishing emails by guessing or randomly generating a shadow email address to bypass EM. We call such phishing attempts as EM engineering attack. To formalize the detection process, let's assume that R is the real email address list, and $\overline{S}$ is the set of shadow email address lists of all VIP users.

Lateral Spear-phishing and Spoofing Attack. By compromising a VIP user's email account or impersonating a VIP user, the adversary sends a phishing email to another VIP user. Formally:

$$\{sender : x, \; recipient : y; \; where, \; x, y \in R\}$$

That means both the sender and receiver email address is enlisted in the VIP user list. EMG immediately detects such an email as a phishing email.

EM Engineering Attack. The adversary sends a phishing email to any VIP user by randomly *guessing* a shadow email address as the sender's address. Formally:

$$\{sender : x, \; recipient : y; \; where, \; x \in \overline{S} \; and \; y \in R\}$$

To evade EM, adversaries may randomly guess or mimic the mutation mechanism to generate a legitimate shadow email address. However, EM creates shadow email addresses from a space of at least 16 byte long alphanumeric sequence. Therefore, the probability of guessing a correct shadow email address is $1/2^{128}$, which is nearly zero.

5 Email Mutation – Challenges and Solutions

Handling Multiple Shadow Email Accounts. In EM, each VIP user has a set of shadow email accounts for sending emails to another VIP user. However, VIP users only discern about their real email account. Therefore, sending emails from multiple shadow accounts and keeping track of all sent emails into one real email account is challenging. EM overcome this challenge by following means. First, shadow email accounts only used for sending emails while the receiver email address will always be the real email address. Therefore, each VIP user receives all emails into their real email account inbox. Second, while forwarding an email from a shadow account, the EMG uses an IMAP APPEND command to populate that email into the real email sent-box after a successful email delivery to the recipient. Thus, the real account gets a trace of email delivery. If an email gets bounced, the EMG sends the bounce email back to the real email account.

Improving Email Mutation Usability. Existing phishing detectors similar to EM mostly suffer because of low usability. For instance, PGP requires user training on public-key cryptography and the PGP tool itself [25,26]. PGP encryption removes the visibility of the email from end-users. Whereas, EM does not distort the generic user experience of using emails. Every operation such as mutation, verification, and shadow email address communication entirely segregated from the end-users and processed by the cloud EMGs. Users only need to use EMAs, for instance, sending an email by pressing the new "Send email with mutation" button beside the regular "Send" button in the Gmail web client (mail.google.com) illustrated in Fig. 4a. EM does not modify or add anything in the email body or headers makes it transparent to mail servers as well. Therefore, EM can be used with any email service provider and email clients without further usability and configuration overhead. The transparency of EM also makes it compatible to work combining with other email security solutions (even with PGP [6] or S/MIME [24]) and cyber agility frameworks [16,17].

Preserving User Privacy. The secure cloud-based gateways in the EM does not violate the end-to-end user email privacy because of the following reasons. Firstly, EMG does not keep any copy of the email. It just either mutates or verifies the sender's email address if the communications happen between two VIP users. All other emails get bypassed. Secondly, EMA connects with EMGs through secure channels (SSL/TLS) to avoid unauthorized data access during transmission. Finally, the organization of the VIP members can maintain their own EMGs to preserve data privacy. The secret shadow email lists can not be retrievable from any EMGs. Therefore, in a cross-enterprise EM system, EMG from one organization can not reveal the shadow email list of another organization. In recent days cloud-based secure email gateways are becoming popular because of their swift, robust, and effective attack detection with minimal management overhead. Therefore, many organizations are adopting such solutions from Cisco, Microsoft, Barracuda, Mimecast, and others [2].

Adding Custom Email Fields is Insufficient. Adding just a new field in the email headers (such as X-headers [7]) or custom trace on the email body for sender authentication will not help to detect the lateral spear-phishing attack. Because adding any extra information into an email will immediately eliminate its transparency to both the client and the mail server. Second, adversaries may corrupt such additional data by adding noises into it, which will cause an interruption in regular email communication, raising high false-positive rates,

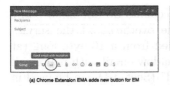  

(a) Chrome Extension EMA adds new button for EM   (c) EMA icon at Chrome Menu Bar   (d) EMA description in Chrome Extension Panel

Fig. 4. EMA in Google Chrome Browser and Thunderbird, (a) "Send email with mutation" button in `mail.google.com`, (b) EMA in Thunderbird, (c) EMA icon at Chrome Menu Bar, and (d) EMA in Chrome Extension Panel.

and opening new security loopholes into the detection system. Finally, motivated adversaries can craft such fields by carefully observing historical emails. To overcome these challenges, EM uses a random selection of the sender email address (shadow address) for each new email delivery without adding anything into the email. This makes the solution transparent to both end-users and mail servers, but hard for adversaries to guess a correct shadow email address.

Addressing Asynchronous Ground Truth Problem. If a VIP user deletes any email from his inbox/sentbox that was sent by another VIP user, then the ground truth between them becomes asynchronous. To solve this problem, EMG keeps the hashed (SHA-512) digest of the last l number of emails between two VIP users. Therefore, EMG stores a maximum of $(v-1)$ hashed ground truth for each VIP user, where v is the number of all VIP users, to prevent asynchronous ground truth problems. Moreover, sender and receiver EMGs perform this hash storing operation asynchronously while sending and/or receiving an email. Thus, the *synchronization* does not require any communication between EMGs.

Handling Insider Attack. A novel contribution of EM is that it can protect VIP users from insider attacks. For instance, John is a VIP user who stoles Alice's email account credentials. Then, John uses his EMA to send a phishing email to Bob impersonating Alice. Formally, an attacker i compromises an email account j and uses i's EMA to send emails to k impersonating j, where $i, j, k \in L$ and L is the list of all VIP users. EM solves this problem by following: every VIP user's EMA is synchronized with its corresponding EMG instance through a unique authentication token (see Sect. 6.1 for details). That means John's EMA can get only his instance of EMG; therefore, it will work only for John himself, not for Alice or Bob. The EMG keeps track who is forwarding the email by examining the authentication token of the EMA, and then verifies if that EMA is associated with the user or not. If the EMA is not assigned for that particular user but delivers an email anyhow, then EMG identifies that email as an insider attack.

Minimizing Shadow Email Account Overhead. The shadow email accounts are only meant to send emails as sender. These accounts do not receive any emails. Creating multiple shadow accounts for VIP users does not increase any inbound email traffic. Besides, these accounts do not impose any memory overhead. Therefore, they create negligible overhead on the service provider. The shadow email addresses can be selected from a 16-byte long (at least) sequence. This ensures no collision between shadow email with real email accounts. Additionally, unique keywords such as "sid" (Sect. 4.1) can be used in shadow accounts creation to make a fine difference from real email accounts

6   Scalable Implementation and Security Measurement

Evaluating EM in a large scale network requires a scalable implementation that is compatible with any existing email clients and email service providers. Moreover, the security measures of each component are necessary to reduce the risk factor in terms of user privacy and data breach. We measure these matrices for the primary components of EM: EMA and EMG.

6.1   Email Mutation Agent

Security Measures. EMA operates alongside with regular Mail user agent [20] or email clients only to deliver or receive new emails from EMGs. It does not communicate with the mail or SMTP server. Therefore, EMAs neither have any storage to collect emails nor requires the user email account credential. The communication between EMA and EMGs happens through a secure channel (SSL/TLS) to protect data breaches during the transaction.

Implementation. Usually, clients use multiple devices, such as cell phones, laptops, desktop, and more, to access their email accounts. Therefore, EMA needs platform-oriented implementation to work on different devices as well. We implemented three types of EMA for three different platforms, 1) browsers extension for web clients that will work in laptops, desktop, where a web browser can run. 2) Shell and python scripts to configure email clients such as Outlook, Thunderbird, and 3) email client (android/iOS) app for cell phones and tabs. Figure 4 shows different implementation of EMAs, such as browser extension (4a) and Thunderbird client (4b). The Chrome browser extension adds a new button called "Send email with Mutation" (Fig. 4a) alongside with the regular "Send" button that `mail.google.com` provides.

Distribution of EMA. A VIP user can get an EMA from their system admin or download it from the web. The admin gives a unique authentication token to each VIP user for their first use of EMA to subscribe with the EMGs. Later on, using that token, they can connect with their corresponding EMG from different EMAs. This ensures users' flexibility to use EMA from different devices and different locations (e.g., public networks). Users can reset the token anytime.

6.2   Email Mutation Gateway

Security Measures. EMG inspects email for detection and modifies for mutation. It does not maintain any mailboxes for users. When a VIP user subscribes
with EMG, it creates an instance for that user. So that later on, the same user
can connect with the EMG from EMAs in different devices. EMG keeps the
arrangement of the shadow email lists secret. Therefore, from an EMA, VIP
users can not retrieve their shadow email list. After a certain mutation interval t
seconds, EMG rearranges all the secret shadow email lits of VIP users randomly.
Besides, an instance of EMG given to a VIP user is not shareable by other VIP
users through EMAs, meaning Alice can not use the EMG instance of Bob from
her EMA. This protects the insider attacks because using her EMA and EMG
instance, Alice can not send emails as Bob, considering that Alice compromises
Bob's email account. Cloud-based solutions like EMGs are secured, and many
providers like Amazon, Microsoft, Cisco, Barracuda, Mimecast, and more are
nowadays providing secure cloud email gateways for phishing detection [2].

Implementation. We implemented the EMGs as an inbound and outbound
Mail transfer agent [20] that works as an SMTP relay to mutate outgoing emails
and proxy gateway to check incoming emails for spear-phishing detection. We
use python libraries such as `smtpd` and `imaplib`, to implement the relay server
and Django framework to make EMG a web service. The code is available on
GitHub.

7   Email Mutation Verification and Evaluation

7.1   System Verification

EM is a new technique; therefore, it is necessary to ensure the design correctness before implementation and deployment over real network. Model checkers
help to formally specify, model, and verify a system in the early design phase
to find any unknown behavior if it exists. This section presents the modeling
of individual components, their interaction, and verification of EM using model
checking tool UPPAAL [22]. The comprehensive system is modeled using timed
automata and verified against user-defined temporal properties. We have illustrated the components of EM using the state machine diagram of the system
modeling language, where the circle represents the state, and the arrow shows
the transition among the states. The transitions are annotated with channels,
guards, and actions. Interaction between components using channel (!, ?) where,
"!" and "?" means the sending and receiving signals, respectively.

Modeling of Client and Mail Server. Figure 5a illustrates the functionality
of a client. The client uses the sending signal $Send(i, j)$! to forward a newly
composed email to the EMG, where i is the sender address, and j is the receiver
address. Using $Fetch\_Email(j)$!, client j request to fetch any new email from

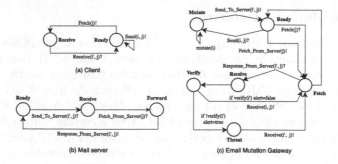

Fig. 5. State machine diagrams of different components in EM.

EMG. As a response, the client receives a new email from EMG by the receiving signal $Receive(i, j)?$, where i is the sender address, and j is the receiver address. Figure 5b shows the basic functionality of a mail server. The channels $Send\_To\_Server(i, j)?$, $Fetch\_From\_Server(j)?$, and $Response\_From\_Server$ $(i, j)!$ represent the transitions for receiving a new email, receiving fetching request for new emails, and responding new emails respectively.

Modeling of Gateway. Figure 5c describes the functionality of the mutation gateway (EMG). EMG receives a new email from clients through the receiving signal $send(i, j)?$ and mutates the sender address i to i' using the function $mutate(i)$. Then forwards the email to the mail server using signal $Send\_To\_Serv$ $er(i', j)!$. EMG goes the $Fetch$ state after receiving a $Fetch(j)$ signal form client j and seeks new emails from the mail server by the signal $Fetch\_From\_Server(j)!$. As a response, EMG receives new emails by the receiving signal $Response\_From$ $\_Server(i', j)?$, where i' is the (mutated) sender address, and j is the receiver address. After that, EMG verifies i' by the function $verify(i')$. If verification pass, then the email will be delivered to the client through the $Receive(i, j)?$, where i is the real address of i'. Otherwise, the email gets flagged as a threat. In case of suspicious email, the invariant $alert$ is set to true; otherwise, it is set to false. Here, the state $Threat$ is presented to flag the email.

Modeling of Adversary. Using channel $Send\_To\_Server(l, j)?$ adversaries send email to recipient j, where l is the adversary chosen sender address. If adversaries make a successful guess, their email will be delivered to the client.

Property Verification. UPPAAL takes the model, and user-defined temporal properties as input to verify the model and generates output, either satisfied or not satisfied. UPPAAL defines temporal properties in the form of computational tree logic (CTL), which is a branch of symbolic logic. To verify EM, we defined the liveness, reachability, and deadlock-freeness as temporal properties. Table 1 describes the properties along with its UPPAAL supported CTL and

Table 1. Temporal properties to verify the correctness of Email Mutation system.

Property	CTL	Result
Reachability	$A[] := \forall\, i \in all\_emg$ $(emg_i.verify \,\wedge\, !emg_i.alert) \rightarrow (emg_i.ready)$	*satisfied*
Liveness	$A[] := \forall\, i \in all\_emg\ (emg_i.alert \rightarrow emg_i.threat)$	*satisfied*
Deadlock-freeness	$A[] := \forall\, i \in all\_emg\ (!emg_i.deadlock)$	*satisfied*

the results of these properties. *Reachability* describes that every good state is reachable, and every bad state is unreachable. In EM, every benign email should be delivered to the destination. *Liveness* describes the system is progressing to achieve a specific goal. For instance, every suspicious email should be flagged as a threat. *Deadlock-freeness* ensures that the system is not stopped, and it is always progressing. The system is in deadlock sate when it stops in a state and does not proceed to other states. The CTL operator $A[]$ represents that every single state on all paths should satisfy the properties, all benign emails are delivered to the destination and every suspicious email is flagged. The reachability property ensures that no suspicious email will be delivered without a threat flag. In reachability and liveness properties, $(\forall\, i \in all\_emg)$ is used for iteration and verification of property against every single email mutation gateway (emg_i).

7.2 Performance Evaluation

We measure the performance of EM in terms of overhead added into existing email infrastructure. EM has a 100% lateral spear-phishing and spoofing detection rate. We compare EM with similar existing solutions to measure the necessity and effectiveness of the system.

Experiment Setup. We evaluated EM in large scale enterprise networks for more than six months and protected 5,000 VIP members over five different organizations. Among them, 46 VIP member was voluntarily from Jet Propulsion Laboratory, NASA (JPL). The JPL red team sends more than half a million attack emails. The VIP members use different mail service providers, including Gmail, Microsoft Exchange, Apple iCloud, and email clients like Outlook, Thunderbird, `mail.google.com` and so on. The shadow email addresses for each VIP user was between ten to one hundred. The mutation interval t was set with different values between 60 s to 2 h to rearrange the secret shadow email lists randomly. All evaluation values have been achieved from real-time email communications.

Shadow Email Selection Overhead. EMG computes shadow email addresses for mutation and verification using Algorithm 1. We measure the selection overhead of a single email over different email sizes. Figure 6a shows the selection

16   M. M. Islam et al.

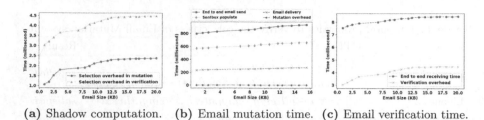

(a) Shadow computation.   (b) Email mutation time.   (c) Email verification time.

Fig. 6. EM gateway performance for mutation-verification of individual emails without attachments.

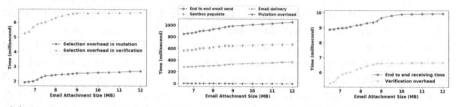

(a) Shadow computation.   (b) Email mutation time.   (c) Email verification time.

Fig. 7. EM gateway performance for mutation-verification of individual emails with attachments.

overhead for mutation is 2.5 ms, and verification is 5 milliseconds for email size range 10–20 KB without attachments. Figure 7a shows the overhead is 3 ms, and 7 ms for email size range 7–12 MB with attachments.

Mutation Overhead. While forwarding an email, EMG 1) mutates the email, 2) delivers the mutated emails to the provider mail server, and 3) populates the real email account sentbox of the sender to keep track of successful email deliveries. Figure 6b and 7b shows the overall forwarding delays over email sizes. Emails in 10–16 KB sizes need 3 milliseconds for mutation, 250 ms for delivery, 650 ms for sentbox population, and overall 950 ms to forward the email. For email sizes 7–12 MB, mutation delay is 4.5 ms, and overall sending time is 1.5 s. In both cases, the mutation overhead is 0.5% compared to the end-to-end email forwarding delay.

Verification Overhead. Figure 6c and 7c shows the end-to-end email receiving time with verification over different email sizes. Emails in 10–20 KB sizes without attachments have overall 8.5 ms receiving delay where the verification delay is 4.5 ms, and emails in 7–12 MB sizes have overall 10 ms receiving delay where the verification delay is 7 ms.

Email Processing Rate by an EMG. We measured the overall performance of an EMG by sending more than thousands of emails at a time to a single EMG

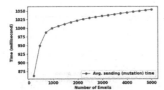

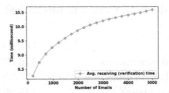

Fig. 8. Multiple email processing overhead for mutation.

Fig. 9. Multiple email processing overhead for verification.

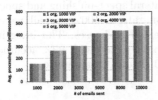

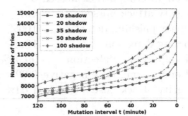

Fig. 10. EMG overhead in cross-enterprise architecture. The increasing number of organization or VIP members do not impact the overall processing time. The number of emails dealt at a time determines the overall delay.

Fig. 11. EM engineering attack, the minimum number of tries adversary needs to break the EM for sending their first successful phishing email.

to process mutation and verification simultaneously. Figure 8 and 9 shows the average processing delay of EM for sending an email with mutation is 1.1 s and receiving an email after phishing detection is 10.9 ms, respectively while dealing with 5000 emails per second.

Cross-Enterprise Architecture Overhead. Adding different organizations into the EM system does not increase additional overheads because the operational cost of each EMG only depends on the total number of emails get processed at a time, not on the size of the VIP user list. Figure 10 depicts that the overall email processing time is the same for one organization having 1,000 VIP users to five organization having 5,000 VIP users. The delays increased when the total number of emails dealt at a time increases. Multiple EMGs can be used to balance these increasing delays.

EM Engineering Attack. If adversaries send a phishing email directly from compromised VIP user accounts or by impersonating a VIP user, they have 0% chance to evade EM. However, adversaries may try to phish by randomly guessing a shadow email address, known as EM engineering attack. A shadow email address is a 16-byte long random alphanumeric sequence, which is practically impossible to guess. Therefore, for the sake of the evaluation, we inform all valid shadow emails to the red team before launching the attack. Figure 11

Table 2. Detection results of EM.

Metric	Data
Total attack emails	516,000
Lateral spear-phishing attack	153,207
Spoofing attack	145,291
EM engineering attack	201,437
Integrity attack	16,065
EM engineering attack missed	3
Integrity attack missed	167
L. spear-phishing detection	100%
Spoofing detection	100%
EM engineering detection	99.99%
EM engineering false negative	0.0015%
Integrity attack false negative	1.04%

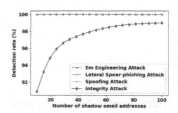

Fig. 12. The detection rate of EM over different shadow email address assigned to a VIP user. Lateral spear-phishing and spoofing detection rate is 100% for all values of shadow email addresses. The integrity attack can be detected with 99% accuracy by using 100 shadow email addresses.

depicts the detection results. With different setups of mutation parameter, the minimum number of tries adversary needs to break EM for sending their first successful phishing email varies. For instance, it takes 7,000 tries to send the first phishing email if a VIP user has 10 shadow emails and 120 min mutation interval. However, the tries dramatically increase to 14,500 (probability 0.000069) if the number of shadows and mutation interval changes to 100 and 1 min, respectively. This indicates that based on user impact, EM can increase the level of protection swiftly.

Detection Results. Table 2 summarizes the performance metrics for EM. From a total of 516,000 attacks, EM detected all of the lateral spear-phishing and spoofing emails with no false positive and false negative rates. Out of 201,437 EM engineering attacks, three were successful, as because we inform prior to the attack generator red team about all valid shadow email addresses. The purpose of EM is to detect lateral spear-phishing and spoofing attacks. However, EM can detect any integrity violation in the email while two VIP user communicates. EM calculates the current shadow email address based on the hashed value of the email and prior l emails (ground truth). Therefore, any changes in the email during transmission will desynchronize the ground truth at the receiver side. Figure 12 shows the integrity attack detection rate is 99% when the shadow address for a user is one hundred. Although this attack is explicitly out of our attack model, however, we add this into the detection results to show the capabilities and completeness of EM.

Comparison with Existing System: *Learning-based.* Existing lateral spear-phishing detectors are mostly learning-oriented; they learn attack signatures, benign users' behavior from the historical data, and create a model to detect phishing emails [10–13, 27]. These solutions require myriad historical data for training, distinct attack signature (e.g., malicious URL or attachment), sufficient number of features, and often shows high false positive and false negative rates because of any lacking of these requirements. False positive means benign emails detected as phishing and false negative means a phishing email detected as benign. For instance, Ho et al. [12] trained their model over 25.5 million emails, and their attack model is limited to malicious URLs embedded in the email body. Gascon et al. [11] showed high false positive (10%) and high false negative rates (46.8%) against detecting lateral spear-phishing attacks. EM does not require any training; it is independent from email content or header and can detect lateral spear-phishing and spoofing attacks with zero false positive and false negative rates.

Agent-based. PGP, S/MIME can ensure sender authenticity by digitally signed the email. However, these solutions are not widely used because of low usability, low transparency, and high manageability issues [25,26]. The end-users require prior knowledge regarding public-key cryptography and proper training to use PGP tools. The encrypted cyphertext eliminates the visibility of the emails, making it incompatible to work with other security extensions such as IDS. Moreover, PGP signatures can be spoofed [23]. In contrast, EM is transparent, has a low management overhead, and highly flexible to use. The end-users do not need any prior knowledge or training to use it. Table 3 shows a comparison of EM with the existing popular PGP solutions in terms of overhead added in a generic mail transfer system. The overhead of EM is negligible (3–7 ms) compared to PGP signature and encryption operations with RSA 2048 bit keys, which is vital for large scale enterprise networks where email processing rate is higher.

Tool	Overhead (ms)			
PGP	GnuPG	Autocrypt	Enigmail	Mailvelope
	760.356	680.65	852.12	785.65
EM	Mutation	Verification		
	3	7		

Table 3. Comparison between existing popular PGP tools and EM.

Authentication-protocol. Standard email spoofing detection protocols such as SPF, DKIM, and DMARC can not detect lateral spear-phishing attacks. Table 4 depicts that, all of our attack data has these security extensions. However, the lateral spear-phishing emails bypass these standard techniques as they are sent from legitimate accounts. Nonetheless, EM detects them all. Therefore, in the prevailing lacking of alternative protection against lateral spear-phishing attacks, the EM system is a valuable extension to existing defenses.

Auth. protocol	Attack data	LSP detect
SPF	100%	0%
DKIM	100%	0%
DMARC	100%	0%
EM	N/A	100%

Table 4. Existing email authentication standards failed to detect lateral spear-phishing (LSP) attacks.

8   Limitations and Future Work

One limitation of EM is that the VIP users' physical machine gets compromised or stolen, where an instance of EMA of that user is installed. In that case, EM can not protect the user. Another limitation regarding usability for EM is to get an EMA instance for every single device VIP members use to access their email account. In the future, we want to enhance EM to protect users if their device gets compromised. Moreover, we want to leverage EM on the server-side to remove the use of EMA.

9   Conclusion

In this paper, we presented a novel approach using sender email address mutation to proactively defend against the most devastating and stealthy spear-phishing called lateral spear-phishing attacks. Our EM system guarantees the phishing emails sent from trusted users will be immediately detected. EM integrates well with existing email infrastructures, and it requires no special handling by users. EM requires an agent to be deployed on the client-side for every user and a central gateway in the cloud. The agent can be a simple plugin installed in email clients. We implemented and evaluated EM in a large scale real-world enterprise network with well-known email service providers (Gmail, for example). Our evaluation showed that EM causes 0.5% overhead on overall email transmission while detecting lateral spear-phishing and spoofing attacks. Moreover, we showed that it is very hard to break EM (probability 0.000069). Unlike the existing spear-phishing detectors, which are limited on malicious content or links, our EM can work beyond email content and headers to detect most stealthy lateral spear-phishing attacks that exploit compromised email account.

Acknowledgement. This research was supported in part by the Defense Advanced Research Projects Agency (DARPA), United States Army Research Office (ARO) and Office of Naval Research (ONR). Any opinions, findings, conclusions or recommendations stated in this material are those of the authors and do not necessarily reflect the views of the funding sources.

References

1. Business email compromise: The $26 billion scam (2019). https://www.ic3.gov/media/2019/190910.aspx
2. Email security gateways. (2020). https://www.expertinsights.com/insights/top-11-email-security-gateways/
3. Multi-factor authentication (2020). https://en.wikipedia.org/wiki/Multi-factor_authentication
4. Spear-phishing email reports (2020). https://www.phishingbox.com/
5. Aggarwal, S., Kumar, V., Sudarsan, S.: Identification and detection of phishing emails using natural language processing techniques. In: Proceedings of the 7th International Conference on Security of Information and Networks. ACM (2014)

6. Callas, J., Donnerhacke, L., Finney, H., Thayer, R.: Openpgp message format. Technical report, RFC 2440, November (1998)
7. Crocker, D.: Rfc0822: standard for the format of ARPA internet text messages (1982)
8. Crocker, D., Hansen, T., Kucherawy, M.: Domainkeys identified mail (dkim) signatures. RFC6376 (2011). https://doi.org/10.17487/RFC6376, https://tools.ietf.org/html/rfc6376
9. Dalton, A., Islam, M.M., Dorr, B.J., et al.: Active defense against social engineering: The case for human language technology. In: Proceedings on Social Threats in Online Conversations: Understanding and Management, pp. 1–8 (2020)
10. Duman, S., Kalkan, K., Egele, M., Robertson, W., Kirda, E.: Emailprofiler: spearphishing filtering with header and stylometric features of emails. In: IEEE 40th COMPSAC, vol. 1, pp. 408–416. IEEE (2016)
11. Gascon, H., Ullrich, S., Stritter, B., Rieck, K.: Reading between the lines: content-agnostic detection of spear-phishing emails. In: Bailey, M., Holz, T., Stamatogiannakis, M., Ioannidis, S. (eds.) RAID 2018. LNCS, vol. 11050, pp. 69–91. Springer, Cham (2018). https://doi.org/10.1007/978-3-030-00470-5_4
12. Ho, G., et al.: Detecting and characterizing lateral phishing at scale. In: 28th {USENIX} Security Symposium ({USENIX} Security 19), pp. 1273–1290 (2019)
13. Ho, G., Sharma, A., Javed, M., Paxson, V., Wagner, D.: Detecting credential spearphishing in enterprise settings. In: 26th {USENIX} Security Symposium ({USENIX} Security 17), pp. 469–485 (2017)
14. Hu, H., Wang, G.: End-to-end measurements of email spoofing attacks. In: 27th {USENIX} Security Symposium ({USENIX} Security 18), pp. 1095–1112 (2018)
15. Hu, X., Li, B., Zhang, Y., Zhou, C., Ma, H.: Detecting compromised email accounts from the perspective of graph topology. In: Proceedings of the 11th International Conference on Future Internet Technologies, pp. 76–82 (2016)
16. Islam, M.M., Al-Shaer, E.: Active deception framework: an extensible development environment for adaptive cyber deception. In: 2020 IEEE Cybersecurity Development (SecDev). IEEE (2020)
17. Islam, M.M., Duan, Q., Al-Shaer, E.: Specification-driven moving target defense synthesis. In: Proceedings of the 6th ACM Workshop on Moving Target Defense, pp. 13–24 (2019)
18. Khonji, M., Iraqi, Y., Andrew, J.: Mitigation of spear phishing attacks: a content-based authorship identification framework. In: 2011 International Conference for ITST, pp. 416–421. IEEE (2011)
19. Kitterman, S.: Sender policy framework (spf). RFC7208 (2014). https://tools.ietf.org/html/rfc7208
20. Klensin, J., et al.: Simple mail transfer protocol. Technical report, rfc 2821 (2001)
21. Kucherawy, M., Zwicky, E.: Domain-based message authentication, reporting, and conformance (dmarc). RFC7489 (2015). https://tools.ietf.org/html/rfc7489
22. Larsen, K.G., Pettersson, P., Yi, W.: Uppaal in a nutshell. Int. J. Softw. Tools Technol. Transf. 1(1–2), 134–152 (1997)
23. Müller, J., Brinkmann, M., Böck, H., Schinzel, S., Schwenk, J., et al.: "johnny, you are fired!"-spoofing openpgp and s/mime signatures in emails. In: 28th {USENIX} Security Symposium ({USENIX} Security 19), pp. 1011–1028 (2019)
24. Ramsdell, B., et al.: S/mime version 3 message specification. Technical report, RFC 2633 (1999)
25. Ruoti, S., Andersen, J., Seamons, K., et al.: "we're on the same page" a usability study of secure email using pairs of novice users. In: Proceedings of the 2016 CHI Conference on Human Factors in Computing Systems, pp. 4298–4308 (2016)

26. Sheng, S., Broderick, L., Koranda, C.A., Hyland, J.J.: Why johnny still can't encrypt: evaluating the usability of email encryption software. In: Symposium On Usable Privacy and Security, pp. 3–4. ACM (2006)
27. Stringhini, G., Thonnard, O.: That ain't you: blocking spearphishing through behavioral modelling. In: Almgren, M., Gulisano, V., Maggi, F. (eds.) DIMVA 2015. LNCS, vol. 9148, pp. 78–97. Springer, Cham (2015). https://doi.org/10.1007/978-3-319-20550-2_5
28. Thomson, I.: Who's using 2fa? sweet fa. less than 10% of gmail users enable two-factor authentication. The Register (2018)
29. Verizon: 2018 data breach investigations report (2018). https://enterprise.verizon.com/resources/reports/DBIR_2018_Report_execsummary.pdf

ThreatZoom: Hierarchical Neural Network for CVEs to CWEs Classification

Ehsan Aghaei(✉), Waseem Shadid, and Ehab Al-Shaer

University of North Carolina at Charlotte, Charlotte 28223, USA
{eaghaei,wshadid,ealshaer}@uncc.edu

Abstract. The Common Vulnerabilities and Exposures (CVE) represent standard means for sharing publicly known information security vulnerabilities. One or more CVEs are grouped into the Common Weakness Enumeration (CWE) classes for the purpose of understanding the software or configuration flaws and potential impacts enabled by these vulnerabilities and identifying means to detect or prevent exploitation.

As the CVE-to-CWE classification is mostly performed manually by domain experts, thousands of critical and new CVEs remain unclassified, yet they are unpatchable. This significantly limits the utility of CVEs and slows down proactive threat mitigation tremendously.

This paper presents *ThreatZoom*, as the first automatic tool to classify CVEs to CWEs. *ThreatZoom* uses a novel learning algorithm that employs an adaptive hierarchical neural network that adjusts its weights based on text analytic scores and classification errors. It automatically estimates the CWE classes corresponding to a CVE instance using both statistical and semantic features extracted from the description of a CVE.

This tool is rigorously tested by various datasets provided by MITRE and the National Vulnerability Database (NVD). The accuracy of classifying CVE instances to their correct CWE classes is 92% (fine-grain) and 94% (coarse-grain) for NVD dataset, and 75% (fine-grain) and 90% (coarse-grain) for MITRE dataset, despite the small corpus.

Keywords: Hierarchical neural network · CVE to CWE classification · Vulnerability analysis · Proactive cyber defense

1 Introduction

Cyber-attack actions allow malicious actors to violate the intended security policies by bypassing the protection mechanisms or manipulating the resources or the system's behaviors. Thus, the consequence of the attack is a behavior that violates the intended security policies of the victim. Such action, if it is made accessible to the attacker, is called weakness. Weaknesses are flaws, fault, bugs, and errors occur in software's architecture, design, code, or implementation that can lead to exploitable vulnerabilities. A vulnerability is defined as a set of one or more weaknesses within a specific product or protocol, which allows an attacker to access the behaviors or resources to compromise.

© ICST Institute for Computer Sciences, Social Informatics and Telecommunications Engineering 2020
Published by Springer Nature Switzerland AG 2020. All Rights Reserved
N. Park et al. (Eds.): SecureComm 2020, LNICST 335, pp. 23–41, 2020.
https://doi.org/10.1007/978-3-030-63086-7_2

The Common Weakness Enumeration (CWE) is a hierarchically-designed dictionary of software weaknesses for the purpose of understanding software flaws, their potential impacts, and identifying means to detect, fix, and prevent errors [6]. CWEs are non-disjoint classes, and they are organized in a hierarchical (tree) structure to reflect this relationship in which every non-root CWE node inherits the whole characteristics of its parents. Therefore, a CWE in the higher level represents a more general definition of weakness, and every lower-level node adds more details to that CWE node of interest. Meanwhile, the Common Vulnerabilities and Exposures (CVE) reports are a list of publicly disclosed computer security vulnerabilities where every report is assigned by an ID. CVEs are brief and low-level descriptions, representing the standard means for sharing cybersecurity vulnerabilities within a particular product or system [5]. CVE IDs are assigned to those vulnerabilities that satisfy three criteria: (1) system bugs and its negative impact on security must be acknowledged by the vendor, or vulnerability report and security policy violation of the affected system must be documented by the reporter, (2) bug can be fixed independently of any other bugs, (3) bug must affect only one codebase and those impact more than one system get separate IDs.

In general, CWE is a dictionary of software vulnerabilities addressing the underlying error, while CVE is a set of known instances of vulnerability for specific systems or products. CWEs mainly explain *how* (conditions and procedures) and *why* (cause) a vulnerability can be exploited, and *what* (impact) are the consequences. When the vulnerability is unpatchable, the classification of CVE into CWE becomes extremely important since only CWEs can provide the means to develop countermeasure techniques and understand the CVE implications. In this paper, we present a novel approach that employs a hierarchical neural network design to automatically estimate the CWE classes corresponding to a CVE instance using both statistical and semantic features from the description of CVEs.

1.1 Motivation Example

Given 'CVE-2004-0366: *SQL injection vulnerability in the libpam-pgsql library before 0.5.2 allows attackers to execute arbitrary SQL statements.*', the description shares the attack action (execute arbitrary SQL statement) within a particular object (libpam-pgsql library) and specifies the consequence (SQL injection). Although this low-level and product-oriented definition demonstrates the exploitation of SQL injection, it fails to adequately specify the characteristic of this malicious behavior, which is necessary to address potential prevention and/or detection methods. The complementary associated CWE (CWE-89: SQL Injection)[1] provides a high-level and beyond-the-product knowledge by answering three key questions: (1) why the attack is exploited: *the system does not or incorrectly neutralized special elements*, (2) how this is exploited: *by modifying*

---

[1] https://cwe.mitre.org/data/definitions/89.html.

the intended SQL command, and (3) what the possible consequences are: *read or modify application data*, and *bypass protection mechanism*.

The above-mentioned case is a confirmatory example to show how a CWE can paint a clear picture of the existing holes in the systems and reveals potential factors that cause vulnerability exploitation. Obtaining these factors is closely associated with the paradigm of pinpointing applicable mitigation or detection methods. For example, we can apply an "accept known good" input validation strategy, i.e., using a set of legit inputs that strictly conform to specifications and rejects the rest, to mitigate SQL injection. Besides, we can detect SQL injection by performing an automated static analysis (e.g., bytecode or binary weakness analysis), dynamic analysis (e.g., database or web service scanners), or design review (e.g., formal methods). Figure 1 shows the hierarchical representation of the CWEs. Analyzing the path from the root all the way to any node in the lower levels is indispensable since each node reveals different functional directions to learn a weakness. For example, by tracking the path from the root node, CWE-707, to CWE-89, we realize that the SQL injection (CWE-89) is a result of an improper neutralization of special elements in data query logic (CWE-943), where both weakness are associated with injection (CWE-74), and the injection itself is the result of improper formation and neutralization of a message within a product before it is read from an upstream component or sent to a downstream component (CWE-707). Incorporating this thorough knowledge graph helps to maintain countermeasures from different senses, even if the most fine-grain node is not available. For example, assume that only two coarse-grain candidates in different levels of hierarchy, CWE-707, and CWE-74, are available for CVE-2004-0366, while the most fine-grain weakness (CWE-89) is not discovered yet. Although fine-grain SQL injection characteristics is not exposed, investigating the coarse-grain candidates helps to find the common consequences

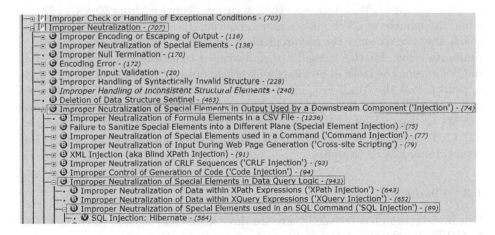

Fig. 1. It depicts the hierarchical representation of the CWEs. The red boxes show the CWE-89's relatives in the higher levels. This hierarchy plays an important role in understanding the character of the weaknesses from different levels.

and impacts, and accordingly extract defense actions against improper neutralization and injection (e.g., filtering control-plane syntax from all input). This example explicitly highlights the significance of the existing hierarchical structure of CWEs and shows how useful it is in perceiving the defense actions.

1.2   Related Works

AA great effort has been made initially by MITRE and NVD[2] to manually classify some CVEs to one or more CWE classes. Considering the growing number of CVEs and the high labor cost of manual classification, MITRE has classified 2553 CVEs (out of 116K) to 364 CWE classes (out of 719) [6]. On the other hand, NVD has [1] attempted to increase the quantity of CVE classification by mapping about 85,000 CVEs. Although MITRE has classified smaller number of CVEs compared with NVD, it covers a higher number of CWEs, and performs a more fine-grain classification in hierarchical fashion. In the meantime, NVD classified more CVEs but it includes smaller number of CWEs, without addressing the hierarchy. The further investigation about the characteristics of each effort is discussed in Sect. 3.1.

In the meantime, there have been several research efforts other than MITRE and NVD to analyze CVEs to enhance the searching process and to perform CVE categorization. Neuhaus et al. [10] proposed a semi-automatic method to analyze the CVE descriptions using topic models to find prevalent vulnerability types and new trends. The test result reports 28 topics in these entries using Latent Dirichlet Allocation (LDA) and assigned LDA topics to CWEs. This approach shows very limited accuracy, depending on the CWE type.

Na et al. [9] proposed Naïve Bayes classifier to categorize CVE entries into the top ten most frequently used CWEs with the accuracy of 75.5%. However, the accuracy of this limited classification significantly decreases as the number of the considered CWEs increases (i.e., accuracy decreased from 99.8% to 75.5% when the number of CWE classes increased from 2 to 10). In addition, this approach does not consider the hierarchical structure for CWEs, which significantly limits its value. Another classifier was developed to estimate the vulnerabilities in CVEs using the basis of previously identified ones by Rahman et al. [12]. This approach uses the Term Frequency-Inverse Document Frequency (TF-IDF) to assign weights to text tokens form the feature vector and Support Vector Machine (SVM) to map CVEs to CWEs. However, they use only six CWE classes and 427 CVE instances. In addition, their classifier does not follow the hierarchical structure for CWEs as well.

1.3   Challenges

Our investigation has revealed there are three main challenges to solve the CVE-to-CWE classification as follows:

---

[2] National Vulnerability Database.

First, CWEs are organized in a hierarchical (tree) structure, in which, a CVE instance can be classified into one or more interdependent CWEs that belong to the same path. In the meantime, a CWE class can be accessed from more than one path in the CWE tree structure [6]. For instance, CWE-22 (Path Traversal)[3] can be reached from two different paths, started by either CWE-435 (Improper Interaction Between Multiple Correctly-Behaving Entities)[4] or CWE-664 (Improper Control of a Resource Through its Lifetime)[5].

Second, there is a semantic gap in and between the language of CVEs and CWEs that makes the feature extraction phase challenging. Thus, performing an efficient semantic analysis is inevitable in order to identify the connection between similar concepts used in the CVE and CWE context.

Third, a considerably small percentage (about 2%) but high-quality classification (fine-grains in the CWE hierarchy) of CVEs are provided by MITRE. On the other hand, NVD delivers a higher percentage of CVE classification (71%), but it used a considerably lower portion of CWEs (about 32% of CWEs used by MITRE). Hence, there should be a trade-off to process small and imbalanced datasets and classify CVEs into the most fine-grain CWE along with exploring the entire nodes in the path. In addition, the feature extraction, feature selection, and training process must be robust to handle the overfitting problem as well.

1.4 Contribution

Our research aims at finding a solution for this challenging problem by offering a novel automated system, so-called ThreatZoom, to estimate the CWE classes corresponding to a CVE instance. ThreatZoom takes the CVE's description as input and assigns a list of CWE classes along with the path connecting the roots of the tree to the lowest possible level class. This classification procedure comprises three steps: preprocessing (Sect. 2.1), feature extraction (Sect. 2.2) , and hierarchical decision-making process (Sect. 2.3). The feature extraction algorithm extracts the textual features from the name and the description of all existing CWE classes and their associated CVEs. Leveraging synonym vector coding and n-gram analysis, we extract both statistical and semantic features and process them to create feature vectors. Each feature is assigned by a TF-IDF score that reflects its importance in the feature space.

The main novelty of this framework is in how TF-IDF scores are incorporated into the neural network design. TF-IDF scores are set to be the initial weights of the neural network at each level such that, the weights of the neural network at one level is the sum of all TF-IDF scores found in its children CWE classes. Then, the neural network framework is trained to adjust these scores to reduce the classification error during backpropagation. This unique technique of using TF-IDF scores within a neural network framework has three advantages: (1)

---

[3] https://cwe.mitre.org/data/definitions/22.html.
[4] https://cwe.mitre.org/data/definitions/435.html.
[5] https://cwe.mitre.org/data/definitions/664.html.

it allows the neural network to learn experts perspectives in classifying CVE instances using his knowledge, and the provided descriptions about the CVE, (2) helps in reducing the effect of having a small number of training samples, and (3) increases the chances for the neural network to converge at the minimum point, which is highly likely is close to the global one in this classification problem.

In summary, this work has four key contributions: (1) the development of the first algorithm that automatically classifies CVEs to CWE classes, (2) a novel design of a hierarchical neural network that is able to trace CWE classes to the most fine-grain in the CWE hierarchical structure, (3) a new approach to extract semantic and statistical features from CVE descriptions and compute the score that reflects the importance of a feature in describing the vulnerabilities at each level in the CWE hierarchical structure, and (4) an adaptive learning technique that incorporates the computed feature scores by TF-IDF in a neural network framework to allow an automatic adjustment for feature scores to reduce classification errors. The algorithm is tested using CVE instances provided by MITRE and NVD. The test results show high accuracy classification and allow for heightening threat understanding of CVE instances to take practical mitigation actions.

To the best of our knowledge, this presented solution is first to offer an automated fine-grain classification of CVE instances to their corresponding CWE classes using a large number of CWE classes and following its hierarchical structure.

2   Methodology

This section describes the algorithm to estimate the CWE classes associated with CVE instances. The algorithm takes as input a CVE instance, and produces a set of plausible CWE classes that might be associated with the input CVE.

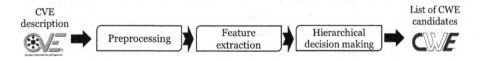

Fig. 2. It shows the three steps for the algorithm to generate a list of plausible CWE classes corresponding to the input CVE instance.

The algorithm consists of three steps namely preprocessing, feature extraction, and hierarchical neural network decision-making process (Fig. 2). The algorithm extracts the text from the description of input CVE instance, and cleans it to generate a normalized version of it. This normalized text is processed to extract n-gram features to characterize the statistical and semantic properties. These features are passed to a trained hierarchical neural network framework to estimate the CWE classes associated with the input CVE. In the following subsections, we describe the details of each three steps in details.

2.1 Preprocessing

This step takes the text provided in the description field of a CVE instance and turns it into a clean and normalized version. This preprocessing phase is accomplished via a five-stage process:

I. **Converting to lowercase**: Convert every letter to its lowercase. This is based on the assumption that each letter conveys the same meaning regardless of its case or encoding.

II. **Filtering the stop words**: Remove words that do not convey valuable information for the classification process. These words are defined in the stop-word list provided by Stanford Natural Language Processing Toolkit (NLTK), e.g., "to", "the", "for", "in".

III. **Text cleaning**: Remove punctuation and special characters that do not convey valuable information (e.g., ",", "!", "?"). Hyphens are kept though, because they may convey information.

IV. **Word stemming**: Reduce each word to its root in order to identify the relationships and commonalities across large text documents. All words are stemmed using snowball stemming model provided by NLTK python library.

V. **Synonym vector coding**: Groups the synonym words in the context, assigns a code word to represent each group, and replace all the synonym words with the code word which represents that group of synonym words in the context. MITRE provides a section for a portion of CWEs called "Alternative Terms" in which it provides the abbreviations or other commonly used advanced terms for that particular weakness. For example, [XEE, XML entity expansion, Billion Laughs Attack, XML Bomb] is a word vector associated with CWE-776 ('XML Entity Expansion'). On the other hand, MITRE provides a "CWE Glossary"[6], which contains more general terminology that is interchangeably used in CWE descriptions to convey similar meanings. Each group of words is represented by a code that is a word from the group, such that any other word in the group will be replaced by this code if found in the text. For example, the word *improper* shares the same meaning with *insufficient* and *incorrect* in cybersecurity domain, therefore they belong to the same vector and represented by code *incorrect*. This helps in reducing the variance within the documents in the same category, and in increasing the distance between different categories.

By conducting this five-stage process, the text is clean and has a unified terminology. This helps in reducing the feature space dimension as described in the next section (Fig. 3).

2.2 Feature Extraction

The input to this component is the preprocessed text and the output is word-level n-grams feature vectors [3,4,11]. The feature extraction is carried out in two stages as follows:

---

[6] https://cwe.mitre.org/documents/glossary/.

Fig. 3. This shows the five CVE description preprocessing stages.

N-Gram Analysis: In this phase, the input text is analyzed to generate a list of unique 1-gram, 2-gram, and 3-gram terms. The window size n in the n-gram analysis is a hyperparameter and set experimentally. We tend to set this value to $1, 2, 3$ to satisfy stability and to avoid overfitting. Longer n-grams dramatically increase the number of terms, i.e., word combination, that are rarely found in CVE instances and may cause over-fitting in the training process. The list of all unique n-gram items, $\mathbf{N}$, is the union of N_1, N_2, N_3, i.e.:

$$\mathbf{N} = \{N_1\} \cup \{N_2\} \cup \{N_3\}$$

This list of unique n-gram terms may contain terms that are rarely found in describing CVE instances or CWE classes. Hence, these terms are removed from the list to generate the feature vector as described next.

Feature Vector Generation: This stage takes the list of unique n-gram terms extracted in the first stage as input and generates a multi-hot representation vector indicating the terms that are likely to be used in describing CVE instances and CWE classes. This vector is referred to as a feature vector. The collection of terms that are likely to be used in describing CVE instances and CWE classes is referred to as a dictionary. This dictionary is generated by the terms found in the descriptions of CVE instances and all CWE classes in the training set. Let the dictionary, denoted by $Dict$, be the set of items in the dictionary. The dictionary is empty at the beginning, i.e., $Dict = \{\}$. Then for each text, x_i, provided either in the description of a CVE instance or in the description of a CWE class in the training set, the preprocessing step described in Sect. (2.1) is performed on it to generate a clean version of the text, $\hat{x}_i$. This clean version is analyzed using the three n-gram levels, i.e., 1-gram, 2-gram, and 3-gram, to generate the list of unique items $\mathbf{N}_i$. This list is added to the dictionary, as described in Eq. (1).

$$Dict = Dict \cup \mathbf{N}_i \tag{1}$$

Equation (1) computes the union between $Dict$ and $\mathbf{N}_i$. After processing the text in the training set, the dictionary $Dict$ includes all unique items that have been found in the context. Notice that any unique item appears only once in $Dict$.

The dictionary items are processed to filter out items with low frequencies (following the power law rule), i.e., a low number of occurrences in the training set. Let $f(t_k)$ be the number of occurrences for the dictionary item t_k in the entire training set. Then the dictionary items are filtered according to the Eq. (2).

$$Dict = Dict \setminus \{t_k\}\&, \ f(t_k) < th, \ \forall k \in 0, 1, 2, \ldots, D-1 \tag{2}$$

The threshold th is the minimum number of occurrences threshold. Equation (2) indicates that an item t_k is removed from the dictionary when its number of occurrences in the entire training set is less than the minimum number of occurrences threshold. This threshold is a prespecified value for the algorithm ($th = 3$). The removed items are assumed to be noise and not conveying any information of interest [7, 8, 13].

The dictionary defines the feature space, and its size determines the size of the feature vector. Let D denotes the number of items in this dictionary. Each unique item in the dictionary is assigned a unique index in the feature vector. The feature vector representing CVE instance x_i is computed as in Eq. (3).

$$F_i[k] = \begin{cases} 1, & t_k \in \mathbf{N}_i \\ 0, & otherwise \end{cases}, \ \forall k \in 0, 1, 2, \ldots, D-1 \tag{3}$$

The F_i is the feature vector representing x_i. t_k is dictionary item associated with index k. $\mathbf{N}_i$ is the list of unique items found in instance x_i. Equation (3) demonstrates that the feature vector has a value of 1 at all indices corresponding to the items found in $\mathbf{N}_i$ and a value of 0 at the other indices. Figure 4 shows the system design for generating feature vectors.

2.3 Hierarchical Decision-Making

Hierarchical decision-making is the third step in the CVE classification algorithm. This step takes the feature vectors computed in the second step (Sect. 3.2) and estimates the CWE classes associated with the CVE instance of interest. It follows a top-down approach by training a classifier per node in the CWE tree. For each node, a decision is made using the classifier that either leads down to a different classification node or to a leaf. This hierarchical architecture allows each classifier to focus on learning two aspects of its children: learning the details that distinguish between the classes of its children and learning the common features between the classes forming each child. This helps to simplify the design of the classifiers to reduce the computational cost, as well as improving the accuracy of the system by making each classifier to focus on its children without getting confused with other nodes.

In the classification procedure, for each node, the neural network takes the feature vector and predicts the label of the class that is associated with a CVE instance in the next level of the tree. In this case, the neural network starts to classify CVEs to CWEs that exist at level 1. In the next level, the neural network takes the predicted CWE classes in the previous level and takes their children for the next level classification. The neural network at each node is unique and independent from the other ones at other nodes [2].

According to the MITRE classification, CWE classes are not unique, which means, a CVE may belong to more than one class. Therefore, the system will miss a portion of the data if it only considers children of one selected node.

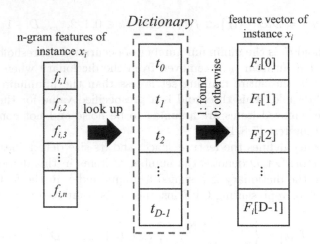

Fig. 4. This shows the system design for generating feature vectors. It simply takes the n-gram feature set from each CVE description and represents (encodes) it in the dictionary space. Given the n-gram feature set for sample x_i, $N(x_i) = \{f_{i,1}, f_{i,2}, ..., f_{i,n}\}$ and the dictionary of features, $Dictionary = \{t_0, t_1, ..., t_{D-1}\}$, for every $t_j \in N(x_i)$, $F_i[j]$ is 1, otherwise 0.

In the best-case scenario, it will reach the correct class in the path, but it is unable to detect other related CWEs that may exist on the other paths since the path to the desired class is not necessarily unique. The neural network employs a multi-hot representation to label the instances to handle this multi-label problem. In this case, every instance can be represented by more than one class in training, and the neural network may output multiple predictions for each as well.

Each neural network consists of one hidden layer. The number of neurons in the hidden layer equals to the number of the classes present at the level L in the CWE tree. Each neuron is fully connected to the input feature vector with no bias. The sigmoid function in every output neuron generates a probability score. If this value is higher than an imposed threshold, it means the input feature vector belongs to the class associated with that neuron. Figure 5 shows the structure of the used neural network.

Let O_i^l be the output of the neuron at index i in hierarchy level l. Then the output of this neuron before applying the Sigmoid function is computed in Eq. 4.

$$O_i^l(x_j) = \sum_{k=0}^{D-1} F[k].w_{ki}^l \qquad (4)$$

where x_j is the text corresponding to the input CVE instance j, and w_{ki}^l is the weight connecting the dictionary element at index k with the neuron at index i at level l.

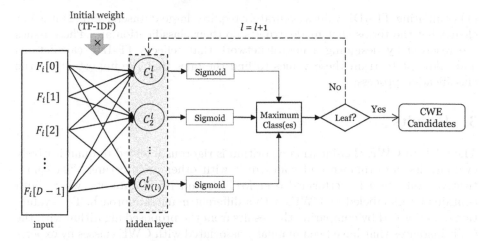

Fig. 5. This shows the hierarchical neural network design of ThreatZoom. The weight of this network is initialized by the TF-IDF score of each entry feature neuron and its corresponding class in the hidden layer. Every node in the hidden layer generates a probability score using sigmoid function and the maximum classes are assigned as the predicted classes for the input CVE. This process continues until the leaf node is reached.

The set of classes with the highest outputs at all levels is the list of candidate CWE classes output by the algorithm.

Each neural network is trained independently from the other ones using the back-propagation procedure. The training process starts by initializing each weight with its corresponding TF-IDF value. Then the weights are iteratively adjusted to reduce the classification error. Thus, the weights of irrelevant features for the classification process keep reduced, while the weights for relevant features get increased. The obtained weights at the end of the training process are assumed to resemble the TF-IDF values that would be calculated if a large enough of training set is available.

The classifier used in this algorithm is a single-layer neural network. This simple classifier has been employed for three main reasons: first, to reduce the computational cost by reducing the number of variables that a neural network needs to learn, second, to avoid the over-fitting problem especially when the size of the training dataset is small, and third, to allow mimicking experts thinking process when classifying CVE to CWE according to the terms mentioned in its description and their knowledge about the CWE classes. Some terms may have higher weights than others in the decision process. This can be interpreted as a score indicating the number of appearances a term occurs in the description of a CWE class, or in the descriptions of the CVE instances classified to that class, as well as, how often this term is used in other classes. This score can be estimated using the TF-IDF technique. However, only taking the TF-IDF scores into the account is error prone and is not the most effective way for two reasons:

(1) computing TF-IDF values accurately requires large datasets, and (2) it is not clear what the terms that made experts do their classification are. These issues are resolved by designing a neural network that reflects TF-IDF calculations and allows it to train these values to find the ones that are important for the classification process.

3   Results

The CVE-to-CWE classification algorithm is rigorously tested to quantitatively evaluate its performance and compare it with other architectures. The quantitative evaluation is performed over MITRE and NVD datasets, where both contains CVEs labeled by CWEs with a different manual approach. The evaluation is performed by comparing the results from the proposed algorithm with the CVE instances that have been manually associated with CWE classes by experts in MITRE or NVD, established as the ground truth. We compute the evaluation metrics including precision, recall, and F_1 score to measure the performance of the algorithm after comparing ThreatZoom's results with the ground truth.

3.1   Dataset Specification

There are two datasets considered in the evaluation process: MITRE dataset and NVD dataset. Each dataset consists of a group of CVE instances that have been classified to one or more CWE classes. The classification process is performed independently, so they may agree or disagree based on the different perspectives of the experts. MITRE dataset comprises 2534 CVE instances that are classified to 364 out of 719 CWE classes. It contains 1546 CVE instances such that, each instance is assigned to one CWE class, while each instance in the remaining CVE instances have been assigned to two or more different CWE classes. On the other hand, NVD datasets contains more labeled CVEs compared with MITRE. However, both data repositories have some major differences. Here, w dig more deeply into the characteristic of both datasets:

1. NVD delivers coarse-grain classification, which provides more general categories for CVEs comparing with MITRE's fine-grain classification.
2. NVD uses the top 116 out of 719 most common CWEs in their classification, while this number for MITRE is 364.
3. Despite MITRE, NVD does not follow the CWE hierarchy in which each CVE is classified to exactly one CWE ID.
4. NVD does not follow MITRE's classification. Out of 2534 CVEs classified by MITRE, NVD has classified only 1092 of them to a particular CWE. Considering all the nodes in the full path MITRE classification for these 1092 CVEs, NVD's classification exists in this path only in 273 cases, (Fig. 6).
5. About 40% of the CVEs are classified to either *Other* or *Categorical CWE*. *Other* represents an unknown CWE class, and *Categorical CWE* is a superclass that covers multiple CWEs.

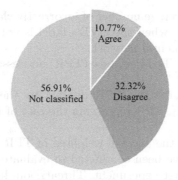

Fig. 6. MITRE and NVD classification comparison

3.2 Experiments

A comparative evaluation experiments have been conducted to evaluate the performance of the CVE-to-CWE classification algorithm on the labeled CVE sets provided by MITRE and NVD. The evaluation compares the estimated candidate list generated by the algorithm with the CWE class associated with the CVE instance in two different levels namely coarse-grain and fine-grain which are defined as follows:

- **Coarse-grain**: if ThreatZoom outputs one or a sequence of CWE classes which are not necessarily full path toward the leaf, it is considered as coarse-grain classification. In this scenario, ThreatZoom may not be able to successfully offer the entire path to the leaf but it provides few candidates for a CVE among existing CWEs. Few candidates simply mean part of the full path that is still very important to learn high-level information about the vulnerability.
- **Fine-grain**: if ThreatZoom successfully predict the full path to the leaf, it is a fine-grain classification.

The performance of the ThreatZoom is evaluated by three standard measurements in both fine-grain and coarse-grain classification [14]:

- *Accuracy*: It computes the number of instances that are correctly classified, divided by the total number of instances. For each input CVE, the neural network offers one or more CWE candidates at each level. According to MITRE, if the CVE label is included in the CWE candidates it is considered as correct classification. This indicates that the algorithm provides a more detailed classification along the right path for classifying the CVE. This can be explained in part by either the CWE sub-class was created by MITRE experts after this CVE has been classified and they classified similar CVEs to this new CWE sub-class, or there is a disagreement between experts, some consider it is acceptable to stop classification, while others classified similar ones to the deeper levels.

- *Error*: It measures average number of incorrectly classified instances. Incorrect classification happens when the CVE's label is not included in CWE candidates generated by the neural network.

- *Recall*: Recall or True Positive Rate (TPR) addresses the average of correct classification per class.

- *Precision*: It represents the TPR divided by the sum of the TPR and False Rate Positive (FPR). FPR represents the rate of the instance mistakenly classified.

- *F-score*: It measures the average weighted of TPR and precision.

Three experiments have been conducted to evaluate different aspects of the proposed design. In the first experiment, ThreatZoom has been evaluated without any modification. According to the results depicted in Table 1, ThreatZoom successfully results 92% and 94% accuracy in fine-grain and coarse-grain classification in the NVD set. In addition, it shows 75% and 90% classification accuracy in MITRE dataset. Although there is 17% gap in accuracy of classification between NVD and MITRE, ThreatZoom shows it is able to learn short corpus and imbalance data with a promising performance, and it can perform even better if it receives more training examples from MITRE.

In the second experiment, the hierarchical neural network framework is replaced by a regular flat one such that the neural network considers all the classes in a one-shot classification process regardless of their hierarchy and initialized the weights randomly during the training process. In the third experiment, the single-layer neural network classifier is replaced by a two-layer one, and the neural network weights initialized randomly during the training process. These experiments have been conducted using MITRE and NVD datasets. For the MITRE dataset, 2131 CVEs are used for training, and 403 CVEs are used for testing. For the NVD dataset, 50000 CVEs have been used in the experiment, 40000 CVEs for training, and 10000 CVEs for testing. In each test, the classification accuracy of the testing is evaluated. In the training process, the maximum number of allowed iterations is set to 500. Figure 7 represents the accuracy of ThreatZoom in all three experiments. The results show that the proposed ThreatZoom approach outperforms all other approaches in classifying CVE instances to their corresponding CWE classes. The proposed ThreatZoom scores 75% and 92% for MITRE and NVD, respectively. The one layer-flat framework scores 18% and 29% for MITRE and NVD, respectively. The model with a two-layer neural network classifier scores 8% and 32% for MITRE and NVD, respectively.

Similarly, ThreatZoom shows a higher performance when it has a single-layer neural network classifier, compared to the two-layer one. This can be explained by the two layers neural network has a lot more weights to learn compared to the single-layer one. This may cause an over-fitting problem when the size of the training is relatively small compared to the number of weights. In this case, the neural network learns the samples correctly in the training set while it is unable to predict correctly unseen ones. The accuracy of the two-layer neural network over the training set is 87% and 92% for MITRE and NVD, respectively,

Table 1. ThreatZoom fine-grain and coarse-grain classification performance over MITRE and NVD datasets

	MITRE (fine-grain, coarse grain)	NVD (fine-grain, coarse grain)
Accuracy	0.75, 0.90	0.92, 0.94
Error rate	0.25, 0.1	0.08, 0.06
Recall	0.73, 0.88	0.90, 0.90
Precision	0.75, 0.88	0.91, 0.93
F1-score	0.74, 0.88	0.89, 0.91

while it is very low on the testing set, i.e., 8% and 32% for MITRE and NVD, respectively. The accuracy of the two-layer neural network is high for NVD compared to MITRE that is because it has a more extensive training set, but it is still not enough to learn all the weights.

ThreatZoom performs better when it has a hierarchical neural network architecture compared to the flat one. The flat neural network uses one classifier to learn the general and the detailed features of all the CWE classes at once. Learning general features deemphasize details to distinguish between dissimilar classes, while learning detailed features deemphasize general features to differentiate similar CWE classes, hence the confusion. On the other hand, in the hierarchical framework, each classifier learns the features that distinguish the CWE classes, which are children to its node in the hierarchical tree, only. Hence, the high performance of the proposed ThreatZoom.

4 Discussion

In this section, we define different scenarios to point out the advantages and practicability of ThreatZoom in dealing with a variety of challenges.

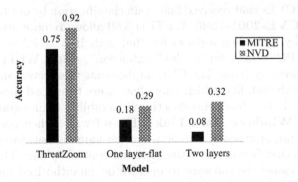

Fig. 7. Comparing ThreatZoom with other models in fine-grain classification performance

4.1   ThreatZoom and Unlabeled CVEs

ThreatZoom is tested by unlabeled CVEs, and the results are evaluated by domain experts to analyze performance consistency. For example, CVE-2019-7632 represents *"LifeSize Team, Room, Passport, and Networker 220 devices allow Authenticated Remote OS Command Injection, as demonstrated by shell meta-characters in the support/mtusize.php mtu_size parameter. The lifesize default password for the cli account may sometimes be used for authentication"*. The proposed classification algorithm result for this CVE is the following sequence: CWE-707 → CWE-74 → CWE-77 → CWE-78. Table 2 shows the ID and the description of the CVE and classified CWEs. The key point in this vulnerability is allowing Remote OS Command Injection. The Command Injection is a type of attack which executes arbitrary commands on the host operating system via a vulnerable application. Thus, the attacker-supplied operating system commands that are usually executed with the privileges of the vulnerable application. Regarding this definition, from the high-level perspective, the Command Injection can be exploited under no or improper enforcement of the password, which is the *lifesize default password* in this CVE. Hence, the CWE-707 clearly reflects this weakness of the system in this context. In the next level, the CWE-74 clearly addresses the *injection*, which is the main action in this CVE. *Command Injection* and finally the *OS Command Injection* are the more specific definition of the *injection* that are explained in CWE-77 and CWE-78.

4.2   More Fine-Grain Classification by ThreatZoom

Reported results show not only ThreatZoom performs as good as the MITRE and NVD engineers, who are well-trained for this task, but also it accumulates their experience to offer even more fine-grain CWEs. Figure 8 shows our approach obtains more fine-grain classification for about 47% and 95% of those CVEs that were correctly matched by MITRE and NVD, respectively. To validate these results, we used our domain expertise to manually inspect 100 randomly selected CVEs that received fine-grain classification by our tool. For example, consider **"CVE-2001-1386**: WFTPD 3.00 allows remote attackers to read arbitrary files by uploading a (link) file that ends in a '.lnk.' extension, which bypasses WFTPD's check for a ".lnk" extension", where WFTPD is an FTP server for Windows systems. The CVE implies that this server contains a directory traversal vulnerability, which may allow users to upload files with a name extension '.lnk'. ThreatZoom classifies this vulnerability to fine-grain class, which is **"CWE-65 (Windows Hard Link)**: The software, when opening a file or directory, does not sufficiently handle when the name is associated with a hard link to a target that is outside of the intended control sphere. This could allow an attacker to cause the software to operate on unauthorized files". It clearly addresses the *windows-based software* flaw that *does not properly validate the name* of the uploaded file that causes unauthorized operation over the data. This CWE is accurate and more specific than the MITRE classification which

Table 2. Example of an unlabeled CVE (CVE-2019-7632) and neural network classification result

ID	Description
CVE-2019-7632	LifeSize Team, Room, Passport, and Networker 220 devices allow Authenticated Remote OS Command Injection, as demonstrated by shell meta-characters in the support/mtusize.php mtu_size parameter. The lifesize default password for the cli account may sometimes be used for authentication
CWE-707: Improper Enforcement of Message or Data Structure	The software does not enforce or incorrectly enforces that structured messages or data are well-formed before being read from an upstream component or sent to a downstream component
CWE-74: Injection	The software constructs all or part of a command, data structure, or record using externally-influenced input from an upstream component, but it does not neutralize or incorrectly neutralizes special elements that could modify how it is parsed or interpreted when it is sent to a downstream component
CWE-77: Command Injection	The software constructs all or part of a command using externally-influenced input from an upstream component, but it does not neutralize or incorrectly neutralizes special elements that could modify the intended command when it is sent to a downstream component
CWE-78: OS Command Injection	The software constructs all or part of an OS command using externally-influenced input from an upstream component, but it does not neutralize or incorrectly neutralizes special elements that could modify the intended OS command when it is sent to a downstream component

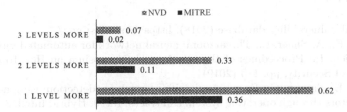

Fig. 8. More fine-grain classification of ThreatZoom over MITRE and NVD classification

is "**CWE-59 (Improper Link Resolution Before File Access ('Link Following'))**: The software attempts to access a file based on the filename, but it does not properly prevent that filename from identifying a link or shortcut that resolves to an unintended resource".

5   Conclusion and Future Work

There are continuous efforts by various organizations to provide a quality CVE-to-CWE classification to enable a deep understanding of vulnerabilities and facilitate proactive threat defense. However, all existing efforts are mainly manual and thereby do not cope with the rate of CVE generation. This paper presents an automated technique for fine-grain classification of CVE instances to CWE classes. To this end, we discuss the existing challenges and shortcomings and introduce ThreatZoom as a novel blend of text mining techniques and neural networks in order to overcome problem. To the best of our knowledge, ThreatZoom is the first automated system that addresses existing challenges and limitations of classifying CVEs to CWEs. Our approach is rigorously evaluated using datasets provided by MITRE and NVD. The accuracy of classifying CVE instances to their correct CWE classes using the MITRE dataset is 75% and 90% for fine-grain and coarse-grain classification, respectively, and 92% for NVD dataset. In many cases, our approach obtains a more in-depth fine-grain classification for 36% for MITRE, and 62% for NVD, as verified by domain experts. This tool is already being developed to leverage word embedding, and deep neural networks to (1) better classify CVEs to CWEs following MITRE standards, (2) extract threat actions out of CTI reports, (3) automatically calculate threat severity scores, and (4) find the potential course of action mitigations and detection, accordingly.

Acknowledgement. This research was supported in part by the Office of Naval Research (ONR) and National Science Foundation (NSF). Any opinions, findings, conclusions or recommendations stated in this material are those of the authors and do not necessarily reflect the views of the funding sources.

References

1. National vulnerability database (2018). https://nvd.nist.gov/
2. Aghaei, E., Al-Shaer, E.: Threatzoom: neural network for automated vulnerability mitigation. In: Proceedings of the 6th Annual Symposium on Hot Topics in the Science of Security, pp. 1–3 (2019)
3. Aghaei, E., Serpen, G.: Ensemble classifier for misuse detection using n-gram feature vectors through operating system call traces. Int. J. Hybrid Intell. Syst. **14**(3), 141–154 (2017)
4. Aghaei, E., Serpen, G.: Host-based anomaly detection using eigentraces feature extraction and one-class classification on system call trace data. J. Inf. Assur. Secur. (JIAS) **14**(4), 106–117 (2019)
5. Corporate, M.: Common vulnerabilities and exposures (2018). https://cve.mitre.org/
6. Corporate, M.: Common weakness enumaration (2018). https://cwe.mitre.org/
7. Egghe, L.: The distribution of n-grams. Scientometrics **47**(2), 237–252 (2000). https://doi.org/10.1023/A:1005634925734
8. Khreisat, L.: A machine learning approach for Arabic text classification using n-gram frequency statistics. J. Inf. **3**(1), 72–77 (2009). https://doi.org/10.1016/j.joi.2008.11.005
9. Na, S., Kim, T., Kim, H.: A study on the classification of common vulnerabilities and exposures using naïve bayes. BWCCA 2016. LNDECT, vol. 2, pp. 657–662. Springer, Cham (2017). https://doi.org/10.1007/978-3-319-49106-6_65
10. Neuhaus, S., Zimmermann, T.: Security trend analysis with CVE topic models. In: Proceedings of the 2010 IEEE 21st International Symposium on Software Reliability Engineering, ISSRE 2010, pp. 111–120. IEEE Computer Society, Washington (2010). https://doi.org/10.1109/ISSRE.2010.53
11. Ogada, K., Mwangi, W., Cheruiyot, W.: N-gram based text categorization method for improved data mining. J. Inf. Eng. Appl. **5**(8), 35–43 (2015)

12. Rehman, S., Mustafa, K.: Software design level vulnerability classification model. Int. J. Comput. Sci. Secur. (IJCSS) **6**(4), 235–255 (2012)
13. Rennie, J.D.M., Shih, L., Teevan, J., Karger, D.R.: Tackling the poor assumptions of naive bayes text classifiers. In: Proceedings of the Twentieth International Conference on International Conference on Machine Learning, ICML2003, pp. 616–623. AAAI Press (2003)
14. Serpen, G., Aghaei, E.: Host-based misuse intrusion detection using PCA feature extraction and KNN classification algorithms. Intell. Data Anal. **22**(5), 1101–1114 (2018)

Detecting Dictionary Based AGDs Based on Community Detection

Qianying Shen and Futai Zou[✉]

Shanghai Jiaotong University, Shanghai, China
{sjtusqy,zft}@sjtu.edu.cn

Abstract. Domain generation algorithms (DGA) are widely used by malware families to realize remote control. Researchers have tried to adopt deep learning methods to detect algorithmically generated domains (AGD) automatically based on only domain strings alone. Usually, such methods analyze the structure and semantic features of domain strings since simple AGDs show great difference in these two aspects. Among various types of AGDs, dictionary-based AGDs are unique for its semantic similarity to normal domains, which makes such detections based on only domain strings difficult. In this paper, we observe that the relationship between domains generated based on a same dictionary shows graphical features. We focus on the detection of dictionary-based AGDs and proposes Word-Map which is based on community detection algorithm to detect dictionary-based AGDs. Word-Map achieved an accuracy above 98.5% and recall rate above 99.0% on testing sets.

Keywords: Algorithmically generated domains · Community detection · Machine learning

1 Introduction

Algorithmically generated domains (AGDs) refer to a group of domains generated in batches based a string of random seeds [1]. According to different generation algorithms, AGDs can be roughly divided into four categories: arithmetic based, hashing based, permutation based and word dictionary based [2]. The first three types of AGDS are often in forms of a random combination of letters and numbers, which is obviously different from the normal domain names in aspects of lexical and semantic characteristics. Dictionary based AGDs discussed in this paper are generated from a random combination of commonly used English words, the lexical and semantic characteristics of which show little difference with normal domains.

In this paper, a new method named Word-Map is proposed to solve the problem that dictionary-based AGDs are difficult to detect using lexical and semantic characteristics. Word-Map is designed to achieve two effects: actively mine DGA dictionaries and

This work is supported by the National Key Research and Development Program of China (No.2017YFB0802300).

© ICST Institute for Computer Sciences, Social Informatics and Telecommunications Engineering 2020
Published by Springer Nature Switzerland AG 2020. All Rights Reserved
N. Park et al. (Eds.): SecureComm 2020, LNICST 335, pp. 42–48, 2020.
https://doi.org/10.1007/978-3-030-63086-7_3

accurately detect dictionary-based AGDs. The key idea of Word-Map is to convert the problem of dictionary-based AGDs detection into a community detection problem on a word map which is constructed based on the co-occurrence of words in a certain set of domains. Data used as training set and test set in this paper are composed of Suppobox domains from DGArchive dataset and Alexa Top 1 M domains. Suppobox domains comes from three different dictionaries. Word-Map has achieved good results in testing set. The accuracy and recall rate of Word-map on domains from same DGA dictionaries, domains from different DGA dictionaries and imbalanced dataset is respectively above 98.5% and 99.0%.

2 Methodology

2.1 Word Graph

Word Graph Construction
For a domain string set D = {d1, d2,......, di,......, dn}, we process each domain name by removing the top-level domain string, and only retaining the second-level domain string. Then we get a second-level domain string set S = {s1, s2,......, si,..., sn}. Then we cut each element in S into single English words. A mature tool named Wordninja [3] can be used to solve this problem efficiently. This paper uses Wordninjia to cut the domain strings into words.

For a domain name set D, after domain string splitting, a word set W can be obtained, and each word in the word set is a vertex. These word vertexes will then be connected by edges according to their co-occurrence relationship in D. In this way, for a domain name set D, a word graph G = (V, E) can be obtained.

An example of the composition process is shown below:

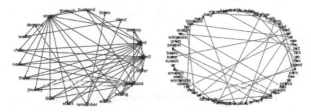

Fig. 1. Word graph of dictionary based AGDs and Alexa domains

Fifty domain strings are respectively randomly chosen from the dictionary based AGDs dataset which are from the same dictionary and Alexa domains dataset. As shown in Fig. 1, there are 21 word nodes and 100 directed edges in DGA-Graph, while there are 72 word nodes and 60 directed edges in Alexa-graph. We can see that the average degree of vertexes in Alexa-graph is less than AGD-Graph. It's because some domains is too short to be cut, therefore becoming isolated vertex in the word graph. It can be intuitively observed that for equivalent amount of dictionary based AGDs and Alexa domains, dictionary based AGDs will be cut into fewer word vertexes, however dictionary based

AGDs word vertexes of are more closely connected, and the average degree of vertexes is higher. This shows that the word vertexes obtained from dictionary based AGDs are more closely related, which makes them easier to be classified into a community

2.2 Community Detection on Word Graph

Introduction of Infomap

The key idea of Word-Map is to convert the detection of dictionary-based AGDs into a community detection problem on word graphs. The key step is to use the Infomap [4] algorithm to perform community detection on word graphs.

Suppose there are M vertexes, which are divided into m communities Infomap. Formula (2) [5] describes the average code length of each step of a random walk on the graph after community division. $q_\curvearrowright$ represents the proportion of community codes in all codes. $H(\mathcal{Q})$ represents the average length of community codes, and $P_\circlearrowleft^i$ represents the proportion of vertexes codes and leaving action codes belonging to community i in all codes. $H(\mathcal{P}^i)$ represents the average length of all vertex codes and leaving action codes of community i. L(M) is the average length of each step of random walk on the graph after community division. Obviously, obtaining the best code is equivalent to minimizing L(M).

$$L(M) = q_\curvearrowright H(\mathcal{Q}) + \sum\nolimits_{i=1}^{m} P_\circlearrowleft^i H\left(\mathcal{P}^i\right) \tag{1}$$

Words Community

Following figures are examples of community detection results of word graphs obtained from dictionary based AGDs, Alexa domains, and mixed domains.

Fig. 2. Communities detected from Alexa-graph

Fig. 3. Communities detected from AGD-graph

As shown in Fig. 2, 46 communities were detected on the word graph obtained from 50 Alexa domains as shown in Fig. 2. The largest community is composed of 6 blue colored vertexes in the center of Fig. 4, of which the total degrees is 14 and the average degree is 2.33. For other communities, The number of vertexes is 1 (isolated vertex), 2 (word vertexes obtained from a same domain string) or 3. It can be seen that words obtained by splitting Alexa domains have no obvious clustering characteristics.

As shown in Fig. 3, 2 communities were detected on the word graph obtained from 50 dictionary based AGDs as shown in Fig. 1. The two communities are composed of 40 and 24 vertexes respectively, of which the total degrees is 739 and 261 respectively and the average degree is 18.48 and 10.88 respectively. Compared to Fig. 2, it can be seen that words obtained by splitting dictionary based AGDs have obvious clustering characteristic. Also, there are obvious differences in aspects of the number of vertexes, the total degrees of vertexes, and the average degree of vertexes between AGD communities and Alexa communities.

Fig. 4. Communities detected from the word graph of mixed domains. (Color figure online)

Mix the 50 Alexa domains and 50 dictionary based AGDs mentioned before and get the word graph of the mixed domains. 48 communities were detected on the word graph. The biggest two communities(blue and green colored vertexes in the center of Fig. 4) have 40 and 24 vertexes respectively. Their total degrees are 739 and 261, and their average degrees are 18.48 and 10.88. The number of vertexes of the remaining communities are all no bigger than 6, and their total degrees are no bigger than 14, while average degrees no bigger than 2.5. Comparing Fig. 4 with Fig. 2 and Fig. 3, it can be seen that dictionary based AGDs and Alexa domains have been effectively distinguished from each other.

It can be seen intuitively that there are the several differences between dictionary based AGD community and Alexa community: 1) The number of vertexes in dictionary based AGD communities is much bigger than that of Alexa communities. 2) The total and average degrees of the vertexes of dictionary based AGD are much bigger than those Alexa communities. Therefore, after community detection, these two features can be collected to train a decision tree to classify whether a community is dictionary based AGD community or not (Fig. 5).

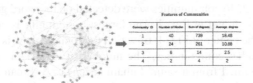

Fig. 5. Extract features of word Communities

3 Experiments and Results

3.1 Dataset

Dataset used in the experiments contains a total of 1,313,571 dictionary based AGDs domains and 1,000,000 benign domains. Dictionary based AGDs come from the Suppobox domains in the DGArchive dataset [6], and benign domains are chosen from Alexa Top 1 M domains.

Ground Truth Data As shown in Table 1., we randomly select 50,000 Alexa domains and 150,000 dictionary based AGDs to make up the training set, where the dictionary based AGDs are composed of words from three different dictionaries named D1, D2, and D3. We randomly select 50,000 Alexa domains and 150,000 dictionary based AGDs from the rest data to make up the testing set, where the dictionary based AGDs are also composed of words from three different dictionaries named D1, D2, and D3.

3.2 Experiments

We designed three different experiments to verify the performance of Word-map on domains from the same DGA dictionary, domains from different DGA dictionaries and imbalanced data sets.

The first group of experiments verifies Word-map's performance on domains from the same DGA dictionary with 3 round independent experiments as shown in Table 1.

Table 1. Experiment on domains from same DGA dictionaries

Dataset	Training set				Testing set			
	Alexa	D1	D2	D3	Alexa	D1	D2	D3
Round 1	50,000	50,000	0	0	50,000	50,000	0	0
Round 2	50,000	0	50,000	0	50,000	0	50,000	0
Round 3	50,000	0	0	50,000	50,000	0	0	50,000

The results of three independent experiments are shown in Table 2.

Table 2. Performance on domains from same DGA dictionaries

	Round 1	Round 2	Round 3
Accuracy	99.7%	99.5%	99.8%
Recall rate	100.0%	99.7%	99.9%

The second group of experiments verifies Word-map's performance on domains from different DGA dictionaries with 3 round independent experiments (Table 3).

Table 3. Experiment on domains from different DGA dictionaries

Dataset	Training set				Testing set			
	Alexa	D1	D2	D3	Alexa	D1	D2	D3
Round 1	50,000	50,000	50,000	0	50,000	0	0	50,000
Round 2	50,000	50,000	0	50,000	50,000	0	50,000	0
Round 3	50,000	0	50,000	50,000	50,000	50,000	0	0

The results of three independent experiments are shown in Table 4.

Table 4. Performance on domains from different DGA dictionaries

	Round 1	Round 2	Round 3
Accuracy	99.3%	99.4%	99.1%
Recall rate	99.7%	99.9%	99.6%

The third group of experiments verifies the performance of Word-map on imbalanced dataset with 3 round of independent experiments as shown in Table 5.

Table 5. Experiment on imbalanced dataset

Dataset	Training set				Testing set			
	Alexa	D1	D2	D3	Alexa	D1	D2	D3
Round 1	50,000	500	500	500	50,000	500	500	500
Round 2	50,000	500	500	0	50,000	0	0	500
Round 3	50,000	500	0	0	50,000	500	0	0

The results of three independent experiments are shown in Table 6.

Table 6. Performance on imbalanced dataset

	Round 1	Round 2	Round 3
Accuracy	98.5%	98.8%	98.6%
Recall rate	99.2%	99.0%	99.1%

Based on the results of the three rounds of experiments, it can be seen that when DGA dictionaries are known in advance, Word-map can accurately detect dictionary based AGDs. The performance of Word-map is not that good when AGDs are from different dictionaries, but its accuracy and recall rates still remains above 99%, indicating that Word-map has sufficient ability to mine new dictionaries. As to imbalanced data sets, the accuracy and recall rate of Word-map are also kept above 98.5% and 99.0% respectively, indicating that Word-map can adapt well to the actual scenarios where the number of dictionary based AGDs is far small than the number of benign domain names.

References

1. Plohmann, D., Yakdan, K., Klatt, M., et al.: A comprehensive measurement study of domain generating malware. In: 25th {USENIX} Security Symposium ({USENIX} Security 16), pp. 263–278 (2016)
2. Sood, A.K., Zeadally, S.: A taxonomy of domain-generation algorithms. IEEE Secur. Priv. **14**(4), 46–53 (2016)
3. wordninja, https://github.com/keredson/wordninja
4. Rosvall, M., Bergstrom, C.T.: Maps of information flow reveal community structure in complex networks. arXiv preprint physics.soc-ph/0707.0609 (2007)
5. Rosvall, M., Axelsson, D., Bergstrom, C.T.: The map equation. Eur. Phys. J. Spec. Topics **178**(1), 13–23 (2009)
6. Plohmann, D., Yakdan, K., Klatt, M., Bader, J., Gerhards-Padilla, E.: A comprehensive measurement study of domain generating malware. In: 25th USENIX Security Symposium, pp. 263–278 (2016)

On the Accuracy of Measured Proximity of Bluetooth-Based Contact Tracing Apps

Qingchuan Zhao$^{(\boxtimes)}$, Haohuang Wen, Zhiqiang Lin, Dong Xuan,
and Ness Shroff

Department of Computer Science and Engineering, The Ohio State University,
Columbus, USA
{zhao.2708,wen.423,lin.3021,xuan.3,shroff.11}@osu.edu

Abstract. A large number of Bluetooth-based mobile apps have been developed recently to help tracing close contacts of contagious COVID-19 individuals. These apps make decisions based on whether two users are in close proximity (*e.g.*, within 6 ft) according to the distance measured from the received signal strength (*RSSI*) of Bluetooth. This paper provides a detailed study of the current practice of *RSSI*-based distance measurements among contact tracing apps by analyzing various factors that can affect the *RSSI* value and how each app has responded to them. Our analysis shows that configurations for the signal transmission power (*TxPower*) and broadcasting intervals that affect *RSSI* vary significantly across different apps and a large portion of apps do not consider these affecting factors at all, or with quite limited tuning.

Keywords: Bluetooth · BLE · Proximity measurement · COVID-19 · Contact tracing

1 Introduction

COVID-19 has created an unprecedented social and economic crisis across the globe. As of August 2020, there are more than 25 million infected patients. and over 840 thousand deaths worldwide. Since COVID-19 will not disappear shortly, practical techniques must be used to fight this pandemic before vaccines are available. Contact tracing, i.e., identifying people who have been in close contact with contagious individuals, has been such a practical technique for a long time. However, existing contact tracing is manual, and is hard to scale to large and rapidly moved populations. Further, manual tracing may result in delays, which could limit its utility. Therefore, recently numerous digital contact tracing systems have been developed and deployed across the globe, by using a variety of sources including locations measured from cellular networks, WiFi hotspots, or GPS, and cryptographic tokens exchanged via Bluetooth Low Energy (BLE).

Among the digital contact tracing systems, BLE has emerged as a promising solution [21] due to its ubiquity (almost everyone holds a smartphone today),

N. Park et al. (Eds.): SecureComm 2020, LNICST 335, pp. 49–60, 2020.
https://doi.org/10.1007/978-3-030-63086-7_4

availability (almost all smartphones have enabled Bluetooth by default), and privacy preserving (e.g., no real location is involved). The idea of using BLE for contact tracing is straightforward. When two users encounter, contact tracing apps automatically exchange information with each other to record such a contact event for both users. A contact event, in general, includes cryptography generated random tokens that represent users, timestamps for duration estimation, and information for distance measurements. In particular, most BLE contact tracing apps use the received signal strength indicator ($RSSI$) of the Bluetooth for distance measurements. In addition, for COVID-19, a close contact refers to a user who has been in within 6 ft range of a contagious individual for more than 15 min according to the recent CDC guidelines [14]. As such, the effectiveness of the Bluetooth-based contact tracing crucially depends on the accuracy of the measured distance from $RSSI$.

Unfortunately, in practice, numerous factors can affect the $RSSI$ that can make the distance measurement inaccurate, such as the power of antenna used for broadcasting (i.e., the $TxPower$) and the obstacles blocking transmission paths. Moreover, Bluetooth-based proximity tracing can also raise false positives because of the potential misinterpretation of various scenarios. For example, a proximity tracing system may interpret two users have a contact even if they are separated by a solid wall, where the risk of infection is much lower than the risk indicated by the measured distance.

Therefore, it is imperative to study how current Bluetooth-based mobile contact tracing systems perform the proximity measurement. To this end, we exhaustively collect 20 Bluetooth-based mobile contact tracing apps from various public sources (e.g., [5,22,31]), systematically inspect the affecting factors that impact the $RSSI$, and examine how each app calculates the proximity distance. Our analysis results have revealed a number of findings:

- Advertising behaviors are highly customized by different mobile apps and the combination of the level of $TxPower$ and advertising interval is inconsistent across mobile apps : our analysis have discovered 8 different combinations of the advertising interval and the level of $TxPower$ from 20 mobile apps (Sect. 3).
- A large portion of apps do not have an accurate and reliable measured distance from Bluetooth: (i) our analysis has identified that 4 apps just use $RSSI$ for distance measurement without any tuning, (ii) 60% of these apps do not consider affecting factors from hardware specifications, and (iii) none of them considers environmental factors (Sect. 4).

2 Background

2.1 BLE-based Contact Tracing

Bluetooth Low Energy (BLE) is a wireless communication technology that is designed to provide basic Bluetooth functionality while consuming considerably low amount of energy. Because of its low energy consumption and its wide availability in almost every smartphone, BLE is considered a promising solution for mobile contact tracing [21].

Using BLE for contact tracing between smartphones is a complicated process. First, a BLE-based contact tracing mobile app will need to be installed. Then, the app will periodically generate a random token for each user as an identifier and constantly advertise this token (which works like a beacon) or BLE-contact tracing service information (in which establishing connection to exchange information is required) to nearby smartphones. Meanwhile, the app also keeps scanning for other smartphones. When two smartphone users encounter each other, the apps on two phones will automatically exchange the necessary information to record this *contact event*, such as the timestamp, the identifier of users, and most importantly, the data used for distance measurements [17]. In addition, data can be exchanged via device connections or by directly reading from the advertising packets. When a user is tested positive, the app will immediately inform all other users who have close contact with this individual. This exposure notification process is implemented differently according to the different architectures, *i.e.*, centralized and decentralized architecture.

- **Centralized.** In a centralized architecture, users receive exposure notifications from the server that remotely determines the risk of infection. In particular, a centralized service will require users who have tested positive to upload their recent contact events to the central server. Then the server will analyze these events to identify all other users who have been exposed to this individual, and notify each of them according to the user contact information (e.g., cell phone number) that is usually collected at user registration. There are several privacy preserving protocols using this type of architecture, such as BlueTrace [4] and ROBERT [24].
- **Decentralized.** In contrast, in a decentralized architecture, it is the client, instead of the server, that determines its own risk of infection. Only the contact events of the contagious users are shared on a public database, and each client will synchronize its own data with the database periodically. Whenever a synchronization is accomplished, the client app will locally check its own contact events against the updated data to determine its own risk of infection. Many privacy preserving contact tracing protocols such as DP-3T [28] and Notification Exposure [3] use such a decentralized architecture.

2.2 Proximity Measurement in BLE-based Contact Tracing

RSSI -based Proximity Measurement. For two BLE devices, their proximity measurement depends on the received signal strength from each other, also known as *RSSI*, which is proportional to the distance of signal transmission in theory. However, in practice, *RSSI* can be impacted by many factors that may result in inaccurate proximity measurements, and these factors can be classified into internal factors and external factors.

(I) Internal Factors Affecting *RSSI*. Factors within a Bluetooth device including the specifications of both hardware and software can influence the *RSSI* value [9]. With respect to smartphones, the internal hardware factors are the Bluetooth chipset and its antenna layout, and the key software factors include both configurations of the operating system and the mobile app itself [6].

- **Factors from Hardware—chipset and antenna**: A Bluetooth chipset determines the maximum transmission power of the signal and maps the received signal strength to *RSSI* values. Such mapping is highly customized by manufacturers [9] that indicates the same signal can be interpreted as heavily different *RSSI* values across different chipsets. Additionally, the antenna layout, orientation, as well as the capability of data transmission can dramatically affect the strength of emitting and receiving signals [7].
- **Factors from Software—OS and App**: Both Android and iOS can significantly change the power consumption of BLE operations [6], *e.g.*, low battery mode, that could impact the transmission power and the *RSSI* value. In addition to the OS, mobile apps can use system APIs to configure its broadcasting attributes, such as *TxPower*, broadcasting interval, and duration. These attributes can also impact the reliability of *RSSI* values.

(II) External Factors Affecting *RSSI*. In addition to the internal factors, factors outside the device can also influence the *RSSI* value. At a high level, these factors can be classified into two categories: invisible radio waves and visible physical objects.

- **Invisible radio waves**: Bluetooth signals can be interfered by other types of radio waves. For example, if WiFi is mis-configured to use channels that overlap with channels used in Bluetooth, both signals may interfere with each other [12] that can make the obtained *RSSI* value less accurate.
- **Visible physical obstacles**: Obstacles on the transmission path can result in fluctuated *RSSI*. In particular, different materials, such as woods, water, and glass, as well as different textures on surface of objects can lead to different levels of signal interference, such as absorption, interference, and diffraction, that may make the *RSSI* unstable [11,12].

3   Analysis of BLE Software Configurations

In this section, we analyze the affecting factors of proximity accuracy from mobile apps. Ideally, we would like to analyze all affecting factors listed in Sect. 2.2. However, it is extremely challenging to analyze the affecting factors from the operating system because of their different battery management strategies that rarely quantitatively clarify the restrictions of BLE usage. Additionally, the affecting factors from hardware specifications have been studied before in TraceTogether [20]. As such, we focus on the available configurations in mobile apps that control either the settings of advertising or the data included in advertising packets.

BLE Advertising Settings. The settings of advertising determine how a device broadcasts BLE advertising packets. In total, there are three configurable behaviors (only in Android) that are relevant to proximity measurement.

- **Level of advertising interval**: The advertising interval is configurable in Android apps and it is controlled by the mode of advertising. In total, there are three modes of advertising: (*i*) LOW_POWER (0) mode, which is the default mode and broadcasts packets every 1 s; (*ii*) BALANCED (1) mode, which broadcasts every 250 ms; and (*iii*) LOW_LATENCY (2) mode, which broadcasts every 100 ms [2].
- **Duration of advertising**: While Android apps can constantly broadcast advertising packets until being terminated, they are allowed to limit the broadcasting duration (up to 3 min). The duration of broadcasting is important for receivers to read a reliable signal as more samples for adjustment are supposed to be received in a longer duration.
- **Level of transmission power (*TxPower*)**: This attribute controls the emission power of signals. In general, a stronger *TxPower* can increase the stability of signal in transmission [11]. In Android, there are four levels of *TxPower*: ULTRA_LOW (0), LOW (1), MEDIUM (2), and HIGH (3), where the HIGH level provides the best range of signal visibility and the default level is LOW [2].

Data Included in Advertising Packets. In addition to configuring broadcasting behaviors, apps are also allowed to customize the data carried within their advertising packets. Among a variety of data that can be included in advertising packets, we focus on the data for proximity measurement, *i.e.*, the level of *TxPower*. In addition, this value is crucial to accurately determine the distance between users since the same signal strength can be interpreted as different *RSSI* values given different levels of *TxPower* [10]. In particular, the *TxPower* value can be included in a separate filed or in a general field, which is integrated with other information.

- **_TxPower_ included in the separated field**: Both Android and iOS allow mobile apps to include the level of *TxPower* in a separate field in advertising packets but with different policies. Specifically, iOS apps are required to include this value in advertising packets and Android apps can choose whether to include this value or not.
- **_TxPower_ included in integration**: Other than being included in advertising packet separately, the level of *TxPower* can also be integrated with other information and stored in general data fields, *i.e.*, the field of manufacture data and service data. In addition, while both fields are allowed for customization in Android, only service data can be customized in iOS.

Table 1. BLE advertising configurations in mobile apps (Note that ∞ represents infinity).

App name	Advertising (Adv.) settings			Adv. Data	
	TxPower	Mode	Duration	Separated	Integrated
COVIDSafe	HIGH	LOW_LATENCY	∞	✔	–
Stopp Corona	HIGH	LOW_LATENCY	∞	✔	–
BeAware	MEDIUM	LOW_POWER	∞	✗	✗
CoronApp	HIGH	LOW_POWER	∞	✔	–
eRouska	MEDIUM	LOW_POWER	∞	–	✗
StopCovid	LOW	BALANCED	∞	✔	–
Aarogya Setu	ULTRA_LOW	LOW_POWER	∞	–	✗
MyTrace	LOW	BALANCED	∞	✗	✗
StopKorona	HIGH	BALANCED	∞	–	✗
Smittestopp	MEDIUM	LOW_POWER	∞	✔	–
Ehteraz	MEDIUM	BALANCED	∞	✗	✗
TraceTogether	HIGH	LOW_LATENCY	∞	✔	-
Mor Chana	MEDIUM	LOW_POWER	∞	–	✗
Hayat Eve Sigar	LOW	BALANCED	∞	✔	–
NHS COVID-19 App	MEDIUM	LOW_POWER	∞	✔	–
Healthy together	ULTRA_LOW	LOW_POWER	∞	✔	–
Bluezone	LOW	LOW_LATENCY	∞	✗	✗
CovidSafePaths	HIGH	LOW_LATENCY	∞	✔	–
Coalition network	HIGH	LOW_LATENCY	∞	–	✗
Covid community alert	HIGH	BALANCED	∞	✗	✗

Results. From 20 apps in our dataset, there are 12 apps that intend to broadcast infinitely until being enforced to close, while 8 have not specified their broadcasting duration. Given the default setting of this attribute is infinity [2], as presented in Table 1, all these apps will constantly broadcast advertising packets. In addition, we have identified that 10 apps have included *TxPower* separately in advertising packets, 5 apps are set to not carry this value in an individual field, and 5 apps have not specified this property. Moreover, neither the manufacturer nor service data fields in the latter 10 apps include *TxPower*.

Observation 1. *All apps in our analysis intend to broadcast advertising packets constantly without time limit and half of them have not included the level of TxPower in advertising packets.*

In terms of advertising interval, we have identified three apps—BeAware, eRouska, and Aarogya Setu—that have not explicitly specified their advertising interval (the default value is lower power mode [2] , while the remaining 17 apps have specified this attribute. Among these 17 apps, there are 6 apps that are set to broadcast advertising packet with minimum intervals, 6 apps that use the balanced mode, and 5 apps that apply the low power mode. Moreover, BeAware, eRouska, and Mor Chana are the only 3 apps that do not explicitly specify their level of *TxPower* in broadcasting (the default value medium will be used in this case). For the remaining 17 apps that specify the *TxPower*, there are 8 apps that specify the highest transmission power, 3 apps that specify it to be medium, 4 apps that set themselves as low level, and 2 apps that apply the lowest level.

Surprisingly, from Table 1, we also observed that the combination of the level of *TxPower* and advertising interval is inconsistent across different apps. In particular, (*i*) among 8 apps that use the high level of *TxPower*, there are 5 apps that broadcast with the minimum interval, 2 apps with medium interval, and 1 app with the maximum interval; (*ii*) among 6 apps using the medium level of *TxPower*, we have identified that 5 apps are set with the maximum broadcasting interval and 1 apps is set with medium interval; (*iii*) for the 4 apps using low *TxPower*, 3 of them broadcast with medium interval and 1 app with the maximum interval; and (*iv*) the remaining 2 apps share the same combination of the lowest level of *TxPower* and the maximum interval.

In general, the combination of *TxPower* and advertising interval can impact the accuracy of *RSSI* value read at receivers [11]. However, in practice, we have not observed a consensus view toward this combination across contact tracing apps. Additionally, the magnitude of the impact on the *RSSI* value from different combinations remains unclear.

Observation 2. *The combination of the level of TxPower and advertising interval is inconsistent across contact tracing apps. Meanwhile, the impact on distance measurement from different combinations is also unclear.*

4   Analysis of Proximity Measurement Approaches

After analyzing the BLE software configurations, we next understand how each app measures the proximity. To this end, we first recognize which type of data is collected in Sect. 4.1, and then uncover how the collected data is used in the proximity measurement in Sect. 4.2.

4.1   Data Collected for Proximity Measurement

The first step to understand how each app measures the distance is to recognize which type of relevant data would be collected. Unfortunately, proximity measurements are rarely mentioned or vaguely expressed in the documentation (*e.g.*, app description and privacy policy) of an app. As such, we need to analyze the code of an app to understand the semantics of its collected data. However, identifying which one is used for proximity measurement is challenging since multiple types of data are processed within an app. Fortunately, we have observed a special feature in BLE-based contact tracing services that can narrow down the scope. That is, the *contact events* will be temporarily stored locally and all necessary data of each event will be stored together as an entry in a database or a local file. Therefore, we focus on the database or file operations, *e.g.*, read and write, of an app to uncover which type of data is collected for proximity measurement.

Table 2. Data collected for distance measurement (Note that ● represents collection).

App name	RSSI	Affecting factors		
		Software	Hardware	Others
COVIDSafe	●	Level of TxPower	modelP; modelC	
CoronApp	●	Level of TxPower	modelP; modelC	
eRouska	●			
StopCovid	●		BuildNumber; Version Manufacturer; Model	
Aarogya Setu	●	Level of TxPower		GPS
StopKorona	●			
Smittestopp	●	Level of TxPower		GPS, Altitude Speed, Accuracy
Ehteraz	●			GPS
TraceTogether	●	Level of TxPower	modelP; modelC	
Mor Chana	●			
NHS COVID-19 App	●	Level of TxPower		
Healthy together	●	Level of TxPower		
Bluezone	●	Level of TxPower		
CovidSafePaths	●	Level of TxPower		
Covid community alert	●		BuildNumber; Version Manufacturer; Model	
Coalition network	●			

Results. We have uncovered the data collected for proximity measurement from 16 apps (note that the rest 4 use native code and reflection to collect data, and we leave them in future work) and present them in Table 2. In addition, we have classified the uncovered data into the following three categories.

- **RSSI**: Our analysis reveals that all 16 apps collect *RSSI* value. In addition, 4 of them collect this value exclusively and the remaining apps collect other types of data such as *TxPower* as well.
- **Affecting Factors**: Our analysis has identified that 9 apps collect the level of *TxPower* and 5 apps gather phone models. Specifically, among these 5 apps, 3 of them collect phone models of senders and receivers, which are required by *BlueTrace* protocol [4], and 2 apps only collect its own (receiver) phone model, which is needed by the AltBeacon library [1] for distance calculation.
- **Other Distance Measurements**: There are 3 apps even collecting GPS coordinates for distance measurement. In particular, unlike Ehteraz and Aarogya Setu that only collect GPS coordinates, Smittestopp also collects altitude, speed, and their degrees of accuracy.

Based on the uncovered data collection from these apps, it would be challenging to obtain an accurate distance. That is, only 5 apps have considered the affecting factors from hardware specifications but the number of specifications is limited. Moreover, 3 apps only use *RSSI* for distance calculation without considering the level of *TxPower*, and none of them considers external affecting factors from the environment, such as having a phone in a pocket.

Observation 3. *Data collection for proximity measurement is inconsistent across different contact tracing apps. Unfortunately, only a few of them consider the affecting factors from hardware specifications, e.g., phone models, some apps do not consider the affecting factors from software configurations, e.g., TxPower, and there is no evidence indicating that external affecting factors have been considered.*

4.2   Data Used in Distance Calculation

In addition to understanding the types of data collected for distance measurement, we also seek to know how such data is exactly used. In this regard, directly checking the formula used for distance calculation is a reliable solution. Because the distance measurement is based on *RSSI*, the formula must use this value in the calculation. As such, we can track the dataflow of *RSSI* value within mobile apps to discover the formula. We follow such an approach in our analysis.

Results. Uncovering this formula from contact tracing apps is challenging. First, in a centralized service, the formula is supposed to exist on the server side whose code is inaccessible to us. Additionally, in a decentralized service, it is also non-trivial to uncover the distance calculation formula from mobile apps because of a variety of obfuscations on the code (*e.g.*, 4 out 6 decentralized apps in our dataset use obfuscation), from variable and method renaming to using reflections. In the end, with our best effort, we have uncovered the distance calculation formula from three apps. Interestingly, they use the same distance measurement model as the following:

$$(\frac{RSSI}{TxPower})^{Coef_1} \times Coef_2 + Coef_3$$

where the three coefficients are used to tune the accuracy for different hardware specifications. Among the apps we analyzed, StopCovid and Covid Community Alert use the AltBeacon library [1] for proximity measurement whose coefficients for 4 phone models are available online[1].

Observation 4. *Different contact tracing apps may use the same formula to measure the proximity. However, their tuning is quite limited to only a few phone models or without tuning at all.*

5   Discussion

From our analysis, a large portion of BLE-based contact tracing apps do not have an accurate and reliable proximity measurement from Bluetooth.

A practical and effective solution to improve the accuracy could be tuning *RSSI* for different phone models, because different models provide a variety of

---

[1] https://s3.amazonaws.com/android-beacon-library/android-distance.json.

BLE hardware specifications and their impacts on the robustness of the *RSSI* values are significant. Fortunately, some groups (e.g., OpenTrace [6] have started conducting experiments and collecting data for this tuning. However, only a limited number of phone models have been involved. More efforts are needed to cover more phone models.

Additionally, we have identified a variety of advertising behaviors with different combinations of the advertising interval and the power of transmission. Unfortunately, it is unclear whether these different behaviors can impact the *RSSI* value as well as their corresponding magnitude of influence. Further studies in this direction could help identify an effective BLE advertising behavior that improves the robustness of *RSSI* values.

6   Related Work

Recently, there are multiple privacy-preserving contact tracing protocols having been proposed. Some of them [4,8] are centralized and some [3,15,19,23,28] are decentralized. Accordingly, there is also a body of research [13] analyzing the potential privacy issues in these protocols. In addition, many studies have focused on the analysis of COVID-19 themed apps. For instance, several studies [16,29] focus on privacy issues of one specific contact tracing app (*e.g.*, Trace-Together [16]), and the rest (*e.g.*, [18,25,27,30]) present empirical analysis with these apps. Similarly, there are also many efforts (*e.g.*, [26,32]) that focus on security issues in BLE mobile apps in general. Unlike these efforts that aim at analyzing privacy and security issues, we focus on the accuracy of proximity measurement in contact tracing apps.

7   Conclusion

To fight COVID-19 pandemic, a large number of BLE proximity tracing apps have been developed and deployed. These apps use the received signal strength indicator, *RSSI*, to measure the proximity between two smartphones. However, multiple factors can impact the *RSSI* value that makes the proximity measurement challenging. In this paper, we provide a detailed study on the accuracy of *RSSI*-based proximity measurements that are applied in 20 BLE-based contact tracing apps. Our study has revealed that different apps configure a variety of BLE broadcasting behaviors and only a small portion of them have tuned *RSSI* to improve the accuracy of measured proximity.

Acknowledgement. This work was supported in part by the National Science Foundation (NSF) under Grant No. CNS 1618520, CNS 1834215, and CNS 2028547. Any opinions, findings, conclusions, and recommendations in this paper are those of the authors and do not necessarily reflect the views of the funding agencies.

References

1. Android beacon library. https://altbeacon.github.io/android-beacon-library/index.html. Accessed 15 Aug 2020
2. Android open source project. https://source.android.com/. Accessed 15 Aug 2020
3. Apple and google partner on covid-19 contact tracing technology. https://www.blog.google/inside-google/company-announcements/apple-and-google-partner-covid-19-contact-tracing-technology/. Accessed 15 Aug 2020
4. Bluetrace. https://bluetrace.io/. Accessed 15 Aug 2020
5. Covid-19 apps - wikipedia. https://en.wikipedia.org/wiki/COVID-19_apps. Accessed 15 Aug 2020
6. Github - opentrace-community/opentrace-calibration: Opentrace calibration. device calibration data and trial methodologies for testing implementations of the bluetrace protocol. https://github.com/opentrace-community/opentrace-calibration/. Accessed 18 Aug 2020
7. Mimo - wikipedia. https://en.wikipedia.org/wiki/MIMO. Accessed 15 Aug 2020
8. Pepp-pt. https://www.pepp-pt.org/. Accessed 15 Aug 2020
9. Proximity and rssi bluetooth®technology website. https://www.bluetooth.com/blog/proximity-and-rssi/. Accessed 15 Aug 2020
10. Transmission power, range and rssi - support center. https://support.kontakt.io/hc/en-gb/articles/201621521-Transmission-power-Range-and-RSSI. Accessed 15 Aug 2020
11. What are broadcasting power, rssi and other characteristics of a beacon's signal? - estimote community portal. https://community.estimote.com/hc/en-us/articles/201636913-What-are-Broadcasting-Power-RSSI-and-other-characteristics-of-a-beacon-s-signal-. Accessed 15 Aug 2020
12. Will wireless interference and wi-fi impact beacons? - estimote community portal. https://community.estimote.com/hc/en-us/articles/200794267-What-are-potential-sources-of-wireless-interference-. Accessed 15 Aug 2020
13. Baumgärtner, L., et al.: Mind the gap: Security & privacy risks of contact tracing apps. arXiv preprint arXiv:2006.05914 (2020)
14. CDC. Public health guidance for community-related exposure. https://www.cdc.gov/coronavirus/2019-ncov/php/public-health-recommendations.html. Accessed 15 Aug 2020
15. Chan, J., et al.: Pact: privacy sensitive protocols and mechanisms for mobile contact tracing. ArXiv arXiv:2004.03544 (2020)
16. Cho, H., Ippolito, D., Yu, Y.W.: Contact tracing mobile apps for covid-19: privacy considerations and related trade-offs. arXiv preprint arXiv:2003.11511 (2020)
17. Crocker, A., Opsahl, K., Cyphers, B.: The challenge of proximity apps for covid-19 contact tracing—electronic frontier foundation (2020). https://www.eff.org/deeplinks/2020/04/challenge-proximity-apps-covid-19-contact-tracing. Accessed 15 Aug 2020
18. Li, J., Guo, X.: Covid-19 contact-tracing apps: A survey on the global deployment and challenges. arXiv preprint arXiv:2005.03599 (2020)
19. Niyogi, S., et al.: Tcncoalition/tcn: Specification and reference implementation of the tcn protocol for decentralized, privacy-preserving contact tracing (2020). https://github.com/TCNCoalition/TCN. Accessed 15 Aug 2020
20. Government of Singapore. Trace together, safer together (2020). https://www.tracetogether.gov.sg. Accessed 15 Aug 2020

21. O'Neill, P.H.: Bluetooth contact tracing needs bigger, better data—mit technology review (2020). https://www.technologyreview.com/2020/04/22/1000353/bluetooth-contact-tracing-needs-bigger-better-data/. Accessed 15 Aug 2020
22. O'Neill, P.H., Ryan-Mosley,T., Johnson, B.: A flood of coronavirus apps are tracking us. now it's time to keep track of them.—mit technology review (2020). https://www.technologyreview.com/2020/05/07/1000961/launching-mittr-covid-tracing-tracker/. Accessed 15 Aug 2020
23. Rivest, R.L., et al.: The pact protocol specification (2020). https://pact.mit.edu/wp-content/uploads/2020/04/The-PACT-protocol-specification-ver-0.1.pdf. Accessed 15 Aug 2020
24. ROBERT ROBust and privacy-presERving proximity Tracing protocol (2020). https://github.com/ROBERT-proximity-tracing. Accessed 12 May 2020
25. Simko, L., Calo, R., Roesner, F., Kohno, T.: Covid-19 contact tracing and privacy: Studying opinion and preferences (2020). arXiv preprint arXiv:2005.06056
26. Sivakumuran, P., Blasco, J.: A study of the feasibility of co-located app attacks against BLE and a large scale analysis of the current application layer security landscape. In: 28th USENIX Security Symposium. USENIX Association. USENIX Sec, Santa Clara (2019)
27. Tang, Q.: Privacy-preserving contact tracing: current solutions and open questions. arXiv preprint arXiv:2004.06818 (2020)
28. Troncoso, C., et al.: Decentralized privacy-preserving proximity tracing (2020). https://github.com/DP3T/documents. Accessed 15 Aug 2020
29. Veale, M.: Analysis of the NHSX contact tracing app 'isle of wight' data protection impact assessment (2020)
30. Wen, H., Zhao, Q., Lin, Z., Xuan, D., Shroff, N.: A study of the privacy of covid-19 contact tracing apps. In: International Conference on Security and Privacy in Communication Networks (2020)
31. Woodhams, S.: Covid-19 digital rights tracker (2020). https://www.top10vpn.com/research/investigations/covid-19-digital-rights-tracker/. Accessed 15 Aug 2020
32. Zuo, C., Wen, H., Lin, Z., Zhang, Y.: Automatic fingerprinting of vulnerable BLE IoT devices with static uuids from mobile apps. In: Proceedings of the 2019 ACM SIGSAC Conference on Computer and Communications Security (2019)

A Formal Verification
of Configuration-Based Mutation
Techniques for Moving Target Defense

Muhammad Abdul Basit Ur Rahim[1]([✉]), Ehab Al-Shaer[2], and Qi Duan[3]

[1] Montana Technological University, Butte, MT 59701, USA
mabdulbasiturrahi@mtech.edu
[2] INI/CyLab, Carnegie Mellon University, Pittsburgh, PA 15213, USA
ehab@cmu.edu
[3] University of North Carolina, Charlotte, NC, USA 28213
qduan@uncc.edu

Abstract. Static system configuration provides a significant advantage for the adversaries to discover the assets and vulnerabilities in the system and launch attacks. Configuration-based moving target defense (MTD) reverses the cyber warfare asymmetry for the defenders' advantage by mutating certain configuration parameters proactively in order to disrupt attacks planning or increase the attack cost significantly.

A key challenge in developing MTD techniques is guaranteeing design correctness and operational integrity. Due to the dynamic, asynchronous, and distributed nature of moving target defense, various mutation actions can be executed in an interleaved manner causing failures in the defense mechanism itself or negative interference in the cyber operations. Therefore, it is important to verify the correctness and operational integrity, of moving target techniques to identify the design errors or inappropriate run-time behavior that might jeopardize the effectiveness of MTD or cyber operations. To the best of our knowledge, there is no work aiming for the formal verification of the design correctness and integrity of moving target defense techniques.

In this paper, we present a methodology for formal verification of configuration based moving target defense. We model the system behaviors with system modeling language (SysML) and formalize the MTD technique using du-ration calculus (DC). The formal model satisfies the constraints and de-sign correctness properties. We use the random host mutation (RHM) as a case study of the MTD system that randomly mutates the IP addresses to make end-hosts untraceable by scanners. We validate the design correctness of RHM using model checking over various configuration-based mutation parameters.

Keywords: Formal specification · Moving target defense ·
Configuration-based mutation · Verification

© ICST Institute for Computer Sciences, Social Informatics and Telecommunications Engineering 2020
Published by Springer Nature Switzerland AG 2020. All Rights Reserved
N. Park et al. (Eds.): SecureComm 2020, LNICST 335, pp. 61–79, 2020.
https://doi.org/10.1007/978-3-030-63086-7_5

1 Introduction

Moving target defense allows the cyber systems to proactively defend against a wide-scale vector of sophisticated attacks by dynamically changing the system parameters and defense strategies in a timely and economical fashion. It can provide robust defense by deceiving attackers from reaching their goals, disrupting their plans via changing adversarial behaviors and deterring them through prohibitively increasing the cost for attacks. MTD is distributed by nature since the processes or actions in MTD are executed in an interleaved manner. It is important to verify the design correctness and integrity otherwise the design error can lead to failure or inconsistencies. The verification of the MTD technique should be performed in an earlier design phase to prevent system failures.

The successful implementation of MTD techniques over numerous mutable and configurable parameters is challenging. Even with the correct design, the system must be correctly configured before performing the simulation and validation. Due to the dynamic nature of MTD, the configurable parameters are dependent on one another. The change in the value of one parameter affects the other parameters. If the parameters are not configured correctly then MTD does not remain conflict-free or system integrity will disrupt. Moreover, MTD design must satisfy the mutation constraints and design properties which make sure that the system is randomized, conflict-free, live and progressive. The reachability, liveness, deadlock-freeness, and fairness are the properties that ensure the design correctness.

In the context of software or hardware, formal verification is the act of proving or disproving the correctness of the underlying system with respect to a certain formal specification [20]. In this work, we present a formal specification and verification methodology to ensure the design correctness and operational integrity of configuration-based MTD techniques. For this purpose, we have simulated and verified the MTD technique, random host mutation (RHM), against the design correctness properties over numerous configurable and mutable parameters. We have designed a generalized model of RHM that ensures the scalability of verification of RHM. Our simulation and verification ensure the design correctness and robustness of RHM.

In this paper, the functionality of individual entities of RHM is graphically presented. The system behaviors and basic functionality are modeled using system modeling language (SysML). The graphical model is helpful to understand the MTD technique. For detailed requirement specification, we use duration calculus which is an interval logic for the specification of a real-time system. DC covers dimensions that are required for specifications and verification for embedded and real-time systems [19]. DC is useful to specify the real-time events and actions such as the one used in the time-based mutation of MTD. Moreover, the DC specifications and constraints are also provable. The RHM is a real-time system as it handles the real-time events which need a real-time response. Therefore, DC best suits for formal requirement specification of RHM.

We use model checking tool for simulation and verification of MTD techniques. Model checking tools formally specify a system and help to find the unknown or inappropriate behavior of a system [23]. We have used UPPAAL for modeling and verification of MTD techniques. UPPAAL is a model checking tool for verification of real-time systems [23,25]. The constraints and properties are specified in temporal format and validated against the formal model to ensure the design correctness.

The rest of the paper is organized as follows. Section 2 briefly describes the preliminaries. Section 3 defines the RHM protocol. Section 4 presents the RHM verification. Section 5 describes the RHM components modeling and Sect. 6 presents the MTD verification. We present the survey of related work in Sect. 7. Section 8 concludes the methodology.

2 Preliminaries

In this section, we have discussed the preliminary concepts required to understand the methodology.

2.1 System Modeling Language

The System modeling language (SysML) is a graphical modeling language which is an extension of a unified modeling language (UML). SysML consists of three types of diagrams which are behavioral diagram, structural diagram, and requirement diagram. The state machine diagram is a behavioral diagram of SysML that we use to describe the functionality of entities associated with RHM. The SMD describes the states of a model and the transitions between the states. The rectangle and arrow represent the state and transition respectively. The transitions are labeled with a guard to enable or disable the transition. The transition executes if the guard is evaluated as true. We have modeled all components of RHM using SMD. SysML covers all modeling aspects require for modeling of MTD. The protocol, triggers, actions, constraints, and parameters can be specified using SysML.

2.2 Duration Calculus

Duration calculus is an interval logic that describes the real-time behavior of dynamic systems. It establishes a formal approach to specify and validate time duration of states in real-time system [13]. DC is also used to specify an interval temporal logic and specify the functionality of the real-time system at the abstraction, concrete and low level.

The duration calculus is designed for specifying and reasoning about embedded and real-time systems [16]. DC is widely practiced and numerous extensions of DC has been proposed for specification and verification of real-time systems [4,17,19,29,30]. The DC expressively specifies the embedded and real-time systems. There are three important dimensions (reasoning about data, communication, and real-time aspects) which are required for verification of embedded hardware and software systems. All these dimensions can be expressed by DC

[19] and these dimensions are required for model checking. Numerous prominent approaches are available that perform verification of temporal specifications by translating the problem into an automata-theoretic setting [13, 19].

DC has a subset which is known as DC-implementable which we have used to describe the detailed RHM model. The DC formal model covers all aspects for modeling of MTD. The MTD protocol, constraints, and parameters are specified using a DC-based formal model. Moreover, the DC formal model is a detailed model as compare to SysML. Even the scenarios for changing the values of parameters can be specified Using DC. The most important reason for using DC is that the DC constraints are mathematically provable.

Table 1 presents some symbols for specification of duration calculus. The ceilings $\lceil \rceil$ is used to specify the state. The right arrow is used for transition. The symbol ε with a right arrow indicates the transition with delay. The right arrow with number zero indicates the control is initially in that state. The appendix describes the DC implementables along-with its use for RHM [6, 13]: DC implementables describe the type of transition among the states, and sets the invariants to make the system stable.

Table 1. Some symbols of duration calculus

Symbol	Description
$\lceil x \rceil$	region,
$\longrightarrow$	followed-by,
$\longrightarrow_0$	followed-by-initially,
$\overset{\varepsilon}{\longrightarrow}$	delay transition,
$\overset{\leq \varepsilon}{\longrightarrow}$	upto,
$\overset{\varepsilon}{\longrightarrow}_0$	followed-by-initially,
;	chop

3   RHM Protocol

The RHM architecture consists of hosts, moving target gateways (MTG), domain name server (DNS), switch and moving target controller (MTC). The MTG is responsible for all interactions of MT hosts with other entities. While the MTC is brain of RHM protocol which mutates *vIP* addresses of MT hosts frequently and updates the MTGs with new *vIP*. There are two types of hosts: mutable and non-mutable hosts. The IP address of the mutable host mutates frequently by MTC to save the MT host from the scanner. The mutable host is also called as MT host. Whereas, the non-MT host is a host whose IP does not mutate. The MTG contains the translation table which contains virtual IP (*vIP*) and real IP (*rIP*) addresses of all MT hosts. It hides the addresses of MT hosts from rest of the entities. While the domain name server (DNS) contains (*rIP*) addresses of all hosts. The DNS directly interacts with MTG and the MT host interacts with DNS through MTG.

Figure 1 illustrates the RHM protocol [22]. We have extended our earlier research and the RHM protocol [3,22]. Initially, the source MT host only knows the name of destination MT host, therefore, source host requests DNS, through source MTG, for the address of destination MT host to start the communication (step 1). The DNS receives the name of destination MT host and responds with *rIP* address of destination MT host (step 2). The source MTG intercepts DNS response and translates the *rIP* address to *vIP* address, rewrites the DNS response, and forwards to source MT host (step 3). The MT host sends a packet to source MTG to forward it to destination MT host (step 4). The source MTG translates the destination MT host *vIP* address to *rIP* address, rewrites the packet, and forwards the packet to the switch with *rIP* addresses of the sender and receiver (step 5). The switch forwards the packet to destination MTG along-with *rIP* address of source and destination MT hosts(step 6). At the end, destination MTG translates the *rIP* address of sender to *vIP* address, forwards the packet to destination MT host using *rIP*, and shares the senders' *vIP* address (step 7). The MT host sends back the packet in the same way however MT hosts can only see the *vIP* address of each other instead of *rIP* address. In both cases, the MTGs translate the *rIP* to *vIP*.

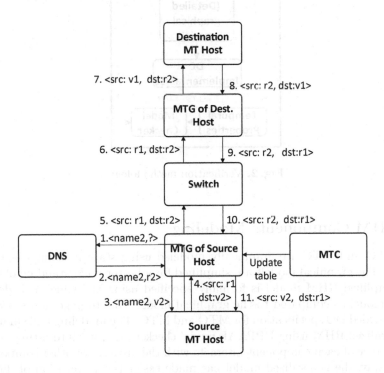

Fig. 1. RHM protocol

4   Verification Methodology

Figure 2 presents the process for specification, modeling, and validation of RHM. The SysML model is used for graphical presentation. We have modeled the behavior of RHM using SMD to present the basic functionality of MTD. The DC is used for formal specification of RHM. The DC formal model contains more details as compared to a SysML model. The DC implementables are used to describe the protocols, mutation function, and mutation and configuration parameters. The user-defined properties are specified using DC constraints. The constraints are specified as temporal properties in model checking tools.

The mapping among SysML, DC, and UPPAAL is done under the proposed mapping rules by researchers in [6,13,24]. Basit Ur Rahim et al. [6] proposed mapping rules from SysML to DC, however, the same rules are also applicable from SysML to DC. We have used the UPPAAL model checking tool for validation of design and the mutation configuration parameter. The model is analysed against the temporal properties which are specified in the form of timed computational tree logic (ECTL) properties. If the property does not hold then model checker shows the counter-example. Then the user can revise the model accordingly.

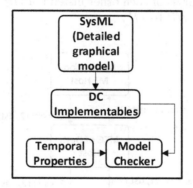

Fig. 2. Verification methodology

5   RHM Components Modeling

The MTG and MTC are graphically modeled using state machine diagram of SysML. The graphical models are simplified for a better understanding of RHM. The simplified RHM model is formally specified using DC which is a detailed formal model as compared to the graphical model. Due to page limits, we have only provided DC specification for MTG and MTC. The modeling and simulation of generalized RHM using UPPAAL model checker are quite interesting because the instance of each component interacts with the instance of other components. In this way, the generalized model has made easier the verification of different sizes of networks.

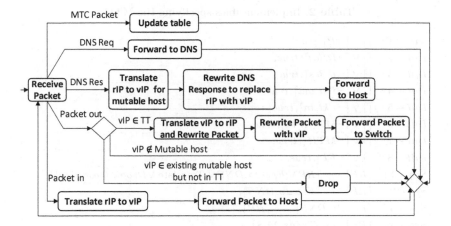

Fig. 3. State machine diagram for MTG

5.1 Moving Target Gateway

The MTG performs an important role for implementation of RHM. MTG is connected with the host, DNS, switch, and MTC. It hides the (rIP) addresses of MT hosts by performing address translation. Figure 3 illustrates the basic functionality of MTG for better understanding of protocol. It describes the input of MTG along-with three different address translations. In Fig. 3, the state Receive Packet is an initial state. The DNS request, DNS response, packet in, packet out, and MTC packets are inputs of MTG. The MTG updates the translation table (TT) on receiving MTC packet which is vIP address of MT host. MTG performs translation on receiving these inputs: DNS response, packet in, and packet out. After translation, the MTG rewrites the packet and forwards to respective entities. Table 2 presents all inputs, the performed address translation, and correspondence with respective entities.

Table 2 is the detailed DC-based formal specification of MTG. It is the detailed formal model as compared to SMD presented in Fig. 3. On receiving inputs, all step-by-step actions shown in 3 are specified using DC implementables. The implementable *Init-1* presents the initial state which is RP (receive packet). Initially, all invariants are set to false as shown by implementables from *Init-2* to *Init-8*. Most of the invariants are self-explanatory. The invariant *DReq* and *DRes* are input that represent the DNS request and DNS response respectively. The invariant *MTC_PKT* is also an input to MTG which is received from MTC to update the translation table. The invariant *MTH* is set to true when a communicating host belongs to MT host and invariant *TT* is set to true when the host is available in the translation table. By Seq-1, there are five possible transitions from initial state *Receive Packet* (RP). Syn-1 states the input for all possible transition from RP state. By Seq-2, Stab-1, and Seq-3, the MT host requests for address of destination MT host. The request is intercepted by MTG and then forwarded to DNS. Figure 3 also illustrates the MT host request with

Table 2. Implementables specifying the MTG

$Init - 1:$	$\bigsqcap \vee \lceil RP \rceil; true,$
$Init - 2:$	$\bigsqcap \vee \lceil \neg DReq \rceil; true,$
$Init - 3:$	$\bigsqcap \vee \lceil \neg DRes \rceil; true,$
$Init - 4:$	$\bigsqcap \vee \lceil \neg Pkt\_out \rceil; true,$
$Init - 5:$	$\bigsqcap \vee \lceil \neg Pkt\_in \rceil; true,$
$Init - 6:$	$\bigsqcap \vee \lceil \neg MTC\_Pkt \rceil; true,$
$Init - 7:$	$\bigsqcap \vee \lceil \neg MTH \rceil; true,$
$Init - 8:$	$\bigsqcap \vee \lceil \neg TT \rceil; true.$
$Seq - 1:$	$\lceil RP \rceil \longrightarrow \lceil RP \vee Frw\_to\_DNS \vee \text{Translate} \vee Drop \vee Update\_table \rceil,$
$Seq - 2:$	$\lceil RP \rceil \longrightarrow \lceil Frw\_to\_DNS \rceil,$
$Seq - 3:$	$\lceil Frw\_to\_DNS \rceil \longrightarrow \lceil RP \rceil,$
$Seq - 4:$	$\lceil RP \rceil \longrightarrow \lceil TransDNS \rceil,$
$Seq - 5:$	$\lceil TransDNS \rceil \longrightarrow \lceil Rewrite\_DNS\_Response \rceil,$
$Seq - 6:$	$\lceil Rewrite\_DNS\_Response \rceil \longrightarrow \lceil Frw\_to\_host \rceil,$
$Seq - 7:$	$\lceil Frw\_to\_host \rceil \longrightarrow \lceil RP \rceil,$
$Seq - 8:$	$\lceil RP \rceil \longrightarrow \lceil TransOut \rceil,$
$Seq - 9:$	$\lceil TransOut \rceil \longrightarrow \lceil Rewrite\_Packet \rceil,$
$Seq - 10:$	$\lceil Rewrite\_Packet \rceil \longrightarrow \lceil Frw\_to\_Switch \rceil,$
$Seq - 11:$	$\lceil Frw\_to\_Switch \rceil \longrightarrow \lceil RP \rceil,$
$Seq - 12:$	$\lceil RP \rceil \longrightarrow \lceil Frw\_to\_Switch \rceil,$
$Seq - 13:$	$\lceil Frw\_to\_Switch \rceil \longrightarrow \lceil RP \rceil,$
$Seq - 14:$	$\lceil RP \rceil \longrightarrow \lceil Drop \rceil,$
$Seq - 15:$	$\lceil Drop \rceil \longrightarrow \lceil RP \rceil,$
$Seq - 16:$	$\lceil RP \rceil \longrightarrow \lceil TransIn \rceil,$
$Seq - 17:$	$\lceil TransIn \rceil \longrightarrow \lceil Frw\_to\_host \rceil,$
$Seq - 18:$	$\lceil RP \rceil \longrightarrow \lceil Update\_table \rceil,$
$Seq - 19:$	$\lceil Update\_table \rceil \longrightarrow \lceil RP \rceil,$
$Syn - 1:$	$\lceil RP \vee DReq \vee DRes \vee Pkt\_in \vee Pkt\_out \vee MTC\_Pkt \rceil \longrightarrow \lceil \neg RP \rceil,$
$Syn - 2:$	$\lceil TransDNS \wedge rIP\_to\_vIP() \rceil \longrightarrow \lceil \neg TransDNS \rceil,$
$Syn - 3:$	$\lceil TransIn \wedge rIP\_to\_vIP() \rceil \longrightarrow \lceil \neg TransIn \rceil,$
$Syn - 4:$	$\lceil TransOut \wedge vIP\_to\_rIP() \rceil \longrightarrow \lceil \neg TransOut \rceil,$
$Stab - 1:$	$\lceil \neg RP \rceil; \lceil RP \wedge (DReq) \rceil \longrightarrow \lceil Frw\_to\_DNS \rceil,$
$Stab - 2:$	$\lceil \neg RP \rceil; \lceil RP \wedge (DRes) \rceil \longrightarrow \lceil TransDNS \rceil,$
$Stab - 3:$	$\lceil \neg RP \rceil; \lceil RP \wedge (Pkt\_out) \rceil \longrightarrow \lceil TransOut \rceil,$
$Stab - 4:$	$\lceil \neg RP \rceil; \lceil RP \wedge (Pkt\_out) \& (vIP \notin MTH) \rceil \longrightarrow \lceil Frw\_to\_Switch \rceil,$
$Stab - 5:$	$\lceil \neg RP \rceil; \lceil RP \wedge (Pkt\_out \& vIP \notin TT) \rceil \longrightarrow \lceil Drop \rceil,$
$Stab - 6:$	$\lceil \neg RP \rceil; \lceil RP \wedge (Pkt\_in) \rceil \longrightarrow \lceil TransIn \rceil,$
$Stab - 7:$	$\lceil \neg RP \rceil; \lceil RP \wedge (MTC\_Pkt) \rceil \longrightarrow \lceil Update\_Table \rceil$

an input DNS Req. Seq-4, Stab-2, and Syn-2 show that the DNS response is intercepted by MTG and then translate the *rIP* to *vIP*. The Seq-5 and Seq-6 lead to rewrite the DNS response and forward to host. By Seq-8, Stab-3, and Syn-4, the host requests for packet out and then MTG translates the destination MT host *vIP* to *rIP*. With Seq-9, Seq-10, and Seq-11, the MTG rewrite the packet, forwards to switch, and comes back to the initial state. Seq-12, Seq-13, and Stab-4 show that if the address does not belong to MT host then forwards the packet to switch without translation. Seq-14, Stab-5, and Seq-15 describe that if the address of destination MT host is not in the translation table (TT) then the will be drooped. Seq-16, Stab-6, Syn-3, and Seq-17 belong to the packet in. When a packet is received, the MTG translates the *rIP* address to *vIP* (Syn-3). Then MTG forwards the packet to MT host. Seq-18, Stab-7, and Seq-19 represent the updating the translation table on MTC response.

After DC specification, MTG is simulated and verified using UPPAAL. Figure 2 is the implementation of MTG using UPPAAL.

5.2 Moving Target Controller

MTC frequently mutates the *vIP* addresses of all MT hosts. Figure 4 is the SMD that illustrates the basic functionality of MTC. The *Check_time* state checks the time and starts mutation if time is above the threshold time value. The *Select_New_vIP* state performs the mutation. The MTC satisfies the constraints while selecting new *vIP*. The mutation function makes sure that all N number of hosts get new and random *vIP*, no host get the same *vIP* consecutively, and no two MT hosts of same subnet will have the same *vIP*. Once mutation process is completed at *Select_New_vIP* state, the MTC clock is reset and an MTC packet is sent to MTG to update the translation table. The mutation process also takes care of liveness and fairness properties that mutation will start after a certain interval and every host will have new *vIP*. Figure 4 represents the timed automaton of MTC where threshold time for mutation is set to 25-time units. It randomly selects an address from a given range.

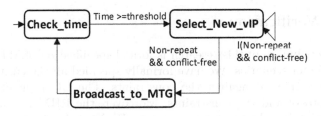

Fig. 4. State machine diagram for MTC

Table 3 presents the DC specification for MTC. The implementable *Init-1* describes the initial state of MTC which is *MTC_Ready* state. By Seq-1 and Prog-1, MTC checks the time, if the time is above the threshold time which is 25 time units then it changes the *vIP* address. Seq-1 and Stab-1 describe the mutation which iterates till all the MT hosts get new *vIP*. Stab-1 makes sure that new *vIP* is no-repeating and conflict-free. The function vIP() in Stab-1 is responsible for mutation. It randomly selects an address and mutates if constraints are satisfied. By Seq-2 and Syn-2, when mutation process completes, the MTC broadcasts the *vIP* to MTG. In a normal system, MTC interval is an important factor and it affects the reachability of the system. We have verified the RHM over various MTC intervals which are up to 100 time units.

Table 3. Implementables specifying the MTC

$Init-1:$	$\lceil\rceil \vee \lceil MTC\_Ready\rceil; true,$
$Seq-1:$	$\lceil Check\_time\rceil \longrightarrow \lceil Select\_New\_vIP\rceil,$
$Seq-2:$	$\lceil Select\_New\_vIP\rceil \longrightarrow \lceil Broadcast\_to\_MTG\rceil,$
$Seq-3:$	$\lceil Broadcast\_to\_MTG\rceil \longrightarrow \lceil Check\_time\rceil,$
$Prog-1:$	$\lceil Check\_time\rceil \xrightarrow{25} \lceil\neg Check\_time\rceil,$
$Stab-1:$	$\lceil\neg Select\_New\_vIP\rceil; \lceil Select\_New\_vIP$ $\wedge(n < N \wedge \neg repeat \wedge \neg conflict \wedge vIP())\rceil \longrightarrow \lceil Select\_New\_vIP\rceil,$
$Syn-2:$	$\lceil Select\_New\_vIP \wedge n = N\rceil \longrightarrow \lceil\neg Select\_New\_vIP\rceil,$

The Eq. (1) is the DC constraint over MTC which specifies that initially MTC is in *MTC_Ready* state, all hosts must initialized with new *vIP* after every 25 time units. This constraint does hold by supported implemetables Prog-1, Stab-1 and Syn-2 respectively. The DC constraints are also mapped to temporal properties of model checking tool.

$$\models MTC \Rightarrow \begin{pmatrix} (\_Ready\rceil \Rightarrow \int M < \varepsilon) \\ \wedge(\lceil Check\_time\rceil \Rightarrow l \geq 25 + \varepsilon) \\ \wedge(\lceil Select\_New\_vIP\rceil \Rightarrow \int (\text{vIP} \wedge n < N) + \varepsilon) \end{pmatrix} \quad (1)$$

6   MTD Verification

The main contribution of this research is formal specification of MTD and verifying the different scenarios. We have formally specified all the entities of RHM protocol and verified it against the constraints. The DC is helpful in specifying the protocol and the constraints. Moreover, the RHM is evaluated over the configuration-based mutation parameters. We have simulated numerous scenarios for verification of RHM. The RHM has proven the robustness during simulation and verification.

6.1   Evaluation Methodology

We have simulated and verified the RHM over networks of various sizes. The DNS entry, routing entry, translation table, size of the network, size of a subnet, and number of MTG are the important parameters that need to be correctly configured. Moreover, a mutable parameter is used to assign the random and non-repeating *vIP* address to all MT hosts. The configuration process makes sure that the network is correctly designed and configured before simulation and implementation. It makes sure that every entity gets an equal opportunity to interact with the respective components. These parameters need to be configured before the simulation and implementation start. In RHM, the MTC interval and, DNS delay are also important parameters that can affect the functionality of RHM. For the implementation of RHM in UPPAAL, the configuration process executes first and the rest of the processes execute accordingly. The configuration parameters must be correctly configured in start otherwise it will disrupt the systems operation. We have created a configuration component in UPPAAL to configure the parameters. In this process, we have defined and configured the parameters for DNS entry, MTG entry, router entry. The mutation interval, and DNS delay, and MTG delay are initialized. The number of MT hosts and MTGs and the size of a subnet are also assigned in the configuration process.

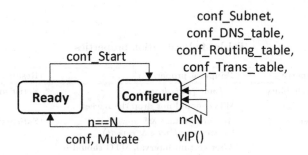

Fig. 5. State machine diagram for Configuration

Figure 5 is the SMD and presenting the configuration process. The *Ready* state is the initial state whereas the *Configure* state performs the configuration. The configuration process configures several tables that belong to MTG, DNS, and Switch which contain information about hosts and their respective MTGs. The invariant *conf_Start* represents the configuration process is started. Initially, this boolean invariant is set to false. The invariant *conf_Subnet* belongs to initialization of MT hosts to their respective subnet. The invariants *conf_DNS_table*, *conf_Routing_table*, and *conf_Trans_table* represent the initialization of DNS, routing, and translation tables respectively. Moreover, all the hosts are initialized with random *vIP* using function vIP(). A loop transition with *Configure* state executes till all N number of MT hosts are initialized with *vIP*. When the configuration process completes the invariant *Conf* and *Mutate* are set to true where the invariant *Mutate* activates the MTC for initiation of mutation process and *conf* represents the completion of configuration process. In UPPAAL, the *Configure* state is set to committed where the time does not elapse during configuration. Moreover, all tables are initialized using user-defined functions *conf_TT()*, *cong_routing_table()*, *cong_DNS()*, *conf_subnet()*, *conf_availability()*, and *vIP()* respectively.

6.2   Properties Verification

The RHM design must satisfy the correctness properties. For this purpose, we have verified the reachability, liveness, and deadlock-freeness of RHM design. Our results prove the correctness, effectiveness, and reliability of RHM. We have found that the RHM satisfies all the correctness properties and ensures the correctness over various configuration parameters.

The RHM design is verified using ECTL temporal properties. The Reachability describes that every good state is reachable and every bad state is unreachable. The liveness describes that system is progressing to achieve a specific goal. Deadlock-freeness ensures that the system is not stopped and it is always in progressing state. The system is in deadlock state when it stops in a state and does not progress to other states [28]. Equal distribution of resources is known as fairness [28].

Table 4. Verification properties

Property	Temporal property	Result
Reachability	$A[]\ not\ (mtg.drop)$	Satisfied
	MTG should not drop the packet	
Liveness	$A[]\ mtc.Mutate\ \&\&\ n < N$ $\&\&\ not(conflict\ \&\&\ repeat)$	Satisfied
	After certain interval, MTC should mutate vIP that should be conflict-free and non-repeatative	
Deadlock-freeness	$A[]\ not\ deadlock$	Satisfied
	Deadlock can prevent MTG from mutation	
Fairness	$A[]\ mtc.Broadcast\ \&\&\ n==N$	Satisfied
	New vIP for every MT host should be broadcast to MTG	

The mutation function *vIP()* of MTC randomly selects the *vIP* from an address range. The RHM satisfies the constraints that no two hosts will have the same *vIP* otherwise the packet will be delivered to the wrong destination or incorrect sender information will be shared with the receiver. It also satisfies the second constraint that no host will have the same *vIP* consecutively. The selection of random *vIP* from a long address range makes scanning difficult for an attacker. Moreover, if the mutation process is faster then even it can be more difficult for the scanner however it can affect the reachability. The system does not stop working and remains live.

The UPPAAL model checking tool verifies the time-based model against the temporal properties and results as satisfied or not-satisfied. The UPPAAL model is the detailed model as compared to MTD specification and SysML model. Table 4 presents the verification properties. The operator ([ ]) is used with temporal properties makes sure that the property is satisfied for all states on all paths.

6.3 Evaluation

While designing and implementing RHM model, we have considered different scenarios. First, the MTG keeps the older *vIP* address which is known as old window. When MTC mutates the *vIP* address, the MTG saves *viPs* of old window. If the MTG has already obtained the *vIP* address, meanwhile, MTC mutates the *vIP* address then MTG forwards the packet to older *vIP* address. Saving the older *vIP* address is also interesting that what will be the size of window. We have simulated this scenario and consider the size of window is one. If the address matches to updated or older *vIP* address then packet will be forwarded to respective address otherwise packet will be dropped. Second, we have also considered another scenario that MTG does not save older *vIP* address then MTG forwards packets to new *vIP* address only. In this case, MTG should not drop the packets. If MT host has old *vIP* address then MTG ask to obtain the new *vIP* address. In this case, if IP mutation is very frequent then it will not affect the reachability and also makes the MT host untraceable. The results presented in this section belong the second scenario.

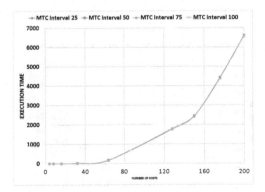

Fig. 6. Reachability analysis over MTC intervals

The analysis figures are based on numerous parameters over various sizes of subnet and networks. Figure 6 describes the reachability analysis of RHM over various mutation intervals of MTC. It shows the execution time of reachability property which is in milliseconds. Figure 6 is based on mutation intervals. For this simulation, the mutation intervals is 25 time units. The size of the subnet

is set to ten. The RHM still satisfies the reachability. The RHM protocol satisfies the reachability property that every packet is delivered to its destination
host and there is no packet loss even we all these parameters. The maximum
time consumed is 6700 ms for a network size of two hundred hosts. The time
consumption is very low which makes verification of RHM scalable. We have
also analyzed the memory usage for properties verification. We have observed
that the UPPAAL model checker uses up to 1.4 GB memory for verification of a
network with 200 hosts and 100 MTGs. Figure 7 presents the memory analysis
of reachability property over MTC intervals.

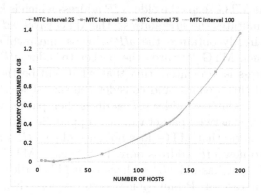

Fig. 7. Memory analysis of reachability property over MTC interval

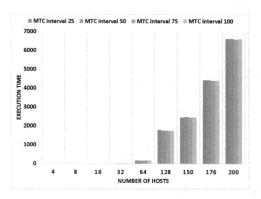

Fig. 8. Liveness analysis over MTC interval

Figure 8 presents the analysis of liveness property over MTC intervals. We
have used the same parameters values as shown in Fig. 6. Although, the execution
time is different, however, the trend of time consuming is almost same. The

maximum time consumed is 6800 milliseconds for network of 200 hosts and 20 MTGs. Figure 9 shows the memory analysis of liveness property over MTC intervals. The parameters for 9 are same as shown in Fig. 7. The maximum memory consumed is 1.23 GB for a network of 200 hosts with 10 MTGs. The trend of memory consumption in both figures (Fig. 7 and Fig. 9) is almost same.

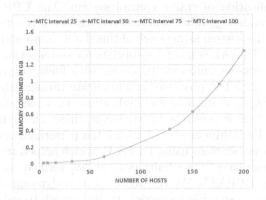

Fig. 9. Memory analysis of liveness property over MTC interval

We have also applied the methodology for formal specification and analysis of random routing mutation (RRM) which is a technique of MTD. In RRM, the router changes the routing path frequently. UPPAAL is useful for the selection of random and un-deterministic routing paths. We use UPPAAL for modeling, simulation, and verification of RRM. The design properties used for verification of RHM are used for validation of RRM.

7 Related Work

In this literature review we have evaluated few techniques for specification and verification. Pedroza et al. [21] propose a SysML profile for designing of an embedded system and perform verification for safety and security of communication links. Perroza uses UPPAAL and ProVerif toolkits for verification of embedded system. Shen et al. [27], Fang et al. [14], and Lugou et al. [18] graphically model the security protocols using unified modeling language (UML), convert it to Spi calculus to perform verification using Profier. Dadeau et al. [9] propose a set of mutation operators for HLPSL models that aim at introducing leaks in the security protocols. The model is analyzed by a tool AVISPA that produce counter-example traces leading to the leaks. Fu et al. [15] propose Security Objectives to Protocol Security Testing, to generate the test cases on-the-fly. He propose the algorithm for the protocol verification. However, the verification of randomized and dynamic system is really challenging especially when size of the network is too large. The researchers of all these proposals use the SysML as a foundation for modeling of their case studies. Then different tools are used to perform the validation of static systems.

Duration Calculus is a specification language for embedded and real-time systems. Basit Ur Rahim et al. [6] and Olderburg [13] use the DC for specification and perform verification using UPPAAL model checker. Schwammberger [26] extended DC and named it as multi-lane spatial logic. The researcher used UPPAAL for verification of traffic control system. The UPPAAL is a model checking tool for modeling, validation and verification of real-time systems [25]. UPPAAL models the system as network of timed automata and performs analysis of the system. UPPAAL is most appropriate for systems that can be modeled as a collection of non-deterministic processes with finite control structure and real-valued clocks [25]. The processes communicate through channels or shared variables [8]. UPPAAL is suitable for applications that include communication protocols and real-time controllers, in particular, those where timing aspects are critical [25]. Basit Ur Rahim et al. [6,7,23,24] has performed verification of various dynamic real-time systems using UPPAAL which helped to find design error in an earlier design phase. Sidra Sultana et al [28] verified the dynamic traffic light system using UPPAAL. As the RHM [3] is a dynamic and randomized, therefore, UPPAAL is suitable to model the framework to validate its correctness, efficiency and reliability.

The notion of mutable networks as a frequently randomized changing of network addresses and responses was initially proposed in [1]. The idea was later extended as part of the MUTE network which implemented the moving target through random address hopping and random fingerprinting [2]. Randomization is a common technique for security. Examples of information randomization include instruction set randomization [5,10], memory address randomization [11], and compiler-generated software diversity [12].

8   Conclusions

In this paper, we present a verification methodology for the correctness and integrity of MTD techniques. We have formalized, modeled, and verified the techniques of MTD over numerous configuration-based mutation parameters. As a case study, we have simulated a class of MTD for conformance of procedures and performed an analysis to ensure the design correctness. The RHM model is validated against reachability, liveness, fairness, and deadlock-freeness properties. The properties ensure that the mutation process does not affect the MTD technique. The mutation process is also evaluated over non-repeating and conflict-free constraints. The mutation process ensures that every MT host address mutates over a certain interval. The results present that dynamic and randomized RHM is correct, effective, and reliable. The verification of RHM does not utilize enough resources that make verification more scalable. The verification of RHM has consumed up to 1.4 GB memory and 6700 ms for verification of TCTL properties for a network with (up to) 200 MT hosts, 100 MTGs, and 40 MT hosts over a subnet. We have designed the generalized model of RHM that also helps to design, simulate, and verify a scalable network.

Acknowledgement. This research was supported in part by the United States Army Research Office (ARO). Any opinions, findings, conclusions or recommendations stated in this material are those of the authors and do not necessarily reflect the views of the funding sources.

Appendix: DC Implementable with Definition

DC implementables	Pattern	Description
Initialisation	$\lceil\rceil \longrightarrow \lceil x\rceil; true,$	Each control automaton is either empty or in initial state
Sequence	$\lceil x\rceil \longrightarrow \lceil x \vee x_1 \vee x_2 \vee .. \vee x_n\rceil$	if the control automaton is in state x it subsequently stays in x or moves to one of the state $x_1, ..., x_n$. e.g. all transition among the states of a component are specified using sequence implementable
Progress	$\lceil x\rceil \xrightarrow{\varepsilon} \lceil\neg x\rceil$	The control automaton stays for ε seconds in state x, it leaves this state and progresses accordingly. e.g. This will be used to define the computational overhead of mutation
Synchronization	$\lceil x \wedge \alpha\rceil \xrightarrow{\varepsilon} \lceil\neg x\rceil$	The control automaton stays for ε second in state x with condition α being true. The time unit ε is a clock that can be either discrete or continuous type. e.g. This will be used to allow the transition iff the mutation criterion is satisfied
Bounded Stability	$\lceil\neg x\rceil; \lceil x \wedge \alpha\rceil \xrightarrow{\leq\varepsilon} \lceil x \vee x_1 \vee x_2 \vee .. \vee x_n\rceil$	When the control automaton changes its state to x with the condition α being true and the time does not exceed ε seconds, it stays in x or it moves to one of states $x_1, ..., x_n$. e.g. Mutate vIP after a certain time interval
Unbounded Stability	$\lceil\neg x\rceil; \lceil x \wedge \alpha\rceil \longrightarrow \lceil x \vee x_1 \vee x_2 \vee .. \vee x_n\rceil$	when the control automaton changes its state to x with the condition α being true, it stays in x or it moves to one of states $x_1, ..., x_n$. e.g. Select new vIP till all MT hosts get a new vIP
Bounded Initial Stability	$\lceil x \wedge \alpha\rceil \xrightarrow{\leq\varepsilon}_0 \lceil x \vee x_1 \vee x_2 \vee .. \vee x_n\rceil$	When the control automaton initially is in state x with the condition α being true and the time does not exceed ε seconds, it stays in x or it moves to one of states $x_1, .., x_n$. e.g. Set values of all parameters in initial phase before mutation starts
Unbounded Initial Stability	$\lceil x \wedge \alpha\rceil \longrightarrow_0 \lceil x \vee x_1 \vee x_2 \vee .. \vee x_n\rceil$	When the control automaton initially is in phase x with the condition α being true, it stays in x or it moves to one of states $x_1, .., x_n$. e.g. Initialise the configuration parameters in initial phase

References

1. Al-Shaer, E.: Mutable networks, National cyber leap year summit 2009 participants ideas report. Technical report, Networking and Information Technology Research and Development (NTIRD) (2009)
2. Al-Shaer, E.: Toward network configuration randomization for moving target defense. In: Jajodia, S., Ghosh, A.K., Swarup, V., Wang, C., Wang, X.S. (eds.) Moving Target Defense, Advances in Information Security, vol. 54, pp. 153–159. Springer, New York (2011). https://doi.org/10.1007/978-1-4614-0977-9_9
3. Al-Shaer, E., Duan, Q., Jafarian, J.H.: Random host mutation for moving target defense. In: Keromytis, A.D., Di Pietro, R. (eds.) SecureComm 2012. LNICST, vol. 106, pp. 310–327. Springer, Heidelberg (2013). https://doi.org/10.1007/978-3-642-36883-7_19
4. An, J., Zhan, N., Li, X., Zhang, M., Yi, W.: Model checking bounded continuous-time extended linear duration invariants. In: Proceedings of the 21st International Conference on Hybrid Systems: Computation and Control (Part of CPS Week), HSCC 2018 pp. 81–90. ACM, New York (2018)
5. Atighetchi, M., Pal, P., Webber, F., Jones, C.: Adaptive use of network-centric mechanisms in cyber-defense. In: Second IEEE International Symposium on Network Computing and Applications, NCA 2003, pp. 179–188 (2003)
6. Basit-Ur-Rahim, M.A., Ahmad, J., Arif, F.: Parallel verification of UML using divine tool. In: 2013 5th International Conference on Computer Science and Information Technology, pp. 49–53 (2013)
7. Basit-Ur-Rahim, M.A., Arif, F., Ahmad, J.: Modeling of real-time embedded systems using SysML and its verification using UPPAAL and DiVinE. In: 2014 IEEE 5th International Conference on Software Engineering and Service Science, pp. 132–136 (2014)
8. Behrmann, G., David, A., Larsen, K.G.: A tutorial on uppaal. In: Bernardo, M., Corradini, F. (eds.) SFM-RT 2004. LNCS, vol. 3185, pp. 200–236. Springer, Heidelberg (2004). https://doi.org/10.1007/978-3-540-30080-9_7
9. Dadeau, F., Héam, P., Kheddam, R.: Mutation-based test generation from security protocols in hlpsl. In: 2011 Fourth IEEE International Conference on Software Testing, Verification and Validation, pp. 240–248 (2011)
10. Droms, R., Bound, J., Volz, B., Lemon, T., Perkins, C., Carney, M.: Dynamic host configuration protocol for IPv6 (2003). https://tools.ietf.org/html/rfc3315
11. Dunlop, M., Groat, S., Marchany, R., Tront, J.: IPv6: now you see me, now you don't. In: The Tenth International Conference on Networks, ICN 2011 (2011)
12. Dunlop, M., Groat, S., Urbanski, W., Marchany, R., Tront, J.: Mt6d: a moving target IPv6 defense. In: 2011 - MILCOM 2011 Military Communications Conference, pp. 1321–1326 (2011)
13. Olderog, E.R., Dierks, H.: Real-Time Systems: Formal Specification and Automatic Verification. Cambridge University Press, Cambridge (2008)
14. Fang, K., Li, X., Hao, J., Feng, Z.: Formal modeling and verification of security protocols on cloud computing systems based on UML 2.3. In: 2016 IEEE Trustcom/BigDataSE/ISPA, pp. 852–859 (2016)
15. Fu, Y., Koné, O.: Validation of security protocol implementations from security objectives. Comput. Secur. 36, 27–39 (2013)
16. Goranko, V., Montanari, A., Sciavicco, G.: A road map of interval temporal logics and duration calculi. J. Appl. Non-Class. Logics 14(1–2), 9–54 (2004)

17. Guelev, D.P., Wang, S., Zhan, N.: Compositional hoare-style reasoning about hybrid CSP in the duration calculus. In: Larsen, K.G., Sokolsky, O., Wang, J. (eds.) SETTA 2017. LNCS, vol. 10606, pp. 110–127. Springer, Cham (2017). https://doi.org/10.1007/978-3-319-69483-2_7

18. Lugou, F., Li, L.W., Apvrille, L., Ameur-Boulifa, R.: SYSML models and model transformation for security. In: 2016 4th International Conference on Model-Driven Engineering and Software Development (MODELSWARD), pp. 331–338 (2016)

19. Meyer, R., Faber, J., Rybalchenko, A.: Model checking duration calculus: a practical approach. In: Barkaoui, K., Cavalcanti, A., Cerone, A. (eds.) ICTAC 2006. LNCS, vol. 4281, pp. 332–346. Springer, Heidelberg (2006). https://doi.org/10.1007/11921240_23

20. Page, R.L.: Engineering software correctness. J. Funct. Program. 17(6), 675–686 (2007)

21. Pedroza, G., Apvrille, L., Knorreck, D.: Avatar: A SYSML environment for the formal verification of safety and security properties. In: 2011 11th Annual International Conference on New Technologies of Distributed Systems, pp. 1–10 (2011)

22. Rahim, M.A.B.U., Duan, Q., Al-Shaer, E.: A formal analysis of moving target defense (2020)

23. Basit ur Rahim, M.A., Arif, F.: Translating activity diagram from duration calculus for modeling of real-time systems and its formal verification using UPPAAL and DiVinE. Mehran Univ. Res. J. Eng. Technol. 35(1), 139–154 (2016)

24. Basit Ur Rahim, M.A., Arif, F., Ahmad, J.: Modeling of embedded system using SysML and its parallel verification using DiVinE tool. In: Murgante, B., et al. (eds.) ICCSA 2014. LNCS, vol. 8583, pp. 541–555. Springer, Cham (2014). https://doi.org/10.1007/978-3-319-09156-3_38

25. Ravn, A.P., Srba, J., Vighio, S.: Modelling and verification of web services business activity protocol. In: Abdulla, P.A., Leino, K.R.M. (eds.) TACAS 2011. LNCS, vol. 6605, pp. 357–371. Springer, Heidelberg (2011). https://doi.org/10.1007/978-3-642-19835-9_32

26. Schwammberger, M.. Introducing liveness into multi-lane spatial logic lane change controllers using UPPAAL, pp. 17–31. CoRR abs/1804.04346 (2018)

27. Shen, G., Li, X., Feng, R., Xu, G., Hu, J., Feng, Z.: An extended UML method for the verification of security protocols. In: 2014 19th International Conference on Engineering of Complex Computer Systems, pp. 19–28 (2014)

28. Sultana, S., Arif, F.: Computational conversion via translation rules for transforming C++ code into UPPAAL's automata. IEEE Access 5, 14455–14467 (2017)

29. Wang, H., Zhou, X., Dong, Y., Tang, L.: Modeling timing behavior for cyber-physical systems. In: 2009 International Conference on Computational Intelligence and Software Engineering, pp. 1–4 (2009)

30. Zhang, M., Liu, Z., Zhan, N.: Model checking linear duration invariants of networks of automata. In: Arbab, F., Sirjani, M. (eds.) FSEN 2009. LNCS, vol. 5961, pp. 244–259. Springer, Heidelberg (2010). https://doi.org/10.1007/978-3-642-11623-0_14

Coronavirus Contact Tracing App Privacy: What Data Is Shared by the Singapore OpenTrace App?

Douglas J. Leith[(✉)] and Stephen Farrell

School of Computer Science and Statistics, Trinity College Dublin, Dublin, Ireland
doug.leith@tcd.ie, stephen.farrell@scss.tcd.ie

Abstract. We report on measurements of the actual data transmitted to backend servers by the Singapore OpenTrace app, with a view to evaluating impacts on user privacy. We have three main findings: 1) The OpenTrace app uses Google's Firebase service to store and manage user data. This means that there are two main parties involved in handling data transmitted from the app, namely Google and the health authority operating the OpenTrace app itself. We find that OpenTrace's use of Firebase Analytics telemetry means the data sent by OpenTrace potentially allows the (IP-based) location of user handsets to be tracked by Google over time. We therefore recommend that OpenTrace be modified to disable use of Firebase Analytics. 2) OpenTrace also currently requires users to supply a phone number to use the app and uses the Firebase Authentication service to validate and store the entered phone number. The decision to ask for user phone numbers (or other identifiers) presumably reflects a desire for contact tracers to proactively call contacts of a person that has tested positive. Alternative designs make those contacts aware of the positive test, but leave it to the contact to initiate action. This may indicate a direct trade-off between privacy and the effectiveness of contact tracing. If storage of phone numbers is judged necessary we recommend changing OpenTrace to avoid use of Firebase Authentication for this. And finally, 3) the reversible encryption used in OpenTrace relies on a single long-term secret key stored in a Google Cloud service and so is vulnerable to disclosure of this secret key.

Keywords: Contact tracing · Covid · Privacy · Firebase

1 Introduction

There is currently a great deal of interest in the use of mobile apps to facilitate Covid-19 contact tracing. More efficient and scalable contact tracing might for example, allow the lockdown measures currently in place in many countries to be relaxed more quickly.

Ensuring that contact tracing apps maintain user privacy has been widely flagged as being a major concern. Bluetooth-based proximity detection

N. Park et al. (Eds.): SecureComm 2020, LNICST 335, pp. 80–96, 2020.
https://doi.org/10.1007/978-3-030-63086-7_6

approaches are appealing from a privacy viewpoint since they avoid the need to record or share user location. However, care is needed in the implementation of these approaches to ensure that privacy goals are actually achieved. In addition, independent evaluation of developed apps is important both to verify privacy claims and to build confidence in users that the apps are indeed safe to use. In this report we take a first step in this direction. We measure the actual data transmitted to backend servers by the Singapore TraceTogether/OpenTrace app with a view to evaluating user privacy.

Mobile apps are already being used in several countries to assist with management of Covid-19 infections. Most of these apps are either used to control the movement of people or to assist people to make an initial self-evaluation of their health based on observed symptoms, rather than for contact tracing. A notable example of the former is the Chinese Health Code app [1], and an example of latter is the Spanish self-evaluation app [8]. It is worth noting that some countries use centralised tracking of mobile phone location, which avoids the need for a specialised app, to control movement of people, e.g. Taiwan's "electronic fence" [3]. In South Korea information on locations visited by infected people are made publicly available and this has prompted the development of apps that display this information e.g. the Corona 100m app [5].

In contrast, in the initial stages of the Covid-19 outbreak the Singapore government developed the TraceTogether app [16] and used this to directly assist with contact tracing. The TraceTogether app uses Bluetooth to broadcast beacons while also logging the signal strength of beacons received from neighbouring handsets. Since received signal strength is a rough indicator of proximity, when a person is detected as being infected the data logged on their phone can be used to identify other people that the person was potentially close in the time preceding discovery of their infection. In Europe Bluetooth-based approaches for contract tracing have also been proposed, e.g. Decentralised Privacy-Preserving Proximity Tracing (DP-3T) [9], while Apple and Google have formed a partnership to develop a contract tracing API based on Bluetooth [2]. However, these initiatives are currently at a relatively early stage whereas the Singapore TraceTogether app is already deployed and operational, plus an open source version, referred to as OpenTrace, has now been released [15]. TraceTogether/OpenTrace is therefore currently the focus of much interest.

This work is solely based on the open-source OpenTrace app and the installable app from the Google Play store without any involvement of the developers of the app or any health authority.

The results of our study can be summarised as follows.

We find that the OpenTrace app uses Google's Firebase service to store and manage user data. This means that there are two main parties involved in handling data shared by the app, namely Google (who operate the Firebase service) and the health authority (or other agency) operating the OpenTrace app itself. As owner of Firebase, Google has access to all data transmitted by the app via Firebase but filters what data is made available to the operator of OpenTrace e.g. to present only aggregate statistics.

The OpenTrace app regularly sends telemetry data to the Firebase Analytics service. This data is tagged with persistent identifiers linked to the mobile handset so that messages from the same handset can be linked together. Further, messages also necessarily include the handset IP address (or the IP address of the upstream gateway), which can be used as a rough proxy for location using existing geoIP services. Note that the Firebase Analytics documentation [11] states that "Analytics derives location data from users' IP addresses". Hence, the data sent by the handset potentially allows its location to be tracked over time. Many studies have shown that location data linked over time can be used to de-anonymise: this is unsurprising since, for example, knowledge of the work and home locations of a user can be inferred from such location data (based on where the user mostly spends time during the day and evening), and when combined with other data this information can quickly become quite revealing [20,21].

The Firebase Analytics documentation states that "Thresholds are applied to prevent anyone viewing a report from inferring the demographics, interests, or location of individual users" [11]. Assuming this is effective (note that the effectiveness of de-anonymisation methods is far from clear when applied to location data over time), then the health authority operating the OpenTrace app cannot infer individual user locations. The primary privacy concern therefore lies with the holding of rough location data by Google itself. It is worth noting that when location history can be inferred from collected data then even if this inference is not made by the organisation that collects the data it may be made by other parties with whom data is shared. This includes commercial partners (who may correlate this with other data in their possession) and state agencies, as well as disclosure via data breaches.

In light of this, and since the potential use of a contract tracing app for large-scale tracking of the population is one of the main privacy concerns highlighted in the media, we recommend disabling use of Firebase Analytics in OpenTrace to avoid this regular transmission of messages to Google.

OpenTrace requires users to enter their phone number in order to use the app, and this number is stored on Firebase and visible to the health authority. It is relatively easy to link a phone number to a users real identity (indeed in some jurisdictions ID must be presented when buying a sim [17]) and so this creates an immediate privacy concern. The BlueTrace white paper [6] notes that storage of user phone numbers is optional and push notifications can be used instead. The decision as to whether to ask for user phone numbers (or other identifiers) therefore really depends on the requirements of the health authority for effectively managing contact tracing. For example, due to the approximate nature of proximity tracking via Bluetooth it is likely that OpenTrace data will be only one of many sources of information used in contact tracing and combining data from different sources may require the use of an identifier such as a phone number. The result may be a direct trade-off between privacy and the effectiveness of contact tracing.

Assuming that recording of phone numbers, or similar identifiers, is judged to be necessary then OpenTrace uses the Firebase Authentication service for this purpose. This use of Firebase Authentication creates an obvious potential conflict of interest for Google whose primary business is advertising based on collection of user personal data. In addition, the data held by Google need not be stored in the country where the app users are located. In particular, the Firebase privacy documentation [4] states that the Firebase Authentication service used by OpenTrace always processes its data in US data centres. Bearing in mind that a successful contact tracing app would be used by a large fraction of the population in a country, use of Firebase Authentication potentially means that their phone numbers may then be available to US state agencies. Such considerations suggest that it might be worth considering changing OpenTrace to make use of backend infrastructure that avoids outsourcing storage of user phone numbers to Google.

2   Threat Model: What Do We Mean by Privacy?

It is important to note that transmission of user data to backend servers is not intrinsically a privacy intrusion. For example, it can be useful to share details of the user device model/version and the locale/country of the device and this carries few privacy risks if this data is common to many users since the data itself cannot then be easily linked back to a specific user [19,22].

Issues arise, however, when data can be tied to a specific user. One common way that this can happen is when an app generates a long randomised string when first installed/started and then transmits this alongside other data. The randomised string then acts as an identifier of the app instance (since no other apps share the same string value) and when the same identifier is used across multiple transmissions it allows these transmissions to be tied together across time.

Linking a sequence of transmissions to an app instance does not explicitly reveal the user's real-world identity. However, the data can often be readily de-anonymised. One way that this can occur is if the app directly asks for user details (e.g. phone number, facebook login). But it can also occur indirectly using the fact that transmissions by an app always include the IP address of the user device (or more likely of an upstream NAT gateway). As already noted, the IP address acts as a rough proxy for user location via existing geoIP services and many studies have shown that location data linked over time can be used to de-anonymise. A pertinent factor here is the frequency with which updates are sent e.g. logging an IP address location once a day has much less potential to be revealing than logging one every few minutes.

With these concerns in mind, two of the main questions that we try to answer in the present study are (i) What explicit identifying data does the app directly request and (ii) Does the data that the app transmits to backend servers potentially allow tracking of the IP address of app instance over time.

3   Measurement Setup

3.1   Viewing Content of Encrypted Web Connections

All of the network connections we are interested in are encrypted. To inspect the content of a connection we route handset traffic via a WiFi access point (AP) that we control. We configure this AP to use mitmdump [18] as a proxy and adjust the firewall settings to redirect all WiFi traffic to mitmdump so that the proxying is transparent to the handset. In brief, when the OpenTrace app starts a new web connection the mitmdump proxy pretends to be the destination server and presents a fake certificate for the target server. This allows mitmdump to decrypt the traffic. It then creates an onward connection to the actual target server and acts as an intermediary relaying requests and their replies between the app and the target server while logging the traffic. The setup is illustrated schematically in Fig. 1.

The immediate difficulty encountered when using this setup is that the app carries out checks on the authenticity of server certificates received when starting a new connection and aborts the connection when these checks fail. To circumvent these checks we use a rooted phone and use Frida [13] to patch the OpenTrace app and Google Play Services (which the app uses to manage most of the connections it makes) on the fly to replace the relevant Java certificate validation functions with dummy functions that always report validation checks as being passed. The bulk of the effort needed lies in deducing which functions to patch since Google Play Services is closed-source and obfuscated (decompiling the bytecode produces Java with randomised class and variable names etc.) plus it uses customised certificate checking code (so standard unpinning methods fail). Implementing the unpinning for OpenTrace is therefore a fairly laborious manual process.

Handset   Laptop configured
                 as WiFi AP and
                 running MITMProxy

Fig. 1. Measurement setup. The mobile handset is configured to access the internet using a WiFi access point hosted on a laptop, use of cellular/mobile data is disabled. The laptop also has a wired internet connection. When an app on the handset starts a new web connection the laptop pretends to be the destination server so that it can decrypt the traffic. It then creates an onward connection to the actual target server and acts as an intermediary relaying requests and their replies between the handset app and the target server while logging the traffic.

3.2   Hardware and Software Used

Mobile handset: Google Pixel 2 running Android 9. Rooted using Magisk v19.1 and Magisk Manager v7.1.2 and running Frida Server v12.5.2. Laptop: Apple Macbook running Mojav 10.14.6 running Frida 12.8.20 and mitmproxy v5.0.1. Using a USB ethernet adapter the laptop is connected to a cable modem and so to the internet. The laptop is configured using its built in Internet Sharing function to operate as a WiFi AP that routes wireless traffic over the wired connection. The laptop firewall is then configured to redirect received WiFi traffic to mitmproxy listening on port 8080 by adding the rule `rdr pass on bridge100 inet proto tcp to any port 80, 443 -> 127.0.0.1 port 8080`. The handset is also connected to the laptop over USB and this is used as a control channel (no data traffic is routed over this connection) to install the OpenTrace app and carry out dynamic patching using Frida. Namely, using the adb shell the Frida server is started on the handset and then controlled from the laptop via the Frida client.

3.3   Test Design

Test design is straightforward since the OpenTrace app supports only a single flow of user interaction. Namely, on first startup a splash screen is briefly displayed and then an information screen is shown that contains a single "I want to help" button. On pressing this the user is taken to a second screen which outlines how OpenTrace works and which has a single button labelled "Great!!!". On pressing this the user is asked to enter their phone number and again there is only a single button labelled "Get OTP". The user is then taken to a screen where they are asked to enter a 6-digit code that has been texted to the supplied number. On pressing the "Verify" button then if this code is valid the user is taken through a couple of screens asking then to give the app needed permissions (Bluetooth, location, disabling of battery optimisation for the app, access to storage) and then arrives at the main screen which is displayed thereafter, see Fig. 2. This main screen has non-functioning buttons for help and sharing of the app, plus a button that is only to be pressed when the user has been confirmed as infected with Covid-19 and which uploads observed bluetooth data to the app backend server hosted on Firebase.

Testing therefore consists of recording the data sent upon installation and startup of the app, followed by navigation through these screens until the main screen is reached. The data sent by the app when left idle at the main screen (likely the main mode of operation of the app) is also recorded. We also tried to investigate the data sent upon pressing the upload function but found that this functionality fails with an error. Inspection of the code suggests that this upload functionality is incomplete.

Although our primary interest is in the open source OpenTrace app, this app is apparently derived from the closed-source TraceTogether app used by the health service in Singapore. We therefore also tried to collect data for the TraceTogether app for comparison with that generated by the OpenTrace app.

Fig. 2. Main screen displayed by OpenTrace following initial setup.

The latest version (v1.6.1) of TraceTogether is restricted to Singapore phone numbers, in our testing we therefore used an earlier version (v1.0.33) without this restriction in our tests.

3.4 Finding Identifiers in Network Connections

Potential identifiers in network connections were extracted by manual inspection. Basically any value present in network messages that stays the same across messages is flagged as a potential identifier. As we will see, almost all the values of interest are associated with the Firebase API that is part of Google Play Services. We therefore try to find more information on the nature of observed values from Firebase privacy policies and other public documents as well as by comparing them against known software and device identifiers e.g. the Google advertising identifier of the handset.

4   Google Firebase

OpenTrace uses Google's Firebase service to provide its server backend. This means that there are at least two parties involved in handling data shared by the app, namely Google (who operate the Firebase service infrastructure) and the health authority (or other agency) operating the OpenTrace app itself. As owner of Firebase, Google has access to all data transmitted by the app via Firebase but filters what data is made available to the operator of OpenTrace e.g. to present only aggregate statistics.

OpenTrace makes use of the Firebase Authentication, Firebase Functions, Firebase Storage and Firebase Analytics (also referred to as Google Analytics for Firebase) services. The app has hooks for Crashlytics and Firebase Remote Config, but the version studied here does not make active use of these two services.

The Firebase Authentication service is used on startup of the app to record the phone number entered by the user and verify it by texting a code which the user then enters into the app. The phone numbers entered are recorded by Firebase and linked to a Firebase identifier.

Firebase Functions allows the OpenTrace app to invoke execution of user defined Javascript functions on Google's cloud platform by sending requests to specified web addresses. The OpenTrace app uses this service to generate tempIDs for broadcast over bluetooth and for upload of logged tempIDs upon the user becoming infected with Covid-19. Firebase Storage is used to hold uploaded tempIDs. The tempIDs are generated by reversible encryption (see below) using a key stored in Google Cloud's Secret Manager service and accessed by the OpenTrace getTempIDs function hosted on Firebase Functions.

Figure 3 shows an example of the Firebase Functions logging visible to the operator of the OpenTrace app. This fine-grained logging data shows individual function calls together with the time and user making the call (the uid value is the user identifier used by Firebase Authentication and so can be directly linked to the users phone number).

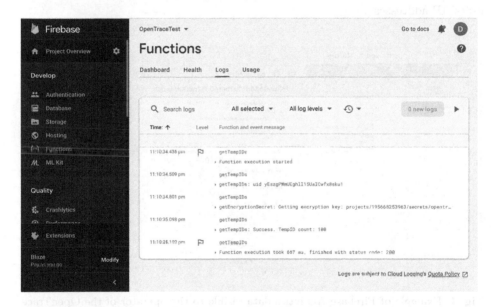

Fig. 3. Example of Firebase Functions logging visible to the operator of the OpenTrace app. Observe that there is fine-grained logging of individual function calls per user (the uid value in these logs is a unique identifier linked to a users phone number). The tempIDs function is, for example, regularly called by the OpenTrace app to refresh the set of tempIDs available for a mobile handset to advertise on Bluetooth.

The app is instrumented to record a variety of user events and log these to the backend server using Firebase Analytics.

The Firebase privacy documentation [4] outlines some of the information that is exchanged with Google during operation of the API. This privacy documentation does not state what is logged by Firebase Storage but notes that Firebase Authentication logs user phone numbers and IP addresses. Also that Firebase Analytics makes use of a number of identifiers including: (i) a user-resettable Mobile ad ID to "allow developers and marketers to track activity for advertising purposes. They're also used to enhance serving and targeting capabilities." [14], (ii) an Android ID which is "a 64-bit number (expressed as a hexadecimal string), unique to each combination of app-signing key, user, and device" [7], (iii) a InstanceID that "provides a unique identifier for each app instance" and "Once an Instance ID is generated, the library periodically sends information about the application and the device where it's running to the Firebase backend." [12] and (iv) an Analytics App Instance ID that is "used to compute user metrics throughout Analytics" [11]. The Firebase Analytics documentation [11] states that "As long as you use the Firebase SDK, you don't need to write any additional code to collect a number of user properties automatically", including Age, Gender, Interests, Language, Country plus a variety of device information. It also states that "Analytics derives location data from users' IP addresses".

Fig. 4. Example of Firebase Analytics data visible to the operator of the OpenTrace app. Observe that data is available on events occurring per individual device.

Figure 4 shows an example of the data made available to the operator of the OpenTrace app by Firebase Analytics. It can be seen that per device event data is available showing for example when OpenTrace is started on the device, when it is viewed etc.

The data collected by Google during operation of its Firebase services need not be stored in the same country as the user of an app is located. The Firebase privacy documentation [4] states that "Unless a service or feature offers data location selection, Firebase may process and store your data anywhere Google or its agents maintain facilities". It also states "A few Firebase services are only run from US data centers. As a result, these services process data exclusively in the United States" and it appears that these services include Firebase Authentication, which OpenTrace uses to stores user phone numbers.

It is important to note that only a filtered version of this data collected by Google is made available to users of its backend Firebase services. The Firebase Analytics documentation states that "Thresholds are applied to prevent anyone viewing a report from inferring the demographics, interests, or location of individual users" [11].

5   Cryptography

The tempIds used in OpenTrace are transmitted in Bluetooth beacons and are an encrypted form of a Firebase user identifier that can be linked to the user phone number using the Firebase Authentication service, together with two timestamps indicating the time interval during which the tempID is valid (to mitigate replay attacks).

In OpenTrace encryption is based on a single long-term symmetric secret that is stored in Google Cloud's Secret Manager service. The encryption is reversible so that the user identifier and timestamps can be recovered from an observed tempID given knowledge of this secret. When a person is detected to be infected with Covid-19 the tempIDs in beacons observed by the app on their phone can therefore be decrypted by the health authority to obtain the phone numbers of people who have been in proximity to the infected person. However, this setup also means that if a data breach occurs and the secret is disclosed then any recordings of tempIDs observed in Bluetooth beacons can also be decrypted by third parties. Alternative designs that ensure that only the tempIds associated with a user testing positive for Covid-19 could be decrypted would seem more desirable. It is also important to add provision for key updates and other key management, which is currently absent in OpenTrace (Table 1).

6   Measurements of Data Transmitted by OpenTrace App

6.1   Data Sent on Initial Startup

Upon installation and first startup the OpenTrace app makes a number of network connections. Note that there has been no interaction with the user beyond startup of the app, in particular no user consent to sharing of information.

The app initialises Firebase upon first startup, which generates the following POST request (standard/uninteresting parameters/headers are omitted):

```
POST https://firebaseinstallations.googleapis.com/v1/projects/opentracetest-4167b/
installations
Parameters:
    key=AIzaSyAB...
```

Table 1. Summary of network connections made by OpenTrace in response to user interactions.

Startup of app
• firebaseinstallations.googleapis.com (sends fid)
• settings.crashlytics.com
• app-measurement.com (sends app_instance_id, Google Advertising Id)
Entering phone number
• www.googleapis.com (sends phone number)
Entering 6-digit code
• www.googleapis.com (sends 6-digit code, receives)
• europe-west1-opentracetest-4167b.cloudfunctions (fetches tempIDs)
Agreeing to app permissions (bluetooth, location, battery)
Agreeing to app storage permission
• europe-west1-opentracetest-4167b.cloudfunctions (fetches tempIDs)
While idle
• app-measurement.com (app_instance_id, Google Advertising Id)

```
Headers:
    X-Android-Cert: 2AE4BED9E4F0...
Request body:
    {"appId": "1:195668253963:android:0e1d8...", <...>
     "fid": "f4vnM2vqSLuOgcpB8FbDd_",<...> }
```

The value of the parameter "key" is hardwired into the app to allow it to access Firebase, and so is the same for all instances of the app. Similarly, the X-Android-Cert header is the SHA1 hash of the app and the "appId" is a Google app identifier and both are the same for all instances of the app. The "key" parameter and X-Android-Cert appear in many of the network requests made by the app but to save space are omitted from now on. The "fid" value appears to be the Firebase Instance ID, discussed above. This uniquely identifies the current instance of the app but is observed to change for a fresh install of the app (i.e. deleting the app and then reinstalling). The response to this request echoes the fid value and includes two tokens which appear to be used to identify the current session.

Next, OpenTrace tries to fetch settings for Crashlytics:

```
GET https://settings.crashlytics.com/spi/v2/platforms/android/apps/io.bluetrace.
opentrace/settings
Parameters:
    instance: da2618e19123d5...
    display_version: 1.0.41-debug-b39f5...
    icon_hash: 8229e07efb...
Headers:
```

```
X-CRASHLYTICS-DEVELOPER-TOKEN: 470fa2b4ae...
X-CRASHLYTICS-API-KEY: 129fa51a5bbee6...
X-CRASHLYTICS-INSTALLATION-ID: e8854e81...
```

The "instance" parameter differs from the fid, its value is observed to changes upon a clean install of the app. Similarly, the X-CRASHLYTICS-INSTALLATION-ID value changes upon a clean install. These two values appear to be used to identify the instance of Crashlytics (and so the app). The "display_version" parameter is the OpenTrace VERSION_NAME value from Build-Config.java in the app source code and is the same for all copies of the app. Its not clear what the X-CRASHLYTICS-DEVELOPER-TOKEN, X-CRASHLYTICS-API-KEY and icon_hash values are, but they are observed to stay unchanged upon fresh install of the app and so do not seem to be tied to the app instance. The response to the request to settings.crashlytics.com is "403 Forbidden" since Crashlytics has not been configured in the Firebase server backend.

OpenTrace now makes its first call to Firebase Analytics:

```
GET https://app-measurement.com/config/app/1%3A195668253963%3Aandroid%3
A0e1d84bec59ca7e66e160e
 Parameters:
    app_instance_id: f67be0634d5102bcfe0352bc0bbeaded
```

```
POST https://app-measurement.com/a
 <...>
\x02_o\x12\x04auto\x07\x03_et\x18\x01\x12\x02_e\x18\xd0\xa4\xdb\x92\x9b. \x00\x1a\
x14\x08\xd0\xa4\xdb\x92\x9b.\x12\x04_fot \x80\x82\xfc\x93\x9b.\x1a\x0e\x08\xd0\xa4
\xdb\x92\x9b.\x12\x03_fi \x01\x1a\x0f\x08\xee\x9a\xdc\x92\x9b.\x12\x04_lte \x01\
x1a\x0e\x08\xef\x9a\xdc\x92\x9b.\x12\x03_se \x01 \xec\x9a\xdc\x92\x9b.(\xd0\xa4\
xdb\x92\x9b.0\xd0\xa4\xdb\x92\x9b.B\x07androidJ\x019R\x07Pixel 2Z\x05en-us'<j\
x0emanual_installr\x16io.bluetrace.opentrace\x82\x01\x191.0.41-debug-b39f57f-F4D3\
x88\x01\xa0\xac\x01\x90\x01\xf9\x8a\x01\x9a\x01$1d2635f5-2af7-4fb3-86e...\xa0\x01\
x00\xaa\x01 f67be0634d5102bcfe0352bc0bbeaded\xb0\x01\xda\x8f\xd6\xd8\xe4\xe5\xa5\
xf4\x8e\x01\xb8\x01\x01\xca\x01-1:195668253963:android:0e1d84bec59ca7e66e160e\xe0\
x01\x01\xf2\x01\x16f4vnM2vqSLuOgcpB8FbDd.\xf8\x01)\x98\x02\x98\x9b\xbe\xa5\xfa\xf8\
xe8\x02\xa0\x02\x00\xe8\x02\xb2\xeb\x86\x0b\xf0\x02\x00
```

The first request appears to be asking about configuration changes and the response is "304 Not Modified". The second request uploads information on events within the app (see below for further discussion). Both requests contain an app_instance_id value which acts to link them together (and also subsequent analytics requests). The second request also contains the Firebase fid value. In addition the second request contains the device Google Advertising Id (1d2635f5-2af7-4fb3-86e...) as reported by the Google/Ads section of the handset Settings app. Unless manually reset by the user this value persists indefinitely, including across fresh installs of OpenTrace, and so essentially acts as a strong identifier of the device and its user. The body of the second request contains a number of other values. Some identify the version of the app, and so are not sensitive, but the provenance of other values is not known to the authors.

6.2 Data Sent upon Phone Number Entry

After initial startup, navigation through the first two information screens generates no network connections. At the this screen the app asks the user to enter their phone number. Upon doing this and pressing the button to proceed the

following network connections are made. The first connection sends the phone
number to Firebase:

```
POST https://www.googleapis.com/identitytoolkit/v3/relyingparty/
sendVerificationCode
Headers:
   X-Goog-Spatula: CjYKFmlvLmJsdWV0cmFjZS5vc...
Request Body:
   1: <phone number>
```

It is not clear how the X-Goog-Spatula value is generated but it seems to consist,
at least in part, of base64-encoded information since base64-decoding yields "6
?io.bluetrace.opentrace? KuS+2eTwbmFXe/8epaO9wF8yVTE=" fol-
lowed by additional binary data.

Firebase now texts a 6-digit code to the phone number entered and the
OpenTrace app asks the user to enter this code. Entering the code generates the
following network connection:

```
POST https://www.googleapis.com/identitytoolkit/v3/relyingparty/verifyPhoneNumber
 Headers:
   X-Goog-Spatula: CjYKFmlvLmJsdWV0cmFjZS5vc...
Request body:
   1: AM5PThB...
   3: <6-digit code entered>
```

The X-Goog-Spatula header value is the same as for the previous request and
so can be used to link them together (perhaps it's a form of short session id).
The AM5PThB... value is from the response to the first request and presumably
encodes the 6-digit value in a way that the server can decode so as to compare
against the value entered by the user.

The response to a correct 6-digit code informs the app of the user id value
yEszgPWm... used by Firebase (which is visible on the Firebase dashboard
and directly linked to the users phone number), together with a number of other
values including what seems to be a user identifier/authentication token that is
used in the body of the following request:

```
POST https://www.googleapis.com/identitytoolkit/v3/relyingparty/getAccountInfo
 Headers:
   X-Goog-Spatula: CjYKFmlvLmJsdWV0cmFjZS5vc...
Request Body:
   1: eyJhbGciOiJSUzI1NiIsI...
```

The response contains the phone number previously entered by the user together
with the user id value yEszgPWm... and some timestamps (presumably associated with account creation etc.).

At this point an account for the user has been successfully created/authen-
ticated on Firebase and OpenTrace now uses the Firebase Functions service to
request a batch of tempIDs:

```
POST https://europe-west1-opentracetest-4167b.cloudfunctions.net/getTempIDs
```

to which the response is 14KB of json:

```
{"result": {"refreshTime": 1587878233, "status": "SUCCESS",
   "tempIDs": [
      { "expiryTime": 1587835873,"startTime": 1587834973,
        "tempID": "RQVK+en..." },
      <...>
```

OpenTrace then makes a call to the getHandshakePin function hosted by Fire-base Functions:

```
POST https://europe-west1-opentracetest-4167b.cloudfunctions.net/getHandshakePin
```

and the response contains the PIN that the health service operating the app needs to present to the user in order to confirm they should ask the app to upload the observed tempIDs to Firebase Storage.

6.3 Data Sent When Permissions Are Granted

After phone number entry and verification, the app asks the user for permission to use bluetooth, location and to disable battery optimisation for OpenTrace. These interactions do not generate any network connections. Finally Open-Trace asks for permission to access file storage on the handset. When this is granted OpenTrace makes a second call to https://europe-west1-opentracetest-4167b.cloudfunctions.net/getTempIDs and receives a further batch of tempIDs in response.

6.4 Data Sent When Sitting Idle at Main Screen

Once startup of OpenTrace is complete it sits idle at a main screen until the user, and it is in this mode of operation that it spends the bulk of its time. Roughly once an hour OpenTrace is observed to make a pair of connections to Firebase Analytics. This is consistent with Firebase Analytics documentation [10] which says that "analytics data is batched up and sent down when the client library sees that there's any local data that's an hour old." and "on Android devices with Play Services, this one hour timer is across all apps using Firebase Analytics". The first connection of the pair:

```
GET https://app-measurement.com/config/app/1%3A195668253963%3Aandroid%3
A0e1d84bec59ca7e66e160e
Parameters:
   app_instance_id: f67be0634d5102bcfe0352bc0bbeaded
```

appears to be checking for updates, to which the response is 304 Not Modified.

The second connection is also to app-measurement.com and appears to send telemetry data logging user interactions with the app. When configured for verbose logging Firebase writes details of the uploaded data to the handset log, which can inspected over the USB connection to the handset using the "adb logcat" command. A typical entry log entry starts as follows:

```
protocol_version: 1
platform: android
gmp_version: 22048
uploading_gmp_version: 17785
dynamite_version: 0
config_version: 1587452740341144
gmp_app_id: 1:195668253963:android:0e1d84...
admob_app_id:
app_id: io.bluetrace.opentrace
app_version: 1.0.41-debug-b39f57f-F4D3
app_version_major: 41
firebase_instance_id: f4vnM2vqSLuOgcpB8FbDd_
```

```
dev_cert_hash: -8149097300642920486
app_store: manual_install
upload_timestamp_millis: 1587823341351
start_timestamp_millis: 1587823321657
end_timestamp_millis: 1587823321670
previous_bundle_start_timestamp_millis: 1587822575641
previous_bundle_end_timestamp_millis: 1587822932936
app_instance_id: f67be0634d5102bcfe0352bc0bbeaded
resettable_device_id: 1d2635f5-2af7-4fb3-86e...
device_id:
ds_id:
limited_ad_tracking: false
os_version: 9
device_model: Pixel 2
user_default_language: en-us
time_zone_offset_minutes: 60
bundle_sequential_index: 14
service_upload: true
health_monitor:
```

Inspection of the message transmitted over the network to Firebase shows a section of the following form:

```
\x07androidJ\x019R\x07Pixel 2Z\x05en-us'<j\x0emanual_installr\x16io.bluetrace.
opentrace\x82\x01\x191.0.41-debug-b39f57f-F4D3\x88\x01\xa0\xac\x01\x90\x01\xf9\x8a
\x01\x9a\x01$1d2635f5-2af7-4fb3-86e...\xa0\x01\x00\xaa\x01
f67be0634d5102bcfe0352bc0bbeaded\xb0\x01\xda\x8f\xd6\xd8\xe4\xe5\xa5\xf4\x8e\x01\
xb8\x01\x03\xca\x01-1:195668253963:android:0e1d84...\xd0\x01\x89\xc7\xdb\x92\x9b.\
xe0\x01\x01\xf2\x01\x16f4vnM2vqSLuOgcpB8FbDd\xf8\x01)\x98\x02\x98\x9b\xbe\xa5\xfa\
xf8\xe8\x02\xa0\x02\x00\xe8\x02\xb2\xeb\x86\x0b\xf0\x02\x00
```

within which many of the values from the log can be identified, including the firebase_instance_id, the app_instance_id, the resettable_device_id (the Google Advertising Id). Each handset log entry also includes a sequence of user_property values of the form:

```
user_property {
  set_timestamp_millis: 1587790361696
  name: first_open_time(_fot)
  string_value:
  int_value: 1587790800000
}
```

followed by a sequence of event entries of the form

```
event {
  name: user_engagement(_e)
  timestamp_millis: 1587823321657
  previous_timestamp_millis: 1587822932919
  param {
    name: firebase_event_origin(_o)
    string_value: auto
  }
  <more param entries>
}
```

and these can also be identified within the body of the message sent by Open-Trace to Firebase Analytics.

6.5 Data Sent by TraceTogether (v1.0.33)

We repeated the above measurements using the closed-source TraceTogether app currently being used by the Singapore government. In summary, we observed similar behaviour to that seen with OpenTrace but with the following differences:

1. TraceTogether was not observed to download tempIDs from Firebase following initial startup. Presumably these are generated locally within the app, at least initially.
2. TraceTogether makes calls to asia-east2-govtech-tracer.cloudfunctions.net/ getBroadcastMessage i.e. to a getBroadcastMessage function hosted on Firebase Functions but which is not present in OpenTrace.
3. TraceTogether makes calls to firebaseremoteconfig.googleapis.com and so presumably makes use of the Firebase Remote Config service (as already noted, there are hooks for this within OpenTrace, but these are not activated).

7 Summary and Conclusions

We have carried out an initial measurement study of the OpenTrace app and of a version of the related closed-source TraceTogether app deployed in Singapore. We find that the use of Google's Firebase Analytics service means the data sent by OpenTrace potentially allows the (IP-based) location of user handsets to be tracked by Google over time. We also find that OpenTrace stores user phone numbers in the Firebase Authentication service. This use of Firebase Authentication creates an obvious potential conflict of interest for Google whose primary business is advertising based on collection of user personal data. In addition, the Firebase Authentication service processes its data in US data centres even if users are located in other countries. Lastly, we note that OpenTrace relies on a single long-term secret key stored in a Google Cloud service and so is vulnerable to disclosure of this secret key. We plan to further investigate this and similar apps for privacy, security and efficacy in the coming weeks but would strongly recommend that anyone planning on using an app based on OpenTrace address these significant issues before deployment.

References

1. In Coronavirus Fight, China Gives Citizens a Color Code, With Red Flags, New York Times, 1 March 2020. https://www.nytimes.com/2020/03/01/business/china-coronavirus-surveillance.html
2. Apple and Google partner on COVID-19 contact tracing technology, 10 April 2020. https://www.apple.com/newsroom/2020/04/apple-and-google-partner-on-covid-19-contact-tracing-technology/
3. Coronavirus: Under surveillance and confined at home in Taiwan, BBC News, 24 March 2020. https://www.nytimes.com/2020/03/01/business/china-coronavirus-surveillance.html
4. Privacy and Security in Firebase, 27 November 2019. https://firebase.google.com/support/privacy

5. Coronavirus mobile apps are surging in popularity in South Korea, CNN, 28 February 2020. https://edition.cnn.com/2020/02/28/tech/korea-coronavirus-tracking-apps/index.html
6. BlueTrace: A privacy-preserving protocol for community-driven contact tracing across borders, 9 April 2020. https://bluetrace.io/static/bluetrace_whitepaper-938063656596c104632def383eb33b3c.pdf
7. Android Reference Guide: Android Id. https://developer.android.com/reference/android/provider/Settings.Secure.html#ANDROID_ID. Accessed 26 Apr 2020
8. CoronaMadrid Covid-19 App. https://www.coronamadrid.com/. Accessed 26 Apr 2020
9. Decentralised Privacy-Preserving Proximity Tracing (DP-3T) Demo App. https://github.com/DP-3T/dp3t-app-android. Accessed 26 Apr 2020
10. Firebase Blog: How Long Does it Take for My Firebase Analytics Data to Show Up? https://firebase.googleblog.com/2016/11/how-long-does-it-take-for-my-firebase-analytics-data-to-show-up.html. Accessed 26 Apr 2020
11. Firebase Help: Automatically collected user properties. https://support.google.com/firebase/answer/6317486. Accessed 26 Apr 2020
12. Firebase Reference Guide: FirebaseInstanceId. https://firebase.google.com/docs/reference/android/com/google/firebase/iid/FirebaseInstanceId. Accessed 26 Apr 2020
13. Frida: Dynamic instrumentation toolkit for developers, reverse-engineers, and security researchers. https://frida.re/. Accessed 26 Apr 2020
14. Google Ad Manager Help: About mobile advertising IDs. https://support.google.com/admanager/answer/6274238. Accessed 26 Apr 2020
15. OpenTrace Source Code. https://github.com/OpenTrace-community. Accessed 26 Apr 2020
16. TraceTogether App Website. https://www.tracetogether.gov.sg/. Accessed 26 Apr 2020
17. The Mandatory Registration of Prepaid SIM Card Users, GSMA White Paper, November 2013. https://www.gsma.com/publicpolicy/wp-content/uploads/2013/11/GSMA_White-Paper_Mandatory-Registration-of-Prepaid-SIM-Users_32pgWEBv3.pdf
18. Cortesi, A., Hils, M., Kriechbaumer, T., Contributors: mitmproxy: A free and open source interactive HTTPS proxy (v5.01) (2020). https://mitmproxy.org/
19. Machanavajjhala, A., Kifer, D., Gehrke, J., Venkitasubramaniam, M.: L-diversity: privacy beyond k-anonymity. ACM Trans. Knowl. Disc. Data (TKDD) 1(1), 3-es (2007)
20. Golle, P., Partridge, K.: On the anonymity of home/work location pairs. In: Tokuda, H., Beigl, M., Friday, A., Brush, A.J.B., Tobe, Y. (eds.) Pervasive 2009. LNCS, vol. 5538, pp. 390–397. Springer, Heidelberg (2009). https://doi.org/10.1007/978-3-642-01516-8_26
21. Srivatsa, M., Hicks, M.: Deanonymizing mobility traces: using social network as a side-channel. In: Proceedings of the 2012 ACM Conference on Computer and Communications Security, pp. 628–637 (2012)
22. Sweeney, L.: k-anonymity: A model for protecting privacy. Int. J. Uncertain. Fuzz. Knowl. Based Syst. 10(05), 557–570 (2002)

The Maestro Attack: Orchestrating Malicious Flows with BGP

Tyler McDaniel[✉], Jared M. Smith, and Max Schuchard

University of Tennessee, Knoxville, USA
{bmcdan16,jms,mschucha}@utk.edu

Abstract. We present **Maestro**, a novel Distributed Denial of Service (DDoS) attack that leverages control plane traffic engineering techniques to concentrate botnet flows on transit links. Executed from a compromised or malicious Autonomous System (AS), Maestro advertises routes poisoned for selected ASes to collapse inbound traffic paths onto a single target link. A greedy heuristic fed by bot traceroute data iteratively builds the set of ASes to poison. Given a compromised router with advantageous positioning in the AS-level Internet topology, an adversary can expect to bring an additional 30% of the entire botnet against vulnerable links. Interestingly, the size of the adversary-controlled AS plays little role in this amplification effect; core links can be degraded by small, resource-limited ASes. To understand the scope of the attack, we evaluate widespread Internet link vulnerability via simulation across several metrics, including BGP betweenness and botnet flow density, and assess the topological requirements for successful attacks. We supplement simulation results with ethically conducted "attacks" on real Internet links. Finally, we present effective defenses for network operators seeking to mitigate this attack.

Keywords: DDoS · Link Flooding Attack · Interdomain routing

1 Introduction

Distributed denial of service (DDoS) attacks direct traffic from many distinct sources on the Internet to overwhelm the capacity of links or end hosts. These attacks proliferate despite extensive academic and economic investment in mitigation, and intensify with the Internet's expansion to new devices and services. A reflection attack fueled by unprotected memcached servers, for example, temporarily disabled Github [35]. *Link Flooding Attacks* or *LFAs* are DDoS attacks against infrastructure links rather than end hosts. Prominent examples in the literature include the Coremelt [52], Crossfire [26], and CXPST [46] attacks. Worryingly, LFAs could be moving from proposed attacks to present threat. In 2016, a Mirai botnet-sourced attack directed over 500 Gbps of traffic to a Liberian infrastructure provider in a real-world LFA [47].

Study supported by the National Science Foundation under Grant No. 1850379.

N. Park et al. (Eds.): SecureComm 2020, LNICST 335, pp. 97–117, 2020.
https://doi.org/10.1007/978-3-030-63086-7_7

In order for an LFA adversary to successfully target a link, the adversary must be able to direct traffic from bots to destinations such that the traffic traverses the target link. However, while end hosts control their traffic's destination, they cannot control the path taken by that traffic. Network operators for the Autonomous System (AS) that bots reside within chose outbound paths for their flows. This means that links have varied exposure to LFAs due to routing choices. For some targets, an attacker may find destinations for individual bots such that the entire botnet sends traffic over some target link; for others, bots may have no such paths.

Prior academic work fails to deeply address this topological constraint. For example, Coremelt [52] only quantified if an adversary could flood *at least one* link of the ten largest ASes by degree, but did not quantify how many links were impacted for those ASes. CXPST [46] targeted links based on control plane properties, and recognized in their results that many likely target links are out of the attacker's reach. Most recently, Crossfire [26] explored the ability of LFAs to disconnect geographic regions. However, their experiments used paths from PlanetLab nodes both as their model for botnet traffic propagation and *overall* topology, meaning that *by definition the only links considered in their model were those their "botnet" could reach.*

In Sect. 3, we quantify the vulnerability of Internet links to LFAs with simulations that join CAIDA's inferred Internet topology with botnet models backed by real-world bot distributions. For one of our link sample sets, we found that just 18% to 23% of links are traversable by the majority of bots in three major botnets, and fewer than 10% of sampled links were vulnerable to >75% of bots. Even if we restrict our set of targets to the 10% most traversed links, the majority are reachable by <20% of the botnet.

In Sect. 4, we investigate how routing-capable adversaries can expose potential LFA targets inadvertently shielded by routing choices. The result is a novel attack, Maestro, that orchestrates remote AS path selection and malicious bot flows to degrade links outside the reach of traditional LFAs. Our attack requires an adversary to have two tools: a botnet and limited control of a Border Gateway Protocol (BGP) speaker. The Maestro attack utilizes a traffic engineering technique called *BGP poisoning* to adjust bots' inbound path to the compromised BGP speaker's network so they include a target link. The attacker then launches a traditional DDoS attack against the compromised BGP speaker's network, resulting in attack flows funneled over the target link.

We demonstrate Maestro's ability to both amplify LFAs for already-vulnerable links and extend a botmaster's reach to previously unexposed targets in simulation. After executing the Maestro attack from a well-positioned adversary, more than 90% of sampled links are exposed to a majority of bots across each botnet, and 85% to 87% of links are exposed to 75% or more bots. Our analysis explores a number of different target link/compromised BGP speaker selection methods to discover how these properties factor into attack success. The results of these evaluations are explored in depth in Sect. 6, where we analyze two Maestro adversary types.

We validate Maestro's underlying mechanisms with experimental "attacks" on the live Internet in Sect. 5. From two different "compromised" routers, we achieved 2x or greater flow density improvement against target Internet links. Following our experiments, we consider defenses to mitigate Maestro, exploring the relative effectiveness of each via simulation, with in-depth discussion of results. Our goal is to give a first look into mitigation techniques network operators can individually deploy to protect their own links from the Maestro attack. Feedback from outreach to the network operator community is also presented.

2   Background

2.1   Border Gateway Protocol

The *Border Gateway Protocol* (BGP) [43] is the Internet's de facto routing protocol. BGP enables 68,000 Autonomous Systems (ASes) to exchange routing information and connect disparate parts of the Internet's infrastructure. BGP routes are defined by a destination IP prefix and a collection of attributes, including the AS PATH, or list of AS-level hops to the route destination. ASes originate routes to hosted IP prefixes via BGP advertisements to neighboring ASes. Each AS chooses its path to a prefix based on attributes of stored paths, most notably LOCAL PREF and AS PATH length. LOCAL PREF represents the AS operator's local policy choices regarding path qualities, and holds precedence over AS PATH length in the decision process. The *longest prefix matching* rule dictates that the stored path with the longest (most specific) IP prefix match is used to forward received packets.

Because the BGP decision process draws on path and policy attributes in route selection, BGP is a path-vector algorithm *with policies*. These policies are informed by *business relationships* between ASes. ASes can have peers, customers, and providers. Peers exchange traffic for free, while customers pay providers to transit traffic. These economic partnerships shape the Internet topology according to the valley-free routing model [18]. In simple terms, the model states that BGP routes will not transit from a customer to a provider after transiting from a provider to a customer, which ensures ASes do not incur monetary costs whenever possible. One important abstraction related to this model is the *customer cone*, defined as an AS and all of its direct/indirect customers. More formally, an AS's customer cone is the set of all ASes that can be reached from the AS transiting only provider to customer links [33].

2.2   BGP Poisoning

The BGP decision process gives local operators control over outbound paths, but operators have little influence over inbound traffic paths. Techniques do exist for next-hop inbound path control, including the MULTI EXIT DISC (exit discriminator) attribute [37] and BGP communities [16], but both are subject to remote AS's policies. This means inbound path control cannot be exerted by a

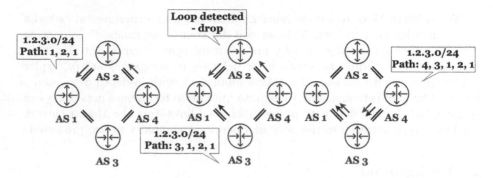

Fig. 1. BGP poisoning. AS 1 advertises a specific prefix (thicker arrow). AS 4's traffic to AS 1 (blue) is moved to the more specific route. AS 2 is said to have been *poisoned*. (Color figure online)

destination AS arbitrarily on the broader Internet. Fortunately, *BGP poisoning*, a traffic engineering technique found in prior work [1,28,48,49,54], allows for inbound route manipulation *without coordination* from other ASes. Recent work demonstrates poisons of non-Tier 1 networks are rarely filtered [48].

BGP poisoning relies on two characteristics of BGP: loop detection and longest-prefix matching. Loop detection is a specified BGP behavior that dictates ASes drop paths that already contain their own AS number (ASN). This prevents loops, but it also enables BGP poisoning (see Fig. 1 for an illustration). An AS that wishes to adjust inbound paths off certain links can falsely include the ASes to be avoided in an advertised path. As a result of being included on the path, the poisoned ASes will drop the incoming update, and routes will propagate around links involving the poisoned ASes. In practice, the poisoned ASes are sandwiched between copies of the originator's ASN to avoid issues with RPKI (see Sect. 2.2 below). Connectivity between poisoner and poisoned ASes can be maintained by using two sets of advertisements: a non-poisoned advertisement for the IP prefix, and poisoned advertisements for more specific (longer) prefixes that cover the original block of IP addresses. Since packets are forwarded on the most specific address match, any AS which has access to the poisoned path will always install it.

RPKI, Path Aggregation, and Poisoning: The Resource Public Key Infrastructure (RPKI) [34] is a feature in partial deployment [6,20] that ties ASNs to their allocated prefixes via Route Origin Authorizations (ROAs). ROAs are designed to prevent prefix hijacking [39] and do not affect BGP poisoning as described above. BGPsec [30] extends BGP with cryptographic hardening of AS PATHs. If fully deployed, BGPsec would prevent BGP poisoning entirely. However, no commercial BGPsec implementations exist [50], and BGPsec is largely ineffective unless widely implemented [21].

AS PATH aggregation as described in [43] allows ASes to aggregate downstream routes for multiple specific prefixes (e.g., many consecutive/24s) into a single, more general prefix (e.g., a/16) originated by the *aggregator*. Operators can apply an AS SET attribute with ASNs of aggregated routes; this step preserves poisons on aggregated routes. The Potaroo project's 2020 routing table analysis found that nearly 40% of aggregate address spans are covered by more specific routes, suggesting that aggregators often allow more specifics to propagate alongside aggregates [19].

2.3 Link Flooding Attacks

Volumetric *Distributed Denial of Service* (DDoS) describes a coordinated availability attack on a target link or end host with overwhelming traffic from multiple sources. A common flow source for these attacks are botnets: networks of compromised end hosts (bots) under an attacker's control. *Link Flooding Attacks* (LFAs) refer to DDoS against network infrastructure rather than end hosts. One of the first such attacks in the literature is Coremelt [52]. Coremelt specifies that a botmaster 1) map which links are present on bot-to-bot paths, 2) target a specific link used between many bots, and 3) direct bot traffic *between bots* over the link. The resulting n^2 flows (for n bots with paths over the link) exhausts target link capacity. The Crossfire attack [26] strategically targets multiple Internet links to isolate an entire region (military installation, university, geographic region, etc.). Rather than directing traffic to one another, bots map paths to publicly available web services (decoys) that transit target links. Bots then send sustained, low-intensity flows to decoys to execute the attack.

3   Can Botnets Target Any Link?

Link Flooding Attacks (see Sect. 2.3 earlier) hinge on the botmaster's ability to drive traffic over a target link. First, the botmaster must find paths from bots to remote destinations that cross the target link. Next, they must direct flows over these paths to aggregate traffic at the target and exhaust its capacity. If the attacker's flows overwhelm the link, "drowning out" benign traffic, the attack is successful. Bots without a path to some destination that includes the target link **cannot participate in the attack**.

This path requirement is largely unaddressed by prior work on LFAs. Researchers often 1) do not perform their measurements with distribution data from a real botnet, notably Kang et al.'s Crossfire [26], 2) assume botnets can direct significant flows over arbitrary links on the Internet without evidence, as in Tran et al.'s examination of the feasibility of re-routing based LFA defenses [54], and/or 3) target links most accessible to botnet flows, as in Coremelt [52], CXPST [46], and Crossfire. In fact, both target selection and attack success for Crossfire is measured via a degradation ratio that *only* considers links exposed to bots. These limitations raise questions about how well LFAs can target arbitrary links in the Internet topology. Here we explore those questions with Internet-scale BGP simulation.

3.1   Simulation Methodology

Our experiments are performed by extending the Chaos BGP simulator from prior work [45,46,49,54] with new modules. Chaos builds the Internet's BGP topology based on publicly available inferred AS relationship data from CAIDA [56]. In the simulator, ASes perform a simplified BGP decision process for path selection that includes longest prefix matching, path selection based on LOCAL PREF and AS PATH, and route export based on local policy. As true local AS policies are private, this is the most accurate simulation of AS behavior we can devise. We model our simulator's poison mechanics on the live Internet's treatment of BGP poisoning [1,28,48].

For each attack, we use three botnet models based on Mirai, Conficker, and Blackenergy botnet IP measurements. Our botnet models are built from passive and active measurements of infected hosts from a variety of sources. The *Mirai* botnet model includes 2.29 million IP addresses in 11,633 ASes. These addresses were recorded by a Chinese CDN as they spread the malware, a process with a unique signature [38]. Our *Conficker* model contains 2.28 million bot IPs from 12,095 ASes found by detecting bot rendezvous points and monitoring traffic to these points [53]. The *Blackenergy* model is a SCADA-focused botnet developed from similar techniques as presented in [5] with a total of 310,943 bot IPs across 4,291 ASes. Note these IP counts may not represent true botnet size given DHCP churn and other factors; in this work, we are primarily concerned with AS distribution of bots rather than counting infected hosts.

3.2   Vulnerability Experiments

Our initial experiments in the simulator measure the vulnerability of Internet links to LFAs. We build the AS-level topology as described above and classify links in two ways - relative usage and vulnerability. We quantify link usage with *betweenness*, defined as the number of times a link appears on paths between any pair of ASes in the simulator. Figure 2a shows the cumulative distribution of betweenness for simulated Internet links. Most links appear on 100 or fewer AS paths. Select links, however, have a betweenness of more than *1 million*. Attacks on these critical links would wreak havoc with upstream and downstream networks, and cause widespread disruption in Internet services. We quantify link vulnerability with *flow density*: the percentage of a botnet's infected hosts with simulated paths over the target link to either 1) another bot-hosting AS, called *bot-to-bot* flow density, or 2) any destination AS, called *bot-to-any* flow density. The bot-to-bot flow density models the effectiveness of a Coremelt-style attack; the bot-to-any flow density roughly follows the Crossfire attack.

To show how link vulnerability and usage are related, Fig. 2b plots bot-to-bot flow density on the x-axis against betweenness on the y-axis. Not unexpectedly, some low betweenness (peripheral) links are wholly outside an LFA attacker's reach. We note that relaxing our attack technique by allowing bots to send traffic to any AS destination does not significantly alleviate these limitations, as shown in Fig. 2c. **Critically, some moderate to high betweenness (core)**

links are also partially or completely devoid of paths between bots.
This experiment provides evidence that botnet-sourced LFAs can be limited by
topological factors. While low betweenness links are most difficult to reach from
the botnet families in our study, even highly trafficked links are not always fully
exposed to botnet flows.

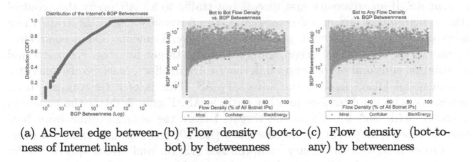

(a) AS-level edge between- (b) Flow density (bot-to- (c) Flow density (bot-to-
ness of Internet links   bot) by betweenness   any) by betweenness

Fig. 2. LFA vulnerability as function of betweenness

4   The Maestro Attack

The prior section demonstrates that most links, including many likely LFA targets, are shielded from the full force of major botnets. This condition arises
from the lack of end host control over traffic routes; bots cannot always find a
destination for their flows that cross a target link. In this section, we introduce
the Maestro attack, the first combination of traffic engineering techniques with
LFAs. Maestro alters the control plane to increase target flow density and extend
a botmaster's reach to previously shielded links.

Threat Model: To execute the attack, an adversary requires 1) command of
a botnet and 2) control of a BGP speaker, i.e., an AS's edge router. The first
item is trivially obtainable, as botmasters routinely monetize their networks by
renting them out in an attack-as-a-service model on the dark web [41]. **Recent
events demonstrate that multiple feasible avenues exist for adversaries
to gain routing capability.** The 3ve fraud operation [22] demonstrated the
most straightforward route - simply registering a new AS. Insider attacks from
disgruntled network operators, e.g. the Canadian bitcoin hijack [32], are another
path to adversarial routing capability. Note that edge routers *themselves* need
not be compromised to launch the attack - it is sufficient to compromise router
configuration systems, as may have occurred in the XLHost ISP breach [17].
However, recent Cisco router vulnerability disclosures show that remote attacks
on edge routers are also a realistic attack vector [7–10]. Finally, BGP has previously been weaponized for intelligence gathering [15] and censorship [14] by
nation states.

Maestro Concept: Since bots are located in disparate ASes, an adversary who seeks to control bot traffic paths must adjust the best path at each bot-containing remote network. Obviously, if the adversary compromised all these ASes, they could change paths directly, but such an adversary is far more powerful than the one in our threat model. Maestro's central insight is that an adversary who controls one edge router in a single AS can influence remote networks' paths *to that AS*. If an adversary first directs bot traffic to an AS/prefix they control (the *compromised AS* or *adversary AS*), the adversary can orchestrate those flows onto a target link with poisoned BGP advertisements (like a conductor, or *maestro*). We call the origin endpoint of the target link the *From AS* and destination endpoint of the target link the *To AS*. In effect, Maestro also executes a traditional DDoS against the adversary AS. This is of little concern to an adversary who compromises another entity's AS. Figure 3 shows the attack in abstract, with link 5 ↦ 8 as the target. Before the attack, traffic from bot-hosting ASes (ASes 0–3) to the adversary (AS 10) flows around (and not over) the target link. Our adversary compromises AS 10, and issues specific prefix advertisements with ASes 4 and 6 poisoned. This causes inbound flows from the bot-hosting ASes to the adversary to concentrate over the target link. After altering these paths, the adversary AS (AS 10) directs bot traffic to itself. The result is a channeled DDoS flowing over 5 ↦ 8.

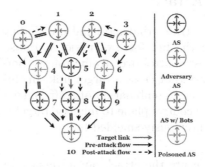

Fig. 3. Maestro: BGP poisons collapse botnet traffic onto a target link.

4.1   Poison Selection Algorithm

BGP poisoning is a primitive that moves inbound traffic *off* a chosen link as seen in prior related work [28,49]. Our adversary's core challenge is different - they want to find a set of poisons (the *poison set*) that focuses traffic *onto* a target link. Finding a poison set that successfully steers bot traffic is non-trivial, because poisons can conflict - successfully steering one AS can block others from traversing the target link. Additionally, each poison extends the poisoning advertisement's AS PATH, and excessively long paths are often filtered [54]. The adversary uses traceroutes [57] to determine bot paths as in [26,52].

The following **iterative poison choice heuristic** represents the core of the Maestro attack. This algorithm finds a poison set for some adversary/target pairing, after which the adversary needs only to issue the poisoned advertisement and direct bot traffic to the poisoned prefix to complete the attack. Our algorithm works by iteratively partitioning ASes into four sets:

Algorithm: Poison Choice Heuristic

---

function ChoosePoisons ($From, To, Adv, Sources, n$)

Input : From AS $From$, To AS To, adversary AS Adv, source ASes $Sources$, poison limit n

Output: poison set $Poisons$

$Poisons = \emptyset$

while $Sources \neq \emptyset$ and $|Poisons| < n$ **do**

$\quad B = \{b \mid b$ is a bgp path $To \mapsto Adv\}$

$\quad Sacred = \{From, To, Adv\} + \bigcap_{i=1}^{|B|} B_i$

$\quad Success \mathrel{+}= \{s \mid s \in Sources$ and $\{From, To\} \in s \mapsto Adv\}$

$\quad Disconn \mathrel{+}= \{s \mid s \in Sources$ and no specific-prefix path $s \mapsto Adv\})$

$\quad Sources \mathrel{-}= \{Sacred \cup Success \cup Disconn\}$

$\quad Score = [0] * |Sources|$

$\quad$ **foreach** $s_i \in Sources$ **do**

$\quad\quad$ **foreach** $s_j \in s_i \mapsto Adv$ **do**

$\quad\quad\quad | \quad Score_j \mathrel{+}= 1$

$\quad\quad$ **end**

$\quad$ **end**

$\quad Poisons \mathrel{+}= \{max(Score)\}$

$\quad Adv$ sends advertisement to poison $Poisons$

end

Sacred ASes are those the adversary cannot poison, as doing so would disconnect the target link from the adversary AS. It is initialized with the From AS, the To AS, and the adversary AS. It is updated at each iteration with every AS that appears on all paths from the To AS to the adversary AS, as determined by traceroutes from bots to the adversary AS. Naturally, we must have a path for traffic from the target link to the poisoning prefix, so these ASes should never be poisoned. *Disconnected* ASes include poisoned ASes and those without a route to the advertising prefix that does not transit a poisoned AS. *Successful* ASes are those hosting bots whose traceroutes transit the target link to the adversary. Lastly, *Source* ASes are those hosting bots that are not yet assigned to another set.

After these sets are updated, we select an AS to poison from the source ASes and add it to the poison set. To accomplish this, we select the AS with the highest vertex betweenness on the directed graph formed by traceroutes from remaining source ASes to the adversary. This is the poison that invalidates the maximum number of source paths that avoid the target link. While no guarantee exists that source ASes will then select a path that *contains* the target link, we at least remove a common hop that *avoids* the link. We update ASes' set membership based on their current traceroutes to the adversary after receiving the update poisoned for all poison set members. Finally, we move to the next iteration. We will terminate iteration once the source set is empty, or if the poison set (which is included in the AS PATH as described in Sect. 2.2) causes the AS PATH to exceed the size AS operators will almost certainly filter in practice: around 254 hops [23,54]. We show in Sect. 7 that this condition is rarely met.

4.2 Evaluation

To evaluate Maestro's impact, we choose thousands of target link/adversary AS pairings for simulated botnet attacks in the framework described in Sect. 3.1. We aim to understand link vulnerability characteristics, and to show how target/adversary topological positions affect flow density. For each attack, we measure pre-attack *flow density* for the target, which represents the target's present vulnerability to LFAs. Next, we execute the Maestro attack to concentrate bot traffic. Finally, we measure post-attack flow density to quantify our success in steering bot-hosting ASes onto the target link. For most experiments, we make bot-to-bot (Coremelt-style) flow density measurements; when using bot-to-any based target link sampling, we will instead measure bot-to-any flow density.

Attacking From the Customer Cone: We initially simulated Maestro on 2,000 randomly selected links with adversaries randomly selected from nearby (1–3 AS-level hops) ASes to illuminate our attack's limits. The attack was generally unsuccessful, but two common success conditions emerged. First, successful attackers were almost universally located in the *customer cone* of the target link destination (the To AS). This is because path export rules are most generous for customers, as ASes provide their customers with all known best paths in hopes of transiting their traffic. So, we expect customer ASes will find the maximum number of *attack paths* - valley-free paths from flow sources to adversary AS that cross the target - among all potential attackers. Second, we observe that flow density improvement for successful attacks varied inversely with attacker distance from the target link. This is an intuitive result; distance increases the number of alternate inbound paths that avoid the target link.

With this knowledge, we next sample 100 links each with relatively low, intermediate, and high betweenness/flow-density. For each target link, we sample three adversaries at each depth from 1–3 in the To AS customer cone. This results in about 1800 adversary/link pairings per link sample set, and about 5400 total simulated attacks. The results are shown in Figs. 5a and 5b. Because we observed similar patterns in success across botnet models, we present only Mirai results here. For direct customers of high betweenness links, on average an additional 30% of the **total bots** in the botnet can target the link (Fig. 5b). For low betweenness links, attack impact is negligible, but these links are not likely targets for LFAs.

A deeper examination of the data yields insights on successful Maestro scenarios. First, target link relationship is critical to attack success. For an adversary

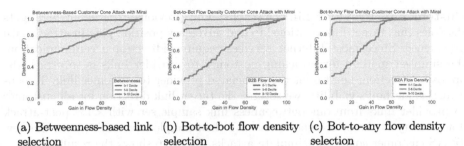

(a) Betweenness-based link selection

(b) Bot-to-bot flow density selection

(c) Bot-to-any flow density selection

Fig. 4. Flow density gain results (post-attack density - pre-attack density) by link selection strategy, **Mirai** botnet model

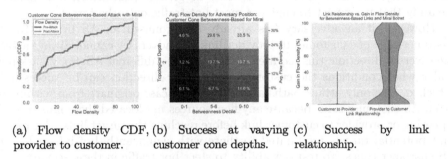

(a) Flow density CDF, provider to customer.

(b) Success at varying customer cone depths.

(c) Success by link relationship.

Fig. 5. Deeper look at the customer attack success, betweenness link sample

in the To AS customer cone, attack paths are most prevalent when the To AS is a customer of the From AS; that is, the target link is a *provider to customer* link. This is an intuitive finding; any bot AS that must transit a provider to customer link to reach the target link *cannot* then transit a customer to provider link and remain valley-free. Like locating the adversary in the To AS customer cone, targeting a provider to customer link removes a potential valley from attack paths, but *at* rather than *after* the target link. The importance of this dynamic is shown in the relative distribution of flow density gains by link relationship in Fig. 5c. Virtually all successful cases for this experiment were on provider to customer links.

Figure 5a displays pre vs. post attack flow density for the same betweenness link sample in Fig. 4a, filtered to include only provider to customer links. Here we see results for the ideal case for the attack: an adversary AS located in the customer cone of the To AS, when the target link is a provider to customer link. The region between the curves in this figure represents the attacker's gain from executing Maestro. Before the attack, most sampled links have flow densities below 10% - that is, most link targets are vulnerable to 10% or fewer bots in a Coremelt LFA. **After Maestro execution, roughly half of sampled links have >50% flow density.**

Customer to Provider Link Attacks: Our previous experiment highlights the roles that target link relationship and adversary position play in attack path prevalence. Since most Internet services require bidirectional communication, the simplest method for attacking customer to provider links is to attack the opposite direction; i.e., target the associated provider to customer link. To confirm this method's viability, we reverse the target link direction for all customer to provider links from our betweenness link sample set with <1% post-attack flow density in the prior experiment. We then sample adversaries from the new To AS customer cones and simulate attacks. Figure 6 shows the results of these reversed attacks. Clearly, link relationship was the primary culprit preventing attack success, as attacking the reversed direction yields drastically improved flow density. For most links, we see 50% or greater post-attack flow density, meaning that we expect to engineer most bot traffic onto the target.

However, if an adversary has already compromised an AS in the To AS customer cone of a customer to provider link, the adversary cannot always attack the reversed direction; this requires compromising a different AS. So, we ask now under what conditions the customer to provider direction can be successfully attacked. The only attack paths available in this case originate from within the From AS customer cone, because any flow sources *not* located there must transit a peering or provider to customer link before reaching the target link. This means that potential targets are limited to those with significantly bot-infected From AS customer cones. To test our ability to steer bot traffic in these scenarios, we randomly sample 300 links from above the 9th deciles for From AS customer cone infection rate from the set of all customer to provider links, simulate attacks, and measured flow density improvement. We find that we can exert significant steering influence on bots in the From AS customer cone as shown in Fig. 7.

While the Maestro attack is most effective for attacking links between customers and providers, the concept of leveraging routing capability to expose links to attack could be extended to peer links, as well. While the details of such an attack fall outside the scope of our paper, we will briefly sketch one possible technique. Peer links (like customer to provider links) are generally only exported within the peers' customer cones, so an adversary wishing to expose such a link would require routing capability at an AS located within the link endpoints' cones. From that position, an adversary could trigger an intentional route leak to a destination that crosses the peering link to expose it to attack; this is analogous to the role of poisoned advertisements in the Maestro attack. Further work could explore the effectiveness of this technique.

5 Internet Experiments

We built an experimental Maestro implementation with the PEERING BGP testbed [44] and the RIPE Atlas framework [51] to 1) validate the basic steering mechanisms behind Maestro and 2) explore what real-world dynamics could affect the attack. PEERING allows us to originate routes from its points of presence (PoPs) worldwide hosting BGP edge routers. RIPE Atlas provides a distributed probe network for data plane measurements including ping, traceroute,

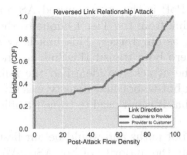

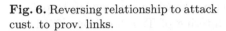

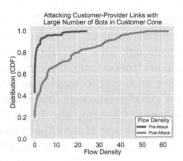

Fig. 6. Reversing relationship to attack cust. to prov. links.

Fig. 7. Attacking cust. to prov. links.

DNS, SSL/TLS and NTP. A subset of these probes, called *anchors*, periodically form a publicly accessible "mesh" measurement of all-to-all traceroutes.

A single PEERING PoP serves as the adversary's compromised AS. All responsive RIPE Atlas anchors ($n \approx 580$) across roughly 470 ASes function as the experimental "botnet". To measure flow density, we combine anchor mesh measurements with traceroutes from anchors to the compromised AS, mapping IP-level hops to AS-level ones using Team Cymru's mapping service [13]. Total flow density includes all anchors with paths to one another or the compromised AS that transit the target.

We conduct the "attack" by first selecting a target from links within three AS-level hops of the compromised AS. Next, we originate an unpoisoned/24 advertisement from the compromised AS and measure pre-attack flow density. Finally, we iteratively select poisons and issue poisoned advertisements for the/24 as described in Sect. 4 to steer traffic over the target link. After the attack, we issue new traceroutes to compare achieved flow density with the original measurement. We perform this procedure on two target links/PEERING PoP pairings.

Ethics: All control plane advertisements are protocol compliant, and all data plane measurements target PEERING prefixes that host only our experimental workstation, so no Internet traffic was affected except our own. Measurements were made with Paris traceroutes [2] using 3 packets of 48 bytes each originating from fewer than 600 RIPE Atlas anchors. The total additional network traffic on any affected link is less than 100KB per measurement. Measurements are spaced by at least one minute. We assess that the potential for our experiments to disrupt normal network operation is minimal, and we did not receive any complaints from operators.

Clemson Results: The Clemson University PoP is the compromised AS for our first experiment. We select 209 ↦ 2722, a link from the Tier 1 clique to the compromised AS's upstream provider AS2722, as our target. This link is two topological hops from the compromised AS. Zero bots transit this link to one another or to the compromised AS prior to the attack; we identified the link from CAIDA's topology [56]. So, the pre-attack bot-to-bot flow density was 0%. This does not indicate the link is unused, only that it is not used to transit traffic between bots and the compromised AS.

AS174 is the most common AS on inbound bot paths and would be our first poison choice, but poisoning this AS disconnects the majority of bot ASes. We observe this behavior in both Internet experiments when attempting to poison Tier 1 ASes, so we suspect that defensive filtering of Tier 1 poisons [24] is to blame. Because AS2722's direct connections are still able to reach the compromised AS, we suspect that filtering occurred at Tier 1 providers. To avoid such disconnections, we skip AS174 and continue the algorithm. After finding 2 poisons, nearly all (533/576 bots) transit the target 209 ↦ 2722. The remaining bots either directly connect to AS2722 (20 bots in AS15169 Google) or were disconnected from the compromised AS (13 bots). **Maestro execution enhances flow density from 0% pre-attack to over 90% after.**

Utah Results: The PEERING PoP behind Utah Education Network (AS210) is our second compromised AS. We selected a Tier 1 to Tier 1 link 3 hops from the compromised AS, 174 ↦ 209, as the target. The original flow density on this link is about 7% - 45/576 bots had bot-to-bot paths that transited this target link before the attack, and none used it to reach the compromised AS.

Our first poison choice would be AS1299, but poisoning this Tier 1 AS triggers the disconnection of most bot ASes as in the Clemson experiment. We again suspect Tier 1 ASes filtering Tier 1 poisons is to blame, so we continue the algorithm without poisoning AS1299 or other Tier 1 providers. The attack finds 3 poisons that steer roughly 16% (91/576) of bots over the target link to the compromised AS. 106 bots transited the target link to reach either another probe or the compromised AS. **Overall, the attack modifies probe flow density from 7% to above 18%, a greater than 2x improvement in flow density.**

Discussion: We find substantial evidence of Tier 1 filtering of Tier 1 poisons during our experiments consistent with a recent BGP interception study, SICO [4]. We note that SICO's path export communities could provide a mechanism to further concentrate traffic when Maestro is limited by Tier 1 poison filtering. We explore filtering in greater detail in Sects. 7 and 9.

6   Attack Scope and Vulnerability

As shown in Sect. 4.2, Maestro adversary is most successful when they 1) target a provider to customer link and 2) compromise a direct/indirect customer of the

To AS. In this section, we explore the Internet's vulnerability to two Maestro attacker types: strategic and opportunistic. The *opportunistic adversary* achieves routing capability at some arbitrary AS, and exploits their position to attack upstream links, e.g. as part of a ransom DDoS. For this attacker, a key question is how many more critical links the adversary can attack with Maestro. The *strategic adversary* targets a specific link or links for broader strategic purposes, e.g. disrupting key services. For this attacker, we want to quantify the pool size of potential attacking ASes given some target link.

Opportunistic Adversary: To answer how Maestro enables the opportunistic adversary, we compare the number of links the adversary can attack with Maestro to the number that can be attacked with a Crossfire LFA. For every AS x in CAIDA's inferred topology [56], we classified upstream links as vulnerable to Maestro if they were provider to customer links where the To AS is 1) a direct/indirect provider of AS x and 2) within 3 topological hops of AS x. We counted links as vulnerable to Crossfire if their simulated pre-attack bot-to-any flow density was over 10%. We call this targeted flow density level the *vulnerability threshold*. We averaged the results by the compromised AS's UCLA classification [40]: stub AS, small ISP, large ISP. Note Tier 1 networks are excluded from these results, as they are not customers of any AS and thus cannot meaningfully execute Maestro. For this analysis, we restrict our focus to core (above 7th decile betweenness) vulnerable links.

The results are displayed in Table 1. In the Maestro columns, we display the average and standard deviation number of Maestro-vulnerable links for each AS classification. The Crossfire columns show the same metrics for links with 10% flow densities without Maestro. **We find that in all AS classes, Maestro increases the pool of potential LFA targets by at least 2x on average.** Small ISPs have the greatest average number of Maestro-vulnerable upstream links (40). This is consistent with our understanding of position-driven vulnerability - small ISPs have, on average, more direct providers than stub ASes and a greater number of provider hops to the Tier 1 clique than large ISPs. This means they have the highest number of provider to customer links within 3 upstream hops, and thus the largest pool of potential Maestro targets.

Table 1. Opportunistic Maestro: key links exposed to Maestro vs. Crossfire.

	Maestro Vuln.		Crossfire Vuln.	
	Avg	**Stddev**	**Avg**	**Stddev**
Stub AS	29	35	14	16
Small ISP	40	49	19	23
Large ISP	35	41	16	18

Strategic Adversary: The strategic adversary is motivated to attack specific links in the topology. For this attacker, Maestro's key capability is its ability to focus traffic on specific upstream targets, including those isolated from LFA flows by topological constraints. Because this attacker seeks to attack a specific link, we want to understand both the number of ASes positioned to attack the target and the attack's potency relative to existing LFAs.

For this analysis, we consider all links in the betweenness link sample set described in Sect. 4.2, which contains randomly selected high, intermediate, and low betweenness links. We analyze the results of the Maestro attack simulations from Sect. 4.2 and determine the proportion of links over a given vulnerability threshold before and after attack execution. The results are presented in Table 2. **Less than 50% of these links have 25% or greater pre-attack flow density across all botnet models; after the attack, greater than 95% of these links are above this threshold.**

In addition to the attack effect, we also want to know how many ASes are positioned to attack each link. The adversary sample set columns in Table 2 display, for each vulnerability threshold, the average set size of potential ASes that an adversary could compromise to perform the attack. To calculate this number, we first note that adversary AS size is not a significant determinant of attack success - the absolute value of the correlation coefficient of CAIDA AS rank [55] and flow density gain for these attacks was always smaller than .01. Success for adversaries in the customer cone is instead dominated by relative topological position. For this reason, if an AS two AS-level hops into the To AS customer cone successfully executes Maestro at some threshold, we expect every other AS at the same or closer depth to likewise succeed at that threshold.

Out of about 600 provider to customer attacks in this sample set, we found that fewer than 3% violated this expectation for any botnet model. So, we estimate the potential adversary pool as the To AS customer cone to the depth of the deepest successful adversary. The standard deviation is also presented for these adversarial sets. Note that the high variance in set size expressed by these statistics illustrates that the potential adversary pool size varies greatly. For target links with large ISPs as the To AS (like core Internet links), the To AS customer cone can include thousands of potential adversaries. For many smaller targets, only a handful of ASes are well-positioned for the attack.

Table 2. Strategic Adversary: Maestro result summary, provider to customer betweenness link selection, customer-only attack

	Vuln. Before			Vuln. After			Avg Adversaries			Stddev Adversaries		
Vuln. Threshold	25%	50%	75%	25%	50%	75%	25%	50%	75%	25%	50%	75%
Mirai	0.44	0.18	0.09	0.97	0.91	0.87	135.45	114.64	91.22	349.69	312.94	215.85
Conficker	0.44	0.21	0.08	0.96	0.91	0.85	151.25	100.01	92.35	360.26	226.39	216.06
Blackenergy	0.38	0.23	0.10	1.00	0.94	0.87	130.61	103.98	92.48	335.06	273.92	217.14

7   Towards Defenses

Two broad categories exist for defense against this attack: general LFA defense solutions and solutions targeting poisoned announcements. Unfortunately, many state-of-the-art LFA defense options are not widely available to network operators, as they require collaboration across ASes [29], deployment of next-generation architectures [12], or additional hardware [25,31,42]. Nyx, a re-routing system [49] could only partially mitigate Maestro by moving traffic between some critical AS and the Nyx deployer AS off the congested target. Here we consider the more relevant mitigations that target Maestro's poisoned advertisements.

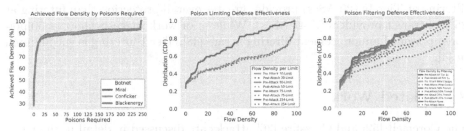

(a) Flow density CDF by number of poisons

(b) Flow density CDF against path filtering

(c) Flow density CDF by various AS filtering sets

Fig. 8. Evaluation of Maestro defenses

The path length defense - rejecting advertisements above some limit - is one easy-to-implement response to this attack. Unfortunately, as shown in Fig. 8a, nearly all of the attack effect is achieved with 5 or fewer poisons; this is partially an artifact of relatively dense botnet distributions as discussed in the next mitigation. Tran et al. [54] observed AS PATH lengths commonly reach 30 hops in legitimate advertisements, indicating that adding 5 hops to the AS PATH is likely insufficient to distinguish attack advertisements. Figure 8b shows the impact if all ASes limited advertisement AS PATH length at various levels, including those observed by prior work (30 and 75) [54] and implemented in common routing hardware (254) [23]. These limits *do not decrease achieved flow density*.

An alternative defense involves detecting and suppressing poisoned BGP advertisements. The current and potential effects of RPKI and BGPSec filtering is discussed in Sect. 2.2. Alternatively, ASes could prevent Meastro with by filtering all poisoned advertisements. This is a feasible approach, because poisoned advertisements have a clear signature. However, as previously discussed, this would prevent benign traffic engineering poisons. ASes are also under unique administrative control, so uniform filter deployment is a challenge.

Figure 8c shows how our betweenness-based link selection/customer only adversary selection experiment responds to different sets of filtering ASes. For this mitigation trial, we ran our attack against four filtering sets. The first two sets place poison filters at 25% and 50% of all transit ASes (those with one or more customers) filtering all poisoned advertisements. The next two sets are smaller but more strategically targeted: filters at all 20 Tier 1 ASes (Hurricane Electric included) to explore how the best-provisioned networks can protect the Internet as a whole, and botnet-specific defenses. The botnet-specific defense springs from the observation that all three botnets in our study are highly concentrated. In the Mirai model, for example, 64% of bots are hosted in just 30 ASes. So, for our final filtering set, we include all providers (58) for these 30 ASes to *cordon* the botnet. While this filtering pattern is botnet-specific, it illustrates the efficient protection that few well-positioned filterers provide relative to many randomly distributed ones. **Both the 50% transit and Mirai cordon filtering sets eliminate virtually all Maestro effect**. Interestingly, filtering at Tier 1s (20 ASes) provides greater overall protection than filtering at 25% of transit providers (2441 ASes). While prior work suggests short (<50 poisons) poisoned announcement filtering is rare [48], Tier 1 filtering is encountered in [4].

8   Related Work

The Coremelt [52] and Crossfire [26] attacks are discussed in detail in the background, Sect. 2.3. Bellovin's link cutting attack [3] discussed strategically cutting topological links to route traffic through colluding ASes. While the purpose of that attack - interception in the presence of path security - is different, the concept of severing links to re-route traffic is similar. Classifying links by BGP betweenness is a technique employed in Schuchard et al.'s Coordinated Cross Plane Session Termination (CXPST) control plane attack [46]. Select LFA mitigation work is presented in Sect. 7. Other uses of BGP poisoning include LIFE-GUARD from Katz-Bassett et al. [27,28] as well as Colitti et al. and Anwar et al.'s policy exploration studies [1,11]. Nyx [49] from Smith et al. employs BGP poisoning for DDoS mitigation. The propagation of poisoned advertisements throughout the Internet is actively measured in [48].

9   Conclusion

In this work we explored both LFA limitations and how adversaries can overcome those limitations. Our experiments show that contrary to assumptions in previous literature, botnet-sourced LFAs cannot target arbitrary links with full force in practice. In fact, many core Internet links can be reached by just a fraction of infected hosts in all three of our botnet models. Our simulations show the Maestro attack can partially overcome topological reach restrictions. Most troublingly, high betweenness links are most vulnerable to this attack, and the rank of AS adversaries plays little role in attack success. Provider to customer targets are most vulnerable to Maestro, but other links with significantly infected From AS customer cones can be affected by the attack. Our mitigation experiments suggest strategic poison filtering drastically reduces vulnerability.

Operator Engagement: We submitted a preprint of this work to the NANOG (North American Network Operators Group) mailing list to solicit feedback on the attack and disseminate mitigations. Responses indicated that operators had not seen any similar attack executed in practice. Some operators suggested that defensive filtering (a "peer lock" mechanism) could provide some protection from the attack [24]. Peer locking validates advertisements against known relationships, an intuitive step in averting path manipulations like those used in Maestro. However, this requires periodic out-of-band information exchange between ASes, and there is little evidence that this feature has penetrated beyond Tier 1 ASes [36]. We encountered some evidence of Tier 1 peer locking in Sect. 5, as did Smith et al. [48] in their measurement study. Our Tier 1 filtering examination from Fig. 8c provides a window into the effect of full Tier 1 peer locking.

References

1. Anwar, R., Niaz, H., Choffnes, D.R., Cunha, Í.S., Gill, P., Katz-Bassett, E.: Investigating interdomain routing policies in the wild. In: ACM IMC (2015)
2. Augustin, B., et al.: Avoiding traceroute anomalies with Paris traceroute. In: ACM SIGCOMM (2006)
3. Bellovin, S.M., Gansner, E.R.: Using Link Cuts to Attack Internet Routing (2003)
4. Birge-Lee, H., Wang, L., Rexford, J., Mittal, P.: SICO: surgical interception attacks by manipulating BGP communities. In: ACM CCS (2019)
5. Chang, W., Mohaisen, A., Wang, A., Chen, S.: Measuring botnets in the wild: some new trends (2015)
6. Chung, T., et al.: RPKI is coming of age: a longitudinal study of RPKI deployment and invalid route origins. In: ACM IMC (2019)
7. Cisco: Cisco IOS and IOS XE Software Cluster Management Protocol Remote Code Execution Vulnerability. https://bit.ly/3aFfFhN
8. Cisco: Cisco IOS XE Software AAA Login Authentication Remote Code Execution Vulnerability. https://bit.ly/2RmkB3o
9. Cisco: Cisco IOS XE Software Static Credential Vulnerability. https://bit.ly/2RnyjmA
10. Cisco: Cisco REST API Container for IOS XE Software Authentication Bypass Vulnerability. https://bit.ly/2NVkIB5
11. Colitti, L., et al.: Internet Topology Discovery Using Active Probing (2006)
12. Cristina, B., et al.: SIBRA: scalable internet bandwidth reservation architecture (2016)
13. Cymru, Team: The Team Cymru IP to ASN lookup page. https://www.team-cymru.com/IP-ASN-mapping.html
14. Dainotti, A., et al.: Analysis of country-wide internet outages caused by censorship. In: ACM SIGCOMM (2011)
15. Demchak, C.C., Shavitt, Y.: China's maxim - leave no access point unexploited: the hidden story of China telecom's BGP Hijacking. Mil. Cyber Aff. (2018)
16. Donnet, B., Bonaventure, O.: On BGP communities. In: ACM SIGCOMM (2008)
17. Madory, D.: BGP Hijack of Amazon DNS to Steal Crypto Currency (2018). https://bit.ly/37vW2Ha
18. Gao, L.: On inferring autonomous system relationships in the Internet. In: IEEE/ACM ToN (2001)

19. Huston, G.: AS65000 BGP Routing Table Analysis Report (2020). http://bgp. potaroo.net/as2.0/bgp-active.html
20. Gilad, Y., Cohen, A., Herzberg, A., Schapira, M., Shulman, H.: Are we there yet? On RPKI's deployment and security. In: NDSS (2017)
21. Goldberg, S.: Why is it taking so long to secure internet routing? CACM (2014)
22. Google Security and White Ops: The Hunt for 3ve (2016)
23. Pepelnjak, I.: Limit the maximum BGP path length (2009). http://wiki.nil.com/ Limit_the_maximum_BGP_AS-path_length
24. Snijders, J.: NTT Peer Locking (2016). http://instituut.net/job/peerlock_manual. pdf
25. Kang, M.S., Gligor, V.D., Sekar, V.: SPIFFY: inducing cost-detectability tradeoffs for persistent link-flooding attacks. In: NDSS (2016)
26. Kang, M.S., Lee, S.B., Gligor, V.D.: The crossfire attack. In: IEEE S&P (2013)
27. Katz-Bassett, E., et al.: Reverse traceroute. In: Usenix NSDI (2010)
28. Katz-Bassett, E., et al.: LIFEGUARD: practical repair of persistent route failures. In: ACM SIGCOMM (2012)
29. Lee, S.B., Kang, M.S., Gligor, V.D.: CoDef: collaborative defense against large-scale link-flooding attacks. In: ACM CONEXT (2013)
30. Lepinski, M., Sriram, K.: RFC 8205 - BGPSEC protocol specification. IETF (2013)
31. Liaskos, C., Kotronis, V., Dimitropoulos, X.: A novel framework for modeling and mitigating distributed link flooding attacks. In: IEEE INFOCOM (2016)
32. Litke, P., Stewart, J.: BGP hijacking for cryptocurrency profit (2014)
33. Luckie, M., et al.: AS relationships, customer cones, and validation. In: ACM IMC (2013)
34. Lepinski, M., Kent, S.: An Infrastructure to Support Secure Internet Routing (2012). https://tools.ietf.org/html/rfc6480
35. Majkowski, M.: Memcrashed-Major amplification attacks from UDP port 11211 (2018)
36. McDaniel, T., Smith, J.M., Schuchard, M.: Flexsealing BGP against route leaks: peerlock active measurement and analysis. In: NDSS (2021, in press)
37. McPherson, D., Gill, V.: BGP MULTI_EXIT_DISC (MED) Considerations (2006)
38. Netlab360: Mirai Scanner (2017). http://data.netlab.360.com/mirai-scanner/
39. Nordström, O., Dovrolis, C.: Beware of BGP attacks. In: ACM SIGCOMM (2004)
40. Oliveira, R., Pei, D., Willinger, W., Zhang, B., Zhang, L.: The (in) completeness of the observed internet AS-level structure. In: IEEE/ACM ToN (2009)
41. Putman, C.G.J., et al.: Business model of a botnet
42. Ravi, N., Shalinie, S.M., Theres, D.D.J.: BALANCE: link flooding attack detection and mitigation via hybrid-SDN. IEEE Trans. Netw. Serv. Manag. **17**, 1715–1729 (2020)
43. Rekhter, Y., Li, T.: A Border Gateway Protocol 4 (BGP-4) (1995)
44. Schlinker, B., Arnold, T., Cunha, I., Katz-Bassett, E.: PEERING: virtualizing BGP at the edge for research. In: ACM CONEXT (2019)
45. Schuchard, M., Geddes, J., Thompson, C., Hopper, N.: Routing around decoys. In: ACM CCS (2012)
46. Schuchard, M., Mohaisen, A., Foo Kune, D., Hopper, N., Kim, Y., Vasserman, E.Y.: Losing control of the internet: using the data plane to attack the control plane. In: ACM CCS. ACM (2010)
47. Scott Sr, J., Winter Summit: Rise of the Machines: The Dyn Attack was Just a Practice Run, December 2016

48. Smith, J.M., Birkeland, K., McDaniel, T., Schuchard, M.: Withdrawing the BGP re-routing curtain: understanding and analyzing the security impact of BGP poisoning through real-world measurements. In: NDSS (2020)
49. Smith, J.M., Schuchard, M.: Routing around congestion: defeating DDoS attacks and adverse network conditions via reactive BGP routing. In: 2018 IEEE Symposium on Security and Privacy (SP) (2018)
50. Sriram, K., Montgomery, D.C.: Resilient Interdomain Traffic Exchange: BGP Security and DDoS Mitigation. NIST (2019)
51. RN Staff: Ripe atlas: a global internet measurement network. IP J. (2015)
52. Studer, A., Perrig, A.: The coremelt attack. In: ESORICS (2009)
53. Thomas, M., Mohaisen, A.: Kindred domains: detecting and clustering botnet domains using DNS traffic. In: WWW (2014)
54. Tran, M., Kang, M.S., Hsiao, H.-C., Chiang, W.-H., Tung, S.-P., Wang, Y.-S.: On the feasibility of rerouting-based DDoS defenses. In: IEEE S&P (2019)
55. UCSD-CAIDA: CAIDA AS Rank dataset (2019). http://as-rank.caida.org/
56. UCSD-CAIDA: CAIDA AS Relationship dataset (2019). https://bit.ly/2RpRWuv
57. Jacobson, V.: Traceroute Man Page. https://linux.die.net/man/8/traceroute

pyDNetTopic: A Framework for Uncovering What Darknet Market Users Talking About

Jingcheng Yang[1], Haowei Ye[2], and Futai Zou[1($\boxtimes$)]

[1] School of Cyper Science and Engineering, Shanghai Jiao Tong University,
Shanghai, China
{amiya_yang,zoufutai}@sjtu.edu.cn
[2] School of Information and Communication Engineering,
University of Electronic Science and Technology of China, Chengdu, China
beicheng@std.uestc.edu.cn

Abstract. Although Dark Net Market (DNM) has attracted more and more researchers' interests, we found most works focus on the markets while ignore the forums related with them. Ignoring DNM forums is undoubtedly a huge waste of informative intelligence. Previous works usually utilize LDA for darknet data mining. However, traditional topic models cannot handle the posts in forums with various lengths, which incurs unaffordable complexity or performance degradation. In this paper, an improved Bi-term Topic Model named Filtered Bi-term Model, is proposed to extract potential topics in DNM forums for balancing both overhead and performance. Experimental results prove that the topical words extracted by FBTM are more coherent than LDA and DMM. Furthermore, we proposed a general framework named pyDNet-Topic for content extracting and topic modeling uncovering DNM forums automatically. The full results we apply pyDNetTopic to Agora forum demonstrate the capability of FBTM to capture informative intelligence in DNM forums as well as the practicality of pyDNetTopic.

Keywords: Darknet market forums · Topic modeling · FBTM · pyDNetTopic

1 Introduction

With the rapid development of Internet based applications, Darknet Markets (DNMs), which are online marketplaces hosted on anonymity networks and are not indexed by any search engine, has become great hotbeds for illicit transactions. DNMs provide escrow services between buyers and sellers transacting using Bitcoin or other cryptocurrencies, usually for illegal and unregulated goods such

This work is supported by the National Key Research and Development Program of China (No. 2017YFB0802300).

N. Park et al. (Eds.): SecureComm 2020, LNICST 335, pp. 118–139, 2020.
https://doi.org/10.1007/978-3-030-63086-7_8

as drugs, weapons and so on. Former researches mostly focus on the services, products on sale (especially drugs) or traders in DNMs [6,9,11] or the functionality and mechanism of DNMs [3,8], from both technical and legal perspectives. But few pay attention to the forums related with markets. In fact, DNM related forums are nonnegligible informative treasuries for researchers. The collecting, mining and analyzing of forum data can reveal valuable information about corresponding DNMs, as well as its users. Researchers can have a quick understanding about the transaction types or goods on sale by finding users in forums talks about "drugs", "cocaine" or "bitcoin", "Monero" frequently. Also, researchers can extract some security-crucial intelligence from discussion between forum users. Recent works explore approaches to extract Cyber Threat Intelligence (CTI) from open or dark web [2,16,24].

According to the value of information hidden in forum data and the lack of relevant researches, we propose to use topic modeling for data mining and topic extraction. Given a large, unstructured collection (or corpus) of documents, topic modeling is an unsupervised machine learning algorithm that estimates the main topics of discussion [4]. As far as we know, former researches simply use LDA for topic modeling and the topical items have poor interpretability and coherence. The purpose of this work is to presenting an effective topic model for darknet market users, as well as an automatic general framework for information mining in DNM forums. Filtered Bi-term Topic Model is presented in this paper not only for generating more coherent and interpretable topical items, but also to reduce consumption and complexity for practical application. The details and experimental results of FBTM will be elaborated in Sect. 3 and 5 respectively. We also propose a general topical mining framework for DNM forums called pyDNetTopic. The functionality of pyDNetTopic lies in forum data extraction and analysis to provide a profile of main items most DNM forum users concern about. Moreover, pyDNetTopic provides an auxiliary and preliminary process for further analysis on darknet. The architecture and implementation of pyDNetTopic will be detailed in Sect. 4.

The contribution of this paper are as follows:

- We propose FBTM, a modified Bi-term Topic Model applicable in large dataset consist of documents with various lengths. FBTM not only handles the sparsity problem when facing short text, but also reduces computational and memory consumption for large corpora, which makes it appropriate for darknet environment. Experimental results show that FBTM has better coherence measures than baseline models LDA and DMM. Comparison of extracted items demonstrates the accuracy and coherence of FBTM surpass baseline models, which indicates FBTM captures the tools used by darknet users and the hot issues visitors discuss that are usually ignored by baseline models.
- We propose pyDNetTopic, a python-based automatic data extraction and topic modeling framework for DNM forums. pyDNetTopic integrate standard pipelined preprocessing steps with FBTM and two alternative baseline models. The functionality of pyDNetTopic is identifying and extracting textual

content from files scraped by web crawler, as well as hot topic detection in darknet. pyDNetTopic aims to provide a general framework for data mining and intelligence extraction for security researchers quicikly understanding underground communities.

– We utilize pyDNetTopic to reveal the latent topics with representative terms from Agora market related forums. Items of interest including the state of darknet markets as well as the security concern of darknet users provide insight to darknet or security researchers.

2   Related Work

The exploration of informative assets beneath darknet have been attracted the interests of security researchers. Topic modeling, as an unsupervised topic derivation method for key information extraction, has been used extensively to gather intelligence directly from darknet informative sources. Grisham et al. [10] analyzes the Alphabay underground marketplace - an anonymous trading grounds for illicit goods and services. This poster uses LDA to determine the providing illicit items and top sellers. Samtani et al. [22,23] proposed a general semi-automatic framework to identify and classify informative assets from underground hacker forums. The hacker assets can be categorized into attachments, tutorials and source code according to Samtani. LDA was utilized in this paper aiming for code analysis by extracting topics and functions of source code, as well as understanding the topics of attachments and tutorial postings. In terms of code analysis, Samtani train a SVM classifier to classify source codes by coding language to provide insight into their implementation. Similar to Samtani, Deliu [7] presents a two-stage, hybrid process to collect CTI from underground hacker forums. Deliu achieves CTI extraction from forums by using a hybrid machine learning model that automatically searches through hacker forums posts, identifies the posts that are most relevant to cyber security and then clusters the relevant posts into estimations of their topics. The first identification stage and second clustering stage use SVM and LDA, respectively. Kyle [19] utilize LDA to reveal states of darknet market and tools users use mostly. Kyle doesn't apply LDA directly on original materials collected from darknet, but on subreddit "DarkNetMarket" in a monthly manner.

Lots of works have been done in topic modeling to improve its accuracy and interpretability, especially in short text environment such as Twitter. Some remarkable modifications include the auxiliary of external knowledge. [17,18] propose to incorporate hidden topics discovered from large-scale external document collections into short sparse documents. Jin et al. [12] propose a novel topic model - Dual Latent Dirichlet Allocation (DLDA) model, which jointly learns two sets of topics on short and long texts and couples the topic parameters to cope with the potential inconsistency between data sets. Recently neural networks are used to learn the prior distribution of document-topic or topic-word from corpus, which are imposed to be Dirichlet distribution in LDA and its modified versions. Deep hierarchical priors, generated from Replicated Softmax Model

[21], Neural Autoregressive Density Estimator [13] or variational autoencoders [26,30] have been developed to generate hierarchical document representations as well as discover interpretable topic hierarchies. But it is worth noting that security studies mining DNM forums only use LDA. We suppose the reasons why security researchers ignore recent achievements on topic modeling lie in:

a) Security researchers focus on the clustering results or extracted keywords from topic modeling while ignoring the accuracy, coherence and interpretability of obtained results;
b) The lack of convenient framework of proposed algorithms hinder security researchers from adopting them into practical application. Most works using LDA may due to the fact that LDA has been integrated into gensim or sklearn packages, which makes it user-friendly.

In view of the development of topic modeling and its relatively backward application in darknet research, this paper is intended to present an algorithm more effective and accurate than commonly used baseline models in darknet forums environment to fill the gap. For ease of use, especially for security researchers who are unfamiliar with machine learning, we propose a general framework for information mining and topic extraction on DNM forums.

3   Background

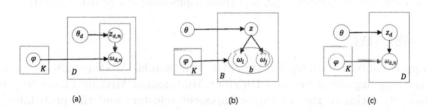

(a)   (b)   (c)

Fig. 1. Graphical representation of three topic models: (a) LDA, (b) BTM, and (c) DMM

3.1   LDA

As a classic algorithm of existing topic models, LDA [4] is a hierarchical parametric Bayesian approach to infer a low dimensional representation that captures the latent semantic topics in a large corpus. LDA models the documents as a mixture of latent topics while each topic can be described as a probabilistic distribution over words. Figure 1(a) illustrates LDA models the generation process of a word $\omega_{d,n}$ in document d within N words corpus composed of D documents and K topics.

a) Draw word mixing distribution $\varphi_k \sim Dir(\beta)$ for each topic $k \in K$
b) For each document d in D:
- Draw topic mixing distribution $\theta_d \sim Dir(\alpha)$
- Generate a topic assignment $z_{d,n}$ from document-topic distribution $Multi(\theta_d)$
- Generate a word $\omega_{d,n}$ from topic-word distribution $Multi(\varphi_{z_{d,n}})$

3.2   BTM

The reliance on word co-occurrence patterns within documents makes LDA model extremely sensitive to the length of documents. When facing short text, LDA model suffers from severe sparsity problem. To handle this, Bi-term Topic Model [28] utilizes a bi-term (a single word co-occurrence pair in a single document) rather than a single word. BTM models topic distribution over the whole bi-terms collections instead of deriving it from Dirichlet prior distribution in each document by LDA. Experimental results demonstrate that BTM exceeds traditional models such as LDA not only in short text, but also in normal text environment. Figure 1(b) illustrates the generation process of a single bi-term (ω_i, ω_j) in the whole bi-terms set B.

a) Draw word mixing distribution $\varphi_k \sim Dir(\beta)$ for each topic $k \in K$
b) Draw topic mixing distribution $\theta \sim Dir(\alpha)$ for B
c) For each bi-term b in B:
- Generate a topic assignment z from topic distribution $Multi(\theta)$
- Generate bi-term $b = (\omega_i, \omega_j)$ from topic-word distribution $Multi(\varphi_z)$

3.3   GSDMM

Collapsed Gibbs Sampling for Dirichlet Multinomial Mixture [29] introduces Gibbs Sampling algorithm into Dirichlet Multinomial Mixture model to probabilistically estimate the mixture component (cluster) and the probability of topic-word distribution based on two assumptions:

a) Each document is generated by a mixture model;
b) Each document originates from only one topic.

These assumptions , especially the second assumption, can indirectly enrich the word co-occurrence pattern in document level. Figure 1(c) illustrates GSDMM models the generation process of a word $\omega_{d,n}$ in document d.

a) Draw word mixing distribution $\varphi_k \sim Dir(\beta)$ for each topic $k \in K$
b) Draw topic mixing distribution $\theta \sim Dir(\alpha)$
c) For each document d in D:
- Generate a topic assignment z_d from document-topic $Multi(\theta)$
- Generate a word $\omega_{d,n}$ from topic-word distribution $Multi(\varphi_{z_d})$

4   Filtered Bi-Term Topic Model

4.1   Motivation

Former researches focus on the sparsity problem topic models confront in short text and solution to it. But in DNM forums, situation seems more complex. The post corpus in DNM forums cannot be regarded as short or long simply. Unlike typical short text collections, such as Tweets2011 or Trec, whose average document lengths are 5.21 and 4.94 respectively. The average document length of DNM forums are longer than 20 words typically. Although on average, DNM forum data seems to fall into the category of long text. However, DNM forum contains a large number of very short posts, while some overwhelmingly long posts increase the average length of the entire dataset. So simply using LDA may receive unsatisfying results. From this point of view, BTM seems to be a propriate choice which produce quite great performance in both short text and long text. However, when performing BTM, another serve problem emerges.

As detailed in Sect. 3, BTM extracts bi-terms from corpus to obtain global word co-occurrence patterns. But with the document length $\bar{l}$ and number $|D|$ increasing, the number of bi-terms increases in square law, which incurs unaffordable memory usage and time consumption. Table 1 illustrates the complexity analysis of three typical topic models: LDA, BTM and DMM, where M and K denotes the number of terms in corpus and the number of topics respectively. The redundancy of bi-terms in BTM makes the model cannot be applied in DNM forums directly, furthermore, in any big dataset with various document lengths.

Table 1. Complexity analysis of LDA, DMM and BTM

Method	Time complexity	Memory complexity
LDA	$O(K|D|\bar{l})$	$|D|K + MK + |D|\bar{l}$
DMM	$O(K|D|\bar{l})$	$D + (M+2)K$
BTM	$O(K|D|\bar{l}^2)$	$K + MK + \frac{1}{2}|D|\bar{l}(\bar{l}-1)$

4.2   Methodology

Since the inefficiency of BTM attributes to the redundancy of bi-terms, an intuitive solution is discarding less indicative bi-terms. Similar work has been done in [27] to discriminate topical terms using document ratio $df(\omega)$, which is calculated in (1).

$$df(\omega) = \frac{m_\omega}{M} \qquad (1)$$

where m_ω represents the number of documents in which term ω is mentioned and M denotes the total number of documents. Xia et al. [27] pointed out that the term belongs to general terms when its $df(\omega)$ is larger than M devided by the maximum number of documents a single topic contains. Besides, a term appears only in single document belongs to document-specific terms while remaining terms are topical terms. Xia's approach seems to have a good performance in headline-based social news clustering, but it cannot be adopted in DNM forums situations. The major drawback lies in the threshold for defining general terms. In DNM forum corpus, it is impossible that we have a prior knowledge of the approximate number of documents the largest topic contains. The "unsupervised" situation in DNM forums makes Xia's approach impractical. Inspired by that, we propose Filtered BTM to select useful bi-terms for topic extraction without any prior knowledge or assumptions.

In FBTM, we propose a novel metric, named "generality" $\gamma(\omega)$, which is formulated as (2).

$$\gamma(\omega) = \frac{f(\omega)}{df(\omega)} = \frac{\frac{n_\omega}{\sum_\omega n_\omega}}{\frac{m_\omega}{M}} \tag{2}$$

where n_ω represent the occurrence number of term ω in the whole corpus and the number of documents which contain term ω. $f(\omega)$ measures the occurrence frequency of term ω in perspective of whole corpus, whereas $df(\omega)$ reflects the document-level distribution range of term ω. So $\gamma(\omega)$ reflects how centrally the term ω distributes in documents. We believe there is a positive correlation between $\gamma(\omega)$ and the degree of how topical term ω is. Firstly, the topic-word distribution ϕ is estimated as (3) in [28].

$$\phi_{\omega|z} = \frac{n_{\omega|z} + \beta}{\sum_\omega n_{\omega|z} + M\beta} \tag{3}$$

where $n_{\omega|z}$ refers to the number of times of term ω assigned to topic z. β is a hyperparameter. The denominator seems to remain almost constant for different term ω. It is intuitive that the term with larger $f(\omega)$ tends to have larger $n_{\omega|z}$. In another word, the term occurs frequently tends to be assigned to one or multiple topics. It can be proved by the observation of output results from many topic models that some frequent words are regarded as top topical words spanning several topics. But only considering the word ratio will make words appearing frequently in most documents dominate the topical words. Although stop words filtering can exclude some commonly used words such as "the", "do" et al., some words appear frequently in darknet context such as "buy", "pay", "from" can still make results confusing. So we introduce the reciprocal of document ratio $df(\omega)$ into the calculation of "generality". If a term appears frequently in corpus, as well as widely in the whole document set, the term belongs to common words so its $f(\omega)$ and $df(\omega)$ will be large simultaneously. Dividing by a large $df(\omega)$ will reduce generality to prevent common word from ranking too high.

Secondly, in the view of Xia's classification approach, the metric generality still makes sense. Xia regards the topical terms and general terms as significant for topic modeling. Due to our observation, the topical terms always appear frequently in a few documents while general terms distribute more broadly than topical terms in document level. The top ranked terms by generality mostly consist of topical terms and general terms. It is worth noting that the so-called document-specific terms, which appear only in one document, still has a relatively low generality, although their document ratio is quite low. Because such terms appear quite rarely and have much lower word ratios. So our proposed generality has capacity to exclude less indicative terms.

The detail of FBTM algorithm is shown in Algorithm 1. After the calculation of $\gamma(\omega)$, FBTM sorts each term in the whole corpus according to its $\gamma(\omega)$ and only retains the bi-terms consist of terms whose $\gamma(\omega)$ is in top η, which is filtering coefficient specified by researcher determining how many terms in corpus are retained. The rest bi-terms are considered as meaningful for topic modeling. The rest bi-terms set B is used by BTM to estimate the topic-word distribution ϕ, as well as some user-determined parameters. Experimental results indicate that by excluding trivial bi-terms extracted topical terms better capture the informative intelligence from darknet corpus.

Algorithm 1. Filtered Biterm Topic Model

Input: number of topics K, preprocessed document set D, hyperparameter α, β, filtering coefficient η, iterations I
Output: topic-word co-occurrence matrix Φ
1: **for** each word ω in D **do**
2:     Compute generality $\gamma(\omega) = \frac{f(\omega)}{df(\omega)}$
3: **end for**
4: Sort each word according to its generality
5: Select the top η words and add them to filtered word set W
6: **for** each document d in D **do**
7:     **for** each $\omega_i, \omega_j \in d$ **do**
8:         **if** $\omega_i, \omega_j \in W$ **then**
9:             Add bi-term (ω_i, ω_j) into bi-term set B
10:         **end if**
11:     **end for**
12: **end for**
13: $\Phi \leftarrow BTM(B, K, \alpha, \beta, I)$

---

5   Framework Architecture

Figure 2 is the overview of framework of pyDNetTopic[1]. The purpose we present pyDNetTopic is extracting the textual content from HTML file obtained by web crawler and uncovering interesting topics with representative words. Based on previous works, we integrate LDA, DMM with FBTM which presented in this paper in pyDNetTopic.

---

[1] The code is available in https://github.com/blade-prayer/pyDNetTopic.

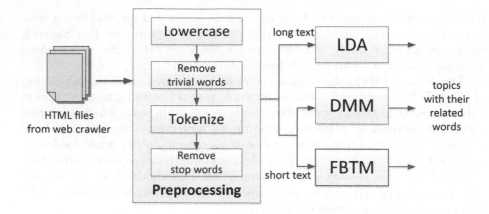

Fig. 2. Overview of architecture of pyDNetTopic

5.1   Data Extraction and Preprocessing

Based on our observation of dataset scraped from darknet, data extraction module utilizes the strategy that choosing files with "topic" in their names and selecting the "inner" elements to get textual content of posts. After filtering the nonrelevant files and finding the requisite content, here with different modes pyDNetTopic provides different text extraction strategies:

a) In long text mode, pyDNetTopic aggregate every single response within a post into one document;
b) In short text mode, pyDNetTopic write every single response into one document.

Aforementioned two modes correspond with different applicable conditions of topic models. LDA model is fit to long texts while FBTM and DMM is suited for short texts. Then pyDNetTopic performs a pipelined preprocessing procedure to the raw bulks of content to transform them into appropriate form for topic model. Such procedure is concluded by our series of experiments combined with related works [19]. We integrate these sequential steps into pyDNetTopic to make it convenient for follow-up studies.

- Lowercase texts
- Remove pure numbers with length less than 2
- Remove words with only one character or longer than 15 characters
- Remove words that appear only once
- Tokenize raw data using regular expression that match with characters a-z0-9
- Remove standard stop words in NLTK Python Library with specific stop words obtained from our observation during series experiments

During the experiments, we find that a mass of posts' topics center in drugs, which contains a lot pure numbers indicating the weights or prices of drugs.

Addition to numbers, such posts always contain a lot ill-formed words with only one character. Another phenomenon we find is that there are many quite long meaningless words stemming from the URL or PGP public keys in generated corpus. These words appearing in extracted topics will make the output confusing. pyDNetTopic removes these meaningless words out of consideration for efficiency and performance.

The selection of localized stop words is inspired by how Kyle did in [19]. When we just use the standard stop words list, we find the results of topic model output revolved around curse and common words, such as "would", "shit", "good". To alleviate this we perform FBTM repeatedly on our generated corpus and choose the top-20 most relevant words within each topic as representative word set. When we find words that add no insight to the potential topics in typical word set, we remove such words from raw corpus by adding them to the stop word list. We repeat this operation until in the top-20 typical word set there are no obviously meaningless words. Appendix A shows our final result of stop words list by performing in typical DNM forums. We believe this stop words list we concluded can be directly applied in future related researches.

5.2 Topic Models

Although FBTM has shown its good performance, we still have some reasons to retain LDA and DMM in pyDNetTopic. Firstly, although after filtering, FBTM still costs longer process time than DMM and LDA when facing a level of tens of thousands data volume. Secondly, we assume that researchers may confront some weird forums consist of abnormally long or short posts. We integrate LDA and DMM as alternative models in pyDNetTopic. The implementation of LDA is LDAMulticore in genism library. For hyperparameters α and β, we simply use the default setting in gensim as the reciprocal of topic number K. pyDNetTopic implements DMM in python. The prerequisite assumption that each document is originated from only one topic makes DMM deal with short text both rapidly and efficiently, however, at the expense of performance and accuracy in DNM forums conditions. We utilize the same default settings as in LDA for model parameters. The default and recommended topic model in pyDNetTopic is our proposed FBTM with short text mode. We set the default values of hyperparameters the same as that in [28]. The default value of filtering coefficient η which controls how many words are retained for topic modeling, is 0.5. The hyperparamter settings in pyDNetTopic are shown in Table 2.

5.3 Relevance Metric

In pyDNetTopic, we choose relevance of each term rather than its topic-word probability to rank the top topical word list of each topic. Relevance is a topical term weighted metric proposed in [25]. The definition of relevance makes a trade-off between the topic-word probability with its corresponding lift (calculated by the

Table 2. Hyperparameter settings in pyDNetTopic

Model	Parameter	Value
LDA	α	$\frac{1}{K}$
	β	$\frac{1}{K}$
	Iterations	100
DMM	α	$\frac{1}{K}$
	β	$\frac{1}{K}$
	Iterations	100
FBTM	α	1
	β	0.01
	Iterations	100
	Filtering coefficient η	0.5

topic-word probability with its marginal probability). The formulation of relevance of term ω belonging to topic t given a weight parameter ε is shown in (4).

$$r\left(\omega,t|\varepsilon\right) = \varepsilon\log\left(\phi_{t\omega}\right) + (1-\varepsilon)\,log\left(\frac{\phi_{t\omega}}{p_\omega}\right) \tag{4}$$

By introducing the lift term, relevance decrease the rankings of globally frequent terms. On the other hand, the topic-word probability term balance the noise introduced by lift term. Parameter ε determines the weight given to the probability of ω under topic t relative to its lift. We set it 0.01 empirically in pyDNetTopic.

6 Experiment

6.1 Evaluation Metrics

In order to perform a quantifying analysis, we choose a series of automatic and unsupervised evaluation metrics, coherence scores, summarized by Roder [20] for topic quality evaluation. Coherence measures do not rely on any human annotators or extrinsic reference collections. The insight of coherence is based on the observation of human expert annotations that pairs of words belong to the same topic clustered by the model tend to co-occur in the same document, while word pairs belonging to different topics have little co-occurrence tendency.

We choose UMass coherence [14], UCI coherence [15] and centroid coherence [1] for topic quality evaluation. The evaluated topic UCI coherence takes the set of top words of a topic and sum a confirmation measure over all word pairs, while UMass coherence uses an asymmetrical confirmation measure between top word pairs (smoothed conditional probability). The formulations of UMass and UCI coherence are shown in (5) and (6) respectively, where $V^{(t)} = \left(v_1^{(t)}, \ldots, v_M^{(t)}\right)$ is a list of the M most probable words in topic t.

$$C_{UMass}\left(t; V^{(t)}\right) = \sum_{m=2}^{M} \sum_{l=1}^{m-1} log \frac{D\left(v_m^{(t)}, v_l^{(t)}\right) + 1}{D\left(v_l^{(t)}\right)} \tag{5}$$

$$C_{UCI}\left(t; V^{(t)}\right) = \sum_{m=1}^{M-1} \sum_{l=m+1}^{M} log \frac{D\left(v_m^{(t)}, v_l^{(t)}\right) + 1}{D\left(v_m^{(t)}\right) D\left(v_l^{(t)}\right)} \tag{6}$$

The calculation of centroid coherence is a bit more complicated. Centroid coherence is formulated based on context vectors for every topic top word. The j-th element of the context vector $\overrightarrow{v_i^{(t)}}$ of topical word $v_i^{(t)}$ is normalized pointwise mutual information (NPMI) and calculated as:

$$v_{ij}^{(t)} = NPMI\left(v_i^{(t)}, v_j^{(t)}\right)^{\gamma} = \left(\frac{log \frac{D\left(v_i^{(t)}, v_j^{(t)}\right) + 1}{D\left(v_i^{(t)}\right) D\left(v_j^{(t)}\right)}}{-log\left(D\left(v_i^{(t)}, v_j^{(t)}\right) + 1\right)} \right)^{\gamma} \tag{7}$$

For topic t, the centroid vector $\overrightarrow{v_c^{(t)}}$ is the sum of each context vector of topical words:

$$\overrightarrow{v_c^{(t)}} = \sum_{v_i^{(t)} \in V^{(t)}} \overrightarrow{v_i^{(t)}} \tag{8}$$

The final coherence is computed as average cosine similarity between top word context vectors and their centroid $\overrightarrow{v_c^{(t)}}$.

$$C_{cen} = \frac{1}{M} \sum_{v_i^{(t)} \in V^{(t)}} cos\left(\overrightarrow{v_i^{(t)}}, \overrightarrow{v_c^{(t)}}\right) \tag{9}$$

6.2 Performance Comparison

In order to make a comprehensive comparison of the clustered topic quality between three topic models: LDA, FBTM and DMM, we choose Agora forum dataset in the Darknet Market Archives[5]. Agora forum dataset is organized in the subfolders whose names indicate the dates when Branwen employed his crawler tools. Valuable intellegence can be obtained from forum user profiles and threads, which began when a forum user created a post that was followed by numerous responding posts. For time limitation, we randomly choose 1000 files from a part of subfolders, which span a whole year in 2014, for topic models in pyDNetTopic respectively and calculate the evaluation metrics. Our setting of topic number is 3 for all models. Another hyperparameters use default settings in pyDNetTopic.

The UMass, UCI and centroid coherence of three topic models in different dates of Agora forum dataset is shown in Figs. 3, 4 and 5 respectively. The average UMass coherence of FBTM fluctuating around 50 is remarkably higher than LDA and DMM. FBTM achieves almost 150% and 250% higher measures than

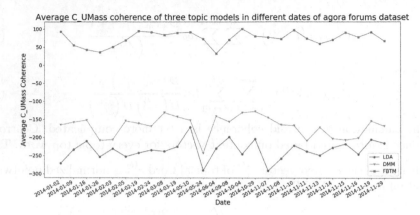

Fig. 3. Average UMass coherence of three topic models in different dates of Agora forums

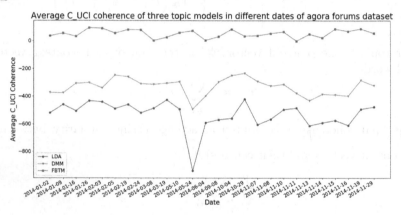

Fig. 4. Average UCI coherence of three topic models in different dates of Agora forums

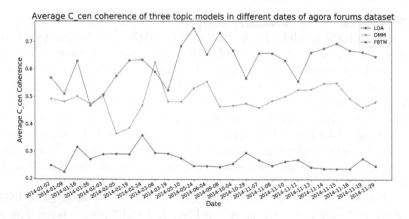

Fig. 5. Average centroid coherence of three topic models in different dates of Agora forums

LDA and DMM. UCI coherence gives a similar result: measures of FBTM is significantly higher than LDA and DMM. Due to our observation of traning files, we attribute the dramatic drop of performance of LDA in "05–24" to the high proportion of short text in dataset, especially some overly short documents. The severely negative affection on performance demonstrates the sparsity problem of LDA, which makes it the worst in all three topic models whereas extensively used in former researches. On the contraty, the stable measures of FBTM demonstrates its capability of handling various length files. About centroid coherence, situation seems a little different. The coherence scores of DMM are slightly lower than FBTM, while LDA still performs worst. We suggest the assumption made by DMM that each document originates from only one topic make the topical words selecting by DMM model much more similar in semantic space.

Table 3 lists some typical topics with their related words selected by three topic models in 02–03. The italic and bold words are related to the transaction and security concerns respectively. As shown in Table 3, FBTM can capture the typical terms of researchers' interests better than DMM and LDA. The topics FBTM extracts can be concluded as topics about "Markets&Drugs", "Trust&Security", "General conversation about markets". According to comparison, the topics FBTM generates consist of more specific words. The word "KUSH", "SDB" and "Sativa", which are kinds of drugs, and the keyword "ddos", "BitcoinFog" are selected only by FBTM. According to that we can have an quick understanding about the majority drugs darknet users prefer, the bitcoin mixing up platform prevalent in darknet(BitcoinFog), as well as the concerns against DDOS attack or business fraud from darknet users. The topics LDA generated is much more ambiguous with a high repetition rate of topical words. Only thing we can see is topic 2 related to the trust issues in darknet market due to some words like "scammer". In general, we can conclude that FBTM can provide a more specific informative intelligence from darknet, which makes it a better choice than LDA that used mostly in previous works Table 3 .

6.3   Result Analysis

Here we give a analysis of topical results listed in detail in Appendix B to show how topic model can help darknet intelligence mining. Owing to space constraints, we choose some of results generated by FBTM according to the date when Branwen applied his crawler in Darknet Market Archives. We show the top twenty most relevant words in each topic. The italic and bold words are related to the transaction and security concerns respectively for more visually appealing results.

Discussion About Transaction and Drug Knowledge. Results in Appendeix B supported the role of Agora market serving as a social platform that enabled users to exchange their goods or reviews for promoting underground transactions. Similar to traditional underground forums, many vendors tend to publish advertisements of their products with introductions and attached links

Table 3. Topics with related words in 02–03

Topic	DMM	FBTM	LDA
Markets& Drugs	shipping item need days5	party *SDB* REAL *KUSH*	*SDB* follows represent number
	add order lt gt	whole traditional generations **TOR**	dealer deposit long either
	last smoke address *MeO*	*Markovich* **AGORA** process *USD*	place invite say status
	new *SDB* bond listing	guide reason funds dedicated	ran people maligan vend
	another last smoke address	priority banks active **SR1**	scammed market chemicals stock
Trust& Security	**onion** market hash vendors	less try let established	either place say invite
	weed fucking back **Tor**	**BitcoinFog ddos** days change	trust index stock along
	squidgy going forum money	around scammer trust work	scammed scammer market still
	far send almost thing	described amp confident clean	chemicals people maligan register
	cannabis lol re black	provide allways *cannabis* squidgy	true wrong tormarket kxevkwmxhe7mby
General conversation about market	**onion** BEGIN register SIGNATURE	REAL *KUSH SDB* Nite	000 dealer number represent
	http LINK **GnuPG** ETw6LBrqv6http	login address **MingW32** hand	long follows deposit vend
	Version END account **MingW32**	Market administrative **TOR** successful	status popular single cool
	v1 REFERRAL please THE	link *Markovich* best outdoors	however **TOR** tormarket wrong
	team top MESSAGE NEW	**GNU** END **GnuPG** *Sativa*	none ksxq wanted topic

in the forums, especially new coming vendors. This can be reflected by the topic with keywords such as "Welcome" paired with the vendors' names. The topical words reveal some active vendors such as "Markovich", "Trim", "SQK". Another fact is active vendors always have business among multiple markets. For example, vendor "SQK" always appearing with another market "Pandora" seems that he does business in both two markets, which can be demonstrated by the content of posts.

An important functionality of underground Agora forums is it build a reputation system as a complement to the market. Forums provide a platform for exchanging evaluation and experience in transaction or drugs with freedom. That makes the forum a best place for customers to receive honest reviews and identify scammers. The common topical words "smell", "Feedback", "QUALITY" come from posts buyers exchange their usage experience or recommendation on the selling drugs. Prevalence of "scam", "scammer"or "trust" reflects the fraudulent conduct in DNM. FBTM also lists some prevalent goods, which are not captured by other models. "delta9", "x25", "KUSH", "meth", "DMT", "Lamas" are all chemical drugs sold in market. "cannabis" is also a prevalent goods while "Sativa" is the most popular species.

Another interesting findings are the transaction means used by darknet users. Topical words such as "address", "drugs", "days", "pack", and "time" seems to indicate discussions focused on purchase and delivery of drugs. The common choice for goods delivery is USPS owing to its high occurence rate in topics around transaction or delivery. Cryptocurrency is another big issue discussed frequently in darknet forums. Mentioned escrow services or tools are bitcoin exchanges or wallets such as "LocalBitcoins", "Multibit", "bitcoinamory", "brainwallet", "Mycelium". Although bitcoin is the most commonly used cryptocurrency in darknet market, the usage of credit card "Pasmo" become prevalent among darknet users after being recommended in "02–24".

Security Concern and Risk Management. Security concern is always a significant issue in darknet forums. Thereinto, anonymity is the most frequently discussed property due to the appearance of terms "anonymous", "anonymizing" or "stealth". We find the most prevalent tool darknet users used for confidential communication is "pgp" (Pretty Good Privacy), which is implemented by a free open source software "GnuPG". A substantial part of posts contains a large list of PGP keys at the end. Another important communication service mentioned in the forums are emailing indicated by words such as "Tormail", "Vmail", "URSSmail", "Thunderbird" and "SMTP". Besides, darknet users also use "Pidgin" for instant messaging. For secrecy, Pidgin is utilized through Tail, a living operating system where all software is configured to connect to the internet through Tor, which is also reflected in our results. As for anonymity of transaction, mixing is a service which attempts to increase the anonymity of cryptocurrency transactions, where a group of users exchange cryptocoins with each other to increase the difficulty in tracing transactions. "Bitcoinfog" is the most prevalent coinjoin platform appearing in the topic about security.

Darknet users also focus on the security of their wallet, account or the market itself. According to the topics, "DDoS" attack from "hacker" are the most probable attack the darknet website may come under. Apart from the external threat, scam in the market is also an important issue. To prevent business fraud, darknet users take measures which can be seen from the terms such as "escrow" and "multisig" which aims to prevent markets scamming users into purchasing items that they will never receive ("exit scamming"). "FEing", which is a transaction form meaning "finalized early" where the buyer has to release the fund kept in the marketplace's wallet to the vendor before the goods were actually shipped, becomes prevalent since "02–24" to protect vendors.

7 Conclusion

We have presented a general framework named pyDNetTopic, which is integrated with prevalent topic models, enabling automatically extracting textual content and uncovering hot topic issues in Darknet Market forums for researchers to have a general understanding on darknet. Especially, in order to adapt to big data scenarios in corpus with diverse text lengths such as Darknet Market forums datasets, we propose an improved topic model with less resource consumption and computational complexity named FBTM. Better coherence measures indicates better quality and interpretability of topical terms generated by FBTM than baseline models. The full results and analysis on real world darknet dataset demonstrate how pyDNetTopic can help by data mining and extracting informative intelligence in darknet researches.

Appendix A   List of Additional Stop Words

The listing words are some common words among all topics that provide no useful information. We regard such words as general stop words in pyDNetTopic and remove them in preprocessing.

fuck, get, got, shit, see, u0e2a, would, use, think, like, xa0, sr, know, u0e3f, good, tquot, u2591, u25ac, make, fe, day, although, ands, soooo, yet, favs, So, ll, went, br, en, often, knowing, liking, one, get, thinking, even, could, go, going, fucking, fuck, shit, also, use, using, much, got, good, make, making, really, see, want, need, sure, right, still, take, taking (Tables 4, 5, 6, 7, 8, 9, 10, 11, 12, 13) .

Appendix B   Full Topic Results of Agora Forums in 2014

Table 4. Result of 2014-01-09

Topic	Terms
Vendor review	Products stupid *vaporizer* referred fees start growing giving roof reading
	ur day5 lost book started terms members refer bank closed
Trust & Security	*TorBay* point products mean months thread fees sad scammer trustable
	described impossible ve buyers selling comes option crooked wasn hand
Transaction issue	Points absolutely *vaporizer* access More *Pandora* kind *SQK* bottom legit
	TorBay crooked strain sell *Tranzcentral* cloning start *Sativa* server week

Table 5. Result of 2014-02-03

Topic	Terms
Markets & Drugs	Party *SDB* REAL *KUSH* whole traditional generations **TOR** *Markovich* **AGORA**
	Process USD guide reason funds dedicated priority banks active **SR1**
Trust & Security	Less try let established **BitcoinFog ddos** days change around scammer
	trust work described amp confident clean provide allways *cannabis* squidgy
General conversation about market	REAL *KUSH* *SDB* Nite login address **MingW32** hand Market administrative
	TOR successful link *Markovich* best outdoors **GNU** END **GnuPG** *Sativa*

Table 6. Result of 2014-02-24

Topic	Terms
General conversation about market	Partner began **Tormail code** Legit try suddenly buzz browser genetics
	Suite **USB** 2004 Vendors Instruments either Guide Please Requires Do
Anonymity & Security	**URSSMail VPN Gateway** blend *Passmo* **SMTP** log privacy Using **TrueCrypt**
	bitmessage FEing Audio green encrypt **Tormail** items compound anonymous
Vendor review	**www** *Passmo* items BEST recommended testing protect Walther genetic Japan
	Information anonymous *Indica* x4 larger pretty trusted straight person **Tormail**

Table 7. Result of 2014-03-19

Topic	Terms
Transaction tools and items	**Tormail LocalBitcoins** *meth* protects *USPS* DrEarnhardt **Tails Pidgin** House shared
	paper parental deeper experiences delivery Interways called NOW *Enanthate Purps*
General conversation about transaction	Located **bitcoinarmory** integrity replaced *Trim* Japan pack smells Interways thick
	Feedback spread contains genetics lovely via forums worth *Blotters Dawg*
Anonymity	Use **VPN Vmail** Information interest Cert **Tormail** consider **bitmessage** anonymous
	additional **Pidgin** hidden given part admin right **SMTP** began integrity

Table 8. Result of 2014-05-10

Topic	Terms
Unknown	Obviously patients consistently wouldn commissions writing ad_listing pages user inch
	generate **Pidgin** low Sunday Sign March *Morrissons* hardly Grape situation
General conversation about market	*Lotus* won flooring anymore nlm quick Vendors usb previous words
	id Wallets **Thunderbird** specific asked beautiful geometric p1http recognized *CBG*
General conversation about transaction	Boguu inch commissions **LocalBitcoins** offers brand almost improved *cannabinoids*
	privacy sensitive bred Wallets seeking priority pain posting stealth partner known

Table 9. Result of 2014-06-04

Topic	Terms
Security	Id *blotters* numerous **agora** comedown security package sells priced **Vmail**
	clear price b1t **ddos VPN Tormail** privacy *blotter* kind **truecrypt**
Privacy	Thirty hour unsigned Liquid **truecrypt** finished crushed Use nowhere privacy
	trying id headers deal ocbruins encryption register webmail client basically
General conversation about markets	*Lotus* p1http bizarre nowhere comedown activity *x25* unfortunately **Linux** labor
	Download low confirmed opportune kinda secure worried transaction park combined

Table 10. Result of 2014-09-08

Topic	Terms
Drugs	Laid trusted activity asserted smooth *delta9* tv *cannabisrelief* crystal matter
	welcome eaten set mcg 110ug bag March writing system found
General conversation about markets	*Lotus* universe asked flooring news weeks regularly *Blotters* American bizarre
	tv crystal writing Vendors trusted confirmed online situation activity stable
Vendor review	Bogu numb box previous *cannabinoids* indeed outside messaged parents July
	deeper pages brand preview coin seconds moment community known index

Table 11. Result of 2014-10-29

Topic	Terms
Vendor advertisement	*Lamas* Vendors ups thought focus opinion inch white truly asked
	dark presences *drugs* setting bizarre weeks offer **php** forum Jim
Vendor review	Words *Xanax* partner leave work answer old quick unsigned outside
	perception universe comedown lower comeup sbizarre information feeling truly USD
Drug	*Lamas* anyone white reccomend contains quotes *drugs* info thoroughly amount
	Other *Sativa Shamrock* trusted *DMT* stable allows fun line looked

Table 12. Rresult of 2014-11-11

Topic	Terms
Transaction tools	Public *Paypal* **Multibit Mycelium** buys really cash Using someone **Blockchain**
	signed *silver* certain Love lower amazing Offline watching buyer blotter
Vendor advertisement	**LocalBitcoins** welcome anyone unsigned however understanding put refund prejudice
	page three forums connects tried **brainwallet** funds longer big Jim untested
Drug review	Password *blotter* lectures packs left paper nature *BMR* wall want
	documentaries set jar site ready world Any Vendors Guide White

Table 13. Result of 2014-11-19

Topic	Terms
Vendor review	Numb indeed *USPS* container snoopy recommended *Sativa* Even *Floyd* Go
	Low hot March **Pidgin** Some re Twins Cheap Vendors solution
Mailing discussion	**Tormail** asked deeper Jim crazy **VPN Vmail** actually ask truly
	writing **SMTP** yesterday old spread spice hacked disk network **bitmessage**
Unknown	Won bizarro overall soft inch **Linux** hope writing bonus words
	comeup yesterday connected action posts spread tripped unsigned universe numb

References

1. Aletras, N., Stevenson, M.: Evaluating topic coherence using distributional semantics, pp. 13–22, March 2013
2. Almukaynizi, M., Grimm, A., Nunes, E., Shakarian, J., Shakarian, P.: Predicting cyber threats through hacker social networks in darkweb and deepweb forums, pp. 1–7, October 2017. https://doi.org/10.1145/3145574.3145590
3. Biddle, P., England, P., Peinado, M., Willman, B.: The darknet and the future of content protection. In: Feigenbaum, J. (ed.) DRM 2002. LNCS, vol. 2696, pp. 155–176. Springer, Heidelberg (2003). https://doi.org/10.1007/978-3-540-44993-5_10
4. Blei, D., Ng, A., Jordan, M.: Latent dirichlet allocation. J. Mach. Learn. Res. **3**, 993 (2013)

5. Branwen, G., et al.: Dark net market archives, 2011–2015. www.gwern.net/ Blackmarket%20archives (2015)
6. Christin, N.: Traveling the silk road: a measurement analysis of a large anonymous online marketplace, pp. 213–224, May 2013. https://doi.org/10.1145/2488388. 2488408
7. Deliu, I., Leichter, C., Franke, K.: Collecting cyber threat intelligence from hacker forums via a two-stage, hybrid process using support vector machines and latent dirichlet allocation, pp. 5008–5013, December2018. https://doi.org/10.1109/ BigData.2018.8622469
8. Dittus, M., Wright, J., Graham, M.: Platform criminalism: The 'last-mile' geography of the darknet market supply chain, pp. 277–286, April 2018. https://doi.org/ 10.1145/3178876.3186094
9. Eimer, T., Luimers, J.: Onion governance: Securing drug transactions in dark net market platforms, August 08 2019
10. Grisham, J., Barreras, C., Afarin, C., Patton, M.: Identifying top listers in alphabay using latent dirichlet allocation, p. 219, September 2016. https://doi.org/10.1109/ ISI.2016.7745477
11. Hout, M.C., Bingham, T.: 'Surfing the silk road': a study of users' experiences. Int. J. Drug Policy **24**, 524–529 (2013). https://doi.org/10.1016/j.drugpo.2013.08.011
12. Jin, O., Liu, N., Zhao, K., Yu, Y., Yang, Q.: Transferring topical knowledge from auxiliary long texts for short text clustering, pp. 775–784, October 2011. https:// doi.org/10.1145/2063576.2063689
13. Larochelle, H., Lauly, S.: A neural autoregressive topic model. In: Advances in Neural Information Processing Systems, vol. 4, pp. 2708–2716, January 01 2012
14. Mimno, D., Wallach, H., Talley, E., Leenders, M., Mccallum, A.: Optimizing semantic coherence in topic models, pp. 262–272, January 2011
15. Newman, D., Lau, J., Grieser, K., Baldwin, T.: Automatic evaluation of topic coherence, pp. 100–108, January 2010
16. Nunes, E., et al.: Darknet and deepnet mining for proactive cybersecurity threat intelligence, July 2016
17. Phan, X., Nguyen, L., Horiguchi, S.: Learning to classify short and sparse text & web with hidden topics from large-scale data collections. In: Proceedings 17th International Conference on World Wide Web, pp. 91–100, February 2020
18. Phan, X.H., Nguyen, C.T., Le, D.T., Nguyen, L., Horiguchi, S., Ha, Q.: A hidden topic-based framework toward building applications with short web documents. IEEE Trans. Knowl. Data Eng. **23**, 961–976 (2011). https://doi.org/10. 1109/TKDE.2010.27
19. Porter, K.: Analyzing the DarkNetMarkets subreddit for evolutions of tools and trends using LDA topic modeling. Digit. Invest. Int. J. Digit. Forensics Incid. Response **26**, S87–S97 (2018)
20. Röder, M., Both, A., Hinneburg, A.: Exploring the space of topic coherence measures. In: WSDM 2015 - Proceedings of the 8th ACM International Conference on Web Search and Data Mining, pp. 399–408, February 2015. https://doi.org/10. 1145/2684822.2685324
21. Salakhutdinov, R., Hinton, G.: Replicated softmax: an undirected topic model. pp. 1607–1614, January 2009
22. Samtani, S., Chinn, R., Chen, H.: Exploring hacker assets in underground forums, pp. 31–36, May 2015. https://doi.org/10.1109/ISI.2015.7165935
23. Samtani, S., Chinn, R., Chen, H., Nunamaker, J.: Exploring emerging hacker assets and key hackers for proactive cyber threat intelligence. J. Manag. Inf. Syst. **34**, 1023–1053 (2017). https://doi.org/10.1080/07421222.2017.1394049

24. Sapienza, A., Bessi, A., Damodaran, S., Shakarian, P., Lerman, K., Ferrara, E.: Early warnings of cyber threats in online discussions, January 2018
25. Sievert, C., Shirley, K.: Ldavis: A method for visualizing and interpreting topics, June 2014. https://doi.org/10.13140/2.1.1394.3043
26. Srivastava, A., Sutton, C.: Autoencoding variational inference for topic models, March 2017
27. Xia, Y., Tang, N., Hussain, A., Cambria, E.: Discriminative bi-term topic model for headline-based social news clustering. In: FLAIRS Conference (2015)
28. Yan, X., Guo, J., Lan, Y., Cheng, X.: A biterm topic model for short texts. pp. 1445–1456, May 2013. https://doi.org/10.1145/2488388.2488514
29. Yin, J., Wang, J.: A dirichlet multinomial mixture model-based approach for short text clustering. In: Proceedings of the ACM SIGKDD International Conference on Knowledge Discovery and Data Mining, August 2014. https://doi.org/10.1145/2623330.2623715
30. Zhang, H., Chen, B., Guo, D., Zhou, M.: Whai: Weibull hybrid autoencoding inference for deep topic modeling, March 2018

MisMesh: Security Issues and Challenges in Service Meshes

Dalton A. Hahn$^{(\boxtimes)}$, Drew Davidson, and Alexandru G. Bardas

EECS Department, ITTC University of Kansas, Lawrence, KS, USA
{daltonhahn,drewdavidson,alexbardas}@ku.edu

Abstract. Service meshes have emerged as an attractive DevOps solution for collecting, managing, and coordinating microservice deployments. However, current service meshes leave fundamental security mechanisms missing or incomplete. The security burden means service meshes may actually cause additional workload and overhead for administrators over traditional monolithic systems. By assessing the effectiveness and practicality of service mesh tools, this work provides necessary insights into the available security of service meshes. We evaluate service meshes under skilled administrators (who deploy optimal configurations of available security mechanisms) and default configurations. We consider a comprehensive set of adversarial scenarios, uncover design flaws contradicting system goals, and present limitations and challenges encountered in employing service mesh tools for operational environments.

Keywords: Service mesh · DevOps · Containers · Consul · Istio · Linkerdv2

1 Introduction

The widespread enthusiasm of large enterprises for *microservice* system architectures [2], where many lightweight containers are managed and deployed via automation tools [20], lacks a matching evaluation of their security. A number of academic works have examined the security of individual containers [6,30,34]. However, the *service meshes* of interdependent microservices, are largely unstudied. Service meshes aid the microservice design philosophy of refactoring monolithic applications into distinct components that collaborate at scale [24].

Service meshes ease the complexity of managing microservice architectures by allowing the administrator to express the structure and relationships between services using configuration files [16,23]. State-of-art service mesh tools such as Consul [13], Istio [22], and Linkerdv2 [19] launch collections of microservices automatically. Furthermore, these tools automate *service discovery*, the process of locating and binding services together. Service discovery is a non-trivial process under the DevOps [2,3] ideology to support a range of flexible deployments. As such, service discovery is decentralized with dependencies satisfied dynamically.

N. Park et al. (Eds.): SecureComm 2020, LNICST 335, pp. 140–151, 2020.
https://doi.org/10.1007/978-3-030-63086-7_9

In studying service mesh security, we discover that misconfiguration issues and lack of security mechanisms enable numerous attacks. We view these as consequences of design flaws in service mesh security. When facing these attacks, service meshes either offer no defense or require significant manual intervention on the part of the system administrator. The latter effectively undermines a core goal of service meshes: ease of automation.

Current practices such as infinite-lifetimes and shared encryption keys [14] indicate that the design of service meshes has overlooked important security concerns. Nonetheless, deployment of immature service meshes is growing in production environments [5,9,10,25,39]. Moreover, the context-dependent scope and implementations of service meshes are so diverse that establishing a meaningful comparison between different tools is difficult.

Despite the building importance of defending service meshes, we are unaware of any systematic assessment of their security. To the best of our knowledge, this paper presents the first study to specifically focus on existing security mechanisms in service meshes. Our assessment indicates service mesh security implementations and maintenance mechanisms are incomplete, or even non-existent. Additionally, we discovered that even though service mesh tools advertise their security contributions, they are either not enabled by default, or are left to third-party tools to implement.

Our contributions can be summarized as follows:

- We present the first study to examine the security design and analyze the available security mechanisms within current service meshes
- We propose a relevant threat model to the service mesh domain and assess the effectiveness of existing tools to mitigate these threats
- We assess the impact and the effort of utilizing available security features in current service mesh tools

2   Background

Microservice architectures consist of a complex web of narrowly-scoped, interacting services in place of a monolithic architecture. This structure better enables incremental changes, resilience to cascading failures, and quicker update/release cycles [3,11,35] at the cost of complexity; it is a significant challenge to maintain synergy between services. Systems such as Kubernetes [26] provide a framework to deploy, scale, and manage microservices quickly, magnifying the need to coordinate services. Service meshes seek to address this gap between fast deployments and collaborating webs of microservices. In this section, we describe some of the enabling tools and design concepts that underlie service meshes.

Service Mesh Tools: Service meshes enable a service to be registered to a cluster, discovered dynamically by other dependent services, and to have configuration state maintained. Consul, Istio, and Linkerdv2 are the current state-of-art service mesh tools with full, production-ready releases. A major cause of complexity in coordinating services is to determine cluster membership and

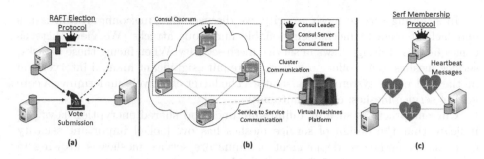

Fig. 1. Model Consul Service Mesh – Using Consul, the creation and operation of a model service mesh are shown. **(a).** RAFT elections occur periodically among Consul servers to determine cluster leadership. **(b).** Proxies present on each node route cluster- and service-level communications to nodes. Proxies may be installed on a variety of platforms including virtualized, containerized, and physical machines with little restriction on operating system [1]. **(c).** The Serf membership protocol occurs with high frequency to send heartbeat messages among nodes to track health and membership.

node operation status. Consul implements the Serf [17] membership and node health protocol (an extension of SWIM [8]) and the RAFT consensus protocol. The basic process is illustrated in Fig. 1. Leveraging the cluster membership logic, Consul creates a membership hierarchy to organize the permissions that members of the cluster possess to take action within the cluster. The Consul quorum is responsible for maintaining a consistent membership registry and holding cluster elections for the cluster permission hierarchy.

Istio and Linkerdv2 both require an underlying Kubernetes platform to provide cluster membership logic. In contrast, installation of Consul is supported on a range of operating systems and architectures as well as virtualized and physical instances [1]. Without a previously created and configured Kubernetes cluster of *pods*; collections of containers with shared resources [27,28], Istio and Linkerdv2 are unable to provide any of their promised features or security benefits. By imposing the initial requirement of a properly installed, configured, and secured Kubernetes infrastructure, in addition to the overhead of configuring and maintaining the service mesh, Istio and Linkerdv2 demonstrate a higher burden on system administrators than that of Consul. In contrast to Consul, Istio and Linkerdv2 do not maintain a hierarchical structure for permissions and state management, instead, they rely upon a star topology-like system where the Kubernetes master controls the cluster's pods either remotely, or locally, and sets the configuration and permissions of specific members within the cluster.

Service Mesh Security: The paradigm shift from monolithic systems to microservice systems has caused a change from *intra*-service issues to *inter*-service issues. This transitions the burden of security from within the operating system of a machine to across network connections. Issues previously addressable by trusted security measures within the operating system must now be addressed with network-level security measures. These issues include the need to protect

Table 1. Adversarial Goals on a Consul Deployment – Presents experimental results of achieved adversarial goals on a properly configured Consul service mesh deployment. Disruption: Interruption to service availability. Manipulation: Infiltration or exfiltration of data to cluster. Takeover: Adversary assumes the leadership position in cluster.

	Datacenter Label as a Secret	UDP Encryption	ACLs (Access Control Lists)	TLS Encryption	All Mechanisms Combined (Datacenter Label, UDP, ACLs, TLS)
Unprivileged Threat	D M T	—	D	—	—
Client Compromise	D M T	D M T	D	M	—
Server Compromise	D M T	D M T	D	M	—
Leader Compromise	D M T	D M T	D M T	D M T	D M T

cluster-level communications, service-level communications, and access permissions, both at the cluster-level as well as the service-level.

3 Threat Model and Experimental Design

To evaluate the security of modern service mesh tools, we used Consul as a model for service mesh design and implementation. We constructed a proof-of-concept environment using Consul to conduct our experiments. We consider the available security mechanisms for administrators and examine a deployment utilizing all available mechanisms as well as one using default configurations. Under these setups, we conduct a series of active attacks and report our results. We also present a comparison of available and default security mechanisms within Istio and Linkerdv2 and provide our findings. We utilize these findings to frame a discussion of the shortcomings and overhead system administrators should expect when attempting to secure service mesh clusters within their infrastructure.

Consul provides a meaningful representation of service meshes and the maturity of these tools. Of the current state-of-art service meshes, Consul is the most feature-rich and flexible tool available in this domain. As mentioned previously, Consul can be used with any other tools or forms of virtualization such as containers or virtual machines whereas Istio and Linkerdv2 are dependent upon an underlying Kubernetes implementation to provide necessary features for the mesh. Additionally, as of the writing of this work, Consul appears to be the most actively developed tool, enjoying the largest number of GitHub contributors (594) of the tools we encountered, and a comparable number of GitHub repository stars to the runner-up tool, Istio [15,21]).

Threat Model: The threat model we employ in this work considers common attacker goals of disruption of services and exfiltration of sensitive data. However, we also consider adversarial targets that are unique to the service mesh domain. For example, an attacker may often desire to infiltrate the cluster and gain privilege rather than destroying the functionality of a system. By infiltrating the cluster, the attacker may inject malicious service configurations to possibly redirect benign service requests to externally controlled endpoints. In Table 1, we denote these high-level goals as **D**isruption, **M**anipulation, and **T**akeover for disruption to services and cluster activities, tampering of sensitive data via manipulation, and gaining privilege through service mesh takeover, respectively.

Experimental Setup: We deployed our model cluster upon a Dell R540 server configured with 128 GB of RAM, Xeon Gold 5117 processor, and 10 TB of SSD storage. We believe this hardware to be comparable to what would be utilized in production environments, both in on-site and remote, cloud datacenters.

The proof-of-concept Consul service mesh consists of an initial leader node or "bootstrapper" responsible for initializing the cluster and connecting the initial nodes. Alongside the leader node are two server nodes, forming the quorum, and a singular client node. Using Fig. 1 as our model, we manually deployed and configured these four Consul nodes (one leader, two servers, and one client node). We utilize only one client node due to the equivalent functionality of subsequent clients. Due to the architecture of Consul service mesh clusters, it is recommended to have 3 nodes acting as servers (one leader node and 2 server nodes) to manage the quorum and maintain the cluster state and log files [14]. Nodes are the main structural components of service mesh clusters, hosting ephemeral or long-lived microservices on permanent, virtual, or physical instances.

4   Evaluation of Modern Service Meshes

We consider an administrator with deep knowledge of the employed tool and its available security mechanisms. We present an experimental assessment of this "idealized" scenario and compare the results against default offerings of the tool.

With deep knowledge of available security mechanisms and their correct configuration, an administrator can leverage these protections to their greatest potential. To study how varying degrees of attacker strength can affect the level of compromise under these security mechanisms, we position the adversary at different levels of initial compromise. The lowest initial power we consider an attacker to have is that of an "Unprivileged Adversary" who has not yet compromised any node within the cluster. The highest initial level of power we consider is that of "Leader Compromise" where an adversary has the preliminary position of a node considered to be the leader of the Consul quorum. Under the assumption of a knowledgeable administrator and the preconditions placed upon the adversary, we evaluate the experimental results and provide our assessment.

Consul – Datacenter Label as a Secret: The first means of potential defense we consider within our proof-of-concept Consul service mesh is the datacenter label. We consider this a potential security mechanism due to the fact that if a prospective cluster node is configured with a datacenter label that differs from the target cluster, the prospective node will be denied membership to the cluster.

As shown in Table 1, under all adversarial scenarios, using strictly "Datacenter Label as a Secret" is insufficient in thwarting attacks against the cluster. Specifically, when using datacenter label alone, communication messages are exchanged in plaintext between nodes of the cluster. Due to the realistic possibility of an adversary to capture a *single* packet exchanged between the nodes of the cluster, they may extract the datacenter label from the packet. The malicious join operation is, subsequently, made possible and once a member of the cluster, all high-level attacker goals can be achieved.

Consul – UDP Message Encryption: Next, we consider the Consul service mesh deployed using UDP message encryption as the sole mechanism of defense. As shown in Table 1, enabling UDP message encryption thwarts an unprivileged adversary from achieving any of their goals, but fails to provide protection under compromise of any cluster members. By enabling UDP encryption, the adversarial joins previously possible are prevented because an attacker is unable to decrypt packets from the legitimate nodes.

All nodes within a Consul service mesh share the <u>same</u> encryption key. To exacerbate this concern, Consul, as of the writing of this work, fails to provide any means of key revocation or rotation. In order to provide key rotation within the cluster, even through a separate "recovery" mechanism such as an SSH [36] session, all nodes must be stopped, configurations adjusted, and the cluster recreated. While the managed services of the cluster may be transient and possibly short-lived, the underlying service mesh infrastructure is intended to be long-living. Therefore, support for key rotation capabilities is vital for managing and maintaining a secure service mesh architecture.

Consul – ACLs: As shown in Table 1, Access Control Lists (ACLs) are highly effective at thwarting the adversarial goals of manipulation and takeover within the cluster. However, ACLs prove futile against disruption of cluster activities and service availability. In order for a system administrator to enable ACLs as a defense mechanism, extensive permission policies must be created and access tokens exchanged using a third-party, secure channel such as SSH. With a lack of support for distributing security objects safely within Consul itself, the implementation of ACLs, and subsequently the policies and tokens generated, demonstrates that security mechanisms within service meshes have been "bolted-on" to existing software, rather than incorporated into system design.

In order to secure the simple, four node service mesh used for our evaluation, as advised by the Consul tutorials [14], an administrator would need to generate unique access policies, generate tokens, and distribute and assign the generated tokens to proper recipients. All of these actions must be conducted from the single leader node due to the advised "operator-only" policy. Under the "operator-only" policy, permissions to edit the ACLs are restricted to the leader, meaning a singular node is responsible for all creation and distribution of policy materials. In direct contrast to the decentralized, distributed nature of the service mesh, the security structure implemented has been consolidated to a single point of control, the Consul leader. Augmenting the burden placed upon system administrators, the current implementation of Consul ACLs have no token rotation policy in place. Therefore, either the created access tokens within the cluster will exist for the lifetime of the cluster, or are revoked after a period of time, but with no means of redistributing fresh tokens to nodes.

When ACLs are the sole mechanism of defense for a Consul service mesh cluster, they prove ineffective at mitigating adversarial disruption efforts. Due

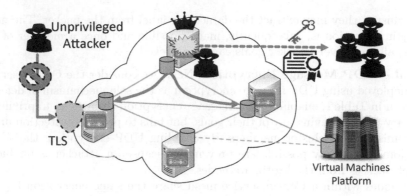

Fig. 2. TLS Message Encryption – Encrypting service traffic with TLS prevents an unprivileged attacker influencing the cluster. However, a leader node compromise allows an adversary to generate malicious TLS key pairs and exfiltrate them to other adversary nodes. Once additional adversaries join they may join the quorum and cast votes due to their server-permissioned certificates.

to implementation of processing access control policies within the service mesh, unauthorized messages must be confirmed as illegitimate by the cluster. Using around 25 adversarial nodes, we were able to disrupt operations within the service mesh by overwhelming the consensus protocol.

Consul – TLS Message Encryption: In order to protect service-level communication within the Consul cluster, a system administrator may enable TLS message encryption. To provide nodes the capability to sign messages, they must first have signed certificates from the certificate authority. When constructing the service mesh, the administrator would create a certificate authority from one of the server nodes of the cluster. Afterwards, the certificate authority is responsible for generating all server and client certificates. Distribution of certificates must be completed through a separate channel before cluster creation.

By enabling TLS encryption, the unprivileged adversary is unable to maliciously join the cluster, preventing any goals from being achieved in this case. Despite this, there are no protections for the key/value storage system. Accessing the key/value storage allows an adversary to manipulate configurations or secrets stored within the cluster. Figure 2 shows how, should the leader node ever be compromised in the lifetime of the cluster, an adversary may leverage the signing privileges of the certificate authority to generate illegitimate certificates and keys for malicious nodes.

The implementation of the certificate hierarchy within Consul once again shows a disconnect between the desired decentralized and distributed nature of service meshes with a centralized, consolidated security structure. Within Consul, the only node able to sign certificates of any privilege is the certificate authority (commonly created on the quorum leader node). Additionally, should the leader node fail, barring replication of the certificate authority key, the cluster loses the ability to sign new certificates, once again conflicting with the flexibility goal of the DevOps ideology. Lastly, a lack of revocation and rotation mechanisms within Consul itself necessitates a third-party tool such as HashiCorp's Vault [18] or SSH be used to distribute fresh certificates to nodes, which triggers the need for widespread edits to configurations in order to return to a secure state.

Consul – All Mechanisms Combined: By enabling and combining all available security mechanisms, Table 1 shows a clear improvement in mitigating adversarial goals. However, employing all mechanisms presents administrators with a daunting amount of manual configuration. Considering the cost required to establish a secure model example with trivial functionality, the requirements to successfully deploy and secure enterprise-level systems is unreasonable. Also, due to the implementation of the available security mechanisms, should the leader of the cluster ever be compromised across the lifetime of a cluster, all configuration effort must be repeated to redeploy securely. By lacking necessary revocation and rotation mechanisms, Consul has limited the ability to construct dynamic service mesh clusters that are resilient to compromise events. Service mesh tools, while aiming to fill the niche of microservice architecture discovery, connection, and management, may, in fact, lead to substantial overhead for administrators who wish to deploy these tools in a secure fashion.

Nacos: While not directly considered a service mesh, Nacos provides many of the same features as the service meshes considered and has the ability to be configured in a way to accomplish many of the same high-level goals as service mesh tools. However, it is important to note that Nacos is technically a service discovery and management tool. As of the writing of this work, Nacos is in version 1.1.4, and is available for public use. However, Nacos has very little, if any security mechanisms available to its users. In its current state, Nacos depends primarily upon external security mechanisms such as firewalls, subnetting, and other perimeter defenses for protection.

Default Security Mechanisms: Table 2 outlines the available security mechanisms of service meshes and Kubernetes and the default state of these mechanisms. While Consul offers all of the necessary security capabilities to administrators, it *fails* to enable any of them by default and lacks rotation support for all mechanisms. With an extensive list of configurations to create and assign, such as node permissions, key creation and distribution, and certificate hierarchy, the overhead for system administrators is significant.

Additionally, Istio and Linkerdv2 fail to provide means of securing the cluster-level functionality and service-level access control by default. However, Linkerdv2 does enable service-to-service message encryption via mutual TLS by default, representing a valuable design decision that benefits security. In Istio, to provide the same service-level security, an administrator would be required to modify configurations of the cluster and provide additional authentication rules for individual pods and services in order to provide proper, secure functionality.

Table 2. Security Mechanisms in Service Mesh Tools – A summarized view of the security mechanisms available in each service mesh tool analyzed, which mechanisms are enabled by default, and additional details about the actual implementations. *Pod-to-pod encryption left to third-party implementation [27]. **Inherited from Kubernetes' Role-Based Access Control system [19, 23].

Tool	Security Mechanism	Available in Tool?	Enabled by Default?	Default Lifetime	Revocation	Redistribution
Consul	Cluster Message Encryption	Yes	No	∞	No	No
	Service Message Encryption	Yes	No	1 year	Yes	No
	Cluster Access Control	Yes	No	∞	Yes	No
	Service Access Control	Yes	No	∞	Yes	No
Linkerdv2	Cluster Message Encryption	No	No	N/A	N/A	N/A
	Service Message Encryption	Yes	Yes	24 hours	Yes	Yes
	Cluster Access Control	No	No	N/A	N/A	N/A
	Service Access Control	Yes	No	∞**	No**	No**
Istio	Cluster Message Encryption	No	No	N/A	N/A	N/A
	Service Message Encryption	Yes	No	Ext Tool [23]	Ext Tool [23]	Ext Tool [23]
	Cluster Access Control	No	No	N/A	N/A	N/A
	Service Access Control	Yes	No	∞**	No**	No**
Kubernetes	Cluster Message Encryption	No*	No	N/A	N/A	N/A
	Service Message Encryption	Yes	No	1 year	Beta	Beta
	Cluster Access Control	Yes	No	∞	No	No
	Service Access Control	Yes	No	∞	No	No

5 Related Work

To our knowledge, this work is the first systematic study of service mesh security. Many of our attacks are inspired by existing work, and many of the implications of our work build upon previous studies of microservice security and networked systems. We discuss some works most closely related to our own below.

Microservice Security: Automation and the decentralized nature of microservice security has been observed or utilized by a number of previous works. Rastogi, *et al.* [31] evaluate an automation system for dismantling a monolithic software deployment into a collection of collaborating microservices in order to better adhere to the principle of least privilege [33]. Yarygina, *et al.* [40] note the comparative lack of security protections for Docker containers, and propose a container security monitor. In Sun, *et al.* [38], the authors study how the trust relationship between deployed microservices may result in the compromise of an entire system and they propose a system for deploying network security monitors in microservice environments to detect and block threats to clusters.

A number of previously published works focus on the security of individual Docker containers, which are frequently used for microservices. A representative example is Enck, *et al.* [34], which studies the risk of deploying containers automatically from 3rd-party container repositories. In Lin, *et al.* [29] and Martin, *et al.* [30], the authors examine attacks and countermeasures to the security of containers, as well as the ecosystems of repositories and orchestration tools. Our work assumes that individual containers and repositories are secure, instead focusing on external threats to the mechanisms by which microservices interact.

Analysis of Consensus Protocols: Some of the attacks that we propose target the RAFT protocol used to form a service mesh. Some previous work, most notably by Sakic, *et al.* [32], examines the availability and response time of nodes participating in RAFT. However, previous work does not consider the influence of an adversary, and is instead concerned with the performance of RAFT in a purely-benign setting.

The considerable interest around blockchain technologies has driven the development of security studying microservice clusters specifically for running consensus protocols, such as Hyperledger Fabric [12,37]. These studies observe the threat of sybil attacks on collaborative network services, as does our work. However, blockchain technology can defeat traditional sybil attacks via proof-of-work or related protocol-level mechanisms, whereas our attacks require low-latency communication and collaboration between microservices.

Microservice Attacks: The attack vectors that we present are (to our knowledge) unreported. The actual attacks themselves, and the goals of the adversaries that we articulate in our threat model are inspired by previous work on attacks against more traditional systems. One of the most relevant studies is that of Cherny, *et al.* [4], which also proposes the use of microservice containers as a vector of attacks, thus providing a motivation for services as a target. In Csikor, *et al.* [7], the authors study how specially tailored access control policies crafted by an attacker may result in an exhaustion of cloud resources resulting in a denial-of-service to a cluster.

6 Conclusions

Due to the increase of deployed microservices, service mesh tools appear to be an enticing solution to manage and maintain these deployments. However, it is necessary to assess the available security mechanisms and their strength in deterring adversarial efforts. As the initial study of service mesh tools used for microservice deployments, we examine the three most popular, state-of-art offerings in the service mesh domain and articulate a threat model tailored to concerns within the service mesh domain.

Through experimentation, we find that under configuration by a skilled administrator, in 10 of the 20 studied scenarios, complete cluster compromise is possible for an attacker. Further, in 5 additional scenarios, at least one adversarial goal is achievable. Under default configuration, all studied tools, except Linkerdv2, fail to enable *any* of their security mechanisms. These results and our observations in usability of these mechanisms indicate important design flaws in the security of service mesh tools requiring further research and development.

Acknowledgments. The authors would like to acknowledge Seena Saiedian for their contributions in proofreading and revising this work.

References

1. HashiCorp. Download Consul. https://www.consul.io/downloads. Accessed 06 2020
2. Balalaie, A., Heydarnoori, A., Jamshidi, P.: Microservices architecture enables DevOps: migration to a cloud-native architecture. IEEE Softw. **33**(3), 42–52 (2016)
3. Chen, L.: Microservices: architecting for continuous delivery and DovOps. In: 2018 IEEE International Conference on Software Architecture (ICSA), pp. 39–397, April 2018
4. Cherny, M., Dulce, S.: Well, that escalated quickly! how abusing docker api led to remote code execution, same origin bypass and persistence in the hypervisor via shadow containers. In: BlackHat 17 (2017)
5. Christopherson, J.: Spaceflight uses HashiCorp consul for service discovery and runtime configuration in their hub-and-spoke network architecture. https://www.hashicorp.com/blog/spaceflight-uses-hashicorp-consul-for-service-discovery-and-real-time-updates-to-their-hub-and-spoke-network-architecture/. Accessed 02 2020
6. Combe, T., Martin, A., Di Pietro, R.: To docker or not to docker: a security perspective. IEEE Cloud Comput. **3**(5), 54–62 (2016)
7. Csikor, L., Rothenberg, C., Pezaros, D.P., Schmid, S., Toka, L., Rétvári, G.: Policy injection: a cloud dataplane DoS attack. In: Proceedings of the ACM SIGCOMM 2018 Conference on Posters and Demos, pp. 147–149 (2018)
8. Das, A., Gupta, I., Motivala, A.: SWIM: scalable weakly-consistent infection-style process group membership protocol. In: Proceedings International Conference on Dependable Systems and Networks, pp. 303–312. IEEE (2002)
9. Fishner, K.: How BitBrains/ASP4all uses Consul for Continuous Deployment across Development, Testing, Acceptance, and Production. https://www.hashicorp.com/blog/how-bitbrains-asp4all-uses-consul/. Accessed 02 2020
10. Fishner K.: Using Consul at Bol.com, the Largest Online Retailer in the Netherlands and Belgium. https://www.hashicorp.com/blog/using-consul-at-bol-com-the-largest-online-retailer-in-the-netherlands-and-belgium/. Accessed 02 2020
11. Cloud Native Computing Foundation. CNCF Cloud Native Interactive Landscape. https://landscape.cncf.io. Accessed 01 2020
12. Gupta, D., Saia, J., Young, M.: Peace through superior puzzling: an asymmetric sybil defense. In: 2019 IEEE International Parallel and Distributed Processing Symposium (IPDPS), pp. 1083–1094. IEEE (2019)
13. HashiCorp. Consul by HashiCorp. https://www.consul.io/index.html. Accessed 01 2020
14. HashiCorp. Consul Docs. https://www.consul.io/docs. Accessed 02 2020
15. HashiCorp. Github hashicorp/consul. https://github.com/hashicorp/consul. Accessed 02 2020
16. Hashicorp. Modern Service Networking for Cloud and Microservices. https://www.hashicorp.com/resources/modern-service-networking-cloud-microservices. Accessed 01 2020
17. HashiCorp. Serf. https://www.serf.io/. Accessed 02 2020
18. HashiCorp. Vault by HashiCorp. https://www.vaultproject.io/. Accessed 02 2020
19. Buoyant Inc., Linkerd. https://linkerd.io. Accessed 01 2020
20. Docker Inc., Docker Home. https://docker.io. Accessed 02 2020
21. Istio. Github istio/istio. https://github.com/istio/istio. Accessed 02 2020
22. Istio. Istio. https://istio.io. Accessed 01 2020

23. Istio. Istio Docs. https://istio.io/latest/docs/. Accessed 02 2020
24. Jamshidi, P., Pahl, C., Mendonça, N.C., Lewis, J., Tilkov, S.: Microservices: the journey so far and challenges ahead. IEEE Softw. **35**(3), 24–35 (2018)
25. Grant Joy. Distil Networks securely stores and manages all their secrets with Vault and Consul. https://www.hashicorp.com/blog/distil-networks-securely-stores-and-manages-all-their-secrets-with-vault-and-consul/. Accessed 02 2020
26. Kubernetes. Kubernetes - Production-Grade Container Orchestration. https://kubernetes.io/. Accessed 01 2020
27. Kubernetes. Kubernetes Pods. https://kubernetes.io/docs/concepts/workloads/pods/. Accessed 02 2020
28. Lewis, I.: What are Kubernetes Pods Anyway? https://www.ianlewis.org/en/what-are-kubernetes-pods-anyway. Accessed 02 2020
29. Lin, X., Lei, L., Wang, Y., Jing, J., Sun, K., Zhou, Q.: A measurement study on linux container security: attacks and countermeasures. In: Proceedings of the 34th Annual Computer Security Applications Conference, pp. 418–429 (2018)
30. Martin, A., Raponi, S., Combe, T., Di Pietro, R.: Docker ecosystem-vulnerability analysis. Comput. Commun. **122**, 30–43 (2018)
31. Rastogi, V., Davidson, D., De Carli, L., Jha, S., McDaniel, P.: Cimplifier: automatically debloating containers. In: Proceedings of the 2017 11th Joint Meeting on Foundations of Software Engineering, pp. 476–486 (2017)
32. Sakic, E., Kellerer, W.: Response time and availability study of RAFT consensus in distributed SDN control plane. IEEE Trans. Netw. Serv. Manage. **15**(1), 304–318 (2018)
33. Saltzer, J.H.: Protection and the control of information sharing in multics. Commun. ACM **17**(7), 388–402 (1974)
34. Shu, R., Gu, X., Enck, W.: A study of security vulnerabilities on docker hub. In: Proceedings of the Seventh ACM on Conference on Data and Application Security and Privacy, pp. 269–280. Association for Computing Machinery, New York (2017)
35. Singleton, A.: The economics of microservices. IEEE Cloud Comput. **3**(5), 16–20 (2016)
36. SSH.COM. Ssh (secure shell). https://www.ssh.com/ssh. Accessed 02 2020
37. Sukhwani, H., Martínez, J.M., Chang, X., Trivedi, K.S., Rindos, A.: Performance modeling of PBFT consensus process for permissioned blockchain network (hyperledger fabric). In: 2017 IEEE 36th Symposium on Reliable Distributed Systems (SRDS), pp. 253–255. IEEE (2017)
38. Sun, Y., Nanda, S., Jaeger, T.: Security-as-a-service for microservices-based cloud applications. In: 2015 IEEE 7th International Conference on Cloud Computing Technology and Science (CloudCom), pp. 50–57. IEEE (2015)
39. Thomson, R.: LogicMonitor uses terraform, packer & consul for disaster recovery environments. https://www.hashicorp.com/blog/logic-monitor-uses-terraform-packer-and-consul-for/. Accessed 02 2020
40. Yarygina, T., Bagge, A.H.: Overcoming security challenges in microservice architectures. In 2018 IEEE Symposium on Service-Oriented System Engineering (SOSE), pp. 11–20. IEEE (2018)

The Bitcoin Hunter: Detecting Bitcoin Traffic over Encrypted Channels

Fatemeh Rezaei[1]([✉]), Shahrzad Naseri[1], Ittay Eyal[2], and Amir Houmansadr[1]

[1] University of Massachusetts Amherst, Amherst, USA
{frezaei,shnaseri,amir}@cs.umass.edu
[2] Technion, Haifa, Israel
ittay@technion.ac.il

Abstract. Bitcoin and similar blockchain-based currencies are significant to consumers and industry because of their applications in electronic commerce and other trust-based distributed systems. Therefore, it is of paramount importance to the consumers and industry to maintain reliable access to their Bitcoin assets. In this paper, we investigate the resilience of Bitcoin to blocking by the powerful network entities such as ISPs and governments. By characterizing Bitcoin's communication patterns, we design classifiers that can distinguish (and therefore block) Bitcoin traffic even if it is tunneled through an encrypted channel like Tor and even if Bitcoin traffic is being mixed with background traffic, e.g., due to browsing websites. We perform extensive experiments to demonstrate the reliability of our classifiers in identifying Bitcoin traffic even despite using obfuscation protocols like Tor Pluggable Ttransports. We conclude that standard obfuscation mechanisms are not enough to ensure blocking-resilient access to Bitcoin (and similar cryptocurrencies), therefore cryptocurrency operators should deploy tailored traffic obfuscation mechanisms.

Keywords: Bitcoin · Traffic analysis · Blocking-resistance

1 Introduction

Bitcoin and similar blockchain-based currencies [35] have seen rapid adoption by consumers and industry because of their many applications in electronic commerce and other trust-based distributed systems. Bitcoin supports $1–$4.2B worth of transactions per day, growing steadily. Bitcoin and similar virtual currencies offer significant advantages compared to traditional electronic currencies, which include open access to a global e-commerce infrastructure, lower transaction fees, cryptographically supported contracts [3] and services [32], and transnational operations.

Given this significant importance of electronic currencies, they need to be resistant to embargoes by governments. That is, people investing in cryptocurrencies (by running businesses that rely on such currencies) should be assured that their Internet providers or governments are not able to prevent them from

© ICST Institute for Computer Sciences, Social Informatics and Telecommunications Engineering 2020
Published by Springer Nature Switzerland AG 2020. All Rights Reserved
N. Park et al. (Eds.): SecureComm 2020, LNICST 335, pp. 152–171, 2020.
https://doi.org/10.1007/978-3-030-63086-7_10

using their cryptocurrencies if they decide too. For the sake of argument, consider what happens if the Great Firewall of China decides to block all Bitcoin traffic overnight.

In this paper, we investigate the resilience of Bitcoin to blocking by powerful network entities, including ISPs and governments. Note that identifying standard (non-encrypted) Bitcoin traffic is trivial as Bitcoin messages use specific packet contents and formats. Therefore, a trivial countermeasure to prevent an ISP from identifying Bitcoin traffic is to tunnel Bitcoin over an encrypting tool, e.g., VPN, SSH, or Tor. However, previous studies [7,46] show that encryption is *not enough* to conceal the nature of communications, as the characteristics of encrypted traffic may leak sensitive information. Such attacks are broadly known as *traffic analysis*.

In this paper, we investigate if and how Bitcoin's traffic can be identified through traffic analysis despite being tunneled through an encrypted channel. First, we characterize Bitcoin's traffic patterns such as rates, timings, and sizes. Comparing with other protocols, we show that Bitcoin has traffic patterns that are unique, because of the specific types of messages sent by Bitcoin peers. Leveraging such unique features of Bitcoin traffic, we design a toolset of classifiers in order to distinguish Bitcoin traffic over encrypted channels. We perform extensive evaluations of our classifiers by capturing Bitcoin traffic in the wild. Particularly, we use several months of Tor traffic tunneled through Tor [12] and three major Tor pluggable transports [40], namely, FTE [14], meek [31], and obfs4 [39], to evaluate our classifiers. Our experiments show that while such obfuscation mechanisms modify Bitcoin's traffic by changing packet sizes timings, they are not able to hide the presence of Bitcoin traffic.

In summary we make the following main contributions:

1. We evaluate Bitcoin's traffic and characterize its patterns such as its packet sizes and traffic shape. We compare Bitcoin's traffic patterns to other popular protocols showing the uniqueness of Bitcoin traffic.
2. Based on our characterization of Bitcoin traffic, we design a range of classifiers whose goal is to identify Bitcoin traffic despite being tunneled through an encrypted channel (like Tor) and in the presence of background noise (e.g., open browser tabs).
3. Using several months of Bitcoin traffic and other protocols, we perform experiments to evaluate the performance of our classifiers when Bitcoin traffic is tunneled over Tor and three major Tor pluggable transports of FTE [14], meek [31] and obfs4 [39], and in the presence of background noise. Our classifiers are able to identify Bitcoin traffic in all cases with only 10 min of traffic with more than 99% true positive and negligible false positives.

2 Background on Bitcoin Traffic and Its Network Traffic

Bitcoin communications involve various protocol messages that are created by Bitcoin peers. We divide Bitcoin protocol messages into two classes: *synchronization messages*, which are used for propagating user addresses and transactions in the Bitcoin network, and *block-related messages*.

Synchronization Messages: These messages are aimed at keeping Bitcoin peers synchronized with the rest of the Bitcoin network.

addr: Each peer advertises the information and IP addresses of other peers via addr message in the network.

inventory(inv): Peers send inv to advertise their knowledge about the known objects, like transactions and blocks.

getdata: A peer sends getdata message in response to the inv to retrieve information about the content of an object, which can be a block or a transaction.

tx: This message describes a transaction in response to a getdata message.

Block-Related Messages: Such messages are used to exchange Bitcoin blocks among the peers. The current Bitcoin network is supporting two ways of propagating blocks, full block and compact block propagation.

Full Block Propagation: The sender node first validates the block completely, then it advertises the possession of block by an inv message. The receiving peer which does not have the block asks for it by sending an getdata message. Finally, the sender node sends the block via a block message. A block message consists of block version information, previous block hash, and the merkle root value related to this block.

Compact Block Propagation: In 2016, Bitcoin rolled out a new propagation mechanism (version 0.13.0). In this new approach, only a sketch of each block is sent to the peers instead of full blocks. The sketch include 80-byte block's header, the short transactions IDs used for matching already-available transactions and a selection of transactions which sending peer expect that a receiving peer may be missing. The following are the specific messages exchanged to run Bitcoin in the compact block mode.

sendcmpct: This message informs the receiving peer about the mode of communication the sending peer has chosen (low or high bandwidth).

cmpctblock: This message introduced in the compact block relaying and is presenting a sketch of block.

getblocktxn: This message is introduced in compact block relaying and is used to request for the transactions that are missed by sending a list of their indexes.

blocktxn: This message is introduced in compact-block relaying and is used to provide some of the transactions in a block, as requested.

3   Characterizing Bitcoin Traffic

We start by characterizing Bitcoin's traffic patterns.

3.1   Proportion and Distribution of Messages

Bitcoin peers generate various kinds of messages as introduced in the previous section. We show that the distribution and sizes of such messages are quite unique to the Bitcoin protocol, making Bitcoin traffic easily distinguishable from other protocols.

Distribution of Packet Sizes. Figures 1a to 1h illustrate the packet size histogram of different types of Bitcoin messages in our collected Bitcoin traffic. As can be seen, each type of message has a distinguishing traffic pattern. Note that through our experiments, we find out that `tx` and `inv` are dominating with 43.6% and 27.2% of all packets, respectively. Therefore, the characteristics of these messages will shape the pattern of a Bitcoin peer's traffic.

Histogram of Packet Sizes in Aggregate Traffic. Figures 2a and 2b show the histogram of packet sizes in the upstream and downstream directions, respectively, in compact block relaying. As mentioned before, `tx` and `inv` dominate the messages sent by a typical Bitcoin peer, therefore their sizes (shown in Figs. 1a and 1h) strongly shape the histogram of Bitcoin traffic, making it uniquely distinguishable from other protocols.

We also show the histogram of Bitcoin traffic in the full block relaying mode in Figs. 2c and 2d. These histograms have a larger spike close to the MTU, unlike the case of compact block relaying. These are because of the larger block sizes (around 1 MB) in the full block relaying.

Comparing to Other Protocols: Figures 2e to 2l show the histogram of other popular protocols, collected as described in Sect. 5. Note that we look at the traffic after going through an encryption tunnel, e.g., a VPN or SSH tunnel, so the histogram includes the (small) TCP ACK packets. As we can see, the packet size distribution of Bitcoin is uniquely different from these other protocols, since a Bitcoin connection is composed of unique messages with specific size distributions shown before. For instance, the large number of `inv` messages shapes the overall distribution of sizes in Bitcoin traffic.

Ratio of Downstream to Upstream. We also measured the ratio of downstream to upstream traffic volumes, which is shown in Fig. 3a. Unlike other protocols like HTTP (shown in Figs. 3b to 3f), Bitcoin traffic has a *symmetric* traffic volume in upstream and downstream. This is due to the fact that Bitcoin peers broadcast most of the bulky protocol messages they receive such as block and transaction announcements.

3.2   Shape of Traffic

Above we showed that the counts and sizes of packets in Bitcoin demonstrate a unique behavior. Here we show that, additionally, the shape of Bitcoin traffic is distinguishable from other protocols.

Full Block Relaying Mode: Figure 4a shows the traffic of a Bitcoin client operating in the full block relaying mode. As can be seen, the small protocol packets, mostly corresponding to `inv` and `tx` messages, appear uniformly over the time. On the other hand, the Bitcoin full blocks appear as large spikes of roughly 1 MB at specific points in time, i.e., once a new block is generated in the network.

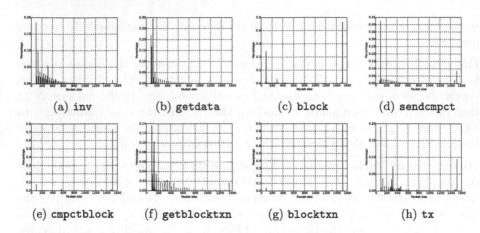

(a) inv   (b) getdata   (c) block   (d) sendcmpct

(e) cmpctblock   (f) getblocktxn   (g) blocktxn   (h) tx

Fig. 1. Packet size distribution of Bitcoin communication messages in compact block relaying

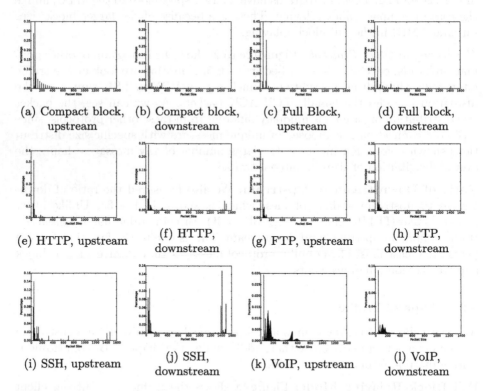

(a) Compact block,   (b) Compact block,   (c) Full Block,   (d) Full block,
upstream   downstream   upstream   downstream

(e) HTTP, upstream   (f) HTTP,   (g) FTP, upstream   (h) FTP,
                      downstream   downstream

(i) SSH, upstream   (j) SSH,   (k) VoIP, upstream   (l) VoIP,
                      downstream   downstream

Fig. 2. Upstream and downstream packet size distribution of Bitcoin and several popular protocols

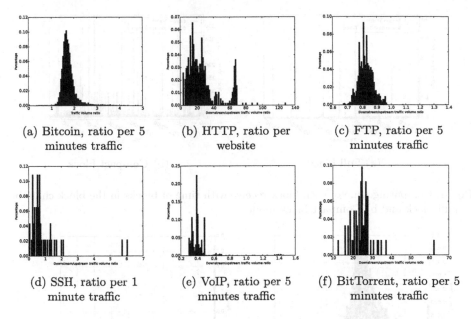

(a) Bitcoin, ratio per 5 minutes traffic

(b) HTTP, ratio per website

(c) FTP, ratio per 5 minutes traffic

(d) SSH, ratio per 1 minute traffic

(e) VoIP, ratio per 5 minutes traffic

(f) BitTorrent, ratio per 5 minutes traffic

Fig. 3. Ratio of downstream to upstream traffic volume

Compact Block Relaying Mode: In the compact block relaying mode, it is harder to notice the block spikes since only a sketch of the blocks is transmitted. In this mode, transmitting a compact block in the network results in smaller spikes of 100 KB. Spikes of such small sizes may also occur when unverified transactions are transmitted, which will increase the detection's false positive. Also, a Bitcoin client may operate in the high bandwidth mode, in which the receiver node asks its peers to send new blocks without asking for permissions first. This will lead to more than one peer sending the same block at the same time. This and the large volume of missed transactions result in having spikes with more than 100 KB in the traffic. Figure 4b illustrates when and how compact blocks appear on a peer's traffic. As can be seen, compact blocks appear at smaller amplitudes than the actual block size, but the behavior is also nondeterministic, since it depends on whether the client has previously received some of the transactions in that block. This intuitively makes detection of compact blocks less reliable than full blocks, as shown later in our experiments.

We also measure the size of compact blocks by measuring the *length* field of cmpctblock messages, which is shown in Fig. 5a. As can be seen, most of the compact blocks are as small as 15 KB (in contrast to 1 MB in full blocks).

Finally, we measure the volume of transactions missing from an announced compact block (we do so based on the payload length of blocktxn messages). As described earlier, a Bitcoin client operating in the compact block mode will

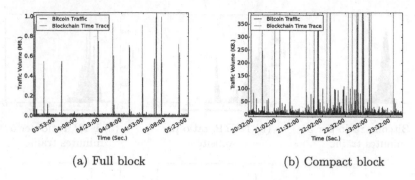

(a) Full block   (b) Compact block

Fig. 4. Comparing time of each block receive with time of blocks in the block chain in a) Full block and b) Compact block modes

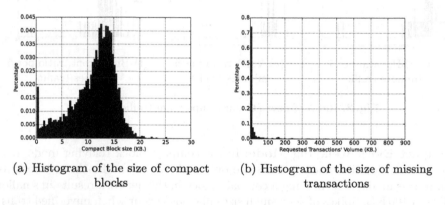

(a) Histogram of the size of compact   (b) Histogram of the size of missing
              blocks   transactions

Fig. 5. Histogram of compact block mode components

download such missing transactions. This is shown in Fig. 5b. As we can see most of the transactions have volumes less than 100 KB.

Block Propagation Latencies. The propagation delay in the Bitcoin network is due to transmission delays and block verification by the receiving node at each hop. The transmission delay is the time to exchanging `inv` and `get data` messages, and sending the block via a `block` message. We measure block propagation delay by subtracting the receiving time of the block message and the time stamp in the header of the block message. Figures 6a and 6b show the histogram of propagation delay for 6000 blocks in compact block and full block relaying, respectively. As shown in the figures, we can model this empirical data using a Beta distribution [13].

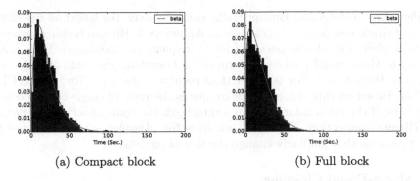

(a) Compact block   (b) Full block

Fig. 6. Histogram of block propagation delays

4 Designing Bitcoin Classifiers

We leverage the features described above to build robust classifiers for Bitcoin traffic. We aim for our classifiers to work even in the presence of encryption and background traffic, e.g., when the machine running Bitcoin is used for web browsing and runs other applications, or when the Bitcoin traffic is tunneled over Tor.

4.1 Size-Based Classifier

As noted in Sect. 3.1, the histogram of Bitcoin packet sizes has a unique pattern. Based on this, we designed classifiers to distinguish Bitcoin traffic from other protocols.

Size Histogram Classifier (SizeHist). This classifier correlates the packet size histogram of a target user's traffic with the packet size histogram of Bitcoin traffic captured by the adversary. By histogram of packet sizes we mean number of each packet size from 1 to MTU size. To do so, the classifier first divides the given traffic into upstream and downstream directions, then it calculates the histogram of packet sizes in each direction. The baseline (real-time Bitcoin traffic) is also divided in upstream and downstream directions. In the next step, the classifier calculates the cosine similarity between the histogram of the target traffic and several Bitcoin traces in both upstream and downstream direction. If both of the upstream and downstream averaged correlation values are above their thresholds, the target traffic is detected as Bitcoin traffic.

Tor-Specific Classifier (SizeTor): Tor [12] reformats traffic into constant-sized segments called *cells*. However, as the size of a cell is smaller than the MTU of IP packets, depending on the volume of traffic, multiple cells can merge into one single packet. This makes the number of single-cell packets and multiple-cell packets different for different protocols tunneled over Tor. Our SizeTor classifier aims at detecting Bitcoin traffic tunneled over Tor based on the distribution of single-cell packets. As shown in Appendix 3, Bitcoin traffic consists of a large number of small-size packets (due to frequent inv messages). Tor will add padding to these small packets to form cells. Therefore, the ratio of single-size packets in Bitcoin over-Tor is larger than regular traffic over Tor, e.g., HTTP-over-Tor. Based on this, our classifier compares the ratio of single-cell packets to all packets; if the ratio is larger than a threshold, the connection will be flagged as a Bitcoin connection. Note that our SizeTor classifier can be adjusted for other protocols that similarly change the size of packets.

4.2   Shape-Based Classifier

The main intuition of our shape-based classifier is looking for changes in the traffic volume of a target user around the times of block announcements. Therefore, we assume that the classifier obtains the times and sizes of Bitcoin blocks, e.g., from the public blockchain.info repository, or even by running a local Bitcoin client.

For each confirmed Bitcoin block, the algorithm analyzes the volume of the target traffic two time windows with size ω_i around the block time, one before $(t_{block_i} - \omega_i, t_{block_i})$ and one after the block time $(t_{block_i}, t_{block_i} + \omega_i)$. The size of the window depends on the size of the block, the target client's bandwidth, etc., as evaluated later. For an actual Bitcoin traffic with no noise, the difference should be close to the size of the block. If the difference is within the bound (J), the algorithm considers that block to be *detected* in the traffic of the suspected user. The algorithm performs the same for a number of blocks and evaluates the ratio of such "detected" blocks. If the ratio is above a threshold η, the target user is declared to be a Bitcoin client.

Choosing the Threshold η. The threshold should be chosen based on the target user's specific network conditions such as background traffic, network noise, and bandwidth.

To do so, the classifier generates N (e.g., $N = 100$) synthetic block series, which we call *ground falses*. The classifier then correlates the target traffic with each of the N ground false instances using the correlation function. Finally, the threshold η is chosen to be larger than the largest correlation value.

Choosing Other Parameters. The window shape classifier also needs to choose the values of the parameters ω and J. Parameter ω needs to be big enough to contain the most of the traffic of a block during block propagation. Moreover, Parameter J is chosen to take into account that some of the block propagation traffic might not be downloaded in that time window. This parameters needs to be selected based on user's bandwidth and the volume of background traffic, and therefore it needs to be chosen for each client specifically.

4.3   Neural Network-Based Classifier (NN-Based)

As done in similar applications [36], we use a neural network-based classifier to detect Bitcoin in presence of a more complex background noise, e.g., browsing more than one website simultaneously. In following, we explain the feature selection phase, and then describe the design of our neural network.

Feature Selection. To create each sample data, we divide time into intervals and use the volume of traffic in each interval as our features, which is presented in equation vlm $= v_1, v_2, ..., v_n$. Note that v_I is the volume of traffic in interval I. We choose 10 min as the *sample size*, which is the smallest length to have at least one peak of traffic. Furthermore, to choose the interval length, we try different values of 1, 5, 10 and 20 s. From our experiments, we find out that the interval length of 10 s results in the best performance. Therefore, we choose 10 s as the interval length (l). Since the length of each sample is 10 min (600 s), using equation $n =$ sample size$/l$, we get an array of length 60 as our feature.

Designing the Model. For our neural network model, we use a combination of convolutional and fully-connected network that consists of an input layer, an output layer, and three hiden layers: one convolutional layer, and two dense layers. The input layer has $n = 60$ number of neurons, which is the size of each sample data, the hidden layers have $n_1 = 64$, $n_2 = 32$ and $n_3 = 16$ number of neurons, respectively, and the output layer has 1 neuron which represents if the sample data contains Bitcoin traffic or not. We use Relu as the activation function of the hidden layers and sigmoid [19] for the output layer. Also, we use binary cross-entropy as our loss function, and Adam optimization [28].

4.4 Combined Classifier

In this classifier, we combine all the attributes used in the above classifiers. More specifically, we are using the size histogram of the packets, downstream to upstream traffic volume ratio, and volume over time. Our final feature set has a length of 1576 (1 for downstream to upstream, 60 for volume over time, and 1515 for size histogram). Note that the feature that we use in sizeTor classifier is a subset of size histogram, and volume over time is capturing the shape of traffic that we utilized in the shape-based classifier. The model that we use has three convolutional layers and one dense layer with sizes: 1024, 128, 64, and 32 for the dense layer. We use the same activation functions and loss function as the NN-based classifier.

5 Experimental Setup

We use Bitcoin Core software[1] to run full node Bitcoin clients on 5 virtual machines on a campus network. Each virtual machine is connected to the Internet with high bandwidth. Before starting the experiments, we leave our Bitcoin clients for a few days to make sure they have downloaded an up-to-date blockchain ledger. The Bitcoin client is passively receiving blocks and participating in the Bitcoin network, but it is not doing any transactions. We capture Bitcoin traffic under different scenarios on a Linux 16.0.4 virtual machine.

---

[1] https://bitcoin.org/en/bitcoin-core/.

5.1 Datasets

Collecting Bitcoin Traffic: We use Bitcoin version 0.12.0 to capture Bitcoin traffic in the full block relaying mode and Bitcoin version 0.14.0 to capture traffic in the compact block relaying mode. We capture Bitcoin traffic for each version for a period of a month.

Bitcoin Tunneled Through Tor: We captured Bitcoin traffic behind Tor [12] for both compact and full block modes. We also captured Bitcoin traffic in the compact block mode behind Tor and popular Tor pluggable transports of obfs4 [47], FTE [14], and Meek-amazon [31].

Bitcoin with Background Traffic: We captured Bitcoin traffic in presence of HTTP background traffic by browsing the top 500 Alexa websites using the Selenium[2] tool while running Bitcoin software. We also collected Bitcoin traffic with HTTP background for the same set of websites behind Tor and its three pluggable transports using Selenium.

CAIDA Background Traffic: We use CAIDA's 2018 anonymized traces[3] as a dataset for additional background traffic.

HTTP Traffic: We collect top 500 Alexa websites using Selenium tool. Also, we capture these websites over Tor, and three pluggable transports. Moreover, we use the dataset by [36] which has collected the top 50,000 Alexa websites over Tor (Table 1).

Table 1. Traffic class breakdown for CAIDA dataset

Traffic class	Port numbers	Number of connections	% of total
http, https	80, 8080, 443	745262	0.318
dns	53	1073758	0.457
smtp	25	2646	0.001
telnet	23	6958	0.003
ssh/scp	22	4928	0.002
other	–	511700	0.219
all	–	2345252	1.0

5.2 Metrics

We use following metrics to measure the performance of our classifiers:

- **True positive:** True positive shows the proportion of the data which contain Bitcoin, and our model correctly identified as Bitcoin traffic.

---

[2] http://www.seleniumhq.org.
[3] https://www.caida.org/data/monitors/passive-equinix-nyc.xml.

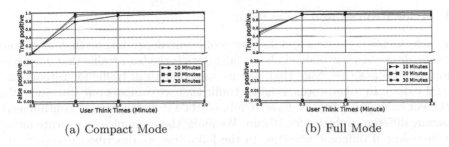

(a) Compact Mode   (b) Full Mode

Fig. 7. Result of `sizeHist` classifier on noisy Bitcoin traffic

- **False positive:** False positive shows the proportion of the data which did not contain Bitcoin traffic, and our model incorrectly classified as Bitcoin.
- **Accuracy:** Accuracy shows the proportion of the data which was correctly classified.

5.3   Modeling Normal Users

In this section, we describe four different types of users' profile that we use to evaluate the performance of our Bitcoin classifiers against.

- Simple User: A simple user is a Bitcoin client with no background noise and traffic. This type of user does not generate any network traffic except the Bitcoin client application traffic. Therefore, all traffic of the simple user is Bitcoin traffic.
- Simple Noisy User: A simple noise user is a Bitcoin client who browses only **one** webpage. To control the background traffic, we introduce a parameter named think time, T, representing the amount of time that the user spends on a particular website.
- Complex Web (Complicated/Sophisticated) User: A complex user is a Bitcoin client who browses **multiple** websites simultaneously.
- Complex CAIDA User: A complex CAIDA user is a Bitcoin client who is running 1–5 number of CAIDA applications, which is introduced in Table 2 simultaneously in the background.

6   Results

In this section, we implement our classifiers to evaluate their performance on user profiles described in part Sect. 5.3 writing more than a thousands lines of code in Python. First, for each classifier, we declare the user profile(s) that we use for evaluation of its performance and the false data that we use for computing its false positive. Second, we describe the result of each classifier and give a summary and comparison of them at the end of this section.

6.1   User Profiles and False Data

For each classifier, we use a specific user profile and depending on that we choose the false data. As we explained above, false data is the base traffic that we use to compute false positive. Note that, we use same length of traffic for Bitcoin and the false data. In other words, it is the traffic that we compare our Bitcoin traffic with. For example, when we have 10 min of HTTP traffic, we are continuously browsing different websites for 10 min. We make these samples by concatenating the browsing of different websites. In the following, we describe these pairs for each classifier(s).

– For shape-based classifier, we use the simple user profile. Furthermore, we use HTTP which is the typical user behavior as the false data. This experiment evaluates if Bitcoin traffic can be differentiated from browsing an HTTP website.
– For the rest of the binary classifiers in this section, we use simple noisy user profile and attempt to detect the presence of Bitcoin. Note that, similar to the window-based classifier, we use HTTP for the false data. This experiment attempts to evaluate if browsing an HTTP website is enough to hide the Bitcoin traffic.
– For the neural network-based and combined classifiers, we use the complex web and complex CAIDA user for training and testing.

Note that, for these two classifiers, we evaluate our model using 10, 000 number of test data, and report the false positive, true positive and accuracy. For rest of the classifiers, we use 500 number of test data for evaluation. Also, the data is balanced, which means we have the same number of data for each category.

6.2   Size-Based Classifiers

SizeHist Classifier. We implement the sizeHist classifier on Bitcoin traffic in compact and full block modes using the noisy user model described in Sect. 5.3. Figure 7 shows the performance of this classifier. We control the noise using think time (T). Increasing T decreases the noise and enhances the classifier's performance. Figure 7 shows that we can reach more than 90% true positive and 0% false positive for both modes when we have 10 min of traffic and set T to 2 min. It is worth stating that we could reach similar results when we set T to 0.5 min and have 20 min of traffic.

6.3   Shape-Based Classifier

To implement this classifier, we set J and ω introduced in Sect. 4.2 to 100 kilo-bytes and 20 s, respectively. To set η, we compute block detection rate for Bitcoin using ground false shown in Fig. 8. We need to set η to be larger than all the detection rate values for Bitcoin using ground false. Note that each point for Bitcoin using ground false in the figure is the average for 25 different ground falses.

Using this figure, we set η to 0.4. Moreover, Fig. 8 shows the block detection rate for HTTP using ground truth and block detection rate for Bitcoin using ground truth too. Using the η, we can detect all Bitcoin traffic through (August 28–October 5) as Bitcoin. Also, we did not classify any of the HTTP traffic as Bitcoin, which results in 0% false positive. Furthermore, the performance of shape-based classifier quickly diminishes in the presence of a small HTTP background noise. Also, we fail to detect Bitcoin traffic in compact mode because of small block sizes, which makes it impossible to distinguish them.

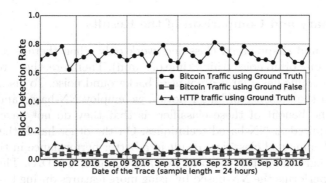

Fig. 8. Block detection rate using shape-based classifier

6.4 Neural Network-Based Classifier

We implement the NN-based classifier using Keras [10] with Tensorflow [1] backend. We use complex web and complex CAIDA user to evaluate its performance. Table 2 shows the result of NN-based classifier for different sizes of training data. As the table indicates, the accuracy of the classifier improves from 62% to 96% when we increase the size of training data from 1000 to 40,000. Note that, true and false positive improves from 44% to 92% and 20% to 2% respectively when we increase the size of training data.

Table 2. Result of neural network classifier.

Training size	False positive (%)	True positive (%)	Accuracy (%)
1000	20	44	62
5000	11	80	85
10,000	6	84	89
40,000	2	92	95

6.5   Combined Classifier

To extend the neural network-based classifier, we defined combined classifier, which uses all of the attributes used in previous classifiers. Using this classifier, we reach 99.84% accuracy with false positive of 0 and true positive of 99.74% having 40,000 of training data and sample size of 10 min. This result is very promising and shows that having enough data and using the attributes that distinguishes Bitcoin from other traffic, we are able to train a neural network model that gives us 0% false positive and more than 99% accuracy.

6.6   Summary and Comparison of the Results

The SizeHist and shape-based classifiers work only when there is a very small background noise or no noise (think time of 2 min). Therefore, they are not useful when Bitcoin traffic has a large amount of background noise. To distinguish Bitcoin traffic in the presence of larger noises, we employ NN-based and combined classifiers. The benefit of these classifiers is that they do not have the training phase required in NN-based techniques. On the other hand, the NN-based classifier and combined classifiers result in a better performance in the presence of higher background noise (complex web and complex CAIDA). The combined classifier outperforms the NN-based by using more features during training. This classifier detects Bitcoin traffic using the complex web and complex CAIDA user explained in Sect. 5.3 with 0% false positive and much higher accuracy (99.84%).

7   Countermeasures

A possible countermeasure against Bitcoin detection is to tunnel Bitcoin traffic over an anonymity system like Tor. We tunnel Bitcoin traffic over Tor to disguise its patterns. We evaluate the invisibility that Tor provides by designing a new classifier (SizeTor) which is tailored for Tor. Also, we use our strongest classifiers (NN-based and combined) to evaluate if Tor succeeds in hiding Bitcoin traffic.

7.1   Bitcoin over Tor

Tor sends traffic in *cells*. If the packets sizes is below the cell size, it will add padding to the packets to reach the fixed cell sizes. This modifies the traffic patterns of Bitcoin traffic, e.g., its packet sizes, therefore it may increase resistance to traffic classification. In the following we evaluate our classifiers against Tor and three state-of-the-art Tor pluggable transports [40] namely *obfs4*, *FTE*, and *Meek* explained in the following.

Pluggable Transports: We evaluated against the following major transports:

- **Obfs4:** obfs4 is a widely used Tor pluggable transport, which is based on *ScrambleSuit* [44]. It differs with ScrambleSuit in public key obfuscation and its protocol for one-way authentication, which makes it faster.

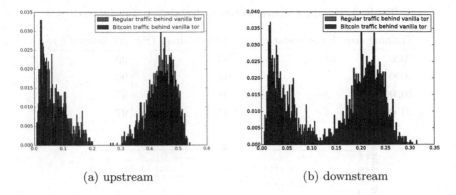

(a) upstream   (b) downstream

Fig. 9. Histogram of one cell packet ratio for HTTP traffic and Bitcoin traffic

- **FTE:** The FTE transport re-encrypts Tor packets in order to match the regular expressions of a benign protocol like HTTP.
- **meek:** Meek uses *domain fronting* [18] to tunnel traffic through public CDN or cloud platforms.

Bitcoin traffic has a larger ratio of one-cell packets compared to Tor. This is due to a large number of small Bitcoin messages (e.g., inv) that are each put into a single-cell packets. Figures 9a and 9b show the histogram of one cell size packets ratio in the upstream and downstream directions.

7.2 Evaluating Bitcoin Over Tor

SizeTor Classifier. We implement SizeTor classifier on noisy Bitcoin on compact mode for Tor and its three pluggable transports. As it is displayed in Fig. 10, we could detect Bitcoin traffic with high accuracy for the complex user model when the background noise is one open tab. As Fig. 10 indicates, having a traffic size of 10 min is enough to detect Bitcoin traffic with around 90% true positive and 0% of false positive. Moreover, the Figure states that the result of classifier quickly diminishes when we increase the background noise from one to 2 or 3 open tabs. Note that this figure shows the average result of this classifier on Tor and three pluggable transports.

Neural Network-Based Classifier. Table 3 presents the result of NN-based classifier for the complex web user over Tor for 10,000 numbers of test data. As the table suggests, performance of our classifier improves when we increase the size of training data. More specifically, our false positives enhances from 11% to 4% when we increase the training data from 1000 to 40,000. Moreover, when using 40,000 training data, we reach 99% and 4% true and false positive, respectively (97% accuracy). Note that the reason we get better results from this classifier on Tor dataset is that this dataset only contains the complex web user since we did not have CAIDA application over Tor to use for our evaluation.

Table 3. Result of neural network classifier on Tor dataset.

Training size	False positive (%)	True positive (%)	Accuracy (%)
1000	11	98	93
5000	6	98	96
10,000	3	98	97
40,000	4	99	97

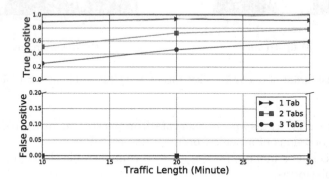

Fig. 10. Detecting Bitcoin compact mode traffic behind Tor (Tor and its three pluggable transports: meek, obfs, fte) using SizeTor

Combined Classifier Over Tor: We apply the combined classifier on our Tor dataset, which consists of Bitcoin traffic with up to 5 number of open tabs on the background. Our experiments show that having 40,000 of training data is enough to achieve more than 99.72% accuracy with 0.04% false positive and 99.5% true positive. Our combined classifier outperforms the previous classifiers (SizeTor and NN-based) on the Tor dataset as well. This is because we are using a more complex model and a more significant number of features.

8   Related Work

In this section, we overview previous work on classifying different protocols and discuss previous attacks on Bitcoin cryptocurrency.

8.1   Protocol Classification

There is extensive work in literature attempting to classify different applications or protocols in the network. Previously, researchers were focused on classification according to the port numbers [23,24,30,42] and payload [9,20,34,42]. Since many applications use uncertain port numbers [23], or some encrypt their payloads, researchers adopted new methods for protocol classification. Recent techniques use statistics such as packet sizes and timings for classification [5,8,11,15,16,25,48].

In some of the studies, researchers apply machine learning techniques on these statistics to classify different applications. For example, in [15], authors take a semi-supervised approach to classify a variety of applications such as FTP, HTTP, P2P. In [8,48], authors use SVM classifier to distinguish different applications such as WWW, Mail, and FTP. Also, in [48], authors use SVM to classify a broad application category such as mail, buck traffic, service. Moreover, in [27,38], authors survey the papers on Internet traffic classification using machine learning techniques.

8.2 Attacks on Bitcoin Cryptocurrency

In this section, we discuss the previous attacks on the Bitcoin network. In [4], the authors discuss routing attacks, their impact, and possible countermeasures. In [21], authors design an eclipse attack in which the attacker isolate a victim from its peers by monopolizing its all incoming and outgoing connections.

In [2,41], authors use Bitcoin transaction patterns to link users (or link transactions) using some side information. In [6], the authors propose a technique to link the public key of a user to her address or link her transactions. In [26], they analyze the security of using Bitcoin for fast payments and show that the current Bitcoin system is not secure unless they integrate Bitcoin network with some detection mechanism. Also, they study double-spending attacks on fast payments and implement a method to prevent it. Attacks on the blockchain system as a whole [17,29,33,37], and against second-tier payment networks [22,43,45] are not directly affected by single participant detection and hacking.

9 Conclusions

The reliable access to Bitcoin and similar cryptocurrencies is of crucial importance due to their consumers and the related industry. In this paper, we investigated the resilience of Bitcoin to blocking by a powerful network entity such as an ISP or a government. By characterizing Bitcoin's communication patterns, we designed various classifiers that could distinguish (and therefore block) Bitcoin traffic even if it is tunneled over an encrypted channel like Tor, and even when it is mixed with background traffic. Through extensive experiments on network traffic, we demonstrated that our classifiers could reliably identify Bitcoin traffic despite using obfuscation protocols like Tor pluggable transports that modify traffic patterns. In order to disguise such patterns, an obfuscating protocol needs to apply significant cover traffic or employ large perturbations, which is undesirable for typical clients.

Acknowledgement. The work was supported by the NSF CAREER grant CNS-1553301 and BSF.

References

1. Abadi, M., et al.: TensorFlow: large-scale machine learning on heterogeneous systems (2015). http://www.tensorflow.org

2. Androulaki, E., Karame, G.O., Roeschlin, M., Scherer, T., Capkun, S.: Evaluating user privacy in bitcoin. In: Sadeghi, A.-R. (ed.) FC 2013. LNCS, vol. 7859, pp. 34–51. Springer, Heidelberg (2013). https://doi.org/10.1007/978-3-642-39884-1_4
3. Andrychowicz, M., Dziembowski, S., Malinowski, D., Mazurek, L.: Secure multi-party computations on bitcoin. In: S & P (2014)
4. Apostolaki, M., Zohar, A., Vanbever, L.: Hijacking bitcoin: routing attacks on cryptocurrencies. In: 2017 IEEE Symposium on Security and Privacy
5. Bar-Yanai, R., Langberg, M., Peleg, D., Roditty, L.: Realtime classification for encrypted traffic. In: Festa, P. (ed.) SEA 2010. LNCS, vol. 6049, pp. 373–385. Springer, Heidelberg (2010). https://doi.org/10.1007/978-3-642-13193-6_32
6. Biryukov, A., Khovratovich, D., Pustogarov, I.: Deanonymisation of clients in bitcoin P2P network. In: CCS (2014)
7. Cai, X., Zhang, X., Joshi, B., Johnson, R.: Touching from a distance: website fingerprinting attacks and defenses. In: CCS (2012)
8. Cao, J., Fang, Z., Qu, G., Sun, H., Zhang, D.: An accurate traffic classification model based on support vector machines. Int. J. Network Manage. **12**, 301 (2017)
9. Choi, T., et al.: Content-aware internet application traffic measurement and analysis. In: Managing Next Generation Convergence Networks and Services, IEEE/IFIP Network Operations and Management Symposium, NOMS (2004)
10. Chollet, F.: keras. https://github.com/fchollet/keras (2015)
11. Crotti, M., Dusi, M., Gringoli, F., Salgarelli, L.: Traffic classification through simple statistical fingerprinting. Comput. Commun. Rev. **37**(1), 5–16 (2007)
12. Dingledine, R., Mathewson, N., Syverson, P.: Tor: the second-generation onion router. In: USENIX Security (2004)
13. Durrett, R.: Probability: Theory and Examples. Cambridge University Press, Cambridge (2010)
14. Dyer, K., Coull, S., Ristenpart, T., Shrimpton, T.: Protocol misidentification made easy with format-transforming encryption. In: CCS (2013)
15. Erman, J., Mahanti, A., Arlitt, M.F., Cohen, I., Williamson, C.L.: Offline/realtime traffic classification using semi-supervised learning. Perform. Eval. **64**, 1194–1213 (2007)
16. Erman, J., Mahanti, A., Arlitt, M.F., Williamson, C.L.: Identifying and discriminating between web and peer-to-peer traffic in the network core. In: WWW (2007)
17. Eyal, I., Sirer, E.G.: Majority is not enough: bitcoin mining is vulnerable. ACM Commun. **61**, 95–102 (2018)
18. Fifield, D., Lan, C., Hynes, R., Wegmann, P., Paxson, V.: Blocking-resistant communication through domain fronting. In: PETS (2015)
19. Goodfellow, I., Bengio, Y., Courville, A.: Deep Learning. MIT Press, Cambridge (2016)
20. Haffner, P., Sen, S., Spatscheck, O., Wang, D.: ACAS: automated construction of application signatures. In: MineNet (2005)
21. Heilman, E., Kendler, A., Zohar, A., Goldberg, S.: Eclipse attacks on bitcoin's peer-to-peer network. In: USENIX (2015)
22. Jona Harris, A.Z.: Flood & loot: a systemic attack on the lightning network (2020)
23. Karagiannis, T., Broido, A., Brownlee, N., Claffy, KC., Faloutsos, M.: Is P2P dying or just hiding? [P2P traffic measurement]. In: GLOBECOM (2004)
24. Karagiannis, T., Broido, A., Faloutsos, M., Claffy, K.C.: Transport layer identification of P2P traffic. In: IMC (2004)
25. Karagiannis, T., Papagiannaki, K., Faloutsos, M.: BLINC: multilevel traffic classification in the dark. In: Proceedings of the 2005 Conference on Applications, Technologies, Architectures, and Protocols for Computer Communications (2005)

26. Karame, G., Androulaki, E., Capkun, S.: Double-spending fast payments in bitcoin. In: CCS (2012)
27. Kim, H., Claffy, K.C., Fomenkov, M., Barman, D., Faloutsos, M., Lee, K.: Internet traffic classification demystified: myths, caveats, and the best practices. In: CoNEXT (2008)
28. Kingma, D.P., Ba, J.: Adam: a method for stochastic optimization. CoRR (2014)
29. Kwon, Y., Kim, D., Son, Y., Vasserman, E.Y., Kim, Y.: Be selfish and avoid dilemmas: Fork after withholding (FAW) attacks on bitcoin. CoRR (2017)
30. Madhukar, A., Williamson, C.L.: A longitudinal study of P2P traffic classification. In: MASCOTS (2006)
31. Meek Pluggable Transport. https://trac.torproject.org/projects/tor/wiki/doc/meek
32. Miller, A., Juels, A., Shi, E., Parno, B., Katz, J.: Permacoin: repurposing bitcoin work for data preservation. In: S&P (2014)
33. Mirkin, M., Ji, Y., Pang, J., Klages-Mundt, A., Eyal, I., Jules, A.: BDoS: blockchain denial of service. arXiv preprint arXiv:1912.07497 (2019)
34. Moore, A.W., Papagiannaki, K.: Toward the accurate identification of network applications. In: PAM (2005)
35. Nakamoto, S.: Bitcoin: a peer-to-peer electronic cash system (2008)
36. Nasr, M., Bahramali, A., Houmansadr, A.: Deepcorr: strong flow correlation attacks on tor using deep learning. In: CCS (2018)
37. Negy, K.A., Rizun, P.R., Sirer, E.G.: Selfish mining re-examined. In: Bonneau, J., Heninger, N. (eds.) FC 2020. LNCS, vol. 12059, pp. 61–78. Springer, Cham (2020). https://doi.org/10.1007/978-3-030-51280-4_5
38. Nguyen, T.T., Armitage, G.: A survey of techniques for internet traffic classification using machine learning. IEEE Commun. Surv. Tutorials **10**(4), 56–76 (2008)
39. A Simple Obfuscating Proxy. https://www.torproject.org/projects/obfsproxy.html.en
40. Tor: Pluggable Transports. https://www.torproject.org/docs/pluggable-transports.html.en
41. Reid, F., Harrigan, M.: An analysis of anonymity in the bitcoin system. In: SocialCom/PASSAT (2011)
42. Sen, S., Spatscheck, O., Wang, D.: Accurate, scalable in-network identification of p2p traffic using application signatures. In: WWW (2004)
43. Tsabary, I., Yechieli, M., Eyal, I.: MAD-HTLC: because HTLC is crazy-cheap to attack. arXiv preprint arXiv:2006.12031 (2020)
44. Winter, P., Pulls, T., Fuss, J.: Scramblesuit: a polymorphic network protocol to circumvent censorship. In: Proceedings of the 12th ACM Workshop on Privacy in the Electronic Society. ACM (2013)
45. Winzer, F., Herd, B., Faust, S.: Temporary censorship attacks in the presence of rational miners. IACR Cryptol. ePrint Arch. (2019)
46. Wright, C., Ballard, L., Monrose, F., Masson, G.: Language identification of encrypted VoIP traffic: Alejandra y Roberto or Alice and Bob? In: USENIX Security (2007)
47. Yawning. Obfsproxy4 (2015). https://github.com/Yawning/obfs4/blob/master/doc/obfs4-spec.txt
48. Yuan, R., Li, Z., Guan, X., Xu, L.: An svm-based machine learning method for accurate internet traffic classification. Information Systems Frontiers (2010)

MAAN: A Multiple Attribute Association Network for Mobile Encrypted Traffic Classification

Fengzhao Shi[1,2,3], Chao Zheng[1,3]([✉]), Yiming Cui[1,2,3], and Qingyun Liu[1,2,3]

[1] Institute of Information Engineering, Chinese Academy of Sciences, Beijing, China
zhengchao@iie.ac.cn
[2] School of Cyberspace Security, University of Chinese Academy of Sciences, Beijing, China
[3] National Engineering Laboratory for Information Security Technology, Beijing, China

Abstract. With the rapid development of mobile applications and the rising concern over user privacy, cryptographic protocols, especially Secure Socket Layer/Transport Layer Security (SSL/TLS), are widely used on the Internet. Many networking and security services call for application-level encrypted traffic classification before conducting related policies. Exiting methods exhibit unsatisfying accuracy using the partial handshake information or only the flow-level features. In this paper, we propose a novel encrypted traffic classification method named Multiple Attribute Associate Network (MAAN). MAAN is a unified model that automatically extracts features from handshake messages and flows. Moreover, the MAAN has acceptable time consumption and is suitable to apply in real-time scenarios. Our experiments demonstrate that the MAAN achieves 98.2% accuracy on a real-word dataset (including 59k+ SSL sessions and covering 16 applications) and outperforms the state-of-the-art methods.

Keywords: Encrypted traffic classification · SSL/TLS · Handshake messages · Application Data · Network management

1 Introduction

Mobile encrypted traffic classification, which classifies mobile encrypted traffic into specific applications, plays a very significant role in many areas, such as Quality of Service (QoS), network management, intrusion detection, and prevention systems [26]. Taking intrusion detection as an example, network administrator needs to identify the applications before analyzing user behavior. Hence, it has gained significant interest in both academia and industry.

Traditional port-based and payload-based traffic classification methods are inappropriate for mobile encrypted traffic classification because of encryption and dynamic port technology [16]. Machine learning methods, which don't need

© ICST Institute for Computer Sciences, Social Informatics and Telecommunications Engineering 2020
Published by Springer Nature Switzerland AG 2020. All Rights Reserved
N. Park et al. (Eds.): SecureComm 2020, LNICST 335, pp. 172–189, 2020.
https://doi.org/10.1007/978-3-030-63086-7_11

port and payload information, are suitable to solve this task. Although many excellent methods have been proposed, there still remain several problems. Firstly, traditional machine learning methods need sophisticated feature engineering, and model optimization cannot optimize the feature extraction process [19]. Secondly, traditional machine learning is difficult to convert all TLS handshake messages into feature vectors, thus missing part of handshake message features [10]. Thirdly, some networking and security services need early prediction results to conduct related policies before the transmission of communication payloads. However, the previous methods are unable to solve this problem effectively based on the characteristics of a single flow. For example, current methods using sequence features require complete flow information, which leads these methods to get results at the end of the flow [16, 18, 19, 26, 27].

In this paper, we try to apply some deep learning methods to overcome the above challenges. Deep learning methods have drawn widespread attention in many areas, such as speech recognition, visual object recognition, machine translation, etc. Some deep neural networks show impressive performance in dealing with natural language. Since the handshake messages can be seen as a kind of character language, we can use deep learning methods for mobile encrypted traffic classification [17]. Motivated by the above idea, we propose a novel approach named the Multiple Attribute Associate Network (MAAN). MAAN takes a hierarchical neural network to extract message-level and flow-level features from handshake messages and flows. Moreover, MAAN achieves an acceptable time delay for real-time classification.

Our contributions can be briefly summarized as follow:

- We propose a unified MAAN model for mobile encrypted traffic classification. MAAN automatically learns representative features from raw encrypted traffic and doesn't need manual feature engineering.
- MAAN combines handshake messages with flows to extract message-level and flow-level features. In a real-world dataset, MAAN achieves satisfactory results and outperforms several state-of-the-art methods. Meanwhile, MAAN performs an acceptable time delay and is suitable for real-time classification.

2   Background

2.1   SSL/TLS Basics

The Secure Socket Layer (SSL) protocol and its successor Transport Layer Security (TLS) protocol are the encryption standards of two largest mobile markets, the App Store and the Google Play [1, 2]. As a result, most of the applications use the SSL/TLS to communicate with servers, which leads to a high proportion of the SSL/TLS traffic in mobile networks. Figure 1 shows an example of the SSL/TLS protocol communication session. It consists of two processes that are the handshake process and the data transfer process. In the handshake process, the client first sends Client Hello to the server and try to initiate a connection.

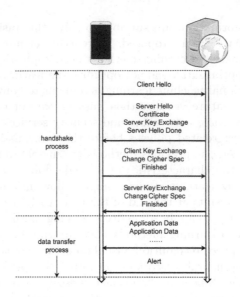

Fig. 1. Example of the SSL/TLS Protocol Communication Session

Then, the server sends **Server Hello** and **Certificate** to the client for authentication and encryption parameter negotiation. Next, the two sides use four kinds of messages, **Server Key Exchange**, **Client Key Exchange**, **Change Cipher Spec**, and **Finished** Message to agree on a master secret and complete handshake. In the data transfer process, the two sides transfer **Application Data**, which has been encrypted with a master secret. Finally, the session terminates with an **Alert** Message from the server. Moreover, SSL/TLS uses session reuse to reduce resource consumption during the handshake phase. For brevity, we refer to SSL/TLS as SSL in this paper.

2.2   Related Work

We have briefly stated the drawbacks of convolutional traffic classification methods, the port-based and the payload-based, in the introduction. The merits and defects of the machine learning methods for encrypted traffic classification will be elaborately discussed below. For a clear comparison, we categorize the related work into two classes: statistical machine learning methods and deep learning methods.

Statistical Machine Learning Methods: Statistical machine learning methods contain two processes that are feature engineering and classifier selection. At present, researchers mainly focus on feature engineering. We summarize three kinds of features widely used in the encrypted traffic classification: statistical features, flow sequential features, and original message features.

Statistical Features: Statistical features are used to solve encrypted traffic classification problems combined with traditional machine learning methods, such as random forest, SVM. Taylor et al. [30] proposed AppScanner, which uses the packet lengths or some statistical features of packet lengths as features and takes the SVM or random forest as the classifier. To get the best results, AppScanner uses the classification validation technique. Then, Taylor et al. optimized AppScanner by the technique of ambiguity detection [31]. Al-Naami et al. [7] extracted statistic features from the packet, uni-burst and bi-burst (e.g., packet length, uni-burst size). They also propose a new method to overcome concept drift. Hayes et al. [14] generate a more robust web fingerprint from some statistical features by random forest. And Shi et al. [28] take a deep learning method to optimize the statistical features and enhance the performance of traffic classification. However, these methods require manual feature designing that is mainly based on rich experiences, professional knowledge, and lots of human effort.

Flow Sequential Features: Message type sequence and packet length sequence are two widely used flow sequential features. Korczyński et al. [16] first use a message type sequence to establish a one-order Markov chain for application traffic classification. Shen et al. [26] incorporate attribute bigrams into the second-order Markov chain to solve the misclassification problem of the one-order Markov chain. Liu et al. [18] combine message type sequence one-order Markov chain with Length Block sequence one-order Markov chain to generate probability feature vectors and use the random forest as the classifier. Due to the need for adequate sequence information, these methods are hard to classify encrypted traffic in real-time.

Original Message Features: These methods take advantage of the differences in SSL protocol. Sengupta et al. [25] exploit the diversity in SSL implementations for application traffic classification. Whereas, this method is unsuitable for real-time classification due to the high computational complexity of feature extraction. Chen et al. [10] take Domain Name, Common Name, Organization, and Application Data lengths as the features and combine the contextual reference to improve the performance of classification. However, some features of the method are difficult to extract in practice.

Deep Learning Methods: The deep learning methods combine feature engineering and classifier optimization into a unified model. These methods mainly contain two categories: packet-based methods and flow-based methods.

Packet-Based Methods: These methods take raw packet as input and design deep neural network for classification. Wang et al. [35] achieve protocol identification andanomalous protocoldetection with DNN and SAE. Datanet [34] designs three neural networks for encrypted traffic classification. Zeng et al. [37] combine three neural networks to adapt to different network environments. Lotfollahi et al. [21] adopt the stacked autoencoder and one-dimensional convolutional neural network to extract features from packet payload. Li et al. [17] transform the raw network datagram into several segments and use a hierarchical attention encoder to extract features. However, these methods only focus on the packet level features and do not consider the flow level information.

Flow-Based Methods: Yang et al. [36] adopt autoencoder and CNN with manual extraction features for encrypted traffic classification. However, the method doesn't take advantage of the automatic feature extraction of the neural network, and it can't be applied in real-time classification by reason of features' limitation. Aceto et al. [5] propose MIMETIC, a new architecture that can incorporate multiple inputs and multiple models to improve the performance of classification. Whereas, the MIMETC requires a through design which cannot ignore network expertise's help. And Liu et al. [19] adopt autoencoder to establish an end-to-end model that learns features from the raw flow sequences. This method is no more suitable for real-time classification than the flow sequential features methods mentioned above.

3   Architecture of MAAN

MAAN extracts features from encrypted traffic flow, which contains a complete SSL session. According to the SSL protocol, handshake messages and Application Data messages contain application identity information. For handshake messages, we consider Client Hello, Server Hello, and end-entity certificate, which is the final certificate signed for servers, as inputs. For Application Data messages, the message lengths of Application Data reflect the application layer's transmission logic, which can be used to classify. Therefore, we use the message lengths of first N Application Data, named as Application Data lengths, as inputs.

MAAN is a hierarchical model that consists of 5 layers, as shown in Fig. 2. In our method, a segment preprocessor first breaks three handshake messages into three integer sequences. Next, the message feature extractor transforms three integer sequences and Application Data lengths to $N + 3$ message-level representation vectors. Then, a flow feature extractor extracts a flow-level representation vector from $N + 3$ message-level representation vectors. After this, a dense layer compresses the flow-level representation vector and creates the final fingerprint. Finally, the fingerprint of the flow is introduced to a classification layer to predict the class of the flow. Herein, the details of each layer are as follows.

3.1   Segment Preprocessor

Segment preprocessor is designed to convert three handshake messages into three integer sequences (named as S_{client}, S_{server} and $S_{certificate}$) that can

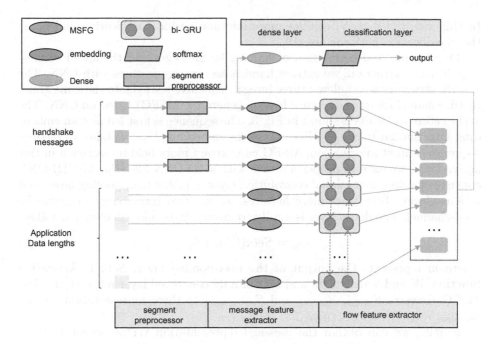

Fig. 2. The architecture of MAAN

be calculated by the deep learning models. We refer to each handshake message as a datagram. Firstly, segment preprocessor cuts the datagram into 2-byte chunks. Then, every chunk is transformed into an integer between 1 to 65536. Besides, each type of datagram is transferred into a sequence with fixed length (S_{client} and S_{server} are set to 300, and $S_{certificate}$ is set to 5000). In the case of sequences longer (resp. shorter) than the considered fixed-length data formats, these sequences are truncated (resp. padded with zeros) to the designed length. To be specific, for these session-resumed flows, we set the end-entity certificate to a sequence of zero.

3.2 Message Feature Extractor

The message feature extractor takes three integer sequences (S_{client}, S_{server}, $S_{certificate}$) and Application Data lengths (named as S_{length}) as the inputs, extracting message-level features.

We embed each element of the S_{length} to a vector via embedding layer [23]. The embedding layer is a lookup table essentially. For the element $s_i, i \in [1, N]$ in S_{length}, the corresponding embedding vector of s_i is the s_i-th row of matrix $E \in \mathbb{R}^{k \times d}$, where E, k, and d represent the embedding matrix, the size of S_{length}'s element set and the dimension of embedding vectors respectively. The embedding matrix E is trainable and contains the context information of s_i [23]. Finally, we can obtain N representation vectors $[l_1, l_2, ..., l_N]$ where $l_i = E_{s_i}$.

In this way, $l_i, i \in [1, N]$ can get more information for classification and boost the classification performance [19].

Due to the local correlation of handshake messages and the speed of message feature extraction, we extract handshake message features with CNN. The specific structure is as follows: three integer sequences are fed into the same architecture named message sequence feature generator (MSFG) based on CNN. The architecture of MSFG is shown in Fig. 3. The sequence is first fed into an embedding layer similar to S_{length}. Because of the embedding layer's ability to retrieve sequence context information, MSFG can extract more field information in this layer. Then, we extract deeper features with a 1D-CNN like [15]. The 1D-CNN consists of a one-dimensional convolution layer, a global max-pooling layer, and a dense layer. To extract more features, we use two kernel sizes to make the dual-channel. The dense layer is a fully connected layer and calculated as follow:

$$m_d = Selu(Wm + b) \qquad (1)$$

where m represents the output of the max-pooling layer, $Selu$ is Activation function, W and b are weight and bias of fully connected layer respectively. The MSFG converts S_{client}, S_{server} and $S_{certificate}$ to three representation vectors m_{client}, m_{server} and $m_{certificate}$.

Finally, we can obtain the message representation vector sequence $M = [m_1, m_2, ..., m_{N+3}]$ where m_1, m_2, m_3 denote $m_{client}, m_{server}, m_{certificate}$ respectively and $m_j, j \in [4, N+3]$ represent $l_i, i \in [1, N]$.

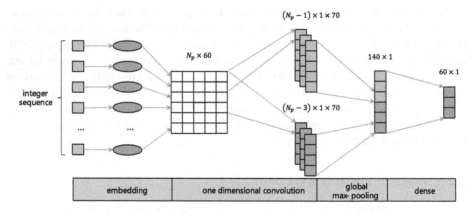

Fig. 3. The Architecture of MSFG. N_p represent integer sequence length (Subscript p represents Client Hello, Server Hello and end-entity certificate).

3.3 Flow Feature Extractor

The network flow conforms to the sequence characteristics with time correlation, so RNN is suitable for extracting flow-level features. Due to the vanishing gradient problem [9] and lacking backward information of traditional RNN, we use the bidirectional GRUs (bi-GRU) in this layer. Meanwhile, we use single bi-GRU to achieve acceptable time consumption. Given a message representation vector sequence $M = [m_1, m_2, ..., m_{N+3}]$, the bi-GRU contains a forward GRU network $\overrightarrow{GRU}$ which reads M from m_1 to m_{N+3} and a backward GRU network $\overleftarrow{GRU}$ which reads M from m_{N+3} to m_1:

$$\overrightarrow{h}_t = \overrightarrow{GRU}(\overrightarrow{h}_{t-1}, m_t), t \in [1, N+3] \tag{2}$$

$$\overleftarrow{h}_t = \overleftarrow{GRU}(\overleftarrow{h}_{t+1}, m_t), t \in [1, N+3] \tag{3}$$

where $\overrightarrow{h}_t$ and $\overleftarrow{h}_t$ are the forward and backward hidden states respectively, and the initial hidden state vectors $\overrightarrow{h}_0$ and $\overleftarrow{h}_{N+4}$ are both zero vectors. Then, the bi-GRU conbines the forward hidden state $\overrightarrow{h}_t$ and the backward hidden state $\overleftarrow{h}_t$ to create a two direction outputs like: $o_t = [\overrightarrow{h}_t, \overleftarrow{h}_t]$. Finally, we concatenate the all output o_t to obtain the flow based feature vector z as follows:

$$z = [\overrightarrow{h}_1, \overleftarrow{h}_1, \overrightarrow{h}_2, \overleftarrow{h}_2, ..., \overrightarrow{h}_t, \overleftarrow{h}_t], t \in [1, N+3] \tag{4}$$

3.4 Dense Layer

To compress the dimension of flow-based feature z and overcome the risk of over-fitting, we take a dense layer similar to Eq. 1 (*tanh* is Activation function in this layer) and create a higher representation of the entire flow, named as z_c.

3.5 Classification Layer

The flow fingerprint z_c is input into a softmax classifier to generate the probability distribution over different applications:

$$p(i) = \frac{exp(\theta_i z_c + b_i)}{\sum_{a=1}^{A} exp(\theta_a z_c + b_a)} \tag{5}$$

where $p(i)$ is the probability that z_c is application $i(i \in [1, A])$. With the distribution, we take the application with the maximum probability as the prediction label.

4   Experiment

In this section, we introduce our experiments to evaluate the MAAN. All experiments are conducted on a PC with an Intel Xeon E5-2682V4 CPU, Nvidia Tesla P4 GPU, and 16 GB RAM running Ubuntu 18.04. We conduct all experiments with python.

4.1 Dataset

To the best of our knowledge, active dataset collection and passive dataset collection are widely used data collection schemas. Considering that passive dataset collection is hard to label comprehensively, we only use active dataset collection schema in this paper. Meanwhile, we take a manual collection schema to reflect the users' real usages. In this scheme, an iOS phone connects to a laptop's Wifi network and only run one application at a time. When the iOS phone is running an application, the laptop captures all the flows generated by this application using Wireshark [4], and the operator labels them with the application name. Then, we extract the SSL encrypted traffic by matching 443 port. Some flows generated by iOS system don't belong to any app in dataset. To get a purer dataset, we filter out these flows by pattern matching, which uses two pattern strings (*.icloud.* and *.apple.*) to match SNI values.

With the collection scheme above, we collect over 59 thousands encrypted traffic flows corresponding to 16 applications from January 1, 2020 to January 20, 2020. Table 1 shows detailed information about each application.

Table 1. Overview of dataset

Application	Flows	Packets	Bytes
Alipay	4298	219035	374 MB
Amap	4084	81486	252 MB
Ele	3825	484892	559 MB
Baidu Tieba	3978	459833	528 MB
Baidu Map	4025	281585	299 MB
Zhihu	4349	814797	1019 MB
Meituan	4066	273988	311 MB
Weibo	3636	774925	957 MB
Youdao	3872	684298	888 MB
Linkin	2091	528350	550 MB
Douyin	3899	1235634	1586 MB
Jd	4375	1294364	1593 MB
Booking	2567	115650	105 MB
Airbnb	2027	327338	374 MB
Evernote	4165	644703	798 MB
Bilibili	3808	211843	211 MB
Total	59065	8432721	10094 MB

4.2   Experiment Setting

Setting of MAAN: We take Client Hello, Server Hello, end-entity certificate, and the message lengths of the first 10 Application Data as the inputs (the quantities of Application Data messages will be discussed in Sect. 4.4). The dimension of the embedding layer is set as 60. We set the kernel sizes of the convolutional network to 2 and 4, and the filter of each kernel to 70. We set the dimension of hidden states of each GRU as 50. Moreover, we take a dropout with 0.1 ratios to avoid over-fitting, and we set epochs to 10. Our model is implemented with TensorFlow [3]. We detail the parameters selection in Appendix A.

Cross Validation: To obtain a reliable and stable model, we establish 5-fold cross-validation. More specifically, we split the total dataset into five parts, and every time four parts are used for training while one part is used for testing. All the process repeats five times with different parts. Finally, we use the average value of five-fold cross-validation results as the final result.

Assessment Criteria of Model: We evaluate all the methods with three metrics, Precision (Prec.), Recall (Rec.), and Accuracy (Acc.). For app a, Precision is the proportion of real encrypted flows belonging app a in the encrypted flows classified as app a, while Recall is the proportion of encrypted flows correctly classified as app a in the total app a encrypted flows [10]. Accuracy is the proportion of encrypted flows correctly classified in total flows.

4.3   Comparisons with Existing Approaches

Comparative Experiments: We use three state-of-the-art methods as comparison experiments. The description and setup of these experiments are shown below:

- **MaMMF:** MaMMF [18] constitutes probability feature vectors with the message type Markov chain and Length Block Markov chain, taking Random Forest as the classifier. We set Length Block to cover 90% of the whole packets.
- **MAAF-SFF:** MAAF [10] takes Domain Name, Common Name, Organization, and Application Data lengths as features. Meanwhile, it uses the context reference to improve the classification performance. Some features of MAAF are hard to be used in practice (e.g., Domain Name is confusing to associate with the corresponding flow). Therefore, we only consider the single flow's characteristics (Common Name, Organization, and Application Data lengths) in this method and abandon the context reference. We call it as MAAF-Single Flow Features (MAAF-SFF). We set the parameters same as the paper and take XGBoost as the classifier.
- **FS-Net:** FS-Net [19] uses an encoder-decoder structure to extract features from raw flow sequences and classify them with neural network. We use the packet length sequence as the FS-Net' input and set the parameters same as the paper.

Table 2. Experimental results of different approaches

Application	MaMMF		MAAF-SFF		FS-Net		MAAN	
	Prec.	Rec.	Prec.	Rec.	Prec.	Rec.	Prec.	Rec.
Alipay	0.8719	0.8328	0.9394	0.8954	0.9471	0.9523	**0.9830**	**0.9540**
Amap	0.9297	0.9699	0.9910	0.9705	0.9822	**0.9851**	**0.9962**	0.9850
Ele	0.8400	0.7038	0.9091	0.9161	0.9347	0.9361	**0.9466**	**0.9836**
Baidu Tieba	0.8210	0.8326	0.8791	0.7387	0.9068	0.9305	**0.9829**	**0.9765**
Baidu Map	0.8912	0.8301	0.8213	0.8473	0.9408	0.9188	**0.9911**	**0.9749**
Zhihu	0.7217	0.9218	0.9788	0.9399	0.9803	**0.9826**	**0.9976**	0.9821
Meituan	0.8783	0.9059	0.9842	0.9712	0.9753	0.9893	**0.9857**	**0.9904**
Weibo	0.8621	0.7015	0.8312	0.9561	0.9532	0.9587	**0.9862**	**0.9944**
Youdao	0.8084	0.8574	0.8951	0.8894	0.9723	0.9412	**0.9853**	**0.9906**
Linkin	0.7379	0.6161	0.8806	0.8130	0.9322	0.8603	**0.9710**	**0.9327**
Douyin	0.8570	0.8525	0.8836	0.8494	0.9536	0.9578	**0.9743**	**0.9850**
Jd	0.6937	0.9177	0.8724	0.8734	0.9752	0.9708	**0.9828**	**0.9924**
Booking	0.9529	0.7613	0.7966	0.8766	0.9790	0.9378	**0.9842**	**0.9862**
Airbnb	0.6746	0.8661	0.6984	0.8432	0.8369	0.9789	**0.9662**	**0.9856**
Evernote	0.9522	0.9430	0.9357	0.9774	**0.9916**	0.9839	0.9850	**0.9988**
Bilibili	0.8655	0.6096	0.9667	0.9414	0.9786	0.9700	**0.9847**	**0.9847**
Accuracy	0.8308		0.8984		0.9557		**0.9822**	

Results: Table 2 shows the experimental results of different approaches. We can obtain the following conclusions:4

1) MAAN outperforms all the other methods. According to Table 2, MAAN obtains the best precision performances on 15 of 16 applications except for Evernote, but its recall is the best. For the overall performance, MAAN achieves the best performance on accuracy. In comparison with other methods, MAAN's advantages are credited to the multiple features association and the unified learning structure.

2) Handshake messages have many representative features that can improve the accuracy of classifier. MaMMF, FS-Net, and MAAN all extract flow-level features, and our method outperforms the other methods, according to Table 2. MAAN benefits from the handshake messages, which contain much plaintext of application identity.

3) The unified framework leads MAAN to achieve a better performance than the two-stage method. Our MAAN outperforms the MAAF-SFF, although they all use handshake messages and Application Data lengths as inputs. The MAAF-SFF needs to extract features from the handshake messages manually, so it is challenging to make use of all the handshake information. By contrast, MAAN uses a unified structure that can automatically extract comprehensive handshake information. Meanwhile, MAAF-SFF ignores the flow-level based features.

4.4 Analysis of MAAN

Segment Lengths: To convert the handshake messages into the integer sequences that can be calculated by neural networks, we must segment handshake messages with a fixed length. There are two viable segment lengths, 1-byte and 2-byte. In this experiment, we focus on the effectiveness of two segment lengths for classification. Table 3 shows the accuracy of two segment lengths. We figure out that the accuracy of 2-byte segment was 0.94% higher than that of 1-byte segment. We believe the reason is that 1-byte segment divides all the fields of messages, making it difficult for the classifier to extract features. Meanwhile, 2-byte segment can produce a shorter integer sequence than 1-byte segment, which can improve classification speed.

Table 3. Comparison of 1-byte and 2-byte segment

Segment length	1-byte	2-byte
Accuracy	0.9728	0.9822

Combination of Messages: This experiment studies the contribution of each handshake message and the collaboration between the handshake messages. We traverse all combinations of the three handshake messages and study the classification accuracy for each combination. Based on the experimental results, we can optimize the combination of the handshake messages to suit the actual network scenario.

The experimental results are presented in Fig. 4. Due to the limited space, we replace the message names by abbreviations. We use CL, SH and EC to represent Client Hello, Server Hello and end-entity certificate respectively. We use ALL to represent the combination of three messages.

According to the experimental results in Fig. 4, three handshake messages improve the classification accuracy, which verifies the original intuition that handshake messages can effectively classify applications. In detail, Client Hello contributes the most information for classification, while Server Hello contributes the least. We think the reason for this situation is that Server Hello contains fewer protocol parameters than Client Hello. Furthermore, we found that Client Hello and end-entity certificate can be harmoniously combined to improve the accuracy significantly.

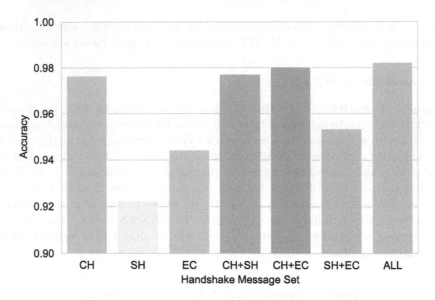

Fig. 4. Clssification Accuracy under Different Handshake Message Sets

Quantities of Application Data Messages: This experiment studies the classification accuracy under different quantities of Application Data messages. We iterate over the quantities of Application Data messages, from zero to twenty, with an interval of two. Figure 5 shows the upward trend of the classification accuracy with the increase of the quantities of Application Data messages. Obviously, as the quantities of Application Data messages increase, the accuracy is rising, too. When the quantities of Application Data messages increase to 10, the accuracy reaches its maximum and does not increase afterwards. Therefore, we consider 10 to be the optimal value for the quantities of Application Data messages.

4.5 The Efficiency of MAAN

In this section, we study the ability of MAAN for real-time classification. We first illustrate online classification ability of MAAN by comparing with other approaches. Then, we discuss the performance of MAAN in a real-time scenario.

Table 4 lists the comparison results of different approaches. The classification time of single flow in MAAN is 1.5 ms, which is 10 times faster than that of MaMMF and FS-Net. Although the classification time of MAAN is longer than that of MAAF-SFF, MAAN has a five-fold reduction of error rate compared to MAAF-SFF. Therefore, we believe that MAAN is more suitable for online classification than other methods.

In real-time scenarios, the classifier is expected to classify the traffic as soon as possible. MAAN can obtain earlier predictions with fewer Application Data messages. Because handshake messages contain many identity information, MAAN

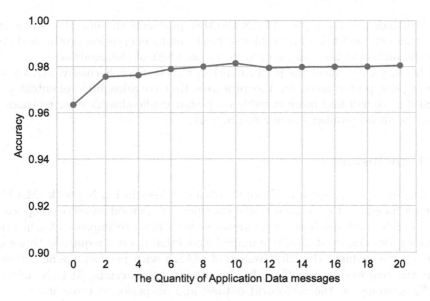

Fig. 5. Classification Accuracy under Different Quantities of Application Data messages

can achieve 96.34% accuracy with zero Application Data messages, which outperforms other methods.

Table 4. Efficiency of Approaches. Classification Time of Single Flow is the ratio of test time to total number of test samples. Error Rate is the ratio of misclassified simples to all.

Approaches	MAAN	MaMMF	FS-Net	MAAF-SFF
Classification Time of Single Flow	1.5 ms	19.9 ms	19.0 ms	0.1 ms
Error Rate	1.8%	16.9%	4.4%	10.2%

5 Discussion

In this section, we will discuss how to apply our method in other encryption protocol. Firstly, most encryption protocols exchange keys with a handshake protocol, which is plaintext and contains many identity information (e.g. encryption parameters), so we can take the plaintext handshake messages as the first part of the input. Then, the message length field cannot be obtained in some encryption protocols, we can substitute it with burst, which is the sum of the data packets's lengths in the same direction. Finally, we can build a model with similar architecture to MAAN for classification.

Although we can apply MAAN to other protocols through the above process, there still exist several problems: firstly, many encryption protocols do not contain authentication information in the plaintext of the handshake (e.g. ssh), which will greatly affect the performance of the classifier. Secondly, MAAN will obtain poor performance for the protocols that contains little plaintext (e.g. TLS1.3). We will find more suitable encrypted traffic classification methods to solve the above problems in our future work.

6   Conclusion

In this paper, we propose a Multiple Attribute Association Network (MAAN), which is an efficient encrypted traffic classification method based on deep learning. MAAN combines handshake messages with flows to improve classification accuracy. Besides, it establishes a unified model that doesn't require feature engineering. We evaluate the effectiveness of MAAN with network traffic collected from the real-world. According to the experimental results, MAAN achieves 98.2% accuracy on the real-world dataset and outperforms three state-of-the-art approaches. Moreover, the experiments demonstrate the effectiveness of the attributes employed by MAAN and reveal that MAAN is suitable for real-time classification.

A   Parameters Selection

We use grid search method to find the optimal parameters. The specific results are shown in the Table 5.

Table 5. Parameters selection

Architecture	Parameter	Range	Step	Optimal parameter
Message feature extractor	embedding dimension	$[10, 100]$	10	60
	kernal size	$2, 3, 4, 5$		$2, 4$
	CNN activation	$Relu, Selu, tanh, None$		$None$
	CNN filters	$[10, 100]$	10	70
	Dense activation	$Relu, Selu, tanh$		$Selu$
Flow feature extractor	GRU hidden states	$[10, 100]$	10	50
	GRU activiation	$Relu, Selu, tanh$		$tanh$
Dense layer	dense dimension	$[50, 200]$	50	100
	dense activiation	$Relu, Selu, tanh$		$tanh$
	optimizer	$Adam, RMSProp$		$Adam$
	dropout	$[0.05, 0.3]$	0.05	0.1

References

1. App transport security. https://developer.apple.com/library/archive/documentati on/General/Reference/InfoPlistKeyReference/Articles/CocoaKeys.html#//apple ref/doc/uid/TP40009251-SW33
2. Network security configuration. https://developer.android.com/training/articles/ security-config
3. Tensorflow. https://www.tensorflow.org/
4. Wireshark. https://www.wireshark.org/
5. Aceto, G., Ciuonzo, D., Montieri, A., Pescapè, A.: MIMETIC: mobile encrypted traffic classification using multimodal deep learning. Comput. Netw. **165**, 106944 (2019)
6. Aceto, G., Ciuonzo, D., Montieri, A., Pescapé, A.: Mobile encrypted traffic classification using deep learning: experimental evaluation, lessons learned, and challenges. IEEE Trans. Netw. Serv. Manage. **16**(2), 445–458 (2019)
7. Al-Naami, K., et al.: Adaptive encrypted traffic fingerprinting with bi-directional dependence. In: Proceedings of the 32nd Annual Conference on Computer Security Applications, pp. 177–188 (2016)
8. Anderson, B., McGrew, D.: Machine learning for encrypted malware traffic classification: accounting for noisy labels and non-stationarity. In: Proceedings of the 23rd ACM SIGKDD International Conference on Knowledge Discovery and Data Mining, pp. 1723–1732 (2017)
9. Bengio, Y., Simard, P., Frasconi, P.: Learning long-term dependencies with gradient descent is difficult. IEEE Trans. Neural Networks **5**(2), 157–166 (1994)
10. Chen, Y., Zang, T., Zhang, Y., Zhouz, Y., Wang, Y.: Rethinking encrypted traffic classification: a multi-attribute associated fingerprint approach. In: 2019 IEEE 27th International Conference on Network Protocols (ICNP), pp. 1–11. IEEE (2019)
11. Conti, M., Mancini, L.V., Spolaor, R., Verde, N.V.: Analyzing android encrypted network traffic to identify user actions. IEEE Trans. Inf. Forensics Secur. **11**(1), 114–125 (2015)
12. Draper-Gil, G., Lashkari, A.H., Mamun, M.S.I., Ghorbani, A.A.: Characterization of encrypted and VPN traffic using time-related. In: Proceedings of the 2nd International Conference on Information Systems Security and Privacy (ICISSP), pp. 407–414 (2016)
13. Fu, Y., Xiong, H., Lu, X., Yang, J., Chen, C.: Service usage classification with encrypted internet traffic in mobile messaging apps. IEEE Trans. Mob. Comput. **15**(11), 2851–2864 (2016)
14. Hayes, J., Danezis, G.: k-fingerprinting: a robust scalable website fingerprinting technique. In: 25th USENIX Security Symposium (USENIX Security 16), pp. 1187–1203 (2016)
15. Kim, Y.: Convolutional neural networks for sentence classification. arXiv preprint arXiv:1408.5882 (2014)
16. Korczyński, M., Duda, A.: Markov chain fingerprinting to classify encrypted traffic. In: IEEE INFOCOM 2014-IEEE Conference on Computer Communications, pp. 781–789. IEEE (2014)
17. Li, R., Xiao, X., Ni, S., Zheng, H., Xia, S.: Byte segment neural network for network traffic classification. In: 2018 IEEE/ACM 26th International Symposium on Quality of Service (IWQoS), pp. 1–10. IEEE (2018)

18. Liu, C., Cao, Z., Xiong, G., Gou, G., Yiu, S.M., He, L.: MaMPF: encrypted traffic classification based on multi-attribute Markov probability fingerprints. In: 2018 IEEE/ACM 26th International Symposium on Quality of Service (IWQoS), pp. 1–10. IEEE (2018)
19. Liu, C., He, L., Xiong, G., Cao, Z., Li, Z.: FS-Net: a flow sequence network for encrypted traffic classification. In: IEEE INFOCOM 2019-IEEE Conference on Computer Communications, pp. 1171–1179. IEEE (2019)
20. Liu, J., Fu, Y., Ming, J., Ren, Y., Sun, L., Xiong, H.: Effective and real-time in-app activity analysis in encrypted internet traffic streams. In: Proceedings of the 23rd ACM SIGKDD International Conference on Knowledge Discovery and Data Mining, pp. 335–344 (2017)
21. Lotfollahi, M., Siavoshani, M.J., Zade, R.S.H., Saberian, M.: Deep packet: a novel approach for encrypted traffic classification using deep learning. Soft. Comput. 24(3), 1999–2012 (2020)
22. Mandic, D.P., Chambers, J.: Recurrent Neural Networks for Prediction: Learning Algorithms, Architectures and Stability. Wiley, New York (2001)
23. Mikolov, T., Sutskever, I., Chen, K., Corrado, G.S., Dean, J.: Distributed representations of words and phrases and their compositionality. In: Advances in Neural Information Processing Systems, pp. 3111–3119 (2013)
24. Razaghpanah, A., Niaki, A.A., Vallina-Rodriguez, N., Sundaresan, S., Amann, J., Gill, P.: Studying TLS usage in android apps. In: Proceedings of the 13th International Conference on emerging Networking Experiments and Technologies, pp. 350–362 (2017)
25. Sengupta, S., Ganguly, N., De, P., Chakraborty, S.: Exploiting diversity in android TLS implementations for mobile app traffic classification. In: The World Wide Web Conference, pp. 1657–1668 (2019)
26. Shen, M., et al.: Classification of encrypted traffic with second-order Markov chains and application attribute bigrams. IEEE Trans. Inf. Forensics Secur. 12(8), 1830–1843 (2017)
27. Shen, M., Wei, M., Zhu, L., Wang, M., Li, F.: Certificate-aware encrypted traffic classification using second-order Markov chain. In: 2016 IEEE/ACM 24th International Symposium on Quality of Service (IWQoS), pp. 1–10. IEEE (2016)
28. Shi, H., Li, H., Zhang, D., Cheng, C., Cao, X.: An efficient feature generation approach based on deep learning and feature selection techniques for traffic classification. Comput. Netw. 132, 81–98 (2018)
29. Sirinam, P., Imani, M., Juarez, M., Wright, M.: Deep fingerprinting: Undermining website fingerprinting defenses with deep learning. In: Proceedings of the 2018 ACM SIGSAC Conference on Computer and Communications Security, pp. 1928–1943 (2018)
30. Taylor, V.F., Spolaor, R., Conti, M., Martinovic, I.: AppScanner: automatic fingerprinting of smartphone apps from encrypted network traffic. In: 2016 IEEE European Symposium on Security and Privacy (EuroS&P), pp. 439–454. IEEE (2016)
31. Taylor, V.F., Spolaor, R., Conti, M., Martinovic, I.: Robust smartphone app identification via encrypted network traffic analysis. IEEE Trans. Inf. Forensics Secur. 13(1), 63–78 (2017)
32. Velan, P., Čermák, M., Čeleda, P., Drašar, M.: A survey of methods for encrypted traffic classification and analysis. Int. J. Network Manage. 25(5), 355–374 (2015)
33. Wang, P., Chen, X., Ye, F., Sun, Z.: A survey of techniques for mobile service encrypted traffic classification using deep learning. IEEE Access 7, 54024–54033 (2019)

34. Wang, P., Ye, F., Chen, X., Qian, Y.: DataNet: deep learning based encrypted network traffic classification in SDN home gateway. IEEE Access **6**, 55380–55391 (2018)
35. Wang, Z.: The applications of deep learning on traffic identification. BlackHat USA **24**(11), 1–10 (2015)
36. Yang, Y., Kang, C., Gou, G., Li, Z., Xiong, G.: TLS/SSL encrypted traffic classification with autoencoder and convolutional neural network. In: 2018 IEEE 20th International Conference on High Performance Computing and Communications; IEEE 16th International Conference on Smart City; IEEE 4th International Conference on Data Science and Systems (HPCC/SmartCity/DSS), pp. 362–369. IEEE (2018)
37. Zeng, Y., Gu, H., Wei, W., Guo, Y.: $deep-full-range$: a deep learning based network encrypted traffic classification and intrusion detection framework. IEEE Access **7**, 45182–45190 (2019)
38. Zhang, J., Chen, X., Xiang, Y., Zhou, W., Wu, J.: Robust network traffic classification. IEEE/ACM Trans. Networking **23**(4), 1257–1270 (2014)
39. Zou, Z., Ge, J., Zheng, H., Wu, Y., Han, C., Yao, Z.: Encrypted traffic classification with a convolutional long short-term memory neural network. In: 2018 IEEE 20th International Conference on High Performance Computing and Communications; IEEE 16th International Conference on Smart City; IEEE 4th International Conference on Data Science and Systems (HPCC/SmartCity/DSS), pp. 329–334. IEEE (2018)

Assessing Adaptive Attacks Against Trained JavaScript Classifiers

Niels Hansen[1], Lorenzo De Carli[2(✉)], and Drew Davidson[1]

[1] University of Kansas, Lawrence, USA
{nahansen,drewdavidson}@ku.edu
[2] Worcester Polytechnic Institute, Worcester, USA
ldecarli@wpi.edu

Abstract. In this work, we evaluate the security of heuristic- and machine learning-based classifiers for the detection of malicious JavaScript code. Due to the prevalence of web attacks directed though JavaScript injected into webpages, such defense mechanisms serve as a last-line of defense by classifying individual scripts as either benign or malicious. State-of-the-art classifiers work well at distinguishing currently-known malicious scripts from existing legitimate functionality, often by employing training sets of known benign or malicious samples. However, we observe that real-world attackers can be *adaptive*, and tailor their attacks to the benign content of the page and the defense mechanisms being used to defend the page.

In this work, we consider a variety of techniques that an adaptive adversary may use to overcome JavaScript classifiers. We introduce a variety of new threat models that consider various types of adaptive adversaries, with varying knowledge of the classifier and dataset being used to detect malicious scripts. We show that while no heuristic defense mechanism is a silver bullet against an adaptive adversary, some techniques are far more effective than others. Thus, our work points to which techniques should be considered best practices in classifying malicious content, and a call to arms for more advanced classification.

Keywords: JavaScript security · Web security · Adversarial ML

1 Introduction

Developments in adversarial machine learning are deeply affecting the science of computer security. In recent years, the research community has shown how a variety of classification techniques are vulnerable to *adversarial samples*. An adversarial sample is a malicious object—its type depending on the classification task—which exhibits features causing a target classifier to misclassify it. Adversarial samples apply naturally to a special form of classification in which there are two categories: *malicious* and *benign* (we consider software defense frameworks to be instances of classifiers in this regard, and we will use the term classifier to

© ICST Institute for Computer Sciences, Social Informatics and Telecommunications Engineering 2020
Published by Springer Nature Switzerland AG 2020. All Rights Reserved
N. Park et al. (Eds.): SecureComm 2020, LNICST 335, pp. 190–210, 2020.
https://doi.org/10.1007/978-3-030-63086-7_12

refer to such systems throughout this work). By subverting the training sets of security mechanisms to misclassify attacks as benign, adversarial samples have been shown to be effective against such classifiers in several contexts [2].

The potential impact of adversarial samples is significant in the domain of website protection. In this context, the task is to analyze each individual script, particularly JavaScript, being served from a page. The analysis deems a script as allowed if the script is legitimate content, or disallowed otherwise. The research community has produced classification techniques that can (i) learn descriptive features for benign and malicious JavaScript samples from a corpus, and (ii) efficiently use these features to distinguish scripts from the two classes, so that malicious scripts can be stopped before they are executed or served to the user. A key benefit of these classifiers is that they do not need to have access to an explicit whitelist of scripts, but can instead rely on heuristics or learned models. Indeed, such a classifier labels a script as benign as long as it is sufficiently similar to other scripts that are known to be benign (and, in the case of some classifiers, if it is sufficiently dissimilar from a script that it known to be malicious). In other words, the power of the classifier comes from its ability to learn general characteristics of benign code, and look for those characteristics in unknown scripts. However, trained classifiers may misclassify a script with malicious behavior but descriptive features similar enough to the benign training. An *adaptive* adversary may attempt to exploit this limitation by altering an attack script to encourage misclassification.

The degree to which an adaptive adversary can succeed in forcing misclassification in the context of JavaScript has not been fully investigated. Although previous work has been successful by proposing specific ways to mask malicious scripts, more work is needed to understand the effect of factors such as the type of classifier being attacked, the knowledge the adversary has about the benign scripts, and the type of malicious content that the adversary wants to inject. While the security literature presents various instances of adaptive attacks (e.g., [9,19]), their effectiveness relative to each other has been understudied. In this work, we analyze several forms of adaptive attacks, and evaluate their strength against different styles of classifier. Our goal is to build a more complete characterization of the landscape of threats faced by trained classifiers, and to better characterize their ability to withstand various attempts at evasion. We consider two types of classifiers, those that directly use a script's syntactic structure for classification, and those that use scalar features indirectly derived by the syntactic structure. As representative and recently-proposed examples of classifiers, we consider CSPAutoGen, which is a structural classifier [19], and JaSt, which is a feature-based classifier [9]. We choose CSPAutoGen and JaSt for two reasons. First, they both achieve near-0% false negative rate (against a non-adaptive adversary), and they can be considered the state-of-art in malicious JavaScript detection. Second, they are based on fundamentally different mechanisms, allowing us to compare two distinct approaches to classification. Both approaches use syntactic features derived from a script's abstract syntax tree: CSPAutoGen generates a whitelist of generalized ASTs served from a website, while JaSt uses frequencies of n-grams extracted from ASTs to train a tree ensemble classifier to distinguish between malicious and benign email JavaScript snippets.

A key insight of our paper is that the strength of an adaptive adversary depends on his or her knowledge about the target. We present three threat models, corresponding to attackers with different levels of knowledge about the target site. We also introduce three novel, domain-specific mimicry attacks: the *subtree editing mimicry attack*, the *gadget composition attack*, and the *script stitching attack*.

This Paper Makes the Following Contributions:

- We examine state-of-the-art algorithms for malicious JavaScript code detection, determining their vulnerability to mimicry attacks.
- We articulate a number of threat models for attacks against current syntax-based JavaScript classifiers. These threat models both explore the design space of attacks and highlight realistic adversarial capabilities.
- We identify three classes of adaptive attacks at the AST level: *subtree editing*, *script stitching*, and *gadget composition*.
- We implement and evaluate the above attacks, characterizing their effectiveness in realistic scenarios.

The rest of this paper is structured as follows. Section 2 provides background on malicious JavaScript detection. Section 3 presents our characterization of various threat models that correspond to our domain. Section 4 describes our newly-discovered attack techniques, and Sect. 5 describes their implementation. Section 6 experimentally validates these attacks on a realistic JavaScript corpus. Section 7 reviews related work, and Sect. 8 concludes the paper.

2   Problem Overview

There are a variety of attack scenarios in which automatic JavaScript classification might be deployed. In order to focus the discussion on the case most commonly proposed in the literature, we consider the case of malicious JavaScript code injected in a website or web application, and served to the web application's users. Such malicious code may have various goals, such as extracting information from the webpages visited by the user, or downloading and executing additional payloads. The first line of defense against these attacks is to prevent the code from being added to the victim website. However—as recently demonstrated by the outbreak of infections due to the MageCart attack code [16]—relying on injection prevention alone is insufficient.

Due to the persistent vulnerability of web applications to code injection, the security community has produced forms of defense-in-depth. The goal of these defenses is to render injected JavaScript harmless. The most popular of such solutions is the content security policy (CSP) - a set of directives that can be added to a webpage to limit the set of scripts that can run in the context of that webpage. Unfortunately, CSP has been plagued by a perceived lack of flexibility and semantics that do not match the way web applications are developed in practice, and has seen limited adoption [3]. For these reasons, researchers have also investigated heuristic- and machine learning-based classifiers that automatically learn what scripts are acceptable on a webpage, and prevent anything that does not fit the model from reaching the end-user. Those classifiers are our object of study, and we discuss them next.

2.1 Existing Classification Approaches

Existing approaches to JavaScript classification cannot rely on an exhaustive list of scripts to whitelist. Indeed, in many cases websites generate scripts dynamically in a content-dependent manner, which means that the set of benign scripts may potentially be infinite [19]. Instead, the classifier labels scripts as benign if they are *similar* to a training set of benign scripts, which is usually a subset of all of the benign scripts that may be served. Some tools also use a training set of known attack scripts to serve as negative examples. These detectors are necessarily approximate, and can incur both false positives and false negatives during deployment. In order to be usable, automatic classifiers need to make allowances to reduce both types of errors. In practice, tools have attempted to recognize aspects of benign scripts that are characteristic of acceptable functionality in order to reduce false negatives. To reduce false positives, they allow some tolerances for similarity to a benign script. To illustrate these tradeoffs, we describe our two representative classifiers.

CSPAutoGen [19] is a defense framework which aims at preventing execution of malicious injected JavaScript code. Although (as the name implies), CSPAutoGen automatically generates Content Security Policies, it also includes a core template-based algorithm recognizing and allowing benign scripts (for brevity's sake we refer to this algorithm as "CSPAutoGen"). CSPAutoGen automatically learns a model of which scripts are benign using only a training set of allowed sample scripts, for which it builds generalized templates that capture the structure of the benign script's abstract-syntax tree (AST). At runtime, a client-side library component of CSPAutogen determines whether each loaded script should be allowed to run. This library parses the script under test, extracts its AST, and checks for a match against a template. Ultimately, the framework considers a script to be benign if it has a template match, and malicious otherwise. Based on its template behavior, we view CSPAutoGen as effectively solving the benign/malicious script classification problem. To our knowledge, CSPAutoGen is the most recent of classifiers based on the syntactic structure of scripts. As such, CSPAutoGen is a good representative of structural classifiers. Although it is intended to run with client and server components, its core algorithm can be evaluated in a command-line batch mode through tooling included in its open-source distribution.

JaSt [9] is representative of feature-based classifiers. It trains a random forest classifier on a corpus of labeled benign and malicious scripts. Vectorization is accomplished by computing the frequency of various n-grams in each script's

AST. In order to reduce feature sparsity, only n-grams appearing in the evaluation dataset are considered, and only n-grams of length ≤ 5 are considered.

2.2 Objectives and Challenges

Consider a classifier $f : P \rightarrow \{M, B\}$ mapping any JavaScript program $p \in P$ to one of two possible classes: malicious (M) or benign (B). Given a malicious program p_M s.t. $f(p_M) = M$, an adaptive attack is a transformation $T(p_M)$ which generates a second program p_M^* which is functionally equivalent to p_M but $f(p_M^*) = B$.

There are two important points to note about our attacker's goal. First, as program equivalence is in general undecidable, care must be taken so that the transformation $T(p_M) = p_M^*$ maintains the semantic effect of the original p_M. In practice, we use a weak form of program equivalence that postulate that two programs are identical *if, when run under the same conditions, they accomplish the same security exploit*. Second, the above formulation is different from the ones traditionally used in adversarial machine learning [2,25], which tend to stress minimization of some notion of distance $d(p_M, p_M^*)$ in feature space. In fact, in our case p_M and p_M^* can be arbitrarily distant as long as they are functionally equivalent, and a good attack sample does not necessarily lie in the vicinity of p_M (intuitively, this is a consequence of syntactic features not being a good proxy for program behavior and semantics).

3   Threat Models

A key contribution of our work is that we consider various ways in which an adversary might attack a JavaScript classifier. These threat models are intended to explore the range of scenarios that a website maintainer should consider when evaluating defense measures against an adaptive adversary.

We note that a common capability shared by adversaries in all of our threat models is the ability to inject an arbitrary script onto the target page. Thus, we assume that the adversary is capable of bypassing any form of script sanitization or input validation. While the ability to embed malicious content onto a benign page is a strong capability for overall web security, it is exactly the threat model in which malicious JavaScript classifiers operate: if a malicious script is never embedded, the classifier is unnecessary. As noted in Sect. 2, these tools are designed to be a last line of defense when input validation and sanitization has failed. Furthermore, the prevalence of such attacks in the wild show that real adversaries can and do hold the capability to inject content.

We differentiate our different threat models based on the knowledge that an attacker has about the system that they are attempting to evade, as well as the power of the system itself. In adversarial machine learning, the knowledge that an attacker may have about a system is typically classified as knowledge about the following aspects of the target system [2]:

- The dataset $\mathcal{D}$ upon which the classifier was trained. We note that it is highly likely that the attacker will have at least partial knowledge of $\mathcal{D}$, because the adversary has interactive access to the website that they are attacking. It is reasonable to assume that the classifier will be trained on the benign scripts that it is serving, and those scripts are freely accessible to the adversary, either by crawling the site or by recording the results of reconnaissance sessions of browsing the target site. If $\mathcal{D}$ also include sample malicious scripts, an attacker may attempt to replicate this by collecting publicly-available JavaScript exploit datasets (e.g., [1]).
- The (weighted) feature set $\mathcal{X}$ that the classifier uses to determine syntactic similarity between scripts. This information is valuable to an attacker, as they may choose to mount their mimicry by prioritizing similarity to those features that are most highly valued by the classifier.
- The learned model $\mathcal{F}$ that is used by classifier f to label a script as benign or malicious. Implicit in the $\mathcal{F}$ is the style of classification used by f.

We articulate several threat models that correspond to various levels of knowledge that the adversary has about the classifier under attack.

Scenario 1: Non-adaptive Attacker. For the sake of comparison, we first consider the case of an attacker with no knowledge of the target site. This attacker essentially serves as a baseline for adaptive attacks: although the attacker may attempt to obfuscate their malicious script to make it appear more benign, the obfuscation must, by definition, be done without knowledge of what constitutes a benign script in the context of the victim. The non-adaptive attacker threat model constitutes limited evasion capabilities: the attacker has no access to the dataset $\mathcal{D}$, the learned model $\mathcal{F}$, or the feature set $\mathcal{X}$. Nevertheless, this attacker is the one modeled (implicitly or otherwise) by most classifiers.

Scenario 2: Reconnaissance Attacker. The next attacker that we consider is designed to represent realistic capabilities for an attacker with regular access to the target website. This attacker has the ability to observe the behavior of pages on the victim site, including the ability to collect scripts embedded in the site such as inline JavaScript, event handlers, and callbacks. This reconnaissance phase allows the attacker to collect a partial dataset of benign scripts $\mathcal{S}'^B$, which were observed during interaction with the target. We assume that $\mathcal{S}'^B$ is nearly a proper subset of $\mathcal{S}^B$, because we expect that the classifier will necessarily be trained on the benign scripts that are served to the user (modulo minor variations, such as those caused by dynamic scripts) in order to ensure the lowest possible rate of false alarms. However, because the attacker only has access to the data served from the pages visited during the reconnaissance phase, and makes no attempt to make inferences about the target classifier through aggregate observations on the scripts in $\mathcal{S}'^B$, the attacker has no knowledge of $\mathcal{F}$ or $\mathcal{X}$. We believe that the reconnaissance attacker should be considered the minimal bar for a classifier to address in order to be considered effective. For most web sites and web apps, the target site will be publicly accessible, and therefore the reconnaissance phase can be achieved by crawling public pages or by simply collecting all scripts encountered during a regular browsing session on the target site. We note any attacker that encounters a script classifier is likely to have gone through a reconnaissance phase in the due course of finding a vulnerability that allows for malicious content to be injected onto a page. As such, attacker access to S'^B should be expected.

Scenario 3: Classifier-Aware Attacker. The third attack scenario we consider extends the capabilities of the reconnaissance attacker with (potentially partial) knowledge of the classifier being used to defend the target site. Because of this access, we call the attacker in this threat model the classifier-aware attacker. The classifier-aware attacker seeks to mount more sophisticated attacks than the prior two threat models. Rather than being constrained to mimicry of exactly those scripts that are observed during reconnaissance, the classifier-aware attacker can construct a mimicry attack based purely on a notion of what the classifier will accept. Note that the classifier-aware attacker is stronger than the attacker in the previous two threat models. However, this attacker still represents a realistic set of capabilities. As noted in the previous scenario, the attacker has interactive access to the target site. Thus, the attacker can build a *surrogate* by training a classifier similar to the one used to protect the site on the set S'^B that was collected during reconnaissance. While a training set S^M of malicious scripts (only necessary for some classifiers) cannot be directly obtained from the target, an attacker may build a surrogate S'^M from public sources as discussed above. In a typical attack scenario, it is unlikely that the attacker will have direct access to $\mathcal{F}$ or to $\mathcal{X}$. However, the attacker can make reasonable assumptions about $\mathcal{X}$ based on training a surrogate classifier on S'^B (and if necessary S'^M). Furthermore, previous work on *model inversion* [10] has shown that interactive attacker can gain significant details about the classifier (and indeed the underlying model) by making repeated queries to the classifier. In this case, the attacker can simply make naive attempts to inject content into the page and observe the success of the attack. In doing so, they can likely infer the type of classifier $\mathcal{F}$. Coupled with the ability to train on the surrogate data, the attacker can likely build a classifier which is quite close to that used by the site. We note that the classifier-aware attacker represents a strong adversary. Nevertheless, we feel that this model is important to consider if a classifier is to be relied upon in a real deployment, and to assess the strength of a classification system.

4   Attacks

In this section, we introduce several types of adaptive attacks against JavaScript classification. We ignore the non-adaptive, non-adversarial attacker (ref. Sect. 3) as this is the attacker normally assumed by target classifiers [9,19]. The *subtree editing* and *script stitching* attacks are within the capabilities of a reconnaissance attacker (ref. Sect. 3), while the *gadget composition* attack assumes a classifier-aware attacker (ref. Sect. 3). We discuss each attack below.

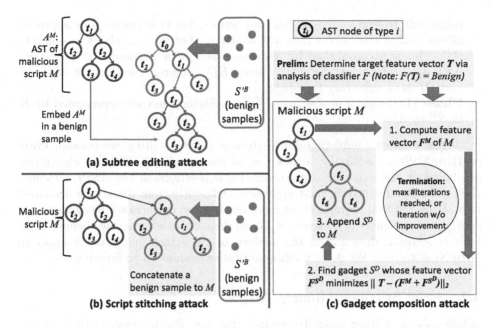

Fig. 1. Attacks discussed in this paper

4.1   Subtree Editing Mimicry Attack

The *subtree editing* mimicry attack assumes the attacker has partial knowledge of the dataset D. In particular, the attacker knows a subset of the benign scripts used for training, $\mathcal{S}'^B \subseteq \mathcal{S}^B$. Consider a malicious script M the attacker wishes to be classified as benign by the target classifier $\mathcal{F}$. The core idea of this attack, depicted in Fig. 1a, is to find a benign script whose AST contains a subtree which is isomorphic to the AST of M, and replace such AST with that of M.

More formally, let $\mathcal{S}'^B = \{S_1^B, S_2^B, \ldots, S_n^B\}$ be the set of benign scripts present upon a target website, where each S_i^B induces AST A_i. The attack seeks to inject a malicious script S^M onto the page with an AST indistinguishable from some A_j. If the attack succeeds, then the matching defense must either mark both S^M and S_j^B as benign, or mark both S^M and S_j^B as malicious. The attack takes part in two phases:

- **Phase I:** Let M be a JavaScript snippet that realizes the attacker's goal, and let A^M be the AST for M. Note that M need not be a self-contained JavaScript program. Find a benign script $S_j^B \in \mathcal{S}'^B$ s.t. its AST A_j is isomorphic to A^M. In the most basic formulation of the attack, A^M needs only exhibit a subtree isomorphism to a subtree K of S_i^B. However, the search for a satisfying K can be subject to additional constraints if the web defense mechanism employs extra attributes in script matching. For example, the search for K may also require that nodes of K exhibit the same AST type as A^M. In practice, requiring ASTs A^M and A_j to be isomorphic may make it impossible to find viable benign host scripts. For that reason, our approach allows benign candidates that are similar to, but not exactly isomorphic to A^M. This is accomplished by requiring that, for a viable candidate benign AST A_j, $TED(A_j, A^M) < DT$, where TED computes the tree-edit distance, and DT is an arbitrary threshold.

- **Phase II:** Create a new script S^M by replacing the code represented by K in S_j^B by M.

While we were completing our analysis of subtree editing, we became aware of HIDENOSEEK, a similar attack due to Fass et al. [8]. The two algorithms are based on the same principle (replacing subsections of the AST), although they differ significantly in their approach. Differently from the attack described here, HIDENOSEEK requires exact matching but can perform swaps against non-contiguous sequences of statements. Given these considerations, we believe high-level conclusions drawn from the analysis of our attack qualitatively apply to HIDENOSEEK too. We defer a full quantitative evaluation to future work.

4.2   Script Stitching Mimicry Attack

While subtree editing generates scripts that are, feature-wise, virtually indistinguishable from benign ones, it relies upon the existence of a suitable benign host script within a targeted website, which may not always exist. In practice, we found that for certain classifiers simpler forms of mimicry, which relax the reliance on the existence of suitable host scripts, are sufficient.

Like the subtree editing attack, the *script stitching* attack (summarized in Fig. 1b), assumes partial knowledge of the training dataset $\mathcal{D}$. In particular, it is sufficient to have access to a subset $\mathcal{S}'^B \subseteq \mathcal{S}^B$ of benign samples used for training (which in the domain of interest can typically be obtained by crawling the target website).

Let $\mathcal{S}'^B = \{S_1^B, S_2^B, \ldots, S_n^B\} \in \mathcal{S}^B$ be the set of benign scripts available to the attacker, and M a JavaScript snippet that realizes the attacker's goal. In a script stitching attack, the attacker randomly select a benign script $S_C^B \in \mathcal{S}'^B$ and generate an adversarial sample $S^M = M \cdot S_C^B$, i.e. she concatenates the selected benign script to the malicious code. Although this attack is simple, in Sect. 6 we show that a script generated with this approach can bypass a state-of-the-art classifier.

4.3   Gadget Composition Mimicry Attack

One limitation of script stitching is that it does not provide guidance to the attacker in selecting benign scripts in a manner that maximizes the probability of success. This limitation is unavoidable if the attacker does not have knowledge of the classifier model $\mathcal{F}$. However, in some cases it may be possible to gain such knowledge, e.g. by training a model on a surrogate dataset. In this case, the model can offer guidance on selecting appropriate transformations to the malicious code M to increase the probability of success. We leverage this insight for the *gadget composition* attack, depicted in Fig. 1c. This attack assumes knowledge of the model $\mathcal{F}$, and specifically of (i) ranking of features by their importance (e.g. using Gini importance), and (ii) full or partial knowledge of the values of such features should achieve for a sample to be classified as benign (this can be inferred by repeatedly querying a model, or using model-specific attacks such as the one by Kantchelian et al. [17] for random forests). Assume the attacker has access to the set of N highest-ranked features for $\mathcal{F}$, and define F^S as the vector containing the values of such features for a given script S. Furthermore, assume the attacker is able to produce a target vector T containing values of features in H that cause a script to be classified as benign with high probability. Finally, assume the attacker has a dictionary $\mathcal{D}$ of *gadgets*, i.e. self-contained snippets of JavaScript code. Given a malicious snippet M, at every iteration, this attack "grows" M by appending the gadget $S^D \in \mathcal{D}$ whose feature vector F^{S^D} minimizes $\|F^B - (F^M + F^{S^D})\|_2$. In other words, at every iteration the attack chooses the gadget S^D that brings the concatenation $M \cdot S^D$ closest to the target T (according to the Euclidean distance), and then updates M to $M \cdot S^D$. Note that $\mathcal{D}$ does not have to be limited to the corpus $\mathcal{S}^B$ of benign scripts for the domain, and indeed does not even have to contain any such scripts. This makes the attack also viable for the case where the attacker has access to the target model $\mathcal{F}$ but not the training dataset $\mathcal{D}$ (which is only relevant from a theoretical point of view, because in our domain of interest building $\mathcal{D}$ can trivially be achieved by crawling the victim website.)

4.4 Correctness

An important question is whether the generated adversarial code successfully executes the exploit. Script stitching concatenates two valid programs, generating code which is syntactically correct by construction. Similarly, gadget composition grows a script by adding syntactically correct program snippets. We empirically verified syntactic correctness by parsing each stitched script; this resulted in only a handful of corner cases being discarded. We note that both operations may still introduce semantic inconsistencies (e.g., variable aliasing); however, due to the dynamic nature of JavaScript interpretation, any such issue will cause an error *after* the malicious code has been executed. For subtree editing, we parse each generated script to ensure syntactic correctness. We also manually checked a number of generated samples and determined that the script would indeed execute up to the entrypoint of the malicious code. We note that all methods can generate multiple adversarial samples from a single malicious one, maximizing the probability of obtaining one or more working scripts.

The only tricky point concerns the generation of the gadget dictionary $\mathcal{D}$ for the gadget composition attack. In our experiments, we generated such dictionary by randomly extracting 250,000 AST subtrees, ranging in size from 1 to 100 nodes, from our script dataset (ref. Sect. 6). To reduce the chance of breaking JavaScript semantic by concatenating malformed gadgets, when mining gadgets the algorithm only considers AST subtrees whose root node can appear as child of the AST root node type. The set of suitable AST node types is automatically learned by analyzing the structure of scripts in the JavaScript dataset.

5   Implementation

In order to generate the script corpus used for our evaluation (Sect. 6), we adapted the web scraper open-sourced by the CSPAutoGen project [19]. This scraper crawls a list of target websites, saving extracted JavaScript snippets into a MongoDB instance. For convenience, we used the same approach to store adversarial scripts generated by our attacks; all of our attack tools store their output as MongoDB collections.

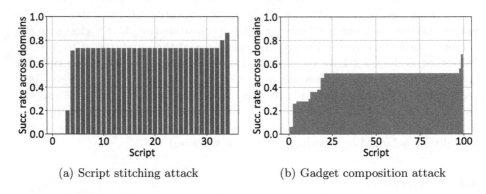

(a) Script stitching attack   (b) Gadget composition attack

Fig. 2. Success rate of each script against JaSt for different attacks

The components implementing our subtree editing attack (ref. Sect. 4.1) and the dictionary generation for our gadget composition attack (Sect. 4.3) were implemented as a set of Java classes totaling 7222 lines of code. This codebase also includes a suite of AST analysis tools by Falleri et al. [7], which we used for their efficient implementation of tree-edit distance computation. Internally, our program analysis routines leverage Java's Nashorn JavaScript parser. Interestingly, Nashorn defines a set of AST node types which is both quantitatively and qualitatively different from that defined by Esprima, which is the parser used by the JaSt classifier for feature computation. However, we found that this fact does not prevent isomorphic scripts generated by our tool to be effective against JaSt. This observation suggests that the effectiveness of this attack may not depend on the specific choice of AST-based features, instead reflecting an inherent fragility of such features in general. The script-stitching attack (Sect. 4.2) and gadget composition attacks were implemented as suite of Python tools totaling ~300 lines of code.

In order to evaluate the performance of CSPAutoGen [19] and JaSt [9] in identifying malicious JavaScript code, we used the respective implementations open-sourced by their authors.

6 Experimental Evaluation

In this section we evaluate the robustness of two state-of-the-art techniques for malicious JavaScript detection, CSPAutoGen [19] and JaSt [9]. We aim to answering the following questions:

1. **Are the attacks identified in this paper effective in generating adversarial scripts?** Section 6.3 shows that subtree editing, script stitching, and gadget composition can generate adversarial scripts that go undetected by JaSt and CSPAutoGen between 3% and 47% of the cases, depending on the combination of classifier and attack method.
2. **What is the degree to which different domains are vulnerable to adversarial JavaScript samples?** Our analysis in Sect. 6.4 shows that a per-domain JaSt classifier would be vulnerable to one or more attack script in 96% of the domains under consideration. A CSPAutoGen classifier would be vulnerable for 27% of the domains.
3. **Does knowledge of classifier model lead to the creation of more effective adversarial scripts compared to knowledge of training dataset alone?** Section 6.5 shows that knowledge of the model leads to a small but significant increase in the number of successfully obfuscated scripts (45 additional adversarial variants across 50 domains).

Table 1. JavaScript dataset summary

Dataset	#Domains	#Scripts	Avg script len [char]
Benign	306	35632	2763
Malicious	N/A	1327	5068

6.1 Dataset and Infrastructure

To extensively evaluate the robustness of the target classifiers, we randomly selected 300 websites from Alexa's Top-500 and crawled them as described in Sect. 5. To ensure a realistic corpus of malicious JavaScript snippets, we used a publicly-available collection by the security collective GeeksOnSecurity [1]. Both datasets (benign and malicious) are summarized in Table 1. Our tooling and implementation are described in Sect. 5. We ran all experiments on a MacBook Pro laptop with a quad-core 2.6 Ghz Intel Core i7 CPU, 16 GB of RAM, and 500 GB of storage. The laptop runs MacOS Mojave 10.14.

6.2   Baseline Classifier Performance

JaSt: In order to evaluate the best-case performance of JaSt in the absence of adaptive adversarial samples, we trained it on 303 domains from our dataset (the remaining 3 domains triggered bugs in the classifier code which prevented their evaluation). In each instance, we used all the scripts scraped from a domain as the benign dataset, and our collection of malicious scripts as the malicious dataset. We first used the same dataset for training and evaluation, asking JaSt to re-label each script on which it was trained. JaSt performs consistently well in this experiment, achieving on average **0% false negatives (evasion rate)** and a **2.3% false positives (false alarm rate)** across all domains.

Since assuming that JaSt has access of the entirety of both the benign and malicious script sets of interest is unrealistic, we also performed a round of experiments where we split the dataset in disjoint training and evaluation subsets using 10-fold cross validation. This results in a **0.5% evasion rate** and a **6% false alarm rate**.

CSPAutoGen: We generated CSPAutoGen templates for each of 227 domains. We could not test the remaining 79, as the current implementation of CSPAutoGen crashes while processing their scripts. Since CSPAutoGen generates templates using benign scripts exclusively, no malicious script was used for training. We then used CSPAutoGen to analyze each script in the training corpus, and all the scripts in the malicious corpus. CSPAutoGen achieves on average **0.06% evasion rate** and a **1.5% false alarm rate** across all domains. Splitting the dataset in training and evaluation and performing 10-fold cross-validation results in **0.06% evasion rate** and **11% false alarm rate**.

Discussion: Although the evasion rate remains negligibly low for both classifiers, both suffer from a somewhat high false alarm rate. This is a significant hurdle to deployment, as even a handful of false positives may disrupt website functionality. Even when using the same dataset for training and evaluation, we note that both classifiers present occasional significant deviations from the false alarm average. This results in extremely high false alarm rates for some domains. For JaSt, these occurrences mostly occur for pathological domains where the scraper could only successfully extract a few scripts. The most extreme case is `theglobeandmail.com`, which only includes 2 benign scripts, both misclassified, giving a 100% false positive rate. CSPAutoGen occasionally exhibits unacceptably high false positive rate even for domains for which a significant amount of data is available. For example, CSPAutoGen misclassifies 29 of the 70 benign scripts scraped from `360.cn`, yielding a false positive rate of 41%.

6.3   Evaluation of Attacks

Attacks Setup. To launch subtree editing and script stitching attacks for a given domain, we simply attempted to combine each malicious script of interest with each benign script in the domain, according to each attack's semantics. This involves attempting to perform a suitable tree-swap in subtree editing - we include each distinct point of the benign script at which an attack can be injected as a separate sample. For script stitching, combination consists of concatenating the given attack script and the target benign one. The tree-edit distance threshold for subtree editing was set to 20.[1] For gadget composition, we mutated each malicious script towards a target feature vector by adding gadgets from the dictionary described in Sect. 4.4. We generate the target feature vector by extracting the highest-ranked (by feature importance) 35 features from each model, and computing the average value of each feature across the benign scripts for that domain. We note that this is a rather crude way to generate adversarial feature vectors, however it serves as a lower-bound on attack effectiveness.

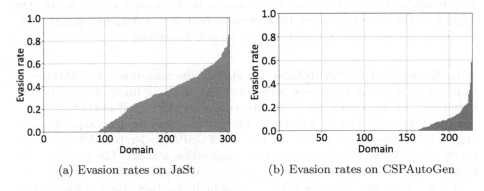

(a) Evasion rates on JaSt   (b) Evasion rates on CSPAutoGen

Fig. 3. Evasion rates for subtree editing attack

Attacks Against JaSt. While the performance of our current toolchain is practical for attack generation (see Sect. 6.7), the unoptimized nature of the code and the file-based interface used for some operations result in high sample generation times for some combinations of attacks/domains. To keep experiment times manageable, we used different randomly selected sets of malicious scripts in each attack: 1291 malicious scripts for subtree editing, 34 for script stitching, and 100 for gadget compositions. For gadget composition, we also limited the number of considered domains to 100. Figure 2 depicts, for each malicious script, the number of domains for which the corresponding JaSt classifier is vulnerable. We consider a domain to be vulnerable to a script if one or more adversarial variants of that script successfully go undetected. Figure 2a depicts the results for script stitching, and Fig. 2b for gadget composition. On average, script stitching results in a **15% evasion rate** (considering adversarial scripts only) across domains. Gadget composition achieved **47% evasion rate** across domains.

---

[1] Experimentally, we determined that increasing the maximum tree-edit distance above 20 results in a sharp increase in the detection rate for the generated samples. This applies to both classifiers in our examination.

In practice, the low evasion rate result for script stitching is misleading as the attack generates numerous variants of each malicious script; even if most of those variants are not successful, the attack is still effective when at least one working variant is found. Indeed, on average script stitching can generate at least one successful adversarial variant for **68%** of all considered scripts. The percentage is **46%** for gadget composition (note that gadget composition only generates one variant per script per domain, so this result is identical to the evasion rate above.)

We do not plot per-script results for subtree editing as that attack only generates successful adversarial samples from 8 scripts out of 1291. 7 of these scripts generate one or more samples for 237 (out of 304) domains, and 1 for 236 domains. The set of vulnerable domains is the same for each script. On aggregate, this attack achieves **46% evasion rate** across domains against JaSt. Figure 3a shows evasion rate per domain for subtree editing.

Attacks Against CSPAutoGen. To analyze the robustness of CSPAutoGen to adversarial samples, we only considered the subtree editing attack. By construction, CSPAutoGen looks at the structure of the AST itself and not at feature counts, therefore feature-based attacks like stitching and gadget composition are largely ineffective (moreover, access to a set of CSPAutoGen templates does not provide useful guidance for the gadget composition attack). The price for this increased robustness is the high false positive rate highlighted in Sect. 6.2.

Figure 3b shows the evasion rate per domain for this attack. Overall, this attack achieves **3.1% evasion rate** across domains against CSPAutoGen. Note that this value, and the evasion rates shown in Fig. 3b, are likely to *underestimate* the attack effectiveness. The implementation of CSPAutoGen appears to have a bug that occasionally results in partial crash and a reported evasion rate of 0% for some domains.

Number of Variants. We now consider the overall number of successful variants generated by each method, i.e., the number of malicious scripts that successfully get misclassified as benign by the victim classifier. For the attacks against JaSt, we found, on average **891** working attack variants per domain using subtree editing, **606** using script stitching, and **47** using gadget composition. For CSPAutoGen, subtree editing generated on average **43** successful variants per domain. While the ability to generate even a single working variant per domain is troubling, these numbers indicate a highly-effective set of attacks.

6.4   Per-domain Analysis

Given that the attacks above prove to be effective in a significant percentage of cases, we move to looking at how these attacks affect different domain. We first evaluated JaSt. We only consider the 34 attack scripts and 49 domains on which we executed all attacks in our evaluation. Figure 4a plots the cumulative distribution of the number of adversarial scripts per domain which go undetected by JaSt. In this case, we aggregate scripts produced by all three attack methods. Overall, **47 out of 49** domains (96%) are vulnerable to one or more attacks. The maximum number of working attack scripts per domain is **16515**.

We then performed the same evaluation for CSPAutoGen; in this case we only considered the subtree editing attack. Our data cover 227 domains. Figure 4b plots the cumulative distribution of number of working attack scripts per domain. Overall, **62 out of 227** domains (27%) are vulnerable to at least one attack script. The maximum number of working attack scripts per domain is **702**.

6.5 Knowledge of Dataset vs Model

The final part of our evaluation asks whether knowledge of both the training dataset $\mathcal{D}$ and a victim model $\mathcal{F}$ can provide an attacker with an advantage over knowledge of $\mathcal{D}$ only. For this, we look at our results for both the stitching and the gadget composition attack, considering a set of 34 scripts and 50 domains on which both attacks were executed.

Due to its simplicity, our gadget composition attack is likely to achieve a lower bound for a model-aware attack. In particular, the current version of the algorithm attempts to generate at most one malicious variant per domain; due to this limitation, gadget composition generates *less* working adversarial variants per domain than the simpler script stitching attack[2]. Even with this limitation, we find **45** combinations of script and domain for which stitching could not generate any working adversarial variants, while gadget composition could. We therefore conclude that knowledge of $\mathcal{F}$ can provide an attacker with additional power to generate undetectable script mutations.

6.6 Impact of Adversarial Training

While a full discussion of defenses is outside the scope of this paper, we briefly consider the approach which is most readily available to a defender, which is *adversarial training*. With adversarial training, adversarial scripts generated via an attack method of interest are added back into the training dataset and labeled as malicious. The typical drawback of adversarial training is that it tends to decrease the discerning power of a classifier, increasing the false alarm rate, due to the fact that some malicious samples in the dataset have features are by construction very similar to those of benign samples.

In order to assess the effectiveness of adversarial training, we evaluate JaSt against subtree editing, before and after adding a subset of the generated attack scripts to the training set. Since it is unrealistic to assume that a defender could generate all possible adversarial samples of interest, we used 10-fold cross validation on the dataset.

While adversarial training does allow the classifier to identify most adversarial samples, it also causes the (already high) false alarm rate to double from **6%**

---

[2] It is in principle possible to extend the algorithm with backtracking during the gadget search process, enabling it to generate an arbitrary number of variants.

to 12%. Since false alarms have the potential to break website functionality (by preventing legitimate scripts from being served), this result suggests that adversarial training cannot protect against this class of attacks.

6.7   Execution Times

Our subtree editing can compare a malicious script with a candidate benign host (and embed the malicious script in the benign one, if successful) at a rate of 1 comparison per second. For script stitching, adversarial scripts can be generated at 1 per 5.7 s, and for gadget composition, 1 per 57 s.

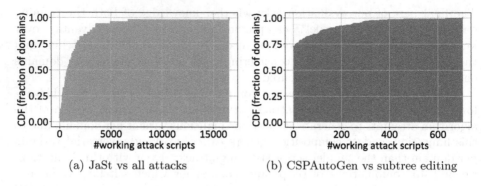

(a) JaSt vs all attacks   (b) CSPAutoGen vs subtree editing

Fig. 4. CDF of successful number of attacks per domain

6.8   Analysis of Results

The results in this section highlight two important observations. First, existing state-of-the-art AST-based classifiers are extremely effective in identifying non-adversarial malicious scripts, although they also appear to incur a high false positive rate which may hamper their use in practice. Second, the same classifiers appear to be relatively fragile to low-complexity adversarial attacks. The considered attacks were able to generate tens to hundreds of successful adversarial scripts per domain, without requiring any customization of the source code of the seed scripts. There are also specific findings related to the type of classifier:

Structural Classifiers. As we show in Sect. 6, mimicry of structural properties of benign scripts can frequently be achieved on a variety of sites. Through the use of our subtree editing attack, we show that 27% of sites can admit a structural replacement that is undetectable by our representative structural classifier. We also note that the only successful attack against the structural classifier was the subtree editing attack, which uses the threat model of the reconnaissance attacker, which relies on a weak set of capabilities. Indeed, note that denying the attacker the capabilities requires restricting the access of a visitor to benign scripts on a page, which is likely to break the public functionality of the site.

Feature-Based Classifiers. In the conceptual framework proposed by Maiorca et al. [18], classifiers may exhibit *learning vulnerability*, *feature vulnerability*, or both. Learning vulnerabilities stem from artifacts of the training process: if the region of feature space mapped to benign classes is unnecessarily large, an attacker has significant freedom in generating malicious samples. However, this vulnerability can generally be remediated by adversarial training (which causes the boundaries of benign classes to tighten around actual practical benign samples). Feature vulnerability instead derives from the classifier features being intrinsically unable to separate benign and malicious classes; i.e., it is possible for an attacker to generate malicious samples that are, for the classifier purpose, indistinguishable from benign ones. This second class of vulnerabilities cannot be prevented without changing the features themselves. Results in Sect. 6.6 suggest that the feature-based classifier under consideration may suffer, at least in part, of the latter type of vulnerability (i.e., there exist some attack scripts which are feature-wise indistinguishable from benign ones).

7 Related Work

To our knowledge, our work is the first to systematically build and apply a system of threat models against JavaScript syntactic detectors. We also believe that our attacks constitute novel techniques to cause misclassification by existing JavaScript detectors. In this section, we discuss previous work that is similar in spirit or approach to various aspects of this paper.

Malicious JavaScript Classifiers. Our work is inspired by the proliferation of tools to identify malicious JavaScript. While we focus on [9, 19], we use these tools as representative of a broad range of previous work in the area. Some related tools include the feature-based Bayesian analysis classifier [4,13], which operate over features of the AST or lexical tokens. CuJo [20] uses Support Vector Machines (SVM) trained over static script features. Synode [24] is another template-based JavaScript security tool, though it is intended to work server-side to identify malicious NPM packages. Although Synode is a multi-component system for defending from injections, it does use a template-based mechanism to restrict what code can be run by injection. Although we note that the SyNode templates may fall victim to the same attacks we describe, defeating other components (such as script injection sanitization) is out of scope for this work.

Ultimately, we focused on CSPAutoGen and JaSt because they represent the most recent and distinct work. We believe that our results are likely to translate to these other systems, though we leave the analysis to future work.

Mimicry Attacks. Attempts to fool automatic security classification tools are by no means new. Wagner et al. introduced the term mimicry attacks to describe an intrusion that is obfuscated in order to avoid detection [26] and automatic mimicry attacks have also been used to mask malicious system call sequences [11]. Conceptually-related attacks have also been demonstrated against PDF [23] and Flash-based [18] classifiers. Ersan et al. [6] evaluate AST-based evasion of detectors for HTML-based malware; however their approach by design does not guarantee that semantic correctness of malicious code is preserved.

Finally, HIDENOSEEK by Fass et al. [8] is a work of which we became aware immediately after it was published, and subsequently after the development of our attacks. The HIDENOSEEK attacker fits within the general framework of our reconnaissance attacker (ref. Sect. 3), but their paper does not consider the other threat models. The HIDENOSEEK attack itself is conceptually similar to the subtree-editing attack described here (the differences are discussed in Sect. 4.1). A preliminary evaluation of HIDENOSEEK on a subset of our data suggests that their attack has a higher success rate than subtree editing (on a set of 100 randomly-selected malicious/benign scripts pairs, HIDENOSEEK found one or more embeddings in 66 cases), at the price of a higher execution time (2 orders of magnitude slower than subtree editing, with execution times affected by script size; we discarded one additional pair on which HIDENOSEEK executed for 17 h without terminating). This is consistent with the designs of both algorithms: HIDENOSEEK can split a malicious AST into subtrees and embed each separately; this relaxes the constraints on the candidate benign host but increases complexity and computation time. Conversely, subtree editing needs to find a near-exact AST match for the malicious script, but can leverage decades of research in efficient tree-edit distance algorithms to quickly find a candidate.

Adversarial Machine Learning. Related work in AML has already shown the fragility of program classifiers in other domains [5,12,15,18]. However, features in these work typically consist of presence/absence of context-independent entities—such as specific system calls [15] or entries in an application's manifest [12]. In these cases, there tend to be trivial mappings between an adversarial feature vector and a concrete attack program (e.g., add appropriate entries to a malicious manifest to masquerade it as a benign one). In our case, features include presence or absence of specific subtrees in a program's abstract syntax tree. When restructuring a program to alter its features, the set of transformations is bound by the requirement that the resulting AST must be correct. For example, it is not possible to alter features by appending a function subtree to a integer variable, as the latter is bound to appear exclusively as leaf node. Our solution is to ensure that the procedure used to generate candidate adversarial programs guarantees correctness by construction.

Finally, there exist a number of works that focus on altering *dynamic* program behavior in order to evade classifiers [14,21,22]. None of these works focus on JavaScript, and they are orthogonal to the goal of this paper.

8   Conclusion

In this work, we show that adversaries can leverage their knowledge of the target to better disguise malicious JavaScript code as benign, and propose a framework of threat models to capture different real-world adversarial capabilities. We believe that this work makes an important contribution in motivating the creation of new defensive measures and best practices for classifiers in realistic settings.

Acknowledgments. We thank the anonymous reviewers and our shepherd, Yuan Zhang, for their insightful comments. We further thank: Louis Narmour and Devin Dennis for their help in building infrastructure and dataset; Bruce Kapron and Somesh Jha for informative early discussions on the problems tackled in this paper.

References

1. GitHub - geeksonsecurity/js-malicious-dataset, December 2019. https://github.com/geeksonsecurity/js-malicious-dataset
2. Biggio, B., Roli, F.: Wild patterns: Ten years after the rise of adversarial machine learning. Pattern Recogn. **84**, 317–331 (2018)
3. Calzavara, S., Rabitti, A., Bugliesi, M.: Content security problems?: evaluating the effectiveness of content security policy in the wild. In: CCS (2016)
4. Curtsinger, C., Livshits, B., Zorn, B.G., Seifert, C.: ZOZZLE: fast and precise in-browser javascript malware detection. In: USENIX Security Symposium (2011)
5. Demontis, A., et al.: Yes, machine learning can be more secure! a case study on android malware detection. IEEE Trans. Dependable Secure Comput. **PP**, 1 (2018)
6. Ersan, E., Malka, L., Kapron, B.M.: Semantically non-preserving transformations for antivirus evaluation. In: FPS (2016)
7. Falleri, J.R., Morandat, F., Blanc, X., Martinez, M., Monperrus, M.: Fine-grained and accurate source code differencing. In: ASE (2014)
8. Fass, A., Backes, M., Stock, B.: HideNoSeek: camouflaging malicious JavaScript in benign ASTs. In: CCS (2019)
9. Fass, A., Krawczyk, R.P., Backes, M., Stock, B.: JaSt: fully syntactic detection of malicious (Obfuscated) JavaScript. In: DIMVA (2018)
10. Fredrikson, M., Jha, S., Ristenpart, T.: Model inversion attacks that exploit confidence information and basic countermeasures. In: CCS (2015)
11. Giffin, J.T., Jha, S., Miller, B.P.: Automated discovery of mimicry attacks. In: RAID (2006)
12. Grosse, K., Papernot, N., Manoharan, P., Backes, M., McDaniel, P.: Adversarial examples for malware detection. In: ESORICS (2017)
13. Hao, Y., Liang, H., Zhang, D., Zhao, Q., Cui, B.: JavaScript malicious codes analysis based on naive bayes classification. In: International Conference on P2P, Parallel, Grid, Cloud and Internet Computing (2014)
14. Hu, W., Tan, Y.: Black-box attacks against RNN based malware detection algorithms. arXiv:1705.08131 [cs], May 2017. http://arxiv.org/abs/1705.08131
15. Hu, W., Tan, Y.: Generating adversarial malware examples for black-box attacks based on GAN. arXiv:1702.05983 [cs], February 2017
16. Leyden, J.: Payment-card-skimming Magecart strikes again: Zero out of five for infecting e-retail sites, October 2018. https://www.theregister.com/2018/10/09/magecart_payment_card_malware/
17. Kantchelian, A., Tygar, J.D., Joseph, A.D.: Evasion and hardening of tree ensemble classifiers. In: ICML (2016)
18. Maiorca, D., Biggio, B., Chiappe, M.E., Giacinto, G.: Adversarial detection of flash malware: limitations and open issues. arXiv:1710.10225 [cs], October 2017

19. Pan, X., Cao, Y., Liu, S., Zhou, Y., Chen, Y., Zhou, T.: CSPAutoGen: black-box enforcement of content security policy upon real-world websites. In: CCS (2016)
20. Rieck, K., Krueger, T., Dewald, A.: Cujo: efficient detection and prevention of drive-by-download attacks. In: ACSAC (2010)
21. Rosenberg, I., Shabtai, A., Elovici, Y., Rokach, L.: Query-efficient GAN based black-box attack against sequence based machine and deep learning classifiers. arXiv:1804.08778 [cs] (Apr 2018), http://arxiv.org/abs/1804.08778
22. Rosenberg, I., Shabtai, A., Rokach, L., Elovici, Y.: Generic black-box end-to-end attack against state of the art API call based malware classifiers. In: RAID (2018)
23. Srndic, N., Laskov, P.: Practical evasion of a learning-based classifier: a case study. In: IEEE S&P (2014)
24. Staicu, C.A., Pradel, M., Livshits, B.: Synode: Understanding and automatically preventing injection attacks on node. js. In: NDSS (2018)
25. Szegedy, C., et al.: Intriguing properties of neural networks. In: ICLR (2014)
26. Wagner, D., Soto, P.: Mimicry attacks on host-based intrusion detection systems. In: CCS (2002)

An Encryption System for Securing Physical Signals

Yisroel Mirsky[1,2]([✉]), Benjamin Fedidat[3], and Yoram Haddad[3]

[1] Georgia Institute of Technology, Atlanta, GA, USA
[2] Ben-Gurion University, Beer Sheva, Israel
yisroel@post.bgu.ac.il
[3] Jerusalem College of Technology, Jerusalem, Israel
ben@fedidat.com, haddad@jct.ac.il

Abstract. Secure communication is a necessity. However, encryption is commonly only applied to the upper layers of the protocol stack. This exposes network information to eavesdroppers, including the channel's type, data rate, protocol, and routing information. This may be solved by encrypting the physical layer, thereby securing all subsequent layers. In order for this method to be practical, the encryption must be quick, preserve bandwidth, and must also deal with the issues of noise mitigation and synchronization.

In this paper, we present the Vernam Physical Signal Cipher (VPSC): a novel cipher which can encrypt the harmonic composition of any analog waveform. The VPSC accomplishes this by applying a modified Vernam cipher to the signal's frequency magnitudes and phases. This approach is fast and preserves the signal's bandwidth. In the paper, we offer methods for noise mitigation and synchronization, and evaluate the VPSC over a noisy wireless channel with multi-path propagation interference.

Keywords: Physical channel security · Vernam Cipher · Harmonic encryption · FFT · Signal encryption · Waveforms

1 Introduction

Knowledge is power. It is in the interest of two communicating parties to secure their communication channel to the degree that no information about the channel or the communication is revealed. Today it is common practice to encrypt the payloads of higher level protocols in the communication protocol stack (*Layer 4 and above in the OSI model*). This is analogous to encrypting the content of a letter but not the envelope itself. Doing so allows onlookers (eavesdroppers) to see the frame's header information in plaintext and even modify it. This is an even more serious problem for radio transmissions over public domains [22]. For

Y. Mirsky—Part of this author's work was done in the Jerusalem College of Technology.

© ICST Institute for Computer Sciences, Social Informatics and Telecommunications Engineering 2020
Published by Springer Nature Switzerland AG 2020. All Rights Reserved
N. Park et al. (Eds.): SecureComm 2020, LNICST 335, pp. 211–232, 2020.
https://doi.org/10.1007/978-3-030-63086-7_13

instance, by targeting specific bits, an attacker is able to perform energy-efficient jamming [14].

Solutions to this problem have been investigated thoroughly [3,18,27]. A common solution is to encrypt the data-link layer (*Layer 2*) before it is passed on to the physical layer (*Layer 1*). MACSec [20] is an example of such a protocol for multi-hop wired networks while the most common wireless encryption protocols are WEP and WPA/2. However, encrypting the *Layer 2* bit-stream does not provide secrecy for all information obtainable from the physical channel's characteristics. Examples of this information include traffic statistics, data rates, number of physical channels, service priorities, data size, data packet frequency, baud rate, modulation, and channel bandwidth. Knowledge of this information can be used to infer the transmission equipment, message importance, channel content, and channel capacity. This information leakage is analogous to writing letters in code and mailing them to a friend. One who sees these letters cannot explicitly determine the content, however the shape (bandwidth), address (protocol) and transmission frequency (bit-rate) can reveal significant information. Another advantage to securing the physical signal is that doing so protects the channel from all attacks that require observation of the bits. For example, protocol manipulation, timing inference, and replay attacks.

Therefore, in order to make a communication channel completely secure, the channel in its entirety should be protected, like a curtain over the entire operation. By extension, it should also be impossible to determine whether the intercepted signal was originally of a digital or analog origin. This level of security can only be achieved by acting at *layer 1* of the OSI protocol stack. For this reason, research on the topic of physical layer security (*Layer 1*) has gained attention over the years [3].

In this paper, we propose an application of the Vernam Cipher to analog signals, which we call the Vernam Physical Signal Cipher (VPSC). The VPSC is unique because it encrypts waveform signals on the frequency domain while achieving a high degree of secrecy on *Layer 1*.

There are several notable advantages to working on the frequency domain:

1. **Complete Information Privacy:** By encrypting the raw signal itself, no information about the channel is exposed. Regardless of waveform, the encrypted signal appears as white noise.
2. **Bandwidth Preservation:** This aspect is particularly desirable for radio applications where spectrum is a commodity. This is in contrast to performing modulo-based encryption on samples from the temporal plane, since doing so adds energy to all frequencies in the spectrum. In order to preserve the original signal's bandwidth, transformation in the frequency domain is necessary.
3. **Selective Band Encryption:** This process is similar to a band-pass filter since an entire signal's spectrum can be presented to the VPSC, but only selected frequency bands will be encrypted (regardless of the bands' content).
4. **Hardware Parallelization:** The signal's spectrum can be split and then encrypted in parallel by independent processors in real-time. This is useful when dealing with very large bands and weak processors. This modularity

makes the technology highly scalable to the consumer's needs. When operating directly on the temporal plane, this type of parallelization cannot be achieved when targeting specific frequency bands.

Although some of these advantages are present in current wireless security channels, the advantages altogether are unavailable in any single one [18,22,27]. The aim of the VPSC is to provide a secure connection (one that does not leak any information, even about the channel itself) between two communicating parties over a single physical link – such as a radio channel or an optical trunk line. The VPSC can also be applied to a multi-hop network if each link is protected separately, and the routing nodes are considered trusted.
Altogether, this paper has three main contributions:

1. **A Generic Physical Layer Cipher:** A method for applying the One-Time Pad [21]/Vernam Cipher [24] to the frequency domain, enabling all of the advantages listed above.
2. **Noise Mitigation for Modulo Operation on Waveforms:** We propose two noise mitigation techniques which enable modulo-based signal encryption (on both the time and frequency domains), and a method which combines the two into one. These noise mitigation techniques are necessary because modulo operations on analog signals are extremely sensitive to the presence of noise.
3. **Simulations, Source Code, and Prototyping:** We evaluate the VPSC's practicality by simulating a realistic wireless channel with distortions, interference, and noise. We also provide the Python source code for researchers to reproduce our work.[1] Finally, we demonstrate the technology by implementing the VPSC over two Arduino Duo development boards.

2 Related Work

In 1919, Gilbert Vernam patented a XOR-based cipher known as the Vernam Cipher [24]. This cipher works by applying the XOR operation between a message and a secret pseudo-random key. In 1949, Claude Shannon published a historical paper [21] in which communication secrecy was studied from the perspective of information theory. He proved the theoretical significance of the Vernam Cipher and proposed the one-time pad (OTP), also known as the Shannon Cipher System (SCS), a cipher capable of perfect secrecy. The OTP is essentially a Vernam Cipher which uses a truly random key.

Later in 1975, Wyner wrote his seminal paper that describes a degraded wiretap channel and provides information-theoretic concepts needed for the domain [25]. Loosely speaking, a wiretap channel (WTC) is one where the sender (Alice) transmits a signal to the legitimate receiver (Bob) while an eavesdropper (Eve) intercepts it. However, the signal Eve intercepts is noisier than Bob's, allowing Bob to obtain information that Eve cannot.

---

[1] The Python source code to the VPSC can be found online: https://github.com/ymirsky/VPSC-py.

We can relate the SCS to the WTC because both can be directly applied to quantized signal samples. However, there is an inherent difference between the SCS and the WTC. The SCS's secrecy is solely based on information theory, while the WTC's secrecy is based on exploiting the physical traits of communication media [5,25]. In [26], the authors find the secrecy capacity of a shared-key WTC in the presence of noise. Later, the authors in [12] generalized [26] by considering any channel (not necessarily noisy). It can be seen in these works that a secret-key WTC without the presence of noise and with maximum secrecy is essentially an SCS. Therefore, in our work, we focus on the SCS since its theory forms the basis for the VPSC.

In [13], the author proposes two methods for encrypting a physical signal: amplitude log masking (ALM) and sample-wise RSA encryption. In ALM, each signal sample in the time-plane is encrypted by taking the logarithm of the sample multiplied by a random value (a key). However, the ALM method does not provide a high degree of secrecy since ALM simply masks (obfuscates) the samples with a key, and attacks such as correlation analysis [10] can be used to reveal the masked message. Moreover, ALM is very sensitive to noise since errors are exponentially multiplied during the decryption process. This makes ALM impractical to use in noisy channels.

In the RSA method, the RSA [19] cipher is applied to each sample from the time-plane. The RSA method requires that the samples be quantized to discrete values. This is necessary in order to perform the power operation of RSA without float-point overflows. As a result, the RSA method is highly susceptible to even the slightest amount of noise. This is because RSA has a non-linear relationship between the cipher-text and the plain-text. As a consequence, every single rounding error in the cryptogram results in a completely different deciphered value. This behavior is similar to how the output of a hash map is sensitive to changes in its key. This means that the RSA method is not a practical solution for real-world channels.

Both the ALM and RSA methods use a significant amount of energy over the entire spectrum. These are undesirable side effects, especially for wireless channels. The VPSC, on the other hand, uses the same amount of bandwidth as the original signal, and a similar amount of energy as well. Furthermore, the VPSC is much more robust to noise and interference, since the modulo operation of the SCS maps noise close to the original sample's value (discussed further in Sect. 8).

In [16], the authors propose frequency component scrambling (FCS) via a Fast Fourier Transform (FFT) to protect audio channels. Their method is to scramble the frequency components (f.c.) of the given signal to obfuscate its contents. However, scrambling does not provide a high level of secrecy. Regardless of the number of f.c.s, it is possible to descramble the signal by analyzing the correlation of the f.c. magnitudes, similarly to what was done in [10]. For example, if a 16-QAM modulation is applied to the carrier frequency f_c, FCS is used to encrypt the band surrounding f_c, then FCS would simply move the contents of f_c to a neighboring bin (see Fig. 1). This is similar to frequency hopping

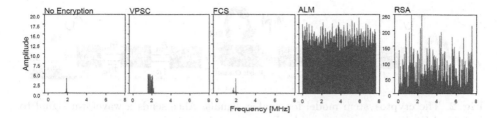

Fig. 1. The spectrum of a 16-QAM channel, with a carrier wave of 1.9 MHz, encrypted by the various methods.

except applied to a much smaller band, and with only one hop. Therefore, FCS is only applicable to the prevention of casual eavesdroppers.

Figure 1 shows the spectrum of an encrypted 16-QAM signal carried on 1.9 MHz wave, using each of the methods. It can be seen that the methods either do not sufficiently secure the channel (FCS), or use the entire spectrum with a large amount of energy (ALM and RSA).

Therefore, to the best of our knowledge, the VPSC is the first physical layer encryption system capable of perfect secrecy that operates directly on the frequency domain, and is also robust to noise.

3   Cryptographic Model

In this Section, we introduce the notations which will be used throughout this paper. We also apply the standard cryptographic model to the waveform message space.

In this paper, we assume that we are dealing with discretely sampled and quantized real signals. Let there be Q discrete levels of quantization such that the highest level is Q_U and the lowest is Q_L. Let $S \subseteq \mathbb{Z}^N$ be the collection of all possible signal segments to be encrypted from some particular channel T, where $N = 2^k, k \in \mathbb{N}$ and $s \in S$ has the form

$$s = \begin{bmatrix} v_1 \\ \vdots \\ v_N \end{bmatrix} \tag{1}$$

where $Q_L \leq v_i \leq Q_U$ for every i. In other words, s is a frame of N quantized samples, taken from the time domain, which we want to encrypt.

Let f_s be the sample rate of the system such that $f_s \geq 2B$, where B is the essential bandwidth of the selected signals from S (Nyquist rate). Let the message space M (the collection of all possible plaintext messages) of the cryptosystem be defined as the collection of all discrete Fourier transforms (DFT) of the vectors in S, in polar form, such that

$$M = \left\{ (m_m, m_a) \middle| \begin{array}{l} m_m = |DFT[s]| \\ m_a \angle DFT[s] \end{array} \right\} \tag{2}$$

Fig. 2. The cryptosystem model for analog signals. Alice sends a waveform signal to Bob, and Eve's interception provides her with no information about it.

It is helpful to view the message $m \in M$ as the polar form of the DFT of N consecutive samples of a real-time signal segment found in S. In other words, m_m represents the frequency magnitudes and m_a denotes the frequency angles (phases) of the signal segment s.

Let ϕ be a scalar parameter which defines the maximum frequency magnitude of the cryptosystem. It is restricted to the inequality

$$\phi \geq max(m_m[i] + \varepsilon), \forall i, m_m \tag{3}$$

where ε is a small value. Let the key space K (the collection of all possible keys) of the cryptosystem be defined as a collection of all possible tuples in the form

$$k = (k_m, k_a) \tag{4}$$

where k_m and k_a are random N-length vectors which are used to encrypt magnitudes and angles respectively. Since we are dealing with real signals, k_m and k_a must be structured to conform to the DFT output from real signals.

Specifically, k_m has the structure

$$k_m = concatenate\left(0, v, \texttt{mirror}\left(v\left[2:\frac{N}{2}\right]\right)\right) \tag{5a}$$

where v is a $^N/_2$ length vector of random values on the range $[0, \phi)$, $\texttt{refl}$ is the mirror rearrangement operation on the values of some vector, and the symbol ":" indicates a range of indexes. Similarly, k_a has the structure

$$k_a = concatenate\left(a, -\texttt{refl}(a)\right) \tag{5b}$$

where a is also a $^N/_2$ length vector of random values, but on the range $[-\pi, \pi)$.

Let the key space K (the collection of all possible keys) of the cryptosystem be defined as the collection of all possible k.

The cryptogram space of the system C is equivalent to the collection of all possible real signals found in M. This is necessary in order to obtain perfect secrecy, since it must be possible to map any cryptogram $c \in C$ back to any message $m \in M$ [21].

Let the inverse-DFT (DFT^{-1}) of the cryptogram c be referred to as s', such that

$$DFT^{-1}(c) = s' \tag{6}$$

Let the general encryption function be defined as

$$e_k(m) = c \tag{7a}$$

and the general decryption function be defined as

$$d_k(c) = m \tag{7b}$$

where the key $k \in K$ is used to encrypt the message $m \in M$ and decrypt the ciphertext $c \in C$.

Now that some notation has been defined, we can present the cryptographic model used in this paper, as depicted in Fig. 2. Consider a case in which Alice wants to transmit s (a segment of some analog signal) securely to Bob so that Eve cannot obtain any information about s as it travels across the public medium. First, Alice obtains the tuple $m = (m_m, m_a)$ by converting the DFT of s into polar form. Next, Alice encrypts the frequency components (m) with (7a) by performing $e_k(m) = c$. Finally, Alice performs a DFT^{-1} on the cryptogram c and transmits the result s' over the public medium towards Bob.

Once Bob has received s' he can obtain the original s from it by performing the same steps which Alice performed, while using the decryption function (7b) instead.

This process is repeated continuously in real-time for each set of N samples that Alice wishes to send. However, each key k is selected at random from K (key generation is further described in the next Section).

4 The Vernam Physical Signal Cipher

In this Section, we define the VPSC by detailing its implementation of the encryption and decryption functions (7a, 7b). We also introduce two methods of noise mitigation which are essential for the VPSC to work in the real world. Afterwards, we review possible key-sharing options.

Let the VPSC encryption function be defined as

$$e_k(m) = \begin{Bmatrix} e_{k_m}(m_m) + \lambda \\ e_{k_a}(m_a) \end{Bmatrix} = \begin{Bmatrix} ((m_m + k_m) \bmod \phi) + \lambda \\ m_a + k_a \end{Bmatrix} = \begin{Bmatrix} c_m + \lambda \\ c_a \end{Bmatrix} = c \tag{8a}$$

and let the VPSC decryption function be defined as

$$d_k(c) = \begin{Bmatrix} d_{k_m}(c_m) - \lambda \\ d_{k_a}(c_a) \end{Bmatrix} = \begin{Bmatrix} ((c_m - k_m) \bmod \phi) - \lambda \\ c_a - k_a \end{Bmatrix} = \begin{Bmatrix} m_m - \lambda \\ m_a \end{Bmatrix} = m \tag{8b}$$

where mod is the element-wise modulo operation, k is a purely random vector selected from K, and λ is a required amplification of the encrypted signal. The parameter λ is a constant defined by the user such that $\lambda > 0$. The purpose of λ is to ensure that the phase of component n will not be lost, in the chance that $c_m[n] \approx 0$. This can legitimately occur at random, based on k_m. We note that λ does not affect the secrecy of c because we are simply amplifying the final signal.

4.1   Noise Mitigation

Since the VPSC is a physical signal cipher, it must operate according to physical constraints. One of those is ϕ; the maximum frequency magnitude of the cryptosystem. This parameter must be larger than the largest possible frequency magnitude in M, by a small amount ε, as described in (3). Setting ϕ to a value less than the largest magnitude will result in a loss of information due to the modulo operation.

The functions (8a, 8b) can provide a high level of security since they are essentially an OTP (discussed later in Sect. 5). However, their implementation in reality (as-is) does not function. This is because every communication medium adds some noise to the channel, whether it is natural noise or some other signal interference. Therefore, under normal circumstances, some energy always gets added or subtracted from some of the frequency magnitudes in c_m. This incurs an undesirable effect in the decryption process.

Depending on the amount of energy, the subtraction and then modulo of the cryptogram in (8b) can send values in m_m that were close to 0 or ϕ to the opposite extreme.

To illustrate this issue we can track the usage of the VPSC over some noisy channel. Let's say that $m_m[n]$ is the nth frequency magnitude from the original signal segment s, and that $m_m[n] = \phi - \varepsilon$, where ε is some relatively small number. Suppose that the encryption key to be used on the magnitude $m_m[n]$ is $k_m[n] = \alpha$, where $0 \leq \alpha < \phi$. Encrypting m_m with (8a) results in:

$$c_m[n] = (m_m[n] + k_m[n]) \bmod \phi = (\phi - \varepsilon + \alpha) \bmod \phi \qquad (9a)$$

Now c_m is converted into s' by (6) and transmitted over the communication medium. Assume that by doing so, the magnitude $c_m[n]$ (of s') receives some additional energy γ from noise in the channel, where $\gamma > \varepsilon$. The result is that Bob now receives a noisy cryptogram,

$$c_m[n]^* = (\phi - \varepsilon + \alpha) \bmod \phi + \gamma \qquad (9b)$$

and Bob cannot analytically determine γ since the original message magnitude $m_m[n] = \phi - \varepsilon$ is unknown to him. When Bob tries to decrypt (9b) using (8b), assuming $\gamma - \varepsilon < \phi$ the following will occur:

$$d_{k_m[n]}(c_m[n]^*) = (c_m[n]^* - k_m[n]) \bmod \phi \qquad (9c)$$

If $\alpha < \varepsilon$ then (9c) evaluates to

$$(\phi - \varepsilon + \alpha + \gamma - \alpha) \bmod \phi = (\phi - \varepsilon + \gamma) \bmod \phi = \gamma - \varepsilon \text{ since } \gamma > \varepsilon \qquad (9d)$$

If $\alpha \geq \varepsilon$ then (9c) evaluates to

$$(\alpha - \varepsilon + \gamma - \alpha) \bmod \phi = (\gamma - \varepsilon) \bmod \phi = \gamma - \varepsilon. \qquad (9e)$$

In both cases (9d, 9e), Bob will interpret s's n^{th} frequency magnitude to be a near-zero value, as opposed to the correct near maximum value (ϕ). Similarly,

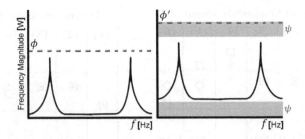

Fig. 3. A sine wave signal undergoing the PR technique. The image on the right shows the new signal after the procedure where the shaded areas provide a modulo-error "buffer zone" with a width of ψ watts each.

the same issue can be shown for near-zero values being interpreted as maximum values as well.

These unavoidable errors add a tremendous amount of noise to the decrypted signal. Therefore, since a small amount of noise energy γ can cause a large signal to noise ratio (SNR), it is impractical to implement the VPSC as-is by simply using the encryption and decryption functions (8a, 8b) without any noise mitigation. Therefore, we propose two methods of noise mitigation for the VPSC: preemptive-rise and statistical-floor.

Preemptive-Rise. The preemptive-rise (PR) technique is implemented both in the encrypter (transmitter) and decrypter (receiver). The idea is to make a buffer zone above and below the original signal's range of frequency magnitudes. This ensures that the addition of random noise will not cause any of the magnitudes to fall out of bounds during the subtraction step of (8b) as depicted in Fig. 3. This is not a conventional signal boost since non-relevant frequencies within the encrypted band will be boosted as well.

Let ψ be the width of each buffer zone in watts where $\psi \equiv u \times \sigma_0$ such that $u \in \mathbb{N}$ and σ_0 is the standard deviation of the channel's noise energy.

In order to implement PR, the encrypter and decrypter must use a larger ϕ than previously required due to the larger range of magnitude values. This larger version ϕ' can be defined as

$$\phi' = \phi + 2\psi \tag{10}$$

where ϕ is determined from (3). Furthermore, the range from which the magnitude keys can be selected (5a) must be changed to $[0, \phi')$.

The implementation of PR is equivalent to modifying the magnitude encryption function in (8a) to

$$e_{\boldsymbol{k}_m}(\boldsymbol{m}_m) = (\boldsymbol{m}_m + \boldsymbol{k}_m + \psi) \bmod \phi' \tag{11}$$

and magnitude decryption function in (8b) to

$$d_{\boldsymbol{k}_m}(\boldsymbol{c}_m) = (\boldsymbol{c}_m - \boldsymbol{k}_m) \bmod \phi' - \psi \tag{12}$$

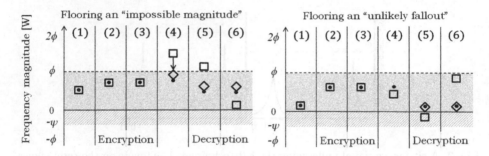

Fig. 4. A single frequency magnitude undergoing SF. Each step of the VPSC encryption/decryption is shown for when the system has no noise (filled circle), noise but no SF (square frame), and noise with SF (diamond frame). Steps are **(1)** original value, **(2)** key added, **(3)** modulo step, **(4)** transmission over channel, **(5)** key removed, and **(6)** modulo step.

Although PR can completely eliminate the noise distortions, its cryptogram (12) requires a greater transmission power than the original cryptogram (8a) due to the power change in (10).

Statistical-Floor. Unlike the PR technique, statistical-floor (SF) is implemented in the decrypter alone. The idea is to try and correct those values which have erroneously been shifted over the boundaries by the noise energy. The method tries to clean the signal by correcting erroneous fallouts before and after the subtraction step in (8b).

There are two cases which we consider erroneous: impossible magnitudes and unlikely fallouts. When there is no added noise to the signal, it is impossible to receive an encrypted magnitude above a certain value. Therefore, when we receive these "impossible magnitudes" the only conclusion we can have is that they were affected by some positive noise. More specifically, when there is no noise, the largest frequency magnitude possible is $\phi - \varepsilon$.[2] When there is noise, it is possible to receive a magnitude above ϕ. Therefore, we can conclude that any received magnitudes greater than or equal to ϕ should be floored to $\phi - \varepsilon$ before the subtraction step (8b). An illustration of this technique can be found at the top of Fig. 4.

This flooring procedure can be done without any prior knowledge about the original signal. However, after the subtraction step, some values end up just above or below 0. Without knowing the original signal, it is impossible to determine if the values had initially been just above 0 or had been altered as a result of noise. As discussed earlier, these values could add a large amount of noise to the signal after the modulo step. Fortunately, if we have some statistical information about the original signal, then we can attempt to correct these values (unlikely fallouts).

---

[2] The largest magnitude of the system is $\phi - \varepsilon$ and not *phi*, similar to how in *nmodm*, the largest n can be is $m - 1$.

For instance, let us assume that it is known that the original signal has most of its magnitude values close to 0 (like the signal in Fig. 3). In this case, after the subtraction step, we will assume that all values in the range $[-\psi, 0)$ were supposed to be just above 0 but were shifted down by noise. To correct them, we will floor them to 0. The same idea can be applied if we have prior knowledge that the original signal is mostly made up of large magnitudes. An illustration of this technique can be found at the bottom of Fig. 4. This figure shows that the error is minimized by SF in both cases. Furthermore, in the case of "impossible magnitudes", a potentially high level of noise can be mitigated.

In Algorithm 1 the pseudo-code for the SF magnitude decrypter modified from (8b), where ε is a very small number, and we assume that the original signal has mostly small magnitudes.

Algorithm 1. Pseudo-code for the magnitude decryption function using the SF technique, under the assumption that the original signal has mostly small frequency magnitudes.

```
 1: function STATISTICAL-FLOOR(mm, km)
 2:     for i ← 1 to N do
 3:         if mm[i] ≥ φ then                          ▷ impossible magnitude
 4:             mm[i] ← φ − ε
 5:         end if
 6:         mm[i] ← cm[i] − km[i]
 7:         if −ψ ≤ mm[i] < 0 then                     ▷ unlikely fallout
 8:             mm[i] ← 0
 9:         end if
10:         mm[i] ← (mm[i]) mod φ
11:     end for
12: end function
```

Algorithm 2. Pseudo-code for the VPSC's magnitude encryption, using the combined noise mitigation technique.

```
 1: function e_{km}(mm)
 2:     cm ← mm
 3:     for i ← 1 to N do
 4:         cm[i] ← cm[i] + λ                          ▷ add energy buffer
 5:         cm[i] ← mod(mm[i] + km[i], φ + 2λ)         ▷ encrypt
 6:         cm[i] ← cm[i] + λ                          ▷ add carrier energy
 7:     end for
 8: end function
```

Algorithm 3. Pseudo-code for the VPSC's magnitude decryption, using the combined noise mitigation technique.

1: **function** $d_{k_m}(c_m)$
2:     $m_m \leftarrow c_m$
3:     **for** $i \leftarrow 1$ to N **do**
4:         **if** $c_m[i] > \phi + 3\lambda$ **then**   ▷ remove impossible magnitudes
5:             $c_m[i] \leftarrow \phi + 3\lambda$
6:         **end if**
7:         $c_m[i] \leftarrow c_m[i] - \lambda$ ▷ remove carrier energy
8:         **if** $c_m[i] < 0$ **then**
9:             $c_m[i] \leftarrow 0$
10:        **end if**
11:        $m_m[i] \leftarrow \mathrm{mod}(c_m[i] - k_m[i], \phi + 2\lambda)$ ▷ decrypt
12:        $m_m[i] \leftarrow m_m[i] - \lambda$ ▷ remove energy buffer
13:    **end for**
14: **end function**

Although SF does not require more power to transmit a cryptogram (unlike PR), it sometimes incorrectly floors values that happen to be below 0 that should not have been modified. Since this error is unavoidable when using this technique, it is impossible for SF to completely eliminate the modulo noise distortions without adding some of its own.

Combined Method. It is clear that the PR and SF techniques have their advantages and disadvantages, as mentioned above. To obtain the *best of both worlds*, one may use a combination of both PR and SF techniques. Such a combination can eliminate almost all distortions while using less transmission power than PR to achieve the same noise reduction. The pseudo-code for performing encryption and decryption with the combined method can be found in Algorithms 2 and 3.

4.2 Key Sharing

Since the VPSC is a specific case of the OTP, the length of the VPSC's key must equal the length of the streamed message. Sharing this key as a prior secret between two parties is impractical. In this type of situation it is common for both parties to agree upon a secret seed to initialize a key-stream generator. This makes the shared key finite as opposed to virtually infinite in length. Another consideration is how two communicating parties with only public channels can share a secret key (or seed) before any secure channel has been established. This subject has been well researched [8] and there are several common solutions. One solution is to form a hybrid cryptosystem using public-key cryptography [23]. In hybrid cryptosystems, a symmetric-key system (such as the VPSC) is initiated with an asymmetric key exchange.

5   Cryptanalysis

The VPSC is unconditionally secure (unbreakable) when using truly random keys. Claude Shannon proved that if truly random numbers are used to generate this cipher's encryption keys, it then becomes what is known as a One-Time-Pad (OTP), which is unconditionally secure [21].

The typical OTP operates by performing bitwise XOR operations on two binary vectors of equal length: the message and the key. The cryptographic behavior of the XOR operation, performed on each bit in the vector, can be applied to each element in an n-ary vector as well. This is because the XOR operation can be viewed as a modulo-2 operation. For instance, if $a, b \in \{0, 1\}$ then the XOR operation $a \oplus b$ is equivalent to performing $(a+b) \bmod 2$. Similarly, with an n-ary vector, if $c, d \in \{0, \ldots, n-1\}$ then the same cryptographic behavior is observable from $(a + b) \bmod n$.

This means that the OTP cipher can be applied to any system which uses n-ary vectors such as m_m, k_m, c_m and m_a, k_a, c_a from our cryptographic model described in Sect. 3. Therefore, the VPSC can be viewed as an extension of the OTP, and if the selection of $k = (k_m, k_a) \in K$ is purely random then the VPSC is unconditionally secure. The complete proof can be found in appendix 11.

Since no amount of cryptograms $c[i]$ may provide any information about the original plaintext $m[i]$, an encrypted signal s' has the appearance of random noise (completely random samples with zero correlation).

It is also important to note that public knowledge of ϕ or ϕ' does not compromise the system; rather it is the secrecy of the key which protects the message (see the proof in appendix 11). Therefore, knowledge of the setting of ϕ may not compromise the system. This conforms with Kerckhoffs's principle since ϕ is part of the cryptosystem and does not belong to the secret key.

Finally, the strength of symmetric stream ciphers depends on random number generator [15]. Therefore, to secure the VPSC, one must use a cryptographically secure pseudo random number generator (CSPRNG) [17] such as elliptic curve generators [2] or the use of integer factorization like the Blum-Blum-Shub number generator [4].

6   Signal Synchronization

In this Section, we propose a direct analytical method of synchronizing a VPSC decrypter to an encrypter at any arbitrary point in its key sequence. We will assume that the VPSC has been implemented with a cipher in counter (CTR) mode, such as AES-CTR [6]. This is usually done in the manner shown in [9]. The counter mode, while being secure and fully parallelizable (which is a performance advantage) [7], also offers the ability to access any value in the key stream independently from previous ones.

In order to initialize their cryptographic systems, both the encrypter and decrypter must use the same secret configuration. Let D be the collection of all possible initial configurations for a system such that

$$D = (sc, st, g)|sc, st, g \in N \tag{13}$$

where sc is the CSPRNG's initial counter (seed counter), st is the start time of the encryption relative to the encrypter's world-clock t_{tx}, and g is the key generation rate (values per time unit). This initial configuration can be used by a decrypter to calculate the current CSPRNG-counter (cc) which can be used to generate the current key-frame k.

To synchronize using time references, the decrypter must take into account the propagation delay ρ and the drift between its world-clock (t_{rx}) and the encrypter's (t_{tx}). This time delay δ can be described as $\delta = (t_{rx} - t_{tx}) + \rho$. Once δ is known, the decrypter can calculate the current CSPRNG-counter value as follows

$$cc = [((t_{rx} + \delta) - st) \times g] \bmod P \tag{14}$$

where P is the counter's period for the CSPRNG.

To account for δ, we propose that the decrypter seek it out from the received signal. This can be achieved by (1) using (14) without δ to find a nearby counter, and then (2) finding the spot in the current signal where the autocorrelation of the decrypted signal is the least like white noise. In order to measure the similarity of a decrypted signal to white noise we use the metric

$$\alpha = \frac{\sum_{k=1}^{N-1} R_{d,d}[k]}{R_{d,d}[0]} \tag{15}$$

where $R_{x,x}[n]$ is the discrete autocorrelation of the vector x at index n, and d is the decrypted frame.

Since we have temporally found the frame for the respective key, we can now calculate δ. This can be done by solving

$$cc_k = [((t_{usedRx_k} - t_{peak_k}) - st) \times g] \bmod P \tag{16}$$

where cc_k and t_{usedRx_k} are the counter and "current time" used when creating k and t_{peak_k} is the timestamp where (15) is maximized. Moreover, one can increase the precision by averaging the results over several consecutive counters. Figure 5 demonstrates this on a signal captured between two Arduino development boards.

7   Complexity and Performance

As mentioned in Sect. 4, the operations that take place at each end are: DFT, DFT^{-1}, modulo-add or modulo-subtract and key generation. The most computationally expensive operations are the DFT and DFT^{-1} operations performed on each frame. Since the VPSC operates on real-valued signals, a trick can be performed to reduce complexity. The trick is to put $N/2$ samples into each both real and complex inputs of a $\frac{N}{2}$ DFT [11]. Therefore, the complexity of the encryption function e_k and decryption function d_k is $O\left(N\log\left(\frac{N}{2}\right)\right)$ Today it is possible to find inexpensive hardware-accelerated DSP chips capable of performing them at high speeds. For example, the processor shown in [1] calculates a

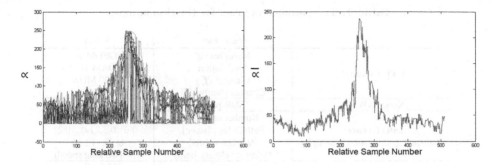

Fig. 5. Receiver synchronization to handle propagation and sender-receiver world clock delays though autocorrelation over several consecutive counters (left) and when averaged together (right).

1024-point complex FFT at a 32-bit precision in 23.2 µs. Using optimizations for real signals, it is possible to achieve even lower processing times. The same processor can also perform the division required for the modulo operations in 8.75 ns, which is negligible compared to the FFT processing time. Therefore, a frame of 1024-samples could undergo encryption and decryption on this chip in about 92.8 µs

To increase the speed further, or handle larger frames, one can use several VPSC encrypters and decrypters in parallel. This would be done by having each pair operate on a slice of the signal's spectrum and by combining the slices back together in the time plane.

8 Evaluation

In this Section, we verify the VPSC's practicality in realistic scenarios, such as both wired and wireless channels. We accomplish this by first evaluating the VPSC in a realistic channel simulator, and then by implementing the VPSC on actual hardware as a proof-of-concept.

8.1 Wireless – Simulation

The most practical use for a physical signal cipher, is to protect channels which (1) are easily accessible by an eavesdropper/attacker, and (2) do not require third parties to interpret and relay the signal (e.g. switches and routers). For these reasons, we evaluate the VPSC's performance in a wireless channel. We also note that wireless channels are significantly more challenging than in wired channels due to multi-path propagation and other distortions.

Experiment Setup: To evaluate VPSC in a wireless channel, we developed a simulator in Python which uses the configuration of an LTE OFDMA

Table 1. The parameters taken for the simulations.

	Parameter	Value
LTE Channel	Multiplexing	OFDMA
	Modulation	QAM 16
	Channel (f_c)	1900 MHz
	Channel Bandwidth	1.4 Mhz
Noise: AWGN	SNR [dB]	10
Interference: Multi-path propagation + Doppler	Number of paths	4
	Path Delays [μsec]	0.0, 0.5, 1.0 , 0.2
	Path Gains [dB]	0, -9, -12, -6
	Relative velocity [m/s]	1.4 (walking speed)
Signal Processing	Sample Rate (f_s)	15.3 Mhz
	Frame size (N)	1024
	VPSC/FCS Encryption band	1899.3 – 1900.7 MHz
Simulation	Number of bits	40,000
	Number of QAM symbols	10,000

mobile wireless channel.[3] The simulator can apply additive Gaussian white noise (AWGN), multi-path propagation (MPP) interference based on Rayleigh fading, and the Doppler effect (assuming a mobile receiver). The default configurations are listed in Table 1 unless mentioned otherwise. Furthermore, in all simulations, we applied the VPSC's combined method of noise mitigation from Algorithms 2 and 3, and set $\lambda = (N_0)^{-10}$, where N_0 represents the mean of the AWGN energy.

As a baseline comparison, we evaluated the VPSC against an unencrypted channel and three other physical signal ciphers: FCS, ALM, and RSA (see Sect. 2). For the VPSC and FCS, we encrypted the channel's bandwidth only, while the other methods had to encrypt the entire spectrum.

For each simulation, the following steps are performed until 40k bits are sent: (1) four random bits are modulated into a QAM-16 symbol, (2) the corresponding signal is generated on carrier frequency f_c for 66.7 μs (the LTE OFDMA symbol duration), (3) the raw signal is encrypted and sent over the noisy channel, (4) the received signal is decrypted, (5) the symbol is demodulated, and (6) the bit error rate (BER) is updated.

Results–Signal Quality: In Fig. 6, we present the BER plots for all methods of encryption after passing through an AWGN channel, and a channel with both AWGN and MPP. The figure shows that the VPSC is more robust to AWGN than the other methods up to about 8dB SNR. Moreover, the VPSC is more robust than all other methods in the case of MPP, making the VPSC a better choice for wireless channels. The reason why the VPSC performs better than an unencrypted signal up to 6dB SNR is because the noise mitigation adds some energy for the buffers.

Note that FCS is robust to AWGN, but not to MPP. This is because FCS shifts the majority of the signal's energy to the left or right of the carrier wave,

---

[3] The Python source code to the VPSC can be found on online: https://github.com/ymirsky/VPSC-py.

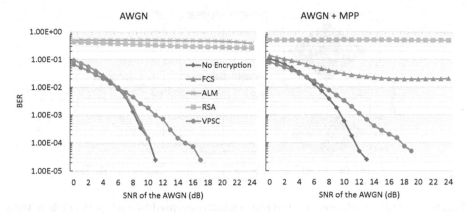

Fig. 6. The bit error rate plots for all ciphers when introduced to AWGN (left) and both AWGN with multipath propagation and Doppler effect (right).

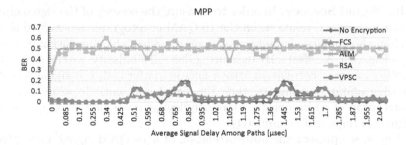

Fig. 7. The bit error rate plots for all ciphers when introduced to multipath propagation and Doppler effect, with increasing propagation delays.

thus increasing the interference of MPP and the Doppler effect across the channel's band. The ALM and RSA methods fail completely even in the presence of a minute amount of noise (24 dB SNR), requiring 300 dB SNR for zero errors. ALM fails because the logarithm operations increase the noise. RSA fails because the function acts like a hash map, resulting in large discrepancies for small input variations. To visualize the effect of the encryption, we provide a 16-QAM constellation plot of the demodulated symbols for various channels encryption methods in Fig. 10 of the appendix.

In Fig. 7, we examine the effect of the propagation delay in an MPP channel. In this simulation, we scaled up the propagation delays of the signal paths (Table 1). As a result, interference increases when there are symbols that overlap (ISI) which can be seen in the plot. The figure shows that the VPSC is nearly as robust to MPP as the original signal (without encryption). We note that FCS never has a 'peak' of interference, but rather always stays at a non-zero BER. This is because most of the signal's energy falls on a single frequency component, and the random shift of this component's location helps mitigate ISI.

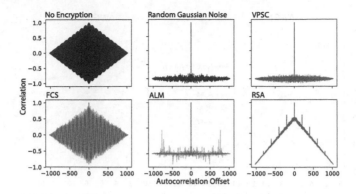

Fig. 8. The autocorrelation of a 16-QAM signal, encrypted by each of the ciphers three times (each time with a different key).

Results–Signal Secrecy: In order to measure the secrecy of the signal ciphers, we performed autocorrelations on the 16-QAM cryptograms (encrypted signals) for each of the ciphers. An autocorrelation measures the correlation of a signal with itself at various offsets. By measuring this self similarity, we can see evidence on whether or not a correlation attack may be performed. If a signal reveals no information about its contents, then the signal is essentially white noise. The autocorrelation of white noise is extremely low at every offset, except for when the signal overlaps itself completely.

In Fig. 8, we present the autocorrelation of a 16-QAM signal, encrypted by each of the signal ciphers three times: each time with a different key. The plots reveal that the VPSC has the same autocorrelation as random noise. This makes sense since each of the FFT's frequency components holds a random magnitude and phase as a result of the selected key. The figure also shows that the FCS does not protect the channel's content, but rather only obfuscates it. This is also apparent from the spectrum of the FCS's cryptograms, illustrated earlier in Fig. 1. The ALM cipher provides a relatively good encryption since it resembles white noise. However, the ALM has *spikes* in its autocorrelations. This means that some information is being leaked. This imperfection is likely due to the fact that ALM multiplies each sample with a value which is never zero. As a result, the cryptogram's distribution can reveal a portion of the contents. Given enough cryptograms, it may be possible to correlate out the ciphered signal. Finally, the RSA method fails to protect the signal's contents. This is due to an oversight in the cipher's implementation. Specifically, the RSA method encrypts the samples with the same private key, otherwise the complexity (of finding prime numbers and exchanging public keys in real-time) would be too high. As a result, all samples with the same value are mapped to the same location after encryption. Although this process obfuscates the ciphered signal, some of its original frequencies are still retained. An illustration of this effect can be seen in Fig. 11 in the appendix.

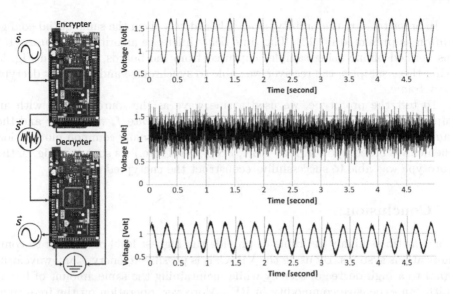

Fig. 9. The encryption and decryption of 4 Hz sine wave using the prototype, with the original signal, (top) the intercepted encrypted signal (middle), and the decrypted signal (bottom).

In summary, the VPSC is suitable for encrypting physical signals which traverse real-world channels. The VPSC is significantly more secure than other physical signal ciphers.

8.2 Wired – Proof of Concept

We implemented a hardware proof of concept for the VPSC to (1) illuminate any overlooked issues with the concept, and (2) demonstrate that the system works in practice. The VPSC prototype was implemented across two Arduino Due development boards. These boards embed 32-bit ARM core microcontrollers clocked 84 MHz with 512 KB of flash memory and numerous embedded digital I/O pins. One board was designated as the encrypter and the other as the decrypter (left side of Fig. 9). The boards contain both digital-to-analog converters (DAC) and analog-to-digital converters (ADC), which were used for transmitting and receiving signals respectively. We implemented the VPSC in C++ and open-source libraries were used for the Fast Fourier Transforms and the PRNG (SHA-1 as a counter-mode cipher).

In order to start the prototype, each board was given the same initial configuration as presented in (13). The time delay inference algorithm that uses (15) was verified offline using samples captured from the boards, plotted in Fig. 5. Using these samples, the receiver was able to synchronize and correctly decrypt every frame.

To test the prototype, we used a sine wave as the source signal, with an amplitude 1 V and a frequency of 4 Hz. The sample rate f_s was 1 kHz and the frame size N was 256. We chose a sine wave because many common modulation schemes are based upon it (e.g., ASK, FSK, QAM, etc.) As shown in Fig. 9, the prototype was able to successfully reconstruct the encrypted signal.

9   Conclusion

It is sometimes highly desirable to provide the highest level of security to communications systems. By using the VPSC, it is possible to encrypt any waveform signal to a high degree of secrecy while maintaining the same amount of bandwidth (an expensive commodity in RF). Moreover, operation on the frequency domain has many advantages such as parallelization on the hardware level. To ensure the stability of the VPSC, we have proposed two mitigation techniques when noise is introduced, and recommend using a combination of both.

To evaluate the VPSC, we implemented three other known physical signal ciphers. We then simulated an LTE OFDMA wireless channel, with noise and interference, and measured the ciphers' performance in carrying a 16-QAM modulation. Furthermore, we explored the secrecy of each of the ciphers by examining the autocorrelations of their respective encrypted signals. Our evaluations demonstrated that the VPSC is not only the most suitable physical signaling cipher in noisy channels, but also the most secure.

In summary, the VPSC offers a powerful method of encrypting any waveform signal (as well as complex), with a trade-off between security and power efficiency.

Acknowledgements. This research was partly funded by the Israel Innovations Authority under WIN - the Israeli consortium for 5G Wireless intelligent networks.

10   Appendix - Additional Figures

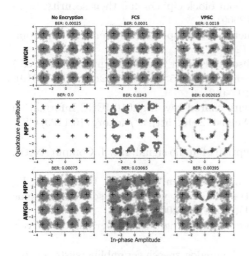

Fig. 10. QAM-16 constellation plots of the deciphered and demodulated symbols (1900 MHz LTE OFDMA), with various types of noise and interference, where red indicated incorrectly demodulated symbols. (Color figure online)

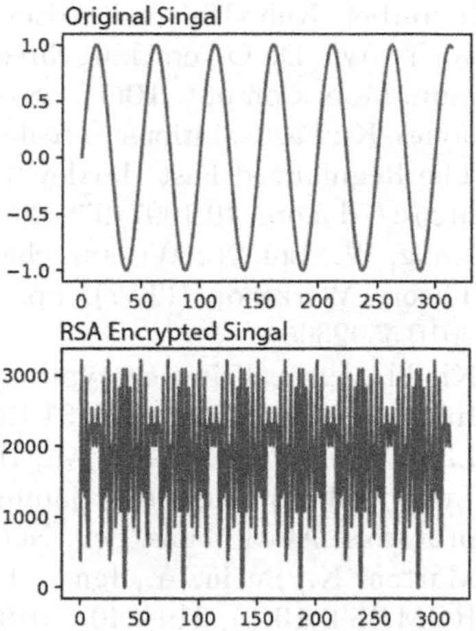

Fig. 11. The RSA method's failure demonstrated by a sine wave on the top (plaintext) and the encrypted RSA signal on the bottom (ciphertext).

The proof that the Vernam Cipher and OTP can be extended from binary to N-ary values with out loss of secrecy, can be found here: https://github.com/ymirsky/VPSC-py/blob/master/Additional%20Proofs.pdf.

References

1. Sharc processor adsp-21367 reference, datasheet (2013). http://www.analog.com/static/imported-files/data_sheets/ADSP-21367_21368_21369.pdf
2. Barker, E.B., Kelsey, J.M.: Recommendation for random number generation using deterministic random bit generators. NIST Special Publication 800–90A (2012)
3. Bloch, M., Barros, J.: Physical-Layer Security: From Information Theory to Security Engineering. Cambridge University Press, Cambridge (2011)
4. Blum, L., Blum, M., Shub, M.: A simple unpredictable pseudo-random number generator. J. Comput. **15**(2), 364–383 (1986)
5. Csiszar, I., Korner, J.: Broadcast channels with confidential messages. IEEE Trans. Inf. Theory **24**(3), 339–348 (1978). https://doi.org/10.1109/TIT.1978.1055892
6. Dworkin, M.: Recommendation for block cipher modes of operation-methods and techniques. NIST Special Publication 800–30A (2001)
7. Ferguson, N., Schneier, B., Kohno, T.: Cryptography Engineering: Design Principles and Practical Applications, p. 70. Wiley, Hoboken (2012). Chap. 4

8. Garrett, P., Lieman, D.: Public-key Cryptography: Baltimore (Proceedings of Symposia in Applied Mathematics) (Proceedings of Symposia in Applied Mathematics). American Mathematical Society, Boston (2005)
9. Hudde, H.C.: Building stream ciphers from block ciphers and their security. Seminararbeit Ruhr-Universität Bochum (2009)
10. Jo, Y., Wu, D.: On cracking direct-sequence spread-spectrum systems. Wirel. Commun. Mob. Comput. **10**(7), 986–1001 (2010)
11. Jones, K.: Fast solutions to real-data discrete Fourier transform. In: Jones, K. (ed.) The Regularized Fast Hartley Transform, pp. 15–25. Springer, Dordrecht (2010). https://doi.org/10.1007/978-90-481-3917-0_2
12. Kang, W., Liu, N.: Wiretap channel with shared key. In: 2010 IEEE Information Theory Workshop (ITW), pp. 1–5, August 2010. https://doi.org/10.1109/CIG.2010.5592665
13. Khalil, M.: Real-time encryption/decryption of audio signal. Int. J. Comput. Netw. Inf. Secur. (IJCNIS) **8**, 25–31 (2016)
14. Law, Y.W., Palaniswami, M., Hoesel, L.V., Doumen, J., Hartel, P., Havinga, P.: Energy-efficient link-layer jamming attacks against wireless sensor network mac protocols. ACM Trans. Sen. Netw. **5**(1), 6:1–6:38 (2009)
15. Marton, K., Suciu, A., Ignat, I.: Randomness in digital cryptography: a survey. ROMJIST **13**(3), 219–240 (2010)
16. Matsunaga, A., Koga, K., Ohkawa, M.: An analog speech scrambling system using the FFT technique with high-level security. IEEE J. Sel. Areas Commun. **7**(4), 540–547 (1989). https://doi.org/10.1109/49.17718
17. Menezes, A., van Oorschot, P., Vanstone, S.: Handbook of Applied Cryptography. Discrete Mathematics and Its Applications. Taylor & Francis, Boca Raton (1996)
18. Nichols, R., Lekkas, P.: Wireless Security: Models, Threats, and Solutions. McGraw-Hill Telecom Professional. McGraw-Hill, New York (2002)
19. Rivest, R.L., Shamir, A., Adleman, L.: A method for obtaining digital signatures and public-key cryptosystems. Commun. ACM **21**(2), 120–126 (1978)
20. Romanow, A.: IEEE standard for local and metropolitan area networks-media access control (MAC) security. IEEE Std 802.1AE-2006, pp. 1–142 (2006). https://doi.org/10.1109/IEEESTD.2006.245590
21. Shannon, C.E.: Communication theory of secrecy systems. Bell Syst. Tech. J. **28**(4), 656–715 (1949)
22. Shiu, Y.S., Chang, S.Y., Wu, H.C., Huang, S.H., Chen, H.H.: Physical layer security in wireless networks: a tutorial. IEEE Wirel. Commun. **18**(2), 66–74 (2011). https://doi.org/10.1109/MWC.2011.5751298
23. Vacca, J.: Computer and Information Security Handbook. Elsevier Science, Amsterdam (2012)
24. Vernam, G.S.: Secret signaling system, July 1919. US Patent 1,310,719
25. Wyner, A.D.: The wire-tap channel. Bell Syst. Tech. J. **54**(8), 1355–1387 (1975)
26. Yamamoto, H.: Rate-distortion theory for the Shannon cipher system. IEEE Trans. Inf. Theory **43**(3), 827–835 (1997). https://doi.org/10.1109/18.568694
27. Zhou, X., Song, L., Zhang, Y.: Physical Layer Security in Wireless Communications. Wireless Networks and Mobile Communications. Taylor & Francis, Boca Raton (2013)

A Cooperative Jamming Game in Wireless Networks Under Uncertainty

Zhifan Xu[1(✉)] and Melike Baykal-Gürsoy[2]

[1] Department of Industrial and Systems Engineering, Rutgers University,
Piscataway, NJ 08854, USA
zhifan.xu@rutgers.edu
[2] Department of Industrial and Systems Engineering, Rutgers University,
RUTCOR and CAIT, Piscataway, USA
gursoy@soe.rutgers.edu

Abstract. Considered is a multi-channel wireless network for secret communication that uses the signal-to-interference-plus-noise ratio (SINR) as the performance measure. An eavesdropper can intercept encoded messages through a degraded channel of each legitimate transmitter-receiver communication pair. A friendly interferer, on the other hand, may send cooperative jamming signals to enhance the secrecy performance of the whole network. Besides, the state information of the eavesdropping channel may not be known completely. The transmitters and the friendly interferer have to cooperatively decide on the optimal jamming power allocation strategy that balances the secrecy performance with the cost of employing intentional interference, while the eavesdropper tries to maximize her eavesdropping capacity. To solve this problem, we propose and analyze a non-zero sum game between the network defender and the eavesdropper who can only attack a limited number of channels. We show that the Nash equilibrium strategies for the players are of threshold type. We present an algorithm to find the equilibrium strategy pair. Numerical examples demonstrate the equilibrium and contrast it to baseline strategies.

Keywords: Non-zero sum game · Cooperative jamming · Physical layer security · Incomplete channel state information

1 Introduction

Wireless communication networks are vulnerable to eavesdropping attacks due to the multi-cast nature of wireless communication. Considering the fast development of various forms of wireless communication networks, such as wireless sensor networks and vehicle communication networks, information secrecy against

This material is based upon work supported by the National Science Foundation (Grant No.1901721).

N. Park et al. (Eds.): SecureComm 2020, LNICST 335, pp. 233–254, 2020.
https://doi.org/10.1007/978-3-030-63086-7_14

eavesdropping attacks has become more and more critical. Traditionally, securing messages transmitted through wireless networks depends on encryption and randomness in coding schemes [25,32]. It is shown that the difference between the legitimate channel and the eavesdropping channel capacities, which is defined as *Secrecy Capacity*, decides the secrecy level of transmitter-receiver pairs [19].

During the last decade, various efforts have been made to investigate the security of wireless communication networks at the physical layer, which is coined as *Physical Layer Security*. It is shown that intentionally generated interference signals, either mixed into the signal by the transmitter or sent by a third party helper, can decrease the channel capacity between the transmitter and the eavesdropper at the physical layer [11,23,27–30]. Thus, the secrecy capacity of the transmitter-receiver channel can be increased by employing intentional interference signals at the transmitter-eavesdropper channel. This approach is usually referred to as *Cooperative Jamming* when interference signals are sent by helpers or other components (i.e., idle relays) in a wireless network [29,30].

Researchers have studied the power control strategies and configurations of cooperative jamming signals under various setups [4,16]. Traditional power allocation schemes for cooperative jamming on a multi-channel network usually consider passive eavesdroppers listening in all channels. However, considerable portion of cooperative jamming power is wasted under such schemes if some channels are not actually attacked by eavesdroppers. Besides, due to other constraints on the number of antennas or on the available power, an eavesdropper may not be able to attack all channels at the same time. Instead of simply assigning an arbitrary probability to each channel for being under eavesdropping attack, a game-theoretic model leaves that decision to the eavesdropper who tries to maximize her eavesdropping capacity. In fact, in such game-theoretic settings, an eavesdropper could be a strategic player or nature. A strategic player tries to maximize his/her own payoff function while nature is always assumed to work against its adversary. As shown in [13] and [20], a natural disaster is considered to have been caused by an intelligent player who targets the weakest point of the system, while the defender uses limited resources to harden valuable assets. In [35], Yolmeh and Baykal-Gürsoy investigated the optimal patrolling policy against potential terrorist attacks for a railway system. Wei *et al.* [31] studied the protection strategy of a power system against an attacker who has enough knowledge of how power systems operate.

This paper considers the optimal power allocation strategy for cooperative jamming on a multi-channel wireless communication system. Such problems arise, for example, in military operations, where a frequency division multiplexing (FDM) communication system is used to transmit confidential messages in an adversarial environment. Particularly, we focus on the scenario in which the presence of eavesdroppers at each communication channel is uncertain and the state information of the eavesdropper's channels is not completely known. In previous works, the assumption of complete channel state information (CSI) has been widely used to analyze the optimal power allocation strategy for cooperative jamming. However, as argued in [6,15], CSI may not be easily obtained since eavesdropping channels' state information is closely related to eavesdroppers' private information such as their hidden location and antenna setups. It is unrealistic to assume complete CSI when the existence of an eavesdropper is even unknown.

A non-zero-sum Nash game for the multi-channel wireless communication system describes the confrontation between a friendly interferer and a strategic eavesdropper. Thus, the eavesdropper is also a decision maker who can select a communication channel to attack. In addition, the game-theoretic model incorporates the probability distributions of the eavesdropper's fading channel gains into the players' payoff functions instead of using simple estimators such as the mean. Moreover, there is a cost for the usage of cooperative jamming power since the friendly interferer may be a third party service provider. We show that the Nash equilibrium (NE) strategy of each player is of threshold type. We present an algorithm to compute the equilibrium strategy, and apply it to numerical examples to demonstrate its usage and contrast NE to baseline strategies. If the friendly interferer naively assigns the jamming power without taking into account the presence of a strategic eavesdropper, the system may not reach its ultimate secrecy capacity.

1.1 Related Works

Due to limitations on battery and power technologies in their current state, finding optimal power control strategies has been a crucial problem for cooperative jamming. Dong et al. [7] studied a wireless wiretap channel, with a single source-destination pair and an eavesdropper, aided by a friendly interferer equipped with multiple antennas. The authors presented the optimal configuration of all jamming antennas to maximize secrecy capacity under a total power constraint. Yang et al. [34] considered a multi-user broadcast network where a single eavesdropper with multiple antennas attacks all data streams simultaneously. They proposed and solved an optimization problem for a friendly interferer to maximize the minimum secrecy rate of all data streams under total power and minimum rate constraints. Cumanan et al. [5] investigated a secrecy capacity maximization problem for a single source-receiver pair in the presence of multiple eavesdroppers and multiple friendly interferers. They derived the optimal power level of each friendly interferer by taking into account the detrimental effect of interference also on the intended receiver. Zhang et al. [37] studied wireless cooperative jamming for an orthogonal frequency-division multiplexing (OFDM) communication system, in which the friendly interferer needs to optimally assign the limited jamming power to all subcarriers in order to maximize the total secrecy capacity. In these models, communication networks are controlled by a single decision maker such as a friendly interferer or a transmitter, since the eavesdroppers are assumed to be present at every existing communication channel.

In reality, wireless network secrecy may not only depend on the strategy of one decision maker. A strategic eavesdropper may also be an active decision maker. Game-theoretic models arise naturally when conflict of interest exists among different decision makers, as discussed in the survey by Manshaei *et al.* [21]. Altman *et al.* [1] obtained a transmitter's optimal power allocation strategy against a hostile jammer using game-theoretic models. The authors later extended the model to incomplete information CSI case [2]. Han *et al.* [12] studied a pricing game for the negotiation of security service price between transmitters and multiple friendly interferers. Yuan *et al.* [36] derived the optimal strategy for a two-user Gaussian interference channel in which each user can decide to activate cooperative jamming by themselves. Gradually, researchers started to use game-theoretic approaches to explore attack scenarios in which not all communication channels will be eavesdropped. Garnaev and Trappe [10] proposed a type of active eavesdropper who strategically attacks a limited number of wireless channels. In [8], Garnaev *et al.* considered a target selection game between a friendly interferer and an eavesdropper with players working on a single channel at a time. Recently, we have investigated a power control game for cooperative jamming against a strategic eavesdropper who can only attack one of N parallel channels [33]. A threshold type power allocation plan is obtained under the complete CSI assumption.

Most works mentioned above, except [2], which considers a hostile jammer instead of eavesdroppers, assume complete CSI obtained either instantaneously or statistically from historical data, ignoring the fact that it may actually be difficult to get complete CSI of eavesdropping channels since eavesdroppers are hiding and listening passively. Various efforts have been made to overcome this assumption in traditional setup when eavesdroppers are assumed to attack every existing communication channel. Garnaev and Trappe [9] presented a zero-sum anti-eavesdropping game for transmission power allocation on a multi-channel communication network, in which the environment is regarded as a hostile player that makes CSI as bad as possible. Hu *et al.* [14] investigated a cooperative jamming aided multiple-input-single-output (MISO) communication system with network defenders working together to maximize secrecy capacity under a constraint on the secrecy outage probability (SOP). Si *et al.* [26] studied the power control problem under SOP constraints for cooperative jamming against another type of active eavesdroppers who can listen and send hostile jamming signals at the same time. In cases that complete CSI is not available, some historical information might be acquired to infer the probability distributions of the eavesdroppers' CSIs.

To the best of our knowledge, this is the first paper studying the cooperative jamming game against a strategic eavesdropper under the incomplete CSI assumption. The NE strategy derived leads to a more intelligent power allocation strategy that can handle complex, uncertainty environments.

1.2   Summary of Contributions

This paper

1. introduces a non-zero sum cooperative jamming game considering a strategic eavesdropper, uncertain CSIs, and jamming costs;

2. incorporates the probability distributions of the eavesdropper's CSIs into the players' payoff functions instead of using estimators directly;
3. derives a threshold type power allocation policy, and presents an algorithm to compute the NE strategy pair.

The structure of the paper is as follows. Section 2 presents the model setup. Section 3 proposes two basic optimization problems, one for the defender and the other for the eavesdropper. Section 4 introduces a non-zero sum game model when the fading channel gains of eavesdropping channels are characterized by discrete distributions. Section 5 demonstrates numerical examples and compares the game-theoretic model in Sect. 4 with the method of approximating fading channel gains using mean values. Section 6 summarizes conclusions and discusses possible future research.

2 System Model and Game Formulation

2.1 System Model

Consider a wireless communication network with N parallel channels, such as the frequency division multiplexing (FDM) communication system as shown in Fig. 1. Each channel occupies a different frequency and the interference from adjacent channels is mitigated via techniques like pulse-shaping filters. An eavesdropper, due to budget limitations, or to reduce the risk of Local Oscillator (LO) leakage power emitted from eavesdropping antennas that may reveal her hidden location(see [24,38]), is using hardware with limited capability and can only listen on n of N different frequencies at the same time. A friendly interferer can simultaneously send cooperative jamming signals to N communication channels, and is tasked to enhance the overall secrecy performance against the eavesdropper. Let SINR represents the throughput on each channel, which is very often used, especially for systems operating under low SINR regime [17,18]. Thus, the Shannon capacity can be approximated by SINR, and the communication capacity for each channel $i \in \{1, ..., N\}$, is

$$C_{L_i} = \ln\left(1 + \frac{g_i T_i}{\sigma_i}\right) \approx \frac{g_i T_i}{\sigma_i},$$

with T_i as the transmission power, σ_i as the background noise, and g_i as the fading channel gain from the transmitter to the legitimate receiver at channel i. We assume that cooperative jamming signals will not interfere with the legitimate receiver, which might be achieved when jamming signals are designed to be nullified at the receiver or the friendly interferer is carefully positioned to be away from the receiver [11,16,23]. The eavesdropper can intercept encrypted messages on channel i through a degraded eavesdropping channel with capacity

$$C_{E_i}(J_i) = \ln\left(1 + \frac{\alpha_i T_i}{\sigma_i + \beta_i J_i}\right) \approx \frac{\alpha_i T_i}{\sigma_i + \beta_i J_i},$$

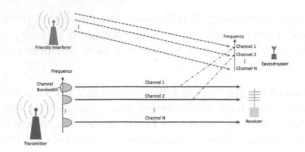

Fig. 1. FDM network with N channels, aided by a friendly interferer.

with J_i as the cooperative jamming power assigned to channel i, α_i as the fading channel gain from transmitter i to the eavesdropper and β_i as the fading channel gain from the friendly interferer to the eavesdropper at channel i.

If channel i is not under an eavesdropping attack, the full communication capacity can be used to transmit secret information. However, if channel i is attacked, information can be transmitted secretly only when the receiver's channel is more capable than the eavesdropper's channel. The difference of these capacities is called channel i's secrecy capacity, $C_{S_i}(J_i)$, given as

$$C_{S_i}(J_i) = \left[C_{L_i}(J_i) - C_{E_i}(J_i) \right]^+.$$

We assume that the friendly interferer does not know the fading channel gains of eavesdropping channels with certainty, but has a belief about the distributions of fading channel gains according to her knowledge of the communication environment and possible locations of the eavesdropper. Let A_i be the random variable representing the fading channel gain of transmission signals at eavesdropping channel i such that

$$\Pr(A_i = \alpha_i^m) = q_i^m, \quad \forall m \in \{1, ..., M_i\},$$

with M_i denoting the number of possible transmission gains. Let B_i be the random variable representing the fading channel gain of jamming signals at eavesdropping channel i such that

$$\Pr(B_i = \beta_i^k) = p_i^k, \quad \forall k \in \{1, ..., K_i\},$$

with K_i denoting the number of possible eavesdropping channel gains. Assume A_i and B_i are independent. Thus, with probability $p_i^k q_i^m$, the eavesdropping capacity at channel i is

$$C_{E_i}^{k,m}(J_i) \approx \frac{\alpha_i^m T_i}{\sigma_i + \beta_i^k J_i},$$

and the expected eavesdropping capacity at channel i is

$$\mathbb{E}\left[C_{E_i}(J_i)\right] = \sum_{k=1}^{K_i} \sum_{m=1}^{M_i} p_i^k q_i^m C_{E_i}^{k,m}(J_i) \approx \mathbb{E}\left[A_i\right] \mathbb{E}\left[\frac{T_i}{\sigma_i + B_i J_i}\right],$$

where $\mathbb{E}\left[A_i\right] = \sum_{i=1}^{M_i} q_i^m \alpha_i^m$ and $\mathbb{E}\left[\frac{T_i}{\sigma_i + B_i J_i}\right] = \sum_{k=1}^{K_i} p_i^k \frac{T_i}{\sigma_i + \beta_i^k J_i}$. The case when A_i's and B_i's are continuous random variables is left for future discussion. Also, for the sake of simplicity, assume $\mathbb{E}\left[C_{E_i}(0)\right]$'s are all distinct.

Note that, every eavesdropping channel should always be a degraded version of the corresponding communication channel, so assume

$$g_i > \max\{\alpha_i^m, m = 1, ..., M_i\}, \quad \forall i = 1, ..., N. \tag{1}$$

Under assumption (1), it will always be true that $C_{L_i} > C_{E_i}^{k,m}(J_i)$. Thus, with probability $p_i^k q_i^m$, the secrecy capacity for each channel i is

$$C_{S_i}^{k,m}(J_i) = C_{L_i} - C_{E_i}^{k,m}(J_i) \approx \frac{g_i T_i}{\sigma_i} - \frac{\alpha_i^m T_i}{\sigma_i + \beta_i^k J_i}.$$

Then, the expected secrecy capacity for channel i under cooperative jamming power J_i is

$$\mathbb{E}\left[C_{S_i}(J_i)\right] = \sum_{k=1}^{K_i} \sum_{m=1}^{M_i} p_i^k q_i^m C_{S_i}^{k,m}(J_i) \approx \frac{g_i T_i}{\sigma_i} - \mathbb{E}\left[A_i\right] \mathbb{E}\left[\frac{T_i}{\sigma_i + B_i J_i}\right],$$

which is a positive concave function w.r.t. $J_i \geq 0$.

Assume that the friendly interferer incurs \$$c$ per unit power used for jamming. Meanwhile, it earns \$$r$ from network users per unit secrecy capacity achieved. Thus, the payoff at channel i after applying J_i level of cooperative jamming is

$$\tilde{\mu}_i(J_i) \equiv \begin{cases} r\frac{g_i T_i}{\sigma_i} - cJ_i, & \text{if channel } i \text{ is not attacked,} \\ r(\frac{g_i T_i}{\sigma_i} - \mathbb{E}\left[A_i\right] \mathbb{E}\left[\frac{T_i}{\sigma_i + B_i J_i}\right]) - cJ_i, & \text{if channel } i \text{ is attacked.} \end{cases}$$

Remaining sections use the following simplified payoff function obtained by substituting $\gamma = c/r$.

$$\mu_i(J_i) \equiv \frac{\tilde{\mu}_i(J_i)}{r} = \begin{cases} \frac{g_i T_i}{\sigma_i} - \gamma J_i, & \text{if channel } i \text{ is not attacked,} \\ \frac{g_i T_i}{\sigma_i} - \mathbb{E}\left[A_i\right] \mathbb{E}\left[\frac{T_i}{\sigma_i + B_i J_i}\right] - \gamma J_i, & \text{if channel } i \text{ is attacked,} \end{cases}$$

Note that, it is not beneficial to send cooperative jamming signals to channel i if:

1. channel i is not being eavesdropped, or
2. it is too expensive to enhance secrecy capacity by applying cooperative jamming.

The eavesdropper can only attack n out of N channels. Let y_i be the probability that channel i is under an eavesdropping attack, so the expected payoff to the friendly interferer at channel i is

$$\mathbb{E}\left[\mu_i(J_i)\right] = \frac{g_i T_i}{\sigma_i} - y_i \mathbb{E}\left[A_i\right] \mathbb{E}\left[\frac{T_i}{\sigma_i + B_i J_i}\right] - \gamma J_i.$$

Note that $\mathbb{E}\left[\mu_i(J_i)\right]$ is a concave function of J_i, since

$$\frac{d}{dJ_i}\mathbb{E}\left[\mu_i(J_i)\right] = y_i \sum_{k=1}^{K_i} p_i^k \frac{\mathbb{E}\left[A_i\right]\beta_i^k T_i}{(\sigma_i + \beta_i^k J_i)^2} - \gamma,$$

is a decreasing function of J_i. It is optimal not to jam channel i unless

$$\frac{d}{dJ_i}\mathbb{E}\left[\mu_i(J_i = 0)\right] = y_i \frac{\mathbb{E}\left[A_i\right]\mathbb{E}\left[B_i\right] T_i}{\sigma_i{}^2} - \gamma > 0, \tag{2}$$

where $\mathbb{E}\left[B_i\right] = \sum_{i=1}^{K_i} p_i^k \beta_i^k$. Inequality (2) provides a lower bound on y_i that makes the friendly interferer jam channel i.

2.2 Formulation of the Game

The proposed non-zero sum Nash game solves the friendly interferer's problem of effectively responding to an eavesdropper who strategically picks some channels to attack. The game is played between the friendly interferer as the defender, who decides on the jamming power allocation plan, and a strategic eavesdropper as the attacker. That is, the defender's strategy is $\boldsymbol{J} = (J_1, ..., J_N)$ with $J_i \geq 0$, $\forall i = 1, ..., N$ such that $\sum_{i=1}^{N} J_i \leq J$, where $J > 0$ is the total power available to the friendly interferer. The attacker's strategy is $\boldsymbol{y} = (y_1, ..., y_N)$ with $0 \leq y_i \leq 1$, $\forall i = 1, ..., N$ such that $\sum_{i=1}^{N} y_i = n$, with y_i representing the probability of targeting channel i. Both the friendly interferer and the eavesdropper have complete knowledge about the system parameters.

While the attacker tries to choose n channels to attack in order to maximize her total expected eavesdropping capacity, the defender tries to send cooperative jamming signals to channels to maximize the overall utility of the whole network. Thus, for a given pair of strategy pair, $(\boldsymbol{J}, \boldsymbol{y})$, the defender's payoff is

$$v_D(\boldsymbol{J}, \boldsymbol{y}) = \sum_{i=1}^{N}\mathbb{E}\left[\mu_i(J_i)\right] = \sum_{i=1}^{N}\frac{g_i T_i}{\sigma_i} - \sum_{i=1}^{N} y_i \mathbb{E}\left[A_i\right]\mathbb{E}\left[\frac{T_i}{\sigma_i + B_i J_i}\right] - \gamma\sum_{i=1}^{N} J_i, \tag{3}$$

and the eavesdropper's payoff is

$$v_E(\boldsymbol{J}, \boldsymbol{y}) = \sum_{i=1}^{N} y_i \mathbb{E}\left[C_{E_i}(J_i)\right] = \sum_{i=1}^{N} y_i \mathbb{E}\left[A_i\right]\mathbb{E}\left[\frac{T_i}{\sigma_i + B_i J_i}\right]. \tag{4}$$

Note that increasing the total expected eavesdropping capacity will result in the decrease of the total expected secrecy capacity, so the defender and the eavesdropper are playing a game with conflicting interests. Also note that only $\mathbb{E}[A_i]$ but not $\mathbb{E}[B_i]$ appears in both payoff functions.

The Nash Equilibrium (NE) provides a pair of power allocation and attack plans $(\boldsymbol{J}^*, \boldsymbol{y}^*)$ such that no player has an incentive to unilaterally change its policy, i.e.,

$$v_D(\boldsymbol{J}, \boldsymbol{y}^*) \leq v_D(\boldsymbol{J}^*, \boldsymbol{y}^*), \quad \forall \boldsymbol{J} \in \mathcal{J},$$

$$v_E(\boldsymbol{J}^*, \boldsymbol{y}) \leq v_E(\boldsymbol{J}^*, \boldsymbol{y}^*), \quad \forall \boldsymbol{y} \in \mathcal{Y},$$

where $\mathcal{J}$ is the region containing all possible power allocation strategies $\boldsymbol{J}$ and $\mathcal{Y}$ is the region containing all probabilistic attack strategies $\boldsymbol{y}$ in this game.

3 Best Response Functions

We present two optimization problems each corresponding to the best response for each player when the other player's strategy is fixed.

First consider the case when the defender's cooperative jamming strategy, $\boldsymbol{J} = (J_1, ..., J_N)$, is fixed and is known to the eavesdropper. In this case, the eavesdropper solves the following optimization problem to maximize the total expected eavesdropping capacities,

$$
\begin{aligned}
\max_{\boldsymbol{y}} \quad & v_E(\boldsymbol{J}, \boldsymbol{y}) = \sum_{i=1}^{N} y_i \mathbb{E}\left[A_i\right] \mathbb{E}\left[\frac{T_i}{\sigma_i + B_i J_i}\right] \\
\text{s.t.} \quad & \sum_{i=1}^{N} y_i \leq n, \\
& 0 \leq y_i \leq 1, \quad \forall i = 1, ..., N.
\end{aligned}
\tag{5}
$$

Clearly, (5) is a linear optimization problem w.r.t $\boldsymbol{y}$ since $v_E(\boldsymbol{J}, \boldsymbol{y})$ is a linear function of $\boldsymbol{y}$ for fixed $\boldsymbol{J}$, with linear constraints. Thus, the response of the eavesdropper can be found as given in the next theorem.

Theorem 1. *For a fixed cooperative jamming strategy, $\boldsymbol{J}$, the optimal strategy for the active eavesdropper is to eavesdrop on the channels that have the top n largest expected eavesdropping capacities $\mathbb{E}\left[A_i\right] \mathbb{E}\left[\frac{T_i}{\sigma_i + B_i J_i}\right]$.*

Proof. It is easy to see that

$$\frac{\partial v_E(\boldsymbol{J}, \boldsymbol{y})}{\partial y_i} = \mathbb{E}\left[A_i\right] \mathbb{E}\left[\frac{T_i}{\sigma_i + B_i J_i}\right], \quad \forall i = 1, ..., N,$$

which are constants for fixed $\boldsymbol{J}$. Thus, to maximize $v_E(\boldsymbol{J}, \boldsymbol{y})$, we should increase y_i's with the largest $\frac{\partial v_E(\boldsymbol{J}, \boldsymbol{y})}{\partial y_i}$ as much as possible. $\qquad\square$

Next, consider the case when the defender knows the eavesdropper's attack strategy ahead of time, i.e., $\boldsymbol{y} = (y_1, ..., y_N)$ is fixed and is revealed to the defender. In this case, the defender solves the following optimization problem to maximize the total utility of secrecy performance,

$$
\begin{aligned}
\max_{\boldsymbol{J}} \quad & v_D(\boldsymbol{J}, \boldsymbol{y}) = \sum_{i=1}^{N} \frac{g_i T_i}{\sigma_i} - \sum_{i=1}^{N} y_i \mathbb{E}\left[A_i\right] \mathbb{E}\left[\frac{T_i}{\sigma_i + B_i J_i}\right] - \gamma \sum_{i=1}^{N} J_i \\
\text{s.t.} \quad & \sum_{i=1}^{N} J_i \leq J, \\
& J_i \geq 0, \quad \forall i = 1, ..., N.
\end{aligned}
\tag{6}
$$

Note that $v_D(\boldsymbol{J}, \boldsymbol{y})$ is a convex function w.r.t. $\boldsymbol{J}$. Thus, problem (6) is a convex optimization problem w.r.t. $\boldsymbol{J}$. Next theorem provides the best response of the defender.

Theorem 2. *The best payoff of the defender against the eavesdropper's strategy,* $\boldsymbol{y} = (y_1, ..., y_N)$ *is*

$$v_D^* = \sum_{i=1}^N \frac{g_i T_i}{\sigma_i} - \sum_{i=1}^N \Big[\sum_{k=1}^{K_i} p_i^k \frac{y_i \mathbb{E}\,[A_i]\,T_i}{\sigma_i + \beta_i^k J_i^o(w_D)} - \gamma J_i^o(w_D) \Big],$$

where $w_D \geq 0$ is a threshold value and $(J_1^o(w_D), ..., J_N^o(w_D))$ is the optimal power allocation strategy such that
(a) if

$$y_i T_i \frac{\mathbb{E}\,[A_i]\,\mathbb{E}\,[B_i]}{\sigma_i{}^2} - \gamma > w_D$$

then $J_i^o(w_D)$ is the unique root of the following equation

$$F_i(x) = w_D,$$

where

$$F_i(x) := y_i T_i \sum_{k=1}^{K_i} \frac{\mathbb{E}\,[A_i]\,\beta_i^k p_i^k}{(\sigma_i + \beta_i^k x)^2} - \gamma,$$

(b) if

$$y_i T_i \frac{\mathbb{E}\,[A_i]\,\mathbb{E}\,[B_i]}{\sigma_i{}^2} - \gamma \leq w_D.$$

then $J_i^o(w_D) = 0$.
Moreover, the threshold value $w_D \geq 0$ is a real number such that if

$$\sum_{i=1}^N J_i^o(0) > J,$$

then w_D is the unique root of the equation

$$\sum_{i=1}^N J_i^o(w_D) = J,$$

otherwise $w_D = 0$.

Proof. Note that

$$F_i(J_i) = \frac{\partial v_D(\boldsymbol{J}, \boldsymbol{y})}{\partial J_i},$$

and

$$F_i(0) = y_i T_i \frac{\mathbb{E}\,[A_i]\,\mathbb{E}\,[B_i]}{\sigma_i{}^2} - \gamma.$$

By the KKT conditions for problem (6), a vector $\boldsymbol{J} = (J_1, ..., J_N)$ is the optimal solution if there exists a Lagrange multiplier $w_D > 0$ and non-negative coefficients $\lambda_1, ..., \lambda_N$ such that

$$\begin{cases} w_D(J - \sum_{i=1}^{N} J_i) = 0, \\ \lambda_i J_i = 0, \quad \forall i = 1, ..., N, \\ w_D = F_i(J_i) + \lambda_i, \quad \forall i = 1, ..., N. \end{cases}$$

Consider the last equality $w_D = F_i(J_i) + \lambda_i$. Since $\lambda_i \geq 0$ and $F_i(J_i)$ is decreasing in J_i, if $F_i(0) > w_D$, then J_i must be positive. Furthermore, since $\lambda_i J_i = 0$, then $F_i(J_i) = w_D$ if $F_i(0) > w_D$. On the other hand, if $F_i(0) \leq w_D$, then $J_i = 0$ and $\lambda_i = w_D - F_i(0)$.

Let $\boldsymbol{J}^o(w_D)$ denote the solution to the above KKT conditions as a function of w_D. If $\sum_{i=1}^{N} J_i^o(0) \leq J$, then $\boldsymbol{J}^o(0)$ is a feasible solution. Thus, $w_D = 0$ and $\boldsymbol{J}^o(0)$ is the optimal solution. But, if $\sum_{i=1}^{N} J_i^o(0) > J$, then $\boldsymbol{J}^o(0)$ is not a feasible solution. It follows that $w_D > 0$. Thus,

$$\sum_{i=1}^{N} J_i^o(w_D) = J,$$

since $w_D(J - \sum_{i=1}^{N} J_i^o(w_D)) = 0.$ $\qquad\qquad\square$

4   Nonzero-Sum Game Under Uncertainty

This section considers the general case and derives conditions for the Nash Equilibrium (NE). Since $v_D(\boldsymbol{J}, \boldsymbol{y}^*)$ given $\boldsymbol{y}^*$ is a concave function w.r.t. $\boldsymbol{J} \in \mathcal{J}$ and $v_E(\boldsymbol{J}^*, \boldsymbol{y})$ given $\boldsymbol{J}^*$ is a linear function w.r.t. $\boldsymbol{y} \in \mathcal{Y}$, a NE exists [3]. By the Karush-Kuhn-Tucker Theorem, the NE cooperative jamming strategy $\boldsymbol{J}^*$ should satisfy the KKT conditions:

$$\left. \frac{\partial v_D(\boldsymbol{J}, \boldsymbol{y}^*)}{\partial J_i} \right|_{\boldsymbol{J}=\boldsymbol{J}^*} = y_i^* \sum_{k=1}^{K_i} p_i^k \frac{\mathbb{E}[A_i]\beta_i^k T_i}{(\sigma_i + \beta_i^k J_i^*)^2} - \gamma \begin{cases} = w_D, & if \ J_i^* > 0, \\ \leq w_D, & if \ J_i^* = 0, \end{cases} \quad (7)$$

for all $i = 1, ..., N$, and

$$w_D \left(\sum_{i=1}^{N} J_i^* - J \right) = 0,$$

where $w_D \geq 0$ is a Lagrange multiplier. Similarly, the NE attack strategy $\boldsymbol{y}^*$ should satisfy the KKT conditions:

$$\left. \frac{\partial v_E(\boldsymbol{J}^*, \boldsymbol{y})}{\partial y_i} \right|_{\boldsymbol{y}=\boldsymbol{y}^*} = \sum_{k=1}^{K_i} p_i^k \frac{\mathbb{E}[A_i]T_i}{\sigma_i + \beta_i^k J_i^*} \begin{cases} \geq w_A, & if \ y_i^* = 1, \\ = w_A, & if \ 0 < y_i^* < 1, \\ \leq w_A, & if \ y_i^* = 0, \end{cases} \quad (8)$$

for all $i = 1, ..., N$, where $w_A \geq 0$ is a Lagrange multiplier.

In this paper, we limit the capability of the active eavesdropper to $n = 1$ and leave the case $n > 1$ for future discussion. Next theorem describes the case in which the active eavesdropper adopts a pure strategy in the NE, that is, $y_i^* = 1$ for a single channel $i \in \{1, ..., N\}$.

Theorem 3. *Let m be a positive integer such that*

$$\mathbb{E}\left[C_{E_m}(0)\right] = \max\left\{\mathbb{E}\left[C_{E_i}(0)\right], i = 1, ..., N\right\}.$$

Let $\boldsymbol{y}^o$ be an attack strategy such that

$$y_i^o = \begin{cases} 1, & i = m, \\ 0, & \forall i \neq m, \end{cases}$$

and $\tilde{w}_D$ and $\boldsymbol{J}^o(\tilde{w}_D)$ be the corresponding threshold value and the optimal power allocation strategy, respectively, as discussed in Theorem 2. If

$$\mathbb{E}\left[C_{E_m}(\tilde{J}_m^o(\tilde{w}_D))\right] \geq \mathbb{E}\left[C_{E_i}(0)\right], \quad \forall i \neq m,$$

then $(\boldsymbol{J}^*, \boldsymbol{y}^*) = (\boldsymbol{J}^o(\tilde{w}_D), \boldsymbol{y}^o)$ is a pair of NE strategies with a pure eavesdropper's strategy.

Proof. We provide a proof in Appendix A. □

When such a pure attack strategy is not in the Nash Equilibrium, $\boldsymbol{y}^*$ will be a mixed strategy such that $0 \leq y_i^* < 1$, $\forall i = 1, ..., N$. Thus, KKT conditions (8) can be simplified to

$$\left.\frac{\partial v_E(\boldsymbol{J}^*, \boldsymbol{y})}{\partial y_i}\right|_{\boldsymbol{y} = \boldsymbol{y}^*} = \sum_{k=1}^{K_i} p_i^k \frac{\mathbb{E}\left[A_i\right] T_i}{\sigma_i + \beta_i^k J_i^*} \begin{cases} = w_A, & \text{if } y_i^* > 0, \\ \leq w_A, & \text{if } y_i^* = 0, \end{cases} \tag{9}$$

for all $i = 1, ..., N$. The next theorem describes the general NE strategy pair.

Theorem 4. *Let w_A be a Lagrange multiplier with a given value and $\boldsymbol{J}(w_A)$ be a cooperative jamming strategy such that*

$$J_i(w_A) = \begin{cases} \text{the unique root of } R_i(x) = w_A, & \text{if } \frac{\mathbb{E}[A_i]T_i}{\sigma_i} > w_A, \\ 0, & \text{if } \frac{\mathbb{E}[A_i]T_i}{\sigma_i} \leq w_A, \end{cases} \tag{10}$$

for all $i = 1, ..., N$, with

$$R_i(x) := \sum_{k=1}^{K_i} p_i^k \frac{\mathbb{E}\left[A_i\right] T_i}{\sigma_i + \beta_i^k x},$$

and the capacity constraint

$$\sum_{i=1}^{N} J_i(w_A) \leq J.$$

Let w_D be another Lagrange multiplier such that

$$w_D = \begin{cases} \text{the unique root of } \sum_{i \in I(w_A)} y_i(w_A, w_D) = 1, & \text{if } \sum_{i=1}^{N} J_i(w_A) = J, \\ 0, & \text{if } \sum_{i=1}^{N} J_i(w_A) < J, \end{cases} \quad (11)$$

where

$$I(w_A) = \{i = 1, ..., N : J_i(w_A) > 0\},$$

and $\boldsymbol{y}(w_A, w_D)$ is an attack strategy such that

$$y_i(w_A, w_D) = \begin{cases} H_i(w_A, w_D), & \text{if } J_i(w_A) > 0, \\ 0, & \text{if } \frac{\mathbb{E}[A_i]T_i}{\sigma_i} < w_A, \quad (12) \\ \min\left\{\left[1 - \sum_{j \in I(w_A)} y_i(w_a, w_D)\right]^{+}, H_i(w_A, w_D)\right\}, & \text{if } \frac{\mathbb{E}[A_i]T_i}{\sigma_i} = w_A, \end{cases}$$

for all $i = 1, ..., N$, where

$$H_i(w_A, w_D) = \frac{\gamma + w_D}{T_i \sum_{k=1}^{K_i} \frac{p_i^k \mathbb{E}[A_i] \beta_i^k}{(\sigma_i + \beta_i^k J_i(w_A))^2}}.$$

Then, $(\boldsymbol{J^*}, \boldsymbol{y^*}) = (\boldsymbol{J}(w_A), \boldsymbol{y}(w_A, w_D))$ is a pair of NE strategies if

1. $w_D \geq 0$, and
2. $\sum_{i=1}^{N} y_i(w_A, w_D) = 1$.

Proof. We provide a proof in Appendix B. □

Let us now analyze the process to find the value of w_A. Note that $w_A \geq \bar{w}_A$ where $\bar{w}_A$ is the unique root of

$$\sum_{i=1}^{N} J_i(w_A) = J.$$

If $w_A = \bar{w}_A$ and $w_D \geq 0$ as the solution of Eqs. (11) and (12), then a pair of equilibrium strategies has been found.

However, it is possible that $w_D < 0$ when $w_A = \bar{w}_A$. But, this means

$$\sum_{i=1}^{N} y_i(\bar{w}_A, 0) = \sum_{i \in I(\bar{w}_A)} y_i(\bar{w}_A, 0) > 1,$$

suggesting that one should look for $w_A > \bar{w}_A$ that leads to $w_D = 0$ and smaller $y_i(w_A, w_D)$'s.

Clearly, $J_i(w_A)$ is decreasing in w_A. It then follows that $y_i(w_A, w_D)$ is also decreasing w.r.t. $w_A > \bar{w}_A$. Thus, for a given w_A, if $\sum_{i=1}^{N} y_i(w_A, w_D) > 1$, one should look for the NE with $w_A' > w_A$; if $\sum_{i=1}^{N} y_i(w_A, w_D) < 1$, one should look for the NE with $w_A' < w_A$.

Here we present an algorithm to approximate a pair of Nash Equilibrium strategies $(\boldsymbol{J}^*, \boldsymbol{y}^*)$ within a given tolerance, ϵ. The algorithm starts searching from $w_A = \bar{w}_A$ and uses a bisection search scheme to converge.

Algorithm 1. Finding NE Strategies $(\boldsymbol{J}^*, \boldsymbol{y}^*)$ under incomplete CSI.
Inputs. State information of the communication network: $T_i, \mathbb{E}[A_i], \beta_i^k, p_i^k$, $\forall k = 1, ..., K_i, \forall i = 1, ..., N$. The background noise σ_i, $\forall i = 1, ..., N$; the total available power J; and the explicit tolerance $\epsilon \leq 0.01$.
Step 1. Sort $\mathbb{E}[C_{E_i}(0)]$ in descending order.
Step 2. Let $w_A \leftarrow \bar{w}_A$. Find $(\boldsymbol{J}(w_A), \boldsymbol{y}(w_A, w_D))$ using Eqs. (10), (11) and (12).

> **Step 2a.** If $w_D \geq 0$, then $(\boldsymbol{J}^*, \boldsymbol{y}^*) = (\boldsymbol{J}(w_A), \boldsymbol{y}(w_A, w_D))$ is a pair of NE strategies and the algorithm is terminated. Otherwise, go to step 2b
> **Step 2b.** If $w_D < 0$, let $w_A^{LB} \leftarrow w_A$ and h be the largest integer such that $J_i(w_A) > 0$. Go to step 3.

Step 3. Let $w_A \leftarrow \mathbb{E}[C_{E_h}(0)]$. Find $(\boldsymbol{J}(w_A), \boldsymbol{y}(w_A, w_D))$ using Eqs. (10), (11) and (12).

> **Step 3a.** If $|\sum_{i=1}^{N} y_i(w_A, w_D) - 1| \leq \epsilon$, then $(\boldsymbol{J}^*, \boldsymbol{y}^*) = (\boldsymbol{J}(w_A), \boldsymbol{y}(w_A, w_D))$ is a pair of NE strategies and the algorithm is terminated. Otherwise, go to step 3b
> **Step 3b.** If $\sum_{i=1}^{N} y_i(w_A, w_D) > 1 + \epsilon$, then let $w_A^{LB} \leftarrow w_A$ and $h \leftarrow h - 1$. Go to step 3. Otherwise, go to step 3c.
> **Step 3c.** If $\sum_{i=1}^{N} y_i(w_A, w_D) < 1 - \epsilon$, then let $w_A^{UB} \leftarrow w_A$. Go to step 4.

Step 4. Let $w_A \leftarrow \frac{1}{2}(w_A^{UB} + w_A^{LB})$. Find $(\boldsymbol{J}(w_A), \boldsymbol{y}(w_A, w_D))$ using equations (10), (11) and (12).

> **Step 4a.** If $|\sum_{i=1}^{N} y_i(w_A, w_D) - 1| \leq \epsilon$, then $(\boldsymbol{J}^*, \boldsymbol{y}^*) = (\boldsymbol{J}(w_A), \boldsymbol{y}(w_A, w_D))$ is a pair of NE strategies and the algorithm is terminated. Otherwise, go to step 4b
> **Step 4b.** If $\sum_{i=1}^{N} y_i(w_A, w_D) > 1 + \epsilon$, then let $w_A^{LB} \leftarrow w_A$. Go to step 4. Otherwise, go to step 4c.
> **Step 4c.** If $\sum_{i=1}^{N} y_i(w_A, w_D) < 1 - \epsilon$, then let $w_A^{UB} \leftarrow w_A$. Go to step 4.

5   Numerical Illustrations

This section compares the following four different power allocation strategies for the friendly interferer:

1. Strategy 1: the game-theoretic power allocation strategy derived by Theorem 4, which takes into account the uncertainty of the eavesdropper's fading channel gains.

2. Strategy 2: the game-theoretic power allocation strategy that uses mean values of the eavesdropper's fading channel gains as estimators. It can be calculated following Theorem 4 with $R_i(x) = \frac{\mathbb{E}[A_i]T_i}{\sigma_i + \mathbb{E}[B_i]x}$ and $H_i(w_A, w_D) = \frac{(\gamma + w_D)(\sigma_i + \mathbb{E}[B_i]J_i(w_A))^2}{T_i\mathbb{E}[A_i]\mathbb{E}[B_i]}$.

3. Strategy 3: the power allocation strategy of a friendly interferer who expects eavesdropping attacks at every channel with equal probability but still takes into account the uncertainty of the eavesdropper's fading channel gains. This strategy can be derived following Theorem 2.

4. Strategy 4: the power allocation strategy of a friendly interferer who expects eavesdropping attacks at every channel with equal probability, but this time the friendly interferer uses mean values of the eavesdropper's fading channel gains as estimators. This strategy can be calculated following Theorem 2 with $F_i(x) := y_i T_i \frac{\mathbb{E}[A_i]\mathbb{E}[B_i]}{(\sigma_i + \mathbb{E}[B_i]x)^2} - \gamma$.

Consider a wireless communication network with 5 parallel channels. Let A_i's be the random eavesdropping channel gains of transmission signals whose mean values are $\{\mathbb{E}[A_i], i = 1, ..., 5\} = (0.75, 0.6, 0.4, 0.275, 0.25)$. Let B_i's be the random eavesdropping channel gains of jamming signals such that

$$[\beta_i^k] = \begin{bmatrix} 0.4 & 0.8 & 1.2 \\ 0.4 & 0.7 & 1.0 \\ 0.1 & 0.5 & 0.9 \\ 0.25 & 0.6 & 0.95 \\ 0.15 & 0.45 & 0.75 \end{bmatrix}, [p_i^k] = \begin{bmatrix} 0.33 & 0.34 & 0.33 \\ 0.33 & 0.34 & 0.33 \\ 0.33 & 0.34 & 0.33 \\ 0.33 & 0.34 & 0.33 \\ 0.33 & 0.34 & 0.33 \end{bmatrix},$$

where the ith row stands for channel i and the kth column stands for scenario k. Note that the mean values of B_i's are $\{\mathbb{E}[B_i], i = 1, ..., 5\} = (0.8, 0.7, 0.5, 0.6, 0.45)$. Also, let $\{g_i, i = 1, ..., 5\} = (1.2, 1.0, 0.9, 0.75, 0.7)$, $\gamma = 1.5$, $J = 1$, $T_i = 1$ and $\sigma_i = 0.12$, $\forall i = 1, ..., N$.

For strategy 1, the optimal power allocation plan is $\boldsymbol{J}_I^* = (0.292, 0.218, 0.129, 0, 0)$ with payoff $v_D(\boldsymbol{J}_I^*, \boldsymbol{y}_I^*) = 34.668$, as shown in Fig. 2a. The eavesdropper's

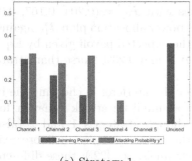 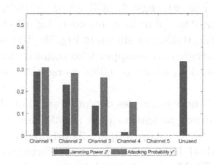

(a) Strategy 1.   (b) Strategy 2.

Fig. 2. Plots of $\boldsymbol{J}^*$ and $\boldsymbol{y}^*$ for strategies 1 and 2.

best response is $y_I^* = (0.317, 0.272, 0.307, 0.104, 0)$. Due to the cost coefficient γ, channel 4 is not protected by cooperative jamming even when there is unused power.

For strategy 2, the optimal power allocation plan is $J_{II}^* = (0.288, 0.229, 0.134, 0.014, 0)$ as shown in Fig. 2a. Compared to strategy 1, the friendly interferer adjusts the jamming powers to cover channel 4. If the friendly interferer uses J_{II}^* to face the eavesdropper who is still using the NE strategy y_I^* given by Theorem 4, then the payoff given by Eq. (3) is $v_D(J_{II}^*, y_I^*) = 34.661$, which is 0.02% worse than the payoff brought by strategy 1.

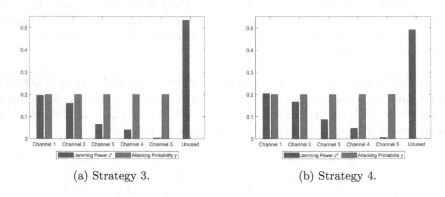

(a) Strategy 3.   (b) Strategy 4.

Fig. 3. Plots of J^* and y for strategy 3 and 4.

For strategy 3, let $y = (0.2, 0.2, 0.2, 0.2, 0.2)$. The optimal power allocation plan is $J_{III}^* = (0.197, 0.160, 0.065, 0.040, 0.004)$, as shown in Fig. 3a. Compared to strategies 1, the friendly interferer covers every channel instead of using a threshold policy. To use this power allocation plan J_{III}^* against a strategic eavesdropper who commits to y_I^*, the friendly interferer will waste cooperative jamming power on channel 5, and the expected payoff given by Eq. (3) is 34.566, which is 0.29% worse than strategy 1.

For strategy 4, still let $y = (0.2, 0.2, 0.2, 0.2, 0.2)$. The optimal power allocation plan is again covering all channels with $J_{IV}^* = (0.204, 0.167, 0.087, 0.047, 0.006)$, as shown in Fig. 3b. To use this power allocation plan J_{IV}^* against a strategic eavesdropper who commits to y_I^*, the expected payoff given by Eq. (3) is 34.581, which is 0.25% worse than strategy 1 and 0.23% worse than strategy 2.

These examples demonstrate that the friendly interferer in choosing the best resource allocation plan should not assume a simplistic attack behavior for a strategic eavesdropper. Additionally, even though strategies 1 and 2 (also 3 and 4) have quite similar performance in the given examples, in more realistic FDM systems involving more than 100 channels (see [22]), these differences are expected to be more significant.

6   Conclusions and Future Research

In this paper, we consider a cooperative jamming game for a multi-channel wireless communication network against an active eavesdropper when the eavesdropping channel gains are uncertain. We present a non-zero sum game to help the defender find the optimal cooperative jamming power allocation strategy under the assumption that the eavesdropper will strategically pick her targets. It turns out that the optimal power allocation strategy follows the classic water-filling scheme. An algorithm to approximate the optimal strategy to within a given error threshold is also presented. We show that the channel gains of cooperative jamming signals should not be simply approximated using mean values if the defender wants to use the optimal power allocation strategy.

Of interest for future research is an extension of this model to the case in which the strategic eavesdropper can attack more than a single channel. Another possible extension is to include the transmission power control problem as part of the defender's decision.

Appendix A: Proof of Theorem 3

Note that

$$\mathbb{E}\left[C_{E_i}(J_i)\right] = \frac{\partial v_E(\boldsymbol{J}, \boldsymbol{y})}{\partial y_i}.$$

Given $y_m^o = 1$ and $y_i^o = 0$, $\forall i \neq m$, Theorem 2 implies

$$y_i^o T_i \sum_{k=1}^{K_i} \frac{\mathbb{E}\left[A_i\right] \beta_i^k p_i^k}{\sigma_i{}^2} - \gamma = -\gamma < w_D, \ \forall i \neq m,$$

which leads to $\tilde{J}_m^o(\tilde{w}_D, \boldsymbol{y}^o) = 0$, $\forall i \neq m$.

Assume $(\tilde{\boldsymbol{J}}^o(\tilde{w}_D), \boldsymbol{y})$ is a pair of NE strategies. It is required that

$$w_A \geq \mathbb{E}\left[C_{E_i}(0)\right], \ \forall i \neq m,$$

by KKT conditions (8). Also, since $y_m^o > 0$, then

$$w_A = \mathbb{E}\left[C_{E_m}(J_m^o(\tilde{w}_D))\right] \leq \mathbb{E}\left[C_{E_m}(0)\right],$$

by KKT conditions (8). Thus, it must be true that

$$\mathbb{E}\left[C_{E_m}(0)\right] \geq \mathbb{E}\left[C_{E_i}(0)\right], \ \forall i \neq m,$$

$$\mathbb{E}\left[C_{E_m}(J_m^o(\tilde{w}_D))\right] \geq \mathbb{E}\left[C_{E_i}(0)\right], \ \forall i \neq m,$$

for the assumption to be true.   □

Appendix B: Proof of Theorem 4

Let w_A be the Lagrange multiplier for the eavesdropper's optimization problem (6). Note that

$$R_i(J_i) = \frac{\partial v_E(\boldsymbol{J}, \boldsymbol{y})}{\partial y_i},$$

$$R_i(0) = \frac{\mathbb{E}\left[A_i\right] T_i}{\sigma_i},$$

and $R_i(J_i)$ is decreasing w.r.t. $J_i \geq 0$. Let $\boldsymbol{J^*}$ be the cooperative jamming strategy in the NE. Note that

$$R_i(J_i^*) \leq w_A, \quad \forall i = 1, ..., N,$$

as required by KKT condition (9). Thus, if $R_i(0) > w_A$, then $J_i^* > 0$. Let w_D be the Lagrange multiplier for the defender's optimization problem (5) and $\boldsymbol{y^*}$ be the attack strategy in the NE. By KKT condition (7), if $J_i^* > 0$, then

$$y_i^* T_i \sum_{k=1}^{K_i} \frac{\mathbb{E}\left[A_i\right] \beta_i^k p_i^k}{(\sigma_i + \beta_i^k J_i^*)^2} - \gamma = w_D \geq 0,$$

thus giving $y_i^* > 0$. But, if $y_i^* > 0$, then

$$R_i(J_i^*) = w_A,$$

by KKT condition (9). In summary, if $R_i(0) > w_A$, then J_i^* is the unique root of the equation,

$$R_i(x) = w_A.$$

If $R_i(0) \leq w_A$, then

$$w_A \geq R_i(0) > R_i(J_i), \quad \forall J_i > 0,$$

which leads to $J_i^* = 0$ since $R_i(J_i^*) < w_A$ if $J_i^* > 0$. Thus, let us define $\boldsymbol{J}(w_A) := \boldsymbol{J^*}$ to show that the NE cooperative jamming strategy is dependent on w_A.

Note that $H_i(w_A, w_D)$ is the unique root of the equation,

$$\left. \frac{\partial v_D(\boldsymbol{J}, \boldsymbol{y^*})}{\partial J_i} \right|_{\boldsymbol{J}=\boldsymbol{J^*}} = w_D,$$

w.r.t. y_i^*.

If $R_i(0) > w_A$, then $J_i^* > 0$, which leads to $y_i^* = H_i(w_A, w_D)$ by KKT condition (7).

If $R_i(0) < w_A$, then $R_i(J_i^*) = R_i(0) < w_A$ since $J_i^* = 0$. It follows that $y_i^* = 0$ by KKT condition (9).

If $R_i(0) = w_A$, then $J_i^* = 0$, but it is possible to have $y_i^* > 0$ in a NE as long as

$$\begin{cases} \left. \frac{\partial v_D(\boldsymbol{J}, \boldsymbol{y^*})}{\partial J_i} \right|_{\boldsymbol{J}=\boldsymbol{J^*}} \leq w_D, \text{ by KKT condition (7)}, \\ y_i^* \geq 0, \\ y_i^* + \sum_{j \in I(w_A)} y_j^* \leq 1. \end{cases}$$

Thus, $\boldsymbol{y}(w_A, w_D)$ in (12) is correctly defined to satisfy KKT conditions (7) and (9). Note that it is possible to have

- $y_i(w_A, w_D) = H_i(w_A, w_D) < 1 - \sum_{j \in I(w_A)} y_j(w_A, w_D)$, or
- $\sum_{j \in I(w_A)} y_j(w_A, w_D) > 1$.

So the constraint $\sum_{i=1}^{N} y_i(w_A, w_D) = 1$ is not guaranteed by (12).

Finally, it is required that

$$w_D (J - \sum_{i=1}^{N} J_i(w_A)) = 0.$$

Thus, if $\sum_{i \in I(w_A)} J_i(w_A) < J$, then $w_D = 0$. In this case, the only requirement missing for $(\boldsymbol{J}(w_A), \boldsymbol{y}(w_A, w_D))$ to be a pair of NE strategies is to satisfy

$$\sum_{i=1}^{N} y_i(w_A, w_D) = 1.$$

Now look at the case when $\sum_{i \in I(w_A)} J_i(w_A) = J$. Following (11) and (12) when $\sum_{i \in I(w_A)} J_i(w_A) = J$, it is guaranteed that $\sum_{i=1}^{N} y_i(w_A, w_D) = 1$. However, it is possible that $w_D < 0$, so the only requirement for $(\boldsymbol{J}(w_A), \boldsymbol{y}(w_A, w_D))$ to be a pair of NE strategies is to satisfy $w_D \geq 0$.

In summary, following (10), (11) and (12), if

1. $w_D \geq 0$, and
2. $\sum_{i=1}^{N} y_i(w_A, w_D) = 1$,

then (w_D, w_A) is a proper pair of Lagrange multipliers for the Nash equilibrium, $(\boldsymbol{J}(w_A), \boldsymbol{y}(w_A, w_D))$. $\qquad \square$

References

1. Altman, E., Avrachenkov, K., Garnaev, A.: A jamming game in wireless networks with transmission cost. In: Chahed, T., Tuffin, B. (eds.) NET-COOP 2007. LNCS, vol. 4465, pp. 1–12. Springer, Heidelberg (2007). https://doi.org/10.1007/978-3-540-72709-5_1
2. Altman, E., Avrachenkov, K., Garnaev, A.: Jamming in wireless networks under uncertainty. Mob. Netw. Appl. **16**(2), 246–254 (2011)
3. Arrow, K.J., Debreu, G.: Existence of an equilibrium for a competitive economy. Econometrica J. Econometric Soc., 265–290 (1954)
4. Atallah, M., Kaddoum, G., Kong, L.: A survey on cooperative jamming applied to physical layer security. In: 2015 IEEE International Conference on Ubiquitous Wireless Broadband (ICUWB), pp. 1–5. IEEE (2015)
5. Cumanan, K., Alexandropoulos, G.C., Ding, Z., Karagiannidis, G.K.: Secure communications with cooperative jamming: optimal power allocation and secrecy outage analysis. IEEE Trans. Veh. Technol. **66**(8), 7495–7505 (2017)

6. Ding, Z., Leung, K.K., Goeckel, D.L., Towsley, D.: Opportunistic relaying for secrecy communications: cooperative jamming vs. relay chatting. IEEE Trans. Wirel. Commun. **10**(6), 1725–1729 (2011)
7. Dong, L., Han, Z., Petropulu, A.P., Poor, H.V.: Cooperative jamming for wireless physical layer security. In: 2009 IEEE/SP 15th Workshop on Statistical Signal Processing, pp. 417–420. IEEE (2009)
8. Garnaev, A., Baykal-Gürsoy, M., Poor, H.V.: Incorporating attack-type uncertainty into network protection. IEEE Trans. Inf. Forensics Secur. **9**(8), 1278–1287 (2014)
9. Garnaev, A., Trappe, W.: An eavesdropping game with SINR as an objective function. In: Chen, Y., Dimitriou, T.D., Zhou, J. (eds.) SecureComm 2009. LNICST, vol. 19, pp. 142–162. Springer, Heidelberg (2009). https://doi.org/10.1007/978-3-642-05284-2_9
10. Garnaev, A., Trappe, W.: Secret communication when the eavesdropper might be an active adversary. In: Jonsson, M., Vinel, A., Bellalta, B., Belyaev, E. (eds.) MACOM 2014. LNCS, vol. 8715, pp. 121–136. Springer, Cham (2014). https://doi.org/10.1007/978-3-319-10262-7_12
11. Goel, S., Negi, R.: Guaranteeing secrecy using artificial noise. IEEE Trans. Wirel. Commun. **7**(6), 2180–2189 (2008)
12. Han, Z., Marina, N., Debbah, M., Hjørungnes, A.: Physical layer security game: interaction between source, eavesdropper, and friendly jammer. EURASIP J. Wirel. Commun. Netw. **2009**, 1–10 (2010)
13. Haphuriwat, N., Bier, V.M.: Trade-offs between target hardening and overarching protection. Eur. J. Oper. Res. **213**(1), 320–328 (2011)
14. Hu, L., Wen, H., Wu, B., Tang, J., Pan, F., Liao, R.F.: Cooperative-jamming-aided secrecy enhancement in wireless networks with passive eavesdroppers. IEEE Trans. Veh. Technol. **67**(3), 2108–2117 (2017)
15. Hyadi, A., Rezki, Z., Alouini, M.S.: An overview of physical layer security in wireless communication systems with CSIT uncertainty. IEEE Access **4**, 6121–6132 (2016)
16. Jameel, F., Wyne, S., Kaddoum, G., Duong, T.Q.: A comprehensive survey on cooperative relaying and jamming strategies for physical layer security. IEEE Commun. Surv. Tutor. **21**(3), 2734–2771 (2018)
17. Kim, S.L., Rosberg, Z., Zander, J.: Combined power control and transmission rate selection in cellular networks. In: Gateway to 21st Century Communications Village. VTC 1999-Fall. IEEE VTS 50th Vehicular Technology Conference (Cat. No. 99CH36324), vol. 3, pp. 1653–1657. IEEE (1999)
18. Koo, I., Ahn, J., Lee, J.A., Kim, K.: Analysis of erlang capacity for the multimedia DS-CDMA systems. IEICE Trans. Fund. Electron. Commun. Comput. Sci. **82**(5), 849–855 (1999)
19. Leung-Yan-Cheong, S., Hellman, M.: The Gaussian wire-tap channel. IEEE Trans. Inf. Theory **24**(4), 451–456 (1978)
20. Majumder, R., Warier, R.R., Ghose, D.: Game theory-based allocation of critical resources during natural disasters. In: 2019 Sixth Indian Control Conference (ICC), pp. 514–519 (2019)

21. Manshaei, M.H., Zhu, Q., Alpcan, T., Başar, T., Hubaux, J.P.: Game theory meets network security and privacy. ACM Comput. Surv. (CSUR) **45**(3), 1–39 (2013)
22. National Instruments Measurement Fundamentals: OFDM and Multi-Channel Communication Systems (2015). https://www.ni.com/en-us/innovations/white-papers/06/ofdm-and-multi-channel-communication-systems.html
23. Rabbachin, A., Conti, A., Win, M.Z.: Intentional network interference for denial of wireless eavesdropping. In: 2011 IEEE Global Telecommunications Conference - GLOBECOM 2011, pp. 1–6 (2011)
24. Salem, A., Liao, X., Shen, Y., Jiang, X.: Provoking the adversary by detecting eavesdropping and jamming attacks: a game-theoretical framework. Wireless Communi. Mob. Comput. **2018** (2018)
25. Shannon, C.E.: Communication theory of secrecy systems. Bell Syst. Tech. J. **28**(4), 656–715 (1949)
26. Si, J., Cheng, Z., Li, Z., Cheng, J., Wang, H.M., Al-Dhahir, N.: Cooperative jamming for secure transmission with both active and passive eavesdroppers. arXiv preprint arXiv:2002.06324 (2020)
27. Tang, X., Liu, R., Spasojevic, P., Poor, H.V.: Interference assisted secret communication. IEEE Trans. Inf. Theory **57**(5), 3153–3167 (2011)
28. Tang, X., Liu, R., Spasojevic, P., Poor, H.V.: The Gaussian wiretap channel with a helping interferer. In: 2008 IEEE International Symposium on Information Theory, pp. 389–393. IEEE (2008)
29. Tekin, E., Yener, A.: The Gaussian multiple access wire-tap channel: wireless secrecy and cooperative jamming. In: 2007 Information Theory and Applications Workshop, pp. 404–413 (2007)
30. Tekin, E., Yener, A.: The general Gaussian multiple-access and two-way wire-tap channels: achievable rates and cooperative jamming. IEEE Trans. Inf. Theory **54**(6), 2735–2751 (2008)
31. Wei, L., Moghadasi, A.H., Sundararajan, A., Sarwat, A.I.: Defending mechanisms for protecting power systems against intelligent attacks. In: 2015 10th System of Systems Engineering Conference (SoSE), pp. 12–17. IEEE (2015)
32. Wyner, A.D.: The wire-tap channel. Bell System Technical Journal **54**(8), 1355–1387 (1975)
33. Xu, Z., Baykal-Gürsoy, M.: A friendly interference game in wireless secret communication networks. In: Forthcoming in the Proceedings of the 10th International Conference on NETwork Games, COntrol and OPtimization (NETGCOOP), Cargèse, France (2021). https://hal.archives-ouvertes.fr/hal-02870629
34. Yang, J., Kim, I.M., Kim, D.I.: Joint design of optimal cooperative jamming and power allocation for linear precoding. IEEE Trans. Commun. **62**(9), 3285–3298 (2014)
35. Yolmeh, A., Baykal-Gürsoy, M.: Urban rail patrolling: a game theoretic approach. J. Transp. Secur. **11**(1–2), 23–40 (2018)
36. Yuan, Z., Wang, S., Xiong, K., Xing, J.: Game theoretic jamming control for the gaussian interference wiretap channel. In: 2014 12th International Conference on Signal Processing (ICSP), pp. 1749–1754. IEEE (2014)

37. Zhang, G., Xu, J., Wu, Q., Cui, M., Li, X., Lin, F.: Wireless powered cooperative jamming for secure OFDM system. IEEE Trans. Veh. Technol. **67**(2), 1331–1346 (2017)
38. Zhao, G., Shi, W., Li, L., Li, S.: Passive primary receiver detection for underlay spectrum sharing in cognitive radio. IEEE Signal Process. Lett. **21**(5), 564–568 (2014)

SmartSwitch: Efficient Traffic Obfuscation Against Stream Fingerprinting

Haipeng Li[1], Ben Niu[2], and Boyang Wang[1]($\boxtimes$)

[1] Department of EECS, University of Cincinnati, Cincinnati, USA
li2hp@mail.uc.edu , boyang.wang@uc.edu
[2] Institute of Information Engineering, Chinese Academy of Sciences, Beijing, China
niuben@iie.ac.cn

Abstract. In stream fingerprinting, an attacker can compromise user privacy by leveraging side-channel information (e.g., packet size) of encrypted traffic in streaming services. By taking advantages of machine learning, especially neural networks, an adversary can reveal which YouTube video a victim watches with extremely high accuracy. While effective defense methods have been proposed, extremely high bandwidth overheads are needed. In other words, building an effective defense with low overheads remains unknown. In this paper, we propose a new defense mechanism, referred to as *SmartSwitch*, to address this open problem. Our defense intelligently switches the noise level on different packets such that the defense remains effective but minimizes overheads. Specifically, our method produces higher noises to obfuscate the sizes of more significant packets. To identify which packets are more significant, we formulate it as a feature selection problem and investigate several feature selection methods over high-dimensional data. Our experimental results derived from a large-scale dataset demonstrate that our proposed defense is highly effective against stream fingerprinting built upon Convolutional Neural Networks. Specifically, an adversary can infer which YouTube video a user watches with only 1% accuracy (same as random guess) even if the adversary retrains neural networks with obfuscated traffic. Compared to the state-of-the-art defense, our mechanism can save nearly 40% of bandwidth overheads.

Keywords: Encrypted traffic analysis · Machine learning · Feature selection

1 Introduction

Millions of Internet users steam videos from service providers, such as YouTube, Amazon Prime, Netflix, Hulu, etc., on a daily basis. As streaming videos has become a routine to Internet users, privacy of streaming services has become one of the primary concerns to both service providers and customers. For example, all the network traffic between a service provider and a user are encrypted to prevent eavesdroppers from learning the content of video streams.

© ICST Institute for Computer Sciences, Social Informatics and Telecommunications Engineering 2020
Published by Springer Nature Switzerland AG 2020. All Rights Reserved
N. Park et al. (Eds.): SecureComm 2020, LNICST 335, pp. 255–275, 2020.
https://doi.org/10.1007/978-3-030-63086-7_15

However, recent research studies [5, 11, 18, 20, 21, 28] have shown that steaming services are vulnerable under encrypted traffic analysis. An attacker can compromise user privacy due to the use of adaptive bitrate streaming technique (e.g., Dynamic Adaptive Streaming over HTTP), which is the key for service providers to offer high quality streaming. Specifically, the side-channel information of encrypted traffic (e.g., packet size) has a *strong correlation* with the content of a video. As a result, an attacker, who can eavesdrop a user's network traffic, can infer which video a user watches based on the side-channel information of encrypted traffic and achieve extremely high accuracy with machine learning. For example, an attacker can achieve 99% accuracy by leveraging Convolutional Neural Networks [21, 28]. Revealing users' sensitive information and interests through streaming fingerprinting can lead to unintended disclosure and can be leveraged by other cyberattacks, such as email phishing [16] and targeted advertising [25], which will cause more severe damages to individuals.

Traffic obfuscation, which adds noise (i.e., dummy data) to preserve real packet size, is one of the primary approaches to mitigate privacy leakage against encrypted traffic analysis [7, 17, 28]. However, it is often challenging for traffic obfuscation to be both efficient and effective in defense. Namely, producing small noise would introduce low bandwidth overheads but is often not effective. On the other hand, significant amounts of noises can effectively preserve user privacy but could easily introduce high bandwidth. For instance, Zhang et al. [28] proposed an effective defense to obfuscate packet sizes. Unfortunately, their method produces over 600% bandwidth overheads. The extremely high overhead is an enormous burden to both service providers and users, and impedes the implementation of traffic obfuscation in streaming services.

In this paper, we develop a new defense mechanism, referred to as SmartSwitch. The main idea of our proposed mechanism is to *smartly switch* the noise level in traffic obfuscation. More specifically, our proposed method obfuscates side-channel information of each packet (i.e., the size of each packet) differently, where more significant packets are obfuscated with higher noises while others are obfuscated with lower noises. The reason that switching the noise level can optimize efficiency while remain effective in defense is because *not every packet leaks privacy equally*. In other words, adding higher noises to more significant packets can maintain efficacy in defense and applying lower noises on less significant packets can save bandwidth overheads.

To identify which packets are more critical and need to be protected with higher noises, we formulate this problem as a feature selection problem ([3, 4, 15, 27]), where packet sizes are considered as features. However, addressing feature selection in the context of encrypted traffic is not trivial as the number of dimensions (i.e., the number of packets) is over hundreds or even thousands, which faces the *curse of dimensionality* [3, 4, 15, 27]. In this study, we investigate and customize several feature selection methods to examine their different trade-offs in the context of encrypted traffic. The main contributions of this paper are summarized below:

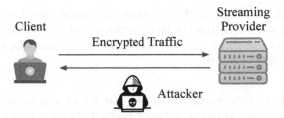

Fig. 1. The system model.

- To advance the understanding of privacy leakage in stream fingerprinting, we collect a large-scale encrypted traffic dataset of YouTube videos. The dataset consists of 100 classes (i.e., 100 YouTube videos) with 200 traffic traces per classes. Our dataset has a greater number of classes and a greater number of traces per class compared to datasets examined in previous studies [21,28].
- We build a Convolutional Neural Network (CNN) for stream fingerprinting. Our CNN is more comprehensive than the CNN used in previous studies, and outperforms it in attack accuracy. Specifically, our CNN achieves 91.4% accuracy while the previous one achieves 80.1% accuracy over our dataset.
- We investigate a fundamental research problem—*which packets are more critical against encrypted traffic analysis?*—and leverage feature selection to address it. We leverage and customize several feature selection methods, including feature permutation importance and mutual-information-based algorithms, to evaluate which packets are more critical than others and should be protected with higher noises.
- While our mechanism is generic, we leverage d^*-privacy used in [26,28] as the underlying noise generation algorithm to demonstrate its efficacy and efficiency. Specifically, even an attacker retrains neural networks with obfuscated traffic, our mechanism reduces attack accuracy to around 1%, which is the same as random guess over 100 classes. Compared to the previous research [28], our mechanism can reduce nearly 40% of bandwidth overhead.
- Our study promotes the *interpretability* of encrypted traffic analysis as many of the recent attacks [12,19,21–23,28] utilize neural networks as *black boxes* and do not reason which parts of an encrypted traffic trace leak more privacy. Our study also sheds lights on optimizing overheads of defenses against other encrypted traffic analysis, such as website fingerprinting.

2 Background

System Model. In the system model, which is described in Fig. 1, we assume there is a client and a streaming service provider. The network traffic between the client and service provider is encrypted with AES (Advanced Encryption Standard) with TLS (Transport Layer Security) protocol. The streaming service provider utilizes Dynamic Adaptive Streaming over HTTP (MPEG-DASH) technique in order to delivery high quality streaming services. MPEG-DASH creates different sizes of segments from a video and the service provider sends those segments to the client through TLS [21]. We assume the client watches a single YouTube video each time.

Threat Model. In this study, we assume an attacker is an eavesdropper who has *passive on-path access* to the network traffic between a client and the service provider [9]. For instance, an adversary could be someone who can sniff a client's WiFi traffic or on the same local-area network as the client. We also assume an attacker knows the IP addresses of the client and the service provider. The network packets between the client and the service provider are encrypted. The attacker dose not have the secret key to decrypt the content of traffic packets.

We denote the packets sent by the client as outgoing packets and packets received by the client as incoming packets. We assume that the attacker knows the start time of each traffic trace. Note that this is feasible to learn in the context of streaming traffic as outgoing packets usually locate at the beginning of each trace to initiate the connection and a significant amount of incoming packets would be received by the client when a video starts to play.

Closed-World Setting. We measure stream fingerprinting attacks and defenses in the *closed-world setting* by following the literature in this line of research. Specifically, the closed-world setting assumes that an attacker knows a list of stream videos that a client could watch (e.g., popular videos on YouTube). In addition, the closed-world setting assumes a traffic trace that is captured from a victim is associated with one of the stream videos in the attacker's list.

The attacker collects labeled traffic traces by itself to train its machine learning models, and then infers the label (i.e., which video) of a captured traffic trace from a victim. We leverage the *accuracy* of the classification to measure the privacy leakage of stream fingerprinting. A higher accuracy indicates more privacy leakage in encrypted stream traffic.

3   Stream Fingerprinting Attack

To advance our understanding of privacy leakage in stream fingerprinting, we collected a dataset in a greater scale and built a more comprehensive neural network compared to previous studies.

Data Collection. We collected a large-scale dataset of encrypted traffic traces from YouTube videos. The dataset consists of 20,000 traffic traces in total. Specifically, we selected 100 videos (classes), played each selected video 200 times and captured a traffic trace each time. For the 100 videos we investigate in this study, we selected videos recommended by YouTube in five categories, including gaming, music, talk, news and sports. In each category, we selected 20 different videos. For each video, we collected the encrypted traffic for the first 3 min and

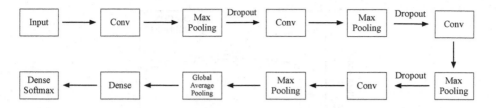

Fig. 2. Structure of our CNN model.

discarded the rest if a video lasts longer than 3 min. If there are advertisements at the beginning of each video, we keep the corresponding traffic of advertisements in our data collection.

We implemented a traffic crawler in `Python` and ran it on a Linux machine (Ubuntu 18.04, 3.40 GHz CPU, 16 GB Memory) to collect traffic. In our traffic crawler, we leveraged `Selenium` to automatically open a YouTube video page and utilized `pyshark` to capture the corresponding traffic. We used `Chrome` (Version 80.0) as the web browser during our data collection. It took one month of efforts (from September 2019 to October 2019) to complete the data collection.

Compared to the largest YouTube encrypted traffic dataset in the existing literature [28], where this dataset has only 40 classes and 100 traces per class, our dataset outperforms it in both the number of classes and the number of traces per class. The increases in those two aspects are critical to advance the understanding of the privacy leakage under stream fingerprinting in the real world.

Data Format. Raw traffic traces in our dataset are further processed to extract side-channel information of traffic, such that they can be used as inputs for neural networks. Existing studies [21,28] in stream fingerprinting aggregate packets into *bins* and use the size of aggregated traffic in a bin as a feature, where each bin contains all the packets in a fixed interval.

We follow the same method to extract bins from raw traffic traces. For example, given a 180-second traffic trace and an interval size of $w = 1$ s, a traffic trace is transformed into a vector of 180 elements, where each element is the size of aggregated traffic in a bin. When interval size $w = 0$, it indicates that there is no bins anymore and we use the size of each packet as a feature in that case. As the majority of packets (over 99% packets) are incoming packets in each trace, *we only keep incoming packets by following previous studies.*

Convolutional Neural Networks. We built a new Convolutional Neural Network and leveraged it as the classifier in stream fingerprinting. As shown in Fig. 2, our CNN consists of 11 layers, including 1 input layer, 4 convolutional layers, 5 pooling layers, and 1 output layer. It is more comprehensive than the CNN used in previous studies. For instance, the CNN used in [21,28] has only 6 layers at most.

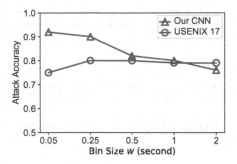

Fig. 3. Comparison of Our CNN and USENIX17 CNN in attack accuracy.

Attack Results in Stream Fingerprinting. Similar as [28], we studied the attack results of stream fingerprinting over a dataset by considering different bin sizes. Specifically, we applied five different bin sizes, $w = \{0.05, 0.25, 0.5, 1, 2\}$ seconds on our YouTube dataset, and obtained 5 versions of the dataset, where each version maps to a bin size. The number of elements n in a vector in each version depends on the corresponding bin size w and can be computed as $n = 180/w$.

To implement our CNN, we used `Keras` (front end) and `Tensorflow` (back end). We trained our CNN on a Linux machine with Ubuntu 18.04, 2.80 GHz CPU, 16 GB Memory and a GPU (NVIDIA Titan RTX). We used 64% of data for training, 16% of data for validation, and 20% of data for test. We also performed 5-fold cross-validation in our evaluation. In addition, we used `BatchNormalization()` function from `Keras` to normalize the data. We tuned hyperparamters of our CNN using NNI (Neural Network Intelligence) [1], a free toolkit offered by Microsoft. Specifically, we ran at most 50 epochs with NNI or stopped the search if the accuracy did not further improve after 10 consecutive epochs. It took us about 6 h to tune hyperparameters for bin size $w = 0.05$. These tuned hyperparameters are described in Appendix. If a different bin size was used, we retuned hyperparameters in our experiments. The hyperparameters for other bin sizes are skipped in this paper due to space limitations.

The attack results of our CNN on test data are summarized in Fig. 3. Overall, the attack achieves high accuracy and successfully infers user privacy across different bin sizes. For instance, given $w = 0.05$ s, our CNN achieves 91.4% accuracy in stream fingerprinting compared to 1% of random guess over 100 classes. We also noticed that the accuracy decreases if we increase the bin size. This is reasonable as a greater bin size leads to more coarse side-channel information, which reveals less privacy over encrypted traffic analysis.

To compare with previous attacks, we also implemented the CNN used in [21] and [28], which we referred to as USENIX17 CNN in this paper. As the tuned hyperparameters rendered in [21] only achieved 1% of accuracy over our YouTube dataset, we retuned the parameters of USENIX17 CNN again based on our YouTube dataset, and the attack results are reported in Fig. 3. As we can

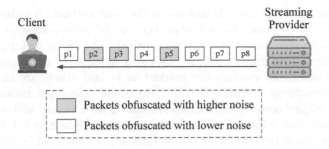

Fig. 4. A high-level overview of SmartSwitch.

MarkFeature(F, D): Given a set of features $F = \{f_1, ..., f_n\}$ over a traffic dataset D, where D has m traffic traces and each trace has n elements, run and output a binary vector $\boldsymbol{b}$

$$\boldsymbol{b} = (b_1, ..., b_n) \leftarrow \mathsf{FeatureSelectAlgo}(F)$$

where $b_i = 1$ if f_i is a selected feature and $b_i = 0$ otherwise.

ObfuTraffic($\boldsymbol{a}, \boldsymbol{b}$): Given a traffic trace $\boldsymbol{a} = \{a_1, ..., a_n\}$ and a binary vector $\boldsymbol{b} = \{b_1, ..., b_n\}$, generate two noise parameters e_0 and e_1, where e_0 represents for a lower noise level and e_1 represents for a high noise level, for $1 \leq i \leq n$, run

$$a_i' = \begin{cases} a_i + \mathsf{NoiseGeneAlgo}(e_0) \text{ if } b_i = 0 \\ a_i + \mathsf{NoiseGeneAlgo}(e_1) \text{ if } b_i = 1 \end{cases}$$

and output an obfuscated traffic trace $\boldsymbol{a'} = (a_1', ..., a_n')$.

Fig. 5. The Details of SmartSwitch.

observe, our CNN outperforms USENIX17 CNN in almost each bin size except $w = 2\,\text{s}$. For instance, given bin size $w = 0.05\,\text{s}$, the attack accuracy of our CNN is 11.4% higher than the one derived by USENIX17 CNN.

We would like to point out that the USENIX17 CNN achieved 94.4% accuracy on the dataset of 40 classes in [28] and 99% accuracy on the dataset of 20 classes in [21]. The accuracy of USENIX17 CNN dropped over our dataset as our evaluation involves more classes. For a machine learning problem, it is common to see that the accuracy of a same model decreases when the number of classes increases.

4   SmartSwitch: Our Proposed Defense Mechanism

We present our defense mechanism in this section. It consists of two building blocks, including a feature selection method and a noise generation algorithm. A feature selection method decides which packets are more significant, and can be one of the methods we will discuss in the next section. A noise generation algorithm produces noises to obfuscate the size of each packet using privacy-preserving techniques, such as differential privacy [26,28] or padding [6,7].

SmartSwitch first runs a feature selection method to distinguish packets, where more significant packets are marked as 1s and others are marked as 0s. Then, to generate an obfuscated traffic trace, the noise generation algorithm will apply a higher noise level to packets marked with 1s and add a lower noise level to packets marked with 0s. The high-level idea of SmartSwitch is illustrated in Fig. 4. The more rigorous technical details are summarized in Fig. 5. We use MarkFeature to describe the feature selection step and use ObfuTraffic to illustrate the generation of an obfuscated trace. We denote the two underlying building blocks as FeatureSelectAlgo and NoiseGeneAlgo.

Discussion. SmartSwitch is a *generic* defense mechanism, which can be integrated with concrete feature selection methods and noise generation algorithms. It is also feasible to apply it to defend against other fingerprinting attacks over encrypted traffic, such as website fingerprinting [6,10,13,14,19,22].

5   Which Packets Are More Significant?

In this section, we investigate a fundamental research problem—*which packets are more significant against encrypted traffic analysis?* Specifically, we consider the side-channel information of each bin as a feature, and formulate the question above as a feature selection problem. However, evaluating important features over encrypted stream traffic is not trivial as the number of features could be more than hundreds or even thousands. For instance, if the bin size is $w = 0.05\,\mathrm{s}$, then our dataset has $3,600$ dimensions, which is challenging to identify critical features from others.

As how to effectively and accurately select features over high dimensional data remains open in the current literature, we explored and customized two approaches, including permutation feature importance and mutual-information-based algorithms, in the context of encrypted traffic analysis.

5.1   Permutation Feature Importance

Feature selection methods can be grouped into two categories, wrapper methods and filter methods. A wrapper method modifies data associated with one feature each time and evaluates the corresponding change of accuracy of a trained classifier. A greater change in accuracy suggests a feature is more important.

Permutation Feature Importance (PFI) is one of the most common wrapper methods. It modifies the input to a classifier by permuting data in one feature each time. However, *directly permuting data in one feature each time in our problem is not effective as the number of dimensions in our dataset is high.*

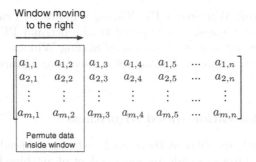

Fig. 6. An example of Sliding Window PFI, where a window include 2 features. In this figure, Sliding Window PFI permutes data inside the window to evaluate the importance of the 2 features.

Specifically, in our preliminary experiments, we did not notice changes of accuracy on a classifier and failed to evaluate the importance of a feature when we only permuted data related to one feature each time.

To overcome this limitation, we customize the algorithm of PFI by permuting data within a *sliding window* each time, where a sliding window consists of multiple consecutive features. In addition, the permutation within each sliding window is performed both vertically (i.e., across traces) and horizontally (i.e., across features) to create differences in data in order to examine the potential change of accuracy of a classifier. We refer our method as Sliding Window Permutation Feature Importance (Sliding Window PFI). An example of Sliding Window PFI is illustrated in Fig. 6.

Details of Sliding Window PFI. Given a dataset with m traces and n features, which can be represented as a $m \times n$ matrix, Sliding Window PFI initiates from the very left and takes a $m \times p$ submatrix, where p is the width of the sliding window and $p < n$. Within the sliding window, Sliding Window PFI first performs row-permutation to shuffle data across traces and then operates column-permutation to shuffle data across features. The rest of the matrix outside the current window keeps unchanged. The entire dataset after this permutation is fed into the trained CNN to measure the change in terms of accuracy in classification. This accuracy change is recorded to indicate the importance of the p consecutive features within the sliding window. A greater change on accuracy indicates the consecutive features within the sliding window is more significant. Our method keeps the size of the window the same but strides the sliding window to the right with one feature to measure the importance of the p features inside the sliding window for the next iteration. Our method iterates until it records the accuracy change of the last p features on the right in the matrix.

Tradeoff of Sliding Window PFI. Sliding Window PFI can effectively evaluate the changes of a classifier compared to the original PFI. As a necessary tradeoff, the significant features selected by Sliding Window PFI are groups of *consecutive* features, where each group of consecutive features is derived from one sliding window.

5.2 Mutual-Information-Based Algorithms

Unlike wrapper methods, filter methods analyze features based on statistic information. Therefore, filter methods are independent of machine learning classifiers and they are more efficient and generic. Mutual Information (MI) is a primary metric to measure the importance of features in filter methods. Given two random variables F, C, the mutual information of these two random variables can be calculated as below:

$$I(F;C) = H(C) - H(F|C) \tag{1}$$

where $H(F)$ is the entropy of random variable F and $H(F|C)$ is the conditional entropy for F given C. Mutual information of two random variables is greater than zero, and a higher mutual information indicates two random variables are more dependent.

In the context of feature selection, F is a random variable over data in a feature (or a subset of features) and C is a random variable over all the classes. A greater mutual information between F and C suggests that the feature (or the subset of features) is more important to classify the data. Given the number of features k that a method would like to select, the goal of this method is to maximize the mutual information of random variable F based on a subset of k selected features and target variable C [2].

As feature selection over high dimensional data using mutual information is a NP-hard problem [12], we leveraged three greedy algorithms, including Max-Relevance [2,15], Minimal-Redundancy-Maximal-Relevance [15] and Joint Mutual Information Maximisation [3,27], to address feature selection over encrypted stream traffic. The main idea of each greedy algorithm is briefly discussed below. More details can be found in the references.

Max-Relevance (MR). MR [2,15] evaluates the *relevance* between features and classes. It first calculates the MI score between each single feature and classes. Then, the features with top-k highest MI scores will be selected.

Given a set of features $F = \{f_1, ..., f_n\}$, the MI score of feature f_i and random variable of classes C can be computed as $I(f_i, C)$. MR selects a set of features $S = \{f_{s_1}, ..., f_{s_k}\}$, where $S \subset F$ and $f_{s_j} \in F$ for $1 \leq j \leq k$, such that

$$\arg\max_{S} D(S, C) \tag{2}$$

where $D(S, C) = \frac{1}{|S|} \sum_{f_{s_j} \in S} I(f_{s_j}; C)$.

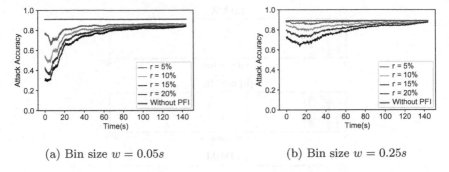

(a) Bin size $w = 0.05s$ (b) Bin size $w = 0.25s$

Fig. 7. The results of Sliding Window PFI. The x-axis is the time difference compared to the starting point of traffic traces.

Minimal Redundancy Maximal Relevance (mRMR). In addition to measuring the relevance between features and classes as in MR, mRMR [15] also measures the *redundancy* among features. When two features highly depend on each other, classification accuracy would not change significantly if only one of them is selected. Therefore, the other feature is considered as redundant and can be removed from the result of feature selection.

Specifically, given a set of features $F = \{f_1, ..., f_n\}$, the MI score of feature f_i and random variable of classes C is denoted as $I(f_i, C)$. mRMR selects a set of features $S = \{f_{s_1}, ..., f_{s_k}\}$, where $S \subset F$ and $f_{s_j} \in F$ for $1 \leq j \leq k$, such that

$$\arg \max_{S} D(S, C) - R(S), \tag{3}$$

where redundancy $R(S) = \frac{1}{|S|^2} \sum_{f_{s_i}, f_{s_j} \in S} I(f_{s_i}; f_{s_j})$. mRMR uses a greedy selection, which iterates each feature to find these top-k features.

Joint Mutual Information Maximisation (JMIM). JMIM [3,27] utilizes joint mutual information score to examine redundancy. Specifically, given two features f_i, f_j and random variable of classes C, the joint mutual information can be evaluated as

$$I(f_i, f_j; C) = I(f_i; C|f_j) + I(f_j; C) \tag{4}$$

Given a set of features $F = \{f_1, ..., f_n\}$ and an empty set $S = \varnothing$, JMIM first selects the feature with the maximum mutual information and adds it to set S. Then, JMIM adds one feature to set S in each iteration. Specifically, an unselected feature $f_u \in \{F - S\}$ is selected in an iteration such that it maximizes the minimum joint mutual information of itself, any selected feature $f_s \in S$ and random variable C, which can be formulated as below:

$$\arg \max_{f_u \in \{F - S\}} (\min_{f_s \forall S} (I(f_u, f_s; C))) \tag{5}$$

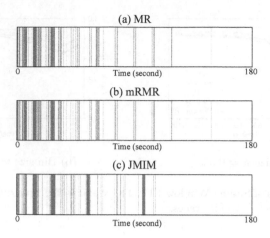

Fig. 8. Spectrum of selected features given bin size $w = 0.05$ s and $t = 10\%$. If a feature is selected, it is marked with red; otherwise, it is marked with white. (Color figure online)

Table 1. Attack accuracy with data from selected features only

	$n = 3600$ (bin size $w = 0.05$ s)		$n = 720$ (bin size $w = 0.25$ s)	
	$k = 180$	$k = 360$	$k = 72$	$k = 144$
Sliding window PFI	**35.1%**	48.5%	46.4%	**61.7%**
MR	30.5%	**57.7%**	39.8%	47.6%
mRMR	30.1%	57.5%	39.7%	46.7%
JMIM	32.2%	52.3%	**47.8%**	50.2%

Feature f_u is added to set $S = S \cup f_u$ and removed from the unselected set $\{F - S\}$ at the end of this iteration. JMIM continues the iterations until a total number of k features is selected.

6 Evaluation of Feature Selection

Next, we evaluate the results of feature selection over our YouTube dataset and show that each packet is not equally significant in stream fingerprinting.

Results of Sliding Window PFI. We examine Sliding Window PFI over our dataset by examining different sizes of sliding windows. Specifically, given the overall number of features n of a dataset, we examine sliding window size p, where $p = r \cdot n$ and parameter r is the ratio of the sliding window size to the overall number of features.

Given each n, which is decided by bin size, we examine parameter $r = \{5\%, 10\%, 15\%, 20\%\}$. We implemented Sliding Window PFI in Python and utilized our CNN described in Sect. 3 as the trained classifier. Specifically, after each permutation within a sliding window is completed, the accuracy change of classification on test data is recorded.

Due to the limitation of space, we only report the results of Sliding Window PFI when bin size is $w = 0.05$ and $w = 0.25$ s as our CNN achieves higher attack accuracy given these two bin sizes. As we can observe from Fig. 7, significant accuracy changes introduced by the permutation on data are identified at the first 40 s of traffic traces. This indicates that the beginning of encrypted traffic traces are more significant and leaks more privacy.

In addition, we can observe that, given the same bin size (or the number of features), a wider sliding window (i.e., a greater value of r) will cause more changes in attack accuracy. This is expected as a wider sliding window will cause more data to be permuted in each iteration. Moreover, we notice that permutation on data over a smaller bin size will cause more differences in the classification results. This is consistent with our attack results, where data over a smaller bin size leaks more privacy.

Results of Mutual-Information-Based Algorithms. Next, we examine the results of the three mutual-information-based greedy algorithms. Compared to the evaluation of Sliding Window PFI, where the feature importance is reported based on each sliding window, the three greedy algorithms report feature important based on each feature.

We implement the three methods using `feast` in Matlab [4]. `feast` is an open source framework for mutual-information-based feature selections. For each bin size, we select the top $t\%$ of features by following each greedy algorithm. The results of feature selection for bin size $w = 0.05$ and $t = 10\%$ are described in Fig. 8. Given $w = 0.05$ s and $t = 10\%$, there are $3,600$ features in total and 360 features are selected. As we can see that, all the three greedy algorithms indicate the features at the beginning of traffic traces are more significant. We have the same observation for other bin sizes. We skip further details due to space limitation. In addition, we observe that although the selected top $t\%$ of features from each greedy algorithm might be different, but overall the selected feature set is relatively similar.

Validation of Results with CNN. In addition to visualizing the selected features, we also run experiments to valid selected features are more significant to the classification in stream fingerprinting. Specifically, we perform stream fingerprinting, retune hyperparameters and re-train CNN based on data that is associated with selected features. As shown in Table 1, by selecting a much smaller number of features, the CNN model can achieve an accuracy that is much higher than random guess of 1%. For instance, give $n = 3600$ (bin size $w = 0.05$ s), selecting top $k = 360$ ($t = 10\%$) features can achieve more than 50% of accuracy in stream fingerprinting. In addition, we can also confirm that Sliding Window PFI and the three greedy algorithms obtain similar attack accuracy if they select a same number of features on the same dataset. We also notice that mRMR is outperformed by other methods in most of the cases shown in Table 1.

7   Evaluation of SmartSwitch

In this section, we use a concrete noise generation algorithm, named d^*-privacy [26], as a case study to demonstrate that our proposed defense mechanism Smart-Switch can effectively mitigate privacy leakage against fingerprinting attacks but can also significantly save bandwidth overhead.

To prove the advantage of our defense mechanism, we compare SmartSwitch with an existing defense [28], which also leverages d^*-privacy as the underlying noise generation algorithm but applies the same level of noise on all packets. We denoted this defense mechanism as NDSS19 in the rest of this paper. To conduct a fair comparison, we report the efficacy and efficiency of the two defense mechanisms over the same dataset—our YouTube dataset and utilize the same classifier—our CNN.

Details of d^*-privacy can be found in Appendix. The security analysis of it can be found in [26]. We would like to point out that applying the same level of noise in the context of d^*-privacy means that using the same privacy parameter ϵ to generate noise for all the packets in a traffic trace. In our evaluation, we assume a *strong attacker* who can adapt in aware of a defense and can re-train CNN with obfuscated traffic generated by a defense.

7.1   Defense Performance of NDSS19 on YouTube Dataset

We first reproduce the results of the defense mechanism, NDSS19, on our dataset. By reproducing it, we aim to validate that NDSS19 is effective against our CNN model, but not efficient in bandwidth. This evaluation will be used as the baseline in our comparison. We examine YouTube dataset with bin size $w = \{0.05, 0.25\}$ seconds, and we choose privacy parameter $\epsilon = \{5 \times 10^{-7}, 5 \times 10^{-6}, 5 \times 10^{-5}, 5 \times 10^{-4}, 5 \times 10^{-3}, 5 \times 10^{-2}\}$ to obfuscate data with each bin size by using NDSS19. We would like point out that a smaller privacy parameter indicates a higher level of noise in differential privacy. We skip other bin sizes ($w = \{0.5, 1, 2\}$ seconds) investigated in Sect. 3 as those bin sizes derived lower attack accuracy.

Attack Accuracy on Obfuscated Traffic Generated by NDSS19. We performed the attack on obfuscated traffic by using our CNN model. We re-tuned hyperparameters and re-trained CNN over each obfuscated dataset for each combination of bin size w and privacy parameter ϵ. The attack accuracy is shown in Fig. 9. As we can observe, NDSS19 is effective on our dataset when we choose privacy parameter $\epsilon \leq 5 \times 10^{-5}$, which we denote it as *privacy parameter threshold*. When choosing a greater privacy parameter than the threshold, the noise level is no longer effective against the attack using CNN. In addition, given the same privacy parameter, a smaller bin size leads to a higher attack accuracy, which is expected.

The overall observations in Fig. 9 are consistent with the results in the paper of NDSS19, which suggests that we successfully reproduced the results

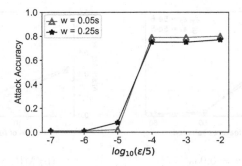

Fig. 9. Attack accuracy on obfuscated traffic generated by NDSS19.

Table 2. Bandwidth overhead of NDSS19

Privacy parameter ϵ	$w = 0.05\,\text{s}$	$w = 0.25\,\text{s}$
5×10^{-4}	50.8%	8.7%
5×10^{-5}	487.5%	87.6%
5×10^{-6}	4895.1%	881.4%

of NDSS19 on our dataset. It is worth to mention that, in the paper of NDSS19, the defense remains effective when privacy parameter $\epsilon \leq 5 \times 10^{-6}$, which is different from our privacy parameter threshold $\epsilon \leq 5 \times 10^{-5}$. This is likely because our dataset is different from the dataset used in their paper.

Bandwidth Overhead of NDSS19. We report the bandwidth overhead of NDSS19 on our YouTube dataset. As shown in Table 2, given bin size $w = 0.25\,\text{s}$ privacy parameter $\epsilon = 5 \times 10^{-5}$, NDSS19 introduces, on average, 87.6% (14.9 MB) bandwidth overhead per trace to generate obfuscated traffic traces. If we keep the bin size the same but change the privacy parameter to privacy parameter $\epsilon = 5 \times 10^{-6}$, the bandwidth overhead increases to 881.4% (149.8 MB) per trace on average. We also observed that a smaller bin size will need more bandwidth overhead given the same privacy parameter. The observation we have in bandwidth overhead is also consistent with the results in the paper of NDSS19. Given a same privacy parameter, *the degree of bandwidth overhead* is similar. The actual numbers are different due to the difference in datasets.

7.2 Defense Performance of SmartSwitch on YouTube Dataset

Next, we report the defense performance of SmartSwitch using d^*-privacy as the underlying noise generation algorithm. In terms of the underlying feature selection algorithms, we investigate Sliding Window Permutation Feature Importance, Max-Relevance, and Joint Mutual Information Maximisation, respectively. We skip Minimal Redundancy Maximal Relevance in the rest of this

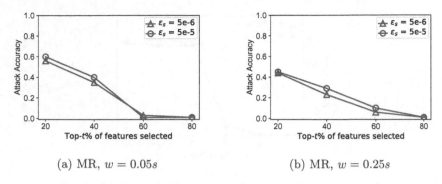

(a) MR, $w = 0.05s$ (b) MR, $w = 0.25s$

Fig. 10. Attack accuracy on obfuscated dataset generated by SmartSwitch with Max-Relevance.

evaluation as it has a similar but weaker results in feature selection than the other two mutual-information-based algorithms as we shown in Table 1.

The Number of Selected Features. While we have addressed how Smart-Switch can select features and how SmartSwitch can apply noise to obfuscate packets, another critical question we have not answered yet is—*how many features should SmartSwitch select?* To answer this question, given bin size $w = 0.25$ s, we selected top-$t\%$ of features using different feature selection algorithms on YouTube dataset, where $t = \{20, 40, 60, 80\}$. We applied privacy parameter $\epsilon_u = 5 \times 10^{-3}$ to generate noise for unselected features and privacy parameter $\epsilon_s = \{5 \times 10^{-5}, 5 \times 10^{-6}\}$ respectively to produce noise for selected features. We re-tuned hyperparameters and re-trained CNN over each obfuscated dataset for each combination of bin size w, privacy parameter ϵ and the proportion of selected features t.

As we can see from Fig. 10, if Max-Relevance is the underlying feature selection algorithm, SmartSwitch should select more than top-60% features to effectively defend against stream fingerprinting. For instance, given $\epsilon_s = 5 \times 10^{-5}$, SmartSwitch can reduce the attack accuracy close to 1%. We can also observe that, if we compare the defense performance between $\epsilon_s = 5 \times 10^{-5}$ and $\epsilon_s = 5 \times 10^{-6}$, a higher noise level on selected feature is more effective in defense. If Sliding Window PFI serves as the underlying feature selection algorithm, as shown in Fig. 11, our observations are consistent.

Note that we did not report the cases with Joint Mutual Information Maximization for bin size $w = 0.05$ s (i.e., $3,600$ features), as it is computationally challenging to select more than top-20% of features from a total number of $n = 3,600$ features. For example, after running 2 days with Joint Mutual Information Maximization, our desktop ran out of memory. Thus, we only used JMIM to analyse the datasets with $w = 0.25$ s which is shown in Fig. 12. As we shown above, SmartSwitch in that case needs to obfuscate top-60% of features to be effective in defense.

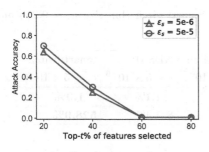
(a) Sliding Window PFI, $w = 0.05s$

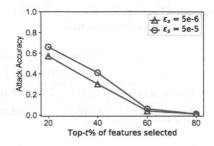
(b) Sliding Window PFI, $w = 0.25s$

Fig. 11. Attack accuracy on obfuscated dataset generated by SmartSwitch with Sliding Window PFI.

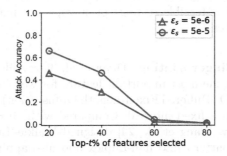

Fig. 12. Attack accuracy on obfuscated dataset generated by SmartSwitch with Joint Mutual Information Maximisation (bin size $w = 0.25$ s).

Bandwidth Overhead of SmartSwitch. As SmartSwitch only needs to primarily protect top-60% of all the features, it can save bandwidth overhead compared to NDSS19. As shown in Table 3, SmartSwitch can reduce the overhead from 87.6% to 52.9% when $w = 0.25$ s. And also, when $\epsilon_s = 5 \times 10^{-6}$, which is the threshold to make the defense effective in [28], SmartSwitch can reduce the overhead from 881.4% to 528.9%. In other words, SmartSwitch can save nearly 40% ($\approx \frac{881.4\% - 528.9\%}{881.4\%}$) bandwidth compared to NDSS19.

8   Related Work

Website Fingerprinting. During the early stage, researchers focused on using traditional machine learning methods to identify encrypted traces [6,10,13,14], These studies rely on hand-crafted features as inputs. Panchenko et al. [13] proposed the state-of-art fingerprinting method which leverages the cumulative size of traffic data as features and their proposed method is able to achieve an accuracy of 93%. Recently, researchers adapted deep learning model as attack which can automate the feature extraction process and achieve a very high accuracy. [19,22] used a carefully designed and tuned Convolutional Neural Network

Table 3. Comparison between NDSS19 and SmartSwitch (bin size $w = 0.25$ s and $\epsilon_u = 5 \times 10^{-3}$ in SmartSwitch)

	NDSS19	SmartSwitch	NDSS19	SmartSwitch
	$\epsilon = 5 \times 10^{-5}$	$\epsilon_s = 5 \times 10^{-5}$	$\epsilon = 5 \times 10^{-6}$	$\epsilon_s = 5 \times 10^{-6}$
Attack accuracy	8.1%	**4.5%**	1.1%	**1.0%**
Bandwidth	87.6%	**52.9%**	881.4%	**528.9%**

(CNN) and achieved 98% accuracy. Besides website fingerprinting, Schuster et al. [21] demonstrated that fingerprinting video streaming traffic is also feasible. They applied CNN on video streams collected from different service providers and their classification accuracy can reach as high as 99%. Recent studies [8,23] also demonstrated that it is feasible to fingerprint voice commands from encrypted traffic of smart speakers.

Defense Against Fingerprinting. Dryer et al. [6] revealed that burst-related information is one of the most important feature for website fingerprinting and they proposed BuFLO (Buffered Fixed-Length Obfuscation) which sends packets at a fixed size within a fixed interval. Compared with BuFLO, WTF-PAD [7] introduces no latency. Wang et al. [24] designed Walkie-Talkie, which changes the communication pattern into half-duplex and also apply burst-modeling to change the burst patterns of traffic. However, both WTF-PAD and Walkie-Talkie can be compromised by deep learning model based attacks. The attack in [22] can achieve 90% accuracy against WTF-PAD and 49.7% against Walkie-Talkie with their CNN model. In [28], Zhang et al. explored differential privacy in order to against the deep learning based attacks. They applied d^*-privacy on video streaming traffic and is able to reduce the accuracy to nearly 1%.

Feature Selection. In general, feature selection methods can be divided into two different categories, classifier dependent (wrapper methods) or classifier independent (filter methods). Wrapper methods analyse feature space by evaluate the classifier's results on each subset [12]. Therefore, the performance of Wrapper methods heavily relies on a well-designed and fine-tuned classification model.

Filter methods use information theory to estimate the relevance between features and class labels. Mutual Information is one of the most popular approaches. Battiti [2] proposed mutual information based feature selection. This method leverages the mutual information between candidate features and labels to select the informative subset. Yang et al. [27] proposed a feature selection method based on JMI (Joint Mutual Information), which estimates the relevance between pairs of features and class labels. Compared to MI, JMI considers conditional mutual information between each two individual features such that JMI treats features dependently. Peng et al. [15] devised a MI-based feature selection criterion, called mRMR (Minimal-Redundancy-Maximal-Relevance). The redundancy and relevance of candidate features are both considered for the purpose of reducing the dimension of feature set. Bennasar et al. [3] proposed JMIM (Joint Mutual Information Maximisation) which selects features based on JMI. The major difference between mRMR and JMIM is that, JMIM considers labels when it estimates the redundancy of features. In general, relevance and redundancy are two major factors for MI and JMI based filter methods when they evaluate candidate features.

9 Conclusion

We propose a novel defense mechanism to reduce the bandwidth overhead against stream fingerprinting. Our analysis results show that not every encrypted packet leaks privacy evenly, and protecting more significant packets with higher noise level is sufficient to maintain the efficacy in defense. Our defense mechanism is generic and can also be extended to defenses again other encrypted traffic analysis, such as website fingerprinting.

Acknowledgement. Our source code and datasets can be found on GitHub (https:// github.com/SmartHomePrivacyProject/SmartSwitch). Authors from the University of Cincinnati were partially supported by National Science Foundation (CNS-1947913), UC Office of the Vice President for Research Pilot Program, and Ohio Cyber Range at UC.

Appendix

Hyperparameters of CNN. The tuned hyperparameters of our CNN are described in Table 4. For the search space of each hyperparameter, we represent it as a set. For the activation functions, dropout, filter size and pool size, we searched hyperparameters at each layer. The tuned parameters we report in the table are presented as a sequence of values by following the order of layers we presented in Fig. 2. For instance, the tuned activation functions are selu (1st Conv), elu (2nd Conv), relu (3rd Conv), elu (4th Conv), tanh (the second-to-last Dense layer).

d^*-**privacy.** Xiao et al. [26] proposed d^*-privacy, which is a variant of differential privacy on time-series data, to preserve side-channel information leakage. They proved that d^*-privacy can achieve $(d^*, 2\epsilon)$-privacy, where d^* is a distance between two time series data and ϵ is privacy parameter in differential privacy.

Let $\boldsymbol{x} = (x_1, ..., x_n)$ and $\boldsymbol{y} = (y_1, ..., y_n)$ denote two time series with the same length. The d^*-distance between $\boldsymbol{x}$ and $\boldsymbol{y}$ is defined as:

$$d^*(\boldsymbol{x}, \boldsymbol{y}) = \sum_{i \geq 2} |(x_i - x_{i-1}) - (y_i - y_{i-1})| \tag{6}$$

d^*-privacy produces noise to data at a later timestamp by considering data from an earlier timestamp in the same time series. Specifically, let $D(i)$ denote the greatest power of 2 that divides timestamp i, d^*-privacy computes noised

Table 4. Tuned hyperparameters of CNN When $w = 0.05\,\text{s}$

Hyperparameters	Search Space	CNN $(w = 0.05)\,$s
Optimizer	{Adam, SGD, Adamax, Adadelta}	Adam
Learning rate	{0.001, 0.002, ..., 0.01}	0.006
Decay	{0.00, 0.01, 0.02, ..., 0.90}	0.71
Batch size	{32, 64, 128, 256, 512}	64
Activation function	{softsigh, tanh, elu, selu, relu}	[selu; elu; relu; elu; tanh]
Dropout	{0.1, 0.2, ..., 0.7}	[0.3; 0.4; 0.4; 0.7]
Dense layer size	{100, 110, ...,200}	170
Convolution number	{32, 64, 128, 256, 512}	[256; 128; 128; 512]
Filter size	{4, 6, ..., 26}	[14; 20; 16; 24]
Pool size	{1, 3, 5, 7}	[1; 3; 1; 3]

data $\tilde{x}_i$ at timestamp i as $\tilde{x}_i = \tilde{x}_{G_{(i)}} + (x_i - x_{G_{(i)}}) + r_i$, where $x_1 = \tilde{x}_1 = 0$, function $G(\cdot)$ and r_i are defined as below

$$G(i) = \begin{cases} 0 & \text{if } i = 1 \\ i/2 & \text{if } i = D(i) \\ i - D(i) & \text{if } i > D(i) \end{cases} \tag{7}$$

$$r_i = \begin{cases} \text{Laplace}(\frac{1}{\epsilon}) & \text{if } i = D(i) \\ \text{Laplace}(\frac{\lfloor \log_2 i \rfloor}{\epsilon}) & \text{otherwise} \end{cases} \tag{8}$$

References

1. NNI: An open source AutoML toolkit for neural architecture search and hyper-parameter tuning. https://github.com/Microsoft/nni
2. Battiti, R.: Using mutual information for selecting features in supervised neural net learning. IEEE Trans. Neural Netw. **5**, 537–550 (1994)
3. Bennasar, M., Hicks, Y., Setchi, R.: Feature selection using joint mutual information maximisation. Exp. Syst. Appl. **42**, 8520–8532 (2015)
4. Brown, G., Pocock, A., Zhao, M.J., Lujan, M.: Conditional likelihood maximisation: a unifying framework for information theoretic feature selection. J. Mach. Learn. Res. **13**, 27–66 (2012)
5. Dubin, R., Dvir, A., Hadar, O., Pele, O.: I know what you saw last minute – the Chrome browser case. In: Black Hat Europe (2016)
6. Dyer, K.P., Coull, S.E., Ristenpart, T., Shrimpton, T.: Peek-a-Boo, I still see you: why efficient traffic analysis countermeasures fail. In: Proceedings of IEEE S&P'12 (2012)
7. Juarez, M., Imani, M., Perry, M., Diaz, C., Wright, M.: Toward an efficient website fingerprinting defense. In: Proceedings of ESORICS 2016 (2016)
8. Kennedy, S., Li, H., Wang, C., Liu, H., Wang, B., Sun, W.: I can hear your alexa: voice command fingerprinting on smart home speakers. In: Proceedings of IEEE CNS 2019 (2019)

9. Kohls, K., Rupprecht, D., Holz, T., Popper, C.: Lost traffic encryption: fingerprinting LET/4G Traffic on Layer Two. In: Proceedings of ACM WiSec 2019 (2019)

10. Liberatore, M., Levine, B.N.: Inferring the source of encrypted HTTP connections. In: Proceedings of ACM CCS'06 (2006)

11. Liu, Y., Ou, C., Li, Z., Corbett, C., Mukherjee, B., Ghosal, D.: Wavelet-based traffic analysis for identifying video streams over broadband networks. In: Proceedings of IEEE GLOBECOM 2008 (2008)

12. Molnar, C.: Interpretable machine learning a guide for making black box models explainable. (2019). https://christophm.github.io/interpretable-ml-book/

13. Panchenko, A., et al.: Website fingerprinting at internet scale. In: Proceedings of NDSS 2016 (2016)

14. Panchenko, A., Niessen, L., Zinnen, A., Engel, T.: Website fingerprinting in onion routing based anonymization networks. In: Proceedings of Workshop on Privacy in the Electronic Society (2011)

15. Peng, H., Long, F., Ding, C.: Feature selection based on mutual information: criteria of max-dependency, max-relevance, and min-redundancy. IEEE Trans. Pattern Anal. Mach. Intell. **27**(8), 1226–1238 (2005)

16. Peng, P., Yang, L., Song, L., Wang, G.: Opening the blackbox of virustotal: analyzing online phishing scan engines. In: Proceedings of ACM SIGCOMM Internet Measurement Conference (IMC 2019) (2019)

17. Rashid, T., Agrafiotis, I., Nurse, J.R.C.: A new take on detecting inside threats: exploring the use of hidden markov models. In: Proceedings of the 8th ACM CCS International Workshop on Managing Insider Security Threats (2016)

18. Reed, A., Klimkowski, B.: Leaky streams: identifying variable bitrate DASH videos streamed over encrypted 802.11n connections. In: 13th IEEE Annual Consumer Communications & Networking Conference (CCNC) (2016)

19. Rimmer, V., Preuveneers, D., Juarez, M., Goethem, T.V., Joosen, W.: Automated website fingerprinting through deep learning. In: Proceedings of NDSS 2018 (2018)

20. Saponas, T.S., Lester, J., Hartung, C., Agarwal, S.: Devices that tell on you: privacy trends in consumer ubiquitous computing. In: Proceedings of USENIX Security 2007 (2007)

21. Schuster, R., Shmatikov, V., Tromer, E.: Beauty and the burst: remote identification of encrypted video streams. In: Proceedings of USENIX Security 2017 (2017)

22. Sirinam, P., Imani, M., Juarez, M., Wright, M.: Deep fingerprinting: understanding website fingerprinting defenses with deep learning. In: Proceedings of ACM CCS 2018 (2018)

23. Wang, C., et al.: Fingerprinting encrypted voice traffic on smart speakers with deep learning. In: Proceedings of ACM WiSec 2020 (2020)

24. Wang, T., Goldberg, I.: Walkie-Talkie: an efficient defense against passive website fingerprinting attacks. In: Proceedings of USENIX Security 2017 (2017)

25. Weinshel, B., et al.: Oh, the places you've been! user reactions to longitudinal transparency about third-party web tracking and inferencing. In: Proceedings of ACM CCS 2019 (2019)

26. Xiao, Q., Reiter, M.K., Zhang, Y.: Mitigating storage side channels using statistical privacy mechanisms. In: Procedings of ACM CCS 2015 (2015)

27. Yang, H.H., Moody, J.: Feature selection based on joint mutual information. In: Proceedings of International ICSC Symposium on Advances in Intelligent Data Analysis (1999)

28. Zhang, X., Hamm, J., Reiter, M.K., Zhang, Y.: Statistical privacy for streaming traffic. In: Proceedings of NDSS 219 (2019)

Misreporting Attacks in Software-Defined Networking

Quinn Burke[✉], Patrick McDaniel, Thomas La Porta, Mingli Yu, and Ting He

The Pennsylvania State University, State College, PA 16801, USA
qkb5007@psu.edu, mcdaniel@cse.psu.edu, {tfl12,mxy309}@psu.edu,
t.he@cse.psu.edu

Abstract. Load balancers enable efficient use of network resources by distributing traffic fairly across them. In software-defined networking (SDN), load balancing is most often realized by a controller application that solicits traffic load reports from network switches and enforces load balancing decisions through flow rules. This separation between the control and data planes in SDNs creates an opportunity for an adversary at a compromised switch to *misreport* traffic loads to influence load balancing. In this paper, we evaluate the ability of such an adversary to control the volume of traffic flowing through a compromised switch by misreporting traffic loads. We use a queuing theoretic approach to model the attack and develop algorithms for misreporting that allow an adversary to tune attack parameters toward specific adversarial goals. We validate the algorithms with a virtual network testbed, finding that through misreporting the adversary can draw nearly all of the load in the subnetwork (+750%, or 85% of the load in the system), or an adversary-desired amount of load (a target load, e.g., +200%) to within 12% error of that target. This is yet another example of how depending on untrustworthy reporting in making control decisions can lead to fundamental security failures.

Keywords: Network security · SDN · Load balancing

1   Introduction

Today's dynamic, cloud-centric marketplace demands faster and more reliable services. In order to meet these demands and maintain a specified quality of service, scaling out infrastructure has become a necessity. Key network functions, like load balancing, then provide the support necessary to keep these larger networks afloat. Load balancers split traffic fairly across equivalent backend servers or links to enable more efficient use of available network resources. In software-defined networking (SDN), however, load balancing typically manifests differently. The load balancer is divided into two components: the application logic (e.g., load balancing algorithm) that does the decision making and the network switches that enforce the decisions via flow rules. Here, the network switches are employed to report traffic loads (switch statistics) to the controller application

© ICST Institute for Computer Sciences, Social Informatics and Telecommunications Engineering 2020
Published by Springer Nature Switzerland AG 2020. All Rights Reserved
N. Park et al. (Eds.): SecureComm 2020, LNICST 335, pp. 276–296, 2020.
https://doi.org/10.1007/978-3-030-63086-7_16

to decide where to route incoming flows. While offering scalability and reliability benefits, this separation also creates an opportunity for an adversary at a compromised switch to misreport the traffic loads to influence load balancing.

In this paper, we evaluate an adversary's ability to control the amount of traffic flowing through the compromised switch (for eavesdropping and traffic analysis) by misreporting traffic loads. We take a queuing theoretic approach to model the attack and develop algorithms for misreporting that allow the adversary to tune attack parameters toward specific adversarial goals. We introduce two attacks against SDN load balancers: the *max-flooding* attack to draw as much load as possible and the *stealthy* attack to draw a target amount (an adversary-desired amount) of traffic through the compromised switch. We then evaluate them against four widely used load balancing algorithms: *least-loaded, weighted least-loaded, least-connections,* and *weighted least-connections,* which are included in the widely used Floodlight's [1] and OpenDayLight's [2] load balancing modules, and relied upon by several other specialized load balancing solutions [23,30]. We note that most dynamic load balancers in practice inevitably perform some form of *least-X* selection (e.g., least-loaded in bytes, least-connections) to select the most suitable path or endpoint for a flow [24]. The wide reliance on this calculation provides motivation for its effectiveness in a setting where the load balancer is subject to malicious inputs—in the form of false load reports.

Additionally, as the network traffic characteristics depend on the services offered by a subnetwork, we consider in our analyses two distinct traffic models that are representative of workloads most commonly found in modern cloud and datacenter networks: short and long flows (in terms of flow duration) [8,27]. The adversary must therefore calibrate the attack parameters appropriately based on the environment. We validate the attack algorithms with a virtual network testbed, finding that through misreporting the adversary can draw 750% additional load (85% of the load in the subnetwork) through aggressive misreporting, or draw a target amount of additional load to within 12% error of that target. We also find that the queuing model accurately describes the network behavior in response to misreporting to within 12% of the predicted throughput and 7% of the predicted number of misreports. Thus it is an effective tool for performing reconnaissance and provides a means of planning attacks on real SDNs. This demonstrates that misreporting extends to other services beyond those discussed in prior work. This is yet another example of how depending on collecting faithful information from untrustworthy sources leads to vulnerabilities, the results here being potentially disastrous, besides being difficult to detect in real-time. Our key contributions are:

- An attack model for analysis and planning of misreporting attacks against SDN-based load balancers.
- Development of two attacks against SDN load balancers that allow an adversary to control the volume of traffic through a compromised switch.
- Evaluation of misreporting attacks against four widely used load balancing algorithms and two distinct traffic patterns.

Prior work has partially addressed the issue of compromised switches with regards to eavesdropping, message integrity, and malicious link-discovery messages [16,20]; however, they have not considered the effects of malicious control messages in the context of load balancing. Here, we evaluate the performance of SDN-based dynamic load balancers in the presence of compromised switches who may misreport traffic loads (by under-reporting them). Several questions are raised concerning the performance of dynamic load balancers in adversarial settings: (1) *To what extent* can an adversary degrade the performance of load balancers by misreporting? (2) *When* must the adversary misreport? And (3), by *how much* must they misreport in order to accomplish their goal? We seek to address these key questions to highlight and quantify adversarial capabilities with regards to critical SDN services such as load balancers.

2   Background

Software-defined networks provide a framework that allows a more reliable and scalable alternative to traditional hardware- and software-based load balancers which sit in front of network resources. In the following, we discuss how load balancing is typically realized in SDNs.

Load-Balancing Algorithms. Existing load balancing solutions for traditional networks come in two categories: static and dynamic. Static solutions implement proactive techniques for splitting incoming flows evenly across network resources (i.e., servers or links). Since the client mappings are known ahead of time, these techniques cannot exploit run-time knowledge of bandwidth utilization, often resulting in a negative impact on network performance (e.g., underutilization, increased latency). Common implementations of static load balancing include Randomized, Round-Robin, and hash-based solutions like equal-cost multipath (ECMP) [5,19,29]. In contrast, dynamic solutions implement various reactive techniques for connection assignment and provide a means for connection affinity by maintaining a per-connection state. They allow more flexible and favorable decision making by exploiting knowledge about resource utilization learned during normal operation of the network. Widely used implementations of dynamic load balancers include least-response-time, least-loaded, and least-connections, along with their weighted counterparts [1,22,23].

Load-Balancing Architecture in SDN. Dedicated software-based load balancers offer scalability and reliability benefits over traditional hardware-based load balancers, which are often expensive and suffer from poor horizontal scalability. Previous work has already demonstrated the ability of load balancers to be implemented as software running on commodity hardware [13,25]. In SDNs, however, load balancing typically manifests slightly differently. The load balancer is abstracted from the physical infrastructure that it is deployed on by moving the load balancing logic to the control plane and distributing decision to network switches in the form of flow rules.

To enable dynamic load balancing in SDNs, the network administrator first defines a *pool*: a list of *switch ports* connected to links to load balance for (see

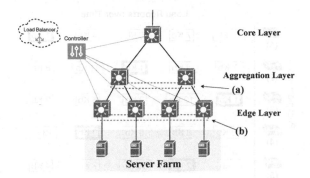

Fig. 1. Pool members for SDN-based load balancing across (a) links and (b) servers.

Fig. 1). These switch ports, or pool members, then become participants in the load balancing of the pool. The load balancer requests traffic load reports from them at each time epoch t, where epochs may be separated by one or more seconds. We will refer to this epoch length, the time between load-report collections, as the *collection interval.*

Under the OpenFlow [3] protocol, the reports come in the form of *switch statistics.* The loads represent the total activity at the switch ports since the last report, and may be measured in terms of Kb, number of active flows (or connections), etc., depending on the algorithm in use. The loads are then used to fairly route new incoming flows (that are destined for the resources offered by the pool); for example, with a variant of *least-X* selection.

As shown in Fig. 2, when a switch reports the minimum load at any epoch, the load balancer will temporarily route new flows through it. For example, switch (3) reports 1Kb of activity in the first epoch, has new flows routed through it to a backend server or link, and reports 12Kb of activity in the following epoch. Importantly, in the general case of the considered algorithms, all incoming flows are routed through the same pool member until the next load report is collected[1]; as the load balancer is removed from the data plane, it can only respond to the information given in load reports.

Notation for Load Balancing. Consider a network composed of N pool members, where the load balancer requests a load report R_t^i at each time epoch t for each member $1 \leq i \leq N$. For the case of least-loaded and least-connections [23], the load balancer temporarily routes new flows through the member who reported the minimum load (in bytes or number of active flows/connections), until the next load report is collected. More formally, the new flows will be routed through some member m in epoch t if:

$$R_t^m = \min_{1 \leq i \leq N} R_t^i, \tag{1}$$

If multiple members report the minimum load, random selection is done.

---

[1] We leave to future work analyzing more specialized variants of these algorithms.

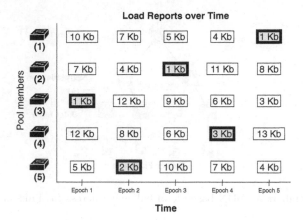

Fig. 2. Load reports (R_t^i) used for routing new incoming flows. Bolded reports are where switches reported the minimum load to the load balancer.

For weighted least-loaded and weighted least-connections, an exponentially-weighted moving average of loads is used for balancing. Weights are applied to the historical load values (α, where $0 \leq \alpha \leq 1$) and the current load value $(1 - \alpha)$, which are then summed together, allowing the load balancer to smooth out sudden bursts which may lead to inefficient balancing. Then, the new load $R_t^{i'}$ computed for each member at time t is:

$$R_t^{i'} = \alpha R_{t-1}^{i}{}' + (1 - \alpha)R_t^i, \tag{2}$$

and new flows will be temporarily routed through the member with the minimum load as in (1), with R_t^m and R_t^i replaced by $R_t^{m'}$ and $R_t^{i'}$. Again, random selected is applied in the case of multiple members with the minimum.

Related Work. This work focuses on modelling and evaluating misreporting attacks against load balancers in SDN. We draw from prior work on the security of SDN services [4,28] to identify vulnerable points in the control plane, which observe that an adversary at a compromised switch can manipulate link-discovery (LLDP) packets [16] to poison the topology information used by the controller for tracking network hosts and performing routing functions. Moreover, other works have found that adversaries can directly launch denial-of-service attacks against the control plane to saturate functions at the controller, for example, the service that computes routes for incoming flows [12]. Other works evaluate other vulnerabilities, including data modification and leakage, malicious control applications, lack of security features such as encryption, etc. [11]. Recent work also proposed a load-balancer attack in more traditional network architectures which requires sending probes from a network host [15]. Our work differs in that we consider misreporting (switch statistics) in the context of load balancing. problem Lastly, others have proposed defense systems to protect against some of these different classes of attacks [11,18,21,31], but these systems are not applicable to this attack scenario.

3   Attacking the Load Balancer

Misreporting switch statistics allows adversaries to directly control the volume of traffic flowing through a compromised switch for larger-scale eavesdropping and traffic analysis, which have been established as significant threats in modern cloud networks (e.g., to uncover browsing histories [14]). Here, we introduce two attack methods against two distinct network traffic patterns.

3.1   Threat Model and Overview

Threat Model. We assume switches report aggregate (i.e., port-level) statistics to a trusted load balancer, as balancing is typically done at a coarser level than individual flows [6]. Of these switches, we assume that one becomes compromised. If there is a single switch reporting for an entire pool (as with dedicated load balancers) and the switch becomes compromised, then load balancing integrity is clearly lost. We consider the situation where multiple switches faithfully report statistics for the pool and one becomes compromised[2]. Switches may be compromised by either an insider or external adversary [4,28]; however, methods for carrying out attacks are outside the scope of this work. The adversary may also be located at either the edge (balancing across servers) or aggregation layer (balancing across links) of the network.

In the context of load balancing, we define the general adversarial goal as misreporting to induce the load balancer into sending a *target* volume of traffic (on average) through the compromised switch. The adversary's capabilities are limited to recording its own load reports and sending misreports. Note that misreporting is necessary to draw more traffic regardless if packets on the switch ports are actually dropped; although, the adversary may drop an equivalent amount of traffic to evade detection systems that may leverage downstream switches to find inconsistencies in reports. We focus on adversaries under-reporting their true load to obtain an unfair proportion of traffic, and we leave over-reporting attacks (to deny service downstream or overload other switches) to future work.

Overview. Studies of modern datacenter and cloud networks have identified two distinct patterns in network traffic among different cloud services. The first consists of a majority of small (in bytes) and short (in seconds) flows that exist only momentarily in the network. This traffic is representative of applications such as web servers. The second consists of a majority of relatively longer and larger flows that persist in the network for several seconds or minutes; for example, for applications like video streaming. We draw from these studies [8,27] to generate packet traces for each pattern, consisting of flows with sizes and durations randomly selected along two pareto curves (Sect. 4). Preliminary observations shown in Fig. 3 with the Floodlight [1] SDN controller are representative of well-known traffic loads observed in the wild [8,27]. Note that load balancing occurs

---

[2] Note that switches may have multiple pool members (ports), but here we just consider a single pool member per switch and use *switch* and *pool member* interchangeably.

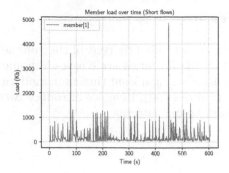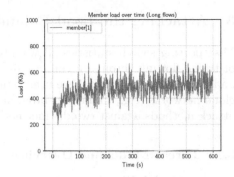

Fig. 3. 10-min captures of load reports of a single switch in two different scenarios. With traffic dominated by short flows (left) the switch observes momentary load spikes, and for long flows (right) a more stable load over time as active flows persist.

on a per-pool basis, and since pool members would be serving similar kinds of services, they would see similar traffic characteristics [8]. Nonetheless, our preliminary observations of these traffic patterns across a pool of servers reveal two threat vectors for an adversary to compromise the load balancer.

Short Flows. In the context of short flows, a majority (>80%) of flows entering the network lasts less than one second [8,17]. The result is network switches periodically observing momentary *load spikes* [8] as batches of incoming flows are temporarily routed through them. The load at such a switch will fall back down to normal levels (i.e., only overhead from control traffic) within just a few epochs (and load reports) as the flows expire quickly, and while the load balancer selects a different member as the minimum. This can be seen in Fig. 3 (left), where the load may be very high at one epoch (e.g., 1000 Kb) and then very low by the next (e.g., <10 Kb).

The key insight here is that the load reported by pool members is constituted by these momentary load spikes, as opposed to showing a more stable (or flatter) observed load over time. The rest of the load reports will show low activity, until more flows are routed through the switch. Thus, for an adversary to draw more traffic through the compromised switch, they must misreport (under-report) to induce more load spikes. Misreporting can exploit the load balancer's *least- X* calculation to cause the load balancer to immediately begin routing new flows through the switch, creating another load spike. The challenge is determining an appropriate number of misreports to draw the target load through the switch.

Long Flows. In the context of long flows, the observed loads of pool members are dominated by persistent activity of longer-lived flows rather than momentary bursts. As a result, pool members observe a steadier (or flatter) load distribution over time. The behavior in Fig. 3 (right) is consistent with this. The key insight here is that since the load reported by pool members is constituted by longer-lived flows, drawing more load is based on increasing the number of flows actively sending data through the compromised switch. The challenge here then becomes finding a suitable number of times to misreport to induce a certain number of active flows traversing the switch at any given moment.

We formalize misreporting in terms of a target utilization at a port on the compromised switch. We will refer to this target as ρ_{tar}. We then introduce two misreporting attacks with respect to ρ_{tar}. In the trivial attack, the *max-flooding* attack, the goal is to draw as much traffic as possible (e.g., $\rho_{tar} = 1.0$ utilization) through the switch port. In the *stealthy* attack, the goal is to draw a target volume of traffic (e.g., $\rho_{tar} = 0.2$) through the switch. This allows the adversary to manage the risk they are exposing themselves to by only misreporting the necessary amount to increase the utilization to the target.

With this formulation, the adversary must calibrate two parameters to draw the target utilization. $\overline{L}$ is the average load, the meaning of which differs slightly depending on the considered traffic pattern. It is used to determine *how many* misreports must be sent in order to draw ρ_{tar} through the switch port. The second parameter is δ, the misreported amount (e.g., in Kb) sent to the load balancer. It determines *by how much* to misreport by, and the choice of which will affect the success rate of misreporting; i.e., if the load balancer immediately begins routing new flows through the switch.

3.2   Attack Model

We introduce an M/D/1-based discrete-time queueing model (following prior work [15]) to approximate the behavior of the output switch port, and later validate the model accuracy on an experimental network. Here, we assume flow arrivals are determined by a Poisson process and service times are fixed (to transmit each bit). The model allows the adversary to derive attack parameters from model parameters for a given ρ_{tar}, and also serves to assess the effect of the attack on network performance.

Under an M/D/1 model, the utilization ρ of the switch port is given by:

$$\rho = \frac{\lambda}{\mu}, \tag{3}$$

where λ is the arrival rate (in bits per second, or bps) at the network interface card on the port, and μ is the service rate (in bps) of the card, fixed across all pool members as they serve similar services. For a given target utilization ρ_{tar}, there exists some target arrival rate of bits λ_{tar} that the adversary wishes to draw through the switch port:

$$\rho_{tar} = \frac{\lambda_{tar}}{\mu} \tag{4}$$

The adversary must then estimate the necessary number of misreports to draw λ_{tar} through the switch port.

Short Flows. Let M denote the number of misreports required to achieve the goal. As network traffic dominated by short flows is characterized by momentary load spikes, whenever the member reports the minimum load, a load spike will occur (see Fig. 3). Note that a load spike occurs whether the reported value was a misreport or not. However, a single successful misreport therefore corresponds with a single load spike. Then, the required number of misreports M to draw λ_{tar} can be approximated with knowledge of the amount of load (in bits or number of flows) contained in a load spike, or its *amplitude*. If $\overline{L}$ is the average load spike amplitude, then the number of misreports necessary to draw an average of λ_{tar} on the switch port over an attack window of W epochs is given by:

$$M = \frac{\lambda_{tar} \times W}{\overline{L}} \tag{5}$$

For offline analysis, we can approximate $\overline{L}$ for the least-connections algorithms by first considering an average flow inter-arrival rate of R flows per second [8]. Note that the adversary will compute the actual value at runtime. Since all of the flows are temporarily routed through the compromised switch for the next epoch, then the average load spike amplitude $\overline{L} = R$ flows. For the least-loaded algorithms, we also consider that the network flows have an average size of $\overline{f}$ bytes, based on characteristics of network flows observed in prior work [8]. Then, the average load contained in any load spike is $\overline{L} = 8R\overline{f}$ bits.

Long Flows. For network traffic dominated by long flows, the load in the network depends more on the number of active flows sending data through a switch rather than the amplitude of momentary load spikes, which are not as significant in this scenario compared to the number of active flows. Here, a single successful misreport corresponds with a set of long-lived flows being scheduled through the compromised switch. We therefore propose a heuristic method to drawing λ_{tar} on the port: *batch misreporting*. Specifically, the adversary will report consecutively a fixed number of times starting at the beginning of every t_{long}-second time slot, where t_{long} represents the average duration of the long-lived flows [27]. By misreporting in batches, or in consecutive epochs, the adversary can influence the load balancer to schedule an additional set of flows through the switch whose lifespan will nearly overlap in time. Then, the next batch of misreports will replace those expiring flows with new ones.

If we let $\overline{L}$ represent the average load observed at the switch port, the number of consecutive misreports to send, or the batch size B, is computed as the multiplicative factor of λ_{tar} over $\overline{L}$:

$$B = \frac{\lambda_{tar}}{\overline{L}} \tag{6}$$

For example, if the target load is $2\,\mathrm{Mb/s}$, the average load is $1\,\mathrm{Mb/s}$, and flows have an average duration of $10\,\mathrm{s}$, the adversary will misreport in batches of 2 at the beginning of every 10-s time slot to double the number of active flows traversing the switch. The required number of misreports M is:

$$M = \frac{B}{t_{long}} \times W \tag{7}$$

where the adversary misreports B times out of every t_{long} seconds, for the duration of the attack window.

We can approximate $\overline{L}$ for the least-connections algorithms by $\overline{L} = R \times t_{long}/N$ flows, where N is the number of pool members, and $\overline{L}$ represents the steady-state average load at any pool member. Note that for short flows we assume an average flow size $\overline{f}$ as the entire flow is consumed before the next epoch. If network flows have an average flow rate of $\overline{p}$ bytes [8,27], then for the least-loaded algorithms, we have similarly: $\overline{L} = 8R\overline{p} \times t_{long}/N$ bits. Note that the adversary will compute the actual value of $\overline{L}$ at runtime.

3.3   Max-Flooding Attack

In this attack, the goal of the adversary is to maximize the volume of traffic flowing through the compromised switch ($\rho_{tar} = 1.0$). The adversary can trivially perform the attack by misreporting every time the load balancer requests a load report. Specifically, here the number of misreports is $M = W$, each epoch for the entire duration of the attack window. Without loss of generality, we denote the compromised switch by switch N. To maximize the probability that the misreported load will be the minimum in (1), the adversary will set δ to zero (0 bytes, 0 flows, etc.), sending a new load ($R_t^{N''}$) in each epoch:

$$R_t^{N''} = \delta = 0 \tag{8}$$

The goal is to draw all flows arriving during the attack window through the compromised switch for larger scale eavesdropping and traffic analysis, and also may create congestion at the server connected by the switch port. Although feasible, the attack may also become readily observable.

3.4   Stealthy Attack

In the second attack, we generalize the max-flooding approach to allow the adversary to more stealthily attack the load balancer. A stealthy attack is one in which the adversary manages their detectability by drawing a λ_{tar} that is less than the maximum (less than maximum utilization). It is up to the attacker to assess the environment and decide what an appropriate undetectable load would be; i.e., how much load can they misreport before they are observable to some detection system. Thus, what we provide here is a method for configuring the attack such that the adversary can target a specific load (to within reasonable bounds) that they have decided is stealthy. Then, to meet the idea of stealthy, the adversary must reduce the amount of misreporting to only that required to draw λ_{tar} on the switch port. To accomplish this, we divide the attack into two phases: the reconnaissance phase and the attack phase.

Phase 1: Reconnaissance. In contrast to the max-flooding attack, here, $\overline{L}$ plays the critical role in determining the number of misreports that must be sent for a given λ_{tar}. Depending on what traffic conditions are present in the network—which we assume the adversary has some knowledge of or can infer from its own load distribution—$\overline{L}$ is computed in one of two ways. With an estimate for $\overline{L}$, the adversary must then find an appropriate δ.

Estimating $\overline{L}$: Short Flows. To estimate the amplitude of any load spike, we propose a heuristic method for detecting load spikes, then take the average as the estimate. The adversary first must select a threshold P at which an observed load should be considered a load spike. For example, if an observed load is greater than the 99th percentile of all observed loads seen thus far, it will be considered a load spike, since the majority of observed loads are much lower (and spikes are short-lived). We first let the adversary perform a warm-up phase (e.g., 10 min) to fill a list *observed_loads* of observed loads before detecting load spikes. Then, the adversary maintains a list S of load values considered load spikes, until D load spikes have been detected. The average is then taken as the estimated amount of load concentrated in any momentary load spike whenever a pool member reports the minimum load. If the list of detected load spikes S has size D, then the average load spike amplitude $\overline{L}$ is given by:

$$\overline{L} = \frac{\sum_{i=1}^{D} S_i}{D} \tag{9}$$

Given the average load spike amplitude (Kb or number of new flows) calculated during reconnaissance, the adversary computes the required number of misreports with (5). Note that misreports can be spaced out evenly with a misreporting period of T_m, or randomized with an average misreporting period of T_m:

$$T_m = \frac{\overline{L}}{\lambda_{tar}} \tag{10}$$

After the period is set, the adversary exits the reconnaissance phase.

Estimating $\overline{L}$: Long Flows. In this network setting, to draw more load, the adversary must increase the number of active flows sending packets through the switch. $\overline{L}$ can similarly be computed as simply the average load observed over an arbitrary window of time. If this window for reconnaissance is D epochs long, then $\overline{L}$ is given by:

$$\overline{L} = \frac{\sum_{i=1}^{D} observed\_loads_i}{D} \tag{11}$$

Given this, the number of misreports required to draw λ_{tar} through the switch is then given by (7). Unlike the network dominated by short flows, here misreports must be batched to have the target number of flows active as soon as possible.

Estimating δ. We previously assumed that whenever the adversary sent a misreport, the load balancer would certainly begin routing new flows through the compromised switch. Although guaranteeing a 100% misreporting success rate is difficult, sending a load of zero in each misreport will provide the highest probability of success. However, sending a load of zero in each misreport may likely raise alarms, especially if the desired load is very high (e.g., +500% load than usual) and thus so is the misreporting frequency. To meet the idea of stealthy, a better approach is for the adversary to simulate activity at the switch by mis-reporting (setting δ) to very low loads *which have been observed previously* and which have nearly the same probability of drawing a load spike as a load of zero. This is less likely to raise flags as it would be difficult to discern a legitimate report from a falsified one in this case.

To this end, we first observe that the observed-load distributions of all pool members (for either network traffic pattern) show small differences, which reflects observations made in prior work [8,9] of network switches observing similar traf-fic characteristics. Given this, we approximate the load distribution observed at other pool members by that observed and recorded by the adversary during reconnaissance. Then, if we first let U denote a cumulative probability of the load distribution, then there is an associated load value U_L (in Kb/s or num-ber of flows) with that cumulative probability: U percent of observed loads fall within $[0, U_L]$. Then, if there are N pool members, we can express the number of switches expected to report within some $[0, U_L]$ at any given time epoch as a binomial experiment on random variable X, with probability U of reporting within $[0, U_L]$:

$$E(X) = (N - 1) * U, \quad U > 0 \tag{12}$$

For example, if $N = 100$ and $U = 0.01$, approximately 1 switch (not the adver-sary) is expected to report within the given range (or percentile) any time the load balancer requests a report. The goal of the adversary then becomes select-ing a sufficiently low U to misreport to within, to reduce the expectation and therefore have a higher probability of (mis)reporting the minimum load. The adversary will randomly set δ to a previously observed load in $[0, U_L]$. Note that the adversary may not know the pool size; in this case, they should assume a large pool (and a small U), which will still be advantageous if the pool is actually smaller.

Phase 2: Sending the Misreport. After determining $\overline{L}$, then with a suitable misreporting period T_m or batch size B, along with a proper δ that should provide a reasonably high misreporting success rate, the adversary can then send the misreport. The adversary would first verify that the current load report collection time epoch falls at the beginning of a t_{long} time-slot for the case of long flows, or if it falls on a misreporting period (T_m) boundary for short flows. If so, the adversary may update the load to an under-reported value satisfying $\delta \in [0, U_L]$:

$$R_t^{N''} = \delta \tag{13}$$

If the actual load at the switch port is already below the determined threshold load U_L, the adversary will simply report that amount instead of modifying it. The key idea here is that the adversary can significantly reduce (to nearly a minimum) the amount of misreporting that must be done to reach the target load rate via simple analyses of the steady-state behavior.

3.5   Assessing the Impact

To assess the effects of the proposed attacks, we first want to measure the direct impact of misreporting. We then evaluate the effects of the attack on network performance across the compromised switch using an analytical attack model.

Measuring Attack Effectiveness. To describe the direct impact of the attack with regards to drawing more traffic through the switch, we define a damage metric D. It represents the ratio of the average load on the compromised switch during the attack window to the average load observed under normal conditions. If we denote the average load during the attack by L_{attack}, and under normal conditions by L_{normal}, then the relative damage is:

$$D = \frac{L_{attack}}{L_{normal}} - 1 \tag{14}$$

To concretely quantify misreporting effectiveness, we introduce a potency metric P that represents the average load increase obtained per misreport:

$$P = \frac{D}{\# \; misreports} \tag{15}$$

Note that M is an upper bound for the number of misreports, as the actual load may be within the misreporting range and the adversary can send the report without modification. Nonetheless, we also measure the rate and success rate of misreporting, which describes how often a misreport resulted in more traffic being routed through the compromised switch.

Measuring the Impact on Network Performance. A natural effect of shifting a large volume of traffic onto the switch port is congestion at the port, which will have a large impact on the throughput of flows traversing the switch port. However, as the utilization is significantly lower (less than 5%) on the servers or links in subnetworks dominated by many short flows, even shifting all of the traffic onto the link will not cause measurable impacts on throughput. Here, we just consider the effect of the attack on the changes in throughput for the long traffic pattern, where the servers and links are continuously being stressed by persistent flows. We measure the throughput as a function of the target ρ_{tar}, as well as a function of the number of misreports.

For a specified ρ_{tar}, the average time spent waiting in an M/D/1 system for each bit (delay per bit) is given by:

$$T_w = \frac{1}{\mu} + \frac{\rho_{tar}}{2\mu(1 - \rho_{tar})} \tag{16}$$

Since we know the number of misreports in this network scenario from (7), we can now measure the throughput changes as the target utilization increases.

4   Evaluation

With the formulation of the reconnaissance and attack phases, here, we explore
the effects on the performance of the load balancer in several scenarios (shown in
Table 1) and address the last research question: to what extent can the adversary
degrade the performance of the load balancer? We consider 4 widely used load-
balancing algorithms: least-loaded, weighted least-loaded, least-connections, and
weighted least-connections. We then provide an analysis of the effectiveness of
the two attacks in each scenario and the effects on the network performance when
considering long-lived flows (for example, in video streaming applications).

4.1   Experimental Setup

Network Setup. For experimentation, we employ the latest version of the
widely used Floodlight [1] SDN controller, along with its load balancing module.
To configure the virtual network, we use the popular Mininet emulator [10] to
create a similar topology of virtual switches and hosts to that shown in Fig. 1.
New flows will originate from a source connected to the "top-most" switch in the
figure, which represents a common gateway from which flows split paths in the
network (e.g., an aggregation switch in a three-tiered network). Each switch runs
the latest version of Open vSwitch (v2.12.0) and is invoked to connect to and
receive forwarding instructions from the Floodlight controller. And the directly
connected hosts act as sinks for the incoming network flows. The attacks are
then carried out by designating one switch as the adversary.

We configure the load balancer to have a single pool consisting of 10 SDN-
enabled switches, which is a realistic pool size for small clusters based on real
configurations used in the wild [26]. We note that our experimentation with larger
pool sizes yielded qualitatively similar results, where the load is scaled propor-
tionately for the same arrival rate of flows. The switches are directly connected
to a single backend resource (which represent either servers, or more switches).
We also configure the load balancer to have a load-report collection period of
1 s, which is suitable for providing reasonably low load-error rates [6]. We then
consider an average arrival rate of 250 flows/s and 100 flows/s for short and
long flows, respectively. Note that smaller or larger arrival rates yielded qualitatively similar results. We set the load spike detection percentile for the short-flow
traffic pattern to $P = 0.9$, the 90th percentile load. We set the load threshold
for misreporting $U = 0.01$, meaning the adversary will misreport to within the
bottom 1th percentile of loads (over a training window of 10 min). Note that
the success rate decreases with a power-law relationship to the threshold U, and
therefore flexibility in parameter choice is limited. We also set the attack window
to $W = 300$ epochs. Simulations are averaged over 25 independent executions.
Without loss of generality, the adversary is designated by switch number N.

Traffic Models. In evaluating our attacks, we draw from prior work to generate packet traces for each of the short and long traffic patterns. The sizes and
durations of flows are randomly distributed amongst the probability distribution defined by two pareto curves, which are widely accepted approximations

Table 1. Experimental network results with the Floodlight [1] SDN controller.

		Short flows				Long flows			
		LL	WLL	LC	WLC	LL	WLL	LC	WLC
Control	Average load	251.42 Kb/s	247.64 Kb/s	26 flows/s	27 flows/s	1017 Kb/s	929.6 Kb/s	83 flows/s	84 flows/s
Max-flooding	Average load	2142 Kb/s	2104 Kb/s	206 flows/s	209 flows/s	8277 Kb/s	8210 Kb/s	694 flows/s	688 flows/s
	Misreport rate	100%	100%	100%	100%	100%	100%	100%	100%
	Success rate	100%	100%	100%	100%	100%	100%	100%	100%
	Damage	+752%	+749%	+692%	+674%	+714%	+783%	+736%	+719%
	Potency	+2.51%	+2.49%	+2.31%	+2.25%	+2.38%	+2.61%	+2.45%	+2.39%
Stealthy	Target load	750 Kb/s	750 Kb/s	75 flows/s	75 flows/s	3000 Kb/s	3000 Kb/s	250 flows/s	250 flows/s
	Average load	866.70 Kb/s	834.67 Kb/s	93 flows/s	72 flows/s	2630 Kb/s	2650 Kb/s	223 flows/s	220 flows/s
	Misreport rate	32.3%	32.0%	30.3%	29%	23.7%	23%	24.8%	23.1%
	Success rate	96.9%	94.1%	98.6%	96.1%	97.1%	94.3%	98%	97.4%
	Damage	+245%	+237%	+244%	+167%	+159%	+157%	+169%	+162%
	Potency	+2.53%	+2.47%	+2.69%	+1.92%	+2.23%	+2.23%	+2.27%	+2.34%

for network traffic behavior [9]. Following these prior works, for the short traffic pattern we generate a set of flows with an average size of about 1 KB and average duration of about 100 ms. For longer flows, we generate flows with an average duration of about 10 s (for a flow size of about 10 KB). Note that experiments with longer flows (and therefore larger in terms of total size) yielded qualitatively similar results. Flow packets are transmitted at an average rate equal to the flow size divided by the duration.

Note that while switches may observe many flows of different types and patterns at any given time, load balancing is application-based (or switch-port based). Therefore, the load reports are only collected from those switch ports in the load balancing pool. Thus, we assume the same traffic pattern across pool members (i.e., either short or long flows) as downstream resources may serve similar services and should therefore see similar traffic patterns [8].

4.2   Experimental Results

Short Flows. In the first part of the evaluation, we considered short traffic flows. In this scenario, the adversary performed reconnaissance on the load spike amplitude (averaged over 10 load spikes) to compute the required number of misreports to draw the target load through the compromised switch. In Table 1, compared to the average load observed under normal conditions (the control experiment), running the max-flooding attack against the load balancer (using the least-loaded algorithm) was able to effectively draw nearly 85% of the load in the system (i.e., across the pool members) toward the adversary. In fact, the max-flooding attack proved to be successful across all four of the considered load balancing algorithms, drawing from 600–800% additional load through the switch compared to normal conditions. The misreporting rate for each was 100% of the attack window, and since the misreported load was zero (and loads must be non-negative), the misreporting success rate was also maximal. This means that each misreport resulted in at least one new flow being routed through the compromised switch, although multiple pool members may have all shared the minimum load at some time epochs.

The stealthy attack showed similar results with respect to misreporting success. Nearly all misreports resulted in the load balancer routing new flows through the compromised switch, allowing the adversary to maintain approximately the target amount of load at the switch port for the duration of the attack, to within 13% of the target (and almost always above the target). We note that the target load was specified to be three times that observed under normal conditions, although the adversary is not restricted to just that. Depending on the choice of P, the computed load spike amplitude may have been lower or higher, resulting in either more or less misreports (respectively). A persistent adversary may take a dynamic approach to misreporting by analyzing the effects and re-calibrating P appropriately to better meet the target.

Interestingly, the misreporting success remained the same even in the case of weighted load balancing. Even with a significantly high weight factor α for weighted balancing (e.g., $\alpha = 0.5$) [7], where the misreported load only has half the significance toward the smoothed value, the adversary was able to misreport low enough for the load balancer to consider it the minimum and begin routing flows through it. Certainly, a much higher α would place more weight on the historical load value and thus dampen the effects of misreporting.

In terms of direct damage to the system, the results indicate that the attack was successful in drawing approximately the target amount of traffic through the switch. Regardless of the algorithm in use, the adversary computed a required number of misreports (or alternatively, the misreporting period) that was nearly the same across all algorithms at approximately 30% of the attack window. It follows that the potency of misreports was also approximately the same across all algorithms at about 2% average increase in load per misreport, revealing that neither attack proved to be more or less resistant to the misreporting attack.

Long Flows. Next we consider a network dominated by longer flows. At runtime the adversary computed a batch size $B = 3$ from the given target and average load observed. As with short flows, the max-flooding attack shifted nearly 83% of the load in the system toward the compromised switch for an increase of more than 700% load than under normal conditions. The success rate was also at a maximum against each algorithm.

The stealthy attack in the context of long flows also proved to be successful against all four load balancing algorithms. In this case, the adversary was able to draw an amount of load through the switch to within 12% of the target. As with short flows, using the results as a feedback mechanism for a more dynamic attack is possible for adjusting parameters to better meet the goal. However, there is one difference here from the case of short flows: the average load was always under the target. In contrast to short flows, where the attack exploited the fact that load was concentrated in load spikes, here the fact that a fixed (average) number of flows arrive each second means that the batch misreporting will take longer to reach steady-state at the target load. This delayed effect of misreporting also scales up as the target (and therefore batch size) increases. Regardless, with a longer attack, the adversary would be able to reduce the error rate, although our evaluated attack window proves to be effective still.

The misreporting success showed a similar pattern across all of the algorithms, where none proved to be more or less resistant to misreporting. The potency of misreports also aligned with that observed under the short flows scenario.

4.3   Effects on Network Performance

As flow throughputs can be significantly larger in a long-flow environment (for example, when streaming high-definition multimedia), for example when streaming media, utilization on the switch port increases significantly relative to the available capacity (typically 100 Mb [9]). Higher utilizations begin to impose non-negligible delay overheads for active flows. Therefore, the adversary can directly control the congestion at the server connected by the switch port. Note that the goal is not to cause denial-of-service at the switch itself.

As the imposed delay increases with a power-law (under an $M/D/1$ system) as utilization increases, the throughputs for flows traversing the port thus decrease similarly as the adversary draws more load toward the compromised switch. We configure a network with a larger arrival rate of 10K new flows per second and show in Fig. 4 (left) how the average throughput for flows changes as the adversary's target utilization increases and more traffic is shifted onto the compromised switch. We also plot the predicted changes according to the proposed queuing model, demonstrating that the model is a reasonable approximator of the shape and scale of the plot from the experimental results.

The results demonstrate that throughput loss becomes significant quickly. At 20% utilization, flows suffer a nearly 20% throughput loss; similarly, at 40% utilization, which is not uncommon in modern cloud and datacenter networks [8], nearly 40% of throughput is lost. Although, the extent to which an adversary can degrade the throughput for active flows depends heavily on the number and arrival rate of flows in the network. Nonetheless, the ability of the adversary to impose throughput losses on flows in the network exists. In Fig. 4 (right), we measure the throughput changes as a function of the number of misreports sent. Note that pool members observed an average utilization of 10% under normal conditions in this scenario, therefore a goal of either 0% or 10% utilization resulted in approximately the same throughput although a single misreport was sent once every t_{long} seconds when the goal is 10% utilization.

Throughput loss is related to utilization. For example, the adversary misreports in batches of 2 consecutive misreports at the beginning of every 10-s time window (t_{long}), for a total of about 60 misreports over the 300-s attack window to draw nearly 20% utilization and induce a 20% throughput loss. As the

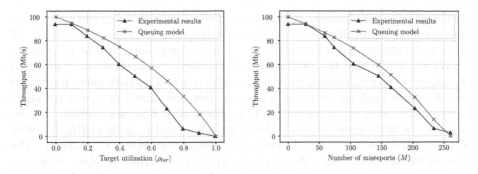

Fig. 4. Throughput vs. target utilization and number of misreports for least-loaded.

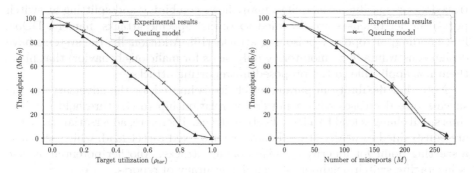

Fig. 5. Throughput vs. target utilization and number of misreports for least-connections.

steady-state load is already significantly high (about 10% utilization), misreporting will indeed draw more and heavier flows through the switch, meaning that the throughput loss per misreport is significant. In contrast, in networks with a lower flow inter-arrival rate and a smaller number of active flows in the network, the throughput loss per misreport is significantly less, and thus the adversary would have to misreport significantly more to cause a similar effect.

The key insight from Fig. 4 is that the proposed attack model (with the approximated $\overline{L}$) accurately describes the network behavior as a function of misreporting, to within 12% and 7% of the predicted behavior, respectively. In the least-connections case in Fig. 5, the model was within 10% and 5% error, respectively. In this way, we show that the attack model is an effective tool for performing reconnaissance and planning attacks on real networks, besides providing a means for further analysis defensively.

4.4   Discussion

The key insight from our experimentation is that an adversary can in fact feasibly subvert the load balancer by sending false load values in the load reports collected by the load balancer. Note that the chosen heuristics (for computing the number of misreports) are not necessarily optimal, and a persistent threat can tune attack parameters dynamically to meet their goals. However, the chosen heuristics still prove to be effective as a first exploration into misreporting attacks in general.

We also found that the analytical model accurately reflects what we observed experimentally, which makes the model an effective tool for both planning attacks and defensive analysis (without having to test the attack in a real network). Further, the need for a general security framework becomes obvious. Recent advances in SDN-based anomaly detection have tried to address this problem, however, the approaches are not designed to detect this attack [11,18,21,31]. The state-of-the-art detection system Sphinx [11] relies on trusting edge switches to detect inconsistencies along flow paths, and it operates only at flow-level where load balancing is typically done at port-level (and thus inconsistencies cannot be traced along specific paths due to many flows combining and splitting at switch ports). Other defenses are designed to thwart specific attacks, namely: DDoS, link-flooding, or topology poisoning attacks [16]. Additionally, the systems have design constraints (e.g., monitoring only *hosts* for malicious behavior) that make them not applicable to the proposed misreporting attacks.

Note that flexibility in parameter choice is limited for the adversary (as the success rate decreases with a power-law relationship to the threshold U), and thus small changes lead to a less-effective attack. Therefore, adversarial strategies are constrained to nearly-static behavior for a fixed target load, which serves as a starting point for identifying misreporting attacks. Another potential avenue is leveraging switch neighbors to vet the accuracy of reports.

5 Conclusion

As load balancers are a key feature of modern networks, protecting the integrity of their decisions is critical. To provide this, it is necessary that traffic measurements accurately reflect the true state of the network. In this paper, we proposed a new model and methods for attacking SDN-based load balancers. Our analytical model very accurately described the network conditions as a function of different attack parameters, providing both a means of planning attacks for the adversary, as well as a tool for analysis defensively.

Acknowledgements. This research was sponsored by the U.S. Army Combat Capabilities Development Command Army Research Laboratory and was accomplished under Cooperative Agreement Number W911NF-13-2-0045 (ARL Cyber Security CRA). The views and conclusions contained in this document are those of the authors and should not be interpreted as representing the official policies, either expressed or implied, of the Combat Capabilities Development Command Army Research Laboratory or the U.S. Government. The U.S. Government is authorized to reproduce and distribute reprints for Government purposes notwithstanding any copyright notation here on. This work was also supported in part by the National Science Foundation under award CNS-1946022.

References

1. Project floodlight (2011). http://www.projectfloodlight.org/floodlight/. Accessed 19 Oct 2018
2. Opendaylight project (2013). https://www.opendaylight.org/. Accessed 19 Oct 2018
3. OpenFlow switch specification (2015). https://www.opennetworking.org/software-defined-standards/specifications/. Accessed 19 Oct 2018
4. Arbettu, R.K., Khondoker, R., Bayarou, K., Weber, F.: Security analysis of Open-Daylight, ONOS, Rosemary and Ryu SDN controllers. In: 2016 17th International Telecommunications Network Strategy and Planning Symposium (Networks) (2016)
5. Aslam, S., Shah, M.A.: Load balancing algorithms in cloud computing: a survey of modern techniques. In: 2015 National Software Engineering Conference (NSEC), pp. 30–35. IEEE (2015)
6. Aslan, M., Matrawy, A.: On the impact of network state collection on the performance of SDN applications. IEEE Commun. Lett. **20**(1), 5–8 (2016)
7. Aweya, J., Ouellette, M., Montuno, D.Y., Doray, B., Felske, K.: An adaptive load balancing scheme for web servers. Int. J. Network Manage **12**(1), 3 39 (2002)
8. Benson, T., Akella, A., Maltz, D.A.: Network traffic characteristics of data centers in the wild. In: Proceedings of the 10th ACM SIGCOMM Conference on Internet Measurement, pp. 267–280. ACM (2010)
9. Benson, T., Anand, A., Akella, A., Zhang, M.: Understanding data center traffic characteristics. In: Proceedings of the 1st ACM Workshop on Research on Enterprise Networking, pp. 65–72. ACM (2009)
10. De Oliveira, R.L.S., Schweitzer, C.M., Shinoda, A.A., Prete, L.R.: Using Mininet for emulation and prototyping software-defined networks. In: 2014 IEEE Colombian Conference on Communications and Computing (COLCOM), pp. 1–6. IEEE (2014)
11. Dhawan, M., Poddar, R., Mahajan, K., Mann, V.: SPHINX: detecting security attacks in software-defined networks (2015)
12. Dridi, L., Zhani, M.F.: SDN-Guard: DoS attacks mitigation in SDN networks. In: 2016 5th IEEE International Conference on Cloud Networking (Cloudnet) (2015)
13. Eisenbud, D.E., et al.: Maglev: A fast and reliable software network load balancer. In: 13th USENIX Symposium on Networked Systems Design and Implementation (NSDI 16), pp. 523–535 (2016)
14. Feghhi, S., Leith, D.J.: A web traffic analysis attack using only timing information. IEEE Trans. Inf. Forensics Secur. **11**(8), 1747–1759 (2016)
15. Guirguis, M., Bestavros, A., Matta, I., Zhang, Y.: Reduction of quality (RoQ) attacks on dynamic load balancers: vulnerability assessment and design tradeoffs. In: IEEE INFOCOM 2007–26th IEEE International Conference on Computer Communications, pp. 857–865. IEEE (2007)
16. Hong, S., Xu, L., Wang, H., Gu, G.: Poisoning network visibility in software-defined networks: new attacks and countermeasures (2015)
17. Hong, S., Xu, L., Wang, H., Gu, G.: Poisoning network visibility in software-defined networks: new attacks and countermeasures (2015)
18. Kang, M.S., Gligor, V.D., Sekar, V., et al.: SPIFFY: inducing cost-detectability tradeoffs for persistent link-flooding attacks (2016)
19. Kang, N., Ghobadi, M., Reumann, J., Shraer, A., Rexford, J.: Niagara: scalable load balancing on commodity switches. Technical report, Technical Report (TR-973-14), Princeton (2014)

20. Khan, S., Gani, A., Wahab, A.W.A., Guizani, M., Khan, M.K.: Topology discovery in software defined networks: threats, taxonomy, and state-of-the-art. IEEE Commun. Surv. Tutorials **19**(1), 303–324 (2016)
21. Lee, S., Kim, J., Shin, S., Porras, P., Yegneswaran, V.: Athena: a framework for scalable anomaly detection in software-defined networks. In: 2017 47th Annual IEEE/IFIP International Conference on Dependable Systems and Networks (DSN), pp. 249–260. IEEE (2017)
22. Mahmood, A., Rashid, I.: Comparison of load balancing algorithms for clustered web servers. In: ICIMU 2011: Proceedings of the 5th International Conference on Information Technology & Multimedia, pp. 1 6. IEEE (2011)
23. Mesbahi, M., Rahmani, A.M.: Load balancing in cloud computing: a state of the art survey (2016)
24. Neghabi, A.A., Jafari Navimipour, N., Hosseinzadeh, M., Rezaee, A.: Load balancing mechanisms in the software defined networks: a systematic and comprehensive review of the literature. IEEE Access **6**, 14159–14178 (2018). https://doi.org/10.1109/ACCESS.2018.2805842
25. Patel, P., et al.: Ananta: cloud scale load balancing. In: ACM SIGCOMM Computer Communication Review, vol. 43, pp. 207–218. ACM (2013)
26. Qian, H., Medhi, D.: Server operational cost optimization for cloud computing service providers over a time horizon. In: Hot-ICE (2011)
27. Rao, A., Legout, A., Lim, Y.s., Towsley, D., Barakat, C., Dabbous, W.: Network characteristics of video streaming traffic. In: Proceedings of the Seventh Conference on Emerging Networking Experiments and Technologies, pp. 1–12 (2011)
28. Scott-Hayward, S., O'Callaghan, G., Sezer, S.: SDN security: a survey. In: 2013 IEEE SDN For Future Networks and Services (SDN4FNS), pp. 1–7. IEEE (2013)
29. Wang, R., Butnariu, D., Rexford, J., et al.: OpenFlow-based server load balancing gone wild (2011)
30. Zhang, J., Yu, F.R., Wang, S., Huang, T., Liu, Z., Liu, Y.: Load balancing in data center networks: a survey. IEEE Commun. Surv. Tutorials **20**(3), 2324–2352 (2018)
31. Zhang, Y.: An adaptive flow counting method for anomaly detection in SDN. In: Proceedings of the Ninth ACM Conference on Emerging Networking Experiments and Technologies, pp. 25–30. ACM (2013)

A Study of the Privacy of COVID-19 Contact Tracing Apps

Haohuang Wen[(✉)], Qingchuan Zhao, Zhiqiang Lin, Dong Xuan, and Ness Shroff

Department of Computer Science and Engineering, The Ohio State University, Columbus, USA
{wen.423,zhao.2708,lin.3021,xuan.3,shroff.11}@osu.edu

Abstract. The COVID-19 pandemic has spread across the globe and resulted in substantial loss of lives and livelihoods. To effectively fight this pandemic, many digital contact tracing mobile apps have been developed. Unfortunately, many of these apps lack transparency and thus escalate concerns about their security and privacy. In this paper, we seek to perform a systematic and cross-platform study of the privacy issues in official contact tracing apps worldwide. To this end, we have collected 41 released apps in total, many of which run on both iOS and Android platforms, and analyzed both their documentation and binary code. Our results show that some apps expose identifiable information that can enable fingerprinting of apps and tracking of specific users that raise security and privacy concerns. Further, some apps have inconsistent data collection behaviors across different mobile platforms even though they are designed for the same purpose.

Keywords: Contact tracing app · Program analysis · COVID-19 · Privacy

1 Introduction

The COVID-19 pandemic has rapidly spread across more than 180 countries around the world and the death toll has passed 846,000 [6] within only a few months after it first appeared in December 2019. Though governments and healthcare authorities around the world have quickly responded to this pandemic, at the time of this writing, only a few countries have successfully brought it under control. From their practices, *contact tracing* is a widely recognized and effective strategy to monitor and control the spread of the virus.

Contact tracing is an infectious disease control strategy that aims at identifying people who may have come into contact with an infected individual. It is not a new technique and has been performed in past pandemics including SARS in 2003 and H1N1 in 2009. Conventionally, contact tracing is conducted manually starting from collecting the necessary information from infected patients,

© ICST Institute for Computer Sciences, Social Informatics and Telecommunications Engineering 2020
Published by Springer Nature Switzerland AG 2020. All Rights Reserved
N. Park et al. (Eds.): SecureComm 2020, LNICST 335, pp. 297–317, 2020.
https://doi.org/10.1007/978-3-030-63086-7_17

such as locations they visited and people they had met, via an extensive interview. Unfortunately, manual contact tracing can result in inaccuracies because of the unreliable human memory as well as contacts with strangers. Further, manual contact tracing can also result in large delays, which could reduce its effectiveness.

In order to overcome the above problems in manual tracing, numerous digital contact tracing systems have been recently developed using camera footage, or credit card transaction, or information in cellular network (e.g., cellular tower) or smartphones. Among these, using information exchanged and stored in the smartphone for automated contact tracing is considered one of the most promising solutions for at least two reasons. First, smartphones are ubiquitous. Today, there are 3.5 billion smartphone users (1/3 of the entire population) worldwide, and more than 77% of Americans have smartphones [1]. Second, smartphones have many sensors and communication channels. For instance, a smartphone can easily acquire location information from GPS sensors, communicate with the Internet through the cellular network or Wi-Fi, and exchange information among themselves directly using Bluetooth.

While smartphone-based digital contact tracing is quite promising, it has raised privacy concerns since it can easily become a surveillance system if not properly designed and implemented. To operate, contact tracing apps require their devices to collect a large amount of privacy information (e.g., identifiable information of users). However, such data collection process lacks transparency. That is, according to our observation, only a few official contact tracing apps have been open-sourced and the majority of them remain close-sourced as of June 2020. Though many of these apps have announced to apply privacy-preserving protocols, these publicly disclosed protocols have also been criticized as sacrificing privacy in certain levels. For example, even with Bluetooth Low Energy (BLE) in which no real location is used, it could have various data leakages [17,19], and meanwhile the identity of an infected user could be de-anonymized by authorities or other users [16].

Motivated by such lack of transparency as well as the privacy concerns, we would like to conduct a systematic study of the official mobile contact tracing apps that have been released by governments and healthcare authorities. While there are many aspects to consider, we focus on the following ones: (i) which type of privacy-related information (i.e., information that reveals one's identity) has been collected for contact tracing? (ii) are these apps designed and implemented correctly to avoid privacy leakage? (iii) is the data being transmitted to other parties, e.g., servers or other users, privacy preserving (e.g., has the data been protected against eavesdropping, tracking, and de-anonymization attacks)? and (iv) do these apps behave consistently in different mobile platform?

To this end, we have collected a set of 41 official mobile contact tracing apps on both Android and iOS platforms (26 unique ones in total) as of June 15, 2020 and used a set of techniques to analyze the data privacy of the contact tracing apps. Specifically, for each app, we first recognize contact tracing relevant APIs to detect whether the app uses GPS or BLE to track users. Next, we de-compile the app and analyze the code to identify the privacy-related data collected for contact tracing, including those for BLE broadcasting and those collected along with the GPS data. Finally, we cross-compare the results from the same app between Android and iOS to investigate its behavior discrepancy.

Contribution. In summary, in this paper, we make the following contributions:

- **Systematic Study.** We conduct the first cross-platform study on the user privacy of 41 official contact tracing mobile apps, by analyzing their binary code to reveal the type of privacy-related data collected for the contact tracing purpose.
- **Novel Discovery.** We have uncovered that many of the apps can be fingerprinted with static UUIDs, and two apps are vulnerable to user tracking due to their fixed user IDs.
- **Cross-platform Comparison.** We compared the behaviors of an official app in both the iOS version and the Android version, and we found discrepancies in two apps across the two platforms.

2 Background

2.1 Digital Contact Tracing

Contact tracing has been used by public health authorities to monitor and control the spread of infectious diseases for a long time [24]. Being essentially a tracking system, it has to collect relevant data (*e.g.*, location) to track the contact. Unlike most location-based tracking, such as map navigation, that have to pinpoint users to a specific physical area, *e.g.*, a specific building with the exact physical location labelled by the latitude and longitude, not all digital techniques used in contact tracing request for such precise data, because the goal of contact tracing is just to understand whether two persons are in close proximity. Accordingly, we can classify the types of data used for tracing into the following two categories.

(I) Data for Location Tracing. Collecting the exact locations a person has visited and linking these locations together with timestamps is the most straightforward way to track users (*e.g.*, geo-locating drivers [44]). Meanwhile, a smartphone can provide a variety of data, by either reading from the hardware layer, *e.g.*, GPS sensors, or software layer, *e.g.*, information about a Wi-Fi hotspot, that can be used to pinpoint the specific location of a user. Based on how a user is tracked, we can further break the data for location tracing into two subcategories:

- **Continuous Coordinates-based Data.** A location can be recognized by its GPS coordinates. To obtain such data, we can directly read the coordinates of a smartphone from its embedded GPS sensor. In addition, we can also use cell tower and Wi-Fi to estimate an approximate location within an area. Moreover, even IP addresses can also be used to guess locations with coarse precision, *e.g.*, the street address.

- **Discrete Places-based Data.** In addition to tracking users using the continuous coordinates, we can also profile the movements of a user based on discrete places. For example, we can know where a user has visited by using fixed surveillance cameras, requiring users to check-in in certain places via QR code, or even collecting the transaction histories of credit cards that contain location information. By collecting discrete places, we can uncover the places users have visited.

(II) Data for Proximity Tracing. Unlike conventional location tracing, proximity tracing, theoretically, only measures the distance between two encounters without requiring any identifiable location information in any precision level. In addition, it requires data exchanges between users. In this case, Bluetooth Low Energy (BLE) is a well-suited technology because its signal strength can be used to estimate distances as well as its low energy consumption [21].

2.2 BLE in Proximity Tracing

The BLE, short for Bluetooth Low Energy, is a wireless communication technology with considerably lower energy consumption. In recent years, it has been widely deployed in wearable, smart homes, beacons, and car dongles [39]. Its features are well-suited for mobile contact tracing for three reasons. (*i*) BLE only consumes a low amount of energy to keep its normal operations; (*ii*) It can satisfy the requirement of proximity tracing as only a small amount of data is needed to be exchanged by design; (*iii*) The strength of BLE signal power can be used to calculate the distance between two contacts, which is a required functionality of proximity tracing. Additionally, in BLE communication, there are two important components worthy of mentioning, namely GATT and UUID.

- **GATT.** The Generic Attribute Profile (GATT) is the foundation of communication between two BLE devices that defines the procedures and format of data for transmission. GATT has a hierarchical structure with two key attributes: *service* and *characteristic*. In particular, each service represents a specific property and contains a number of characteristics, and each characteristic stores a piece of data of such property. Additionally, a characteristic can include several descriptors to provide its detailed information.
- **UUID.** The universally unique identifier (UUID) is an important component in BLE communication. It is a hexadecimal string used to uniquely represent an attribute, *e.g.*, service, characteristic, and descriptor. In addition, a UUID could be either a SIG-approved one or a vendor-specific one. That is, in theory, each UUID should be globally unique and the Bluetooth SIG has provided a set of standard UUIDs. For example, according to Apple/Google's Notification Exposure protocol, the service UUID 0xFD6F has been assigned by Bluetooth SIG for contact tracing [10]. But in practice, SIG also allows different manufactures to use their customized UUIDs, that must be different from the standard ones, for specific purposes.

Workflow of BLE Communication. The workflow of BLE communication involves three primary procedures: (*i*) Broadcasting and Connection, (*ii*) Pairing and Bonding, and (*iii*) Communication.

- **Broadcasting and Connection.** A connection is established between a BLE central device and a BLE peripheral device. To initiate a connection, the peripheral device needs to broadcast its advertisement packets to declare its existence. Whenever a central device notices such a peripheral device, it can actively establish a connection based on the data carried within the advertisement packets, *e.g.*, UUIDs.
- **Pairing and Bonding.** When a connection is established, the central and peripheral devices need to create a channel for secure communication. The processes to establish such a channel are pairing and bonding. In particular, the pairing process works by exchanging supported pairing protocol as well as negotiating a long term key (LTK) for data encryption. Then the bonding process will ask the two devices to store such LTK and use this key to encrypt the data transmitted through the established channel.
- **Communication.** After pairing and bonding, now two paired devices can communicate with each other by exchanging data whose format follows the GATT hierarchy. In particular, the central device first obtains the list of services and characteristics from either the advertisement packets or directly asking from the peripheral device. Next, with the list of characteristics, the central device can operate on values stored in a characteristic, *e.g.*, read and write, if holding sufficient permissions.

Typically, there are two ways to achieve contact tracing using BLE. In the first approach, a smartphone (when acting as a central) directly uses the received broadcasting packets sent from a peripheral (another smartphone), and records the received random cryptographic IDs parsed from the packets, without really establishing any connection. As such, each smartphone will also work as a BLE beacon, which is a 1-way transmitter that keeps broadcasting its identifiers to nearby BLE-enabled devices. The second approach to achieve contact tracing requires device mutual connection, as what has been done in BlueTrace [5] protocol. To be more specific, the two devices first discover each other based on a static UUID from the broadcast packet, and then establish a connection. Next, they exchange the contact information (*e.g.*, a user ID) by writing and reading from a specific characteristic in turn.

2.3   Centralized vs. Decentralized Mobile Contact Tracing

Depending on where the contact detection is performed, there are two typical architectures among current mobile contact tracing systems: (*i*) centralized in which all the detection is performed at a central server, and (*ii*) decentralized in which each client (*i.e.*, the smartphone) performs the detection. To do so, each user's (including the diagnosed positive patient) encounter record is uploaded to a central trusted server periodically in the centralized architecture, and then the central trusted server performs the contact tracing and notifies those who have been in contact with the patient. However, in the decentralized architecture, only the diagnosed positive patient's record is uploaded to the server, and each smartphone will periodically pull the record from the server and then perform the detection locally. There are still heated debates on which architecture is better, though the trend is moving towards the decentralized one especially given the decentralized industry standard set by Apple and Google [7].

3 Methodology

3.1 Scope and Overview

The goal of this work is to analyze COVID-19 contact tracing mobile apps with a focus on the user privacy (*e.g.*, whether there is any privacy leakage or over collecting of user data) from the program analysis perspective. In the following, we define the scope of our analysis, including the privacy issue and program code of our interest, followed by the overview of our analysis.

Privacy of Our Interest. While there is a broad range of privacy issues that potentially exist in mobile apps, not all of them are of our interest. In fact, many of the them (*e.g.*, information leakage, over-granted permissions) have been well-studied in the literature [41,42]. Consequently, in this work, we particularly focus on the user privacy issues that are resulted from the misuse of the data being collected for contact tracing purpose. For instance, what type of user data is collected? Can such data reveal user identity?

Program Code of Our Interest. Since our analysis is performed on both Android and iOS apps, the program codes of interest are disassembled or decompiled Java bytecode, Objective-C code, or Swift code.

Overview of Analysis. Our analysis can be broken down into three phases. In particular, given an Android or iOS COVID-19 app, we first decompile it and recognize the APIs involved in contact tracing (Sect. 3.2). Next, based on these APIs, we identify the privacy information collected for contact tracing (Sect. 3.3). Finally, we perform a cross-platform comparison analysis of the corresponding apps to further investigate the discrepancies of the same app (Sect. 3.4).

3.2 Contact Tracing Relevant API Recognition

The first step for our analysis is to identify the source information collected for contact tracing in a given app. As described earlier in Sect. 2.1, there are two types of sources for contact tracing: cryptographic tokens exchanged through BLE channel, or GPS coordinates acquired from smartphone sensors. Fortunately, all of these operations have to pass through system-defined APIs provided by the mobile operating systems. Therefore, recognizing these APIs will enable the identification of information sources of our interest. To this end, our analysis first decompiles the app binary, which is achieved through the off-the-shelf tools

Table 1. Relevant APIs for contact tracing in apps.

Platform	Tracking source	API name
Android	GPS	Location: float getAccuracy
		Location: float getAltitude
		Location: double getLatitude
		Location: double getLongitude
		Location: float getSpeed
		LocationManager: void getCurrentLocation
		LocationManager: Location getLastKnownLocation
		LocationManager: void requestLocationUpdates
		LocationManager: void requestSingleUpdate
	BLE	BluetoothLeAdvertiser: void startAdvertising
		BluetoothLeAdvertiser: void startAdvertisingSet
iOS	GPS	void CLLocationManager.requestLocation
		void CLLocationManager.startUpdatingLocation
	BLE	void CBPeripheralManager.startAdvertising

including ApkTool [3] and IDAPro [12]. Next, from the decompiled code, we run a simple script to scan and detect the APIs defined in Table 1, including all the APIs in Android and iOS for BLE and GPS. If any API in the BLE or GPS category is invoked, it implies that very likely the app has used BLE or GPS for contact tracing.

3.3 Privacy Information Identification

Given the recognized APIs, we further identify the privacy information collected for contact tracing. More specifically, we need to analyze where they are defined, and how they are used, *etc..*, in order to recognize the privacy issues. However, since a mobile contact tracing app can use either GPS or BLE to track users, the collected data can be different regarding different techniques. As a result, we correspondingly have two different approaches to identify them. In the following, we first present the approach of how we recognize BLE-specific data, and then how we recognize location tracing related data.

(I) Identifying BLE-Specific Data. Given the nature of the BLE protocol discussed in Sect. 2.2, there are two ways for smartphones to exchange contact information: one is through broadcasting of BLE packets (*e.g.*, BLE beacon [21]), and the other is through reading characteristic values via an established BLE connection. As a result, according to these two ways, we have summarized all the related system APIs for Android and iOS in Table 2. For instance, the `start-tAdvertising` API begins broadcasting of BLE packets, and the `setValue` API

Table 2. Targeted APIs for private data collection for BLE.

Platform	API name
Android	AdvertiseSettings: AdvertiseSettings.Builder setAdvertiseMode
	AdvertiseSettings: AdvertiseSettings.Builder setConnectable
	AdvertiseSettings: AdvertiseSettings.Builder setTimeout
	AdvertiseSettings: AdvertiseSettings.Builder setTxPowerLevel
	AdvertiseData: AdvertiseData.Builder addManufacturerData
	AdvertiseData: AdvertiseData.Builder addServiceData
	AdvertiseData: AdvertiseData.Builder addServiceUuid
	AdvertiseData: AdvertiseData.Builder setIncludeDeviceName
	AdvertiseData: AdvertiseData.Builder setIncludeTxPowerLevel
	BluetoothGattCharacteristic: BluetoothGattCharacteristic
	BluetoothGattCharacteristic: boolean setValue
iOS	void CBPeripheralManager.startAdvertising
	CBMutableCharacteristic CBMutableCharacteristic.init
	CBMutableService CBMutableService.init
	void CBPeripheral.writeValue
	CLBeaconRegion CLBeaconRegion.initWithUUID

sets the value of a BLE characteristic. Given these APIs, we first locate them in the decompiled app code through a searching script by using their names. Next, having identified where these APIs get invoked, we resolve the parameter values since not all of them are directly hardcoded. In particular, since there are quite a number of advertising configurations and data carried by these APIs, we only resolve the parameters that may lead to privacy concerns, such as the advertised data in characteristics and advertisement configurations (*e.g.*, whether the device name is included).

To this end, we have developed a tool to collect the program traces using a backward program slicing algorithm [38], which is based on Soot [13] for Android and IDAPro [12] for iOS. After collecting all necessary program traces, we need to understand the parameter (*i.e.*, their semantics). While there exists systematic approaches to infer semantics of parameters such as ClueFinder [30] that leverages program elements (*e.g.*, variable names), these approaches require a significant amount of data to train their machine learning models. In our case, due to the small number of apps we have, we applied a manual approach instead, in which we extract the data semantics based on the semantic clues (*e.g.*, variable types, names, logs, and API documentations).

BLE configuration identification. Based on the APIs for AdvertiseSettings in Android and startAdvertising in iOS, we are able to obtain the following configurations from the function parameters. Note that in iOS, a broadcasting peripheral device can only configure the device name and service UUID while others are controlled by the system by default [15].

- **(C1) Broadcasting Timeout**: When an app turns the phone into peripheral mode and broadcasts packets, it can set a timeout limit for broadcasting. By default, there is no timeout limit for broadcasting.
- **(C2) Device Connectable:** When turning the phone into a BLE peripheral, not all apps would allow other devices to connect for further communication. By default, this value is set to be connectable, which implies that other devices can connect to it and access (*i.e.*, read and write) the BLE characteristics.
- **(C3) Device Name:** The device name can be involved in the advertised BLE packet, and is by default the device name defined in the OS.
- **(C4) TxPower:** This power value, carried in the advertised packet, is often used in BLE proximity tracing for calculating the distance between two users. By default, this is set to be a medium power strength defined by the OS.

Private BLE data identification. In BLE, the privacy information (*e.g.*, user identifier) can be stored in the manufacture, service, and characteristic data. As such, we leverage the `AdvertiseData` and `setValue` APIs in Android, as well as the `init` APIs in iOS to extract these data. Note that we also need to manually infer the semantics of the extracted data, by using binary code level information such as variable types and names.

- **(P1) Manufacture Data:** The broadcasting packet can carry manufacture data along with the manufacture ID, and the manufacture data can be customized that might contain private information.
- **(P2) Service Data:** Similar to the manufacture data, this value is often customized by each app, and thus it may also carry privacy information.
- **(P3) Characteristic Data:** The value stored in each characteristic is for data exchange among devices, which might be privacy-related. For example, two smartphones may exchange the contact information by reading the user identifier from a characteristic.

Device Fingerprintable Data Identification. Previous studies [20, 45] have demonstrated that several attributes in BLE can be used for device fingerprinting. We thus focus on the following fingerprintable BLE data, which can be identified from the `BluetoothGattCharacteristic`, `addServiceUUID`, `init`, and `initWithUUID` APIs.

- **(F1) Manufacture ID:** The manufacture ID, or company identifier, is uniquely assigned by the Bluetooth SIG [4] for each member. Therefore, it can be potentially used for fingerprinting the device manufacture.
- **(F2) Service UUID:** Since each UUID serves as a unique identifier for a service or characteristic, it can be used to fingerprint a BLE device if it remains static. For instance, a nearby user may know from the broadcast UUID that someone is using a certain contact tracing app. However, in BLE proximity

tracing, UUIDs could be dynamic values that iterate overtime acting as an anonymity of a user.

- **(F3) Characteristic UUID:** Similar to service UUID, a static characteristic UUID can also enable fingerprinting attacks and thus is also of our interest.

(II) Identifying Location Tracking Related Data. Unlike the data collection through BLE proximity tracing, data collected for GPS location tracing needs to be first stored in the local device (*e.g.*, in a database), and then submitted to the central service when the user is tested positive for COVID-19. Therefore, we currently focus on the related APIs for database operations, which are listed in Table 3 to identify these data. In addition, if a piece of privacy data (*e.g.*, system version and device name) is collected and written into a database along with the GPS data, we speculate that such data will be sent to the server ultimately.

Table 3. Targeted APIs for private data collection stored in database.

Platform	API name
Android	void: SQLiteDatabase execSQL
	long: insert
	long: insertOrThrow
	long: insertWithOnConflict
iOS	int sqlite3_finalize
	int sqlite3_prepare
	int sqlite3_prepare_V2
	int sqlite3_execute

As shown in Table 3, the database APIs, such as `executeSQL`, take a SQL statement as input to execute it. Therefore, we infer the data semantics from the SQL statements that create a table (*e.g.*, `CREATE TABLE table_name (column type, ...)`), where the metadata of the table can be understood by an analyst.

3.4 Cross-Platform Comparison

Due to the fact that iOS and Android are the two most dominant mobile operating systems, official contact tracing apps often provide both versions to attract more users. While these apps are released by the same government or healthcare authority, each pair of apps is supposed to behave in the same way, which has been revealed in previous works on other types of apps [40]. However, it is still an open question of whether there are any discrepancies among contact tracing apps across different platforms. Therefore, in the final step of our analysis, we conduct a cross-platform comparison to understand and assess the behavior discrepancies. Specifically, for each pair of apps available in both iOS and Android, we manually compare every perspective of data revealed in the previous phases. For instance, we compare the semantics of the data under the same characteristic (identified with the same UUID) between the two platforms, and observe if there is discrepancy between the app's behaviour.

4 Evaluation

We have applied our methodology to a set of COVID-19 contact tracing apps. In this section, we first describe how we select these apps in Sect. 4.1, and then present the identified privacy information collected by these apps in Sect. 4.2, and finally show the results of our cross-platform study in Sect. 4.3.

4.1 COVID-19 Mobile App Collection

Today, there are numerous COVID-19 themed mobile apps. In this work, we focus exclusively on mobile contact tracing apps. Other types of COVID-19 themed apps (*e.g.*, self-diagnosis apps and treatment guidance apps) are out of scope of this study. In addition, apps under our study should have been released and deployed by governments or healthcare authorities on Google Play and Apple App Store. Therefore, we exclude apps that are still under development or are built for demos, concept proving, or other purposes.

Since there is no centralized repository for COVID-19 contact tracing apps, we have to search through the Internet and app store to know which government or authority has released or planned to roll out an official contact tracing app. Fortunately, there are many efforts that have been made by different groups of researchers to maintain a list of such apps, though there is no single list that has covered all apps. Therefore, we built our dataset by combining the apps from these open lists [8,11] with our own efforts.

In total, we have built a dataset of 41 apps, including 26 Android apps from Google Play and 15 iOS apps from Apple App Store, as of June 15, 2020. Except one app (MyTrace) that exists only in Android, there are 25 apps available in both platforms. However, not all the 25 iOS apps could be downloaded because some of them (*e.g.*, Stopp Corona) have restricted the location for downloading and we were not able to obtain them from our location. Additionally, for the iOS apps, we had to use a jail-broken iPhone to download them and extract the app code from the device. Next, we introduce these 41 apps in the following dimensions:

- **Distribution.** The list of all 41 contact tracing apps is shown in Table 4, and we plot their distribution on the map in Fig. 1. As shown, we can notice that the contact tracing apps are deployed across six continents and most of them are located in Europe, followed by Asia and then North America.
- **Platform.** According to the third column of Table 4, it is indicated that there is one app developed by Malaysia that supports only Android, while the rest supports both Android and iOS.

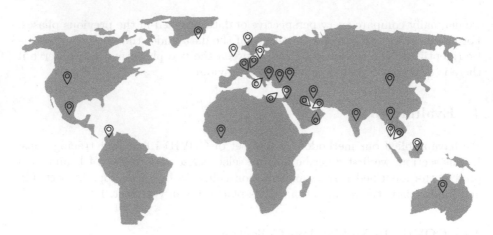

Fig. 1. Distribution of contact tracing apps in our study.

- **Technique.** As indicated in the forth column, among the 26 unique apps in both platforms, there are 20 apps that adopt BLE proximity tracing, 14 apps that use location tracing, and 8 apps that use both for the purpose of accuracy improvement.
- **Architecture.** Based on our best effort, we can identify the corresponding architectures of 18 apps. In particular, 12 apps are implemented using a centralized architecture, while the remaining 6 use a decentralized architecture. This implies that most governments tend to use a centralized server to collect contact tracing data as of this writing.
- **Description.** We also studied the official description of the apps [11]. Specifically, we checked whether the developer has claimed minimized data collection, limited data usage, and data destruction [11], and the results are correspondingly shown in the last three columns. We find that over half of the apps have declared at least one of these claims, which indicate many of these apps are aware of preserving user privacy.

4.2   Evaluation Result

BLE-Specific Data. In total, 20 apps use BLE for contact tracing. We successfully collected all of them from the Android platform but could only downloaded 10 of them from the iOS platform due to location restriction. The collected BLE-specific data can be classified into two categories: broadcasting data sent to all nearby devices, and BLE property data that can be read when the smartphone is being connected. We present the results in terms of their types in the following.

- **Broadcasting Data.** In Table 5, we present the measurement results of the broadcasting parameters, corresponding to the data types defined in Sect. 3.3. According to the tenth column of the table, there are 10 apps that use static

Table 4. Contact tracing apps in our study and their meta information (**M1**: claimed minimized data collection, **M2**: claimed limited data usage, **M3**: claimed data destruction, C: Centralized, D: Decentralized, P: Proximity, L: Location, L*: location with QR code).

App	Country	Plat.	Tech.	Arch.	M1	M2	M3
COVIDSafe	Australia	Both	P	C	✔	✔	✔
Stopp Corona	Austria	Both	P	D	✔	✔	✔
BeAware	Bahrain	Both	P; L	–	–	✔	–
ViruSafe	Bulgaria	Both	L	C	–	✔	✗
Chinese health code system	China	Both	L*	C	–	–	–
CoronApp	Colombia	Both	P	–	–	–	–
CovTracer	Cyprus	Both	L	–	✔	–	✔
eRouska	Czech	Both	P	–	✔	✔	✔
StopCovid	Georgia	Both	P; L	C	–	–	–
GH COVID-19 Tracker	Ghana	Both	L	–	–	–	–
Rakning C-19	Iceland	Both	L	–	✔	✔	✔
Aarogya Setu	India	Both	P; L	C	✗	✔	✗
PeduliLindungi	Indonesia	Both	P	–	–	✔	–
Mask.ir	Iran	Both	L	–	–	–	–
HaMagen	Israel	Both	L	D	✔	✔	✔
MyTrace	Malaysia	Android	P	D	–	–	–
CovidRadar	Mexico	Both	P	C	✗	–	✗
StopKorona	North Macedonia	Both	P	D	–	✔	✔
Smittestopp	Norway	Both	P; L	C	✗	✔	✔
ProteGO	Poland	Both	P	D	✔	–	✔
Ehteraz	Qatar	Both	P; L	C	✗	–	✗
Trace Together	Singapore	Both	P	C	✔	✔	✔
MorChana	Thailand	Both	P; L	–	–	✔	✔
Hayat Eve Sigar	Turkey	Both	P; L	C	✔	✗	✗
TraceCovid	UAE(Abu Dhabi)	Both	P	D	✔	–	–
NHS COVID-19 App	UK	Both	P	C	✔	✗	–
Healthy Together	UTAH(USA)	Both	P; L	C	–	✔	✔

UUIDs (*i.e.*, UUIDs that do not change overtime) for broadcasting. We further extract the UUID values and summarize them in Table 6. We can notice that these UUIDs are highly customized across different apps (*i.e.*, none of the app shares the same UUID with others). As a result, by reading such broadcast UUIDs, one is able to fingerprint the specific contact tracing app, which to some extent compromises user privacy. In addition to these 10 apps, we also find that 6 apps use dynamic UUIDs that rotate periodically. These

UUIDs are generated randomly or through some advanced cryptographic algorithms, which implies that their developers may be aware of such fingerprinting attacks. To summarize, we have the following key finding:

> **Finding 1**: 10 apps broadcast customized and static UUIDs that enable contact tracing app fingerprinting.

Further, we discover that the Aarogya Setu app from India has explicitly included the device name (*e.g.*, Alice's phone) in the broadcast packet, and interestingly, this practice only exists in the Android version. As in the app code, it invokes the setDeviceName API to set the device name with the value of unique_id of a user. Using such device name can raise privacy concern, because it can serve as the unique identifier to track a user.

Table 5. Evaluation result of BLE broadcasting (results separated by/are respectively for Android (left) and iOS (right)).

App	Country	C1	C2	C3	C4	P1	P2	F1	F2
COVIDSafe	Australia	0	✔	0	3	✔	✗	✔	Static
Stop Corona	Austria	0	✔	-	3	✗	✔	✗	Dynamic
BeAware	Bahrain	0	✔	-/-	2	-	✗	✔	Dynamic
CoronApp	Colombia	0	✔	0/1	3	✔	✗	✔	Static
eRouska	Czech	0	✗	0/0	2	✗	✗	✗	Static
Aarogya Setu	India	0	✔	1/0	0	✗	✗	✗	Static
StopKorona	North Macedonia	0	✗	-/1	3	✗	✔	✗	Static
MyTrace	Malaysia	0	✔	1	1	✗	✗	✗	Dynamic
CovidRadar	Mexico	0	✔	-/0	0	✗	✗	✗	Dynamic
Smittestopp	Norway	0	✔	0	2	✗	✗	✗	Static
ProteGO	Poland	0	✔	-/1	2	✗	✗	✗	Dynamic
Ehteraz	Qatar	0	✗	0/0	2	✗	✗	✗	Dynamic
Trace Together	Singapore	0	✔	0/1	3	✗	✗	✗	Static
MorChana	Thailand	0	✔	-	2	✗	✔	✗	Static
Hayat Eve Sigar	Turkey	0	✔	0	1	✗	✗	✗	Static
NHS COVID-19 App	UK	0	✔	1/1	2	✗	✗	✗	Static

- **BLE Property Data.** In Table 6, we present the extracted BLE property data with their semantics. Note that not all the BLE apps have configured such property data, since some apps only configure information in the broadcasting packet (*e.g.*, use UUID as a user identifier). Interestingly, in addition to the user identifier, we also discover that many apps have collected other device information. For instance, as indicated in the table, 4 apps collect the smartphone model, and 1 app collects device OS version, which are set as characteristic values for nearby devices to read. We further investigated their official documentations, and found that these information serve as factors to calculate the proximity distance between devices, which increases the estimation precision [5,43]

Among these results, our key finding is that two apps including Aarogya Setu from India and Hayat Eve Sigar from Turkey directly store fixed user identifier in readable characteristics. Specifically, Aarogya Setu first queries a unique ID from the server and stores it locally. When the `startAdvertising` API is called, the app retrieves the ID, and sets it as both the advertised device name and also the value of a readable characteristic. As for the other app, Hayat Eve Sigar also stores the current user's ID in a readable characteristic. As these property data are not protected and can be read once the smartphone is being connected, such fixed IDs can be obtained by nearby users, which can lead to tracking of a specific user. For instance, if the fixed ID appears again in the same location, or different location, an attacker is able to link these locations and IDs to a specific person. This finding has been disclosed to these two apps' developers.

> **Finding 2**: Two apps store fixed user identifiers in their readable characteristics, which allows tracking of a specific user.

Location Tracking Related Data. Among the 26 unique contact tracing apps, 14 of them have used GPS for tracking. The detailed results of the related data collected and stored into database are shown in Table 7. We then manually categorized the data into 6 types, including ID (*c.g.*, user ID), system version (*e.g.*, Android 7.0), device model (*e.g.*, Samsung Galaxy S6), orientation (*e.g.*, landscape and portrait), UI information (*e.g.*, UI style and brightness), and build number. Similar to the device data collected for BLE, we speculate that these data are also collected to improve the accuracy of distance measurements.

> **Finding 3**: It is surprising that contact tracing apps often collect other device information (*e.g.*, system version, and phone model).

4.3 Evaluation Result of Cross-Platform Comparison

Based on the previous results, we further perform a cross-platform study on the apps available in both platforms. We observe that most of the apps have consistent behaviour, which means they collect the same types of user data on both platforms. Interestingly, we also observe some discrepancies in two apps.

The two apps are Aarogya Setu from India and eRouska from Czech. In particular, the Android version of Aarogya Setu involves a unique ID and a Boolean

Table 6. Evaluation result of BLE properties (S: Service, C: Characteristic, R: Read, W: Write, N: Notify).

App name	Type	UUID	Semantics	Property
COVIDSafe	S	Random	Monitoring Service	
	C	B82AB3FC-1595-4F6A-80F0-FE094CC218F9	ID, model, version, RSSI	R; W
CoronApp	S	92959161-C063-4613-8AF8-9191408DD389	Monitoring Service	
	C	76FE5EB0-F79B-4CE0-8481-59044968DF04	ID, model, version, RSSI	R; W
eRouska	S	1440DD68-67E4-11EA-BC55-0242AC130003		
	C	9472FBDE-04FF-4FFF-BE1C-B9D3287E8F28	Current ID	R
Aarogya Setu	S	45ED2B0C-50F9-4D2D-9DDC-C21BA2C0F825		
	C	8D75EA37-6482-4EF5-9FFE-A5E4F44CBEE5	Unique ID	R; N
	C	91567DDF-9A75-4FE7-A0AB-F83F4DE15E2F	PinggerValue	R; N
	C	5CA2B7AE-EB74-46F4-B161-3C0A6F17F3EC	Device OS	
StopKorona	S	0000FF01-0000-1000-8000-00805F9B34FB		
Smittestopp	S	E45C1747-A0A4-44AB-8C06-A956DF58D93A		
	C	64B81E3C-D60C-4F08-8396-9351B04F7591		R
ProteGO	C	Random	ID, model, version, RSSI	R; W
Trace Together	S	B82AB3FC-1595-4F6A-80F0-FE094CC218F9		
	C	117BDD58-57CE-4E7A-8E87-7CCCDDA2A804	ID, model, version, RSSI	R; W
MorChana	S	000086E0-0000-1000-8000-00805F9B34FB		
Hayat Eve Sigar	S	D28ABA6E-EB1F-4193-8CFF-9EDEA7F9E57F		
	C	98023D4C-DAE7-4D4E-92C5-2800AFC4512E	Exchange Message	
	C	3A8E1D5C-F472-4D41-B33B-C7018CFBAE02	User ID	R
NHS COVID-19 App	S	C1F5983C-FA94-4AC8-8E2E-BB86D6DE9B21		
	C	D802C645-5C7B-40DD-985A-9FBEE05FE85C	Keep alive	R; W; N
	C	85BF337C-5B64-48EB-A5F7-A9FED135C972	Identity	R

Table 7. Device information collected in apps that use GPS tracing.

App	ID	SysVer.	Model	Orientation	UI Info.	Build
BeAware Bahrain	✔	✔				
CovTracer	✔	✔	✔			✔
eRouska	✔			✔		
StopCovid			✔	✔	✔	
GH COVID-19 Tracker	✔	✔	✔		✔	✔
Rakning C-19	✔	✔			✔	✔
Aarogya Setu	✔					
HaMagen	✔	✔	✔	✔	✔	
CovidRadar.mx	✔	✔	✔			
StopKorona	✔	✔	✔	✔	✔	
ProteGO	✔	✔		✔		
Trace Together		✔		✔		
NHS COVID-19 App		✔	✔			
CoronApp	✔	✔	✔			

value in two characteristics, while its iOS version have three characteristics instead: a device ID, device OS, and a field called `PinggerValue`. Obviously, the iOS version exposes the device OS information while the Android version does not. Regarding the app eRouska, its Android version does not specify any characteristic, while its iOS version sets a periodically changed user ID in a readable characteristic. It is interesting to observe these discrepancies, as the same pair of app in different platforms is supposed to behave consistently. We suspect this is due to different development processes between the two platforms.

5 Discussion

5.1 Limitations

While we have performed a cross-platform study on the COVID-19 contact tracing apps, there are still several limitations which need additional work to address. First, the set of apps we collected is incomplete, especially the iOS apps, which is due to the restrictions from the downloading regions. In addition, given the fact that the COVID-19 pandemic continues to spread across the globe, many countries will also likely roll out new contact tracing apps for mitigation. Therefore, it is also important to vet these newly emerged apps to ensure user privacy. Secondly, while our focus has been on privacy aspects of contact tracing apps, there are still open research questions that need to be answered. For example, how secure are these apps, are these apps efficient, *etc.*.

5.2 Mitigation on the Privacy Issues Identified

Ensuring Anonymity. Our findings uncover that some of the apps are vulnerable to fingerprinting and user identity tracking. The root cause is that they use static information such as UUIDs and user IDs that do not change periodically. To mitigate the fingerprinting attack, all contact tracing apps can use a unified UUID for broadcasting. For instance, the `0xFD6F` UUID [10] has been reserved by the Bluetooth SIG for contact tracing purpose. To mitigate user tracking with fixed IDs, developers should integrate dynamically rotatable user IDs, as demonstrated in many of the apps such as eRouska.

Improving Transparency. Our study also uncovers discrepancies between Android and iOS apps. Meanwhile, we find that most devices have collected excessive device information (*e.g.*, device OS and model), whose purposes remain unknown. Additionally, as of June 25th, 2020, only a handful of apps are open-sourced (*e.g.*, NHSX [14], Aarogya Setu [2], and eRouska [9]). Overall, the transparency of these contact tracing apps can still be improved, and many technical details related to user privacy should also be open to public. For instance, the usage of the collected private information, and the algorithm and factor used for distance estimation.

6   Related Work

COVID-19 Contact Tracing App Analysis. Since the emerging of COVID-19 contact tracing apps, many efforts have been devoted to studying the security and privacy of these apps, given the nature that these apps need to collect meaningful identifiable user information. There have been a handful of works summarizing existing contact tracing apps and protocols in the world as well as putting forward the current challenges and research questions. For example, Tang [35] analyzed the existing solutions such as MPC [31] and DP-3T [36], and uncovered drawbacks in terms of precision, authenticity, and transparency. Sun et al. [34] seek to vet the security and privacy of contact tracing apps with a focus on only Android apps. Other works [22,28,33] also mention some of the potential challenges and convey concerns regarding user privacy.

There are also a few works focusing on single contact tracing app or protocol. For instance, one of the earliest released contact tracing apps, TraceTogether has been studied by a number of researchers (e.g., [22,26,28]). In addition, there are also other targets that have been studied, including the NHSX app from UK [37], the contact tracing protocol proposed by Google and Apple [18,27]. Compared to these existing efforts, our work is the first cross-platform study on both the Android and iOS contact tracing apps with a focus on user privacy from a program analysis perspective.

Proximity Tracing with BLE and Its Security. Prior to contact tracing, BLE has been widely used for geo-localization. In particular, as an energy-efficient wireless technology, BLE has been adopted by beacon devices to enable indoor positioning [21,25], where the Received Signal Strength Indicator (RSSI) is measured to estimate the distance between two BLE devices [29]. This technique is later adapted in the contact tracing setting to detect whether two people have been in close contact. However, there are also a few attacks on the BLE protocol and devices, such as eavesdropping attacks [32], identity tracking [23], and more recently device fingerprinting [20,45]. Our analysis with COVID-19 apps also reveals the fingerprinting weaknesses, which may compromise user privacy.

7   Conclusion

In this paper, we present the first cross-platform study of the COVID-19 contact tracing apps, with a focus on user privacy. Starting from the program analysis perspective, we design a methodology to recognize contact tracing relevant APIs, identify the private information collected by the apps, and finally perform a cross-platform comparison on the apps available in both Android and iOS. We have applied our methodology to 41 contact tracing apps (26 Android apps and 15 iOS apps), in which we have obtained a number of privacy concerning findings: one specific app uses default device name for broadcasting which can be used to fingerprint specific users; Two apps store user's fixed IDs in characteristics, which essentially allows user tracking; There are discrepancies across platforms for two apps. Our future work includes improving our analysis to make it more automated, vetting the new emerging apps, and inspecting other issues such as the security of the COVID-19 apps.

Acknowledgement. We would like to thank our shepherd Adwait Nadkarni, and the anonymous reviewers for their valuable feedback. We are also grateful to Juanru Li, Tielei Wang, and Zhi Zhou for their assistance on obtaining the most recent iOS COVID-19 apps. This work was supported in part by the National Science Foundation (NSF) under Grant No. CNS 1618520, CNS 1834215 and CNS 2028547. Any opinions, findings, conclusions, and recommendations in this paper are those of the authors and do not necessarily reflect the views of the funding agencies.

References

1. 60+ revealing statistics about smartphone usage in 2020. https://techjury.net/blog/smartphone-usage-statistics/. Accessed 24 June 2020
2. Aarogyasetu_android.   https://github.com/nic-delhi/AarogyaSetu_Android. Accessed 23 June 2020
3. Apktool. https://ibotpeaches.github.io/Apktool/. Accessed 23 June 2020
4. Bluetooth sig, inc. https://www.bluetooth.com/
5. Bluetrace protocol. https://bluetrace.io. Accessed 23 June 2020
6. Covid-19 map. https://coronavirus.jhu.edu/map.html. Accessed 6 Aug 2020
7. Covid-19 tracing apps now live in Germany, France, and Italy; U.K. rethinks its plans. https://venturebeat.com/2020/06/19/covid-19-tracing-apps-now-live-in-germany-france-and-italy-u-k-rethinks-its-plans/. Accessed 24 June 2020
8. covid19-tracker-apps.   https://github.com/fs0c131y/covid19-tracker-apps. Accessed 23 June 2020
9. erouska-android. https://github.com/covid19cz/erouska-android. Accessed 23 June 2020
10. Exposure notification - Bluetooth specification v1.1. httpoi//www.blog.google/documents/62/Exposure_Notification_-_Bluetooth_Specification_v1.1.pdf. Accessed 24 June 2020
11. A flood of coronavirus apps are tracking us. now it's time to keep track of them. https://www.technologyreview.com/2020/05/07/1000961/launching-mittr-covid-tracing-tracker. Accessed 23 June 2020
12. Ida pro - hex rays. https://www.hex-rays.com/products/ida/. Accessed 23 June 2020
13. Instrumenting android apps with soot. https://github.com/soot-oss/soot/wiki/Instrumenting-Android-Apps-with-Soot. Accessed 23 June 2020
14. Nhsx. https://github.com/nhsx. Accessed 23 June 2020
15. startadvertising(_:) — ios developer documentation. https://developer.apple.com/documentation/corebluetooth/cbperipheralmanager/1393252-startadvertising. Accessed 23 June 2020
16. Bahrain, Kuwait and Norway contact tracing apps among most dangerous for privacy, June 2020. https://www.amnesty.org/en/latest/news/2020/06/bahrain-kuwait-norway-contact-tracing-apps-danger-for-privacy/. Accessed 23 June 2020
17. Qatari contact-tracing app 'put 1m people's sensitive data at risk' (2020). https://www.theguardian.com/world/2020/may/27/qatar-contact-tracing-app-1m-people-sensitive-data-at-risk-coronavirus-covid-19. Accessed 23 June 2020

18. Baumgärtner, L., et al.: Mind the gap: security & privacy risks of contact tracing apps. arXiv preprint arXiv:2006.05914 (2020)
19. BBC: Coronavirus: Security flaws found in NHS contact-tracing app, May 2020. https://www.bbc.com/news/technology-52725810. Accessed 23 June 2020
20. Celosia, G., Cunche, M.: Fingerprinting Bluetooth-low-energy devices based on the generic attribute profile. In: Proceedings of the 2nd International ACM Workshop on Security and Privacy for the Internet-of-Things, pp. 24–31 (2019)
21. Chen, D., Shin, K.G., Jiang, Y., Kim, K.-H.: Locating and tracking BLE beacons with smartphones. In: Proceedings of the 13th International Conference on Emerging Networking Experiments and Technologies, pp. 263–275 (2017)
22. Cho, H., Ippolito, D., Yu, Y.W.: Contact tracing mobile apps for covid-19: privacy considerations and related trade-offs. arXiv preprint arXiv:2003.11511 (2020)
23. Das, A.K., Pathak, P.H., Chuah, C.-N., Mohapatra, P.: Uncovering privacy leakage in BLE network traffic of wearable fitness trackers. In: Proceedings of the 17th International Workshop on Mobile Computing Systems and Applications, pp. 99–104 (2016)
24. Eames, K.T.D., Keeling, M.J.: Contact tracing and disease control. Proc. Roy. Soc. London Ser. B Biol. Sci. **270**(1533), 2565–2571 (2003)
25. Jeon, K.E., She, J., Soonsawad, P., Ng, P.C.: BLE beacons for internet of things applications: survey, challenges, and opportunities. IEEE Internet Things J. **5**(2), 811–828 (2018)
26. Leith, D., Farrell, S.: Coronavirus contact tracing app privacy: what data is shared by the Singapore OpenTrace app? In: International Conference on Security and Privacy in Communication Networks (2020)
27. Leith, D., Farrell, S.: GAEN due diligence: verifying the Google/Apple covid exposure notification API 2020. SCSS Tech Report (2020)
28. Li, J., Guo, X.: Covid-19 contact-tracing apps: a survey on the global deployment and challenges. arXiv preprint arXiv:2005.03599 (2020)
29. Lin, X.-Y., Ho, T.-W., Fang, C.-C., Yen, Z.-S., Yang, B.-J., Lai, F.: A mobile indoor positioning system based on iBeacon technology. In: 2015 37th Annual International Conference of the IEEE Engineering in Medicine and Biology Society (EMBC), pp. 4970–4973. IEEE (2015)
30. Nan, Y., Yang, Z., Wang, X., Zhang, Y., Zhu, D., Yang, M.: Semantics-driven, learning-based privacy discovery in mobile apps. In: NDSS, Finding Clues for Your Secrets (2018)
31. Reichert, L., Brack, S., Scheuermann, B.: Privacy-preserving contact tracing of covid-19 patients. IACR Cryptology ePrint Archive 2020:375 (2020)
32. Ryan, M.: Bluetooth: with low energy comes low security. In: Presented as Part of the 7th USENIX Workshop on Offensive Technologies (2013)
33. Simko, L., Calo, R., Roesner, F., Kohno, T.: Covid-19 contact tracing and privacy: studying opinion and preferences. arXiv preprint arXiv:2005.06056 (2020)
34. Sun, R., Wang, W., Xue, M., Tyson, G., Camtepe, S., Ranasinghe, D.: Vetting security and privacy of global covid-19 contact tracing applications (2020)
35. Tang, Q.: Privacy-preserving contact tracing: current solutions and open questions. arXiv preprint arXiv:2004.06818 (2020)
36. Troncoso, C., et al.: Decentralized privacy-preserving proximity tracing. https://github.com/DP3T/documents. Accessed 23 June 2020
37. Veale, M.: Analysis of the NHSX contact tracing app 'isle of wight' data protection impact assessment (2020)
38. Weiser, M.: Program slicing. IEEE Trans. Software Eng. **4**, 352–357 (1984)

39. Wen, H., Chen, Q.A., Lin, Z.:. Plug-N-Pwned: comprehensive vulnerability analysis of OBD-II dongles as a new over-the-air attack surface in automotive IoT. In: 29th USENIX Security Symposium (USENIX Security 20), Boston, MA, August 2020. USENIX Association (2020)
40. Wen, H., Zhao, Q., Chen, Q.A., Lin, Z.: Automated cross-platform reverse engineering of can bus commands from mobile apps. In: Proceedings of the 27th Annual Network and Distributed System Security Symposium (NDSS 2020), San Diego, CA, February 2020
41. Yang, Z., Yang, M.: LeakMiner: detect information leakage on android with static taint analysis. In: 2012 Third World Congress on Software Engineering, pp. 101–104. IEEE (2012)
42. Yang, Z., Yang, M., Zhang, Y., Gu, G., Ning, P., Wang, X.S.: Appintent: analyzing sensitive data transmission in android for privacy leakage detection. In: Proceedings of the 2013 ACM SIGSAC Conference on Computer & Communications Security, pp. 1043–1054 (2013)
43. Zhao, Q., Wen, H., Lin, Z., Xuan, D., Shroff, N.: On the accuracy of measured proximity of Bluetooth-based contact tracing apps. In: International Conference on Security and Privacy in Communication Networks (2020)
44. Zhao, Q., Zuo, C., Pellegrino, G., Lin, Z.: Geo-locating drivers: a study of sensitive data leakage in ride-hailing services. In: Proceedings of the 26th Annual Network and Distributed System Security Symposium (NDSS 2019), San Diego, CA, February 2019
45. Zuo, C., Wen, H., Lin, Z., Zhang, Y.: Automatic fingerprinting of vulnerable BLE IoT devices with static UUIDS from mobile apps. In: Proceedings of the 2019 ACM SIGSAC Conference on Computer and Communications Security, pp. 1469–1483 (2019)

Best-Effort Adversarial Approximation
of Black-Box Malware Classifiers

Abdullah Ali and Birhanu Eshete$^{(\boxtimes)}$

University of Michigan, Dearborn, USA
{aliabdul,birhanu}@umich.edu

Abstract. An adversary who aims to steal a black-box model repeatedly queries it via a prediction API to learn its decision boundary. Adversarial approximation is non-trivial because of the enormous alternatives of model architectures, parameters, and features to explore. In this context, the adversary resorts to a *best-effort strategy* that yields the closest approximation. This paper explores best-effort adversarial approximation of a black-box malware classifier in the *most challenging setting*, where the adversary's knowledge is limited to label only for a given input. Beginning with a limited input set, we leverage *feature representation mapping* and *cross-domain transferability* to locally approximate a black-box malware classifier. We do so with *different feature types* for the target and the substitute model while also using *non-overlapping data* for training the target, training the substitute, and the comparison of the two. Against a Convolutional Neural Network (CNN) trained on raw byte sequences of Windows Portable Executables (PEs), our approach achieves a 92% accurate substitute (trained on pixel representations of PEs), and nearly 90% prediction agreement between the target and the substitute model. Against a 97.8% accurate gradient boosted decision tree trained on static PE features, our 91% accurate substitute agrees with the black-box on 90% of predictions, suggesting the strength of our purely black-box approximation.

Keywords: Model extraction · Model stealing · Adversarial machine learning

1 Introduction

Recent advances in machine learning (ML), specially in deep learning, have led to significant improvement on the accuracy of image classification, machine translation, speech processing, and malware/intrusion detection. Despite their impressive accuracy, deep neural networks (DNNs) and other traditional machine learning models such as Logistic Regression, Support Vector Machines, and Decision Trees have been shown to be vulnerable to training-time poisoning [8,9], test-time evasion [7,14,25,33], model extraction [24,28,34], and membership inference attacks [11,31].

N. Park et al. (Eds.): SecureComm 2020, LNICST 335, pp. 318–338, 2020.
https://doi.org/10.1007/978-3-030-63086-7_18

With the advent of ML-as-a-Service (MLaaS), ML models are increasingly served via prediction APIs to allow remote submission of input samples to produce predictions or provide pre-trained models as foundations to build up on. While MLaaS enables new frontiers of ML use-cases such as serving models from the cloud with pay-per-query price model, it also exposes models behind prediction APIs to model extraction/approximation attacks via iterative input-output interactions [19,24,28,31,34]. An adversary aiming to game a prediction API of a model to avoid a pay-per-prediction bill or a competitor targeting the trade secret of a model have financial motivations to steal ML models. For instance, adversaries are motivated to steal (approximate) a remote black-box model trained on privacy-sensitive data (e.g., medical records), intellectual property (e.g., stock market trends), or inherently security-sensitive data (e.g., malware/intrusion traces). In general, so long as the cost of approximating an ML model is lower than the potential financial gain from obtaining a close-enough copy of it, MLaaS will continue to be a target of financially motivated adversaries.

More precisely, given a black-box model f_b (e.g., a malware detector) served via a prediction API, the adversary's goal is to perform *best-effort* approximation of f_b's decision boundary by locally training a substitute model f_s. Best-effort in this sense refers to relying on limited seed-set (e.g., 5%–10% of the training set for f_b) to probe f_b and leveraging publicly accessible resources (e.g., features, pre-trained models) for effective and efficient approximation of f_b.

Previous work explored black-box model approximation by leveraging the fidelity (e.g., probability scores) of predictions [19,34], feature and/or model architecture similarity between f_b and f_s [16,25,28,34], and cross-model transferability [25,26]. The approximation formulation spans equation solving [34], optimization methods [18], generative adversarial networks [16], and reinforcement learning [24].

This paper explores adversarial approximation of a black-box malware detector f_b in the *most challenging setting for the adversary*. In particular, we explore a threat model where the adversary aims for a close-enough approximation of f_b in the face of (i) access to limited inputs to f_b, (ii) for a given input sample no additional observations beyond prediction label, (iii) different feature representations for f_b and f_s, and (iv) disjoint training sets for f_b, f_s, and the similarity evaluation set. To that end, beginning with limited seed-set for the black-box classifier, we leverage *representation mapping* and *cross-domain transferability* to approximate a black-box malware classifier by locally training a substitute.

Our work complements prior work [16,19,25,26,28,34] in three ways. First, we do not assume any adversarial knowledge other than prediction label for a given PE. This is a strong adversarial setting, which effectively leaves the adversary no leverage except a best-effort strategy that relies on publicly available vantage points (e.g., input samples, pre-trained models). Second, we approximate f_b with *different feature types* for f_b (e.g., byte sequences) and f_s (e.g., pixel intensities). By mapping the representation of PEs from byte-space to pixel-space, our approach eliminates the need for manual feature engineering. The motivation behind using dissimilar feature representations for f_b and f_s

is to leverage publicly accessible pre-trained models (e.g., Inception V3 [1]) by means of transfer learning, while only training on the last layer. While prior work [25] demonstrated cross-model transferability for image classifiers, we show a different dimension of transferability in a cross-domain setting by re-purposing a pre-trained image classifier to approximate a black-box malware detection model trained on raw-byte sequences of PEs. Third, we deliberately use *non-overlapping data* for training f_b, training f_s, and comparison of similarity between the two. We note that some prior work [19,24–26,34] use disjoint data when f_b is hosted by MLaaS providers. It is, however, hard to verify the disjointedness of f_b's training data against f_s's or the comparison set, because in such a setting f_b's training data is typically confidential.

Against a black-box CNN [27] trained on byte sequence features of Windows PEs, our approximation approach obtained up to 92% accurate CNN on pixel features, and trained based on the Inception V3 [1] pre-trained model (details in 4.3). On a comparison dataset disjoint with the black-box's and the substitute's training sets, our approach achieved nearly 90% similarity between the black-box CNN and the substitute one. In a nutshell, the results suggest that, even if the target model is a black-box, an adversary may take advantage of a limited training data and the underlying knowledge of pre-trained models (Inception V3 in this case) to successfully approximate the decision boundary of a black-box model. An intriguing observation of our results is that, although the training samples used for approximation are disjoint with training samples used to train the black-box CNN, the adversary can still achieve an acceptable approximation of the black-box CNN with minimal efforts. Another intriguing observation is, despite the dissimilarity of the representation of the black-box (i.e., byte sequences) and that of the substitute model (i.e., pixels), our approximation approach still managed to achieve nearly 90% similarity between the target black-box and the substitute model.

We further evaluate our approach on a research benchmark dataset, EMBER [6], which is based on static PE features (details in 4.4). Our approach approximated the LightGBM [20] black-box model supplied with EMBER via a 91% accurate substitute model, which agrees with the black-box on 90% of test PEs. With EMBER, we also explore how our approximation strategy performs on different models by training multiple substitute models, confirming the validity of our approach across model architectures such as Decision Trees, Random Forests, and K-Nearest Neighbours. In summary, this paper makes the following contributions:

- By mapping byte sequence features to pixel representations, we eliminate the need for heuristics-based feature engineering, which significantly reduces adversarial effort towards feature guessing.
- Leveraging a pre-trained model as a foundation, we extend the scope of transferability from a cross-model setting by demonstrating the utility of cross-domain transferability for black-box approximation.

– We demonstrate the feasibility of close-enough adversarial approximation using different feature representations for the black-box and the substitute model, across multiple model architectures, and complementary datasets.

2   Background and Threat Model

2.1   Model Approximation Attacks

In this work, we focus on supervised learning for malware classification models, where input samples are Windows PEs and the output is the class label, i.e., `benign` or `malware`.

Let X be a d-dimensional feature space and Y be the c-dimensional output space, with underlying probability distribution $Pr(X, Y)$, where X and Y are random variables for the feature vectors and the classes of data, respectively. The objective of training an ML model is to learn a parameter vector θ, which represents a mapping $f_\theta : X \to Y$. f_θ outputs a c-dimensional vector with each dimension representing the probability of input belonging to the corresponding class. $l(f_\theta(x), y)$ is a loss of f_θ on (x, y), and it measures how "mistaken" the prediction $f_\theta(x)$ is with respect to the true label y. Given a set of training samples $D_{train} \subset (X, Y)$, the objective of an ML model, f_θ, is to minimize the expected loss over all $(x, y) : L_{D_{train}}(f_\theta) = \sum_{(x,y) \in D_{train}} l(f_\theta(x), y)$. In ML models such as DNNs, the loss minimization problem is typically solved using Stochastic Gradient Descent (SGD) by iteratively updating the weights θ as: $\theta \leftarrow \theta - \epsilon \cdot \Delta_\theta(\sum_{(x,y) \in D_{train}} l(f_\theta(x), y))$, where Δ_θ is the gradient of the loss with respect to the weights θ; $D_{train} \subset (X, Y)$ is a randomly selected set (*mini-batch*) of training examples drawn from X; and ϵ is the *learning rate* which controls the magnitude of change on θ.

Figure 1 depicts a typical setup for model approximation attacks against a MLaaS platform that serves a black-box model f_b via a prediction API. The goal of the adversarial client is to learn a close-enough approximation of f_b using as few queries (x_i''s) as possible.

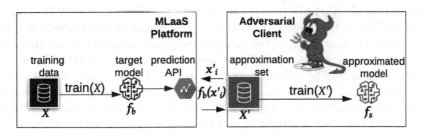

Fig. 1. Typical pipeline for model approximation attacks. MLaaS provider trains a model f_b on confidential/proprietary data X. It then serves f_b via a prediction API to allow clients to issue queries and obtain prediction results. An adversarial client uses f_b as an oracle to label $|X'|$ samples to train f_s such that $f_s \approx f_b$.

Typically, model approximation is used to steal a deployed model (e.g., intellectual property, security-sensitive business logic) [18, 28, 34], trick/bypass pay-per-prediction walls, perform reconnaissance for later attacks that go after the integrity of the victim model through adversarial examples [25], or mount membership inference attacks for models known to be trained on privacy-sensitive data [11, 31].

The success of approximation depends on the adversarial client's knowledge (about details of f_b and its training set) and capabilities (e.g., access to inputs, maximum number of queries). In a *white-box* (full knowledge) setting, the adversary has complete knowledge of the target model architecture and its training data, making it the easiest for the adversary (but the most exposing for the target model). In a *grey-box* (partial knowledge) setting, the adversary has some knowledge about f_b's model architecture (e.g., DNN vs. SVM) and training data (e.g., a subset of the training set), which makes it moderately challenging. In a *black-box* (no/limited knowledge) setting, the adversary knows nothing but prediction labels (and possibly confidence probabilities) for a given input. This is the most challenging setting for the adversary. In this paper, we consider the black-box setting. Next, we describe our threat model.

2.2   Threat Model and Problem Statement

We consider the strongest threat model compared with previous work on adversarial approximation [25, 28, 34]. The adversary interacts with a deployed model f_b, for instance served from MLaaS malware detector. Without loss of generality, we assume that the ML model f_b is a malware detector.

Adversary's Goals: The adversary's goal is to approximate the decision boundary of f_b by training its substitute f_s, beginning with a limited seed-set of PEs.

Adversary's Knowledge: The adversary only knows that f_b accepts Windows PEs as input and returns labels ("benign" or "malicious") as output. The adversary doesn't know f_b's architecture, parameters, hyper-parameters, or features. Besides, the adversary has no access to the training data or the test data used to train and evaluate f_b.

Adversary's Capabilities: The adversary probes f_b with PEs to obtain prediction labels. We assume there is an upper bound on the number of queries the adversary can issue to f_b, but the adversary can workaround the query limit by probing f_b over an extended time-window or from different IP addresses. The adversary has access to a limited seed-set of PEs, but is unable to tell whether or not the PEs in the seed-set overlap with f_b's training set. The adversary is able to continuously collect more PEs to use f_b as an oracle and progressively train f_s with the goal of obtaining a close-enough approximation of f_b.

Problem Statement: Given a deployed malware detection model, f_b, under the threat model stated earlier, the adversary's goal is to find f_b's closest approximation, f_s, with best effort. By "best effort" we mean relying on limited seed-set to probe f_b, and leveraging publicly accessible resources (e.g., feature representations, pre-trained models) towards effective and efficient approximation of f_b.

More formally, given a black-box model f_b trained on dataset X, for a seed-set $|X'| < |X|$ and $X' \cap X = \emptyset$, the adversary's goal is to train f_s using X' such that when compared on dataset X'' disjoint with X and X', $f_b \approx f_s$. The $\approx$ quantifies the percentage of agreement (i.e., number of matching predictions between f_b and f_s on X''). The closer the agreement is to a 100% the more accurate the approximation and vice-versa. The real-life implication of successful approximation of f_b via f_s is that once the adversary obtains a close-enough (e.g., >90%) substitute of f_b, the intellectual property of f_b's owner (e.g., an IDS vendor) is jeopardized. Even worse, the adversary might as well emerge as f_b's competitor by tuning f_s's accuracy with additional training data.

3   Approach

Overview: Figure 2 depicts an overview of our approach. Given a black-box malware detector f_b, the adversary collects benign and malware PEs from public sources to obtain the substitute training set (X'). The adversary then uses f_b as an oracle to label samples in X' (Sect. 3.1). Next, samples in X' are mapped from a source representation: raw-bytes to a target representation: pixel intensities (Sect. 3.2). The progressive approximation step uses the mapped X' to iteratively approximate f_b (Sect. 3.3). It combines *representation mapping* and *cross-domain transferability* to obtain a close-enough approximation of f_b with a limited seed-set to f_b (i.e., $|X'| < |X|$), different feature representations for f_b and f_s, and disjoint training sets for f_b, f_s, and the comparison set used to evaluate similarity between f_b and f_s (i.e., $X \cap X' \cap X'' = \emptyset$). The approximation begins by training an initial substitute model f_s on a fraction (e.g., 20%–25%) of X', and f_s is refined until it achieves acceptable accuracy. Using a dataset X'', the last stage of the approach compares similarity between f_b and f_s (Sect. 3.4). A higher similarity score for f_b and f_s is an indication of the effectiveness of the approach at approximating the decision boundary of f_b.

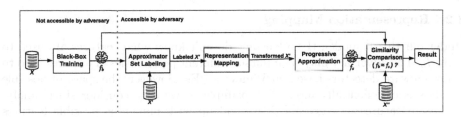

Fig. 2. Approach overview. f_b is accessible by the adversary via a prediction API only.

For the sake of presenting an end-to-end approximation framework, Fig. 2 includes f_b's training at the beginning. In practice, the adversary doesn't have access to the black-box model except through its prediction API. It is also noteworthy that the three datasets (X, X', and X'') shown in Fig. 2 are disjoint.

Again, in reality, with no access to f_b's training set, the adversary has no trivial way to determine if the substitute training set (X') or the model similarity comparison set (X'') have intersection among themselves or with the black-box training set (X). The only motivation of training our own black-box model f_b is to ensure X, X', and X'' are disjoint, and doing so lets us to deterministically examine the most challenging adversarial setting described earlier.

3.1   Approximation Set Labeling

Given a seed-set of Windows PEs collected by the adversary, a first-cut labeling strategy would be to take the ground truth labels that the samples come with (e.g., using VirusTotal [4] as an oracle). Had our goal been to train a malware detector, such an approach would suffice. Our goal, however, is to approximate the decision boundary of a black-box malware detector, and we expect our labeling method to serve this purpose.

Given a set of approximation samples $X' = x'_1, ..., x'_m$ and a learned hypothesis function f_b, we obtain $f_b(x'_i) = y'_i$. The y'_i's may or may not match the ground truth labels. If f_b misclassifies some x'_i's, the misclassified x'_i's will not match the ground truth counter-parts. What should be done with the misclassified samples in the substitute training set? The alternatives we have are (a) drop the misclassified x'_i's and explore approximation with the correctly labeled x'_i's, (b) reinstate labels to ground truth labels and proceed with approximation, or (c) take the labels assigned by f_b for what they are. Alternative (a) is no different from training the substitute without querying f_b. Alternative (b) entails "correcting" the "imperfections" of f_b (note "correcting" could as well mean lower accuracy because we are essentially changing the underlying distribution of f_b's training set). Alternative (c) is the most realistic for our threat model, because it takes f_b for what it is and uses its predictions (y'_i's) to populate the labeled approximation set, which is highly likely to result in a realistic approximation of f_b's decision boundary.

3.2   Representation Mapping

Under our threat model, the adversary doesn't know what features are used to train f_b. The adversary may then pursue different possibilities of features used to train malware detectors based on Windows PEs. However, the space of possible features is exponentially large. For example, if we only consider static analysis based features of a given PE, we end up with numerous possible features such as meta-data, DLL imports/exports, byte sequences, and so on. Similarly, considering the dynamic analysis-based features of PEs results in several candidates such as API/system call traces, instruction sequences, and call graphs. Therefore, given enough resources, while such a strategy of feature guessing may result in a close-enough approximation, it may not be the preferred avenue by the adversary whose goal is to effectively and efficiently approximate f_b.

In-line with the adversary's goals, we map the raw bytes representation of each PE to an image representation (pixel values), analogous to taking a photograph of the PE's raw byte sequences. The main rationale is, instead of searching for the best combination of a set of features to train the substitute, it is plausible to capture the whole PE's bytes via image representations such that the learning algorithm is able to "discover" distinguishing sub-structures from the image representation of PEs. We note that previous work ([15,21,23]) has also explored bytes-to-pixels conversion for malware detection, although not in the exact context of model approximation via cross-domain transferability that we explore in this work. Another equally important rationale for bytes-to-pixels mapping is the accessibility (to the adversary) of acceptably accurate pre-trained image classification models such as Inception V3 [1] which, by way of transfer learning [25], feed knowledge to the substitute model.

Fig. 3. (a) and (b) show EN and CH rendering, respectively, of a benign PE (small02Micro_Card_Reader_Driver_3.11.exe). (c) and (d) show EN and CH rendering, respectively, of a malware PE (Trojan.GenericKDZ.58985).

To realize the bytes-to-pixels mapping, the key intuition is to transform PEs into a colored canvas, such that the colors (pixel intensities) represent the bytes in the PEs, and the color intensities are used as features to train the substitute. To this end, we leverage two types of image representations, the Entropy (EN) representation [30] and the Color Hilbert (CH) representation [13]. CH scans the bytes of a PE and assigns color based on the value of each byte. The assigned pixel intensities are then mapped on a canvas of a chosen dimension. EN uses Shannon Entropy [30] to compute the randomness of bytes in a specific location of the executable as $E = -\sum_{i=1}^{n} \rho_i \log_2 \rho_i$, where ρ_i refers to the probability of appearances of a byte value i and n is the number of possible values ($n = 256$ for possible byte values). Depending on the computed value of E, the corresponding pixel is assigned color intensity in the range black (minimum/zero entropy) to bright pink (maximum entropy). An example that illustrates EN and CH representation for a benign PE is shown in Fig. 3 (a) and (b), respectively. Similarly, Fig. 3 (c) and (d) show EN and CH representations of a malware PE, respectively. Notice the clear visual difference between benign and malware PEs, which seems to support our intuition of mapping bytes to pixels. Looking at the CH representation, the combination of these colors in the images serves best to give the model discriminating features to put apart benign and malware PEs. With regards to the EN representation, we can see that the focus is more on areas instead of specific pixels, and it is not as high-fidelity as the CH representation. In Sect. 4, we evaluate the utility of EN and CH representations via the substitute's accuracy. Next, we briefly describe how the canvas is filled with colors.

To paint the canvas of the image, we leverage a well-known mapping technique called the Hilbert curve [10] (implemented in BinVis [13]), which makes sure that if two bytes are close to each other in the PE, they should be close to each other in the image representation of the PE as well. This property of the Hilbert curve is essential to preserve the semantic structure of PEs when mapping bytes to pixels, and it provides the substitute model an accurate representation of the PE so that, during training, it explores the classification utility of all possible features. A natural question would be, how does the Hilbert curve function? Intuitively, the idea of Hilbert curve is to find a line to fill a canvas that will keep the points which are close to each other on that line at the same distance when it fills the needed space. This, in our case, keeps the features of the PEs intact since separating them would lead to breaking the semantics of the sequence of bytes that represents a part of our feature set in the images we would like to generate at the end of the mapping.

Note that although representation mapping is core to our approach, sometimes, feature guessing may fit the best-effort strategy when the adversary has access to publicly released datasets such as EMBER [6], which reveal details about features. To account for this possibility, in Sects. 4.3 and 4.4, we evaluate our approach with minimal relaxation on our threat model, i.e., the adversary knows features because of public disclosure as in [6]. As we will show, the purely black-box approximation is as strong as the minimally relaxed approximation.

3.3 Progressive Approximation

On the one hand, the adversary has access to limited input samples to the black-box model. On the other hand, the adversary has access to pre-trained and publicly accessible image classification models (e.g., Inception V3 [1]). To obtain an acceptably accurate approximation of the black-box model, the adversary takes advantage of the advances in image classification models to quickly and accurately train a candidate substitute on the mapped features of the PEs via *cross-domain transferability*. The motivation behind leveraging pre-trained models is threefold. First, the fact that our substitute model relies on image classification for which state-of-the-art benchmark datasets are readily accessible. Second, the prospect of using a widely available and acceptably accurate pre-trained model for anyone (including the adversary) is in favor of the constraints the adversary has on collecting enough training samples for the approximation and come up with an effective model architecture tuned to adversarial goals. Third, when using pre-trained models, we are only retraining the last layer, which not only saves us (the adversary) time, but also gives us confidence on the accuracy of the final model because of transferability. Moreover, taking advantage of image representations cuts the effort on feature engineering down to zero because the candidate substitute (e.g., a CNN) would automatically learn the features from its mapped training data, i.e., image representations of PEs.

Algorithm 1: Progressive approximation of f_b.

```
1   τ_acc: accuracy threshold;
2   τ_sim: similarity threshold;
3   num_batches: number of approximation set batches;
4   for i =1 → num_batches do
5   │   acc_i, f_s ← TrainSubstitute(f_s, batch_i);
6   │   sim_i ← GetSimilarity(f_b, f_s);
7   │   if acc_i > τ_acc&&sim_i > τ_sim then
8   │   │   StopApproximation();
9   │   end
10  end
```

Fig. 4. Progressive approximation of f_b.

In order to emulate an adversary who begins with a limited seed-set to bootstrap approximation, we assume that the adversary has $batch_1$ as the first batch (e.g., 20%) of substitute training samples X'. The adversary first trains f_s on $batch_1$ and evaluates its accuracy against a pre-determined threshold, which could be set close-enough to f_b's accuracy for our case. In real-life, one can safely assume that the adversary would estimate the accuracy threshold from public knowledge (e.g., state of the art model accuracy for malware classifiers). Similarly, the adversary can set a similarity threshold based on prediction matches between f_b and f_s over dataset X''. The adversary would then actively collect training data, and progressively re-train and re-evaluate f_s each time they obtain the next batch of approximation examples, until an acceptable accuracy and similarity score is obtained, or the training data is exhausted. Figure 4 shows the details of the progressive approximation.

3.4   Similarity Comparison

Once the substitute model f_s is trained with an acceptable accuracy, its effectiveness is assessed when compared with the black-box model on a separate dataset, disjoint with both the training set of the black-box and the substitute. Figure 5 shows the procedure for similarity comparison of f_b and f_s.

The similarity score is the percentage of matching predictions between f_b and f_s. The higher the similarity score, the closer f_s is to f_b, which means f_s effectively mirrors the decision boundary of f_b. The adversary then probes f_s for further attacks in a white-box setting. Attacks that succeed on f_s, would, by transitivity, succeed on f_b. This is the essence of having an accurate approximation which would be used as a substitute for the black-box. By crafting adversarial examples using methods such as FGSM [33] and CW [12], the adversary can transitively target f_b using f_s as a surrogate white-box model. Comparison of our candidate substitutes with the black-box model is discussed in Sect. 4.4.

Algorithm 2: Similarity comparison between f_b and f_s.

---

1 N: number of samples for comparison;
2 $matches \leftarrow 0$;
3 **for** $i = 1 \rightarrow N$ **do**
4      $y_s^i \leftarrow f_s(x^i)$;
5      $y_b^i \leftarrow f_b(x^i)$;
6   **if** $y_b^i == y_s^i$ **then**
7 | $matches \leftarrow matches + 1$;
8   **end**
9 **end**
10 $similarity\_score \leftarrow \frac{matches}{N} \times 100$;

Fig. 5. Similarity comparison between f_b and f_s.

4   Evaluation

We now describe our datasets, experimental setup, and results on progressive approximation and similarity comparison.

4.1   Datasets

Table 1 summarizes our datasets: Custom-MalConv and EMBER[6].

Custom-MalConv: We collected benign PEs from a Windows freeware site [2] and malware PEs from VirusShare [3]. These two sources are used by prior work [5,6,16,27,29] on adversarial examples and malware detection. Overall, we collect 67.81K PEs with 44% benign and 56% malware. We use 60% for training the black-box CNN, 23% as substitute training set, and 17% as similarity comparison set. Since we control the dataset, we use this dataset to evaluate the effectiveness of our approach on representation mapping and cross-domain transferability.

EMBER: EMBER [6] is a public dataset of malware and benign PEs released together with a Light gradient boosted decision tree model (LGBM) [20] with 97.3% detection accuracy. The dataset consists of 2351 features extracted from 1M PEs via static binary analysis. The training set contains 800K labeled samples with 50% split between benign and malicious PEs, while the test set consists of 200K samples, again with the same label split. The authors of EMBER used VirusTotal [4] as a labeling oracle to label samples in EMBER. We use this dataset to further evaluate the generalizability of our approach. We note, however, that EMBER releases only static analysis based features extracted from PEs, not the PEs themselves, which limits our scope of doing representation mapping. Despite the absence of original PEs, we still evaluate our approach on a different feature space and over multiple candidate substitute models. Of the 200K test set samples, we use 150K as substitution training set, and the remaining 50K (25%) as similarity comparison set.

Table 1. Datasets for Custom-MalConv and EMBER.

Dataset	Benign	Malware	Total
Custom-MalConv			
Black-Box training set	20,000	20,000	40,000
Substitute training set	8,000	8,000	16,000
Similarity comparison set	2,045	9,765	11,810
Total			**67,810**
EMBER [6]			
Black-Box training set	400,000	400,000	800,000
Substitute training set	75,000	75,000	150,000
Similarity comparison set	25,000	25,000	50,000
Total			**1,000,000**

4.2 Experimental Setup

Black-Box Models: The Custom-MalConv black-box is trained on 20K benign and 20K malware PEs. It is based on MalConv [27], a widely used malware detection CNN in adversarial ML literature on malware [22,32]. We use the same architecture as the original MalConv [27] with slight modifications to fit our hardware (NVIDIA 1080 with 8 GB of RAM). MalConv is based on raw bytes of a PE and reads the first 1 MB to extract byte features. To fit our hardware limitations, we fed only $\frac{1}{3}$ MB of each PE to our custom CNN, and got an accuracy of 93% which is acceptable since MalConv [27] used 100K PEs to achieve 98% accuracy. The LightGBM black-box is trained on 400K benign and 400K malware PEs and is shipped with the EMBER [6] dataset with 97.3% accuracy.

Substitute Models: For Custom-MalConv black-box model, our f_s is based on Inception V3 (IV3) [1] and is trained on both CH and EN representations of the substitute training set. In addition, for sanity check, we trained a substitute Custom-MalConv model with exact same features and model parameters as our black-box. For EMBER, we explore 4 candidates for substitute model, namely: decision trees (DT), random forests (RF), k-Nearest neighbors (kNN), and gradient-boosted decision tree model (LGBM).

Progressive Approximation: For Custom-MalConv, we use 16K substitute training set and train f_s progressively on 4K, 8K, 12K, and 16K PEs. For LGBM, we use 150K of the 200K test set with a progression of 30K, 60K, 90K, 120K, and 150K PEs. The metrics we use are *validation accuracy* and *similarity score*. Validation accuracy is the prediction accuracy of the approximated substitute. Similarity score (as shown in Fig. 5) is the percentage of matching predictions between f_b and f_s.

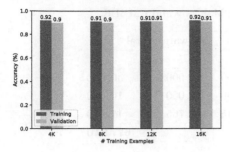
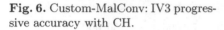
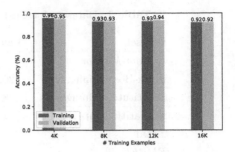

Fig. 6. Custom-MalConv: IV3 progressive accuracy with CH.

Fig. 7. Custom-MalConv: IV3 progressive accuracy with EN.

4.3 Progressive Approximation Results

Custom-MalConv: Figure 6 shows the training accuracy and validation accuracy of each progressive step in training f_s: IV3 with CH representation. It can be seen that the difference between training and validation accuracy narrows as the model progresses with more training data, which is an indication of the real-life effectiveness of the model on training examples it has never seen during training. Similarly, Fig. 7 shows the progressive training of f_s: IV3 with EN representation. Here, the trend persists, where we see a very high training accuracy across the board, but as we train on bigger data sets we get a more accurate model (validation accuracy is close to training accuracy).

For both CH and EN representations, it *takes only 10% the size of* f_b *'s training set to approximate it with* f_s that achieves 0.9 and 0.95 validation accuracy, respectively. On IV3 with CH, quadrupling the substitute training set (4K to 16K) improved its validation accuracy by 0.1 only, showing the *feasibility of approximation under data scarcity by taking advantage of transferability.* IV3 with EN shows a slightly different progress. On 16K approximation samples, it achieves 0.92 validation accuracy, which is 3% less than the IV3 with CH trained on 4K samples. Looking at the difference between the training and validation accuracies (green vs. orange bars in Figs. 6 and 7), we notice that the narrower the gap between training and validation accuracy, the more stable a model would be classifying unknown samples.

EMBER: Figure 13 shows the progressive validation accuracy of the four candidate substitute models against the LGBM black-box. Compared to the progress of Custom-MalConv substitutes (Figs. 6 and 7), the validation accuracies of LGBM, DT, and RF are relatively lower (in the range 0.85–0.88). However, kNN stands out as a clear contender (validation accuracy = 0.91) when compared with Custom-MalConv substitutes. Again, interestingly, the LGBM substitute, despite its architectural similarity to the target black-box LGBM, is not the best in terms of accuracy. From Figs. 8, 9, 10 and 11, it is noteworthy that the gap between training and validation accuracy for EMBER substitutes is comparatively bigger (on average 4%) compared to the narrow differences (on average 0.5%) for Custom-MalConv substitutes shown in Figs. 6 and 7.

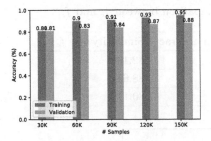

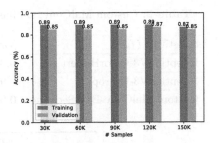

Fig. 8. Progressive accuracy of f_s: LGBM.

Fig. 9. Progressive accuracy of f_s: DT.

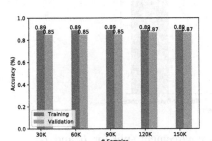

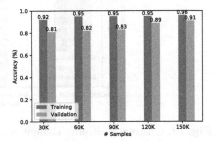

Fig. 10. Progressive accuracy of f_s: RF.

Fig. 11. Progressive accuracy of f_s: kNN.

Looking at the substitute training set size with respect to the LGBM black-box, *to obtain the best performing substitute (kNN), it takes only 18.8% (150K) of LGBM's training set size (800K)*. Interestingly, from Fig. 8, we notice that the LGBM substitute, despite its architectural similarity with the target LGBM, performs relatively poorly, suggesting that *model architecture similarity may not always result in the best approximation.*

4.4 Similarity Comparison Results

Custom-MalConv: As shown in Table 2, we have 3 substitutes, a Custom-MalConv substitute, InceptionV3 with CH, and InceptionV3 with EN. The comparison of these substitutes with the black-box is done on a separate comparison set, disjoint with the b lack-box training set and the substitute training set.

On average, our approach achieved 83.7% similarity score, with the highest similarity score of 89%, on IV3 substitute trained on EN representation. The MalConv substitute that matches the architecture of the black-box Custom-MalConv model is the least accurate, which interestingly indicates that *model architecture similarity may not always result in a substitute that agrees well with a black-box target.* When we compare CH-based and EN-based substitutes, EN-based substitute outperforms the CH-based substitute by about 6.5%, which could be attributed to the canvas coloring schemes of CH and EN.

Table 2. Custom-MalConv: similarity comparison between f_b and f_s.

Substitute (f_s)	Validation accuracy	Similarity (f_b, f_s)
InceptionV3-ColorHilbert	0.91	82.19%
InceptionV3-Entropy	0.92	88.65%
Custom-MalConv-ByteSequence	0.90	80.11%

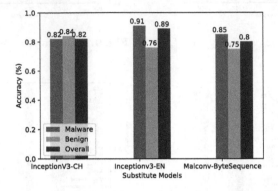

Fig. 12. Custom-MalConv: Benign vs. malware agreement split for f_b and f_s.

Figure 12 shows the details of similarity scores for the three substitute models split into malware and benign. To compute the split, for each label, we divide the number of agreements between f_b and f_s by the total number of samples for that label. Having a malware detection rate higher than the benign detection rate serves us best, since our goal is to be able to identify malware identified as so by the black-box. It can be seen that the EN-based substitute tends to agree with the black-box more on malware, while the CH-based substitute agrees with the black-box more on the benign predictions. Again, this variation is rooted in the canvas coloring methods of the two representations discussed earlier.

EMBER: Table 3 summarizes the similarity comparison between LGBM black-box and candidate substitute models. On average a substitute model agrees with the black-box on 90.3% of the comparison samples. kNN, as the closest approximation with a different model architecture from the black-box, agrees with it on almost 90% of the comparison samples. This result is comparable to the best substitute in Custom-MalConv: InceptionV3-Entropy with 89% similarity score. We also notice from Table 3 that, although it is the least accurate model from Fig. 13, LGBM substitute agrees with the LGBM black-box on over 97% of the comparison instances. This is not surprising, given the exactness of the model architectures. It is, however, in contrast to our observation on the similarity of Custom-MalConv-ByteSequence substitute with the same black-box model architecture, which scores just over 80% similarity (see Table 2).

Figure 14 shows the evolution of similarity scores showing how kNN substitute's similarity improves almost by 10% in the range 90K–150K of approximation instances. RF substitute also shows a similar pattern, but with a smaller

Table 3. EMBER: similarity comparison between f_b and f_s.

Substitute (f_s)	Validation accuracy	Similarity (f_b, f_s)
Decision tree	0.85	86.3%
Random forest	0.87	87.7%
k-Nearest neighbors	0.91	89.9%
LightGBM	0.88	97.1%

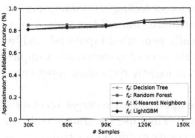

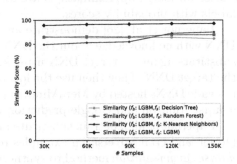

Fig. 13. EMBER: progressive validation accuracy of candidates for f_s.

Fig. 14. EMBER: progressive similarity of f_b with f_s.

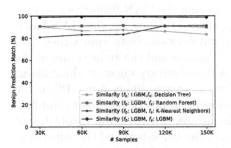

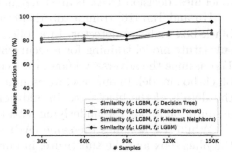

Fig. 15. EMBER: Benign prediction match between f_b and f_s.

Fig. 16. EMBER: Malware prediction match between f_b and f_s.

improvement of 4% (83% to 87%). Note that the LGBM substitute remained stable across the progressive increment of the substitute training set.

Finally, Figs. 15 and 16 show the progression of benign and malware similarity matches as we train the substitutes. It can be seen that, overall, there is high degree of agreement between the LGBM black-box and the substitutes on benign predictions. On benign predictions, the LGBM substitute shows a stable and close to 100% agreement with its black-box counterpart. On malware predictions, it shows variations in the range 83%–95%.

5   Related Work

Tramer et al. [34] show equation-solving and optimization based attacks that approximate target ML models with near-perfect replication for popular learning algorithms including logistic regression, support vector machines, neural networks, and decision trees. They demonstrate their attacks against production MLaaS providers such as BigML and Amazon ML. They note that their most successful model approximations are for MLaaS services that return prediction labels with probability scores.

Papernot et al. [26] demonstrate an adversary controlling a remotely hosted DNN with no knowledge about the DNN and its training data. They train a local substitute against a target DNN using synthetically generated inputs labeled by the target DNN. They then use the local substitute to craft adversarial examples to evade DNNs hosted by MetaMind, and also train logistic regression substitutes against Amazon and Google prediction APIs.

Papernot et al. [25] train substitute models to approximate a target black-box model, and craft adversarial examples to evade it. They use the *Jacobian-based dataset augmentation* method to synthetically generate examples for training the substitute. Similar to [26], they demonstrate transferability within and between different classes of ML models such as DNNs, logistic regression, support vector machines, decision trees, nearest neighbors, and ensembles.

Hu and Tan [16] train a substitute model using the GAN framework to fit a black-box malware detector. In a follow-up work [17], they use the GAN-based substitute model training for a recurrent neural network. Both approaches ([16, 17]) assume the adversary knows the type of features and the architecture of the black-box model. In our case, we assume that the adversary knows nothing about the details of the black-box. In addition, our approach differs from [16] in the assumption about the underlying feature representations of training examples.

While [16] assumes the same (API calls precisely) feature representation of the black-box and the substitute, in our work, the black-box and the substitute have different feature representations. Rosenberg et al. [29] adopt the Jacobian-based augmentation [25] to synthesize training examples to approximate and evade a target black-box malware detector based on API call features. Like Papernot et al. [25] and Hu and Tan [16], Papernot et al. in a different work [26] craft adversarial examples to evade a black-box model.

Orekondy et al. [24] follow a similar threat model to ours where publicly available images from a domain different from the black-box model are used to train a substitute 'Knockoff' model. They show selecting samples from a totally different distribution using reinforcement learning is effective for an approximation attack, while using different model architectures for the victim black-box and the substitute knockoff. We note that, in the cross-domain transferability setting, this work is the closest to ours except that it uses the same pixel features for both f_b and f_s, while we use byte sequences for f_b and pixels for f_s.

Next, we make approach-level comparisons of our work and closely related prior work. Table 4 shows multi-criteria comparison of this work with the state-of-the-art. Since direct quantitative comparison is non-trivial given differences

in assumptions and dataset/task heterogeneity, our comparison is rather qualitative, based on feature representation, model architecture, f_s's training set size,
training set overlap between f_s and f_b, and f_b's prediction output.

Features (f_b, f_s) compares assumptions about features of the black-box
(f_b) and the substitute (f_s). While prior work [16,17,19,25,26,28,29] assumed
similar features for f_b and f_s, we consider raw-bytes for f_b and pixels for f_s.

Model (f_b, f_s) captures assumptions about similarity of model architectures
for f_b and f_s. Unlike most prior work [16,17,19,25,26,28] which assume the same
model architecture for f_b and f_s, we assume the adversary is free to evaluate
different model architectures for f_s (hence could match f_b's architecture or end
up using a different one).

Table 4. Approach-level qualitative comparison with closely related work.

	[19,26]	[34]	[29]	[28]	[16,17]	[24]	[25]	This work
Features (f_b, f_s)	Same	Same	Same	Same	Same	Same	Same	Different
Model (f_b, f_s)	Same	Same/different	Different	Same	Same	Different	Different	Different
Seed-set (f_s)	Moderate	Moderate	Moderate	Limited	Moderate	Moderate	Limited	Limited
Data (f_b, f_s)	Disjoint	Disjoint	N/A	N/A	Disjoint	Disjoint	Disjoint	Disjoint
Output (f_b)	Label+conf.	Label+conf.	Label	Label	Label	Label	Label	Label

Seed-set (f_s) compares assumptions on the size (number of training examples) of the seed-set to train f_s. In [25,26,28], the adversary explores synthetic
data generation techniques such as augmentation to generate more training samples to train f_s. In [16] and [17], the adversary collects enough samples to train
f_s. In this work, we explore approximation with access to a limited seed-set that
we extend with data augmentation techniques.

Data (f_b, f_s) examines whether or not there is overlap in training sets used
for f_b, f_s, and comparison of f_b with f_s. In this work, we use disjoint datasets
for training f_b, f_s, and comparison of f_b with f_s. Doing so enables assessment
of the effectiveness of f_s approximated with a completely new dataset.

Output (f_b) captures whether label only or label with confidence score
(conf.) is returned from f_b. While prior work used label only [16,17,24,28,29]
and label with probability score [19,26,34], our black-box returns only the label
of the PEs, i.e., "benign" or "malware".

6   Conclusion

We presented a best-effort adversarial approximation approach that leverages
representation mapping and cross-domain transferability to obtain a close-
enough approximation of a black-box malware detector. We show that an adversary can obtain nearly 90% similarity between a black-box model and its approximation beginning with a limited input-set to the black-box, different features and
disjoint training sets for the black-box and its substitute. We further demonstrate
that our approach generalizes to multiple model architectures across different

feature representations. This work broadens the scope of adversarial approximation of a black-box ML model in a strictly black-box setting. Our results shade light on the fact that different feature representations may not necessarily hinder close-enough approximation and disjoint datasets still result in successful approximation. More importantly, a pre-trained multi-class image classifier, such as Inception V3, can be re-purposed to approximate a binary malware classifier, demonstrating the scope of transferability beyond cross-model and extending it to a cross-domain setting.

References

1. Advanced guide to inception v3 on cloud TPU (2019). https://cloud.google.com/tpu/docs/inception-v3-advanced
2. Cnet freeware site (2019). https://download.cnet.com/s/software/windows/?licenseType=Free
3. Virus share (2019). https://virusshare.com
4. Virus total (2119). https://www.virustotal.com/gui/home/upload
5. Al-Dujaili, A., Huang, A., Hemberg, E., O'Reilly, U.: Adversarial deep learning for robust detection of binary encoded malware. In: 2018 IEEE Security and Privacy Workshops, SP Workshops 2018, San Francisco, CA, USA, 24 May 2018, pp. 76–82 (2018)
6. Anderson, H.S., Roth, P.: EMBER: an open dataset for training static PE malware machine learning models. CoRR abs/1804.04637 (2018)
7. Biggio, B., et al.: Evasion attacks against machine learning at test time. In: Machine Learning and Knowledge Discovery in Databases - European Conference, ECML PKDD 2013, Prague, Czech Republic, 23–27 September 2013, Proceedings, Part III, pp. 387–402 (2013)
8. Biggio, B., Nelson, B., Laskov, P.: Poisoning attacks against support vector machines. In: Proceedings of the 29th International Conference on Machine Learning, ICML 2012, Edinburgh, Scotland, UK, 26 June – 1 July 2012 (2012)
9. Biggio, B., Roli, F.: Wild patterns: ten years after the rise of adversarial machine learning. Pattern Recognit. **84**, 317–331 (2018)
10. Byrne, A., Hilbert, D.R.: Color realism and color science. Cambridge Univ. Press **26**(1), 3–64 (2003)
11. Carlini, N., Liu, C., Erlingsson, Ú., Kos, J., Song, D.: The secret sharer: evaluating and testing unintended memorization in neural networks. In: 28th USENIX Security Symposium, USENIX Security 2019, Santa Clara, CA, USA, 14–16 August 2019, pp. 267–284 (2019)
12. Carlini, N., Wagner, D.A.: Towards evaluating the robustness of neural networks. In: 2017 IEEE Symposium on Security and Privacy, SP 2017, San Jose, CA, USA, 22–26 May 2017, pp. 39–57 (2017)
13. Cortezi, A.: binviz (2019). https://github.com/cortesi/scurve/blob/master/binvis
14. Goodfellow, I.J., Shlens, J., Szegedy, C.: Explaining and harnessing adversarial examples. In: 3rd International Conference on Learning Representations, ICLR 2015, San Diego, CA, USA, 7–9 May 2015, Conference Track Proceedings (2015)
15. Han, K., Lim, J.H., Kang, B., Im, E.G.: Malware analysis using visualized images and entropy graphs. Int. J. Inf. Sec. **14**(1), 1–14 (2015). https://doi.org/10.1007/s10207-014-0242-0

16. Hu, W., Tan, Y.: Generating adversarial malware examples for black-box attacks based on GAN. CoRR abs/1702.05983 (2017)
17. Hu, W., Tan, Y.: Black-box attacks against RNN based malware detection algorithms. In: The Workshops of the the Thirty-Second AAAI Conference on Artificial Intelligence, New Orleans, Louisiana, USA, 2–7 February 2018, pp. 245–251 (2018)
18. Jagielski, M., Carlini, N., Berthelot, D., Kurakin, A., Papernot, N.: High accuracy and high fidelity extraction of neural networks (2020)
19. Juuti, M., Szyller, S., Marchal, S., Asokan, N.: PRADA: protecting against DNN model stealing attacks. In: IEEE European Symposium on Security and Privacy, EuroS&P 2019, Stockholm, Sweden, 17–19 June 2019, pp. 512–527 (2019)
20. Ke, G., et al.: Lightgbm: a highly efficient gradient boosting decision tree. In: Advances in Neural Information Processing Systems 30: Annual Conference on Neural Information Processing Systems 2017, 4–9 December 2017, Long Beach, CA, USA, pp. 3146–3154 (2017)
21. Khormali, A., Abusnaina, A., Chen, S., Nyang, D., Mohaisen, A.: COPYCAT: practical adversarial attacks on visualization-based malware detection. CoRR abs/1909.09735 (2019)
22. Kolosnjaji, B., et al.: Adversarial malware binaries: evading deep learning for malware detection in executables. In: 26th European Signal Processing Conference, EUSIPCO 2018, Roma, Italy, 3–7 September 2018, pp. 533–537 (2018)
23. Nataraj, L., Karthikeyan, S., Jacob, G., Manjunath, B.S.: Malware images: visualization and automatic classification. In: Proceedings of the 8th International Symposium on Visualization for Cyber Security, VizSec 2011, pp. 4:1–4:7 (2011)
24. Orekondy, T., Schiele, B., Fritz, M.: Knockoff nets: stealing functionality of black-box models. In: IEEE Conference on Computer Vision and Pattern Recognition, CVPR 2019, Long Beach, CA, USA, 16–20 June 2019, pp. 4954–4963 (2019)
25. Papernot, N., McDaniel, P.D., Goodfellow, I.J.: Transferability in machine learning: from phenomena to black-box attacks using adversarial samples. CoRR abs/1605.07277 (2016)
26. Papernot, N., McDaniel, P.D., Goodfellow, I.J., Jha, S., Celik, Z.B., Swami, A.: Practical black-box attacks against deep learning systems using adversarial examples. CoRR abs/1602.02697 (2016)
27. Raff, E., Barker, J., Sylvester, J., Brandon, R., Catanzaro, B., Nicholas, C.K.: Malware detection by eating a whole EXE. In: The Workshops of the the Thirty-Second AAAI Conference on Artificial Intelligence, New Orleans, Louisiana, USA, 2–7 February 2018, pp. 268–276 (2018)
28. Reith, R.N., Schneider, T., Tkachenko, O.: Efficiently stealing your machine learning models. In: Proceedings of the 18th ACM Workshop on Privacy in the Electronic Society, WPES@CCS 2019, London, UK, 11 November 2019, pp. 198–210 (2019)
29. Rosenberg, I., Shabtai, A., Rokach, L., Elovici, Y.: Generic black-box end-to-end attack against state of the art API call based malware classifiers. In: Research in Attacks, Intrusions, and Defenses - 21st International Symposium, RAID 2018, Heraklion, Crete, Greece, 10–12 September 2018, Proceedings, pp. 490–510 (2018)
30. Shannon, C.E.: A mathematical theory of communication. Mob. Comput. Commun. Rev. 5(1), 3–55 (2001)
31. Shokri, R., Stronati, M., Song, C., Shmatikov, V.: Membership inference attacks against machine learning models. In: 2017 IEEE Symposium on Security and Privacy, SP 2017, San Jose, CA, USA, May 22–26, 2017, pp. 3–18 (2017)

32. Suciu, O., Coull, S.E., Johns, J.: Exploring adversarial examples in malware detection. In: 2019 IEEE Security and Privacy Workshops, SP Workshops 2019, San Francisco, CA, USA, May 19–23, 2019, pp. 8–14 (2019)
33. Szegedy, C., et al.: Intriguing properties of neural networks. In: 2nd International Conference on Learning Representations, ICLR 2014, Banff, AB, Canada, 14–16 April 2014, Conference Track Proceedings (2014)
34. Tramèr, F., Zhang, F., Juels, A., Reiter, M.K., Ristenpart, T.: Stealing machine learning models via prediction apis. In: 25th USENIX Security Symposium, USENIX Security 16, Austin, TX, USA, 10–12 August 2016, pp. 601–618 (2016)

Review Trade: Everything Is Free in Incentivized Review Groups

Yubao Zhang[1], Shuai Hao[2(✉)], and Haining Wang[3]

[1] University of Delaware, Newark, DE, USA
ybzhang@udel.edu
[2] Old Dominion University, Norfolk, VA, USA
shao@odu.edu
[3] Virginia Tech, Arlington, VA, USA
hnw@vt.edu

Abstract. Online reviews play a crucial role in the ecosystem of e-commerce business. To manipulate consumers' opinions, some sellers of e-commerce platforms outsource opinion spamming with incentives (*e.g.*, free products) in exchange for *incentivized reviews*. As incentives, by nature, are likely to drive more biased reviews or even fake reviews. Despite e-commerce platforms such as Amazon have taken initiatives to squash the incentivized review practice, sellers turn to various social networking platforms (*e.g.*, Facebook) to outsource the incentivized reviews. The aggregation of sellers who request incentivized reviews and reviewers who seek incentives forms *incentivized review groups*. In this paper, we focus on the incentivized review groups in e-commerce platforms. We perform data collections from various social networking platforms, including Facebook, WeChat, and Douban. A measurement study of incentivized review groups is conducted with regards to group members, group activities, and products. To identify the incentivized review groups, we propose a new detection approach based on co-review graphs. Specifically, we employ the community detection method to find suspicious communities from co-review graphs. Also, we build a "gold standard" dataset from the data we collected, which contains the information of reviewers who belong to incentivized review groups. We utilize the "gold standard" dataset to evaluate the effectiveness of our detection approach.

Keywords: Incentivized review groups · Co-review graph · Community detection

1 Introduction

Online reviews on commercial products and services extensively impact consumers' decision making. As reported, 90% of consumers read online reviews before purchasing a product or service, and 88% of consumers tend to trust online reviews as much as personal recommendations [3]. About 80% of consumers reverse the decisions of product purchase after reading negative reviews, and 87% of consumers affirm a purchase decision based on positive reviews [9].

© ICST Institute for Computer Sciences, Social Informatics and Telecommunications Engineering 2020
Published by Springer Nature Switzerland AG 2020. All Rights Reserved
N. Park et al. (Eds.): SecureComm 2020, LNICST 335, pp. 339–359, 2020.
https://doi.org/10.1007/978-3-030-63086-7_19

Therefore, today's merchants are strongly motivated to fabricate online reviews in order to manipulate custom opinions. One of the most popular ways for fabricating positive reviews is called *incentivized reviews*, *i.e.*, merchants bribe reviewers by providing free products or even offer compensation for favorable reviews (*e.g.*, five-star reviews on Amazon). With incentivized reviews, merchants could gain a competitive advantage over rival merchants, as customers prefer online products with a larger number of favorable reviews.

To further affect people's thoughts and decisions, incentivized reviews nowadays are collected from a group of reviewers (*i.e.*, the *incentivized review groups*) so as to perform opinion spamming. In particular, incentivized review groups are online venues for trading reviews, where merchants can post the products that seek to favorable reviews and reviewers can write such reviews to earn free products or even make extra compensation. Some of the merchants designate well-written reviews to reviewers such that they can guarantee the quality of incentivized reviews. As such, there emerges a shady business that acts as a go-between of merchants and consumers, such as review outsourcing websites.

Apparently, the underground industry of fabricating fake reviews mentioned above violates the rules of most e-commerce platforms. As Amazon's consumer review policy [2] states, the violations include "a seller posts a review of their own product or their competitor's product" and "a seller offers a third party a financial reward, discount, free products, or other compensation in exchange for a review", *etc.* Despite the strict prohibition of Amazon (*i.e.*, banning/closing the accounts of both merchants and consumers), incentivized review groups are still thriving across different platforms, especially the social media such as Facebook and WeChat. This shady industry produces a spate of fake reviews, which mislead the customers, damage the trust of reviews, and even endanger the healthiness of the e-commerce ecosystem.

In this paper, we investigate the incentivized review groups on Amazon, the most popular e-commerce platform. To understand the breadth of the problem, we collect incentivized review groups across several different platforms, including Facebook, WeChat, and Douban. We find that different platforms play different roles in the ecosystem of incentivized review groups. Specifically, incentivized review groups on Facebook act like the blackboards, where a set of merchants (*i.e.*, sellers) post their products directly in these Facebook groups. Meanwhile, incentivized review groups on Douban are of the service for merchants and brokers, which educate them how to effectively obtain incentivized reviews. The incentivized review groups on WeChat are most private and generally are owned by a single person, who recruits reviewers to join the group and posts review requests for a set of products.

To understand the incentivized review groups, we conduct a measurement study to collect and characterize real review groups. We investigate the number and the increment rate of review members, as well as the number of merchants in collected incentivized review groups. In terms of incentivized review requests, we inspect the incentivized review requests in different groups as well as from

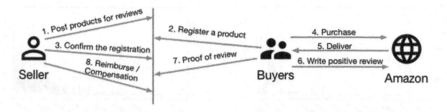

Fig. 1. Amazon incentivized review group

individual merchants. We also examine the categories, questions & answers, and the relationship between merchant and manufacturers of products.

Based on the measurement study, we then propose a graph-based method to detect the incentivized review groups on Amazon by leveraging the co-review behavior among reviewers. *Co-review* reflects the actions that two reviewers post reviews on the same product. By constructing the co-review graphs of reviewers, we then employ the community detection method to identify suspicious communities. Specifically, we consider both the frequency of co-reviews and other important features of the co-review behavior, such as co-reviews in a burst, which could significantly imply the existence of incentivized reviews. Furthermore, we note that the detection of incentivized review groups can be further integrated into the existing spam review detection framework to improve its coverage and effectiveness.

To evaluate our detection method, we construct a "gold standard" dataset by collecting real review requests from popular incentivized review groups, which enables us to validate the effectiveness of our method and shed light on further fake review studies (our dataset has been made publicly available at https://github.com/zhangyubao5/incentivized_review_group). Then, we examine an extensive Amazon review dataset [10,17] ranging from 1996 to 2018 and find that incentivized review groups started to pose serious threats on the ecosystem of online reviews after 2014.

2 Background

Obtaining positive reviews is one major factor of being successful online sellers. When competing with similar products at a similar price, the product with a higher rate or better reviews is more likely to win out.

2.1 Incentivized Reviews

To obtain positive reviews in the short term, sellers provide free products or offer compensation, *i.e.*, the "*incentivized reviews*". With the incentive for reviewers, it is guaranteed that sellers can obtain positive reviews (such as five-star in Amazon) and enhance the rating or recommendation of the products expeditiously. However, incentivized reviews typically violate the policy of online platforms since they are published in exchange for free products or compensation.

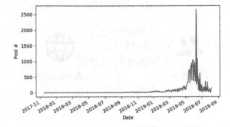

Fig. 2. Facebook review groups.

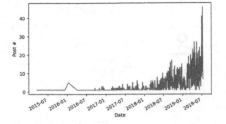

Fig. 3. Douban review groups.

For example, Amazon announced the policy to ban the incentivized reviews in 2016 [1].

2.2   Verified Purchase

Around the same time when Amazon started the crackdown on incentivized reviews, Amazon introduced the "verified purchase" tag. A "verified purchase" tag is labelled with the customer review if Amazon can verify that the review was published by the account who made the purchase. Although the "verified purchase" tag can highlight some authentic reviews and hinder the spam reviews to a certain degree, crooked sellers can bypass the hurdle or even exploit the "verified purchase" through review groups.

2.3   Incentivized Review Group

Incentivized review groups, or incentivized review clubs, are communities created to connect the consumers who want free products or compensation and the sellers who want positive product reviews. Figure 1 illustrates how the incentivized review groups work. First, a seller posts the products that need reviews and reviewers register for particular products of their interest. After the registration is confirmed by the sellers, buyers purchase the products in Amazon and write favorable reviews after the completion of orders. Then, they would show the proof of favorable reviews to the seller and obtain reimbursement or compensation. The registration enables the seller to follow up and ensure that the buyers have posted the reviews and the reviews are favorable.

Since buyers make payments on Amazon at full price, they are eligible for posting "verified purchase" reviews. Once the reviews have been confirmed, sellers send the cost of their purchases back, sometimes with extra compensation. Despite Amazon's strict policy against incentivized reviews, a number of incentivized review groups are still operating on websites or social media platforms. There are a great number of incentivized review groups on Facebook, which are set up specifically for Amazon sellers. Incentivized review groups usually set their groups as private or require sign-up to view the posts. Some of them claim the rules of incentivized review groups, including no scam, no hate speech,

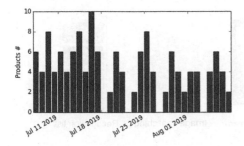

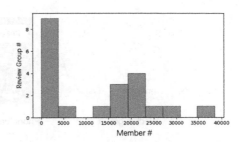

Fig. 4. A review group in WeChat.   **Fig. 5.** Number of group members.

and encouraging users to report invalid posts. Sellers also operate the incentivized review groups on other websites (such as Douban and Reddit) or instant messaging applications (such as WeChat).

3   Data Collection

In this section, we describe the data collection of incentivized review groups and summarize the datasets. We collect incentivized review groups from various social networking platforms, including Facebook, WeChat, and Douban. WeChat is the most popular instant messaging application in China, which allows users to create groups to broadcast events to group members. Douban is one of the most influential social networking service website in China, which allows users to create interest groups to share information.

3.1   Dataset

Facebook: There are many Facebook groups that are abused by incentivized review groups. Some of them are private and only allow group members to view the posts. To obtain good coverage and representativeness, we select 20 most active public incentivized review groups on Facebook, where we observe multiple tasks each day. In addition, we sign up two private groups by sending join requests. Some of the public groups turned into private during our collection and we need to send requests to join. Our collection of the groups ranges from November 1, 2017 to August 7, 2019. We collected a total of 47,148 posts created by 6,260 Facebook accounts. Figure 2 shows the number of posts over the collection period, which indicates the overall activity of these review groups over time.

Douban: Sellers create interest groups in Douban to share review exchange information. We collect the posts from ten incentivized review groups in Douban from May 1, 2015 to August 7, 2019. It covers all the groups that we can obtain through the Douban search engine. We collect a total of 3,762 posts from 1,226 authors and obtain 1,031 WeChat accounts in these posts. Figure 3 shows the

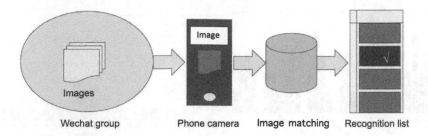

Fig. 6. Amazon product collection. The product images are collected in the WeChat group. Then, we manually search them on Amazon's App via the "camera search" function to identify the corresponding products. If identified in the recognition list, the URLs are collected from the App.

number of posts over time. We find that the incentivized review groups have been becoming increasingly active over time.

WeChat: WeChat group is an ideal place for sellers to broadcast their products since it is private and also offers convenience for further processing and making payments. We send request to join one WeChat group found on Douban and collect the review requests and members' responses over a month from July 7, 2019 to August 7, 2019. In this group, one broker is posting products for several sellers. Figure 4 shows the number of products over time.

3.2 Product Collection

For the purpose of protecting them from detection, sellers are not publishing the URLs of products, but only images and a short introduction. It poses a challenge to the collection of product information involved in the incentivized review groups. To this end, we employ image recognition to collect the corresponding products with the images collected from the group, as shown in Fig. 6. Specifically, we utilize the *Camera Search* feature on Amazon's iOS App to search the products. When searching the products, Amazon may typically pop up a list of products whose descriptions include the image captured from the camera. As such, we need to manually check the product images to ensure that we recognize the correct product in review groups. Note that sellers will copy some parts of product images from other sellers, but scarcely copy all of them. Therefore, we were able to identify such products collected from incentivized review groups. In total, we successfully identify 93 products with image recognition from about 200 products posted in the incentivized review group. We then collect the reviews and product information on these products. For the groups on WeChat, due to significant manual effort and the fact that the review tasks are largely duplicated among the groups, we collect the posts from the largest group which has the most tasks.

Summary. From the above dataset, we find that different platforms play different roles in review groups. The review groups on Facebook are similar to the blackboards, where a set of sellers can post their products directly. In our dataset, there are more than 6,000 sellers who posted products. In the review groups on Douban, most of the posts are to educate sellers on how to obtain incentivized reviews and advertise the brokers who can help sellers. In the review groups on WeChat, there exists a single broker who owns the group. The broker acquires seller members and customer members in many different ways, such as advertisements in Douban. Comparing with review groups on Facebook and Douban, the groups on WeChat are private and hence make members feel sort of close to each other.

4   Measurement

In this section, we examine the collected dataset and characterize incentivized review groups in terms of the group members, review requests, and products.

4.1   Group Members

Figure 5 plots the histogram of member numbers for incentivized review groups we collected from Facebook. We observe that some groups attract a large number of group members (including sellers and reviewers). The largest group has more than 40,000 members. Over a month, there are seven groups that have more than 1,000 new members, indicating that these review groups are remarkably attractive and popular. It also implies that fake reviews from incentivized review groups are still in a considerably large scale.

Sellers: Sellers play a central role in the review groups for posting the review requests that attract members to join the groups. Figure 7 plots the number of sellers for all groups. Note that we label a member as a seller if he/she posts any review request. We can see that there are a number of sellers in most of the review groups, even more than 2,000 sellers in the largest group.

Sellers could join multiple review groups to reach more people and obtain more paid reviews. Figure 8 shows the number of groups that sellers join. We can see that roughly 10% of sellers join more than one group and one of the most aggressive sellers even joins nine review groups at the same time.

4.2   Review Requests

The number of review requests posted in a review group indicates how active the review group is. We observe that some of review groups are notably active during our collection. The most active review group in our dataset has roughly 2,500 review requests every single day.

Figure 9 plots the number of review requests posted by sellers. We can see that some of sellers are notably active, posting more than 100 review requests.

Fig. 7. The number of sellers.

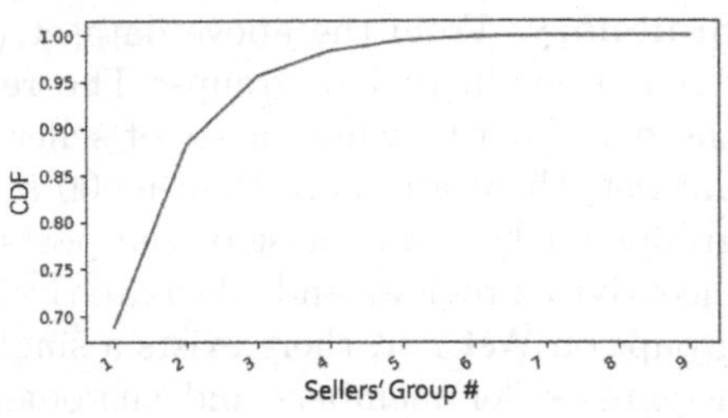

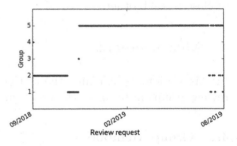

Fig. 8. The number of groups of sellers.

Fig. 9. Review requests of sellers.

Fig. 10. Review requests across groups.

In Fig. 14, we further depict the number of review requests over time for the seller who posts the most review requests. Interestingly, by labeling the review requests posted in different groups (as shown in Fig. 10), we identify that the seller performed a campaign by focusing on a certain group over a period and then switching to another group later on.

Also, sellers typically send duplicate review requests for some products that are urgent for favorable reviews to boost sales. Figure 11 depicts the number of duplicate requests, which could reach as high as eleven in our dataset, indicating the desperate need for positive reviews.

4.3   Products

Categories. We here investigate the categories of products that stand in need of favorable reviews. *Sports & Fitness* has the most review requests, accounting for 6.88% of total requests. It is followed by *Accessories* and *Computers & Accessories*, making up 5.94% and 5.63%, respectively. We find that 69.5% of the products we collect are labeled as "fulfilled by Amazon", which means that the inventory is kept in Amazon's warehouse and will be packed by Amazon. Not only can the sellers utilize Amazon's facility to facilitate their business, but also the potential benefit is to conceal the place of seller's origin.

Questions and Answers. Customers can ask questions in Amazon and the customers who bought the product may be invited to answer the questions.

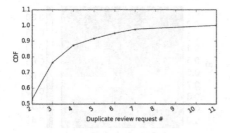

Fig. 11. Duplicate review requests.   **Fig. 12.** Questions & Answers.

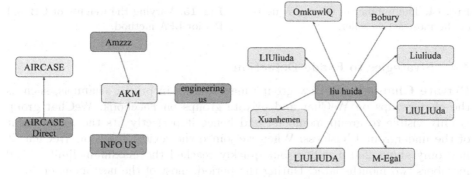

Fig. 13. Relationship types of sellers (blue) and manufacturers (gray). (Color figure online)

Questions & Answers (Q&A) are helpful for addressing customers' concerns and hence could improve the credibility of products. Figure 12 plots the number of the Q&A entries of products collected in the WeChat group. We observe that 16 out of 93 products have at least one Q&A entry, and the largest number of Q&A entries reaches 87. Although the Q&A could also be utilized to promote the products with favorable review requests, we didn't observe the Q&A being manipulated by the review groups.

Sellers and Manufacturers. Manufacturers produce the products which are advertised and listed by sellers on Amazon. We here investigate the relationship between sellers and manufacturers for the products with review requests. Figure 13 shows three different types of relationships. In the left figure, the seller and manufacturer are with a one-to-one relationship and they are usually the same entity. The middle figure reflects a many-to-one model, where multiple sellers work for one manufacturer, and the right figure represents a one-to-many model, where one seller works for multiple manufacturers. Identifying different types of relationship would be useful to understand who is launching the campaign. For example, a many-to-one model implies that it is manufacturers rather than Amazon sellers to request favorable reviews.

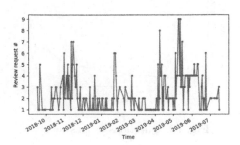
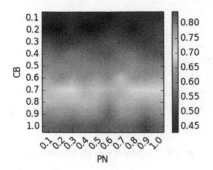

Fig. 14. The number of review requests of the most active seller.

Fig. 15. Varying the weights of CB and PN for LPA method.

4.4 Strategies to Evade Detection

Private Channels. Review groups may operate in private channels, such as the chat groups on WeChat and private groups on Facebook. WeChat group is only visible to group members, and hence it perfectly fits the requirement of the underground business. When we joined the review group on WeChat, it had only about 200 members but quickly reached the maximum limit of 500 members two months later. During the period, most of the new members were invited by the members in the group. The private groups on Facebook are covert and also require permission to join. Due to the effort to discover these groups, the private groups attract the members who are enthused about free product or compensation on the incentivized reviews. Also, the detection of review groups in these private channels is difficult to reach a large scale, and sellers can easily transfer to other review groups.

Without Sharing URLs. Even though sharing URLs of products could simplify the process of review requests and attract more customers, sellers always conceal the URLs of products in the review groups. Even in personal conversations, they are not willing to provide product URLs. The reason is that the URLs from Amazon may include referral information that can be utilized to track the source of sellers. If a number of customers visit a certain product with the same URL that refers to the seller, Amazon can detect the anomaly and probably ban the seller. Concealing URLs in review groups could bring a challenge to our study, which hurdles the collection of products with review requests as well as paid reviews. We utilize an Amazon image recognition procedure to overcome the barrier (Sect. 3).

5 Detecting Incentivized Review Groups with Co-review Graphs

In this section, we model the reviewers as co-review graphs and refer to the identification of incentivized review groups as a community detection problem.

We then employ the graph analysis method to explore the detection. With a "gold standard" dataset collected from real incentivized review groups, we evaluate different community detection algorithms. We also perform a retrospective study on an Amazon review dataset ranging from 1996 to 2018 [10,17].

5.1   Model

We model the reviewers as an undirected graph $G = (V, E)$, where each node $v_i \in V$ represents a reviewer and each edge $\{v_i, v_j\} \in E$ represents a bilateral relationship between v_i and v_j, which indicates that both v_i and v_j write reviews for at least one product. Therefore, we refer to the undirected graph as a *co-review graph*. In the graph, there are $n = |V|$ nodes and $m = |E|$ edges.

To detect the review groups, we employ the graph analysis to detect the communities in the graph and evaluate how accurately the identified communities reflect incentivized review groups. There are more edges inside the communities than the rest of the graph, and the nodes in the same community are considered to be similar to each other. Therefore, the communities of a co-review graph can reveal the cooperation pattern of reviewers in a review graph.

Features. To take various features into our detection, we construct multiple co-review graphs based on different features, such as frequency of co-review and co-review in bursts. Co-review graphs derived from those different features can further improve our detection. Specifically, we consider the following features to construct co-review graphs to perform the community detection:

Frequency of Co-review: The frequency of co-review between two reviewers is one of the most important features for indicating the probability of them belonging to the same incentivized review group. There is no conclusion to draw if two reviewers only occur in one product together. If they occur in more than one product, it is likely that they belong to the same review group, especially when they occur more than three times together. Here, we construct the graph with reviewers occurring more than two times together.

Co-review in Bursts: By checking the time series of reviews of the products that have incentivized reviews, we observe that there exist evident bursts while the products requesting incentivized reviews. Then, we employ Kleinberg's algorithm [12] to detect the burst in the time series. The algorithm models review number in a time series as an infinite hidden Markov model. With the identification of bursts, we collect the co-review of reviewers in the bursts. For the reviewers of review groups, they are required to post the most favorable reviews to obtain free products or compensation. Therefore, we also check the rating of reviewers in the bursts, *e.g.*, five stars in Amazon.

Posting Nearness in Time: The closer in time two reviewers post their reviews, the more possible they belong to the same review group. Also, there exist some legitimate reviews that occur very close to each other. Based on the purchase confirmations in the group, we can identify that most purchases by

incentivized reviewers were made within two days, given these products are all
Amazon Prime products with free 2-day delivery. By collecting reviewers posting
positive reviews (five stars) in the same product within two days, we construct
the co-review graph in terms of posting nearness in time.

Composing Multiple Graphs. We then denote the graph from the frequency
of co-review as **FC graph**, the graph from co-review in bursts as **CB graph**,
and the graph from posting nearness in time as **PN graph**. Multiple graphs
derived from different features are complementary to each other. For example,
CB graphs have some important edges although two nodes of these edges co-
occur only once and hence they do not exist in the FC graph. As such, we
compose multiple graphs according to the following equation:

$$\mathcal{G} = \mathcal{G}_{FC} + W_{CB}\mathcal{G}_{CB} + W_{PN}\mathcal{G}_{PN}. \tag{1}$$

First, we derive the FC graph by taking into account all pairs of nodes co-
occurring more than once. Then, we compose the CB graph into the FC graph
by adding edges that have at least one node in the FC graph with weight W_{CB},
which measures the importance of co-review in burst feature. Similarly, we compose the PN graph into the FC graph with weight W_{PN}, which denotes the
importance of posting nearness in time feature.

5.2 Community Detection

Dataset. For further exploring the community of incentivized review groups, we
collect the products posted in the review groups, including seller information, all
reviews, and questions & answers from customers. As mentioned in Sect. 3, sellers
always conceal the products' URLs and are not willing to provide them even in
personal conversation. We utilize an image recognition procedure to identify
the products on Amazon. We identify 93 products posted in review groups by
searching product images of more than 200 products. These identified products
belong to 48 sellers. We further collect 531 products from these sellers. We find
that sellers usually cooperate with more than one incentivized review groups
and select different products for different time periods or different incentivized
review groups. Therefore, some products from them are likely to be posted in
the incentivized review groups that we do not have access or the periods out of
our collection.

"Gold Standard" Dataset: Since we have knowledge of products and reviews
posted by the incentivized review groups, we can construct a "gold standard"
dataset with these factual incentivized reviews as ground-truth. The dataset consists of 764 incentivized reviews from 737 reviewers. With the dataset, we extract
the co-review connections of reviewers and evaluate the community detection
algorithms. As a result, we obtain 5,950 co-review connections from the "gold
standard" dataset.

Table 1. AMI among algorithms.

	CPM	Louvain	LPA	Infomap
CPM	–	0.80	0.79	0.14
Louvain	–	-	0.83	0.12
LPA	–	–	–	0.14
Infomap	–	–	–	–

Methods. Next, We explore four different community detection methods to detect incentivized review groups:

Clique Percolation Method (CPM): The clique percolation method [20] constructs the communities from k-cliques, which correspond to fully connected sub-graphs of k nodes. Two k-cliques are considered adjacent if they share $(k-1)$ nodes and a union of adjacent k-cliques form a community.

Louvain: Louvain method [4] first finds small communities by optimizing modularity locally on all nodes and then group small communities into nodes. It repeats above the two steps until achieving the optimal modularity. Modularity is a scale value between -1 and 1 that measures the density of edges inside communities to edges outside communities. Optimizing this value theoretically results in the best possible grouping of the nodes in a given network.

Label Propagation Algorithm (LPA): The label propagation algorithm [21] works by propagating labels throughout the network to form communities, where a small subset of nodes have been pre-assigned with labels. Intuitively, a single label can quickly become dominant in a densely connected group of nodes, but it is difficult to cross a sparsely connected region. The nodes that end up with the same label can be considered to be in the same community.

Infomap: Infomap [23] uses community partitions as a Huffman code that compresses the information about a random walker exploring a graph. A random walker exploring the network with the probability that the walker transits between two nodes given by its Markov transition matrix. Once the random walker enters the densely connected regions of the graph, it tends to stay there for a long time, and movements between the regions are relatively rare, which allows us to generate Huffman codes with modularity information. A modular description of a graph can be viewed as a compression of the graph topology.

Clustering Comparison. Here, we compare the results by employing above community detection algorithms to identify the communities corresponding to incentivized review groups. First, we compare the results from different algorithms by measuring the Adjusted Mutual Information (AMI) among different algorithms. AMI accounts for how similar two community detection results are to each other. As shown in Table 1, we can see that the detection results of those algorithms are similar to each other, especially the LPA and Louvain method.

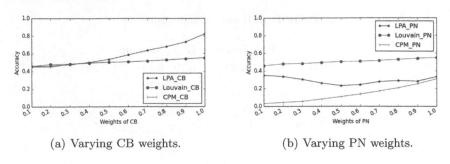

(a) Varying CB weights.   (b) Varying PN weights.

Fig. 16. Varying different weights.

However, the result of Infomap algorithm is remarkably distinct from other algorithms. After careful inspection, we find that Infomap groups most of nodes to one huge community. Therefore, we consider that Infomap is not suitable for this problem. Note that we empirically set $k = 4$ in CPM for the results in Table 1. For example, for $k = 3$, we observe that the AMI between CPM and Louvain drops to 0.43 and the AMI between CPM and LPA falls to 0.40. This inconsistency indicates that $k = 3$ may underperform comparing with $k = 4$.

Varying Weights of Composing Graphs. We then utilize the "gold standard" dataset to evaluate the accuracy of the above algorithms. The accuracy is measured by the proportion of the factual connections extracted from the "gold standard" dataset that are correctly identified by a community detection algorithm. When considering one type of graph alone, the accuracy is prohibitively low. For example, the FC graph produces the accuracy of 0.46 and 0.35 for Louvain and LPA method.

To improve the accuracy, we examine the impact by composing the PN and CB graphs into the FC graph, respectively. First, we empirically determine the composing weights in Eq. (1) by measuring the importance of the PN graph and CB graph, as illustrated in Fig. 16. We can see that composing the CB graph can significantly improve the accuracy of LPA method. When fully composing the CB graph, LPA's accuracy achieves 81%. Meanwhile, the CPM and Louvain method only gains trivial improvement with the CB graph. On the other hand, when composing the PN graph into FC graph, the CPM method gains constant improvement but remains lower than other methods, while the accuracy of LPA method first drops and then rises up. Overall, composing the CB graph achieves higher accuracy than the PN graph. It is probably because although the PN graph is roughly 10 times bigger than the FC graph and CB graph, it may also carry a bunch of unwanted nodes and edges. In the end, we here choose the LPA method to further conduct community detection.

Furthermore, we vary the weights of the CB graph and PN graph at the same time to explore an optimal weight combination of LPA method to achieve the best performance. Figure 15 depicts the heat map of accuracy, where the sidebar represents the scale of accuracy. We can see that $(W_{CB} = 1.0, W_{PN} = 0.9)$

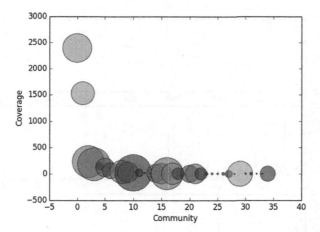

Fig. 17. An example of communities. The size of a circle specifies the number of nodes in the community, and the coverage of communities (y-axis) indicates how many edges from our "gold-standard" dataset they cover.

achieves the best accuracy of 85% in our experiment, although it is just a bit higher than ($W_{CB} = 1.0$, $W_{PN} = 0.1$). It confirms that the CB graph remarkably improves the community partition comparing with the PN graph.

Communities as Incentivized Review Groups. We then investigate the distribution of communities, which could also be used to reflect the performance of community detection method. For example, if the biggest community identified by the community detection method includes most of nodes and covers nearly all of edges from our "gold-standard" dataset, this detection method would achieve a high accuracy but essentially useless. Therefore, we prefer a balanced community detection method. We select LPA method that achieves the best performance above as an example and plot the distribution of communities in Fig. 17. The area of the circle indicates the number of nodes in the community and the coverage of communities (y-axis) represents how many edges from our "gold-standard" dataset they included. We can see that LPA method partitions notably balanced communities. The left two communities which cover most of edges from our "gold-standard" dataset are apparently the communities engaged in incentivized review groups. They are both of moderate size, 1015 and 654 respectively. We then further inspect the nodes of these two communities in the following Sect. 5.3.

5.3   Reviewer Profiles

For the reviewers in two communities mentioned above, we collect their public profiles from Amazon and investigate their ranking, the number of reviews, and the number of helpful votes. Amazon ranks reviewers by a private algorithm,

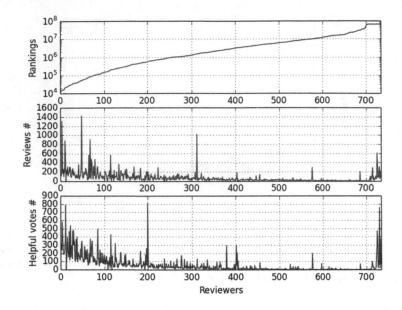

Fig. 18. Ranking, review #, and helpful vote # of reviewers.

where a smaller ranking score represents a higher reputation. Reviewers with higher reputation would be highly preferred by sellers who ask for incentivized reviews, since their reviews would be more authentic and trustworthy. The number of reviews written by a reviewer demonstrates how active the reviewer is, while the number of helpful votes a reviewer received can reflect how helpful the reviews of the reviewer are. In other words, it suggests to what extent the reviewer helps other customers. Figure 18 depicts ranking (top), number of reviews (middle), and number of helpful votes (bottom) of reviewers.

We can observe that, in the left part of those figures, reviewers with higher reputation also produce more reviews and receive more helpful votes. In the middle part, some spikes represent that a few reviewers also have an outstanding amount of reviews or helpful votes. In the right part, some reviewers with relatively lower reputation have an extraordinary amount of both reviews and helpful votes. After inspecting these reviewers, we find that they post a number of reviews within a short period and some of these reviewers actually obtain helpful votes from other customers reciprocally or from suspicious accounts.

5.4   A Retrospect of Amazon Dataset

We here conduct a retrospective study of Amazon review groups with the public datasets [10,17]. The dataset [10] contains product reviews and metadata from Amazon, including 142.8 million reviews from May 1996 to July 2014 (we refer to it as 2014 dataset). We construct the co-review graph and find that there are only 1,022 reviewers in the co-review graph. It indicates that incentivized

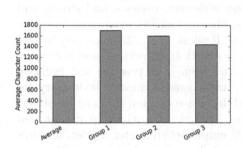

Fig. 19. Average character count per review.

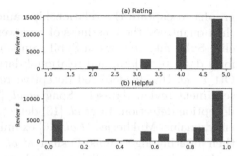

Fig. 20. Rating and helpful index.

review groups were not on an extensive scale before 2014. Then, with the updated version of dataset [17] (we refer to it as 2018 dataset), we extract the new reviews ranging from 2015 to 2018 and construct the co-review graph, which includes 90.3 million reviews. It turns out that we obtain a co-review graph with $197,087$ reviewers, which is significantly higher than the 2014 dataset.

Next, we apply the LPA community detection method for processing the co-review graph with the frequency of co-reviews. We identify 31 groups in the 2014 dataset and $6,278$ groups in the 2018 dataset. To further investigate the groups, we inspect three largest groups, which contain 115, 109, and 71 nodes, respectively, labeled as "Group1", "Group2", and "Group3". Figure 19 plots the average character count per review across different groups. The left bar, "Average" represents the average character count over all the reviews in the dataset. We can see that these three groups have remarkably more characters than the average, which implies that the reviewers from these groups are possibly professional critics who are invited to write professional reviews.

Figure 20 shows the distribution of rating and helpful index of the largest group, *i.e.*, Group1. We observe that there exist a number of average reviews less than 4 and also a spate of reviews' helpful index less than 0.5, which implies that the reviews are not considerably biased. We also inspect the review timestamps and find no anomaly.

Summary: By comparing the datasets ranging from 1996 to 2014 with the dataset ranging from 2015 to 2018, we can see that the co-review graph has shown a significant shift since 2015, indicating that the incentivized review group has become a serious issue for online marketing platforms such as Amazon.

6   Related Work

6.1   Spam Review Detection

Yao *et al.* [29] presented a potential attack against online review systems by employing deep learning to automatically generate fake reviews. They also proposed countermeasures against these fake reviews. Wang *et al.* [24] built review graphs to capture the relationships among reviewers, reviews, and stores, and then quantified the trustiness of reviewers. Zheng *et al.* [30] attempted to detect elite Sybil fake reviews in Sybil campaigns. Rayana *et al.* [22] exploited behavioral data, text data, and relational data to detect spam reviews and reviewers. Ott *et al.* [18,19] detected deceptive reviews from both positive and negative sentiment review datasets. Song *et al.* [7] investigated syntactic stylometry for deception detection. Li *et al.* [13] detected deceptive opinion spam across different domains. Mukherjee *et al.* [16] examined filtered reviews of Yelp and inferred their filtering algorithms. Fusilier *et al.* [8] employed character n-gram features to detect deceptive opinion spam. Harris *et al.* [9] examined a variety of human-based, machine-based, and hybrid assessment methods to detect deceptive opinion spam in product reviews. In [11], Jamshidi *et al.* examined the explicitly incentivized reviews which state their incentives explicitly in the reviews. Different from [11], we investigate the underground economy of incentivized reviews across different social networking platforms and propose a detection method for the incentivized review groups. Also, Mukherjee *et al.* [15] identified opinion spam groups based on a set of spam behavior indicators. These spam behavior indicators could also be applicable to improve our detection of incentivized review groups. Xie *et al.* [25] utilized temporal patterns to detect singleton review spam by identifying the time windows when spam reviews are likely to happen. However, such a method is not suitable for detecting the incentivized review groups since spammers actually collude in a collection of different products. As such, we propose a detection method based on the co-review graph, which can correlate these spammers from different products.

6.2   Reputation Manipulation

In online markets, sellers' reputation is closely related to profitability. Dishonest sellers have been reported to maneuver the reputation system by manipulating the transaction history. Xu *et al.* [28] investigated the underground market by which sellers could easily harness human labor to conduct fake transactions for improving their stores' reputation. They referred to this underground market as Seller-Reputation-Escalation (SRE) markets. Cai *et al.* [5] employed reinforcement learning methods to detect reputation manipulation in online markets. Li *et al.* [14] investigated the manipulation of mobile app reputation by leveraging crowdsourcing platforms. In [6], the authors exploited the unusual ranking change patterns of apps to identify promoted apps and detected the collusive groups who posted high app ratings or inflated apps' downloads. In addition, Xie *et al.* [26,27] inspected the underground market where mobile app developers could misuse positive reviews illegally or manipulate the rating collusively. They also analyzed the promotion incentives and characteristics of promoted apps and suspicious reviews. By contrast, our work focuses on the manipulation of reputation in online markets, which leverages incentivized review groups. The existing detection methods are unable to address this emerging manipulation problem. Therefore, we propose a novel detection method based on the co-review graph for effective defense.

7   Conclusion

In this paper, we revealed a new online reputation manipulation problem existed in the incentivized review groups on Amazon. We first investigated incentivized review groups across different platforms to understand the breadth of the problem and conducted a measurement study by considering group members, review requests, and products. After the measurement study, we proposed a detection method based on co-review graphs. We leveraged the community detection methods to locate the suspicious communities from the co-review graphs with high accuracy. While evaluating our detection method, we also constructed a "gold standard" incentivized review group dataset, which provides the critical ground truth for further study on incentivized reviews.

Acknowledgment. We would like to thank our shepherd Mohammad Mannan and the anonymous reviewers for their detailed and insightful comments, which help to improve the quality of this paper. This work was supported in part by the U.S. ARO grant W911NF-19-1-0049 and NSF grant DGE-1821744.

References

1. Amazon bans incentivized reviews (2016). https://www.usatoday.com/story/tech/news/2016/10/03/amazon-bans-incentivized-reviews/91488702/
2. Amazon consumer review policy (2016). https://www.amazon.com/gp/help/customer/display.html?nodeId=201967050
3. Consumer review survey (2017). https://www.brightlocal.com/research/local-consumer-review-survey/
4. Blondel, V.D., Guillaume, J.-L., Lambiotte, R., Lefebvre, E.: Fast unfolding of communities in large networks. J. Stat. Mech. Theo. Exp. **2008**(10), P10008 (2008)
5. Cai, Q., Filos-Ratsikas, A., Tang, P., Zhang, Y.: Reinforcement mechanism design for fraudulent behaviour in e-commerce. In: The 32nd AAAI Conference on Artificial Intelligence (2018)
6. Chen, H., He, D., Zhu, S., Yang, J.: Toward detecting collusive ranking manipulation attackers in mobile app markets. In: The 2017 ACM on Asia Conference on Computer and Communications Security (2017)
7. Feng, S., Banerjee, R., Choi, Y.: Syntactic stylometry for deception detection. In: The 50th Annual Meeting of the Association for Computational Linguistics: Short Papers, vol. 2, pp. 171–175. Association for Computational Linguistics (2012)
8. Fusilier, D.H., Montes-y-Gómez, M., Rosso, P., Cabrera, R.G.: Detection of opinion spam with character n-grams. In: Gelbukh, A. (ed.) CICLing 2015. LNCS, vol. 9042, pp. 285–294. Springer, Cham (2015). https://doi.org/10.1007/978-3-319-18117-2_21
9. Harris, C.G.: Detecting deceptive opinion spam using human computation. In: Workshops at the Twenty-Sixth AAAI Conference on Artificial Intelligence (2012)
10. He, R., McAuley, J.: Ups and downs: modeling the visual evolution of fashion trends with one-class collaborative filtering. In: Proceedings of the 25th International Conference on World Wide Web (WWW), pp. 507–517 (2016)
11. Jamshidi, S., Rejaie, R., Li, J.: Trojan horses in amazon's castle: understanding the incentivized online reviews. In: 2018 IEEE/ACM International Conference on Advances in Social Networks Analysis and Mining (2018)

12. Kleinberg, J.: Bursty and hierarchical structure in streams. Data Min. Knowl. Disc. **7**(4), 373–397 (2003)
13. Li, J., Ott, M., Cardie, C., Hovy, E.: Towards a general rule for identifying deceptive opinion spam. In: The 52nd Annual Meeting of the Association for Computational Linguistics, vol. 1 (2014)
14. Li, S., Caverlee, J., Niu, W., Kaghazgaran, P.: Crowdsourced app review manipulation. In: The 40th International ACM SIGIR Conference on Research and Development in Information Retrieval (2017)
15. Mukherjee, A., Liu, B., Glance, N.: Spotting fake reviewer groups in consumer reviews. In: The 21st International Conference on World Wide Web (WWW) (2012)
16. Mukherjee, A., Venkataraman, V., Liu, B., Glance, N.S.: What yelp fake review filter might be doing? In: The International AAAI Conference on Web and Social Media (ICWSM) (2013)
17. Ni, J., Li, J., McAuley, J.: Justifying recommendations using distantly-labeled reviews and fine-grained aspects. In: The Empirical Methods in Natural Language Processing and International Joint Conference on Natural Language Processing (EMNLP-IJCNLP) (2019)
18. Ott, M., Cardie, C., Hancock, J.T.: Negative deceptive opinion spam. In: The 2013 Conference of the North American Chapter of the Association for Computational Linguistics: Human Language Technologies (2013)
19. Ott, M., Choi, Y., Cardie, C., Hancock, J.T.: Finding deceptive opinion spam by any stretch of the imagination. In: The 49th Annual Meeting of the Association for Computational Linguistics: Human Language Technologies, vol. 1. Association for Computational Linguistics (2011)
20. Palla, G., Derényi, I., Farkas, I., Vicsek, T.: Uncovering the overlapping community structure of complex networks in nature and society. Nature **435**(7043), 814 (2005)
21. Raghavan, U.N., Albert, R., Kumara, S.: Near linear time algorithm to detect community structures in large-scale networks. Phys. Rev. E **76**(3), 036106 (2007)
22. Rayana, S., Akoglu, L.: Collective opinion spam detection: bridging review networks and metadata. In: Proceedings of the 21th ACM SIGKDD International Conference on Knowledge Discovery and Data Mining (2015)
23. Rosvall, M., Bergstrom, C.T.: Maps of random walks on complex networks reveal community structure. Proc. Nat. Acad. Sci. **105**(4), 1118–1123 (2008)
24. Wang, G., Xie, S., Liu, B., Philip, S.Y.: Review graph based online store review spammer detection. In: 2011 IEEE 11th International Conference on Data Mining (2011)
25. Xie, S., Wang, G., Lin, S., Yu, P.S.: Review spam detection via temporal pattern discovery. In: Proceedings of the 18th ACM SIGKDD International Conference on Knowledge Discovery and Data Mining (2012)
26. Xie, Z., Zhu, S.: AppWatcher: unveiling the underground market of trading mobile app reviews. In: The 8th ACM Conference on Security & Privacy in Wireless and Mobile Networks, p. 10 (2015)
27. Xie, Z., Zhu, S., Li, Q., Wang, W.: You can promote, but you can't hide: large-scale abused app detection in mobile app stores. In: The 32nd Annual Conference on Computer Security Applications (2016)
28. Xu, H., Liu, D., Wang, H., Stavrou, A.: E-commerce reputation manipulation: the emergence of reputation-escalation-as-a-service. In: International Conference on World Wide Web (WWW), pp. 1296–1306 (2015)

29. Yao, Y., Viswanath, B., Cryan, J., Zheng, H., Zhao, B.Y.: Automated crowdturfing attacks and defenses in online review systems. In: Proceedings of the 2017 ACM SIGSAC Conference on Computer and Communications Security (2017)
30. Zheng, H., et al.: Smoke screener or straight shooter: detecting elite Sybil attacks in user-review social networks. In: NDSS (2018)

*Int*egrity: Finding Integer Errors
by Targeted Fuzzing

Yuyang Rong[1(✉)], Peng Chen[2], and Hao Chen[1]

[1] University of California, Davis, Davis, USA
{ptrrong,chen}@ucdavis.edu
[2] ByteDance Inc., Beijing, China
spinpx@gmail.com

Abstract. Integer arithmetic errors are a major source of software vulnerabilities. Since they rarely cause crashes, they are unlikely found by fuzzers without special techniques to trigger them. We design and implement *Int*egrity, which finds integer errors using fuzzing. Our key contribution is that, by targeted instrumentation, we empower fuzzers with the ability to trigger integer errors. In our evaluation, *Int*egrity found all the integer errors in the Juliet test suite with no false positive. On 9 popular open source programs, *Int*egrity found a total of 174 true errors, including 8 crashes and 166 non-crashing errors. A major challenge during error review was how to determine if a non-crashing error was harmful. While solving this problem precisely is challenging because it depends on the semantics of the program, we propose two methods to find potentially harmful errors, based on the statistics of traces produced by the fuzzer and on comparing the output of independent implementations of the same algorithm. Our evaluation demonstrated that *Int*egrity is effective in finding integer errors.

Keywords: Fuzzing · Integer errors · Software security

1 Introduction

Integer arithmetic errors are a significant source of security vulnerabilities [21]. Integer overflow and underflow[1] are undefined behavior in many languages, such as C/C++, and may cause security check bypass or malicious code execution. For example, on April 22, 2018, attackers created a massive number of Beauty Coins (BEC) in two transactions by exploiting an integer overflow in ERC20 [2], which forced the exchange platform OKEx to roll back all the transactions two days later [3]. Divide-by-zero causes the program to crash and so may be used to launch denial of service attacks. The number of reported integer arithmetic

---

[1] The term *underflow* sometimes refers to float point underflow. However, in accordance with Common Weakness Enumeration (CWE) [4], in this paper underflow means that the result of an integer arithmetic operation is smaller than the smallest value that the type can represent.

© ICST Institute for Computer Sciences, Social Informatics and Telecommunications Engineering 2020
Published by Springer Nature Switzerland AG 2020. All Rights Reserved
N. Park et al. (Eds.): SecureComm 2020, LNICST 335, pp. 360–380, 2020.
https://doi.org/10.1007/978-3-030-63086-7_20

Table 1. Verified, unique arithmetic errors that *Integrity* found in real world applications, compared with Angora + UBSan. Note that the total numbers of unique errors at the bottom are fewer than the sums of the rows above because some programs share the same library and therefore we removed these duplicate errors when calculating the totals.

Program	Errors found by *Integrity*			Errors found by	Improvement
	Crashing	Non-crashing	Total(I)	Angora + UBSan(A)	(I - A)
cjpeg	1	12	13	0	+13
djpeg		17	17	14	+3
file		17	17	0	+17
img2txt	3	21	24	2	+22
jhead	2	4	6	4	+2
objdump		5	5	0	+5
readelf		38	38	0	+38
tiff2ps		27	27	1	+26
tiffcp	2	31	33	2	+31
Total	8	166	174	23	+151

bugs has been increasing rapidly in recent years, which account for 104, 232, and 635 Common Vulnerabilities and Exposures (CVE) in 2016, 2017, and 2018, respectively.

Prior work showed how to detect integer overflows *when* they happen. For example, Integer Overflow Checker (IOC) [15,16], which has been included in Undefined Behavior Sanitizer (UBSan) [8] since LLVM 3.5. However, they relied on the programmer to manually create test cases to trigger those bugs, which is laborious and unreliable. We face the challenge of how to generate these test cases automatically and efficiently.

Fuzzing is an automated approach for finding software bugs. Starting with AFL, graybox fuzzers have made great strides in finding bugs fast. They instrument programs with the code for recording program state during execution and use that information to guide input mutation. Fuzzers differ in their strategies for *exploration*, which aims at expanding branch coverage. Previous exploration strategies include matching magic bytes [28], finding sanity checks and checksums [24,35], measuring the distance between the input and target location [11,12], and solving constraints like Angora [13]. Besides exploration, another goal of fuzzing is *exploitation*. In the context of fuzzing, exploitation refers to triggering bugs, regardless if the bug may be used to launch attacks. It is difficult to find good exploitation strategies. As a result, most fuzzers randomly mutate the input to hope that some mutated input might trigger bugs. Given the huge space of input, the probability that a randomly mutated input will trigger a bug is low. Moreover, fuzzers have difficulty in detecting bugs that do not crash the program because they lack reliable signals that indicate bugs in those cases. For example, arithmetic errors cause a program to misbehave (e.g., to produce wrong results), but they rarely cause the program to crash.

Our goal is to allow fuzzers to exploit integer arithmetic errors efficiently. Our key technique is to provide fuzzers with critical information by targeted instrumentation such that the information can later be used to guide fuzzers to exploit potential bugs. For example, to detect overflow when adding two 32-bit signed integers, we extend both the operands to 64 bits, compute their sum (which cannot overflow), and, if the sum is out of the range of 32-bit signed integers, execute a special *guard branch* to send a signal to the fuzzer to indicate the error. This way, if the fuzzer can reach the guard branch, then an integer overflow occurs. The same idea can be used to check for other bugs, such as index out of range, null pointer dereference, etc.

In principle, the above idea works with any fuzzer. However, to find bugs efficiently, we need to overcome three challenges. First, we need to select a fuzzer that efficiently solves the constraints indicating arithmetic errors (Sect. 3.2). Second, the guard branches inserted by the fuzzer have much lower expected reachability than the original branches, because the guard branches indicate arithmetic errors but most arithmetic operations should not have such errors. Therefore, we need to redesign the fuzzer's scheduling algorithm to assign different priorities to the original and guard branches, respectively (Sect. 3.2). Finally, we need to send a unique signal to the fuzzer to indicate arithmetic errors if the guard branches are explored. The fuzzer should let the program continue exploring branches after receiving the signal, in contrast to when the signal indicates a memory violation (Sect. 3.2).

It might be tempting to implement the above idea by simply combining a sanitizer (e.g., UBSan [8]) with a fuzzer. However, because of the challenges described above, such a naive combination would result in poor performance, as we will show in Sect. 5.4. Instead, we implemented our approach in a tool called *Int*egrity. As we will show in Sect. 5, *Int*egrity is effective in finding integer arithmetic errors in both standard test suites and popular open source programs. On the Juliet Test Suite [9], *Int*egrity found all the bugs with no false positive (Table 2). Table 1 shows the bugs that *Int*egrity found on 9 popular open source programs from 6 packages. In total, *Int*egrity found 174 unique arithmetic errors, where 8 caused crash but 166 did not. We define a unique error by a unique (file name, line number, column number) tuple.

Fuzzing is attractive because it provides inputs that witness errors. When an error caused a crash, there is no doubt that the program misbehaved. However, when the error did not cause a crash, verifying whether the error caused the program to misbehave becomes difficult as the decision must take domain knowledge into consideration. We made progress on this problem by proposing two methods. The first method is based on the statistics of the traces generated by the fuzzer. If an integer arithmetic error occurred on most traces generated by the fuzzer where the arithmetic operation executed, then the error was likely benign, as long as the fuzzer had adequate path coverage. The other method is based on comparing the output of independent implementations of the same algorithm on the same input. If an integer error caused one implementation to misbehave, then the other independent implementation of the same algorithm will unlikely generate a similar output, as long as the output is a deterministic function of the input. These two approaches, when applicable, call attention to integer errors that are potentially harmful.

2 Background

2.1 Integer Arithmetic Errors

In statically typed languages such as C, the type of a variable is determined at compile time. An integer type has a fixed width and so can represent only a range of integers. For example, an unsigned 32-bit integer variable can represent only integers in $[0, 2^{32} - 1]$. When the result of an arithmetic operation exceeds the upper/lower bound of its type, overflow/underflow occurs. Another common arithmetic error is divide by zero.

Some compilers have the option to insert code that checks for integer arithmetic error at runtime. However, the checks cause runtime overhead. Moreover, some arithmetic errors are benign because they are intended by the programmer. For example,

$$\texttt{v << (32 - b) >> (32 - b)}$$

is a common idiom to extract the lower b bits from the unsigned 32-bit integer v. As long as b is in $(0, 32]^2$, the implementation correctly achieved the programmer's goal, even though overflow might happen during the left shift. It would be undesirable to terminate the program upon detecting such benign overflows.

2.2 Fuzzing

To avoid runtime overhead or terminating programs upon benign arithmetic errors, we would like to find those errors during testing. Fuzzing is a popular technique for finding bugs automatically with Graybox fuzzing being particularly popular. It instruments programs with the code for recording program state during execution and uses that information to guide input mutation. However, integer overflow/underflow bugs rarely cause crashes, and most fuzzers cannot detect bugs that do not crash the program. In this paper, we propose an approach to instrument arithmetic operations to give the fuzzer critical information to help it find potential errors in arithmetic operations.

---

[2] It is undefined behavior when b is a constant 0. Some architectures only allow 5 bits for the second operand, making shift by 32 bits equivalent to shift by 0 bits, producing v as the result; yet compilers, when $-O2$ optimization is turned on, will optimize this line to 0 if b is compile-time known to be 0.

3   Design

Fuzzers mutate the input to find bugs in the program. They have two goals: (1) exploration: explore different paths; and (2) exploitation: trigger bugs (regardless whether they can be used to launch attacks). Previously, fuzzers were used predominantly to find memory errors. To use fuzzers to find integer arithmetic errors effectively, we need to modify both their exploration and exploitation strategies.

3.1   Exploitation

Arithmetic Operations. We detect integer overflow and underflow during addition (+), subtraction (-), multiplication (*), shift left (<<), and divide by zero during division (/) and remainder (%). We instrument LLVM IR code to detect those errors as follows.

- +, -, *: We promote both the operands to the next longer type (e.g., from int32_t to int64_t, and from uint32_t to uint64_t), evaluate the expression in the longer type, and check if the result is out of the range of the original type. As long as the width of the next longer type is as least doubled (e.g., int8_t, int16_t, int32_t, int64_t), which is the case in C and most C-like languages, the operation in the longer type never overflows. For example, to check if (int8_t)x + (int8_t)y overflows, we compute (int16_t)x + (int16_t)y and check if the sum is out of the range of int8_t.
- <<: A left shift operation x << n overflows if and only if $\mathrm{hp}(x) + n$ is greater than or equal to the width of (number of bits in) the result type, where the function $\mathrm{hp}(x)$ is the position of the highest non-zero bit of x. For example, $\mathrm{hp}(0b00000001) = 0$, $\mathrm{hp}(0b10000000) = 7$.
- / and %: We check if the second operand is 0. For /, we also check if the operands are MININT and -1 because MININT / -1 = MAXINT + 1 overflows.

Range Inference. Integer types have different ranges. To infer the correct integer type, we must determine both the bit width and sign.

Bit Width Inference. For each operation, LLVM promotes every operand shorter than 32 bits to 32 bits, executes the operation, and then truncates the result back to the destination type when necessary. Therefore, if a truncation follows the operation, then we use the destination type of the truncation to infer the bit width; otherwise, we use the left-hand side of the operation.

Sign Inference. LLVM IR does not distinguish between signed and unsigned variables. LLVM determines if an operation on 32 or more bits may have signed overflow or unsigned overflow using the sign information from abstract syntax tree (AST), and encodes that information as a tag in the arithmetic instructions. For example, add nsw (no signed wrap) and add nuw (no unsigned wrap). We use these tags to infer the sign. However, operations on integers shorter than 32 bits carry no such tag because they never overflow in the range of 32-bit integers. In those cases, we infer the sign of each operand using the cast operation before the arithmetic operation. When LLVM casts the shorter type to 32 bits, we examine if the cast is signed or unsigned. If both operands are cast, we take the sign of the operand of the longer type if the operands have different bit widths. If they have the same bit width, and if either operand undergoes an unsigned cast, we infer the sign of the destination type as unsigned; otherwise, we infer the sign as signed.

Instrumentation Reduction. When we instrument an integer arithmetic operation to check for arithmetic errors, we create new branches. When a program has many integer arithmetic operations, the instrumentation would create many new branches for the fuzzer to explore. However, these branches differ from the original branches in the program in a very important way for the fuzzer: we expect most original branches to be reachable but few instrumented branches to be reachable (because the latter represent arithmetic errors). Since unreachable branches waste the fuzzer's computing budget, during instrumentation we eliminate branches that are guaranteed unreachable as follows:

- While we need to check both overflow and underflow of signed operations, we need not check underflow of unsigned operations, because once promoted to a wider type, underflow becomes overflow. For example, when the original type is 8-bit unsigned int, (uint8_t)0-1 = 0xff causes underflow. However, when promoted to 16-bit unsigned int, (uint16_t)0-1 = 0xffff causes an overflow on the original type because the result 0xffff is larger than the upper limit of the original type, 0xff.
- We do not check shift operation on negative integers for the same reason as above.
- When an operation is square, we do not check for underflow because it cannot.
- When a value is added to a negative constant or is subtracted by a positive constant, we do not check for overflow; similarly, when a value is added to a positive constant or is subtracted by a negative constant, we do not check for underflow.

Section 5.5 will show that the above optimization significantly reduced the number of branches that the instrumentation added to the program, and hence the number of constraints that the fuzzer tries to solve.

3.2 Exploration

The instrumentation described in Sect. 3.1 reduces the problem of exploitation to the problem of exploration. At each operation with potential integer arithmetic errors, *Integrity* inserts a conditional statement to check for integer arithmetic errors. When an error happens, the conditional statement executes a branch, called the *guard branch*. In principle, we can use any fuzzer to do the exploration. However, we desire to select a fuzzer that can explore arithmetic errors efficiently. Moreover, since the guard branches are inherently different from the branches in the original program (original branches), the fuzzer must treat them differently: the fuzzer should triage between the original and guard branches when scheduling branches (Sect. 3.2), and should behave differently between when arithmetic errors occur and when other errors occur (Sect. 3.2).

Fuzzer Choice. Section 3.1 provides critical information to the fuzzer by instrumenting the guard branches that represent those errors. While we may use any fuzzer to take advantage of that information, we selected Angora [13] for its two beneficial properties.

First, Angora fuzzes individual branches and can prioritize different branches. With enough computing budget, Angora fuzzes every branch on a path at least once. Since we associate every potential arithmetic error with a guard branch, Angora exploits (tries to trigger) every arithmetic error on the path. Angora also allows us to triage different branches, which is handy because the original branches and guard branches have different expected reachability (Sect. 3.2).

Second, Angora's input mutation strategy fits our goal well. When fuzzing a branch, Angora uses byte-level taint tracking to identify the input byte offsets that flow into the predicate that guards the branch. Then, Angora considers the predicate as a blackbox function on those byte offsets and uses gradient descent to find an input that satisfies the predicate. When the blackbox function is linear or monotonic, this mutation strategy guarantees to find a solution quickly. + and − are linear functions, and ∗ is a monotonic function. When their operands take their values directly from in the input, Angora can solve the predicates of those operations efficiently.

Branch Triage. As discussed in Sect. 3.1, original branches and guard branches have different expected reachability: we expect most original branches to be reachable but few guard branches to be reachable because few arithmetic operations have errors. Moreover, before the fuzzer can reach an original branch b, it cannot explore any guard branch that b dominates.[3] Therefore, we must let the fuzzer assign higher priority to the original branches than to the guard branches.

We replaced Angora's scheduling with the following algorithm:

- At compile time, instrument each branch with a tag to indicate whether it is an original branch or a guard branch.

---

[3] A node d dominates a node n if every path from the entry node to n must go through d.

Algorithm 1. *Int*egrity's scheduling algorithm.

function POP   ▷ Returns the next branch to fuzz
  return priorityQueue.pop()
end function
function PUSH(*b*)   ▷ Pushes a new or existing branch onto the queue
  if *b* is a newly found branch **then**
    if *b.tag = Tag.Original* **then**
      b.priority ← *MAX_PRIORITY*
    else
      b.priority ← *GUARD_INIT_PRIORITY*
    end if
  else
    b.priority ← *b.priority* − 1
  end if
  priorityQueue.push(b)
end function

- At run time, store all the branches to be fuzzed in a priority queue.
- When finding a new branch, assign the branch a priority according to the branch tag (original or guard branch), and then push the branch onto the priority queue (**PUSH** in Algorithm 1).
- When failing to solve a branch, lower the priority of the branch and push it onto the priority queue (**PUSH** in Algorithm 1).
- When ready to explore a new branch, call **POP** in Algorithm 1 to get the branch with the highest priority.

Signal of Errors. When the fuzzer receives a signal indicating an error in the program, it stops the program execution and records the input, and the error and its location. Memory access violation, such as segmentation fault, is the most common signal. To reuse this framework, *Int*egrity lets the instrumented branches send a pre-determined signal to the fuzzer to indicate arithmetic errors.

However, merely sending a signal would be inadequate. Fuzzers stop the program when receiving signals. It makes sense when the signal is triggered by a memory error because the program cannot continue anyway. However, when the signal is triggered by an arithmetic error, the fuzzer should let the program continue to explore more paths, particularly when the error is false positive (see Sect. 5.2 for examples). Without this ability, a false positive arithmetic error early in the program would prevent the fuzzer from exploring most paths because most paths descend from the location of that error. We implemented this desirable function in Angora.

4 Implementation

We implemented *Int*egrity as an LLVM pass in 924 lines of C++. We also modified Angora to do branch triage (Sect. 3.2) and to deal with the new signal of arithmetic errors (Sect. 3.2) in 3419 lines of Rust.

We found that some programs may use 64-bit types (`uint64_t`, for example). However, Angora supported only 64-bit constraints, which was inadequate to check the overflow of the arithmetic operation on two 64-bit integers. To tackle this problem, we extended Angora to support 128-bit constraints. We did so by using `u128` and `__uint128_t` in Rust and C, respectively. In the case of a 128-bit or higher precision integer operation, we created a new struct that has two (or more) 128-bit unsigned integers inside and implemented all the arithmetic traits (`Add`, `Sub`, `Mul`, etc.) for it.

5   Evaluation

We evaluated the performance of *Int*egrity on both the Juliet test suite [9] and popular open source programs. We also evaluated the impact of instrumentation reduction described in Sect. 3.1.

All our experiments ran on a Linux server with two Intel Xeon Gold 5118 CPUs and 256 GB RAM.

We set $MAX\_PRIORITY$ and $GUARD\_INIT\_PRIORITY$ in Algorithm 1 to 65 535 and 65 534, respectively, to guarantee that the fuzzer will try to solve all the original branches at least once before solving the guard branches.

5.1   Juliet Test Suite

The Juliet test suite, developed by the National Security Agency (NSA), contains tests for errors listed in Common Weakness Enumeration (CWE) [4]. It organizes the tests in a hierarchy: at the top level, the suite contains one test set for each CWE. Then, each test set contains many subsets, and each subset contains many tests. Each test is a C or C++ program containing a carefully designed and inserted error. This test suite provides ground truth for evaluating the false positive and false negative of *Int*egrity.

We used Juliet Test Suite v1.3 and selected the following test sets relevant to integer arithmetic errors:

- CWE190_Integer_Overflow
- CWE191_Integer_Underflow
- CWE194_Unexpected_Sign_Extension
- CWE197_Numeric_Truncation_Error
- CWE369_Divide_by_Zero

We excluded the following tests in the above test sets:

- Deterministic errors: These errors always happen regardless of the input, e.g., overflow caused by constant integers.
- Floating point errors, since we focus on integer arithmetic errors only.
- C++ programs. As discussed in Sect. 3.2, we used Angora as the fuzzer, and currently it supports only C programs. This is not an inherent limitation of *Int*egrity.

Table 2. Errors that *Integrity* found on the Juliet test suite. A "–" cell means that the corresponding test set on the top contains no corresponding subset on the left. *Integrity* found all the errors with no false positive. Every test contains one inserted arithmetic error except subset s02 of CWE197, where half of its inserted bugs contain two truncation errors each.

Subset	Set									
	CWE190		CWE191		CWE194		CWE197		CWE369	
	bugs added	bugs found	bugs added	bugs found	bugs added	bugs found	bugs added	bugs found	bugs added	bugs found
s01	114	114	76	76	304	304	152	152	112	112
s02	38	38	38	38	0	0	76	**114**	38	38
s03	190	190	114	114	–	–	–	–	–	–
s04	114	114	190	190	–	–	–	–	–	–
s05	114	114	190	190	–	–	–	–	–	–
s06	190	190	–	–	–	–	–	–	–	–
s07	190	190	–	–	–	–	–	–	–	–

```
1  short CWE_197_s02_trunc_twice(char* inputBuffer){
2    short data = 0;
3    if (fgets(inputBuffer, 14, stdin) != NULL) {
4      data = (short)atoi(inputBuffer);
5    }
6    return (char) data;
7  }
```

Fig. 1. A test in CWE197 s02, which contains two truncation errors on Line 4 and 6.

Two CWEs related to integer arithmetic errors are worth mentioning. One of them is CWE197_Numeric_Truncation_Error. Integer truncation causes an error when the result is out of the range of the destination type. Therefore, to detect this error accurately, we must detect the destination type (both sign and width) accurately. For example, consider x & 0x0000ffff. If the destination type has more than 16 bits or if it is unsigned 16-bit integer, then no overflow can happen. In all the tests of CWE197, it is easy to infer the destination types accurately because of the way how those errors were injected. However, in real world programs, we found that accurately inferring the destination type in the context of integer truncation was difficult. Therefore, we disabled this rule when checking real world programs in Sect. 5.2.

The other one is CWE680_Integer_Overflow_to_Buffer_Overflow. This error happens when calling the function malloc(site_t) and when size_t is defined by uint32_t, which occurs on only 32-bit platforms. Since the fuzzer that we used(Angora) ran only on 64-bit platforms, we did not test this error.

Table 2 shows that *Integrity* found all the bugs in the test sets of the above five CWEs with no false positives. Every test case has one inserted arithmetic

370 Y. Rong et al.

Table 3. Unique errors that *Int*egrity found in common open source programs. Note that the total numbers of unique errors at the bottom are fewer than the sums of the rows above because when calculating the totals we removed the duplicate errors in the libraries shared by different programs.

Package	Version	Program	Unique errors			
			Divide by zero	Overflow crashing	Non-crashing	Benign
libjpeg-ijg	v9a	cjpeg	1		12	63
		djpeg			17	101
file	5.32	file			17	7
libcaca	0.99beta99	img2txt	1	2	21	36
jhead	3.00	jhead		2	4	4
binutils	2.29	objdump -x			5	11
		readelf -a			38	27
libtiff	4.0.7	tiff2ps			27	36
		tiffcp -i	2		31	49
Total			4	4	166	315

error except subset s02 of CWE197. This subset contains 76 tests, where half of the tests contains two truncation errors each as shown in Fig. 1: first truncating the result of `atoi` into `short`, and then further into `char`, both of which cause truncation errors. Therefore, *Int*egrity found a total of $38 + 38 \times 2 = 114$ unique errors in this subset of 76 tests.

We tried Angora and Angora + UBSan on this test set, respectively. Neither of them found any bugs.

5.2 Real World Applications

We evaluated *Int*egrity on popular real world applications. We selected 9 applications from 6 packages that have many integer operations, such as image processing and executable file parsing. Detailed version and command line arguments are shown in Table 3. On each program, we ran *Int*egrity on 12 cores for 72 h.

Table 3 shows all the unique errors that *Int*egrity found. We identified a unique error by the (file name, line number, column number) tuple where the error occurs. We divide those errors into three categories. The first category contains all errors that caused crashes (Sect. 5.2). Then, we manually reviewed the remaining errors to identify benign ones. We determined an error to be benign when we found that the error did not cause the program to misbehave (Sect. 5.2). After excluding those benign errors, the remaining errors belong to the non-crashing error category (Sect. 5.3).

It is also worth mentioning that *tiff2ps* and *tiffcp* share the same underlying library(*libtiff*). As a result, *Int*egrity found 6 duplicate non-crashing errors and

19 benign errors in both program. We removed those duplicate errors from total error count in Table 1 and Table 3.

Benign Errors. An error is benign when we found strong evidence that the error had been expected by the programmer and therefore did not cause the program to misbehave. We classify all the benign errors found into two classes:

Intentional Overflows. The programmer intended to use the result of an overflown value. One example is v << (32 - b) >> (32 - b), where the programmer intended to exact the lower b bits from the unsigned 32-bit integer v, and implemented it by shifting v by $32 - b$ bits to the left and then shifting by $32 - b$ bits to the right. As long as b is in $(0, 32]$, the implementation correctly achieved the programmer's goal, even though overflow might happen during the left shift.

Unused Overflown Values. This class of benign errors is commonly introduced by compiler optimization.

```
while (i--) { /* loop body */ }
```

is an example, Fig. 2 shows the compiled LLVM IR. The loop subtracts 1 from the loop variable (an unsigned integer) and saves the result in another variable just before checking the predicate that if the loop variable is not 0. When the loop variable is 0, the subtraction underflows, but its result will never be used because the loop finishes.

```
1 ; <label>.loop_head:
2 %loop_var = load i32 , i32*%loop_ptr , align 4
3 %next_loop_var = add nsw i32 %loop_var , −1
4 store i32 %next_loop_var , i32*%loop_ptr , align 4
5 %cond = icmp ne i32 %loop_var , 0
6 br i1 %cond , label %loop_body , label %loop_end
7 ; <label>:loop_body: /* body */
8 br label %loop_head
9 ; <label>:loop_end:
```

Fig. 2. An example of benign integer overflow. After LLVM optimization passes, the C program was translated into the IR shown in the figure, the syntax slighted modified for readability. On Line 3, the add instruction overflows when the loop variable %iter_var is 0, but the overflown result will never be used.

Crashes. Arithmetic errors may cause crashes in two different ways. Divide by zero causes a crash immediately, while overflown or underflown values may cause a crash when used as indices to arrays. *Integrity* discovered eight crashes, among which four are divide by zero, and four are overflow.

Figure 3 shows a divide by zero error on Line 4 in the program *libjpeg-ijp*. *Integrity* found an input that caused the parameter `samplesperrow` to become 0, which then caused divide by zero on Line 4.

```
1  // jmemmgr.c:395~435
2  ... alloc_sarray(..., unsigned samplesperrow, ... ) {
3    ...
4    ltemp = ... / ((long) samplesperrow * SIZEOF(JSAMPLE));
5    ...
6  }
```

Fig. 3. Divide by zero error in *jmemmgr.c* of *libjpeg-ijg* happens when the parameter `samplesperrow` is zero.

5.3   Which Non-crashing Error Is Harmful?

An error is said to be *harmful* when it triggers unexpected behavior, e.g. to produce a wrong result. Harmful errors may or may not be exploitable in the context of software security, yet they still cause problems in software correctness and reliability. If an arithmetic error causes a crash, it is definitely a harmful error. However, when it does not cause a crash, it is non-trivial to validate whether it is harmful.

We manually inspected all the 481 non-crashing errors reported by *Integrity* and determined that 315 (or 65 %) were benign. However, manual inspection is tedious and unscalable.

Automatically determining if an arithmetic error is harmful is challenging because it depends on the semantics of the application. Nevertheless, we made progress on this problem by proposing two methods, one based on statistics of the traces generated by the fuzzer, and the other based on comparing the output of independent implementations of the same algorithm on the same input. These two approaches, when applicable, call attention to integer errors that are potentially harmful.

By Statistics of Traces. This method is based on the conjecture that a harmful bug in a popular open source program unlikely occurs during most executions, because otherwise it would have been noticed, reported, and fixed with high probability. By this conjecture, if an integer arithmetic error occurred on most traces generated by the fuzzer where the arithmetic operation executed, then the error was likely benign, as long as the fuzzer had adequate path coverage.

Table 4. Benign arithmetic errors determined by statistics of traces. We use the benign errors found by manual inspection as the ground truth when calculating the precision and recall of the benign errors determined by statistics of traces.

Program	Benign errors found by manual inspection	Benign errors determined by statistics of traces					
		Threshold = 0.95			Threshold = 0.70		
		Count	Precision	Recall	Count	Precision	Recall
cjpeg	63	8	100.0%	12.7%	48	87.5%	66.7%
djpeg	101	19	100.0%	18.8%	42	97.6%	40.6%
file	7	6	83.3%	71.4%	8	87.5%	100.0%
img2txt	36	18	88.9%	44.4%	39	59.0%	69.9%
jhead	4	4	100.0%	100.0%	5	80.0%	100.0%
objdump	11	12	83.3%	90.9%	12	83.3%	90.9%
readelf	27	28	71.4%	74.1%	36	72.2%	96.3%
tiff2ps	36	25	88.0%	61.1%	37	62.2%	63.9%
tiffcp	49	46	67.4%	63.3%	53	67.9%	73.5%
Total	315	149	79.2%	37.5%	280	75.7%	67.3%

To implement the above idea, for each non-crashing arithmetic error, we measured its rate of occurrence on all the traces where the arithmetic operation occurred. When this rate is above a threshold, we consider this error to be benign. We used the benign errors that we manually determined in Table 3 as the ground truth. Then, at each threshold, we counted the number of benign errors using the rule above, and calculated precision and recall based on the ground truth. That is, let G be the set of benign errors that we manually determined, and S be the set of benign errors that we identified by the statistics of traces. Then precision is $\frac{|S \cap G|}{|S|}$ and recall is $\frac{|S \cap G|}{|G|}$.

Table 4 shows the number of benign arithmetic errors and their precision and recall with regard to the ground truth. The overall precision is 79.2% at the threshold of 0.95, and is 75.7% at the threshold of 0.70. The overall recall is 37.5% at the threshold of 0.95, and is 67.3% at the threshold of 0.70. On several programs, this method was quite accurate. For example, at the threshold of 0.95, this method achieved both 100% precision and 100% recall on *jhead*, and 100% precision on *cjpeg*. On 7 out of 9 programs the precision reaches above 80%, which indicates that our method can efficiently rule out part of benign error and thus reduce human labor.

By Comparing Independent Implementations. This method uses two independent implementations P and Q of the same algorithm to evaluate whether an arithmetic error is likely harmful. If P and Q (1) agree (have identical or similar output) on all the inputs that trigger no arithmetic errors but (2) disagree (have different outputs) on the inputs that trigger arithmetic errors in P, then the errors in (2) are likely harmful. This is based on the conjecture that when an input triggers a harmful arithmetic error in P, it unlikely also triggers an arithmetic error in Q, and even if it does, the two errors unlikely cause P

and Q to generate similar output. Obviously, the first property above requires the output to be a deterministic function of the input, i.e., no randomness may affect the output.

We applied the above method on the program *djpeg* in the *libjpeg-ijg* package. A JPEG encoder compresses an image by (1) dividing the image into 8×8 matrices and applying discrete cosine transform (DCT) to each matrix, (2) suppressing the high-frequency signals by element-wise dividing each matrix by a predefined matrix and rounding the result to the nearest integer, and (3) discarding all the tailing zeros. The decoder reverses the above operations, where it can infer the number of discarded zeros based on the size of the small matrix and that of the image.

Since a JPEG decoder uses floating point arithmetic, two independent decoders may create slight different outputs on the same input. However, if the difference is large, then at least one decoder is misbehaving. We measured the difference as the average L^1 distance between two images. More precisely, let

- A and B: two images of dimension $m \times n$.
- $A_{i,j}$: a 3-channel vector representing the RGB values of the pixel at (i, j)
- $A_{i,j}^{(k)}$: the value of the kth channel. This value is in the range $[0, 255]$, and $k \in \{1, 2, 3\}$.

Definition 1. *The* average L^1 distance *between two images A and B of identical size is:*

$$D(A, B) = \frac{\sum_{c \in C(A,B)} \sum_{k \in [1,3]} \mid c^{(k)} \mid}{\mid C(A, B) \mid} \tag{1}$$

where

$$C(A, B) = \{A_{i,j} - B_{i,j} : i \in [1, m], j \in [1, n], A[i, j] \neq B[i, j]\}$$

To evaluate whether non-crash arithmetic errors in *libjpeg-ijg* are harmful, we selected *libjpeg-turbo* as an alternative, independent implementation. *libjpeg-turbo* has the same API as *libjpeg-ijg*; however, its decoder uses SIMD instructions to accelerate arithmetic operations while *libjpeg-ijg* does not.

We prepared two sets of JPEG images as input to the decoders:

- Normal images: We randomly picked 100 JPEG images from Android system images, LaTeX testing images, *libjpeg* testing images, and GNOME 3.28 desktop images. None of them triggered arithmetic errors on either decoder.
- Exploit images: We collected images produced by *Integrity* that triggered arithmetic errors in the program *djpeg* in the package *libjpeg-ijg*, and then removed the following from the collection:
  - Broken images: *Integrity* generated many images that are invalid JPEG and therefore cannot be rendered.

- Images whose width or height is less than 8 pixels. Since JPEG encoder partitions images into 8×8 matrices, the decoder's behavior on those images may be implementation-dependent.
- Images that triggered only the benign errors described in Sect. 5.2

After filtering, we were left with 67 exploit JPEG images.

Figure 4 compares the cumulative distribution functions (CDF) of the average L^1 distance (Eq. 1) between normal and exploit images. The figure cleanly separates the CDF of normal and exploit images with no overlap: the L^1 distance of normal images ranges from 0.0 to 6.0 with a median of 2.4, while the distance of exploit images ranges from 16.9 to 342.4 with a median of 217.2. This implies that those arithmetic errors that *Int*egrity found in *libjpeg-ijg* are harmful.

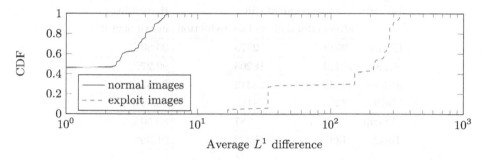

Fig. 4. Cumulative distribution function (CDF) of the average L^1 distance (Eq. 1) between the output of two decoders on the same input JPEG image. The CDF of the normal images is cleanly separable from that of the exploit images.

5.4 Comparison with Angora + UBSan

We compared *Int*egrity with simple combination of Angora and UBSan. We ran Angora with UBSan in the same experimental configuration as we described in Sect. 5.2.

Table 1 compares the number of verified bugs found by *Int*egrity and Angora+UBSan, respectively. *Int*egrity found many more bugs than Angora on each program. On all program together, *Int*egrity found 174 bugs while Angora+UBScan found only 23 bugs. Angora+UBSan found no bug in *file*, *objdump* and *readlef*, but *Int*egrity found a total of 60 bugs in them. This result shows that *Int*egrity performs far superior than simple combination of Angora and UBSan. Without proper information sharing (Sects. 3.2), the fuzzer and the sanitizer cannot cooperate well because the fuzzer would not know where the potential bugs lie and divert computation power accordingly.

As a side note, we had to overcome engineering difficulties to combine Angora and UBSan. Angora compiles two binaries for each program: one uses Data Flow Sanitizer (DFSan) [6] to do taint tracking, and the other monitors the execution traces. DFSan instruments instructions to track data flow. If the program calls a function in third-party libraries, DFSan needs a modeled function to know how to propagate the taint. When we initially compiled the programs using UBSan and DFSan, it failed because DFSan could not find the modeled functions instrumented by UBSan. [31] also warned such issues when using multiple sanitizers. We applied a temporary hack to overcome the compilation problem: we enabled DFSan and disabled UBSan when compiling the binary for taint tracking, and enabled UBSan and disabled DFSan when compiling the binary for monitoring execution traces.

Table 5. Number of instrumented arithmetic operations before and after instrumentation reduction

Library	# of instrumentation		Remaining
	after reduction	before reduction	instrumentation
libpng	2518	2773	90.80 %
binutils	16432	18203	90.27%
libjpeg	14335	15312	93.62%
libtiff	7383	8123	90.89%
libpcap	714	887	80.50%
Total	41382	45298	91.36%

5.5 Instrumentation Reduction

To evaluate the effect of instrumentation reduction described in Sect. 3.1, we instrumented five libraries with and without reduction and compared the number of instrumented arithmetic operations. Table 5 shows that overall this technique eliminated 9% instrumented arithmetic operations.

6   Related Work

6.1 Detecting Integer Overflow

Integer overflow has been extensively studied [15,16,22,27,34,36]. IOC [15,16] instruments AST to test for overflow. It is now part of LLVM's UBSan [8].

IOC tends to generate many benign overflows. IntEQ [34] and IntFlow [27] intend to cut down reported benign overflows. Both use the assumption that an overflown value is benign unless it is used in a sink. IntFlow combines static and dynamic analysis to determine if any overflown value flows into a sink. IntEQ relies on symbolic execution to achieve this goal. It computes a value flown into a sink in both high and low precision and compares the two values. Both these tools rely on the user to provide input (test cases) for finding overflows. *Integrity* overcomes this limitation by triggering arithmetic errors automatically through program instrumentation targeting arithmetic errors.

z3 [22] is a tool for solving integer-related symbolic constraints. IntScope [36] uses symbolic execution to detect integer overflow. Unlike IOC, IntScope does not rely on source code but translates x86 binary to an intermediate representation called PANDA first, then symbolically executes PANDA to detect possible arithmetic errors. Since *Int*egrity uses fuzzing, it inherits the advantages of fuzzing over symbolic execution, such as faster execution and tolerating obscure code (e.g., external libraries, system API, etc.).

6.2   Coverage-Directed Fuzzers

A coverage-directed fuzzer mutates the input to explore paths in the hope to trigger bugs on some of these paths [1, 5, 10–14, 28, 30, 33, 37]. If a mutated input explores a new path, the fuzzer keeps the input as a seed. AFL [1] and Lib-Fuzzer [5] employ evolutionary algorithms to mutate input. Driller [33] and QSYM [37] try to solve complex path constraints by concolic execution. VUzzer [28] and REDQUEEN [10] learn magic bytes and generate satisfying input without symbolic execution. AFLGo [11] and Hawkeye [12] direct fuzzing to a set of target program locations efficiently. Angora [13] models a path constraint as a black-box function, and uses optimization methods such as gradient descent to solve it. NEUZZ [30] also uses gradient descent to explore new paths and approximates the target program's branch coverage by a neural network.

Many coverage-directed fuzzers can turn on various sanitizers to detect bugs during exploration [7, 8, 18, 29, 31, 32]. For example, Address Sanitizer [29], Memory Sanitizer [32], Thread Sanitizer [7], and Undefined Behavior Sanitizer [8] detect invalid memory addresses, use of uninitialized memory, data races, and undefined behavior, respectively. However, those fuzzers only passively detect those bugs when they are triggered by random mutation. By contrast, *Int*egrity instruments arithmetic operations with potential errors to triggers them actively.

6.3   Bug-Directed Fuzzers

Besides integer arithmetic errors, researchers developed fuzzers to exploit other vulnerabilities. SlowFuzz [26] targets algorithmic complexity vulnerabilities guided by resource usage. RAZZER [20] guides fuzzing towards potential data races in the kernel, then deterministically triggers a race. NEZHA [25] exploits the behavioral asymmetries between multiple test programs to focus on inputs that are more likely to trigger semantic bugs. Tensorfuzz [23] use coverage-guided fuzzing methods for neural networks to find numerical errors in a trained neural network. Dowser [17] determines "interesting" array accesses that likely harbor buffer overflow, and triggers overflow by taint tracking and symbolic execution. TIFF [19] infers input types by dynamic taint analysis, and sets input bytes with defined interesting values based on its type to maximize the likelihood of triggering memory-corruption bugs. Compared with those fuzzers, which were built to detect those specific bugs, *Int*egrity reduces the problem of exploitation to the problem of exploration, and therefore can work with most fuzzers and can benefit from the advances of exploration technologies.

7   Conclusion

We designed and implemented *Int*egrity for triggering integer arithmetic errors using fuzzing. By finding and instrumenting integer arithmetic operations with potential errors, *Int*egrity passes critical information to the fuzzer to help it trigger potential bugs. *Int*egrity found all the integer errors in the Juliet test suite with no false positive. On 9 popular open source programs, *Int*egrity found a total of 174 true errors, including 8 crashes and 166 non-crashing errors. To make progress on the challenge of determining if a non-crashing error is harmful, we proposed two methods to find potentially harmful errors, based on the statistics of traces produced by the fuzzer and on comparing the output of independent implementations of the same algorithm on the same input. Our evaluation demonstrated that *Int*egrity is effective in finding integer errors.

Acknowledgment. This material is based upon work supported by the National Science Foundation under Grant No. 1801751 and 1956364.

References

1. American fuzzy lop. http://lcamtuf.coredump.cx/afl/
2. Batchoverflow exploit creates trillions of ethereum tokens, major exchanges halt erc20 deposits—cryptoslate. https://cryptoslate.com/batchoverflow-exploit-creates-trillions-of-ethereum-tokens/
3. Beautychain (bec) withdrawal and trading suspended. https://support.okex.com/hc/en-us/articles/360002944212-BeautyChain-BEC-Withdrawal-and-Trading-Suspended-Update-
4. Cwe - common weakness enumeration. https://cwe.mitre.org/
5. libfuzzer – a library for coverage-guided fuzz testing, https://llvm.org/docs/LibFuzzer.html
6. LLVM dataflowsanitizer https://clang.llvm.org/docs/DataFlowSanitizer.html
7. LLVM threadsanitizer. https://clang.llvm.org/docs/ThreadSanitizer.html
8. LLVM undefinedbehaviorsanitizer. https://clang.llvm.org/docs/UndefinedBehaviorSanitizer.html
9. Software assurance reference dataset. https://samate.nist.gov/SARD/testsuite.php
10. Aschermann, C., Schumilo, S., Blazytko, T., Gawlik, R., Holz, T.: Redqueen: fuzzing with input-to-state correspondence (2019)
11. Böhme, M., Pham, V.T., Nguyen, M.D., Roychoudhury, A.: Directed greybox fuzzing. In: Proceedings of the 2017 ACM SIGSAC Conference on Computer and Communications Security, pp. 2329–2344. ACM (2017)
12. Chen, H., et al.: Hawkeye: towards a desired directed grey-box fuzzer. In: Proceedings of the 2018 ACM SIGSAC Conference on Computer and Communications Security, pp. 2095–2108. ACM (2018)

13. Chen, P., Chen, H.: Angora: Efficient fuzzing by principled search. In: 2018 IEEE Symposium on Security and Privacy (SP), pp. 711–725. IEEE (2018)
14. Chen, P., Liu, J., Chen, H.: Matryoshka: fuzzing deeply nested branches. In: ACM Conference on Computer and Communications Security (CCS), London, UK
15. Dietz, W., Li, P., Regehr, J., Adve, V.: Understanding integer overflow in C/C++. In: 34th International Conference on Software Engineering, ICSE 2012 (2012)
16. Dietz, W., Li, P., Regehr, J., Adve, V.: Understanding integer overflow in C/C++. ACM Trans. Softw. Eng. Methodol. (TOSEM) **25**(1), 2 (2015)
17. Haller, I., Slowinska, A., Neugschwandtner, M., Bos, H.: Dowsing for overflows: a guided fuzzer to find buffer boundary violations. In: USENIX Security, pp. 49–64 (2013)
18. Han, W., Joe, B., Lee, B., Song, C., Shin, I.: Enhancing memory error detection for large-scale applications and fuzz testing. In: Symposium on Network and Distributed Systems Security (NDSS), p. 148 (2018)
19. Jain, V., Rawat, S., Giuffrida, C., Bos, H.: Tiff: Using input type inference to improve fuzzing. In: Proceedings of the 34th Annual Computer Security Applications Conference, pp. 505–517. ACM (2018)
20. Jeong, D.R., Kim, K., Shivakumar, B., Lee, B., Shin, I.: Razzer: finding kernel race bugs through fuzzing. In: Razzer: Finding Kernel Race Bugs through Fuzzing. IEEE (2018)
21. Martin, B., Brown, M., Paller, A., Kirby, D., Christey, S.: 2011 CWE/SANS top 25 most dangerous software errors. Common Weakness Enumer **7515** (2011)
22. Moy, Y., Bjørner, N., Sielaff, D.: Modular bug-finding for integer overflows in the large: Sound, efficient, bit-precise static analysis. Microsoft Res. **11**, 57 (2009)
23. Odena, A., Goodfellow, I.: Tensorfuzz: debugging neural networks with coverage-guided fuzzing. arXiv preprint arXiv:1807.10875 (2018)
24. Peng, H., Shoshitaishvili, Y., Payer, M.: T-fuzz: fuzzing by program transformation. In: 2018 IEEE Symposium on Security and Privacy (SP), pp. 697–710. IEEE (2018)
25. Petsios, T., Tang, A., Stolfo, S., Keromytis, A.D., Jana, S.: Nezha: efficient domain-independent differential testing. In: 2017 IEEE Symposium on Security and Privacy (SP), pp. 615–632. IEEE (2017)
26. Petsios, T., Zhao, J., Keromytis, A.D., Jana, S.: Slowfuzz: automated domain-independent detection of algorithmic complexity vulnerabilities. In: Proceedings of the 2017 ACM SIGSAC Conference on Computer and Communications Security, pp. 2155–2168. ACM (2017)
27. Pomonis, M., Petsios, T., Jee, K., Polychronakis, M., Keromytis, A.D.: Intflow: improving the accuracy of arithmetic error detection using information flow tracking. In: Proceedings of the 30th Annual Computer Security Applications Conference, pp. 416–425. ACM (2014)
28. Rawat, S., Jain, V., Kumar, A., Cojocar, L., Giuffrida, C., Bos, H.: VUzzer: application-aware evolutionary fuzzing. In: NDSS, February 2017
29. Serebryany, K., Bruening, D., Potapenko, A., Vyukov, D.: Addresssanitizer: a fast address sanity checker. In: USENIX ATC 2012 (2012)
30. She, D., Pei, K., Epstein, D., Yang, J., Ray, B., Jana, S.: Neuzz: efficient fuzzing with neural program learning (2019)
31. Song, D., et al.: SoK: sanitizing for security (2019)
32. Stepanov, E., Serebryany, K.: Memorysanitizer: fast detector of uninitialized memory use in C++. In: Proceedings of the 13th Annual IEEE/ACM International Symposium on Code Generation and Optimization, pp. 46–55. IEEE Computer Society (2015)

33. Stephens, N., et al.: Driller: augmenting fuzzing through selective symbolic execution. In: Proceedings of the Network and Distributed System Security Symposium (2016)
34. Sun, H., Zhang, X., Zheng, Y., Zeng, Q.: Inteq: recognizing benign integer overflows via equivalence checking across multiple precisions. In: Proceedings of the 38th International Conference on Software Engineering, pp. 1051–1062. ACM (2016)
35. Wang, T., Wei, T., Gu, G., Zou, W.: Taintscope: a checksum-aware directed fuzzing tool for automatic software vulnerability detection. In: 2010 IEEE symposium on Security and privacy (SP), pp. 497–512 (2010)
36. Wang, T., Wei, T., Lin, Z., Zou, W.: Intscope: automatically detecting integer overflow vulnerability in x86 binary using symbolic execution. In: NDSS. Citeseer (2009)
37. Yun, I., Lee, S., Xu, M., Jang, Y., Kim, T.: QSYM : a practical concolic execution engine tailored for hybrid fuzzing. In: 27th USENIX Security Symposium (USENIX Security 18), pp. 745–761. USENIX Association, Baltimore, MD (2018)

Improving Robustness of a Popular Probabilistic Clustering Algorithm Against Insider Attacks

Sayed M. Saghaian N. E.[1]([⊠]), Tom La Porta[1], Simone Silvestri[2], and Patrick McDaniel[1]

[1] School of EECS, Pennsylvania State University, State College, USA
{sms676,tlp,mcdaniel}@cse.psu.edu
[2] Computer Science Department, University of Kentucky, Lexington, USA
silvestri@cs.uky.edu

Abstract. Many clustering algorithms for mesh, ad hoc and Wireless Sensor Networks have been proposed. Probabilistic approaches are a popular class of such algorithms. However, it is essential to analyze their robustness against security compromise. We study the robustness of EEHCA, a popular energy efficient clustering algorithm as an example of probabilistic class in terms of security compromise. In this paper, we investigate attacks on EEHCA through analysis and experimental simulations. We analytically characterize two different attack models. In the first attack model, the attacker aims to gain control over the network by stealing network traffic, or by disrupting the data aggregation process (integrity attack). In the second attack model, the inducement of the attacker is to abridge the network lifetime (denial of service attack). We assume the clustering algorithm is running periodically and propose a detection solution by exploiting Bernoulli CUSUM charts.

Keywords: Probabilistic clustering algorithm · Anomaly detection · CUSUM test

1 Introduction

Clustering algorithms are widely used in wireless ad hoc and sensor networks to help improve efficacy of performing functions such as routing and data aggregation. Clustering provides scalability, efficient communication, and energy conservation, and prolongs the network lifetime [1,26].

A Wireless Sensor Network (WSN) typically consists of low cost sensor nodes which are not tamper resistant, and are typically left unattended. Consequently, they are susceptible to physical and cyber-attacks. In particular, they are vulnerable to *insider* attacks in which a compromised node retains its full credentials, and is able to operate in compliance with security rules within the network. Likewise, in many ad hoc and mesh network applications nodes are vulnerable to insider attacks. Attackers have different incentives including stealing traffic,

N. Park et al. (Eds.): SecureComm 2020, LNICST 335, pp. 381–401, 2020.
https://doi.org/10.1007/978-3-030-63086-7_21

agitating the data aggregation process, changing routing information, or diminishing the network lifetime. Specifically, the damage from an attack may be more extensive if the compromised node plays the clusterhead role. In this paper, we analyze the impact of node compromise on a probabilistic clusterhead election protocol and propose an algorithm to detect compromised nodes as soon as possible.

Each cluster has a leader called a clusterhead. As opposed to ordinary network nodes which are mainly responsible for sensing or generating data, clusterheads have more responsibilities. Ordinary members of a cluster send their gathered data to their clusterhead. A clusterhead may perform some initial processing on the gathered data, and then forward the data to the base station or possibly other clusterheads. Clusterheads are further responsible for organizing activities within the cluster, maintaining routing tables and paths to ordinary nodes as well as other clusterheads and the base station. Accordingly, the energy resources of a clusterhead are depleted more quickly than ordinary nodes.

In this paper we focus on the robustness of probabilistic clusterhead formation protocols which are very popular. We use EEHCA as an example. We consider two types of attacks. In the first attack, malicious nodes try to gain control over the network by stealing network traffic, or by disrupting the data aggregation process. This attack is known as an *integrity attack* where the attacker inserts itself into the data path and manipulates data. To illustrate the impact of this attack, we derive the percentages of legitimate ordinary nodes served by a malicious clusterhead as a function of the number of compromised nodes. We will observe that even if only a small fraction of nodes are compromised, a considerable number of legitimate ordinary nodes would follow an anomalous clusterhead.

The second attack we consider is called *battery drain attack* under which malicious nodes try to make the energy spent by legitimate ordinary nodes increase. They might further aim to increase the traffic going through legitimate clusterheads. For this attack, we compute the ratio of the expected number of nodes in each cluster under this attack model to the expected number of nodes in each cluster in an honest system. Moreover, since legitimate ordinary nodes in this attack scenario most likely have to join a cluster with a clusterhead positioned at a farther distance, we compute the ratio of the expected energy spent by legitimate ordinary nodes in a cluster under this attack over the expected energy spent by ordinary nodes in a cluster in an attack free environment.

We investigate the effectiveness of these attacks and propose a detection strategy against them which aims to detect malicious nodes as soon as possible. We exploit Bernoulli CUSUM charts to detect misbehaviors rapidly, and discuss how to design an anomaly detection algorithm with a zero false positive rate.

The main contributions of this paper are:

1. We analyze the robustness of EEHCA, a popular probabilistic energy efficient clustering algorithm for WSNs against security compromise.
2. We introduce two types of attack models and analytically characterize the impact of these attack models on the network as a function of the number

of compromised nodes; the scope of the first attack is to gain control over the network (integrity attack). For this attack, we derive the percentage of legitimate ordinary nodes served by a malicious clusterhead as a function of the number of compromised nodes. In the second attack model, the incentive is to abridge the network lifetime (denial of service attack). For this attack, we consider the ratio of the expected energy spent by legitimate ordinary nodes in a cluster under this attack model over the expected energy spent by ordinary nodes in a cluster in an attack free environment.
3. We propose a detection method by exploiting Bernoulli CUSUM charts that results in a rapid anomaly detection while preserving a zero false positive rate. In addition to CUSUM test, we also consider different statistical techniques to detect anomalous sensors including Score test and Likelihood-ratio test.

We begin in the following Section with a review of several key related work.

2   Related Work

Many algorithms for clustering in WSNs have been proposed [1,3,13,26]. One popular class of clustering algorithm takes a probabilistic approach in which nodes become clusterhead with some probability. This class of clustering enables a rapid cluster formation with a low overhead as nodes independently define their role. The objective in this class is to find the optimal probability which results in minimizing the energy spent in the network. This feature is particularly suitable for WSNs where energy conservation is vital to enhancing the network lifetime. LEACH [10], EEHCA [6], HEED [25], and the algorithm proposed by Choi and Lee [8] are examples of this class.

[24] surveyed anomaly detection in WSNs. Perrig et al. [15] proposed a prevention-based scheme which exploits cryptographic primitives such as secret key management, encryption, and authentication. [23] presented a relatively efficient access control method in a sensor network based on public-key and Elliptic Curve Cryptography. However, prevention-based approaches such as cryptographic primitives cannot address security threats due to *insider* attackers. [12] proposed an anomaly detection algorithm that captures insider attackers with a high detection rate and a low false positive rate only when as many as 25% of sensor nodes are compromised and misbehaving. However, we will show that even if only 10% of sensors are compromised, a considerable percentage of legitimate ordinary nodes will follow an anomalous clusterhead.

Our problem of detecting anomalous sensor nodes in the EEHCA clustering algorithm is an instance of a change detection problem. The change detection problem has found many applications from quality control and economics [4] to network security [22] and fraud detection [21]. CUSUM (CUmulative SUM) chart [9,14], sometimes called CUSUM test, is a quickest detection [16] algorithm. CUSUM test is more effective and more popular than other algorithms such as Shewhart control chart [11], Sets method, CUSCORE method and SHDA method [20]. In this paper, in addition to CUSUM test, we also consider different parametric statistical tests to detect anomalous nodes in EEHCA including Score test and Likelihood-ratio test [2], and compare their performance in terms of detection rate and percentages of falsely removed legitimate nodes.

3   Background Material

In this Section, we review EEHCA, a popular probabilistic energy efficient clustering algorithm, two common operations on point processes that we will exploit in our attack model scenarios, namely *thinning* and *superposition*. We further review two parametric statistical tests and Bernoulli CUSUM test as tools and techniques to detect anomalous behavior in the clusterhead formulation process.

3.1   EEHCA

Authors in [6] proposed a distributed energy efficient clustering mechanism named EEHCA in which they assume sensor nodes are distributed as a homogeneous spatial Poisson process in a 2-D square plane. In their scheme, sensor nodes become a clusterhead voluntarily with a same fixed probability, p, independent of their location and each other. These nodes are called *volunteer clusterheads*. Volunteer clusterheads then advertise themselves to nodes within at most k hops.

Nodes that are not volunteer clusterheads themselves join the cluster with the closest volunteer clusterhead within k hops. These nodes are called *ordinary* nodes. As a result, a Voronoi tessellation is formed. A Voronoi tessellation is a partition of a plane into cells (clusters) such that each cell contains only one generating point (volunteer clusterhead) and the distance of other points (ordinary nodes) in a given cell to the corresponding generating point is smallest among the distances to other generating points.

Any other nodes that are neither volunteer clusterheads nor ordinary nodes become *forced clusterheads*. These nodes only serve themselves.

A routing infrastructure is assumed already to exist so that to send data from one node to another node, only the nodes on the routing path forward the data. Moreover, the communication environment is error-free and the nodes do not deal with retransmitting data. In their energy model the energy spent is proportional to the distance and radio range (r) directly and inversely, respectively.

The authors exploit results from independent homogeneous spatial Poisson processes [5] and derive the optimal probability of becoming clusterhead (p_{opt}) and the optimal k that lead to the minimum energy spent in the network.

Below, we review techniques related to point processes as we use them in our performance evaluation of the clustering algorithm against security compromise.

3.2   Two Common Operations on Point Processes

A Point Process [7] is a collection of points randomly scattered in some compact set W. It can be viewed either as a random set or as a random counting measure. A point process is called spatial point process when $W \subset \mathbb{R}^d$ for $d = 2$ or 3. In our setting, each point represents the location of a sensor node.

Poisson point process is the most basic and important point process. A stationary Poisson point process has two properties: The number of points of the process which fall into a bounded Borel set B has a Poisson distribution with mean of $\lambda\|B\|$ for some constant λ, where $\|B\|$ denotes Lebesgue measure of B. Furthermore, the number of points of the process in B_1 is independent from the number points of the process in B_2 for disjoint Borel sets B_1 and B_2.

In the following, we review two main operations on point processes: thinning and superposition. We exploit these operations to characterize our attack models.

3.2.1 Thinning

Thinning is an operation of removing points from a basic point process Φ_b which has intensity of λ_b by some definite rule. *p-thinning* is the simplest thinning operation in which points are removed from Φ_b with probability $(1-p_r)$ independent of location and possible removal of other points in Φ_b. The points remaining after the p-thinning operation are also a point process (*p-thinned* process) that is stationary if the basic point process is stationary. p-thinned process intensity (λ) is related to the intensity of the basic point process (λ_b) by:

$$\lambda = p_r \lambda_b \tag{1}$$

3.2.2 Superposition

Given two stationary non-overlapping point processes Φ_1 and Φ_2 with intensities of λ_1 and λ_2 respectively, define:

$$\Phi = \Phi_1 \cup \Phi_2$$

Then clearly, Φ is point process with intensity of:

$$\lambda = \lambda_1 + \lambda_2 \tag{2}$$

Next, we review some statistical techniques that can be adapted to detect possible anomalous behaviour of the compromised nodes.

3.3   Parametric Statistical Tests

We now provide some background on two main parametric statistical tests: Score and Likelihood-ratio tests. These tests require a fixed number of samples. The larger the sample size, the more accurate results are achieved. When the sample size is large enough, their statistic follow a chi-square distribution, and if the samples are derived from binomial distribution, the degree of freedom is one.

– Score Test: The score statistic for binomial proportion is:

$$S^2 = \left[\frac{\hat{p} - p_{opt}}{\sqrt{\frac{p_{opt}(1-p_{opt})}{n}}} \right]^2$$

where n is the total the number of samples.

– Likelihood-ratio Test: The Likelihood-ratio statistic for binomial proportion is:

$$LR = 2\left[y\log\left(\frac{\hat{p}}{p_{opt}}\right) + (n-y)\log\left(\frac{1-\hat{p}}{1-p_{opt}}\right)\right]$$

where $\hat{p}$ is the estimated probability of success from the observed sample, and y is the number of successes (number of times a node under test volunteered to be clusterhead) out of n trials (election rounds).

3.4 Bernoulli CUSUM Test

When the observations follow a Bernoulli distribution, the Bernoulli CUSUM test [17–19] can be exploited. Define p_0 as the in-control probability (p_{opt}) and p_1 as the out-of-control probability ($p_m = \gamma p_{opt}$). Given a sequence of independent Bernoulli observations $X_1, ..., X_n$, where $X_i = 1$ if the node under test volunteered to be clusterhead in the ith round of clusterhead formation and 0 otherwise, Bernoulli CUSUM aims to detect a shift from p_0 to p_1 as soon as possible.

One advantage of CUSUM test is that it does not need to wait for a fixed number of samples (here, the status of neighbor nodes after each clusterhead formation) to perform the detection process. In contrast, as soon as a sample is available, CUSUM can check whether any changes have been occurred.

To detect an increase ($\gamma > 1$) in the Bernoulli parameter, a sensor node computes the *Increase* CUSUM statistic corresponding to each of its neighbor nodes in each round of clusterhead election:

$$C_i^+ = \max(0, C_{i-1}^+) + (X_i - k) \tag{3}$$

where k is the reference value and is defined by $k = \frac{r_1}{r_2}$ where

$$r_1 = -\log\frac{1-p_1}{1-p_0} \quad and \quad r_2 = \log\frac{p_1(1-p_0)}{p_0(1-p_1)}. \tag{4}$$

Then, it compares the computed result with a control limit (h_h). If $C_i^+ > h_h$, it signals the corresponding neighbor node is declaring to be clusterhead with some probability greater than p_{opt}.

Similarly, to detect a decrease ($\gamma < 1$) in the Bernoulli parameter, a sensor node computes the *Decrease* CUSUM statistic corresponding to each of its neighbor nodes in each round of clusterhead election:

$$C_i^- = \min(0, C_{i-1}^-) + (X_i - k) \tag{5}$$

Then, it compares the computed result with a control limit (h_l). If $C_i^- < h_l$, it signals the corresponding neighbor node is volunteering to be clusterhead with some probability smaller than p_{opt}.

To exploit Markov chains in the performance analyses of CUSUM, it is required to select k such that $k = \frac{1}{m}$, where m is an integer. In practice, one can tolerate a small change from p_1 to $p_{1,a}$ so that m is an integer ($m = \text{round}(\frac{1}{k})$).[1]

The CUSUM statistic (C_i) can be initialized in three different ways. In a *zero-start*, the CUSUM statistic initially starts from 0 ($C_0 = 0$). In the *Fast Initial Response* (FIR), a faster anomaly detection can be achieved by giving the CUSUM statistic a head-start with the cost of a small increase in the false alarm rate. $h/4$ or $h/2$ (fractions of the control limit) are usually used for initial value of the CUSUM statistic. Finally, one can assume that the CUSUM statistic has reached a steady-state or stationary distribution by the time a shift occurs. Before reaching the steady-state, if the CUSUM statistic exceeds the control limit, the generated signal is ignored and the statistic is restarted from 0.

Typically, the Average Number of Observations before Signal (ANOS) is used as a performance metric for CUSUM. $ANOS(p)$ is the expected number of observations needed to signal when the node under test volunteers to be clusterhead with probability of p. The in-control ANOS ($ANOS(p_0)$) measures the average number of observations between two successive false positives. The out-of-control ANOS ($ANOS\ (p \neq p_0)$) indicates the speed of change detection and is defined as the average number of clusterhead election rounds until an alarm is given, indicating a neighbor node is becoming clusterhead with some probability other than the optimal probability. It is desired to have a sufficiently large in-control ANOS and as small as possible out-of-control ANOS. In the case of the steady-state, ANOS is called the Steady State ANOS, $SSANOS$. Simulation results show that convergence to the steady-state distribution occurs long before $1.5ANOS(p_0)$ [20].

A general approach in designing CUSUM is to first select a desired $ANOS(p_0)$ (average number of observations between two successive false positives) and then, find the control limit h that approximately achieves the desire $ANOS(p_0)$. There are two approaches in approximating $ANOS(p_0)$; one method is Corrected Diffusion (CD) approximation and the other approach is by using Markov chain formulation. In the CD approximation, first h^* is computed from[2]:

$$ANOS(p_0) = \frac{\exp(h^*r_2) - h^*r_2 - 1}{|r_2p_0 - r_1|} \tag{6}$$

Once h^* is obtained, h_h for Increase CUSUM and h_l for Decrease CUSUM can be computed from:

$$h_h = \frac{\text{floor}\left[m\left(h^* - \epsilon_{p_0}\sqrt{p_0(1-p_0)}\right)\right]}{m} \tag{7}$$

---

[1] To find such a $p_{1,a}$, Newton-Raphson method with starting point of p_1 for solving the nonlinear equation quickly converges to a solution.

[2] Newton-Raphson method with starting point h_0^* in the range $4 \leq h_0^* \leq 8$ for increase detection scenario or starting point h_0^* in $-4 \leq h_0^* \leq -8$ for decrease detection case can be adopted to solve the nonlinear equation.

$$h_l = \frac{\text{floor}\left[m\left(h^* + \epsilon_{p_0}\sqrt{p_0(1-p_0)}\right)\right]}{m} \qquad (8)$$

where ϵ_p is approximated from:

$$\epsilon_p = \begin{cases} \begin{aligned} &0.410 - 0.0842(\ln(p)) - 0.0391(\ln(p))^3 - \\ &0.00376(\ln(p))^4 - 0.000008(\ln(p))^7 \end{aligned} & \text{if } 0.01 \le p \le 0.5 \\[2ex] \frac{1}{3}\left(\sqrt{\frac{1-p}{p}} - \sqrt{\frac{p}{1-p}}\right) & \text{if } 0 < p < 0.01 \end{cases} \qquad (9)$$

4   Attack Models

We analyze the performance of EEHCA against two attack models by exploiting Thinning and Superposition operations. In the first, the attackers aim to gain control over the network by setting their probability to become volunteer clusterheads to a value greater than p_{opt}. Consequently, they become volunteer clusterheads more often and can gain control over the network by stealing the traffic or by deleting the data sent by ordinary nodes depending on their incentives.

In the second attack model, attackers try to avoid being volunteer clusterheads. In this attack model, the malicious node sets its probability to become volunteer clusterhead to a value less than p_{opt} for the sake of increasing the energy spent by legitimate ordinary nodes as well as overwhelming legitimate clusterheads by increasing the amount of traffic passing through them.

4.1   Attack Model 1

In this subsection, we analyze an attack model where the attacker volunteers to be a clusterhead with a fixed probability (p_m) greater than p_{opt}. This attack is known as *integrity attack*. Clearly, the higher the p_m it chooses, the higher the control it may gain over the network. However, if the attacker becomes a clusterhead too frequently, it may exhaust its own battery lifetime more rapidly. Furthermore, detection of such an extreme attack is easier for the legitimate nodes. Therefore, if the incentive of the attacker is to gain the maximum control over the network during its lifetime (assuming no anomaly detection exits), it would select a p_m equal to 1. However, if the attacker wishes to gain control over the network while conserving its energy for a longer period of time, it will become a volunteer clusterhead with some probability not significantly greater than the optimal. We consider the attacker to have an arbitrary fixed p_m for this attack model in our analyses.

Assume the number of sensor nodes (N) is known and nodes are distributed according to a homogeneous spatial Poisson point process Φ_b with intensity of λ_b. In the following we analyze the percentage of legitimate ordinary nodes that belong to clusters with malicious clusterheads under attack model 1.

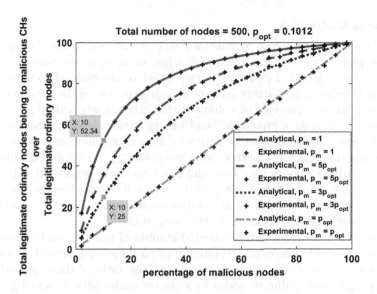

Fig. 1. Percentage of legitimate nodes served by malicious clusterheads for different values of p_m under attack model 1 for a network with 500 sensor nodes (intensity of 5) and $p_{opt} = 0.1012$.

Theorem 1. *In a sensor network with* n *nodes where nodes are distributed as a homogeneous spatial Poisson point process, in order to cause more than 50% of legitimate ordinary nodes to belong to clusters with malicious clusterheads, an attacker needs to be become volunteer clusterhead with probability of* p_m *satisfying:* $p_m \geq (\frac{n}{m} - 1)p_{opt}$ *where* m *is the number of compromised nodes.*

Proof. For proof, see Appendix A.

Figure 1 illustrates the effectiveness of launching an attack under attack model 1 for the sake of gaining control over the network for a network with 500 sensor nodes ($\lambda_b = 5$) where according to [6], $p_{opt} = 0.1012$. In this figure, we show the percentages for 5 different values of p_m selected by malicious nodes. For example, if only 10% of nodes are compromised, 25% of legitimate ordinary nodes will follow a malicious clusterhead if $p_m = 3p_{opt}$. Whereas if the attacker selects $p_m = 1$, the percentage of legitimate ordinary nodes served by a malicious clusterhead would be more than 50%. By setting $p_m = 1$, the attacker can gain the most control over the network with the cost of running out of power rapidly and increasing the chance of being detected by legitimate nodes. Note that the curve is linear for the case where $p_m = p_{opt}$.

We further simulate a network with 500 nodes placed in a square plane with an area of 100 (unit square) and compare the analytical versus experimental percentage of nodes served by malicious clusterheads for different values of p_m selected by the attacker for 100 trials. Our simulation results demonstrate agreement between experimental results and analytical results.

4.2   Attack Model 2

Clusterheads have more responsibilities than ordinary nodes. Consequently, their energy depletes more rapidly. In the following, we analyze the case in which the attackers aim to launch a denial of service attack or alternatively a battery drain attack by abridging the battery-lifetime of legitimate nodes. To achieve this goal, they refuse to play the role of volunteer clusterheads when they are supposed to volunteer. Gaining a "free-ride" and taking advantage of clustering without paying its cost may be another incentive for attackers. They set their probability of becoming clusterhead (p_m) to a value less than p_{opt}. As a result of this attack, legitimate ordinary nodes have to spend more energy to send their data to their clusterhead since they have to join a cluster where its clusterhead is positioned at a farther distance relative to an attack-free environment. Moreover, more traffic is sent to legitimate clusterheads in this scenario.

We compute the ratio of the expected number of nodes in each cluster under this attack model to the expected number of nodes in each cluster in an honest attack free system. Furthermore, we compute the ratio of the expected energy spent by legitimate ordinary nodes in a cluster under attack model 2 over the expected energy spent by ordinary nodes in a cluster in an attack free system.

Theorem 2, characterizes the increase in the number of nodes served by legitimate clusterheads under attack model 2:

Theorem 2. *In a sensor network with* n *nodes where nodes are distributed as a homogeneous spatial Poisson point process, if an attacker who has compromised* m *nodes* $(m \neq n)$ *never becomes a volunteer clusterhead, then:*

$$\mathbb{E}[N_{Ord,Amodel2}|N=n] \approx \frac{1}{(1-\frac{m}{n})}\mathbb{E}[N_{Ord,Afree}|N=n] \qquad (10)$$

where the random variable $N_{Ord,Afree}$ *is the number of ordinary nodes in each cluster in an attack-free system and* $N_{Ord,Amodel2}$ *denotes the number of ordinary nodes in each cluster under attack model 2.*

Proof. For proof, see Appendix B.

Theorem 3, characterizes the increase in the expected energy spent by legitimate ordinary nodes under attack model 2:

Definition 1. *Let* C_1^{Afree} *be the total energy to send 1 unit of data to the clusterhead by ordinary nodes of a cluster in an attack-free system. Similarly, let* $C_1^{Amodel2}$ *be the total energy spent by legitimate ordinary nodes to send a unit of data to the clusterhead when nodes are compromised according to attack model 2.*

Theorem 3. *In a sensor network with* n *nodes where nodes are distributed as a homogeneous spatial Poisson point process, if an attacker who has compromised* m *nodes* $(m \neq n)$ *never becomes a volunteer clusterhead, then:*

$$\frac{\mathbb{E}[C_1^{Amodel2}|N=n]}{\mathbb{E}[C_1^{Afree}|N=n]} \approx \frac{1}{(1-\frac{m}{n})^{1/2}} \qquad (11)$$

Proof. For proof, see Appendix C.

5 Anomaly Detection

In Sect. 4, we observed that a considerable percentage of legitimate nodes may be affected even if only a small fraction of nodes are compromised. Hence, we would like to detect any anomalous behavior in the sense that a node volunteers with some probability other than p_{opt}. On one hand, we want a high detection rate. On the other hand, we desire no false positives. Furthermore, the detection should be done *as soon as possible*.

This problem can be formulated as an anomaly detection problem. *Normal*, in our problem, means nodes volunteer with probability of p_{opt}. Deviation from normal means change in the probability of becoming volunteer clusterhead. Therefore, our problem reduces to detecting changes in the probability distribution. Hence, any detection mechanism for this problem should detect changes in the probability of success p_{opt} of a Bernoulli random variable.

In this Section, we present our strategy to detect malicious nodes that volunteer to be clusterheads with some probability other than p_{opt} as soon as possible. Considering that the clustering algorithm is run periodically, with the existence of even a small false positive rate, falsely removed legitimate nodes accumulate and at some point a significant number of legitimate nodes will be eliminated from the network. Removing legitimate nodes falsely results in degradation in the performance and in the optimality of the clustering algorithm.

At a high level, our detection strategy works as follows: Given in EEHCA, each node becomes a clusterhead voluntarily independent of the other nodes, each legitimate node monitors all of its neighbor nodes by recording their status (clusterhead or ordinary node) for each round of election. Using the observation sequence corresponding to the status of each neighbor node and applying some *quickest detection* algorithm, a node can detect malicious nodes in its neighborhood rapidly. By comparing different statistical tests performance for detecting anomalies, we choose CUSUM chart as our quickest detection method. Legitimate nodes will stop sending traffic or providing services to the detected nodes.

In the following, we provide the design details of CUSUM test, Score test and Likelihood-ratio test. We then compare their performances in terms of detection rate and percentages of legitimate nodes removed incorrectly.

5.1 Design Details and Simulation Results

5.1.1 Parametric Statistical Test

Since the underlying distribution is known here, and samples are expected to come from a Bernoulli distribution with probability of success of p_{opt}, we consider *parametric* statistical tests. Our *null hypothesis* (H_0) and *alternate hypothesis* (H_a) are:

$$H_0 : \text{nodes volunteer with probability of } p_{opt}$$
$$H_a : \text{nodes volunteer with some probability other than } p_{opt}$$

Based on the observed data for each neighbor node (the status of neighbor nodes after each clusterhead formation), we find the P-value. We reject the null hypothesis if P-Value is less than significance level of 5%.

We have two goals; first, a rapid anomaly detection is needed. Second, no legitimate node should be removed incorrectly. In the ideal situation where we have a large number of samples available (e.g. over 100 samples), the parametric statistical tests would have a false positive rate of 5%. However, since we cannot wait until 100 rounds of election to act on detecting malicious nodes, for the parametric statistical tests, we progressively add samples to the tests. Initially, we gather 9 samples before running the tests. From the 10th round on, we perform the tests on all the available data up to that point. Lack of enough sample size would result in a higher false positive rate than the nominal 5%.

5.1.2   CUSUM Test

Setting ANOS to a higher value, results in a higher control limit h_h for Increase CUSUM (or, a lower control limit h_l for Decrease CUSUM) and hence, achieves a lower false positive rate. However, a higher ANOS results in a slower detection rate. We further observed that the zero-start CUSUM has the lowest detection rate as well as the smallest possible false alarm rate relative to the head-start approaches. Moreover, even if a node acts normal and becomes a volunteer clusterhead with probability of p_{opt}, after, on average, $ANOS(p_0)$ clusterhead formation rounds, it will be detected and marked as a malicious node assuming zero-start is used. Removing legitimate nodes falsely results in degradation in the performance and in the optimality of the clustering algorithm. Hence, it is essential to deal with the generated false alarms.

Resetting the CUSUM statistic to zero after every few rounds of cluster formation is one approach to reduce false positives. We call this approach the *resetting method*. A candidate value for the number of rounds before restarting the CUSUM statistic is determine as follows: Suppose we may tolerate up to $x\%$ of traffic to be controlled by an adversary. Considering $\frac{m}{n}\%$ of the sensor nodes are compromised, we find the p_m that results in $x\%$ of legitimate ordinary nodes belonging to a cluster with a malicious clusterhead by using Eq. (22). We set the restarting value to $ANOS(p_m) + 1$.

An obvious drawback of this approach is that it results in a slower anomaly detection. Moreover, our simulation results show that the above approach is not very effective in preventing high false alarm rates even if we increase the tolerance up to 25% which requires $p_m = 3p_0$.

A second approach to reduce the false positives, which we call it the *self-monitoring method*, is to have each legitimate node not only monitor its neighbors by recording their status (clusterhead or ordinary node) and applying the CUSUM method (Increase and Decrease), but also to have it monitor its own status. The intuition behind this method is to prevent legitimate nodes from getting marked as malicious nodes because of crossing the control limits in the CUSUM tests performed by the other nodes.

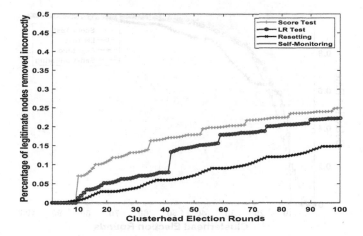

Fig. 2. Percentage of legitimate nodes removed incorrectly under resetting method assuming tolerance of up to 25% ($p_m = 3p_0$) for 100 rounds of elections.

The self-monitoring method works as follows: In each election round, a legitimate node tentatively decides to become a volunteer clusterhead with probability of p_{opt}. If the tentative result is to not become clusterhead, the node computes its own Decrease CUSUM statistic. If its Decrease CUSUM statistic is less than the Decrease CUSUM control limit (h_l), it tentatively becomes a clusterhead. If a legitimate node is tentatively a clusterhead (either as a result of the original decision or as a result of Decrease CUSUM), it computes its Increase CUSUM statistic. Finally, if the Increase CUSUM statistic is less than Increase CUSUM control limit (h_h), then it definitively becomes a volunteer clusterhead for that round of clusterhead formation.

One concern with the self-monitoring method is that a legitimate node might now become a volunteer clusterhead with some probability considerably lower than the optimal probability. However, we find this is not the case. Our simulation results show that as the number of clusterhead election rounds increase, legitimate nodes become clusterhead with some probability very close to the optimal probability. We recorded the status of legitimate nodes in the system for 500 election rounds. On average, a legitimate node volunteered to be a clusterhead with probability of $\overline{p_{leg}} = 0.0994$ (as opposed to $p_{opt} - 0.1012$) where the standard deviation is 0.0072. Hence, the normalized error of the probability of becoming a volunteer clusterhead for a legitimate node is $\frac{(p_{opt} - \overline{p_{leg}})}{p_{opt}} = 0.0783$.

Figure 2 illustrates the percentage of legitimate nodes removed incorrectly for a network with $p_0 = 0.1012$ when 10% nodes are compromised for 100 clusterhead election rounds. For Bernoulli CUSUM we set $ANOS(p_0) = 208$. Assuming tolerance of 25% ($p_m = 3p_0$), the CUSUM statistic is reset to 0 after 19 clusterhead formations. From Fig. 2, we observe that the self-monitoring method eliminates the false alarms. For the other methods, the number of nodes

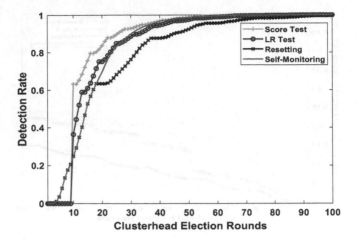

Fig. 3. Comparing detection rates. The network has 500 nodes in which 10% of them are compromised.

incorrectly characterized as compromised nodes accumulates over the rounds of clusterhead formations. Moreover, the parametric statistical tests have a higher percentage of incorrectly removed nodes than the CUSUM test. Although resetting the CUSUM statistic slows the false positive rate, false alarms still result in incorrectly removing a substantial fraction of legitimate nodes.

In Fig. 3, we compare the detection rate of the discussed anomaly detection methods. As expected, the CUSUM self-monitoring approach detects malicious nodes with a higher than the resetting approach. Recall, the CUSUM resetting approach, and the parametric tests result in false positives as shown in Fig. 2 while the CUSUM self-monitoring approach eliminates false positives. Although Score and LR tests have slightly higher detection rates from the round 10 to 40, their high false positive rates offset this advantage as discussed above.

Because of the high detection rate and zero false positive rate, we select the CUSUM self-monitoring approach as our anomaly detection method. To illustrate the performance of our detection method, we run an experiment for 100 trials on a network with $p_{opt} = 0.1012$ in which 10% of nodes are randomly compromised. We set the out-of-control probability $p_{1,a} = 0.1517$ for Increase CUSUM and 0.0478 for Decrease CUSUM. For Increase CUSUM, we set $ANOS_h = 208$ resulting in a control limit of $h_h = 3.1250$. For the Decrease CUSUM, we set $ANOS_l = 195$, which results in a control limit of $h_l = -2.2143$. We evaluate the performance of the proposed anomaly detection method under two different probabilities selected by an attacker, $p_m = 0.9512$ and $p_m = 3p_{opt}$. We depict the percentage of the detected malicious nodes versus the number of the clusterhead election rounds when exploiting zero-start and h/4 head-start CUSUM tests.

Figure 4 exhibits the performance of the self-monitoring approach considering two different probabilities, namely $p_m = 0.9512$ and $p_m = 3p_{opt}$, for an

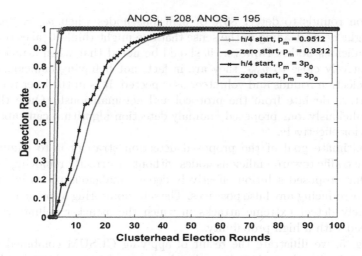

Fig. 4. Detection rate of the Self-Monitoring approach considering two different p_m's for an attacker when CUSUM charts with two different head-starts are exploited. The network has 500 nodes in which 10% of them are compromised.

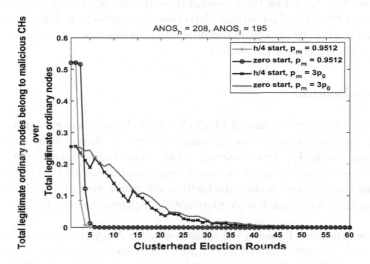

Fig. 5. Percentage of legitimate nodes served by a malicious clusterhead for different values of p_m after integrating CUSUM test into the clustering algorithm.

attacker to become a volunteer clusterhead. As Fig. 4 shows, the more vigorous the attacker, the higher the detection rate. We further compare the performance of CUSUM with different head-starts. CUSUM with a head-start of $h/4$ has a higher detection rate than CUSUM with zero-start because of the provided head-start. Using CUSUM with a head-start of $h/4$, 87% of malicious node were detected in only three rounds of clusterhead formation when the attacker becomes a volunteer clusterhead with $p_m = 0.9512$. On the other hand, it takes

21 election rounds to detect 83% of malicious nodes when $p_m = 3p_{opt}$. This result might be misleading in the sense that one might think it takes too long to detect malicious nodes. However, it should be noted that when attackers chose a p_m relatively close to p_{opt}, they are in fact, not behaving maliciously in the first few election rounds and volunteer as expected. It is in the later rounds that they start to deviate from the protocol and act maliciously. Once they start to act maliciously, our proposed anomaly detection algorithm can capture they misbehavior effectively.

The ultimate goal of the proposed detection strategy is to eliminate any legitimate traffic toward malicious nodes without incorrectly removing legitimate nodes. Our proposed solution effectively detects malicious nodes misbehaviors without introducing any false positives. The self-monitoring approach can almost immediately detect extreme attacks in which the attacker volunteers to be a clusterhead with a high probability.

In Fig. 5, we illustrate the result of applying CUSUM combined with the self-monitoring method. Attackers that become volunteer clusterheads with a probability significantly greater than the optimal probability are almost immediately detected. These attackers gain a higher percentage of traffic control initially. However, they lose their control dramatically after only a few rounds of cluster formation. On the contrary, detection of the attackers that volunteer with a probability close to the optimal probability requires more time, however, these types of attacker have a low impact.

6   Conclusions

We analyzed the performance of EEHCA, a probabilistic energy based clustering algorithm against security compromise. Our results demonstrate a significant vulnerability in EEHCA performance when compromised nodes exist. We then presented a detection strategy to detect anomalous nodes effectively. We showed that when CUSUM test is combined with a self-monitoring approach, anomalous nodes are detected quickly without removing legitimate nodes falsely.

Acknowledgments. Research was sponsored by the Army Research Laboratory and was accomplished under Cooperative Agreement Number W911NF-13-2-0045 (ARL Cyber Security CRA). The views and conclusions contained in this document are those of the authors and should not be interpreted as representing the official policies, either expressed or implied, of the Army Research Laboratory or the U.S. Government. The U.S. Government is authorized to reproduce and distribute reprints for Government purposes notwithstanding any copyright notation herein.

A   Proof of Theorem 1

Proof. Suppose a realization of the random point process Φ_b with number of nodes equal to $N = n$ is given. Arbitrarily compromise m nodes independent of location and each other under attack model 1. One can consider compromising nodes as a p-thinning operation with $p_r = 1 - \frac{m}{n}$. As a result, legitimate nodes and malicious nodes are distributed independently according to a homogeneous spatial Poisson point processes (PPP):

$$PPP_{leg} : \lambda_{leg} = p_r \lambda_b \tag{12}$$

$$PPP_{mal} : \lambda_{mal} = (1 - p_r)\lambda_b \tag{13}$$

Legitimate nodes become volunteer clusterheads with probability of p_{opt}. Hence, legitimate clusterheads and legitimate ordinary nodes are distributed as independent homogeneous spatial Poisson point processes:

$$PPP_{CH,leg} : \lambda_{CH,leg} = p_{opt}\lambda_{leg} \tag{14}$$

$$PPP_{Ord,leg} : \lambda_{Ord,leg} = (1 - p_{opt})\lambda_{leg} \tag{15}$$

Malicious nodes become volunteer clusterheads with probability of p_m and therefore, malicious clusterheads are distributed as a homogeneous spatial Poisson point process:

$$PPP_{CH,mal} : \lambda_{CH,mal} = p_m\lambda_{mal} \tag{16}$$

It should be noted that PPP_{mal} and PPP_{leg} are non-overlapping and independent and hence, $PPP_{CH,mal}$ and $PPP_{CH,leg}$ are independent non-overlapping point processes. Consequently, one can apply the Superposition operation and define:

$$PPP_{CH} = PPP_{CH,leg} \cup PPP_{CH,mal} \tag{17}$$

which is a spatial Poisson point process with intensity of:

$$\lambda_{CH} = \lambda_{CH,leg} + \lambda_{CH,mal} = p_{opt}(1 - \frac{m}{n})\lambda_b + p_m\frac{m}{n}\lambda_b \tag{18}$$

Similarly, one can derive the intensity of $PPP_{Ord,leg}$ as

$$\lambda_{Ord,leg} = (1 - p_{opt})(1 - \frac{m}{n})\lambda_b \tag{19}$$

Denoting the number of $PPP_{Ord,leg}$ process points in each Voronoi cell by the random variable $N_{Ord,leg}$ and applying the results of [5], we get:

$$\mathbb{E}[N_{Ord,leg}|N = n] \approx \mathbb{E}[N_{Ord,leg}] = \frac{\lambda_{Ord,leg}}{\lambda_{CH}} = \frac{(1 - p_{opt})(n - m)}{p_{opt}(n - m) + mp_m} \tag{20}$$

where $\mathbb{E}$ denotes expected value operation.

Since there are m malicious nodes and each of them becomes a clusterhead with probability p_m, there are on expectation mp_m cells having a malicious clusterhead. As a result, the expected number of legitimate ordinary nodes belonging to clusters with a malicious clusterhead is:

$$L_m = mp_m\mathbb{E}[N_{Ord,leg}|N = n] \tag{21}$$

On the other hand, there are a total of $L_{leg} = (n - m)(1 - p_{opt})$ legitimate ordinary nodes on expectation. Hence, one can compute the percentage of legitimate ordinary nodes served by a malicious clusterhead under attack model 1 from:

$$q_{affected} = \frac{L_m}{L_{leg}} = \frac{mp_m}{p_{opt}(n - m) + mp_m} \tag{22}$$

From (22), more than 50% of legitimate ordinary nodes would belong to clusters with malicious clusterheads if the fraction of the compromised nodes satisfies:

$$\frac{m}{n} \geq \frac{p_{opt}}{p_m + p_{opt}} \tag{23}$$

Alternatively, for a given n and m, an adversary causes more than 50% of legitimate ordinary nodes to belong to clusters with malicious clusterheads if it sets its probability of becoming volunteer clusterhead to:

$$p_m \geq (\frac{n}{m} - 1)p_{opt} \tag{24}$$

B   Proof of Theorem 2

Proof. Before any attack has been launched (i.e. nodes become clusterhead with probability of p_{opt}), clusterheads and ordinary nodes form two homogeneous, independent, non-overlapping spatial Poisson point processes with intensities of $p_{opt}\lambda_b$ and $(1 - p_{opt})\lambda_b$, respectively. Consequently, one can derive the expected number of ordinary nodes in each cluster in an attack-free system from [5]:

$$\mathbb{E}[N_{Ord,Afree}|N = n] \approx \frac{\lambda_{Ord,Afree}}{\lambda_{CH,Afree}} = \frac{(1 - p_{opt})}{p_{opt}} \tag{25}$$

Now consider a system under attack model 2. Similar to the analysis presented in Appendix A, legitimate clusterheads form a spatial Poisson process:

$$PPP_{CH,leg} : \lambda_{CH,leg} = p_{opt}(1 - \frac{m}{n})\lambda_b \tag{26}$$

Legitimate ordinary nodes and malicious ordinary nodes are two independent non-overlapping point processes, and hence, their union is also a spatial Poisson point process, PPP_{ord}:

$$PPP_{ord} = PPP_{ord,leg} \cup PPP_{ord,mal} \tag{27}$$

And hence:

$$\lambda_{Ord} = \lambda_{ord,leg} + \lambda_{ord,mal} = (1 - p_{opt})(1 - \frac{m}{n})\lambda_b + (1 - p_m)\frac{m}{n}\lambda_b \tag{28}$$

Denote the number of ordinary nodes in each cluster under attack model 2 by the random variable $N_{Ord,Amodel2}$. Then:

$$\mathbb{E}[N_{Ord,Amodel2}|N = n] \approx \frac{\lambda_{Ord}}{\lambda_{CH,leg}} = \frac{(1 - p_{opt})(n - m) + (1 - p_m)m}{p_{opt}(n - m)} \tag{29}$$

Therefore, the ratio is computed from:

$$\frac{\mathbb{E}[N_{Ord,Amodel2}|N=n]}{\mathbb{E}[N_{Ord,Afree}|N=n]} = \frac{(n-m)+(1-p_m)m}{(n-m)} \tag{30}$$

According to [6], p_{opt} is very small for networks with density higher than 10. Since the attacker selects a p_m even smaller than p_{opt} under attack model 2, one can approximate this ratio by:

$$\frac{\mathbb{E}[N_{Ord,Amodel2}|N=n]}{\mathbb{E}[N_{Ord,Afree}|N=n]} \approx \frac{1}{(1-\frac{m}{n})}, \quad m \neq n \tag{31}$$

C   Proof of Theorem 3

Proof. By applying the results of [6], the total energy to send 1 unit of data to the clusterhead by ordinary nodes of a Voronoi cell in an attack-free system (C_1^{Afree}) is computed from:

$$\mathbb{E}[C_1^{Afree}|N=n] \approx \frac{\lambda_{Ord,Afree}}{2r\lambda_{CH,Afree}^{3/2}} = \frac{(1-p_{opt})}{2rp_{opt}^{3/2}\lambda_b^{1/2}} \tag{32}$$

Likewise, for a system under attack model 2, one can calculate the expected value of the total energy spent by legitimate ordinary nodes in a cluster to send a unit of data to the clusterhead, $C_1^{Amodel2}$ by:

$$\mathbb{E}[C_1^{Amodel2}|N=n] \approx \frac{\lambda_{Ord,leg}}{2r\lambda_{CH}^{3/2}} = \frac{(1-p_{opt})(1-\frac{m}{n})}{2r(p_{opt}(1-\frac{m}{n})+p_m\frac{m}{n})^{3/2}\lambda_b^{1/2}} \tag{33}$$

By assuming p_m is much smaller than p_{opt}, we approximate the total energy spent by legitimate ordinary nodes in a cluster under attack model 2 by:

$$\mathbb{E}[C_1^{Amodel2}|N=n] \approx \frac{(1-p_{opt})}{2rp_{opt}^{3/2}[(1-\frac{m}{n})\lambda_b]^{1/2}} \tag{34}$$

Hence, the ratio of $\mathbb{E}[C_1^{Amodel2}|N=n]$ to $\mathbb{E}[C_1^{Afree}|N=n]$ is computed from:

$$\frac{\mathbb{E}[C_1^{Amodel2}|N=n]}{\mathbb{E}[C_1^{Afree}|N=n]} \approx \frac{1}{(1-\frac{m}{n})^{1/2}}, \quad m \neq n \tag{35}$$

References

1. Abbasi, A.A., Younis, M.: A survey on clustering algorithms for wireless sensor networks. Comput. Commun. **30**(14), 2826–2841 (2007)
2. Agresti, A.: An Introduction to Categorical Data Analysis. Wiley Series in Probability and Statistics. Wiley, Hoboken (2007)

3. Al-Karaki, J.N., Kamal, A.E.: Routing techniques in wireless sensor networks: a survey. Wireless Commun. **11**(6), 6–28 (2004)
4. Andersson, E., Bock, D., Frisén, M.: Some statistical aspects of methods for detection of turning points in business cycles. J. Appl. Stat. **33**(3), 257–278 (2006)
5. Baccelli, F., Zuyev, S.: Poisson-Voronoi spanning trees with applications to the optimization of communication networks. Oper. Res. **47**(4), 619–631 (1999)
6. Bandyopadhyay, S., Coyle, E.J.: An energy efficient hierarchical clustering algorithm for wireless sensor networks. In: INFOCOM 2003, Twenty-Second Annual Joint Conference of the IEEE Computer and Communications, IEEE Societies, vol. 3, pp. 1713–1723. IEEE (2003)
7. Chiu, S.N., Stoyan, D., Kendall, W.S., Mecke, J.: Stochastic Geometry and Its Applications. Wiley, Hoboken (2013)
8. Choi, J., Lee, C.: Energy consumption and lifetime analysis in clustered multi-hop wireless sensor networks using the probabilistic cluster-head selection method. EURASIP J. Wireless Commun. Netw. **2011**(1), 1–13 (2011)
9. Hawkins, D.M., Olwell, D.H.: Cumulative Sum Charts and Charting for Quality Improvement. Statistics for Engineering and Physical Science. Springer, New York (1998). https://doi.org/10.1007/978-1-4612-1686-5
10. Heinzelman, W.R., Chandrakasan, A., Balakrishnan, H.: Energy-efficient communication protocol for wireless microsensor networks. In: Proceedings of the 33rd Annual Hawaii International Conference on System Sciences 2000, p. 10. IEEE (2000)
11. Kang, C.W., Kvam, P.H.: Shewhart control charts. In: Basic Statistical Tools for Improving Quality, pp. 97–124 (2011)
12. Liu, F., Cheng, X., Chen, D.: Insider attacker detection in wireless sensor networks. In: INFOCOM 2007, 26th IEEE International Conference on Computer Communications, pp. 1937–1945. IEEE (2007)
13. Liu, X.: A survey on clustering routing protocols in wireless sensor networks. Sensors **12**(8), 11113–11153 (2012)
14. Page, E.: Continuous inspection schemes. Biometrika **41**, 100–115 (1954)
15. Perrig, A., Szewczyk, R., Tygar, J.D., Wen, V., Culler, D.E.: SPINS: security protocols for sensor networks. Wireless Netw. **8**(5), 521–534 (2002). https://doi.org/10.1023/A:1016598314198
16. Poor, H.V., Hadjiliadis, O.: Quickest Detection, vol. 40. Cambridge University Press, Cambridge (2009)
17. Reynolds, M.R.: The Bernoulli CUSUM chart for detecting decreases in a proportion. Qual. Reliab. Eng. Int. **29**(4), 529–534 (2013)
18. Reynolds, M.R., Stoumbos, Z.G.: A general approach to modeling CUSUM charts for a proportion. IIE Trans. **32**(6), 515–535 (2000)
19. Reynolds Jr., M.R., Stoumbos, Z.G.: A CUSUM chart for monitoring a proportion when inspecting continuously. J. Qual. Technol. **31**(1), 87–108 (1999)
20. Sego, L.H.: Applications of control charts in medicine and epidemiology. Ph.D. thesis, Virginia Polytechnic Institute and State University (2006)
21. Stoto, M.A., et al.: Evaluating statistical methods for syndromic surveillance. In: Wilson, A.G., Wilson, G.D., Olwell, D.H. (eds.) Statistical Methods in Counterterrorism, pp. 141–172. Springer, New York (2006). https://doi.org/10.1007/0-387-35209-0_9
22. Tartakovsky, A.G., Rozovskii, B.L., Shah, K.: A nonparametric multichart CUSUM test for rapid intrusion detection. In: Proceedings Joint Statistical Meetings, 7–11 August 2005

23. Wang, H., Sheng, B., Li, Q.: Elliptic curve cryptography-based access control in sensor networks. Int. J. Secur. Netw. **1**(3–4), 127–137 (2006)
24. Xie, M., Han, S., Tian, B., Parvin, S.: Anomaly detection in wireless sensor networks: a survey. J. Netw. Comput. Appl. **34**(4), 1302–1325 (2011)
25. Younis, O., Fahmy, S.: HEED: a hybrid, energy-efficient, distributed clustering approach for ad hoc sensor networks. IEEE Trans. Mob. Comput. **3**(4), 366–379 (2004)
26. Zhang, Y., Yang, L.T., Chen, J.: RFID and Sensor Networks: Architectures, Protocols, Security, and Integrations. CRC Press, Boca Raton (2009)

Automated Bystander Detection and Anonymization in Mobile Photography

David Darling[1], Ang Li[2(✉)], and Qinghua Li[1]

[1] University of Arkansas, Fayetteville, USA
{dwdarlin,qinghual}@uark.edu
[2] Duke University, Durham, USA
ang.li630@duke.edu

Abstract. As smartphones have become more popular in recent years, integrated cameras have seen a rise in use. This trend has negative implications for the privacy of the individual in public places. Those who are captured inadvertently in others' pictures often have no knowledge of being included in a photograph nor have any control over how the photos of them might be distributed. To address this growing issue, we propose a novel system for protecting the privacy of bystanders captured in public photos. A fully automated approach to accurately distinguish the intended subjects of photos from strangers is first explored. To accurately distinguish these subjects and bystanders, we develop a feature-based classification approach utilizing entire photos. Additionally, we consider the privacy-minded case of only utilizing local face images with no contextual information from the original image by developing a convolutional neural network-based classifier. Considering the face to be the most sensitive and identifiable portion of a bystander, both classifiers are utilized to form an estimation of facial feature locations which can then be obfuscated to protect bystander privacy. We implement and compare three methods of facial anonymization: black boxing, Gaussian blurring, and pose-tolerant face swapping. To validate and explore the viability of these anonymization methods, a comprehensive user survey is conducted to understand the difference in appeal and viability between them.

Keywords: Privacy · Mobile photography · Facial anonymity · Face swapping · Obfuscation

1 Introduction

Digital photography is an enormously growing trend among the general public spurred primarily by the prevalence of smartphones with cameras in the daily lives of users. Attempts at estimating the number of digital photos captured annually have shown significant increases year over year with no sign of slowing down. In 2016, 660 billion photos were estimated to have been captured which

Ang Li was a PhD student at the University of Arkansas at the time of this work.

increased to 1.2 trillion by 2017. Additionally, smartphones were estimated to be primarily responsible for these photos, as they captured roughly 85% of the photos taken. Digital cameras, the next largest device group, made up only 10.3% by comparison [23]. This significant increase in digital photography demonstrates that people are more likely to be taking photos across many scenarios, including in public locations where oftentimes other people are nearby. Due to the crowded nature of public locations, strangers are frequently included in personal photos by circumstance. Figure 1 provides an example of such an image taken in public including both a target person and strangers. These strangers, or bystanders, often are completely unaware of photos being taken of them. Even realizing that a photo was taken, individuals usually have very little recourse to ask to be removed from the photo or have the photo deleted in a public setting.

Extending a preliminary workshop version [7] in which we proposed feature sets and used them to detect bystanders and targets, this work explores beyond feature-based solutions for bystander detection and studies effective ways to obfuscate bystander faces. To this end, we propose both a feature-based classification approach utilizing entire photos and a privacy-minded, convolutional neural network (CNN)-based approach utilizing only local face images with no contextual information from the original photo to investigate how different models learn the intrinsic visual differences between targets and bystanders. In order to train and evaluate our models, a real-world dataset consisting of over 200 photos and over 500 faces has been created to provide a generalized representation of the types of images that commonly can be found uploaded to social media. Generally, the photos provide a mixture of both celebrities appearing in public with bystanders behind them and typical people in front of landmarks or other locations of interest with strangers also inadvertently captured in the photo.

In addition to the classifiers, methods for effective facial obfuscation also are implemented and examined through a user study (with IRB approval) as a part of this work. The methods for anonymizing faces not only include standard methods such as Gaussian blurring and black boxing but also a novel approach of face swapping using a state-of-the-art position map regression network [8]. To gain a more full understanding of how these obfuscation methods impact and are perceived by end users, an in-depth survey is carried out and evaluated to determine the preferred methods of actual users. General opinions on privacy as it relates to digital photos capturing strangers are also collected to validate the assumptions behind this work.

This paper's main contributions are summarized as follows:

- We propose an automated system for protecting bystander's privacy in mobile photography with a unique feature that it can work as a standalone tool on a user's smartphone, without relying on inter-user interaction or any online platform which are commonly needed by previous solutions.
- We propose a novel feature-based classification approach utilizing entire photos and a privacy-minded CNN-based approach utilizing local face images for automatically distinguishing targets from bystanders in mobile photography.

Fig. 1. Example image with target clearly featured in the foreground and bystanders included to the left and right in the background. Image source: http:// mensstreetfashion.weebly.com/home/kanye-west-style

    The two approaches are evaluated and compared to explore the tradeoff between the distinguishing accuracy and privacy.
– We implement three face obfuscation methods for complete face anonymization including black boxing, blurring, and face swapping, and carry out a user study with 89 respondents to evaluate opinions on bystander privacy and on the acceptability of the three face anonymization methods.

    The remainder of this paper is organized as follows. Section 2 provides an overview of related works. Section 3 presents an overview of the design for the system. Section 4 describes the feature-based approach for target/bystander classification. Section 5 describes the convolutional neural network approach. Section 6 provides evaluations of both models. Section 7 provides a technical description of proposed facial obfuscation methods and presents the results from the user survey. Section 8 concludes this paper and discusses future work. Last section offers acknowledgments.

2   Related Work

Works related to improving facial privacy in photography have previously followed trends such as utilizing photographer-bystander cooperation. Li et al. [17,18] design systems for cooperation between smartphone users to blur requesting users' faces. Jung and Philipose [13] utilize a method of gesture recognition to detect a person who wants to be excluded from a photo. *MarkIt* [21] can perform automated covering of user-defined objects in photos, but users must manually predefine objects to be hidden. This work, by comparison, explores a fully automated approach towards the identification of bystanders to be obfuscated and requires no manual interaction from photographers or those captured in photos.

Other approaches in automated anonymization require users interested in having their privacy protected to wear specialized markers. Schiff et al. [24] propose a scheme whereby specialized markers that users wear can be recognized by an automated system which will then blur their faces. Bo et al. [4] similarly utilize worn QR-codes on clothing to automatically determine individual privacy preferences. Our approach does not require any worn markings; only visual attributes of persons within individual images are used to anonymize those who are inadvertently captured.

Some works explore photo privacy protection for individuals in online social network settings [12,19,26] or in individual phones [16]. Li et al. proposed *HideMe* [19], a system for defining scenarios for photo access control and distance-based face blurring. Xu et al. [26] developed a facial identification system to incorporate captured persons into the decision process of sharing photos. Ilia et al. [12] proposed fine grained access control based on face detection to prevent individual faces from being viewed by other users. Each of these works depend upon either accurate facial recognition to identify bystanders for anonymizing or specific scenario definitions from the photographer. Our work circumvents the need for both face recognition and input from the photographer by automating the detection of bystanders and providing low-impact solutions for obfuscating their faces.

One recent work in parallel to ours also explores detection of bystanders utilizing features computed over individuals [10]. However, the features used in our work are different from theirs. Also, that work focuses entirely on feature engineering and effectiveness of predictive models, but our work presents a full system for both detecting and anonymizing bystanders and explores the trade-off between bystander protection and photo quality/usability. Additionally, we consider privacy-aware machine learning with the development of a CNN which does not require access to an entire user photo and can predict solely based on facial images. While Hasan et al. [10] explore both transfer learning on deep neural networks, our approach utilizes a simplified feature-set which allows for simpler and smaller classifiers.

3   System Overview

Our proposed system works on the photographing phone and consists of four main processes that can automatically run over taken photos. The first is an initial pass of face detection which identifies face regions and positions. This process of facial detection is fully automated and requires no manual user input specifying specific photos or regions to be focused by the algorithm. Facial region data from this pass can then be forwarded either to our feature-based or CNN classifiers which automate the detection of targets and bystanders. The classifications along with face landmarks are then used to perform obfuscation processing with the black boxing, blurring, and face swapping methods which can be selected by the user as a system configuration parameter. The resulting anonymized photo is the final output. Figure 2 provides a visualization of this system. We find that both classifiers are robust against nonstandard scenarios where a photo might not include any bystanders or any human targets (pictures of scenery are an example of this.)

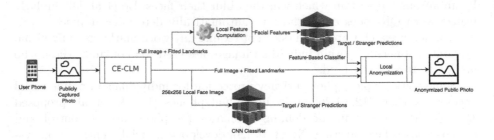

Fig. 2. Architecture of the system.

4   Feature-Based Bystander Classifier

4.1   Feature Identification

In order to begin designing a model for classification of an abstract concept such as who is the desired target of a photo, it is essential to correctly break the problem down into quantitative measurements which provide a suitable amount of information to distinguish classes. Relative face size (the size of a given face relative to the maximum face size in the image) and face deviation from center are identified to model the fact that bystanders are often included in the background or periphery of photos. Local blurriness of a face is also found to regularly indicate a person was not the intended focus of a picture. Beyond these metrics of relative visual differences, additional features are identified to model the fact that bystanders are usually unaware of having their photo captured. Additionally, non-relative features are needed to account for scenarios where photos might exclude any human targets (for example bystanders are captured in an image of scenery or some other non-human target). Head pose angles and gaze deviation from the camera are decided as good indicators of this, as bystanders will commonly not be looking at the camera capturing them if they are unaware of it. Considering all of these metrics in a single model, relative face size, face deviation from photo center, local blurring, head pose, and gaze deviation are identified as a sufficient number of features to capture the complexity of the target/bystander classification problem.

4.2   Feature Extraction and Computation

Relative Face Size. In order to accurately capture face size in an image, traditional bounding box methods used by most state-of-the-art object detection models such as YOLOv3 [22] are not sufficient. These bounding boxes normally have no guarantee of forming a tight bound on the object in question. Instead, we recognize that recent advances in constrained local neural fields (CLNFs) for facial landmark detection are more suited for the task of robust landmark placement for photos taken in the wild due to their resistance to factors such as pose differences, lighting changes, and local facial differences such as hair or accessories. To this end, we adopt a Convolutional Experts Constrained Local Model (CE-CLM) [1,27] to perform accurate facial landmark placement. These types of models function by first capturing landmark shape variations with a point distibution model (PDM) and then modeling the local differences in the visual appearances of fitted landmarks with the use of local patch experts. This model, pretrained over LFPW [3] and Helen [15] training sets, is able to accurately determine landmark positions and provided higher detection rates on smaller faces as well as partially occluded faces as compared to more popular systems such as Dlib [14] during our experimentation.

Figure 3 provides a visualization of the standard collection of facial landmarks which are fitted by networks such as Dlib and the CE-CLM model. Refer to this figure for locating any numbered facial landmarks mentioned subsequently. Once a tight bound has been formed around each face using these landmarks, the maximum size of all faces found in the photo is calculated as:

$$\max_{0 \leq i \leq n} S(i) = (\alpha_i - \beta_i)(\gamma_i - \delta_i) \tag{1}$$

where i refers to the index of the current face in the photo which can have n faces, α_i is the x-coordinate of facial landmark 16, β_i is the x-coordinate of landmark 0, γ_i is the y-coordinate of landmark 24, and δ_i is the y-coordinate of landmark 8. The subscript i for each of these variables indicates that these are specific to the face with index i. Similarly, the relative face size metric for each face is then calculated simply as:

$$R(x) = \frac{s_i}{\mu} \tag{2}$$

where s_i is the size of face i and μ is the maximum face size computed in Eq. 1 Thus, the relative size of any given face will always fall within the bounds of $(0, 1]$.

Deviation of Face from Center. Face position within an image can be extracted and computed in a method similar to the relative face size metric. Facial landmarks are fitted to each detected face in an image with the center of the face treated as landmark 33. By utilizing this landmark, it is possible to accurately extract what region of the image a given face is located assuming the dimensions of the image are known. To create a useful metric for supervised

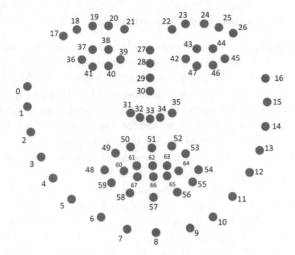

Fig. 3. Standard template of facial landmarks fitted by common face detection networks.

learning models, the face position is computed as the amount of deviation from center of the image. The intuition here is that the feature generally should (but not always) provide a positive correlation with the likelihood that a given face belongs to that of a stranger. To better capture the meaning behind a person's face deviation from the center of a photo, the metric should be normalized such that its range of values carry the same meaning across different photo sizes. To this end, the deviation of a detected face is calculated as:

$$D(i) = \frac{|\epsilon_i - \zeta|}{w} + \frac{|\eta_i - \theta|}{h} \tag{3}$$

Here, ϵ_i is the x coordinate of landmark 30, ζ is the x-coordinate of the computed center of the image, η_i is the y-coordinate of landmark 30, θ is the y-coordinate of the center of the image, w is the width dimension of the image, and h is the height dimension of the image. The subscript i, as in previous equations, refers to the i-th detected face in the image. The deviation in both x and y coordinate axes is summed for this metric because their relative importance towards determining the likelihood of a person being a bystander in an image is unclear. For example, consider a case where a target is featured centrally in front of public stairs, and a bystander is captured farther up the stairs in the image. Although the bystander might be centrally located in the x-axis, their y-axis deviation is more important in this case. Because of this ambiguity in importance across image cases, both axis deviations are weighted the same when computing the overall deviation. The bound of this metric then becomes $[0, 2]$.

Local Blurring. Many methods exist to compute the amount of blurring that occurs over a localized region in an image. One of the most popular methods is to compute a Fast Fourier Transform over an image to break it down into its constituent frequencies and perform frequency domain analysis on the results. This method is not ideal for generating a general metric of blurriness across photos as it is difficult to identify the specific frequencies in the general case which mark a region as blurry vs. another. Instead, the convolution of the Laplacian method proposed by Pech-Pacheco et al. [20] is selected for its ability to provide average edge variance in an image as a single floating point result. This is desirable from a feature engineering perspective, because blurriness, as a measure of edge variance, effectively captures the desired information from an image region without requiring a secondary classifier to convert frequency component information into a blurriness boolean.

To perform this method, the Laplace operator which is defined in 2-dimensional Cartesian space canonically as:

$$\Delta f = \frac{\partial^2 f}{\partial x^2} + \frac{\partial^2 f}{\partial y^2} \tag{4}$$

However, in a discrete grid such as an image, the discrete Laplacian is used which essentially is a convolution of the following kernel:

$$L = \begin{bmatrix} 0 & 1 & 0 \\ 1 & -4 & 1 \\ 0 & 1 & 0 \end{bmatrix} \tag{5}$$

This operation is therefore used to generate a floating point "rating" of the blurriness over each local region of detected faces defined by their bounding boxes extracted by padding the space around the outer facial landmarks. Bounding boxes are used in this case rather than the tight bounds featured in previous features because the wider region around the face contains additional edges for the Laplacian convolution operation. This provides a better idea of how much variance is in the face's surrounding edges.

Head Pose Estimation. Head pose defines the way an individual's head is oriented in 3-dimensional space. Intuitively, being able to extract some measurements of head orientation should capture the trend of strangers having their heads turned away from a capturing camera. To define head orientation, 3 main parameters are needed:

- Pitch: This defines the angle a head is looking up or down. Essentially a measure of vertical tilt.
- Roll: The angle a head is tilted from side to side. Note that this is distinct from yaw in that roll can vary while the face remains looking forward.
- Yaw: The angle a head is turned from left to right. For example, when turning to look at something behind a person, the head yaw angle becomes more extreme.

Each of these angles are intrinsically within the CE-CLM models as they internally keep a 3D representation of the fitted face landmarks. These 3D representations can be utilized to estimate accurate head pose information by solving the n-point in perspective problem [1,2,27]. This procedure essentially allows for accurate estimation of head pose angles in general images. These angles are represented as continuous floating point values which can range both in positive and negative directions.

Gaze Deviation. This feature is intended to provide additional information about whether a given person has awareness of being included in a photograph. Although head pose angles can provide information whether the face in question is oriented toward the camera, these angles do not tell the whole story. A stranger in a photo could very well have their head oriented toward the camera if, for example, they are walking behind someone taking a selfie. To provide more information to learning models about these situations, gaze deviation from the center of the camera focus could be included.

In order to extract gaze angles, a slightly altered method of utilizing CLNFs proposed by [25] is adopted. In the original work, CLNFs were utilized to form a PDM of the eye landmarks for synthesized eyes. This estimation of the shape of the eye can then be used to further estimate what direction the eye is oriented in (and where the eye is looking). The accuracy of the gaze estimation was improved utilizing pre-determined intrinsic camera parameters. However, because photos captured by mobile devices in the wild provide no information about these parameters, we adopt the model to utilize some default values for these camera parameters. These include estimated distance of the face from the camera, focal length, and optical center. This sort of calibration cannot be done for images collected for the training dataset as there simply are too many camera-to-person-positionings to take into account. Therefore, the gaze vectors should be considered rough estimates of whether a given person is looking in the general direction of a camera. The rationale behind this is that a binary value of looking vs. not looking at a camera is still a desirable trait in identifying bystanders in a mobile photo. Example gaze vectors plotted over an image can be seen in Fig. 4.

By utilizing extracted gaze vectors, it is possible to trace a ray from the center of a given face into the estimated camera location. Then, by organizing world coordinates with the camera at the origin $(0, 0, 0)$, it is possible to estimate the position of a face from the camera using coordinates. The tracing process begins by setting up the following equation:

$$\kappa_z + u\boldsymbol{\lambda}_z = 0 \tag{6}$$

Here κ_z refers to the z-coordinate or estimated depth of facial landmark 30, u is a scaling factor which must satisfy the equation, and $\boldsymbol{\lambda}_z$ is the z-coordinate vector of the average gaze angle for a given face. Solving this equation for scaling factor u allows us to then scale the other components of the full gaze vector $\boldsymbol{\lambda}$:

$$\lambda' = u\lambda = u \begin{bmatrix} \lambda_x \\ \lambda_y \\ \lambda_z \end{bmatrix} \tag{7}$$

To compute the point ρ where the ray traced from the face intercepts with the origin or camera z-plane, the scaled gaze vector must be added to κ (landmark 30):

$$\rho = \kappa + \lambda' \tag{8}$$

The value of ρ enables a deviation estimate for anyone looking in the direction of the camera's z-plane. Using the x and y components of ρ, and assuming the camera is the origin of the world coordinates, we can use a simple 2-D distance formula calculation to find the final deviation:

$$D = \sqrt{\rho_x^2 + \rho_y^2} \tag{9}$$

The resulting value of D computed for any given detected face is the final metric for a supervised learning model.

Fig. 4. Gaze vectors from the CLNF model in green with face landmarks from the CE-CLM model on an example image with no bystanders. Original image by Steve Granitz, WireImage. (Color figure online)

4.3 Supervised Learning Model Consideration

Because all of the facial features are collectively designed to fully capture the complexity of the bystander classification problem, they should generalize very well to a wide range of supervised learning models. In our implementation, a collection of diverse classifiers are implemented and evaluated, including Gradient Boosted Decision Tree, Multilayer Perceptron, Random Forest, and Support Vector Machine. Detailed descriptions of these algorithms as well as discussions of their effectiveness in learning from the computed features are presented in the evaluation section.

5   CNN-Based Bystander Classifier

The feature-based bystander classification method needs the entire photo to work, since it considers a target's or a bystander's face in the context of the photo (e.g., whether a face is in the center region of the photo or not). An interesting question is whether it is possible to distinguish target and bystander just based on their faces without relying on the context in the photo. Basing on face only could result in a more privacy-minded classifier which would only require images of faces without revealing their surroundings or even other people nearby. Such a classifier would be especially useful for any application where users might utilize a cloud-based solution for automated bystander training and detection, since the bystander's face itself does not leak his/her privacy (e.g., location) when uploaded to the cloud for analysis. To this end, a CNN architecture is designed and validated on the same dataset as the feature-based models.

5.1   Network Architecture

Figure 5 provides an overview of the complete network architecture. The network utilizes increasingly small convolutions separated by max pooling layers. The activation functions utilized by the network are rectified linear unit (Relu) for the two convolutional layers and sigmoid for the final activation layer. The dense layers in the latter portion of the model are intended to produce meaning from the large feature vector and condense them into more usable, countable features. The final dropout layer is included to reduce overfitting on the training set. It is set to drop inputs at a rate of 0.25 which experimentally achieved best results. The filter size of the convolutional layers is small, at a size of (2,2). This is to ensure that fine-detailed features such as eye direction might be captured, as eyes in the facial dataset can sometimes be very small (only being formed from a few 10s of pixels). Stride for each of these kernels is set to (1,1), such that a direct sweep of the kernel is performed over the image.

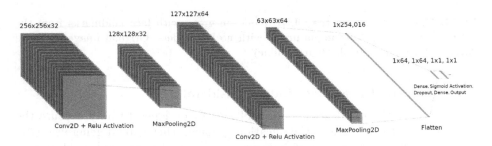

Fig. 5. Overall architecture of the convolutional neural network.

6   Model Evaluation

6.1   Dataset

The dataset for this problem was created specifically for this project due to the fact that no existing datasets could be found at the time which provided the types of required images. The images in the set were automatically collected from freely available online sources including social media platforms, public news sites, and image repository sites. Collected photos were manually reviewed to ensure the dataset would be able to provide a good generalization of the types of images that might be encountered in the wild. To be included, photos were required to have at least one human face. Photos could have all targets, all bystanders, or a mixture of both. The photos are all taken in various settings including indoor/outdoor locations, public venues with varying degrees of crowding, and daytime/nighttime lighting conditions. Photos excluding human targets such as scenery photos were also included to ensure the developed models could generalize to these challenging scenarios. In total, the dataset consists of 515 valid face images extracted from 222 photos. It is worth noting that our dataset is of comparable size to Hassan et al. [10] (515 facial images vs 600). In order to allow other researchers to utilize these images and contribute new images, we have made the dataset publicly available at [6].

6.2   Feature-Based Bystander Classification

Model Selection and Implementation. The following supervised learning algorithms were selected and implemented to provide a good coverage of the varieties of popular classifiers and demonstrate that even with multiple different algorithms, our features generalize well.

Gradient Boosted Decision Tree (GBDT). GBDTs are an enhancement over normal decision trees whereby an ensemble of weaker models are utilized to form a single classifier [9]. The number of estimators or trees used was 300. A maximum depth of 10 was also selected for the classifier. The learning rate was set to 0.03 after multiple training attempts.

Random Forest (RF). Instead of the weak models favored by gradient boosting methods, the RF approach is to make use of deep, fully grown trees and average them together to reduce variance and overfitting [5]. The RF algorithm was selected to offer a good comparison with GBDTs. The number of estimators for this algorithm was selected as 50 with a max depth of 6.

Support Vector Machine (SVM). Because SVMs are considered very suitable for binary classification [11], they were chosen for evaluation alongside other more advanced algorithms. Best results were achieved with a linear kernel, with hyperparameter C set to 10 and gamma set to 0.001.

Multilayer Perceptron (MLP). Neural networks are a logical choice for a feature-based model such as this. The chosen architecture for the MLP is 3 hidden layers of size (7,5,3). The hyperbolic tangent function was selected for activation, and a learning rate of 0.03 is used with alpha parameter set to 0.0001. After multiple training attempts, this coupling of architecture and hyperparameter values provided best results.

Training and Evaluation. Each of the feature-based algorithms was trained over a random 80/20 train/test sample split of 515 feature sets (one set for each face image in the dataset). Validation metrics are shown in Table 1. Of the classifiers we trained, the GDBT and MLP neural network were able to achieve the best validation accuracy at 94.34%. The RF and SVM were still able to achieve acceptable accuracy over 90%. The reasoning for this is that the simpler SVM model had a higher tendency to overfit the training set and resulted in less generalizable models. The RF model suffered from the lower depth of underlying decision trees relative to the GBDT, but required less processing to perform prediction passes.

Different classifiers were able to predict targets and bystanders with varying degrees of effectiveness. This is shown by the precision, recall, and F-1 score of each algorithm. Precision is defined as the number of true positives out of the combined number of true positives and false positives. Recall is defined as the number of true positives out of the combined number of true positives and false negatives. F1-score is the harmonic mean of the two. The MLP actually had the overall highest F1 scores with 0.93 (target positive) and 0.94 (bystander positive). The GDBT actually suffered from significantly worse precision when predicting targets which indicates that it might have difficulty identifying relevant targets in the wild. It actually acheived the same target F1 score as the SVM model which had the lowest scores for both targets and bystander prediction.

In order to determine how effective each of the engineered features was individually to the classifiers, the algorithms were trained over different subsets of the complete feature-set. Each subset had one feature removed and the others included. Table 2 lists the validation accuracies for these models. Of the features tested for exclusion from the models, the gaze deviation metric, when removed, had no real impact on the performance of the GBDT and only a small impact to the other models. By contrast, both the face size and center deviation metrics had significant harmful impacts on all of the classifiers. This could be an indication that the inherent inaccuracy of the gaze metric itself was a problem for training. Additionally, the gaze metric could simply be redundant where head pose information might have been sufficient. For these reasons the gaze deviation metric could be a candidate for removal in the interest of improving training and prediction speed. Appendix A provides a detailed overview of runtime performance for all classifiers. Because of the streamlined set of features used by the classifier, the computational complexity of all classifiers were kept low and should be suitable for direct implementation on resource constrained mobile devices.

Table 1. Accuracy, precision, and recall metrics for all classifier models. (T) and (B) indicate that the metric was computed with target or bystander respectively as the positive class.

Learning Algorithm	Validation Accuracy	Precision (T)	Recall (T)	F1 Score (T)	Precision (B)	Recall (B)	F1 Score (B)
MLP	94.34%	0.98	0.88	0.93	0.90	0.98	0.94
SVM	90.57%	0.94	0.87	0.90	0.87	0.94	0.90
RF	92.45%	0.93	0.95	0.94	0.94	0.92	0.93
GDBT	94.34%	0.83	1.00	0.90	1.00	0.88	0.94

Table 2. Validation accuracy for models trained using feature-subsets

Learning Algorithm	No Gaze Deviation	No Face Size	No Center Deviation	No Head Pose
MLP	90.57%	77.36%	81.13%	85.71%
SVM	92.45%	81.13%	84.91%	86.68%
RF	92.45%	81.13%	77.36%	83.81%
GDBT	94.34%	84.91%	83.02%	84.76%

6.3   CNN-Based Bystander Classification

In order to train the CNN, the same image set was used as for the feature-based model with a similar 80/20 train/test split. However, extracted local face images were used rather than entire photos. As mentioned previously, the goal of analyzing this network is to see if a privacy-concerned model could function well without needing to process entire images. Actual training took place utilizing mini-batch gradient descent with a batch size of 24 samples and 17 steps per epoch. Through experimentation, it was found that the CNN training accuracy generally converged after 15 training epochs. The testing accuracy was 81.55% with target precision and recall of 82.69% and 81.13% respectively which is significantly lower than the best feature-based models. Additionally, the predictive runtime of the model was found to be much higher than the feature based models at around 244ms on an Intel i9 platform (see Appendix A Table 3 for detailed runtime comparisons). However, these metrics are still impressive considering the loss of contextual information about a photo that the CNN experiences in comparison with the feature sets.

Originally, it appeared as though the networks would quickly converge during training due to the relatively stable loss value that was reported for the first 10 training epochs. However, by doubling the training epochs, it was found that true loss convergence did not generally happen until further training occurred. Through multiple experiments, the number of epochs that resulted in the lowest loss without overfitting and harming test accuracy occurred with 15 as mentioned previously. An example of a complete training sequence is provided in Fig. 6 with loss plotted. Additionally, Fig. 8 in Appendix A plots training accuracy over the same number of mini-batches. It is interesting to note that just three epochs were enough to provide significant improvements in loss and training accuracy, but in our experiments the model was not able to effectively generalize to the test set after such short training periods. It is also worth noting that with a training accuracy approaching 89% and test accuracy reaching 81.55%, overfitting still occurs in the model even with a reasonable dropout rate of 0.25.

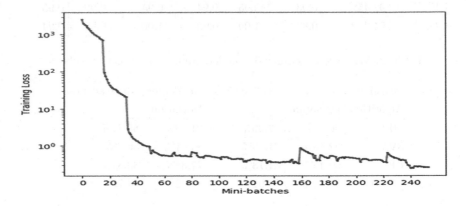

Fig. 6. Progressive loss of the network for each mini-batch.

The main contribution of this model is the fact that, unlike the feature-based approach which will require users to supply entire images to compute contextual features such as relative face size, this model is still able to effectively distinguish bystanders and targets with only face images, as it convolves over a "cropped" facial region. The hope is that users who might not want to supply entire photos to an automated system especially when the system is hosted in the cloud can still make use of a less invasive model which will not see any exposing information at the cost of a significant, flat decrease in performance in terms of accuracy, precision, and recall.

7   Anonymizing Bystander Faces

For a complete system to ensure the privacy of strangers captured in images, it is necessary to automate the obfuscation of faces so that the ease of identifying someone is severely limited. Although there are some methods available to obfuscate faces, it is still unclear how acceptable they are to users. In this section, we implement three different methods for facial anonymization and explore them with a user study. Figure 7 provides a visualization of each method on an example photo from the training dataset.

Fig. 7. From left to right: original image, image with black boxing, image with blurring, image with face swapping. Image source: https://cdn.ebaumsworld.com/2008/08/861915/phelps01.jpg

7.1 Implementation of Obfuscation Methods

Black Boxing. Black boxing of the face is the simplest, and arguably most secure method for facial anonymization. The detected stranger face is completely removed from the image with every pixel RGB value being set to black. In this way, there is not any remaining information which can be gleaned from the face, such as race or face size which the other proposed methods can leave behind. Although this provides the strongest guarantee of privacy, the visual impact to a photo can be very harmful depending on the surrounding lighting conditions.

Gaussian Blurring. Blurring is considered an intermediary between the black boxing and face swapping methods in terms of intended impact to photo quality. Blurring on smaller faces can be relatively unnoticeable in images, especially on persons captured in the far background of an image. Unlike black boxing, information such as race and even hair color can still be preserved depending on the resolution of the photo. However, facial features are always guaranteed to be completely anonymized. Gaussian blurring is used for this system due to its popularity and ease of computation. A kernel size of (70,70) is used and achieves acceptable blurring.

Face Swapping. Pose-tolerant face swapping traditionally required the use of deep CNNs such as the deepfake project which requires specific training for the two faces attempting to be swapped. However, recent advances in automated swapping, specifically the introduction of position map regression networks, have allowed for excellent generalized swapping of 3D face masks without any need for targeted training. Using an implementation of this method introduced by Feng et al. [8] allows for a novel technique of anonymizing bystander faces with any selection of "public" faces. These public faces could be commonly-known celebrities or even artificially generated portraits. Assuming the face is realistic enough and lighting differences are not too extreme, the results can be very believable. For this project, faces taken from stock photos found online were used. To match skin tone for each detected stranger face, it is possible to compute an average pixel color value utilizing facial landmarks within the face region to gain a representation of their overall face color. This color is then compared with the precomputed averages of a collection of public faces. The public face which minimizes the difference is selected for swapping.

7.2   Survey of Users on Face Anonymization

In order to validate our obfuscation methods and demonstrate that they are both effective at anonymizing faces and cause limited impact to user photos, we conduct a comprehensive user survey.

Questions. To gain a better understanding of how actual users regard the protection of privacy for strangers and themselves in photos, one portion of the survey asked participants for their opinions on a series of questions relating to digital photo privacy and stranger protection. These questions were presented as:

- Question 1: Ensuring the privacy of digital photos is important.
- Question 2: You would want your privacy protected if someone took a photo that captures you without you knowing.
- Question 3: It is a good idea to protect strangers' privacy in your photos.
- Question 4: It is sometimes hard to avoid including strangers' faces in photos taken in public places.
- Question 5: If there was an option to protect a stranger's face in your photo without affecting quality, you would use it.
- Question 6: If there was an option to protect a stranger's face in your photo while slightly degrading the quality, you would still use it.
- Question 7: If there was an option to protect a stranger's face in your photo while significantly degrading the quality, you would still use it.

Users were asked to rate their opinions to these questions on a Likert scale.

Another portion of the survey presented an unaltered photo compared with anonymized photos where strangers' faces had been obfuscated using each of the three proposed methods. Participants were asked to rate their opinion on how harmful each method was to the original photo on a sliding scale from 0 to 10, with 0 in this case being not harmful and 10 being extremely harmful. In addition to rating the impact of each method on the photos, participants were also asked to rate their willingness to use each method on their own photos from 0 to 10. At the end of the section, participants could also optionally respond with testimonial as to which method they preferred and why.

In another portion of the survey, participants were presented with timed views of images. One image had strangers anonymized with face swapping and the other did not. The participants had to guess if any face swapping occurred or not in each of the two. This portion of the survey was intended to examine how noticeable face swapping could be in a fast browsing environment such as social media where average users generally only spend a few seconds looking at pictures before moving on.

Responses. In total, the survey received 89 anonymous responses over the course of 1 month. Participants were primarily recruited among university students mainly majoring in computer science and computer engineering although a minority of respondents were working adults. All respondents participated on a completely voluntary basis (no incentives were provided). Exact demographic information was not collected to preserve participant anonymity. The detailed results for questions 1 through 7 are shown in Appendix B Fig. 9. In reviewing the responses to questions 1 through 7, it is clear that respondents had strong feelings in support of digital photo privacy. Most respondents likewise felt that both their privacy and stranger's privacy should ideally be protected in public photographs. Additionally, a large majority of respondents answered positively that they would make use of an anonymization system, assuming the impact to the photo was negligible while a majority responded negatively to any sort of significant impact to photo quality. Clearly, finding obfuscating methods with as little impact as possible to photo quality is paramount in designing a system that would be well-regarded and actually used.

The results of the harmfulness ratings questions are shown in Appendix B Fig. 10. The results of the willingness ratings questions are shown in Appendix B Fig. 11. From these results, black boxing received the most negative feedback with a large majority of participants rating its impact the worst overall and usability the lowest. Interestingly, blurring seemed to score the highest among respondents for both usability and harmfulness. Face swapping had comparable harmfulness, but was rated significantly lower on average for usability. To further examine these results, some participant responses provide helpful insight. Most participants who felt blurring was their preferred method seemed to find that face swapping was either unnatural looking, or felt that they could not trust it to always create a believable swap. For example, one user responded, "The black box hurt the quality of the photo and the swapping was disturbing because you could tell it was the wrong face on the stranger.". Overall, it seemed that blurring would be the best approach from a usability and perceived impact perspective based on this participant feedback.

Analyzing the number of users who were able to detect face swapping in the final survey section demonstrates that face swapping certainly is still detectable among many users despite recent advances in realistic swapping technology. 53.9% of respondents were able to tell that face swapping was used in the photo they were presented compared with 8% detection for the control photo. Many users noticed that something was different about the photo compared with the control photo, although the detection responses were close to random guessing for the photo with swapping.

8   Conclusion and Future Work

In this work, we presented a novel approach for automating the detection and anonymization of bystanders in digital photos, applying both a feature-based model and a privacy-concerned convolutional neural network. Techniques for feature engineering were explored with methods for utilizing metrics such as relative face size and head-pose estimation. Our MLP model achieved the highest validation accuracy at 94.34%, which demonstrates generalizability and promise for future use in an anonymization system for smartphone users. The convolutional neural network also demonstrated promising results with the highest achieved accuracy of 81.55% and limited overfitting of the training set. This work is the first of its kind in being able to offer a fully privacy-concerned approach as all other works previously relied upon contextual information within a full image. Additionally, we eliminate the need for any sort of manual cooperation between photographer and bystanders as most other related works require. The hope is that being able to offer a system that automates the protection of individuals in mobile photos and preserves the privacy of those captured, the user trust and willingness to use such a method in a real-world system is greatly enhanced over any previous methods which all require some form of participation on the bystanders' parts.

Three fully automated approaches for face anonymization (black boxing, blurring, and face swapping) were presented for use with the classifying models. To better understand user opinions around public photo privacy and each of the presented methods, a comprehensive user study was carried out. Participant responses indicated that while privacy of photos and individuals in public settings was definitely a concern for most, developing anonymizing methods which do not harm photo quality is important for creating any sort of real world system. Especially promising were the large number of positive responses on the blurring and swapping methods which indicate that the system has attraction to real-world users.

Due to the lack of available image datasets for the target/bystander detection application, collecting usable images including a good diversity of photo types, locations, lighting, etc. was a time-consuming process that could hardly be fully automated as photos had to be manually reviewed for suitability. The induced small size of the dataset might limit the generality of the results. In the future, we will expand upon this dataset to greatly increase the number of images and faces included. The goal of this is to ensure that models trained over the expanded dataset will be able to better generalize to in-the-wild photos. Making the dataset publicly available will allow other researchers to contribute and refine the images as well. Additionally, we plan to carry out a more significant user study with a larger population to examine the usability of our system in greater detail.

Acknowledgements. We thank Murtuza Jadliwala for shepherding this paper. We also thank the anonymous reviewers for their valuable comments.

Appendix

A   Performance Characteristics of Classifiers

Table 3. Average single prediction forward-pass runtime (Intel i9-10900k)

Learning algorithm	Average runtime (ms)
MLP	0.0743
SVM	0.0541
RF	0.0515
GDBT	0.2028
CNN	244.3

Table 3 shows the measured single forward-pass runtimes for each of the examined classifiers averaged over 1000 runs. All feature-based classifiers have almost negligible runtime requirements for prediction operations on an Intel i9 platform. This indicates they would be excellent candidates to run directly on resource-constrained mobile devices.

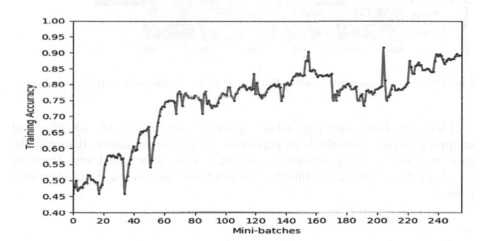

Fig. 8. Progressive accuracy over training mini-batches for the CNN classifier.

Figure 8 shows the accuracy of the CNN as mini-batches progress during training. Taken in conjunction with Fig. 6, the CNN appears to only converge after the 220th mini-batch where loss and accuracy variance is lowest.

B   Detailed Survey Results

Figure 9 shows detailed results of participant responses to survey questions 1–7. It is clear from these results that almost all respondents believe that photo privacy is important. Additionally, the rapid transition in willingness to use a system that does not degrade photo quality shows how paramount developing minimally invasive obfuscation methods is for real-world use.

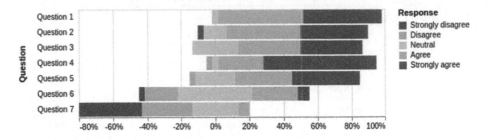

Fig. 9. Survey responses to opinion questions 1–7.

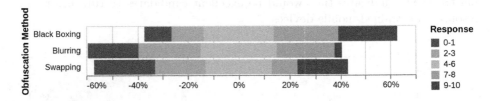

Fig. 10. Survey responses to rating the impact of anonymization methods on photos.

Figure 10 shows that respondents generally believe that the blurring and swapping methods are the least impactful to the sample photos. Interestingly, there was not a strong correlation between responses here and with the next set of questions over user willingness to use these same methods on their own photos.

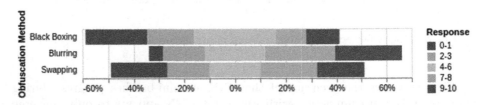

Fig. 11. Survey responses to rating how willing users would be to use each anonymization method.

The responses on willingness to use the obfuscation methods (see Fig. 11) demonstrate that there are more factors in determining what users want to use than perceived impact to photo quality. For example, face swapping, while rated as generally having a low impact to photo quality, received many negative responses from users in their likelihood to actually use it.

References

1. Baltrusaitis, T., Robinson, P., Morency, L.: Constrained local neural fields for robust facial landmark detection in the wild. In: 2013 IEEE International Conference on Computer Vision Workshops, pp. 354–361, December 2013. https://doi.org/10.1109/ICCVW.2013.54
2. Baltrusaitis, T., Zadeh, A., Lim, Y.C., Morency, L.: OpenFace 2.0: facial behavior analysis toolkit. In: 2018 13th IEEE International Conference on Automatic Face Gesture Recognition (FG 2018), pp. 59–66, May 2018. https://doi.org/10.1109/FG.2018.00019
3. Belhumeur, P.N., Jacobs, D.W., Kriegman, D.J., Kumar, N.: Localizing parts of faces using a consensus of exemplars. IEEE Trans. Pattern Anal. Mach. Intell. **35**(12), 2930–2940, December 2013. https://doi.org/10.1109/TPAMI.2013.23
4. Bo, C., Shen, G., Liu, J., Li, X.Y., Zhang, Y., Zhao, F.: Privacy.tag: privacy concern expressed and respected. In: Proceedings of the 12th ACM Conference on Embedded Network Sensor Systems. (SenSys 2014), pp. 163–176. Association for Computing Machinery, New York (2014). https://doi.org/10.1145/2668332.2668339
5. Breiman, L.: Random forests. Mach. Learn. **45**(1), 5–32 (2001). https://doi.org/10.1023/A:1010933404324
6. Darling, D.: Target bystander detection repository (2020). https://github.com/ddarling/target-bystander-detection
7. Darling, D., Li, A., Li, Q.: Feature-based model for automated identification of subjects and bystanders in photos. In: IEEE International Workshop on the Security, Privacy, and Digital Forensics of Mobile Systems and Networks (MobiSec) (2019)
8. Feng, Y., Wu, F., Shao, X., Wang, Y., Zhou, X.: Joint 3D face reconstruction and dense alignment with position map regression network. In: ECCV (2018)
9. Friedman, J.H.: Stochastic gradient boosting. Comput. Stat. Data Anal. **38**(4), 367–378 (2002). https://doi.org/10.1016/S0167-9473(01)00065-2, http://www.sciencedirect.com/science/article/pii/S0167947301000652, nonlinear Methods and Data Mining
10. Hasan, R., Crandall, D., Fritz, M., Kapadia, A.: Automatically detecting bystanders in photos to reduce privacy risks. In: IEEE Symposium on Security and Privacy (S and P), May 2020. https://publications.cispa.saarland/3051/
11. Hearst, M.A., Dumais, S.T., Osuna, E., Platt, J., Scholkopf, B.: Support vector machines. IEEE Intell. Syst. Appl. **13**(4), 18–28 (1998). https://doi.org/10.1109/5254.708428
12. Ilia, P., Polakis, I., Athanasopoulos, E., Maggi, F., Ioannidis, S.: Face/off: preventing privacy leakage from photos in social networks. In: Proceedings of the 22nd ACM SIGSAC Conference on Computer and Communications Security. (CCS 2015), pp. 781–792. Association for Computing Machinery, New York (2015). https://doi.org/10.1145/2810103.2813603

13. Jung, J., Philipose, M.: Courteous glass. In: Proceedings of the 2014 ACM International Joint Conference on Pervasive and Ubiquitous Computing: Adjunct Publication. (UbiComp 2014), pp. 1307–1312. Adjunct, Association for Computing Machinery, New York (2014). https://doi.org/10.1145/2638728.2641711

14. King, D.E.: Dlib-ml: a machine learning toolkit. J. Mach. Learn. Res. **10**, 1755–1758 (2009)

15. Le, V., Brandt, J., Lin, Z., Bourdev, L., Huang, T.S.: Interactive facial feature localization. In: Fitzgibbon, A., Lazebnik, S., Perona, P., Sato, Y., Schmid, C. (eds.) Computer Vision - ECCV 2012, pp. 679–692. Springer, Heidelberg (2012). https://doi.org/10.1007/978-3-642-33712-3_49

16. Li, A., Darling, D., Li, Q.: PhotoSafer: content-based and context-aware private photo protection for smartphones. In: IEEE Symposium on Privacy-Aware Computing (PAC), pp. 10–18 (2018)

17. Li, A., Du, W., Li, Q.: PoliteCamera: respecting strangers' privacy in mobile photographing. In: 2018 International Conference on Security and Privacy in Communication Networks (SecureComm) (2018)

18. Li, A., Li, Q., Gao, W.: PrivacyCamera: cooperative privacy-aware photographing with mobile phones. In: IEEE International Conference on Sensing, Communication, and Networking (SECON), pp. 1–9 (2016)

19. Li, F., Sun, Z., Li, A., Niu, B., Li, H., Cao, G.: HideMe: privacy-preserving photo sharing on social networks. In: IEEE INFOCOM 2019 - IEEE Conference on Computer Communications, pp. 154–162, April 2019. https://doi.org/10.1109/INFOCOM.2019.8737466

20. Pech-Pacheco, J.L., Cristobal, G., Chamorro-Martinez, J., Fernandez-Valdivia, J.: Diatom autofocusing in brightfield microscopy: a comparative study. In: Proceedings 15th International Conference on Pattern Recognition. ICPR-2000, vol. 3, pp. 314–317, September 2000. https://doi.org/10.1109/ICPR.2000.903548

21. Raval, N., Srivastava, A., Lebeck, K., Cox, L., Machanavajjhala, A.: Markit: privacy markers for protecting visual secrets. In: Proceedings of the 2014 ACM International Joint Conference on Pervasive and Ubiquitous Computing: Adjunct Publication. (UbiComp 2014), pp. 1289–1295. Adjunct, Association for Computing Machinery, New York (2014). https://doi.org/10.1145/2638728.2641707

22. Redmon, J., Farhadi, A.: YOLOv3: an incremental improvement (2018)

23. Richter, F.: Infographic: smartphones cause photography boom, August 2017. https://www.statista.com/chart/10913/number-of-photos-taken-worldwide/

24. Schiff, J., Meingast, M., Mulligan, D.K., Sastry, S., Goldberg, K.: Respectful cameras: detecting visual markers in real-time to address privacy concerns. In: 2007 IEEE/RSJ International Conference on Intelligent Robots and Systems, pp. 971–978, October 2007. https://doi.org/10.1109/IROS.2007.4399122

25. Wood, E., Baltruaitis, T., Zhang, X., Sugano, Y., Robinson, P., Bulling, A.: Rendering of eyes for eye-shape registration and gaze estimation. In: 2015 IEEE International Conference on Computer Vision (ICCV), pp. 3756–3764, December 2015. https://doi.org/10.1109/ICCV.2015.428

26. Xu, K., Guo, Y., Guo, L., Fang, Y., Li, X.: My privacy my decision: control of photo sharing on online social networks. IEEE Trans. Dependable Secure Comput. **14**(2), 199–210 (2017). https://doi.org/10.1109/TDSC.2015.2443795

27. Zadeh, A., Baltrušaitis, T., Morency, L.: Convolutional experts constrained local model for facial landmark detection. In: 2017 IEEE Conference on Computer Vision and Pattern Recognition Workshops (CVPRW), pp. 2051–2059 (2017)

SmartWiFi: Universal and Secure Smart Contract-Enabled WiFi Hotspot

Nikolay Ivanov, Jianzhi Lou, and Qiben Yan[✉]

Michigan State University, East Lansing, MI 48824, USA
{ivanovn1,loujianz,qyan}@msu.edu

Abstract. WiFi hotspots often suffer from mediocre security, unreliable performance, limited access, and cumbersome authentication procedure. Specifically, public WiFi hotspots can rarely guarantee satisfactory speed and uptime, and their configuration often requires a complicated setup with subscription to a payment aggregator. Moreover, paid hotspots can neither protect clients against low quality or non-service after pre-payment, nor do they provide an adequate defense against misuse by the clients. In this paper, we propose SMARTWiFi, a universal, secure, and decentralized WiFi hotspot that can be deployed in any public or private environment. SMARTWiFi provides cross-domain authentication, fully automated accounting and payments, and security assurance for both hotspots and clients. SMARTWiFi utilizes a novel off-chain transaction scheme called Hash Chain-based Network Connectivity Satisfaction Acknowledgement (HANSA), which enables fast and low-cost provider-client protocol by restricting otherwise unacceptable delays and fees associated with blockchain interaction. In addition, we present DUPSET, a dynamic user-perceived speed estimation technique, which can reliably evaluate the quality of Internet connection from the users' perspective. We design and implement SMARTWiFi desktop and mobile apps using an Ethereum smart contract. With extensive experimental evaluation, we demonstrate that SMARTWiFi exhibits rapid execution with low communication overhead and reduced fees.

Keywords: WiFi hotspot · Smart contract · Blockchain transaction

1 Introduction

The number of mobile Internet users have been steadily increasing, corroborating a pressing need for reliable wireless connectivity to be available everywhere, all the time. As opposed to cellular communications, WiFi provides a low-cost solution for wireless Internet access with a miniature infrastructure [14]. During the past two decades, WiFi has become the de facto standard for wireless local area networks (WLAN) and Internet-of-Things (IoT) [19].

The WiFi technology has been used to create hotspots to offer Internet access to users in their proximity. WiFi hotspots are typically seen in such venues as airports, cafes, hotels, etc. Private hotspots are often configured in enterprise, personal, and household networks to serve limited number of WiFi-enabled devices.

N. Park et al. (Eds.): SecureComm 2020, LNICST 335, pp. 425–445, 2020.
https://doi.org/10.1007/978-3-030-63086-7_23

Both public and private hotspots often require authentication and/or payment. Two or more hotspots belong to the same *authentication domain* if they share the same authentication server and, if applicable, share a payment server. Although a number of technologies have been introduced for cross-domain authentication, such as Passpoint [7] and eduroam [1], WiFi hotspots are still partitioned into a multitude of incompatible domains, which makes seamless WiFi roaming infeasible. In this work, we introduce a practical solution for a universal (i.e., cross-domain) and decentralized hotspot network, which addresses the domain partitioning problem. **Ultimately, we envision a fully automated cross-domain authentication between wireless APs provided by different businesses and private owners, forming a global permissionless decentralized network of free and paid hotspots.** However, in order to achieve this goal, a number of existing hotspots' shortcomings must be addressed.

Motivation. Despite its obvious benefits and popularity, the current WiFi hotspot technology experiences significant shortcomings: **M1)** *Security:* Public WiFi often eliminates password protection or conveys the passwords insecurely. **M2)** *Unreliable performance:* The speed of a WiFi hotspot largely depends on several unpredictable factors, such as the number of connected users or the bandwidth consumption of each individual user. Moreover, the hotspot owners generally have no incentive for upgrading hardware and service. **M3)** *Limited access:* Traditional WiFi hotspots do not offer a universal service for everyone. To be associated with a hotspot service, a user should be ascribed to a certain role or affiliation. The users' access to the service hinges upon their particular subscriptions. **M4)** *Cumbersome procedure or high infrastructure cost:* Connecting to a WiFi hotspot often requires extensive manual effort, such as: searching for SSID, entering payment details, specifying authentication settings, etc. Although WLAN direct IP access or 3GPP IP access enable easy configurations, they both rely on a heavy-cost cellular authentication infrastructure.

In this research, we envision that transferring the point of centralized trust from hotspot and/or client to a decentralized independent party, i.e., blockchain, enhances security of the connection and payment while simplifying the configuration procedure (to address **M1**). SMARTWiFi hotspot establishes the dependency between the Quality of Service (QoS) and payment, which creates an incentive for hotspot owners to deliver a high QoS (to address **M2**). The proposed hotspot technology is universal and accessible, i.e., it serves all clients who have means to pay, while also supporting unrestricted free WiFi hotspots (to address **M3**). The simplified configuration procedures offer a full automation of handshake, connection control, and checkout using the enforced execution of smart contract protocols without relying on complex server-based or cloud authentication infrastructure (to address **M4**).

Key Challenges. Designing a universal smart contract-enabled WiFi hotspot involves three major challenges. First, blockchain execution incurs significant processing delays, rendering the execution of many operations impossible within reasonable time limits. Second, blockchain offers very limited data storage. Third, blockchain networks charge considerable fees for executing block-modifying operations, e.g., payment transactions, smart contract deployments, smart contract state transitions, etc. In this paper, we present SMARTWiFi, the *first operational smart contract-enabled WiFi hotspot with automated cross-domain authentication*. SMARTWiFi leverages a novel *off-chain protocol* called Hash Chain-based Network Connectivity Satisfaction Acknowledgement (HANSA[1]) to manage secure and reliable connection. An off-chain protocol establishes communication between two entities using blockchain, but executes without any interaction with blockchain, which allows HANSA to enable a fast, low-cost, and low-overhead provider-client interaction with significant reduction of blockchain delays and fees.

In addition, we present DUPSET, a Dynamic User-Perceived Speed Estimation Technique, which reliably estimates the speed of Internet connection for client-side QoS control. Leveraging these novel techniques, we design and implement SMARTWiFi desktop and mobile apps using a smart contract executed by an Ethereum Virtual Machine (EVM). **A video demonstration of the SmartWiFi app is available at** https://youtu.be/jrDl204fGso. **The source code of the SmartWiFi smart contract is available at** https://bit.ly/2X5a4ez.

This paper makes the following main contributions.

– **Protocol Design.** To build SMARTWiFi, we propose HANSA, a novel cryptographic scheme that provides cross-domain authentication and establishes a smart contract-enabled off-chain session arrangement for a hotspot and a client. It provides a fast and low-cost smart contract execution by restricting blockchain transaction delays and fees. We also design DUPSET to quantify the QoS of Internet access provided by SMARTWiFi hotspots to clients. DUPSET allows SMARTWiFi clients to perform low-overhead bandwidth estimation to measure the quality of Internet connection.

– **System Implementation.** We implement operational prototypes of SMARTWiFi router and client that use Ethereum blockchain as a smart contract platform. Both components are cross-platform, hardware-agnostic, and can be easily deployed into existing infrastructure. In addition, we implement a fully-functional SMARTWiFi Android app, demonstrating the feasibility of deploying SMARTWiFi on non-rooted mobile platforms.

– **Experimental Evaluation.** We rigorously evaluate the delays, blockchain fees, and communication overhead of SMARTWiFi on Ropsten and Mainnet Ethereum networks. We also scrutinize the DUPSET technique by juxtaposing its measurements with the results from nine popular bandwidth measurement services. Furthermore, we evaluate the scalability of SMARTWiFi by demonstrating the stability of the system under the load of more than 100 simultaneous client processes connected to a single SMARTWiFi router.

---

[1] The name is inspired by the Hansa Trade League, which successfully operated under the power of mutual trust for over a century in a turbulent political and economic environment of Medieval Europe.

2   Background and Key Insights

2.1   Blockchain and Smart Contracts

Formally, *blockchain* is a distributed abstract data structure (ADS) represented by a list of objects (blocks), which are cryptographically linked in such a way that a modification of any block would require a chain recalculation (validation) of all subsequent blocks in the list. Consequently, any block-modifying operation, except *append*, draws a considerable execution time complexity. The block validation speed is deliberately throttled in the proof-of-work (PoW) consensus protocol employed by Ethereum, Bitcoin, and some other blockchains, making retrospective modifications of these blockchains nearly impossible. Practically, the term blockchain is used to refer to one of many peer-to-peer (P2P) networks that store, synchronize, and cross-validate their respective blockchain data structures. A *smart contract* is a distributed deterministic application, deployed on blockchain, and individually executed by the blockchain participants, with any associated data and results being part of the consensus. Therefore, smart contracts can establish, execute, and unequivocally enforce protocols and agreements between parties.

2.2   Threat Model

We consider a threat model with both malicious clients and malicious hotspots. Malicious clients would attempt to obtain Internet access without payment, which is regarded as *free-rider attack*. They could also try to bring significant performance degradation or complete shutdown of the hotspot. Malicious hotspots, on the other hand, aim to get payment from the clients without providing sufficient QoS.

We assume that hotspots and clients have no knowledge regarding their respective identities, and they have no pre-established trust. Moreover, the blockchain, smart contract, and its underlying cryptography are considered secure and trusted by hotspots and clients, i.e., we do not consider a wide range of attacks towards blockchain [12] and smart contracts [25].

2.3   Overview of Key Insights

Recognizing the shortcomings of existing WiFi hotspots, we bring forth a set of key insights that lead to the design of SMARTWiFi.

Off-Chain Interaction. High delays and fees in blockchain networks make it impossible to query the blockchain frequently for trust renewal. The idea of off-chain interaction, in which a smart contract is used by two or more parties as a guarantor of a protocol, but not as an executor of this protocol, has been proposed for fast and cheap payments [16, 21]. We extend this idea to WiFi hotspots by limiting the blockchain interaction to only handshake (session initiation) and payment resolution (session conclusion).

Cryptographic Satisfaction Acknowledgement. One of the key design goals of SMARTWiFi is to develop a protocol that would deliver a tamper-proof testimony of Internet usage time to the smart contract. The traditional approach is based on connection time and data size measurements performed by the provider itself, which relies on the assumption of its trustworthiness. However, a more comprehensive Internet traffic accounting is needed to ensure proper mutual agreement and non-repudiation. We design such a scheme using periodic cryptographically verifiable acknowledgements sent by the client to the hotspot. Each next acknowledgement testifies the client's satisfaction in the quality of the Internet connection during *a short period of time since the previous acknowledgement*, which we call a *session unit*. Each acknowledgement can be cryptographically verified by the smart contract and exchanged for funds reserved in the contract.

Hash Chain Data Compression. The cryptographically verifiable acknowledgements need to be stored in the smart contract, resulting in fees and consumption of computational time. Our key insight is to represent the set of acknowledgements by a hash chain, which can be generated from one random seed, and the verification of each acknowledgement will only require the head of the hash chain. Therefore, the smart contract only needs to store one hash value, i.e., the hash chain head, to verify a series of acknowledgements. We use hash chain based arrangement instead of signatures to eliminate the need to constantly use the private key by the client, which makes SMARTWiFi a safer option for unattended IoT devices.

Dynamic Speed Measurement. The satisfaction acknowledgement based protocol stipulates that the client evaluates the satisfiability of the Internet connection prior to sending an acknowledgement. Aiming for a fully-automated solution, we quantify the quality of the Internet connection using a dynamic speed measurement technique. Existing bandwidth estimation approaches require the transfer of a large amount of data, while we aim for frequent, fast, and low-overhead speed probes. Here, we simulate Internet activities using a set of HTTP servers deployed globally. The concept of measuring the speed of delivering an average web page, rather than consuming the available bandwidth, creates the possibility for frequent and low-overhead speed probes emulating actual user experience.

3   The SmartWiFi System

In this section, we present the design of the SMARTWiFi system. Unlike traditional WiFi hotspots, SMARTWiFi is a universal infrastructure that supports cross-domain authentication, i.e., anyone can use SMARTWiFi as a client or as a hotspot, while the smart contracts authenticate the users by their Eithereum account (generated offline and stored by user). In this work, we use Ethereum

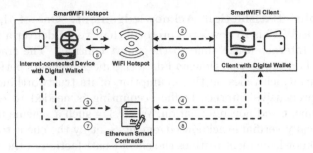

Fig. 1. SMARTWiFi workflow: ① an Internet-connected device (router) provides SMARTWiFi hotspot service; ② the client connects to the hotspot and sends it a hash chain head and its public address; ③ router provides a grace-period Internet access to the client and stores the public address in the smart contract; ④ client funds the smart contract; ⑤ router activates unrestricted Internet access for the client; ⑥ client periodically sends the router satisfaction acknowledgements (links of hash chain); ⑦ router claims payment from the smart contract using the last acknowledgement; ⑧ client is refunded by smart contract. *The dashed lines represent the HANSA protocol communications.*

as the target platform due to its relative maturity and wide popularity. Figure 1 depicts the basic building blocks of the SMARTWiFi system, which consists of six major components: SMARTWiFi router, the router's Ethereum wallet, the hotspot managed by the router, the client, the client's Ethereum wallet, and the smart contract.

SMARTWiFi is enabled by three main ingredients: the HANSA protocol, the DUPSET speed measurement, and the smart contract. The HANSA protocol establishes and maintains an Internet connection, and it includes two major sessions: handshake and service. Payment and refund are processed after the client-router connection terminates. While handshake, payment, and refund require interaction with blockchain, the service session is executed off-chain. DUPSET is a speed measurement technique that allows the clients to quantify their QoS satisfaction and continuously monitor the Internet access quality of SMARTWiFi. The smart contract is designed to process the payment and refund.

3.1   SmartWiFi Setup

SMARTWiFi uses a smart contract to serve as an intermediate trust layer to hold/release the payment and enforce fair behavior between the router and the client. SMARTWiFi also uses the router's firewall policy to control the clients' access privilege. The hotspot initiates SMARTWiFi service after the router performs the following steps: (1) SMARTWiFi router deploys several reusable smart contracts, the number of which equals the maximum number of concurrently-served clients; (2) the router establishes a two-way communication channel with every user; (3) the router activates a default firewall policy that allows every client to have a restricted access to required services, such as the blockchain

API. We define the *service period* as the period the client is connected to the Internet via a SMARTWiFi router, and the *service unit* as the minimum service period that the client will be charged for.

3.2 Hansa Handshake Session

In HANSA handshake session, the router and the client establish a relationship regulated and protected by the smart contract. HANSA protocol begins when the client connects to the hotspot and establishes a TCP connection with the SMARTWiFi router. The router replies with a greeting message, and the client generates a hash chain Υ using a random secret seed Υ_0. The length of the hash chain, denoted as $|\Upsilon|$, is calculated as $|\Upsilon| = \frac{T}{\eta}$, where T is the length of the service period, and η is the length of the service unit. For instance, in our prototype, the length of the service period is 3,600 s, and the length of the service unit is 60 s, i.e., one HANSA session serves a connection up to 1 h in length with per-minute acknowledgements.

The client keeps the seed of the hash chain in secret and sends the head of the hash chain Υ_{head} and the public address A_{pub} to the router. The router then prepares the smart contract by storing the public key of the client's public address and the head of the hash chain in the smart contract. After that, the router replies to the client with the address of the smart contract. Before executing prepayment, the client verifies the bytecode of the smart contract and the price per service unit ξ, which is hard-coded in the smart contract. Then, the client prepays the smart contract with the amount of cryptocurrency Ξ that corresponds to the cost of the entire service period, i.e., $\Xi = \xi \times \frac{T}{\eta}$. Once the prepayment is processed by the blockchain, the client and router enter the HANSA service session. If the price is unacceptable, the client terminates the connection.

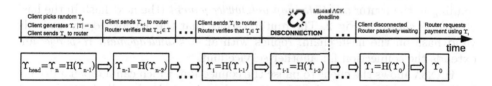

Fig. 2. HANSA timeline with respect to the hash chain Υ. In this scenario, the client disconnects after releasing acknowledgement Υ_i, and the acknowledgement Υ_{i-2} was not released. When the service session timer expires, the router uses the last available acknowledgement Υ_i to request payment from the smart contract.

3.3 Hansa Service Session

The HANSA service session begins after the router verifies that the client has funded the smart contract. Then follows the grace period, which seamlessly switches into an unrestricted Internet access. Meanwhile, the router sends the client a short message signifying the beginning of a service session, and both the client and router start service session timers.

Table 1. Summary of smart contract features required for executing HANSA.

Feature	Type	Access control	Security measure
Υ_{head} (hash chain head)	variable	rw-r--r--	timer
A_{pub} (public address)	variable	rw-r--r--	timer
ξ (price)	constant	rw-r--r--	read only
T (session length)	constant	r--r--r--	read only
τ (refund delay)	constant	r--r--r--	read only
η (session unit length)	constant	r--r--r--	read only
balance check	function	r-xr-xr-x	read only
Υ_{head}-accessor	function	r-xr-xr-x	read only
Υ_{head}-mutator	function	r-xr--r--	timer
A_{pub}-accessor	function	r-xr-xr-x	read only
A_{pub}-mutator	function	r-xr--r--	timer
prepay (fund)	p-function	r-xr-xr-x	none
checkout	function	r-xr--r--	Υ-check
refund	function	r--r-xr--	delay (τ)

Satisfaction Acknowledgement. Traditional paid WiFi hotspots charge users ahead of the service, and if the QoS is unacceptable, requesting refund is often challenging. We use cryptographic satisfaction acknowledgements to allow the client to control its service session and payment. The first service unit of a service session is regarded as a free trial, during which the client confirms that the Internet connection is active and starts measuring speed (described in Sect. 3.4). Before the end of each service unit, the client confirms a satisfactory QoS by sending to the router a *satisfaction acknowledgement* (the next hash in the hash chain), as shown in Fig. 2. The router verifies that the acknowledgement is the valid hash on the hash chain, replies with an *acknowledgement response*, and extends the connection for another service unit.

HANSA allows the client to pause the connection, which can happen automatically as a result of a speed probe, or can be triggered manually by the user. If the router does not receive the next acknowledgement on time, it deactivates the Internet access for the client. During the service period, the client can resume acknowledging the service, which will reactivate the Internet access, with a maximum reactivation delay η. The service session concludes when either the timer reaches the value T, or when the client-router connection breaks.

3.4   DupSet Speed Measurement

We present DUPSET, a bandwidth estimation solution that allows SMARTWiFi clients to quantify hotspots' QoS. SMARTWiFi is designed to operate in a flexible range of speeds and with different number of mobile or stationary users, so the bandwidth estimation should be frequent and with low overhead. Traditional

---

Algorithm 1. Smart contract payment routine

INPUT: Υ_{head}, Υ_i, ξ, t, T, η, A_{pub}
OUTPUT: none
1: **if** $\Upsilon_i \in \Upsilon$ **and** $caller = Router$ **and** $Timestamp \geq t + T$ **then**
2:     $RouterBalance \leftarrow i \times \xi$
3:     $RefundAmount \leftarrow (\frac{T}{\eta} - i) \times \xi$
4:     $TransferFunds(A_{pub}, RefundAmount)$
5: **end if**
6: **return**

---

speed evaluation methods include four metrics: capacity, available bandwidth, TCP throughput, and bulk transfer capacity (BTC) [22]. Although these techniques can provide very accurate results, they are not suitable for SMARTWiFi since they require lengthy probes and transfer of large amounts of data.

The core of DUPSET is a metric called *user-perceived speed*, represented by the transmission component of the throughput when loading an average web page. Measuring the transmission component, instead of the entire end-to-end communication, allows to achieve transparency with respect to different bandwidth uses, such as video streaming services or VPN traffic. DUPSET draws probes from pre-selected servers. Unlike many traditional bandwidth services, such as M-Lab [17] and Ookla [20], the DUPSET servers do not require to deliver high computational and throughput performance. Each probe calculates a statistical summary[2] of readings from all the reachable servers from the list. Then, the current DUPSET reading is calculated using a simple moving average[3].

Each DUPSET server is an HTTP server with two payload files with random information available for download. The size of the first file (P_1 bytes) is much greater than the size of the second file (P_2 bytes). The client loads both the files and calculates the difference between delays of downloading the first and the second file, which extracts the *transmission delay* from the total end-to-end delay. Then, the user-perceived speed reading (in bytes/second) for i^{th} server is determined as $Speed_i = \frac{EPF(P_1 - P_2)}{\Delta D_i}$, where EPF is the *Effective Payload Function* defined as follows:

$$EPF(x) = \begin{cases} 0, & \text{if } x \leq 0; \\ 0, & \text{if request failure;} \\ x, & \text{otherwise.} \end{cases}$$

ΔD_i is the time in seconds needed to load the file from the server i. The EPF function filters out unreliable results and ignores results from inaccessible DUPSET servers, so when one or several DUPSET servers are unavailable or provide unreliable readings, the accuracy of the DUPSET result is not affected.

---

[2] We experimentally found that the third quartile statistic achieves a better measurement accuracy compared to mean, median, and maximum.

[3] We empirically determine that simple moving average over 6 periods (SMA-6) delivers stable and reliable results.

3.5   SmartWiFi Smart Contract

The SMARTWiFi smart contract provides an overarching trust layer between the router and the client to exchange data and payments. The SMARTWiFi smart contract has the following components: a) state variables; b) state changing functions; c) cryptocurrency balance; and d) *payable function (p-function)* for incoming payments. The functions that do not submit transactions (*pure* and *view* functions) are called anonymously, whereas the calls to state changing functions are signed by a specific user (using the account's private key).

The minimal set of the SMARTWiFi smart contract features is summarized in Table 1, which includes constants, variables, functions, and one payable function. The access control to each feature is represented in the Unix-style symbolic access mode format, where the first triple refers to the router's privilege, the second triple is for user's privilege, and the third one is for others. The security column describes protective measures employed for each feature.

The price ξ, session length T, refund delay τ, and service unit length η are set as constants to reduce execution delays and fees. The smart contract has two variables for hash chain head Υ_{head} and client public address A_{pub}; they can only be set by the router using their mutators. The accessor and balance check functions are called without fees since they do not modify the blockchain. Both the mutators use timers to prevent the modification of the values they set. The values are protected using a timer for at least the duration of a HANSA session, including handshake, service session, and checkout. The timer plays two important roles: first, it prevents a malicious modification of Υ_{head} and A_{pub} by the router; second, it facilitates the reuse of the smart contract, thereby reducing blockchain fees and delays. The prepay function funds the smart contract. The checkout and refund functions include additional security checks as depicted in Algorithms 1 and 2, which will be described next.

3.6   Payment and Refund

The fair payment and refund procedures are automatically enforced by the SMARTWiFi smart contract. The smart contract holds the amount of cryptocurrency Ξ, sufficient for funding one HANSA session. The router is prohibited from claiming its payment until the blockchain timestamp reaches the value $t + T$, where t is the saved timestamp at the beginning of the service session. Algorithm 1 shows how the payment is executed. The inputs include: the hash chain head Υ_{head}, last retrieved acknowledgement Υ_i, price ξ (stored as a constant in smart contract), timestamp t (saved during handshake), service session length T (constant), session unit length η, and the user's public address A_{pub}. The router obtains the payment based on the depth of Υ_i, and the remaining funds are transferred back to the client as a refund.

The execution of lines 2–4 in Algorithm 1 can only be triggered by the router. In case when the router does not request any payment, the client may never receive any refund, for which case we design an additional refund routine,

---

Algorithm 2. Smart contract refund routine

INPUT: Υ_{head}, ξ, t, T, η, τ, A_{pub}
OUTPUT: none
1: **if** $caller.address = A_{pub}$ **and** $Timestamp \geq t + T + \tau$ **then**
2:     $RefundAmount \leftarrow \frac{T}{\eta} \times \xi$
3:     $TransferFunds(A_{pub}, RefundAmount)$
4: **end if**
5: **return**

---

described in Algorithm 2. The execution of the actual refund (lines 2–3) is permitted only by the client after the pre-determined refund delay τ, which prevents refund before payment described in Sect. 4.

4   Security Analysis

The security threats of SMARTWiFi come either from malicious clients or from malicious hotspots/routers. In this section, we analyze the security of SMARTWiFi.

Non-service by Malicious Hotspot. The goal of the client is to have a satisfying Internet connection for the money paid. If the high-quality service is not provided, full or partial refund should be guaranteed. A malicious router might refuse a service, i.e., to receive a payment without providing a quality connection. To counteract such a behavior, the SMARTWiFi client uses DUPSET to assess the quality of Internet connection before sending each subsequent acknowledgement, while the SMARTWiFi smart contract guarantees a full or partial refund.

Refund Before Payment. The router expects to be fairly paid after the connection period is over. The goal of the client, who prepaid the smart contract with one whole period worth of money, is to receive a refund for all service units that do not result in satisfaction acknowledgement. *Refund before payment* indicates the case when a malicious client claims no service received and asks for a full refund. In SMARTWiFi, this threat is prevented by the refund delay τ for the router to claim payment, during which the refund is impossible.

Handshake Flooding. The handshake of SMARTWiFi is prone to denial-of-service attacks. The goal of the adversary in the handshake flooding attack is to render the router unavailable or degrade its performance. This can be achieved by initiating multiple incomplete handshakes, in which the attacker, pretending to be a valid client, forces the router to submit values to the smart contract, for which the blockchain charges fees. In SMARTWiFi, this attack is prevented by checking the balance of the client before preparing the smart contract for that client. SMARTWiFi router also curbs the number of clients to serve: once the number of requests exceeds the maximum, SMARTWiFi starts dropping requests.

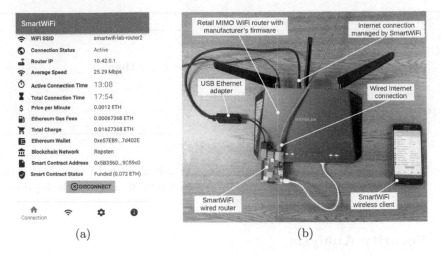

(a)   (b)

Fig. 3. SMARTWiFi prototype: (a) The connection page of the SMARTWiFi Android app; (b) SMARTWiFi configuration with a wired Internet connection, Raspberry Pi as a SMARTWiFi router, retail WiFi router with factory software, and Android smartphone as a SMARTWiFi client.

Free-Rider Attack (Non-payment). The existence of the free trial in SMART-WiFi allows any user who funds the contract to gain one service unit of Internet connectivity without providing an acknowledgement. A dedicated attacker may use multiple client devices to interchangeably connect to the router, use the free trial period (1 min in this paper), disconnect without providing any acknowledgements, tunnel the traffic to the same outlet, and then request a full refund. We define such connection misuse as *traffic hopping*, which is a special case of the free-rider attack. In SMARTWiFi, we prevent such threats by relying on the accruing blockchain fees. As the creation of new malicious nodes (i.e., Sybil nodes) will require the attacker to transfer funds into multiple accounts and pay fees for each funding transaction, such fees, after being summed up from multiple accounts, will nullify the benefits of the free riding. After the free trial, the router expects to receive regular satisfaction acknowledgements. Each acknowledgement from a client is expected to arrive before a strict deadline, otherwise, the Internet connection will be terminated by the router.

5 Implementation

We implement a fully-functional SMARTWiFi prototype on a Netgear router and Raspberry Pi clients for testing the general functionality and performance of the system. In addition, we implement an Android SMARTWiFi client app, as shown in Fig. 3(a), for testing the performance of SMARTWiFi on mobile devices. The client app can be easily ported to iOS. We use Java 11 and Web3j for implementing the software of the router, the desktop/IoT client, and the Android client. We use Infura API [6] to interact with Ethereum blockchain.

Figure 3(b) shows one possible configuration of SMARTWiFi, in which SMART-WiFi router software is installed on Raspberry Pi with two Ethernet interfaces: one for Internet connection, another for delivering the Internet to the WiFi router. The retail WiFi router runs its original software; the configuration of this router includes TCP port 5566 forwarding in order to allow connected devices to access the SMARTWiFi router. The client in this configuration is an ordinary Android smartphone without rooting. This configuration ensures SMARTWiFi's compatibility with legacy systems, i.e., we can easily deploy SMARTWiFi by plugging in a device running SMARTWiFi router software.

We implement a prototype SMARTWiFi Ethereum smart contract using Solidity programming language. In our prototype and evaluation, we use both Mainnet and Ropsten testnet for executing the smart contracts. Furthermore, we build an IoT testbed with five Raspberry Pi clients simultaneously connected to a single-antenna all-in-one SMARTWiFi router (AMD A4 Micro-6400T, 4 GB RAM, Xubuntu 18.04). This setup demonstrates that SMARTWiFi *can be easily adapted to support a diverse variety of IoT configurations.*

6 Evaluation

We thoroughly evaluate the performance of the SMARTWiFi prototype by scrutinizing the following system parameters under different circumstances: blockchain-related delays, Ethereum gas fees, smart contract storage, the accuracy of DUPSET speed probes, the scalability of the system, and the communication overhead. In Ethereum, all blockchain-modifying transactions require the caller to pay fees measured in the unit named *gas*, which is convertible into Ether using a dynamic variable called *gas price*. In our evaluation, the service session lasts for one hour ($T = 3,600\,\mathrm{s}$), and the service unit is one minute ($\eta = 60\,\mathrm{s}$).

6.1 Delays

In this section, we evaluate the blockchain-related delays of SMARTWiFi sessions in both Mainnet and Ropsten Ethereum networks. We add the Ropsten testnet for comparison to demonstrate the performance stability of SMARTWiFi under Ethereum networks with different amounts of mining hash power. Thus, we show that if the parameters of the blockchain change in the future, it will not significantly affect the performance of SMARTWiFi. For each type of blockchain-related delays, ten measurements have been taken. The average delays (with standard deviations) for Ropsten and Mainnet are presented in Table 2, from which we observe similar delays in both the networks.

The connection initiation phase, in which no blockchain interaction occurs, takes a few seconds on average; after this phase the user can start accessing the Internet. The handshake phase, whose average delay is below one minute for both Ropsten and Mainnet, initiates the payment arrangement. The code check phase, which requires only a non-modifying blockchain operation, also takes a

Table 2. Comparison of blockchain-related average delays (in seconds) with relatively high gas price (100 GWei for Ropsten and 5 GWei for Mainnet).

Delay type	Ropsten Testnet		Ethereum Mainnet	
	d_{avg}	σ	d_{avg}	σ
Connection initiation	3.965	0.177	4.161	0.202
Handshake	39.093	18.504	53.161	16.432
Bytecode verification	4.268	0.376	4.291	0.360
Funding	23.629	17.711	25.449	14.519
Payment	30.729	23.208	31.512	17.304
Refund	33.194	23.640	37.521	23.006

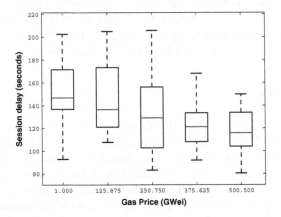

Fig. 4. Full session delays with different gas prices in Ropsten network. The graph has a logarithmic gas price axis, and it shows that while it is empirically true that offering more gas increases the chance of faster transaction, the speed improvement is insignificant.

few seconds in delay. The smart contract funding phase is essentially a cryptocurrency transaction, which requires more time than a read-only blockchain request. Similarly, payment and refund routines, although demanding additional calculations and checks, demonstrate delays just a little longer than a simple Ether transfer. In summary, to connect to a SMARTWiFi router and start Internet access, *the client only experiences a few seconds of connection initiation delay*, which is completely acceptable.

The delay of blockchain execution in the Ethereum network can be further reduced by increasing the gas price offered for a transaction [13]. However, such a performance optimization is not guaranteed [24]. First, the Ethereum blockchain protocol does not enforce the prioritization of incoming transactions, leaving this decision to the discretion of miners. Second, since Ethereum is a decentralized network, the increase of transaction execution speed adopts a best-effort approach. Here, we conduct an empirical testing to evaluate the delays with respect

Table 3. Gas fees for different functions of the SMARTWiFi smart contract. Since SMARTWiFi uses an off-chain execution protocol with infrequent smart contract transactions, the resulting fee overhead drops significantly.

Function	Transaction fee with recommended gas price [2]	
	Gas	Approx. USD
A_{pub}-accessor	0	0
A_{pub}-mutator	28,366	0.11
Υ_{head}-accessor	0	0
Υ_{head}-mutator	33,684	0.13
Balance check	0	0
Payment	50,076	0.20
Refund	42,266	0.17
Fund contract	21,040	0.08
Download contract bytecode	0	0

to different gas prices, the result of which, presented in Fig. 4, demonstrates a slight but consistent reduction of total SMARTWiFi session delays as the gas price increases, which shows the possibility of reducing delays by offering a higher gas price. However, given the increasing cost, the delay reduction may not be worthwhile.

6.2 Fees

In this section, we measure the gas fees per transaction when a public function of the SMARTWiFi smart contract is called. In order to exclude the possibility of variable fees, we take every measurement twice, and confirm that the cost remains the same for both measurements. The summary of gas fees is presented in Table 3. The address accessor, hash chain head accessor, balance check, and bytecode download are read-only blockchain operations, which do not incur any fees. However, the mutators and payable functions require the caller to pay fees. The fees in Table 3 are calculated for one 60-min service session, with 1-min service units.

Ethereum allows the issuer of a transaction to offer an arbitrary gas price to prioritize the transaction. Similar to the delay-measuring experiment in Fig. 4, we record fees over 10 measurements on Ropsten network for a more realistic 10 gas prices equally spread across the interval between 0.5 and 5.0 GWei. The cumulative fee (for both router and client) is less than $0.4, even with the highest gas price and ETH market price. Since the highest gas price is used rarely in production systems, the fee overhead is expected to be significantly lower then the maximum.

It is important to note that the cryptocurrency market price variations have little effect on SMARTWiFi fee overhead. Ethereum is a dynamic self-regulating system, so when the market price of Ether goes up, the users can afford less, and they offer smaller fees for transactions, which results in lower average gas price, and vice versa [13]. The curve of resulting fee in USD is thus smoothed and flattened. Therefore, regardless of any cryptocurrency price fluctuations, SMARTWiFi blockchain *fees paid in USD will remain approximately the same.*

6.3   Smart Contract Storage

Table 4 shows a comparison between data stored in the SMARTWiFi smart contract with and without hash chain compression, from which we can see that the hash chain in HANSA stores about 17 times less data in the smart contract, effectively reducing per-session delays. Moreover, it also reduces per-session fees from \$8 to about 40¢ in USD equivalent, which corroborates the feasibility of SMARTWiFi in terms of low cost.

Table 4. Data stored in the smart contract per session $(T = 3,600, \eta = 60)$.

Data unit	Stored data per session	
	With hash chain	Without hash chain
Acknowledgement data	32 bytes	1,920 bytes
Client identity	20 bytes	20 bytes
Auxiliary data	64 bytes	64 bytes
Total	116 bytes	2,004 bytes

6.4   DupSet Measurement and Overhead

In this section, we evaluate the feasibility of DUPSET by comparing our estimations with the average readings obtained from nine popular Internet speed measurement services, specifically: Bandwidth Place, DSLReports, Fast.com, Google Fiber, Internet Health Test, M-Lab, Ookla, Speed-Of.Me, and Xfinity. We test ten different SMARTWiFi router Internet connections belonging to different speed tiers, and evaluate average speeds of each of these connections by taking six speed test probes at each of the nine services listed above. The six speed test probes consist of three probes per service before running the DUPSET simulation, and three probes per service right after the DUPSET simulation.

In our prototype setup, we deploy ten DUPSET servers in different geographic locations. In order to achieve further diversity in measurements, we use servers provided by two different cloud services, DigitalOcean [5] and Vultr [15]. For each Internet connection, we run 60 probes of DUPSET for measuring the transmission speed component from each of the servers based on the payload of 10 kbytes. The fastest reading from the ten servers represents the speed result of a probe.

The experiment confirms that the low-overhead DUPSET estimations correlate with the high-overhead traditional Internet speed readings. Figure 5 shows

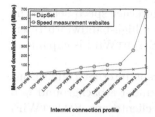

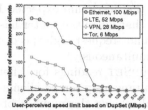

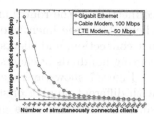

Fig. 5. Correlation between traditional Internet speed measurement (average result from nine websites) and DUPSET probes over 10 different Internet connection profiles.

Fig. 6. Maximum number of clients simultaneously served by the router for 15 min under different Internet connectivities, with random web surfing simulation in the background.

Fig. 7. Average DUPSET readings for different types of Internet connection profiles with different number of clients simultaneously served by a SMARTWiFi router.

that DUPSET speed measurement results accurately reflect the Internet connection speed tier, which quantifies the QoS of user service. The spiked increase in the gap between the two readings at high speeds demonstrates the core difference between traditional bandwidth measurements and user-perceived speed estimation: a drastic increase in available bandwidth after a certain threshold does not trigger a proportional boost in loading web pages. In a high-speed Internet, the performance bottleneck moves from the client to the server.

The overall maximum communication overhead of DUPSET probes depends on the number of DUPSET servers and the size of payload on any of these servers. In our prototype, we empirically select a 10-kbyte DUPSET payload and 10 DUPSET servers, resulting in 100-kbyte maximum overhead per probe, or approximately 6 Mb of overhead per one-hour session. Through this experiment, we demonstrate that DUPSET *probes reflect accurate user-perceived speed with low overhead.*

A SMARTWiFi client uses DUPSET to control minimum expected speed. Since different users may have different minimum speed requirements at different times (e.g, watching stream video needs higher speed than reading e-mail), it is required from the users to explicitly specify their expectations in the client settings. In the SMARTWiFi Android app, for example, we let the user choose between 5 discrete options.

6.5 Scalability

SMARTWiFi is designed to scale to multiple clients connecting to a single router. We evaluate the performance of the system under the load of different numbers of users. For each client, we perform a background web surfing simulation that picks and loads a random website from the Alexa Top 10K list [11] every 10 s. Figure 6 shows the number of clients one router could serve without disconnection. As we can see, this capacity depends on the bandwidth of the Internet connection of the router and the maximum expected Internet speed set by the client. The experiment shows that when the router has a high-bandwidth Internet connection, and clients do not request high speed, SMARTWiFi is capable of serving hundreds of clients simultaneously[4].

Figure 7 shows average DUPSET readings for different Internet connections with different number of simultaneously served clients under a background web surfing simulation. The graph shows the number of clients one SMARTWiFi router can serve based on its Internet connection bandwidth and average speed expectations. For example, it will be overly ambitious for a SMARTWiFi router with 100 Mbps connection to serve 40 users whose average speed expectation is 2 Mbps. However, if the expectation is reduced to 1 Mbps, serving 40 users simultaneously will likely be a realistic projection.

6.6 SmartWiFi Communication Overhead

The *communication overhead* includes the client-router TCP traffic and the Infura blockchain API communication. We measure overhead by capturing network traffic and calculating a cumulative one-hour session TCP payload using Wireshark. Each session's average result is based on 10 measurements. The results in Table 5 demonstrate that the overhead of off-chain communication is low compared to the results for blockchain-related calls.

Table 5. Session communication overhead for different SMARTWiFi calls over 10 measurements. The *local* calls represent off-chain communication between the hotspot and the client, including handshake E_h, connection initiation E_c, connection status check E_s, and acknowledgement E_a. *Blockchain* (B/C) calls use Infura API [6].

Procedure call	Avg TCP payload (bytes)	σ
Local: E_h	580	20
Local: E_c	412	0
Local: E_s	274	9
Local: E_a	334	8
B/C: download bytecode	69,797	32,633
B/C: A_{pub}-accessor	51,597	38,224
B/C: A_{pub}-mutator	51,279	34,389
B/C: Υ_{head}-accessor	50,472	33,205
B/C: Υ_{head}-mutator	60,606	36,489
B/C: balance check	64,487	46,150
B/C: payment	45,326	28,016
B/C: refund	59,500	41,856
B/C: fund contract	56,834	39,542

---

[4] The growing number of users incurs higher rate of physical layer packet collisions. One way to mitigate this is to use MIMO WiFi access point hardware.

7 Related Work

Traditional WiFi Hotspot Solutions. Current non-blockchain WiFi hotspot solutions are represented either by manual setups, or cloud-managed subscription-based proprietary products, such as Cisco Meraki [3], Aruba [4], Ruckus [9], etc. However, none of these approaches addresses the set of objectives achieved by SMARTWiFi, namely: a) enhancing hotspot security against malicious routers *and* clients; b) providing universal authentication and billing; and c) making payment based on service quality.

Blockchain Solutions. The most relevant work to SMARTWiFi is a use case in OPPay [23], a peer-to-peer opportunistic data service system. However, the OPPay-based solution is impractical for a WiFi hotspot, as it incurs high fees and does not offer QoS measurement for sustaining a reliable service. A commercial project WinQ [10] has been in development since 2016. Advertised as a blockchain-enabled mobile WiFi hotspot, the solution was intended to operate on its own blockchain called QLC Chain [8]. We installed both the Android and iOS apps to discover that the system is activated only on testnet blockchain, which was practically unavailable.

Dynamic Speed Evaluation. QDASH was proposed for dynamic speed measurement [18], which is based on the assumption that the user traffic is available to the client connection handler. This requirement makes QDASH and its derivatives unsuitable for use by SMARTWiFi clients. Xylophone [26] observes the behavior of TCP ACK and RST packets for speed measurement. Although the technique accurately estimates the bandwidth, it requires extended permissions for the client to capture TCP packets, which are usually not available on Android and iOS without rooting/jailbreaking.

8 Conclusion

In this paper, we proposed SMARTWiFi, a smart contract-enabled WiFi hotspot system, which provides universal accessibility, cross-domain authentication, association of QoS and payment, and security enhancement. SMARTWiFi utilizes a novel cryptographic mechanism, HANSA, to establish connection. HANSA provides low-cost off-chain execution by restricting otherwise unacceptable smart contract fees, and significantly reduces delays associated with smart contract interaction. To validate the feasibility of SMARTWiFi system, we designed and implemented a SMARTWiFi prototype using an Ethereum smart contract. The experimental results show that SMARTWiFi exhibits low operational delays, minimum communication overhead, and small blockchain fees. We demonstrated that SMARTWiFi is a scalable, secure, and efficient WiFi hotspot solution, which can be easily deployed in a variety of systems with minimal intervention. The limited adoption of cryptocurrencies and the volatility of their market prices can be further addressed through the use of stablecoin tokens, which we leave for future work.

Acknowledgement. We would like to thank the anonymous reviewers for providing valuable feedback on our work. This work was supported in part by National Science Foundation grants CNS1950171 and CNS-1949753.

References

1. eduroam - World Wide Education Roaming for Research & Education. https://www.eduroam.org/. Accessed 10 May 2020
2. ETH Gas Station. https://ethgasstation.info/. Accessed 17 May 2020
3. Cisco meraki for sp public wifi (2019). http://marketo.meraki.com/rs/010-KNZ-501/images/Meraki_for_SP_Public_WiFi.pdf. Accessed 03 Apr 2020
4. Cloud managed networking (2019). https://www.arubanetworks.com/solutions/cloud-managed/. Accessed 10 Apr 2020
5. Digitalocean (2019). https://www.digitalocean.com. Accessed 03 Apr 2020
6. Infura: scalable blockchain infrastructure (2019). https://github.com/INFURA. Accessed 03 Apr 2020
7. Passpoint (2019). https://www.wi-fi.org/discover-wi-fi/passpoint. Accessed 03 Apr 2020
8. Qlc chain (2019). https://medium.com/qlc-chain/chain/home. Accessed 03 Apr 2020
9. Ruckus cloud wi-fi (2019). https://www.ruckuswireless.com/products/system-management-control/cloud-wifi. Accessed 03 Apr 2020
10. Winq (2019). https://winq.net/. Accessed 03 Apr 2020
11. Amazon Web Services, I.: Alexa top sites (2019). https://docs.aws.amazon.com/AlexaTopSites/latest/MakingRequestsChapter.html. Accessed 03 Apr 2020
12. Bonneau, J., Miller, A., Clark, J., Narayanan, A., Kroll, J.A., Felten, E.W.: SoK: research perspectives and challenges for bitcoin and cryptocurrencies. In: 2015 IEEE Symposium on Security and Privacy, pp. 104–121 (2015)
13. Buterin, V.: A next-generation smart contract and decentralized application platform. White paper (2014)
14. Chiang, M.: How WiFi is different from cellular. In: Networked Life: 20 Questions and Answers, pp. 406–409. Cambridge University Press, New York (2012)
15. Corporation, V.H.: Vultr (2019). https://www.vultr.com. Accessed 03 Apr 2020
16. Eberhardt, J., Tai, S.: On or off the blockchain? Insights on off-chaining computation and data. In: De Paoli, F., Schulte, S., Broch Johnsen, E. (eds.) ESOCC 2017. LNCS, vol. 10465, pp. 3–15. Springer, Cham (2017). https://doi.org/10.1007/978-3-319-67262-5_1
17. M-Lab: Measurement lab speed test (2019). https://speed.measurementlab.net. Accessed 03 Apr 2020
18. Mok, R.K., Luo, X., Chan, E.W., Chang, R.K.: QDASH: a QoE-aware DASH system. In: Proceedings of the 3rd Multimedia Systems Conference, pp. 11–22 (2012)
19. Molisch, A.F.: Wireless Communications, 2nd edn., p. 14. Wiley, New York (2011)

20. Ookla, L.: Ookla lab speed test (2019). https://www.speedtest.net. Accessed 03 Apr 2020
21. Poon, J., Dryja, T.: The bitcoin lightning network: scalable off-chain instant payments (2016)
22. Prasad, R., Dovrolis, C., Murray, M., Claffy, K.: Bandwidth estimation: metrics, measurement techniques, and tools. IEEE Network **17**(6), 27–35 (2003)
23. Shi, F., Qin, Z., McCann, J.A.: OPPay: design and implementation of a payment system for opportunistic data services. In: 2017 IEEE 37th International Conference on Distributed Computing Systems (ICDCS), pp. 1618–1628 (2017)
24. Signer, C.: Gas Cost Analysis for Ethereum Smart Contracts. Master's thesis, ETH Zurich, Department of Computer Science (2018)
25. Tsankov, P., Dan, A., Drachsler-Cohen, D., Gervais, A., Buenzli, F., Vechev, M.: Securify: practical security analysis of smart contracts. In: Proceedings of the 2018 ACM SIGSAC Conference on Computer and Communications Security, pp. 67–82 (2018)
26. Xing, X., Dang, J., Mishra, S., Liu, X.: A highly scalable bandwidth estimation of commercial hotspot access points. In: 2011 Proceedings IEEE INFOCOM, pp. 1143–1151 (2011)

ByPass: Reconsidering the Usability of Password Managers

Elizabeth Stobert[1], Tina Safaie[2(✉)], Heather Molyneaux[3],
Mohammad Mannan[2], and Amr Youssef[2]

[1] Carleton University, Ottawa, ON, Canada
elizabeth.stobert@carleton.ca
[2] Concordia University, Montreal, QC, Canada
t_safaie@encs.concordia.ca,m.mannan@concordia.ca,
youssef@ciise.concordia.ca
[3] National Research Council of Canada, Fredericton, NB, Canada
heather.molyneaux@nrc-cnrc.gc.ca

Abstract. Since passwords are an unavoidable mechanism for authenticating to online services, experts often recommend using a password manager for better password security. However, adoption of password managers is low due to poor usability, the difficulty of migrating accounts to a manager, and users' sense that a manager will not add value. In this paper, we present ByPass, a novel password manager that is placed between the user and the website for secure and direct communication between the manager and websites. This direct communication allows ByPass to minimize the users' actions needed to complete various password management tasks, including account registration, logins, and password changes. ByPass is designed to minimize errors and improve usability. We conducted a usability evaluation of ByPass and found that this approach shows promising usability, and can help users to better manage their accounts in a secure manner.

Keywords: Authentication · Usable security · Password manager · API

1 Introduction

Password-based online services are ubiquitous, despite many known security and usability limitations of passwords [10,19]. Password managers can alleviate some of these drawbacks by removing the need for people to memorize a large number of strong passwords, helping users cope with different password policies, creating unique passwords and providing protection features against some attacks (e.g., phishing). However, adoption of password managers is low, and even among password manager users, many still do not use them effectively [27].

Previous studies of password managers [3,5] show that usability issues can contribute to low adoption. While several studies [7,26] have investigated different ways to improve the usability of password managers, the basic wallet

N. Park et al. (Eds.): SecureComm 2020, LNICST 335, pp. 446–466, 2020.
https://doi.org/10.1007/978-3-030-63086-7_24

structure of the password manager has remained the same. In all of them, a password manager is regarded as client-side software that helps users store and fill passwords on a targeted website without the website recognizing whether it is the user who is filling the password field or a software program.

In this work, we investigate how the design of password managers can be rethought to facilitate adoption and minimize usability problems. We design and develop ByPass, a new password manager that sits between the user and the website, reducing friction resulting from usability problems. ByPass uses an API for direct communication between the website and password manager, which allows the password manager to not only directly send credentials to the website, but also to query the website for information such as the password policy. In addition, this communication channel allows the introduction of innovative features, such as automated password changes, and account creation/deletion through the password manager. The primary goal of ByPass is to provide a more usable password management system that encourages users to behave securely. ByPass integrates nudges for secure behaviour, and is designed to make tasks such as account migration and password changes as simple as possible.

No work so far has focused on using APIs within the password manager development. Our key contribution is developing a password manager with new capabilities resulting from different API calls from the websites. Although this approach requires buy-in from websites, it results in increased password manager usability resulting from fewer actions required by the user. Assuming the integration of password-based online services, in ByPass, we shift the focus to comprehensive *account management* instead of current approaches to *password management*, primarily limited to create/save/fill passwords. We address critical security limitations of current password managers, and at the same time, improve ease of use and control over numerous accounts that a typical user needs to manage.

In this paper, we focused on ByPass's impact on end users. We evaluated the usability of our prototype implementation of ByPass by conducting a study with 20 participants. We found that participants were able to quickly and easily add new accounts to ByPass, migrate existing accounts into the manager, and change their passwords. Users were generally positive about the features in ByPass, but expressed concerns about the ways in which ByPass moves the locus of control.

With ByPass, our goal is not to create yet another password manager. We want this new design, along with the results of our prototype evaluation, to act as a vehicle for investigating more fundamental questions about account management. Password managers, while seeming to be one of the most accessible solutions to the password problem, have not been widely adopted. This suggests that a new approach to password management is needed: users need to be empowered with tools to effectively access and manage the security of their accounts by relieving them of tasks more easily completed by a computer.

2   Background

Password managers are software tools primarily designed to save users' passwords. Modern password managers range in sophistication from browser-based managers that save and fill users' passwords, to more complex standalone programs (e.g., 1Password[1], and Lastpass[2]) that integrate features such as customizable password generation, security audits, and family password sharing. Almost all managers are designed based on a *wallet* model, where the central function is to manage a list of passwords, protected by a master password. The security and usability of password managers have been studied extensively.

2.1 Security of Password Managers

By saving all passwords in one place, password managers create a central point of failure in a user's security ecosystem. Although various proposals have been made for password managers that mitigate this problem [16,29,34,36], the majority of commercially-available password managers are vulnerable in this way. The prevalence of such attacks is unclear, but it is compounded by the likelihood that users will choose insecure and easily-guessed master passwords [38].

Silver et al. [33] studied auto-fill password policies among different types of password managers. Although the auto-fill function can increase the usability of password managers, poor implementation of this function can lead to exposure of users' credentials. They also described the *sweep* attack, which requires the attacker to have control over the user's WiFi (e.g., in a public hotspot run/controlled by the attacker); the attacker can extract the user's credentials by injecting malicious JavaScript to the website without the user noticing.

Li et al. [22] analyzed five third-party web-based password managers, revealing four security vulnerabilities—including classical web application vulnerabilities such as Cross Site Scripting (XSS) and Cross Site Request Forgery (CSRF). They also analyzed authorization and user interface vulnerabilities, and proposed guidelines to mitigate these identified issues.

Recently, Carr and Shahandashti [11] revisited various known attacks on password managers, and analyzed whether password managers are still vulnerable to those attacks. They also identified four new vulnerabilities: phishing attacks, clipboard vulnerability, PIN brute force vulnerability (for applications), and brute force via an extension (evaluated against five popular commercial password managers). Their results showed that all of the tested password managers were vulnerable to at least one of the attacks they considered.

2.2 Usability of Password Managers

Chiasson et al. [14] conducted an early usability evaluation of two types of password manager, and found that users' poor mental models of password managers caused them to make dangerous errors. Karole, Saxena and Christin [21] compared a third-party password manager to a phone-based manager and a USB manager. They found that users preferred the control implicit in having passwords stored on a local device.

---

[1] https://www.1password.com/.
[2] https://www.lastpass.com/.

There are a variety of factors leading to the low adoption of password managers. Aurigemma et al. [5] found that insufficient time for installation, lack of immediacy, and users' feeling that using a password manager needs an additional effort that they don't want to spend contributed to password manager non-adoption. Maclean and Ophoff [25] found that trust, habit, and performance expectancy are the three factors that lead to the use of password managers. Pearman et al. [27] interviewed 30 participants, including people who choose not to use a password manager, about their password manager use (and non-use). They found that factors such as lack of awareness and poor understanding of how password managers work prevent people from adopting password managers. They found that users could be divided into two categories: people for whom convenience is a priority, and people for whom security is a priority.

Seiler-Hwang et al. [31] analyzed the usability of smartphone password managers and suggested security, user interaction, and integration with external applications as three key areas for improvement. They mentioned that only knowing about the password manager's existence is not enough to motivate an individual to use it. Users need to be encouraged to install and try password managers. Alkaldi and Renaud [3] identified three phases to user adoption of password managers: searching, trialling, and deciding. They later explored how self-determination theory can be used to encourage users to adopt password managers, and found that recommender tools can cause users to at least search for and try password managers [4].

Lyastani et al. [24] studied whether using a password manager can influence password strength and re-use. They used a browser extension to collect data on different password entry methods. Participants who used technical support for password creation had stronger passwords. They concluded that password generators improve security, but are under-adopted, highlighting the need to rethink password manager workflows.

2.3   Proposals for New Password Managers

A number of studies have designed new tools to address existing problems with password management. McCarney et al. [26] created Tapas, a dual possession, theft-resistant password manager in which an adversary needs to gain access to both devices in order to read the saved credentials. In their design, both devices – a mobile phone and a desktop computer – must be available in order to use the password manager, and the user does not need to have any master password. Barbosa et al. [7] designed UniPass, a password manager for visually impaired users. UniPass allowed users with visual impairment to access their accounts and passwords more effectively and to use public computers. Although not positioned directly as a password manager, Ruoti and Seamons [30] propose a system in which passwords are stored in the operating system, and verified (using zero-knowledge proofs) by an independent password checking service. The system minimizes the interaction between users and passwords, as well as the attack surface for passwords.

3   ByPass: Design and Implementation

ByPass is designed to address usability problems that prevent users from adopting password managers while maintaining good security properties. In this section, we discuss the design of ByPass, features supported and introduced by it, and our prototype implementation.

3.1   Design Overview and Goals

ByPass is designed to reduce friction in password managers resulting from usability problems. Our insight is that many of the usability problems with password managers result from the password manager functioning as an intermediary between the user and the regular login page. Copy/paste errors, form fills happening to the wrong field, leakage of passwords from the paste buffer, all result from placing the password manager as an external resource, accessible only by the user and not the website. Traditional password managers offer little conceptual advantage beyond a list of written passwords, and in doing so, miss an opportunity to genuinely address the usability problems with passwords and add value beyond other password storage mechanisms.

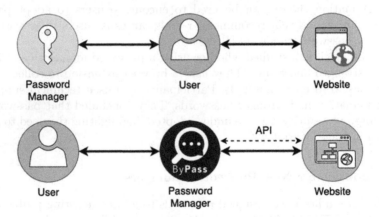

Fig. 1. Top: current password managers rely heavily on users for account interaction, other than storing the passwords. Bottom: ByPass is placed directly between the user and the website, allowing it to mediate communications between them.

As shown in Fig. 1, ByPass communicates directly with websites, thus avoiding errors resulting from user manipulation of passwords and forms. It provides an API for websites to use so that it can pass credentials directly to these websites. This allows users to skip the manual login procedure when using ByPass, improving usability and avoiding errors. Our goal is to design a mechanism to reduce the number of clicks and actions required to complete account/login management tasks.

ByPass is designed to nudge users toward choosing secure options. For example, password generation features in password managers remain mostly unused [24,27,37]. ByPass creates secure randomly-generated passwords by default, and only allows users to select their own passwords by clicking through multiple steps. These generated passwords are secure and unique, and because users usually do not need to interact with these passwords directly, they are encouraged to take advantage of this functionality.

The usability advantages of ByPass are only realized if the website chooses to implement the ByPass API. This is a strong requirement, and we did not want to create a tool that was only usable with affiliated websites. Thus, we designed ByPass to extend the functionality of password managers without taking anything away. ByPass can be used as a repository for copying and pasting passwords in the same way that existing managers can, but adds functionality for websites that implement the needed APIs. Note that when we discuss usability and security of ByPass, we focus on the new design, not this backward-compatibility feature which shares the usual drawbacks of traditional password managers.

Moving the password manager to sit between the user and the website also creates an opportunity to consider other functions that password managers typically exclude, including account creation on third-party websites, account deletion, and automated password changes. The security of ByPass is discussed in Sect. 4, but user authentication to the manager is handled exactly as it is by traditional password managers, i.e., with a username and master password.

3.2 ByPass Features

The key features of ByPass include third-party website account creation, account migration, direct account logins, password changes, and account deletion; more features can also be easily accommodated. Figure 2 shows a flow diagram of user interactions when setting ByPass up for a new account.

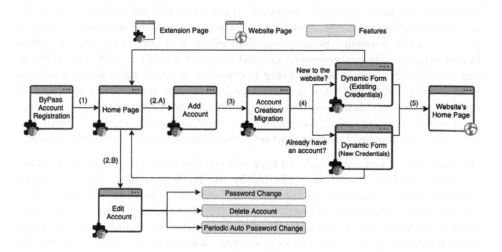

Fig. 2. User flow diagram of ByPass.

Adding Accounts. ByPass provides two options for users when adding new accounts: to register a new account, or to enroll an existing one; both these tasks are abstracted into the same function: "Adding an account". We used a wizard to guide users through the process of choosing what kind of accounts they are adding to ByPass, and to ensure that they enter the correct information.

Because ByPass communicates directly with websites, all user interactions with accounts can be moved to ByPass, including account registration. When users want to create an account on a new website, they search for the website name in ByPass, and ByPass queries the website for the registration fields they want. Users fill these fields, and ByPass automatically populates the password field with a random password conforming to the password policy (also sent by the website). Users can view and regenerate the random password, but must go through an additional confirmation to do so.

To add an existing account, after searching for the website name in ByPass, users simply enter their username and password, similar to standard password managers. If the user enters the name of a website that does not have the ByPass API installed, the password manager will act like a regular password manager, and store credentials for the user to manually enter.

Account Login. After adding an account to ByPass, the user can log into the website by opening ByPass to the account page, and clicking "login". ByPass sends the user's credentials to the website via secure API calls, and opens the site's main page in a browser. The user avoids any direct interaction with login pages, e.g., navigating to intended URLs, and typing usernames and passwords.

Password Changes. Password changes are frequently avoided by users due to serious usability drawbacks [20,37]. While password expiration policies are no longer recommended by NIST [2], they are frequently mandated by organizations. Password changes are particularly onerous to users of password managers, who typically must open the manager to copy the old password, navigate to the password change menu, generate a new password in the manager, ensure it is saved in the password manager account entry, and copied into the website. Because passwords are generally masked to avoid shoulder surfing attacks, it can be difficult to know which string is copied into which field, inviting errors. In ByPass, the direct communication between manager and website elides all of these steps, and makes password changes into a one step process for the user. On the edit account page, users can view their password, change it with the (re)generate password function, and set a timer for automatic password changes.

Account Deletion. Although not typically considered as part of password management, another opportunity afforded by the ByPass architecture is to easily delete website accounts from the password manager. Account deletion is frequently made difficult by website designers [17], but privacy rights (such as the right to be forgotten [6]) indicate that account deletion should be an available straightforward process. In ByPass, account deletion is accessed through the "Edit account" page, and includes a two-step confirmation process.

3.3   Implementation Details

The ByPass implementation has two components: the password manager itself which is implemented as a Chrome browser extension (using JavaScript and HTML, and IndexedDB to store data), and the API that allows secure communication between websites and the password manager. Figure 3 shows the ByPass API interaction between the user's browser and the website backend.

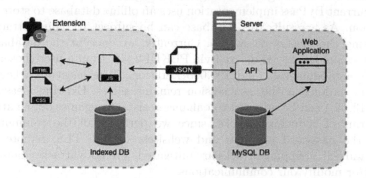

Fig. 3. ByPass API interaction between the user browser and website backend.

We created two fictional websites (an e-commerce portal and a webmail platform) for our study, using a Microsoft IIS server application to handle user requests and communicate with the backend database. The password manager side is a browser extension that directly requests and sends information to and from the website, receives responses, and displays the results in the browser.

We used a REST API for communicating with website backends as it improves the performance, has a simple interface, allows independent modification of the components, and requires low bandwidth [15]. API calls are made via HTTPS using JSON ByPass enables various account management functions, and currently implements API calls for creating an account, logging into an account, editing, and deleting an account. Our prototype API was written in C# using the .NET framework, using the System.Web.Http library.

In our fictional websites, we used JSON Web Tokens [18] for authentication purposes. The tokens contain three parts: header, body, and cryptographic signature. The header consists of a type of the token and signing algorithm, the body contains the claim, which is the value that we want to secure, and the cryptographic signature is formed using the header and body. Our TLS connections for both websites were set up through CloudFlare Keyless SSL [1, 35].

The implementation details described here are specific to our prototype, but ByPass is designed to work with a wide variety of website setups. The API is packaged as a library that can be included by web developers, and the manager is database-agnostic. The password database is stored offline in this particular implementation, which allows users to make easy backups of the (encrypted) password list, but limits portability. In this work, our primary focus was to understand the usability of ByPass, and both the feasibility of this approach, and issues such as portability between devices will be explored in future work.

4   Security and Attack Mitigation

We first discuss the security of the ByPass database, and then explain some attacks that can be mitigated through our design.

Our current ByPass implementation uses an offline database to store account information. As a result, this database can be subject to offline attacks (e.g., via guessing the master password). Currently, we encrypt the database using AES-256, where the key is derived via PBKDF2 [42] from a user-chosen master password, a random salt, and 100,000 iterations. The encryption key is kept in memory as long as the user session remains active. Existing measures (see e.g., [12,13,32]) can be adopted to enhance resistance against offline attacks.

In terms of reducing attacks, since we perform all the communications between the password manager and websites through TLS, remote network attacks, and SSL stripping attacks are mitigated; a remote attacker cannot intercept and/or modify our communications.

Since ByPass communicates directly with web servers (instead of filling forms on client-facing pages), encouraging users to use ByPass for completing account management functions can mitigate HTTP(S) auto-fill vulnerabilities and subdomain equivalence attacks [9,11]. HTTP(S) vulnerabilities happen when the password manager fills the credentials on an HTTP version of the website while the credentials were saved on the HTTPS version, and in this way the password manager makes an opportunity for the attacker to extract the user's credentials from non-HTTPS pages of the website. Avoiding auto-fill also helps us avoid the *sweep* attacks [33], where credentials are filled to invisible fields in a malicious webpage, and exfiltrated using JavaScript.

Copy to clipboard is a feature that most password managers utilize if they cannot auto-fill the credentials. If the password manager doesn't support enough protection for the credentials that were copied to the clipboard, it will lead to clipboard vulnerabilities, e.g., exposing passwords to other sites/processes; see e.g., [11]. In ByPass, passwords and other information are communicated directly to the website, and no password copying/pasting is used for login or other account-related tasks, which avoids leaking passwords from the paste buffer.

User interface-based password brute-force attacks are another vulnerability that affect extension-based password managers [11] if attackers gain access to the password manager user interface. To reduce this vulnerability, we add a delay based on the specific number of wrong master passwords entered by the user (similar to some leading commercial password managers).

5   Usability Evaluation

ByPass is designed to address usability issues that prevent end-users from adopting and using password managers. We conducted two usability evaluations of

ByPass: an inspection-based evaluation of an early prototype, and a lab-based user study of the higher fidelity prototype.

5.1 Cognitive Walkthrough

After creating the first prototype implementation of ByPass, we wanted feedback on the usability of the manager. At that point, the prototype included the main functions (adding accounts, logging in, and a version of password changing), but was not sufficiently functional for a user study. We chose to conduct a cognitive walkthrough [39] because of its focus on learnability and because it allowed us to include the perspective of novice users.

We conducted a pluralistic walkthrough with five evaluators, including the project team leads, the developer, and two volunteers playing the part of a novice ByPass user. One of these volunteers had longtime experience using a password manager, and the other had no password manager experience. We walked through the process of creating a new user account on ByPass, migrating an existing account, registering for a new third-party account, changing a password, and logging into a website.

In general, our novice participants found interacting with the prototype confusing, and were unsure what steps to first take, and what information to enter where. This led us to redesign much of the user interface, and include stronger markers of flow between steps, e.g., the account-adding wizard and more prominent navigation buttons.

Another issue that arose in the walkthrough was that the inexperienced participant seemed to have few mental models for common password tasks, and in particular, had no language for describing them. The abstraction taking place in the password manager was confusing to them, and they had multiple problems entering the right (fictitious) credentials, or choosing the correct menu option.

One of our central questions was whether the features in ByPass made sense to users – would using ByPass seem jarring, given that it departs from the usual interaction with websites? We expected the volunteer with previous password manager experience to question how ByPass worked, but they did not comment until prompted by us. When queried, they spoke to the intuitiveness of the feature set, and said that they did not question how those features were working *because they just worked*.

5.2 User Study

The second phase of our usability evaluation was to conduct an in-lab user study to evaluate the usability of the ByPass prototype with unbiased users. Following the cognitive walkthrough, the ByPass prototype was completely redeveloped into a higher fidelity prototype (described in Sect. 3.3).

The goal of our user study was to gain insight into how easily users learned to use ByPass, their reactions to the functions, and assess how using an API can help the user to deal with password-protected websites. We did not include

Table 1. Descriptive statistics for task completion time in seconds.

Tasks	Mean	SD	Median	Minimum	Maximum	Range
New ByPass account	150.0	125.5	112.5	53.0	578.0	525.0
New web account	188.1	95.4	166.0	73.0	535.0	462.0
Account migration	60.8	25.3	50.5	33.0	128.0	95.0
Login via ByPass	4.4	0.8	4.2	3.2	6.7	3.5
New account via ByPass	161.4	104.5	120.5	52.0	502.0	450.0
Password change	73.1	65.8	43.5	14.0	218.0	204.0
Account deletion	19.6	13.1	13.0	7.0	50.0	43.0

a control condition in this evaluation, because we did not feel that existing managers provided a meaningful comparison to the novel features offered in ByPass. Our goal was to evaluate the usability of ByPass (including the problems that arose). We chose an in-lab study so that we could observe participants' interactions with ByPass, and ask follow-up questions about their experience.

Each study session lasted between 30 min and one h, and was divided into three parts. Participants first completed a pre-test questionnaire asking about existing password habits and demographics. After that, we provided them with a short introduction to password managers and a brief overview of ByPass. They were asked to complete six tasks using ByPass, and then to complete the post-test questionnaire. Participants were paid 15 CAD. The study was approved by our institution's ethics board.

We designed the study to emulate a plausible first-time experience with ByPass. To improve the ecological validity of the study, we created two fictional websites (discussed above) to implement the API and be used for study tasks. These websites were open-source versions of a webmail platform and an e-commerce website, and we gave participants a handout to use in the study with the website URLs and credentials to use in the study. We reminded participants never to use their own passwords in the study.

Participants. We recruited 20 participants (12 female) by posting posters around our university campus. Participants ranged in age from 18 to 46 with a median age of 24. 18 participants were students, and 2 university employees. 15 participants (75%) reported having previous experience with a password manager, though only three participants reported that a password manager was their primary means of saving a password.

6   Results

We structured our usability evaluation around the ISO 9241 definition of usability [8], and evaluated ByPass using three measures: efficiency, effectiveness, and satisfaction. We recorded task completion times, success rates, and errors via instrumented data collection in the prototype, and measured satisfaction using

Likert scale questions on the post-test questionnaire. We evaluated efficiency using the time spent on each task. For effectiveness, we assessed the number and types of errors that occurred during the study, and for satisfaction, we considered findings from the Likert scale questions. We also recorded observations related to task completion, participants' comments, problems, and recommendations.

6.1 Time

Table 1 shows descriptive statistics for the duration of each study task, and Fig. 4 shows the distributions of completion time for all tasks. Times were recorded in the manager logs from the appearance of the first screen to successful completion of the task, and include the time participants spent making errors.

Although there were outliers, the median completion times were less than three minutes for all tasks. Keeping in mind that all participants were completely new to ByPass and were completing all tasks for the very first time, these results are encouraging. Variance was relatively low for most tasks, particularly account migration and login, which we think could form the majority of the users' tasks when setting up the manager for the first time.

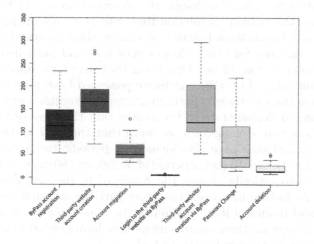

Fig. 4. Boxplots showing the distributions of task completion time in seconds.

ByPass account registration involves the user entering their email address, and choosing a master password. To enhance the ecological validity of the evaluation, we included this task in the study and used a strength meter to encourage participants to choose a strong master password. As mentioned above, participants were warned not to use their real passwords. Ten participants had trouble picking a suitable master password, and the median completion time was 113 s. As the ByPass registration process is no different than regular account creation, participants were not asked to recall this password during the study.

The second task had users register directly on one of our external websites, so that they would have an existing account to add to ByPass in a later step. This step also gave us a baseline for the length of time needed to register on a "regular" website. This task had the highest median completion time at 166 s, and a few participants took much longer to complete it.

Later in the study, participants added that account to ByPass, and this process was considerably faster; the median time to add an account (through ByPass) was just 51 s. Following migration, participants were instructed to log into that account through ByPass and participants had no trouble doing this very quickly, in a median of just 4 s.

The process of creating a new website account via ByPass was new to all users, and the median completion time was 121 s. There was a large interquartile spread, and a few participants struggled considerably with this task, but we expect that times might decrease as users grew more familiar with the manager. In any case, an average of two minutes to register on a new website seems to be an acceptable time. According to our logs, 95% of the participants used the password automatically generated by ByPass, which means that our nudges were successful in encouraging users to use a secure password while keeping convenience.

Participants were asked to change the password on one of their accounts on ByPass, and the median completion time was 44 s. 75% of the participants used the password generation function to change their password and choose a new one. The variance for this task was very low, and participants generally did not encounter any problems. One thing that may have inflated times was that participants clicked on the re-generate password button an average of 4.7 times. It was unclear exactly why participants were doing this, but for some, they seemed to want to demonstrate to themselves that the password was actually changing. Others were looking for a password that appealed to them.

The password change page also included a periodic password auto-change feature, allowing the user to pick a period of 30, 60, and 90 days, so the password manager will automatically change the password as the period ends. We did not include this feature in a task, but most participants expressed interest in this feature, and discussed it in relation to the annoyance of regular password changes. Time spent on these conversations may have also artificially increased the time spent on the password change tasks.

The final study task was to delete an account. At this point, participants were relatively familiar with ByPass, and the median completion time for this task was only 13 s.

6.2   Errors

We were particularly interested in the kinds of errors that participants made while using ByPass, as dangerous errors in computer security can be difficult to undo and can open the user to serious vulnerabilities [41]. Most participants did not make any errors: the median number of errors per participant was zero,

Table 2. Total number of errors committed by usability study task.

Task	Number of errors
ByPass account registration	34
Third-party website account creation	4
Third-party website account creation via ByPass	2
Account migration	1
Password change	0
Account deletion	0
Login to third-party website via ByPass	0

and the maximum was four. We examined errors on two dimensions: the type of error committed, and the incidence of those errors.

Errors were logged by the ByPass software, and then grouped thematically for this analysis. Some errors may have been excluded during this process; e.g., repeated regeneration of a password was not counted as an error, though it is not the intended behaviour.

Table 2 shows the total number of total by task. By far the most error-prone task was the ByPass account registration, incurring a total of 34 errors.

The majority of these errors were password mismatches (i.e., the confirmed password not matching the created one), difficulties in choosing a sufficiently strong master password, and filling in all fields appropriately. The irony that this task had the most errors is not lost on us: we included this step in the evaluation only for the purposes of realism, but we cannot ignore the fact that authenticating to the password manager itself was the most problematic part of the process. The next most error-prone task was the account creation on a third-party website, where participants had a few problems with password mismatches.

Encouragingly, there were few errors in the tasks that actually involved using ByPass. Below is a description of each error type, with the total number of times it occurred in parentheses:

Password Mismatch on the Registration Page (21). This error was unique to the ByPass registration page, and it occurred when the entered master password and the confirm master password were not matched. This error was replicated 21 times in the study with a median of 1 time per participant. The maximum number of errors made by one individual was 3.

Wrong Password (11). We did not expect participants to perform anything other than the tasks described in the study, but some participants took steps to confirm whether or not the tasks they completed in ByPass were really accomplished on the websites. In doing so, these participants made some incorrect password errors when logging into the websites managed through ByPass.

There were a total of eleven incorrect password entries. Participants particularly wanted to check the password change task by visiting the website and

testing the new and old passwords. Since they used the auto-password generation function for changing the password, they sometimes entered their previous
password mistakenly, leading to this error.

All Fields Required (10). Although this validation was included on all the
pages containing different fields, all of these errors happened on the ByPass registration page, and these errors were caused by our design of the login page. Our
extension's window range was not wide enough to accommodate all the fields on
the registration page when the user was typing into the master password field. As
the user typed, the password strength meter gave more feedback and expanded in
size, shifting the password confirmation box below the page break. Although we
included a hint encouraging users to scroll down, several participants missed it.

Choose a Strong Password (4). For study realism, we included a password
strength meter (based on zxcvbn [40]) on the ByPass account creation page, and
required participants to choose a master password with a "strong" rating. Four
users attempted to use a password that did not fill this requirement, and these
problems stemmed from not paying attention to the instruction reminding them
to pick a strong password, from a lack of understanding of what forms a good
password, and from ignoring the feedback from the password strength meter.

Incorrect Master Password (3). Following creation of their master password,
participants were asked to use it to log into ByPass. Three participants made
mistakes in entering their password during login.

Bad Request (1). This error category encompasses several different errors:
when ByPass sends packets containing user information to websites, it waits for
an HTTP response status of 200 (OK) as an approval. Incorrect email addresses,
incorrect passwords, and request timeouts belong to this type of error. In our
study, this happened only once when a participant mistyped an email address.

Unsupported Website (1). Features like creating an account, changing passwords, or deleting an account, can be done only for websites for which we have
their API. This error occurs if the user tries to do any of these functions on an
unsupported website. One participant had a typo while they were entering the
name of the webmail service for the account creation function on ByPass, and
because we did not support that name, this error appeared.

6.3   Usability Perceptions

We were also interested in how our participants perceived the usability and
security of ByPass. We asked participants for their responses to 12 Likert-scale
questions, asking about the ease of use, perceived security, and desire to use
ByPass in future. Participants were asked to rate their agreement on a 7 point
scale where 7 was most positive. Figure 5 shows the distribution of responses for
selected questions.

Participants were universally positive about the ease of use of the password
change process ($med = 7$) and website login processes ($med = 7$) in ByPass.

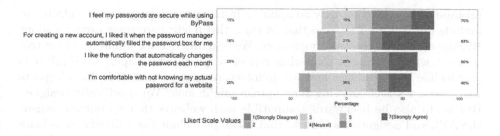

Fig. 5. Responses to Likert scale questions asking about participants' interest in ByPass features.

They were also positive about the ease of creating new accounts through ByPass ($med = 7$) and adding existing accounts ($med = 7$), as well as the ease of deleting accounts ($med = 7$). Participants also found it easy to migrate a third-party account to ByPass ($med = 7$).

The median agreement score for the perceived security of ByPass was 6, indicating general satisfaction with the security of ByPass, though participants expressed more frustration with the process of choosing a master password ($med = 5$). In the discussion, some participants mentioned that they would trust ByPass more if it were a software application from a well-recognized organization like Google. A few of the more technical participants commented that they liked the fact that there is no server-side component to the manager.

Participants were most negative about features that related to user control, see Fig. 5. They were not positive about the concept of not knowing the actual password ($med = 4.5$), and displayed mixed responses about the password generation and auto-change features. 31% of the participants wanted to use their own password, instead of relying on a password generator to create one for them.

7   Discussion

Although widely recommended as a simple step that users can take towards improving their password security, few users adopt password managers. Adoption problems and the extra work of using a manager are thought to be part of the reason that users do not turn to these tools [3,4]. In this paper, we designed and evaluated ByPass, a password manager that rethinks the users' interactions with the password manager, thereby encouraging adoption and encouraging users to make use of security features. ByPass uses an API for secure communication between the password manager and websites, freeing the user from creating and avoiding errors resulting from copying and pasting. ByPass is built to extend traditional password manager features and supports new functionality such as automated password changes and account deletion. ByPass nudges users toward using secure randomly generated passwords.

The downside of the ByPass approach to password management is that it requires buy-in from websites, who must implement the API. We hope that the promise of increased security compliance from users might motivate websites to include the ByPass API, and that in turn, this might encourage users to adopt ByPass over other password managers. We acknowledge the uphill nature of this process, while leaving it somewhat out of scope for this paper; we think it is worthwhile to investigate how an architecture such as that of ByPass impacts users even without knowing how uptake might look. We specifically designed ByPass to also be backwards compatible with websites that do not implement the API, and designed the API so that it can be included as a library by website developers. In future work, we plan to further study the feasibility of ByPass's implementation, as well as the implications for web developers, and how they can be supported in implementing ByPass.

We conducted two early evaluations of ByPass's usability, and found that users were able to understand and use the features in ByPass. Most participants did not encounter major problems, though there is undoubtedly still room for improvement in the ByPass user interface. The results of this study will be used to improve the prototype development. However, through the process of designing, implementing and evaluating ByPass, we made a number of observations that affect the design of not only ByPass, but password management tools in general.

7.1   An Abstraction Layer for Accounts

ByPass adds a layer of abstraction between the user and the website, where all account-management related interactions take place within the password manager. Adding this abstraction layer brings up various design questions: Where should the password manager sit in the physical space of the web browser? How to instrument the browser extension to "correctly" interrupt interactions with websites? How to train users to go to the password manager first for account management-related tasks? What kind of language should be used to correctly convey password tasks when they are de-situated from their website contexts? Our evaluation suggests that while most participants were able to interpret what was happening, some had great problems.

Our goal was to create a space where security could be the users' primary task, and allow them to focus cleanly and consistently on account management tasks. The constancy of the ByPass interface is intended to allow users a greater sense of control over their passwords and accounts. By using the API to move account interactions into this space, we hoped to create an interface where users knew where to address security concerns, and access the controls to address those concerns. Current password managers hint at this functionality (and include innovative tools, such as security audits) but their placement outside the authentication interaction hampers the functionality they are able to support.

7.2 Control vs Automation

ByPass re-architects the password manager to adjust the locus of control for the user. The user is given more control over some aspects of their password management tasks (password changes, account deletion), but less control over passwords themselves. In ByPass, passwords are generated randomly by default, and obscured to the user.

Our contention in ByPass is that the user does not need to know their passwords. With the addition of the API, this is functionally true, but it does not seem to fulfill users' sense of security self-efficacy [28]. In our study, users expressed unhappiness about not knowing their passwords, both in comments and in the post-test questionnaire. We also observed them engaging in "epistemic actions" [23] – actions that serve only to understand a situation rather than to advance a goal, such as repeatedly regenerating passwords, or double-checking on the website that a password had actually changed. Some of these reactions may be due to unfamiliarity, but they echo the findings of previous studies where users have expressed both a desire for control [4,27] and a corresponding sense of responsibility for security [27].

Automating security is often tricky. Solutions such as TLS certificates automate nearly all of the security interaction, turning to the user only when a certificate is not validated, but demonstrate failures when users are unprepared to cope with these situations. Conversely, passwords leave nearly all of the control in the hands of the users, expecting them to exert individual responsibility for all aspects of the password management task. ByPass attempts to find a middle ground for users, removing tasks that needlessly involve users (e.g., reading the password policy, choosing a password that conforms to it). In designing ByPass, we became aware of the myriad corner cases in which the user might need to exert control, and we attempted to leave accessible controls for situations such as assigned passwords, and other unusual contexts.

7.3 Testing a Password Manager

In evaluating ByPass, one difficulty we encountered was creating a realistic testing scenario. Ecological validity, or the realism of the study situation, is of the utmost importance in security studies. Tasks that seem easy or manageable as primary tasks (such as remembering a password) are not always manageable when happening in the context of another more important task. Simulating this for a password manager is difficult – the gold standard evaluation would seem to be a field study where participants use the manager for their own accounts. We would want to collect instrumented data from such an evaluation, and privacy could be a significant concern (not only for data collection, but potentially biasing participants' behaviour). For ByPass, a study of this type carried the additional challenge of needing websites to be implemented with the API, further restricting our ability to have users test the manager with their own accounts.

8   Conclusion

The usability of password managers is a key issue, since there is no benefit in developing a secure password manager when users cannot make use of it. In this paper, we design and implement ByPass, a password management software offering new features to users by reducing the number of required actions for specific task completion. The key idea of our proposed password manager is that API-enabled secure communication between the password manager and websites allows various password management tasks to be streamlined for the end user. ByPass supports third-party account creation, password change, account deletion directly through the password manager.

We constructed a prototype implementation of ByPass and evaluated it in a user study with 20 participants. The results show that the participants found ByPass easy to use, and our concept is effective both in terms of usability and security. ByPass successfully nudged participants towards using automatically generated passwords, and most of the participants were able to learn how to use ByPass efficiently, while making few errors.

In future work, we plan to integrate the findings of this usability evaluation into the ByPass user interface, integrate new features to support users, and further test ByPass in more ecologically valid scenarios. We also plan to address elements of password manager design that were left out of scope in this early prototype, such as portability to multiple devices.

ByPass raises important questions about where security controls should be placed for end-users. Users desire control, but this may be at odds with good usability. The abstraction of password tasks in password manager creates an extra management step for users, and managers must be carefully designed so that users are supported in understanding this abstraction. However, we think that redesigning the password manager could be key to seeing its wide adoption.

References

1. CloudFlare - The Web Performance & Security Company. https://www.cloudflare.com/en-ca/
2. NIST Special Publication 800–63b: Digital Identity Guidelines. SP-800-63b Section 5.1.1.2
3. Alkaldi, N., Renaud, K.: Why do people adopt, or reject, smartphone password managers. EuroUSEC'16 (2016)
4. Alkaldi, N., Renaud, K., Mackenzie, L.: Encouraging password manager adoption by meeting adopter self-determination needs. In: Hawaii International Conference on System Sciences, pp. 4824–4833 (2019)
5. Aurigemma, S., Mattson, T., Leonard, L.: So much promise, so little use: what is stopping home end-users from using password manager applications. 50th Hawaii International Conference on System Sciences (2017)
6. Ausloos, J.: The 'right to be forgotten' - worth remembering. Comput. Law Secur. Rev. **28**(2), 143–152 (2012)

7. Barbosa, N.M., Hayes, J., Wang, Y.: UniPass: design and evaluation of a smart device-based password manager for visually impaired users. In: ACM UbiComp (2016)
8. Bevan, N., Carter, J., Harker, S.: ISO 9241-11 Revised: what have we learnt about usability since 1998? In: Kurosu, M. (ed.) HCI 2015. LNCS, vol. 9169, pp. 143–151. Springer, Cham (2015). https://doi.org/10.1007/978-3-319-20901-2_13
9. Blanchou, M., Youn, P.: Password managers: exposing passwords everywhere. White Paper, iSEC Partners, pp. 1–6 (2013)
10. Bonneau, J., Herley, C., Van Oorschot, P.C., Stajano, F.: The quest to replace passwords: a framework for comparative evaluation of web authentication schemes. In: IEEE Symposium on Security and Privacy, pp. 553–567. IEEE (2012)
11. Carr, M., Shahandashti, S.F.: Revisiting security vulnerabilities in commercial password managers. In: Hölbl, M., Rannenberg, K., Welzer, T. (eds.) SEC 2020. IAICT, vol. 580, pp. 265–279. Springer, Cham (2020). https://doi.org/10.1007/978-3-030-58201-2_18
12. Chatterjee, R., Bonneau, J., Juels, A., Ristenpart, T.: Cracking-resistant password vaults using natural language encoders. In: IEEE Symposium on Security and Privacy. San Jose, CA, USA, May 2015
13. Cheng, H., Zheng, Z., Li, W., Wang, P., Chu, C.H.: Probability model transforming encoders against encoding attacks. In: USENIX Security (2019)
14. Chiasson, S., van Oorschot, P.C., Biddle, R.: A usability study and critique of two password managers. In: USENIX Security, vol. 15 (2006)
15. Doglio, F.: Pro REST API Development with Node. js. Apress, New York (2015)
16. Golla, M., Beuscher, B., Dürmuth, M.: On the security of cracking-resistant password vaults. In: ACM CCS. ACM, Vienna Austria (2016)
17. Habib, H., et al.: It's a scavenger hunt": usability of websites. In: ACM SIGCHI, Opt-Out and Data Deletion Choices (2020)
18. Haekal, M., et al.: Token-based authentication using JSON web token on SIKASIR RESTful web service. In: 2016 International Conference on Informatics and Computing (ICIC), pp. 175–179. IEEE (2016)
19. Herley, C., Van Oorschot, P.: A research agenda acknowledging the persistence of passwords. IEEE Secur. Priv. 10(1), 28–36 (2011)
20. Inglesant, P.G., Sasse, M.A.: The true cost of unusable password policies: password use in the wild. In: CHI'10, pp. 383–392 (2010)
21. Karole, A., Saxena, N., Christin, N.: A comparative usability evaluation of traditional password managers. In: Rhee, K.H., Nyang, D. (eds.) ICISC 2010. LNCS, vol. 6829, pp. 233–251. Springer, Heidelberg (2011). https://doi.org/10.1007/978-3-642-24209-0_16
22. Li, Z., He, W., Akhawe, D., Song, D.: The emperor's new password manager: security analysis of web-based password managers. In: USENIX Security (2014)
23. Liu, Z., Nersessian, N., Stasko, J.: Distributed cognition as a theoretical framework for information visualization. IEEE Trans. Visual. Comput. Graph. 14(6), 1173–1180 (2008)
24. Lyastani, S.G., Schilling, M., Fahl, S., Backes, M., Bugiel, S.: Better managed than memorized. In: USENIX Security, Studying the Impact of Managers on Password Strength and Reuse (2018)
25. Maclean, R., Ophoff, J.: Determining key factors that lead to the adoption of password managers. In: 2018 International Conference on Intelligent and Innovative Computing Applications (ICONIC). IEEE (2018)

26. McCarney, D., Barrera, D., Clark, J., Chiasson, S., Van Oorschot, P.C.: Tapas: design, implementation, and usability evaluation of a password manager. In: ACSAC'12, pp. 89–98 (2012)

27. Pearman, S., Zhang, S.A., Bauer, L., Christin, N., Cranor, L.F.: Why people (don't) use password managers effectively. In: SOUPS'19. USENIX (2019)

28. Rhee, H.S., Kim, C., Ryu, Y.U.: Self-efficacy in information security: its influence on end users' information security practice behavior. Comput. Secur. **28**(8), 816–826 (2009)

29. Ross, B., Jackson, C., Miyake, N., Boneh, D., Mitchell, J.C.: Stronger password authentication using browser extensions. In: USENIX Security, p. 15 (2005)

30. Ruoti, S., Seamons, K.: End-to-end passwords. In: NSPW. ACM (2017)

31. Seiler-Hwang, S., et al.: " I don't see why I would ever want to use it" analyzing the usability of popular smartphone password managers. In: ACM CCS'19 (2019)

32. Shirvanian, M., Jareckiy, S., Krawczykz, H., Saxena, N.: SPHINX: a password store that perfectly hides passwords from itself. In: International Conference on Distributed Computing Systems (ICDCS'17). Atlanta, GA, USA, Jun 2017

33. Silver, D., Jana, S., Boneh, D., Chen, E., Jackson, C.: Password managers: attacks and defenses. In: USENIX Security (2014)

34. Smith, T., Ruoti, S., Seamons, K.: Augmenting centralized password management with application-specific passwords. In: SOUPS'17. USENIX (2017)

35. Stebila, D., Sullivan, N.: An analysis of TLS handshake proxying. In: 2015 IEEE Trustcom/BigDataSE/ISPA, vol. 1, pp. 279–286. IEEE (2015)

36. Stobert, E., Biddle, R.: A password manager that doesn't remember passwords. In: NSPW. ACM (2014)

37. Stobert, E., Biddle, R.: The password life cycle. ACM Trans. Priv. Secur. (TOPS) **21**(3), 1–32 (2018)

38. Wang, D., Zhang, Z., Wang, P., Yan, J., Huang, X.: Targeted online password guessing: an underestimated threat. In: ACM CCS. Vienna Austria (2016)

39. Wharton, C., Bradford, J., Jeffries, R., Franzke, M.: Applying cognitive walk-throughs to more complex user interfaces: experiences, issues, and recommendations. In: ACM SIGCHI (1992)

40. Wheeler, D.L.: **zxcvbn**: low-budget password strength estimation. In: USENIX Security (2016)

41. Whitten, A., Tygar, J.D.: Why johnny can't encrypt: a usability evaluation of PGP 5.0. In: USENIX Security (1999)

42. Yao, F.F., Yin, Y.L.: Design and analysis of password-based key derivation functions. In: Menezes, A. (ed.) CT-RSA 2005. LNCS, vol. 3376, pp. 245–261. Springer, Heidelberg (2005). https://doi.org/10.1007/978-3-540-30574-3_17

Anomaly Detection on Web-User Behaviors Through Deep Learning

Jiaping Gui[(✉)], Zhengzhang Chen, Xiao Yu, Cristian Lumezanu,
and Haifeng Chen

NEC Laboratories America, Inc., Princeton, USA
{jgui,zchen,xiao,lume,Haifeng}@nec-labs.com

Abstract. The modern Internet has witnessed the proliferation of web applications that play a crucial role in the branding process among enterprises. Web applications provide a communication channel between potential customers and business products. However, web applications are also targeted by attackers due to sensitive information stored in these applications. Among web-related attacks, there exists a rising but more stealthy attack where attackers first access a web application on behalf of normal users based on stolen credentials. Then attackers follow a sequence of sophisticated steps to achieve the malicious purpose. Traditional security solutions fail to detect relevant abnormal behaviors once attackers login to the web application. To address this problem, we propose *WebLearner*, a novel system to detect abnormal web-user behaviors. As we demonstrate in the evaluation, *WebLearner* has an outstanding performance. In particular, it can effectively detect abnormal user behaviors with over 96% for both precision and recall rates using a reasonably small amount of normal training data.

Keywords: Web application · Abnormal behavior · Sequence-based attack · Deep learning

1 Introduction

Web applications (or apps) have become an important part of many companies' digital marketing strategy. In 2018, nearly two-thirds of small businesses rely on their web applications to connect with customers [2], not to mention those large enterprises. In spite of business values, web apps can be the target of attackers due to vulnerable interfaces in these apps. We continue to see a trend of increasing number of vulnerabilities in web apps. The overall number of new web-app vulnerabilities in 2018 increased by 23% compared to 2017 and by 162% compared to 2016 [10]. Among all attack targets, web apps are the top two to be hit in 2018 [13].

To defend against web-related attacks, different solutions (e.g., [4,14,16]) have been proposed. Among these solutions, there are two major directions:

© ICST Institute for Computer Sciences, Social Informatics and Telecommunications Engineering 2020
Published by Springer Nature Switzerland AG 2020. All Rights Reserved
N. Park et al. (Eds.): SecureComm 2020, LNICST 335, pp. 467–473, 2020.
https://doi.org/10.1007/978-3-030-63086-7_25

rule-based and learning-based. The former extracts unique patterns from attack traces and design specific rules to detect future attacks that have the same patterns. The latter explores a large amount of attack traces and learns traditional attack patterns. For example, some methods group these attacks into clusters in the hope that future attacks fall into these clusters. Some leverage statistical information (e.g., traffic volume) to detect anomalies related to user behaviors.

Despite the effectiveness of detection on specific web attacks, existing solutions suffer from a critical problem that limits their usability and application. In particular, existing solutions fail to detect sophisticated web attacks that involve multiple steps (as a sequence), since these solutions typically target single-step attacks. For example, in cross-site scripting (XSS), attackers directly inject malicious scripts into benign web applications viewed by other users. To detect such an attack, the solution is straightforward by detecting whether there exists any executable-script keyword in the application. However, there are two key characteristics in sequence-based attacks that existing solutions do not take into account.

The first missing characteristic is the sequence-based patterns. In sophisticated web attacks, a sequence of steps are conducted by attackers to achieve the malicious goal. Each single step may be benign, while as a whole, these steps are suspicious. We call this *local-benign-global-malicious*. For example, in a shopping web app, an infrequent user who makes tens of orders at one time is suspicious. One order itself should be normal but a sequence of such orders are abnormal. The second missing characteristic is to be able to detect attacks with unknown patterns. In the real world, attackers can easily bypass existing solutions once they locate the set of patterns that are leveraged by security solutions. This set of patterns, though can be upgraded iteratively, do not accommodate the dynamic behaviors of attackers. The capability of existing solutions is greatly restricted when new unknown attacks are encountered.

In this paper, we propose *WebLearner*, an intelligent web security system that detects abnormal web-user behaviors through deep learning. In particular, *WebLearner* learns session-based sequences of user visits (e.g., URLs) on a web application. To address the first characteristic, *WebLearner* utilizes a sliding window to generate representations of sequences of user visits. The whole sequence in each window is used for training. In other words, each single visit is not trained individually. To address the second characteristic, *WebLearner* leverages a deep learning technique to model normal user behaviors that takes advantage of information in a guided way. Considering attackers have no access to the web-visit history of normal users, suspicious behaviors from attackers are expected to be different from those normal ones, and thus be detected as abnormal.

The contributions of this paper can be summarized below:

- We propose *WebLearner*, an intelligent web security system that enables UBA on web applications to detect sequence-based anomalies.

- We have implemented *WebLearner* and deployed it into a real-world environment we set up. Our experimental results are promising, demonstrating that *WebLearner* can detect abnormal web-user behaviors effectively.

2   Approach

To detect sequence-based abnormal user behaviors in web attacks (e.g.., credential stuffing, logic attack, and bot-related attacks), *WebLearner* adopts a training-prediction-retraining mode that incorporates feedback from security analysts in an efficient and effective manner. *WebLearner* has following advantages: (1) it takes a representation of web-user behaviors directly from raw user access log, which keeps the inherent relationship among visits in the sequence. (2) it has a flexible framework that can train the model corresponding to each of the groups of user behaviors. (3) it has the capability to detect new, unknown and sophisticated attack behaviors, since *WebLearner* depends on a training data set that consists of sequences of normal user visits on the web app.

In the high level, it has two main components: log parser and deep learning model. There are two different types of inputs: normal user access log for training, and new access log for prediction.

In the first step, the log parser takes as input the normal user access log, and outputs representations of sequences of user visits in different dimensions. In particular, *WebLearner* first extracts effective page requests (in terms of URL) from the user access log, and filters out noisy requests (e.g., resource-related image, JS, CSS). Then *WebLearner* takes into account both the page directory (also known as page topic) and parameters. For example, if a URL is `BrowseCategories.php?nickname=u1&password=p1`, then the page directory of this URL is `BrowseCategories.php`, and parameters are `nickname` and `password`. Let $\mathcal{S}_D = \{d_1, d_2, ...d_m\}$ be the set of all directories in the normal training log, and P_i be the set of all parameters to the directory d_i. *WebLearner* indexes element strings in $\mathcal{S}_D$ according to the alphabetical order. For a new URL with the directory d_n and parameter set P_n, the representation of this new URL is generated according to Eq. 1. Finally, *WebLearner* forms value representations into corresponding vectors.

$$URL\_representation = \begin{cases} i, & \text{if } d_n = d_i \in \mathcal{S}_D \text{ and } P_n \subset P_i \\ n, & \text{if } d_n \notin \mathcal{S}_D \\ max\{int\}, & \text{otherwise} \end{cases} \quad (1)$$

The deep learning model is used to learn complex web-user behaviors in terms of page visits on the web app. To model user-behavioral sequences in terms of URL, we leveraged a recurrent neural network with long short-term memory (LSTM) [8] due to its superior performance in learning long-term dependencies over sequences [5,6,9]. The sequence of page visits is much more diverse than the environmental information. To do the learning, this model utilizes a sliding window to get the input sequence with fixed length, and uses the next visit following the sequence as the output prediction of the sequence.

Finally, after modeling, *WebLearner* can predict whether a new access log has abnormal user behaviors. When new log entries come, the log parser first generates corresponding representations. Then the sequence of page visits goes to the deep learning model. After prediction, if the deep learning model detects the sequence as an anomaly, security analysts further investigate it to take corresponding actions for defense. However, it is possible the sequence that is detected as suspicious is benign. In this case, *WebLearner* uses the sequence to retrain the deep learning model for incremental learning.

3   Evaluation

In this section, we show the performance of *WebLearner* in detecting abnormal web-user behaviors. The high-level research question is how effective *WebLearner* is to detect anomalies.

3.1   Experiment Setup

WebLearner is implemented using JAVA (for log parser) and PyTorch (for deep learning model). We deployed *WebLearner* on a server with 12 cores (Intel Core i7-8700K CPU @ 3.70 GHz) and 32 GB memory.

To evaluate *WebLearner*, we have two requirements on the data set: (1) there are a large amount of user visits on a web app. (2) there is labeling information about normal and abnormal user behaviors. To achieve both requirements, we set up a benchmark based on RUBiS [1], an auction site prototype modeled after eBay.com. To meet the first requirement, we automated the generation of workloads (i.e., user interaction traces) in a large scale. To meet the second requirement, we control the workload generation to create synthetic abnormal behaviors or attack cases. In RUBiS, each group of user behaviors is controlled by a state transition matrix, where each element specifies the probability of page transition that goes from one interaction to another. In the end, we generated five different groups of normal web-user behaviors with in total 11,677 sessions. In the deep learning model, we set the size of sliding window $w = 10$. Table 1 summarizes the values of other relevant parameters. After filtering out the sessions that have no more than ten visits, we have in total 10,910 effective sessions for evaluation.

Table 1. Values of parameters used in deep learning model

# Directories	# Hidden dimensions	# Layers	# Epochs	Batch size
24	64	2	300	2,048

3.2 Effectiveness of *WebLearner*

To validate the effectiveness of *WebLearner*, we randomly selected 30% of sessions in each of the groups for training. The data used for prediction consists of two parts: normal (i.e., the rest 70% of sessions) and abnormal. To collect data related to abnormal behaviors, we randomly generated sessions whose sequence length conforms with the length distribution among those of group behaviors.

For evaluation, we use standard metrics as follows. A false positive (FP) denotes a normal session sequence that is detected as abnormal, and a false negative (FN) denotes an abnormal session sequence that is detected as normal. A true positive (TP) means an abnormal session sequence is detected correctly as abnormal. Metrics for evaluation include: $Precision = \frac{TP}{TP+FP}$, $Recall = \frac{TP}{TP+FN}$, and $F1\text{-}measure = \frac{2 \cdot Precision \cdot Recall}{Precision+Recall}$.

After modeling and predicting, *WebLearner* could achieve the precision 96.75%, the recall 96.54%, and the F1-measure score 96.63%. This indicates that *WebLearner* works well when the training data set is limited.

4 Related Work

In this section, we discuss the overlaps and differences of the related work with our work.

Web Application Defense: Many products or solutions have been implemented to defend against web-related attacks. The Open Web Application Security Project (OWASP) [12], an online community that focuses on web application security, lists the top web attacks (e.g., injection, cross-site scripting) and suggests best practices for developers. In the literature, researchers also propose various methodologies (e.g., [4,14]) for more secure web applications. All pieces of above work focus on traditional web attacks, or model the runtime behavior of web applications. In contrast, our work investigates abnormal web-user behaviors consisting of sequences of visits. We believe our approach is complementary to the related work, and both are beneficial to achieving a more secure web application.

Deep Learning Application: Deep learning models such as LSTM have been widely applied to various scenarios in the real world. Want et al. [15] proposed attention-based LSTM to do sentiment classification in NLP. Du et al. [3] implemented DeepLog, a deep learning model based on LSTM to detect anomalies in system logs. Researchers also use LSTM for other purposes, such as speech recognition [7] and time series study [11]. However, all above studies focus on tasks different from ours. We designed and implemented *WebLearner* to achieve anomaly detection on sequence-based web-user behaviors.

5   Conclusion

In this paper, we propose a novel system, *WebLearner*, to detect abnormal web-user behaviors. This work is motivated by a rising type of web attacks that are based on a sequence of visits. Such an attack is more stealthy than before, and thus cannot be detected by traditional web-security solutions. To address this problem, *WebLearner* utilizes a deep learning model to learn normal user behaviors, and detects abnormal behaviors that are unknown and different from normal ones. Our evaluation results demonstrate *WebLearner* has an outstanding performance. In particular, it can effectively detect abnormal user behaviors with over 96% for both precision and recall rates using a reasonably small amount of normal training data.

References

1. Amza, C., et al.: Specification and implementation of dynamic Web site benchmarks. In: 5th Workshop on Workload Characterization. No. CONF (2002)
2. Clutch: Small Business Websites in 2018. https://clutch.co/website-builders/resources/small-business-websites-2018
3. Du, M., Li, F., Zheng, G., Srikumar, V.: DeepLog: anomaly detection and diagnosis from system logs through deep learning. In: Proceedings of the 2017 ACM SIGSAC Conference on Computer and Communications Security, pp. 1285–1298. ACM (2017)
4. García, V.H., Monroy, R., Quintana, M.: Web attack detection using ID3. In: Debenham, J. (ed.) Professional Practice in Artificial Intelligence. IIFIP, vol. 218, pp. 323–332. Springer, Boston, MA (2006). https://doi.org/10.1007/978-0-387-34749-3_34
5. Gers, F.A., Schraudolph, N.N., Schmidhuber, J.: Learning precise timing with LSTM recurrent networks. J. Mach. Learn. Res. **3**, 115–143 (2002)
6. Graves, A., Schmidhuber, J.: Framewise phoneme classification with bidirectional LSTM and other neural network architectures. Neural Netw. **18**(5–6), 602–610 (2005)
7. Han, S., et al.: ESE: efficient speech recognition engine with sparse LSTM on FPGA. In: Proceedings of the 2017 ACM/SIGDA International Symposium on Field-Programmable Gate Arrays, pp. 75–84 (2017)
8. Hochreiter, S., Schmidhuber, J.: Long short-term memory. Neural Comput. **9**(8), 1735–1780 (1997)
9. Huang, Z., Xu, W., Yu, K.: Bidirectional LSTM-CRF models for sequence tagging. arXiv preprint arXiv:1508.01991 (2015)
10. Imperva: the state of Web application vulnerabilities in 2018. https://www.imperva.com/blog/the-state-of-web-application-vulnerabilities-in-2018/
11. Karim, F., Majumdar, S., Darabi, H., Chen, S.: Lstm fully convolutional networks for time series classification. IEEE Access **6**, 1662–1669 (2017)
12. OWASP: OWASP top ten project. https://www.owasp.org/index.php/Main_Page
13. PTSecurity: cybersecurity threatscape 2018: trends and forecasts. https://www.ptsecurity.com/ww-en/analytics/cybersecurity-threatscape-2018/

14. Seo, J., Kim, H.S., Cho, S., Cha, S.: Web server attack categorization based on root causes and their locations. In: International Conference on Information Technology: Coding and Computing, 2004. Proceedings. ITCC 2004, vol. 1, pp. 90–96. IEEE (2004)
15. Wang, Y., Huang, M., Zhu, X., Zhao, L.: Attention-based LSTM for aspect-level sentiment classification. In: Proceedings of the 2016 Conference on Empirical Methods in Natural Language Processing, pp. 606–615 (2016)
16. Xie, Y., Yu, S.Z.: A large-scale hidden Semi-Markov model for anomaly detection on user browsing behaviors. IEEE/ACM Trans. Netw. **17**(1), 54–65 (2008)

Identity Armour: User Controlled Browser Security

Ross Copeland and Drew Davidson(✉)

EECS Department, ITTC University of Kansas, Lawrence, KS, USA
{rcopeland,drewdavidson}@ku.edu

Abstract. As dynamic technologies are deployed to make the web more responsive and feature-rich, the abuse of these capabilities have given rise to emergent privacy and security concerns. At the same time, the prevalence of targeted advertising-driven revenue streams has built an incentive to amass more information about visitors and little incentive to prevent third-party entities from collecting such data. We create a prototype policy enforcement system called Identity Armour that is purely client-side, requiring no cooperation from the site developer. Our system can enforce policies over the functionality of practical JavaScript, including the ability to prevent data that users consider to be sensitive and to prevent functions that the user considers to be prohibited from being executed. We show that Identity Armour is effective at stopping real privacy leakages, and equips users with modern web protections even when first-party developers fail to supply policies themselves.

Keywords: Web security · User privacy · Cross-site scripting

1 Introduction

An alarming trend exists in web security: although Americans are increasingly concerned about the impact of their private online data being misused [2], they are also increasingly certain that their data will be compromised [11]. A particular focus for user privacy and security is in the browser. As browsers are enhanced to support the needs of increasingly feature-rich websites and web applications, complex new capabilities can serve as vectors for attack on user privacy. As website and web applications evolve to use these capabilities, several factors exacerbate the threat of privacy invasion.

Much of the challenge in mitigating attacks via these vectors is in discerning which capabilities are acceptable operations for a user. Furthermore, enhanced browser capabilities are not without legitimate purpose and their appropriateness depends heavily on context. For example, although HTTP cookies make website more convenient and personalized, they can be used to violate a user's privacy by tracking their browsing behavior. Ultimately, the distinction between what information a user is willing to share with a first-party website (and with

© ICST Institute for Computer Sciences, Social Informatics and Telecommunications Engineering 2020
Published by Springer Nature Switzerland AG 2020. All Rights Reserved
N. Park et al. (Eds.): SecureComm 2020, LNICST 335, pp. 474–480, 2020.
https://doi.org/10.1007/978-3-030-63086-7_26

any third-party embedded content) is a personal decision with no one-size-fits-all solution: some users are willing to give up more privacy than others [8,10].

In recognition of the potential danger of dynamic web content, a number of policy enforcement systems, such as Content Security Policy (CSP), have been developed. These mechanisms allow a web developer to mediate the behavior and provenance of active content, most notably client-side JavaScript, by disallowing functionality. CSP can be used as a mitigation against cross-site scripting attacks (XSS), in which an adversary injects content onto a target website in the hope of exfiltrating data from a victim user of the site. While these defenses exist, their use is sparse, and often deployed in a "report-only mode that does not prevent attacks" [9]. Furthermore, the CSP may not be in the best interest of the user.

To combat the threat of data exfiltration through client-side JavaScript, we create Identity Armour, a prototype policy enforcement mechanism that, unlike the above-mentioned protections, does not rely upon the first-party. The contributions of our work are as follows:

- **Custom policy language**: We develop a novel policy language that allows users to choose what information is shared with first-party and third-party entities, mitigate the behavior of active content such as scripts, and identify possible privacy leaks.
- **Identity Armour prototype**: We implement a prototype version of Identity Armour in order to show that our custom policy language can be enforced in practice.
- **Identity Armour evaluation**: We evaluate our Identity Armour prototype, and show that it is effective at preventing real and synthetic exfiltration attacks. We also show that enforcement overhead is comparable to other methods proposed in the literature.

The rest of our paper is structured as follows: Sect. 2 overviews our technical solution, and discusses our implementation of Identity Armour. Section 3 presents our evaluation of Identity Armour. Section 4 discusses related work, and Sect. 5 concludes.

2   Overview

In this section we outline the use and implementation of Identity Armour. As a broad synopsis, Identity Armour is a Firefox XPCOM extension built on top of the JSFlow taint tracking JavaScript interpreter [3]. Identity Armour's enforcement engine follows a combined policy of a user-defined policy paired with a base policy that defines how JavaScript may act on any given webpage. The next section goes into detail as how this policy language functions within the enforcement engine and what JavaScript behavior the policy controls.

2.1   Policy Language

The policy language is whitelisting based and defines JavaScript behavior on a per domain basis. If any code from the webpage does not behave according to the rules of the defined policy, the enforcement engine stops it from executing. The policy language defines what sources of data are taint tracked, which external JavaScript libraries to load, and which JavaScript functions should be allowed to execute, all at runtime. The user policy is to have a customizable experience on a per webpage basis, and depending on the webpage, the policy can be more restrictive, based on the necessary actions the webpage needs to function correctly. The base policy is used to define actions that are allowed by a webpage that is not defined in the user policy. A webpage not defined in the user policy will still have its JavaScript be restricted by the specifications of the base policy. So that the technologically inexperienced user does not have the burden of implementing these user-defined policies, we implemented a learning aspect in which a user would visit a website and Identity Armour would then create a policy based off of the required actions for the website to perform normally. The system comes with a base policy pre-written, so the user does not have the duty of creating one.

2.2   Implementation Details

We use an extension because they are easily modified and deployed. Additionally, the work of Hedin et al. had already proved JSFlow is an effective taint tracking interpreter [3]. The enforcement engine of Identity Armour uses the dynamic taint tracking of JSFlow to trace individual data flows throughout the website's JavaScript to enforce that no sensitive data leaks. To effectively track data flows through the website's code, we interpose on low-level data propagation operations in JavaScript. Although JSFlow provides an underlying mechanism by which data flow can be tracked throughout execution of a web page (or web application), it does entail some limitations: an older version of Firefox, Firefox 30, must be used as newer browsers disallow implementing a custom JavaScript interpreter as extensions (a core design choice of JSFlow).

2.3   System Workflow

Once a user opens the browser, both policies are read into Identity Armour, and one comprehensive policy is created. When a user visits a website, the web content is loaded and then encountered JavaScript is run by the extension's JavaScript interpreter instead of Firefox's JavaScript engine. While the JavaScript is being parsed, if the externally loaded libraries do not match any of the libraries defined in the combined policy, then it is immediately rejected from the queue of scripts to interpret. If any functions are called which are not within the set of allowed functions specified by the policy, they are then terminated before execution. Finally, throughout this process, sources of information are being tainted and tracked through the system. If any information attempts to leave the user's browser, if be by HTTP request or image request, the user will then be prompted whether or not the information should be sent. The next section describes our evaluation of Identity Armour.

3   Analysis and Evaluation

Our evaluation attempts to answer two questions: how usable Identity Armour is and how secure is Identity Armour against simple and sophisticated attacks.

Experimental Setup. The performance portion of the evaluation was run on Firefox 30.0. All experiments were run on a Dell XPS laptop with an Intel Core i9-9980HK CPU@2.4 GHZ with 16 GB of RAM.

3.1   Performance Evaluation

Our analysis takes Alexa's top 10k websites and records time between page content load and JavaScript interpreted. This system is not compared against a modern browser because we believed the main source of overhead comes from using an interpreter written in an interpreted language. Spidermonkey, Firefox's JavaScript interpreter, being written in C++ [7], just by it's compiled nature is faster than the interpreted language version of a JavaScript engine. For this reason, we compared Identity Armour against a baseline JavaScript interpreter within an extension. By comparing Identity Armour to a JavaScript interpreter, implemented in the same manner, we can see the true cost of Identity Armour while browsing. Around 7% of the Alexa's top 10k websites were not able to be tested because of time-outs or problems with compatibility between the system and the websites being visited.

Table 1 shows Identity Armour has a combined system average JavaScript interpretation time of 6070 ms. There were a number of websites' JavaScript that took minutes to interpret, inflating the combined system average; this is evident by the lesser median and a standard deviation (over fifteen seconds). Next, by comparison Identity Armour on average added 491 ms to the interpretation time of the base JavaScript interpreter. The large difference between the median and mean and the relatively large standard deviation in both experiments show the volatility of JavaScript interpretation.

Table 1. Performance evaluation of Identity Armour vs the baseline JavaScript interpreter across Alexa's top ten thousand websites

	Identity Armour timing (ms)	Base JavaScript interpreter timing (ms)
Average load	6070	5579
Median load	3747	3301
Standard deviation	15228	13418

3.2   Attack Analysis

For the security analysis of the system, we decided to use both custom built malicious scripts and scripts from online resources like metasploit and tech blogs. In the scenarios presented, we assume that a user is visiting a malicious website for the first time, with these exploits intentionally embedded within the page, and only a base policy is used in conjunction with Identity Armour. For this experiment, the policy defines the information that should be taint tracked throughout the system and also defines certain functions that allow dynamic execution of code that should not be allowed to run.

For each exploit, either custom or real-world, we manually confirmed whether Identity Armour could stop malicious code from executing. All of the attacks were thwarted without requiring previous knowledge of the website being visited. To further test Identity Armour, we took the original malicious scripts and obfuscated them to make the behavior of the script unintelligible to the human eye. Since our extension enforces policies at the interpreter level, the same exploits were again defeated because the extension works at a lower root of trust than the served JavaScript. This experiment illustrates how Identity Armour can effectively protect users from information theft.

While Identity Armour adds substantial overhead, we believe the additional security offered by Identity Armour outweighs those costs.

4   Related Work

Given the high-profile nature of web security, there are numerous mechanisms proposed and deployed in academia and industry to protect browsers. We compare our work to the most closely related work, in some cases choosing a representative example for lack of space.

Client-Side Browser Protections: A key design aspect of Identity Armour is that it is purely a client-side protection mechanism. Previous approaches have also been purely client-side such as JSand [1]. JSand is representative of numerous works that use purely client-side enforcement but nevertheless, require the cooperation of web developers to deliver the protection framework and configuration from the server. The main difference between Identity Armour and these systems is that we allow for customizable, client-side policies with no cooperation from the server. We note that our system *does* require active participation on the part of the client, both to acquire policies and to install the protection mechanism. Although this requirement can impact adoption, we believe that future work can automatically craft and distribute policies.

Dataflow For JavaScript: One of the key features of Identity Armour is the use of data flow in order to enforce fine-grained mitigation. Several previous works have focused on detecting and blocking information leaks via dataflow, both statically and dynamically [4–6,12]. The most closely related work to our own is JSFlow [3], which statically defines a set of disallowed flows and dynamically tracks flows from predefined sources to predefined sinks. JSFlow serves as a foundational step in fine-grained privacy protections. As such, the flow-based portion of Identity Armour is inspired by the JSFlow approach, and we build our technology as an extension to the JSFlow codebase. Identity Armour is not limited to purely dataflow-based protections, and allows a user-configurable set of sources and sinks. Identity Armour includes novel user defined policies that then apply features from tools like CSP.

5   Conclusion

With the uncertain intentions of websites, users can not always be sure whether their information is safe. To combat this, we present Identity Armour, a dynamic taint tracking policy enforcement engine easily addable to the browser. We show that many of the most prevalent web security and privacy threats can be mitigated by empowering users to enforce their own policies. With the an average increase of 8.8% in JavaScript interpretation, we believe that our approach is comparable to other, less-flexible browser protections. Our results show that a variety of attacks, both straight forward and obfuscated, can be stopped. To further expand upon this work, we propose that future researchers find a more effective form of automatic policy construction and create an enforcement engine that can be used on a modern system. Ultimately, we hope that Identity Armour will inspire additional work in user-centric policy creation and enforcement.

References

1. Agten, P., Van Acker, S., Brondsema, Y., Phung, P.H., Desmet, L., Piessens, F.: JSand: complete client-side sandboxing of third-party javascript without browser modifications. In: Proceedings of the 28th Annual Computer Security Applications Conference, ACSAC '12, , New York, NY, USA, pp. 1–10. Association for Computing Machinery (2012)
2. Pew Research Center. Americans complicated feelings about social media in an era of privacy concerns. Accessed 06 Aug 2018
3. Hedin, D., Birgisson, A., Bello, L., Sabelfeld, A. JSFlow: tracking information flow in JavaScript and its APIs. In: Cho, Y., Shin, S.Y., Kim, S.W., Hung, C.C., Hong, J., (eds.) Proceedings of the 29th Symposium on Applied Computing, pp. 1663–1671. ACM (2014)
4. Kashyap, V., et al.: JSAI: a static analysis platform for javascript. In: Proceedings of the 22nd ACM SIGSOFT International Symposium on Foundations of Software Engineering, pp. 121–132 (2014)
5. Madsen, M., Livshits, B., Fanning, M.: Practical static analysis of javascript applications in the presence of frameworks and libraries. FSE **2013**, 499–509 (2013)
6. Madsen, M., Møller, A.: Sparse dataflow analysis with pointers and reachability. In: Müller-Olm, M., Seidl, H. (eds.) SAS 2014. LNCS, vol. 8723, pp. 201–218. Springer, Cham (2014). https://doi.org/10.1007/978-3-319-10936-7_13
7. MDN Contributors. SpiderMonkey: The Mozilla JavaScript runtime (2019). Accessed 21 June 2020

8. Norberg, P.A., Horne, D.R., Horne, D.A.: The privacy paradox: personal information disclosure intentions versus behaviors. J. Consum. Aff. **41**(1), 100–126 (2007)

9. Roth, S., Barron, T., Calzavara, S., Nikiforakis, N., Stock, B.: Complex security policy? a longitudinal analysis of deployed content security policies (2020)

10. Schwartz, P.M.: Property, privacy, and personal data. Harv. L. Rev. **117**, 2056 (2003)

11. Stanton, B., Theofanos, M.F., Prettyman, S., Furman, S.: Security fatigue. IT Prof. **18**(05), 26–32 (2016)

12. Tripp, O., Ferrara, P., Pistoia, M.: Hybrid security analysis of web javascript code via dynamic partial evaluation. In Proceedings of the 2014 International Symposium on Software Testing and Analysis, pp. 49–59 (2014)

Connecting Web Event Forecasting with Anomaly Detection: A Case Study on Enterprise Web Applications Using Self-supervised Neural Networks

Xiaoyong Yuan[1]([✉]), Lei Ding[2], Malek Ben Salem[3], Xiaolin Li[4],
and Dapeng Wu[5]

[1] Michigan Technological University, Houghton, MI 49931, USA
xyyuan@mtu.edu
[2] American University, Washington, DC 20016, USA
ding@american.edu
[3] Accenture Labs, Arlington, VA 22209, USA
malek.ben.salem@accenture.com
[4] Cognization Lab, Palo Alto, CA 94306, USA
xiaolinli@ieee.org
[5] University of Florida, Gainesville, FL 32608, USA
dpwu@ufl.edu

Abstract. Recently web applications have been widely used in enterprises to assist employees in providing effective and efficient business processes. Forecasting upcoming web events in enterprise web applications can be beneficial in many ways, such as efficient caching and recommendation. In this paper, we present a web event forecasting approach, DEEPEVENT, in enterprise web applications for better anomaly detection. DEEPEVENT includes three key features: web-specific neural networks to take into account the characteristics of sequential web events, self-supervised learning techniques to overcome the scarcity of labeled data, and sequence embedding techniques to integrate contextual events and capture dependencies among web events. We evaluate DEEPEVENT on web events collected from six real-world enterprise web applications. Our experimental results demonstrate that DEEPEVENT is effective in forecasting sequential web events and detecting web based anomalies. DEEPEVENT provides a context-based system for researchers and practitioners to better forecast web events with situational awareness.

Keywords: Anomaly detection · Event forecasting · Self-supervised learning · Neural networks

1 Introduction

Recently web applications play a major role in many enterprises. Enterprise web applications boost productivity by assisting employees in performing their daily

N. Park et al. (Eds.): SecureComm 2020, LNICST 335, pp. 481–502, 2020.
https://doi.org/10.1007/978-3-030-63086-7_27

tasks. On one side, web events in the enterprise web applications provide insightful sources for analyzing employee behaviors. By forecasting web events based on user behavior, we can provide better recommendation, caching, pre-fetching, and load balancing for enterprise web applications [8,36]. Web event forecasting has been investigated for many years [2,32,35]. However, two critical challenges exist in characterizing the sequence of web events: 1) Although many works have been conducted in forecasting web events, very few works investigated enterprise web applications. Web applications significantly improve productivity in modern enterprises and have become essential components in enterprise operations. Enterprise web applications are more well-organized and closely connected to each other compared to other web applications. Specific patterns of web events exist in the employees' browsing behavior. 2) With the increasing complexity and functionality of web applications, it becomes hard to forecast web events. Browsing a web page can produce a sequence of web events, and the length of the sequence varies a lot for different web pages. For example, a web event is usually made for the HTML of the web page itself, and subsequent events are made for each image, plug-in, audio clip, and other content referenced in the HTML. The web events for each kind of content increase the complexity of the sequence. The format and semantics of web events vary significantly from application to application. It is urgent to develop techniques to automate the process of characterizing web events and representing them in the desired way.

On the other side, enterprise web applications provide extended connectivity to an organization's assets and increase the attack surface of its web-facing infrastructure. Enterprise web applications have become favorite targets of cyberattacks due to easy access and constantly increasing vulnerabilities. Anomaly detection is a critical component to protect web applications against cyber threats. Supervised learning based anomaly detection solutions build detection systems by discovering abnormal behavioral patterns with the use of labeled training data [6,18,29,37]. Unfortunately, high quality annotated data is not easy to obtain, given the velocity, volume, and real-time nature of web events. Usually, labeled data are very imbalanced as it is hard to collect a large number of labeled anomalies as opposed to normal web events. Insufficient and imbalanced training data hinder the performance of machine learning models [12]. Limited labeled data from previous attacks undercut the ability to use supervised models, and constantly evolving attacks make such supervised models irrelevant.

To address the above challenges, we propose a novel deep neural network based approach, DEEPEVENT. By connecting web event forecasting and anomaly detection, DEEPEVENT improves the performance of web event forecasting for complicated web events, while detects anomalies by identifying the most unlikely events in the sequence. We evaluated DEEPEVENT on web events collected from six real-world web applications in a company for three months.

In this paper, we make the following contributions:

1) Context-based web events analysis for better user behavior forecasting: DEEPEVENT characterizes not only the individual web events, but also the relationships among the web events that co-occur within a context, *i.e.*, a

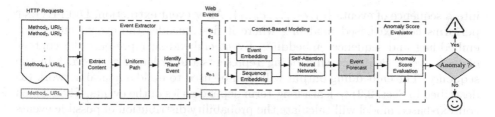

Fig. 1. Workflow of DEEPEVENT.

sequence of events that are commonly produced together for a specific user and web applications' flow characteristics. We leverage deep neural networks to model the context of a web event in a sequence. Based on the context, DEEPEVENT predicts the web events that are likely to appear with associated probabilities.

2) Self-supervised learning to overcome the need for labeled data: By connecting web event forecasting and anomaly detection, we can formulate anomaly detection as a self-supervised learning problem [13,30]. Self-supervised learning tasks do not require any prior knowledge of anomalous web events' features and their sequential relationships, but leverage naturally existing evidence as labeled data for training. Therefore, self-supervised learning overcomes the need for labeled data in anomaly detection. In addition, we leverage a pre-training process that learns the representations of web events to further compensate for the lack of labeled data.

3) Quantitative measures of the anomaly: Different from traditional anomaly detection methods, DEEPEVENT goes beyond binary prediction. Upon encoding the relationship between web events within the vector space, we can quantitatively predict the web events appearing in similar contexts. Therefore, DEEPEVENT predicts if a web event belongs to normal behavior and also measures the deviation of the abnormal event with respect to expected normal events. In such a way, we provide a quantitative measure of the detected anomaly.

We empirically validate that forecasts made by DEEPEVENT are more accurate than baseline solutions. We show that with the assist of web event forecasting, DEEPEVENT can identify anomalous events (*e.g.*, real-world exploits, widely-used web attacks) using the proposed quantitative measures. We find these results encouraging and note that they highlight the benefit of forecasting web events that co-occur within a context for anomaly detection.

2 Workflow of DeepEvent

We design three main components in DEEPEVENT: an event extractor to extract semantic events from web requests, a context-based model for sequential web event forecast as well as an anomaly score evaluator.

Figure 1 illustrates the workflow of DEEPEVENT. DEEPEVENT ingests a sequence of web requests from web applications as its input, *e.g.*, with a length of $n - 1$. Then it extracts the contents from web requests and converts them into a sequence of events $\{e_1, e_2, \ldots, e_{n-1}\}$. After event extraction, DEEPEVENT performs context-based modeling where it first encodes the events into event embedding and sequence embedding. Event embedding represents the content of each event. Sequence embedding represents the order of each event in the sequence. The embedding output will then be used to build a neural network (as described in Sect. 2.2) to learn long-term dependencies of the events. The trained context-based model will calculate the probability distribution of possible events to appear as the next one given $\{e_1, e_2, \ldots, e_{n-1}\}$ and provide the forecast of the upcoming event e_n. In addition, DEEPEVENT uses the predicted probability to evaluate the anomaly score of e_n.

We describe the three main components in the following sections.

2.1 Event Extraction

The purpose of event extraction is to extract semantic events from web requests. We use sequences of events to characterize web requests. For well-formatted web requests (*e.g.*, following REST API design), one can easily map these requests to events by extracting their HTTP methods and well-defined endpoints. However, most web requests may not share a well-organized representation or follow a consistent format. For example, URI paths may not be named around resources. Web developers may use various URI paths for the same resource on the web server. For instance, WordPress provides five different URIs and a custom one for users to access a post[1]. URI paths can be generated by randomized algorithms or encoding algorithms. Diverse web requests impede the effort to extract semantic events from URIs.

We propose a three-step event extraction method, including content extracting, path uniforming, and "rare" event identifying.

- **Extract Content**. We extract three components from web requests: HTTP methods (*i.e.*, GET, POST, UPDATE, etc.), URI paths, and the number of URI parameters. Our experimental results show that using merely these three components are effective in representing user behavior.
- **Uniform Path**. We apply a two-character Markov Chain model to detect the "random" elements in URI paths. We first segment URI paths into "elements" separated by special characters such as "/" and "-". We then investigate every character in the element from left to right. If the likelihood of the upcoming character based on the preceding two characters is lower than a certain threshold, then we consider the element as "random."[2]
- **Identify "RARE" Events**. We consider the events occurring less than T times in the training data as "RARE" events. In this way, we learn the information of "RARE" events during training, which helps us to understand if such rare events are anomalous or not.

---

[1] https://codex.wordpress.org/Using_Permalinks.
[2] We detect randomness in URIs based on a gibberish detection tool (https://github.com/rrenaud/Gibberish-Detector).

The entire process of pre-processing data proceeds as follows:

1. Extract HTTP methods, URI paths, and URI queries from web requests;
2. Segment URI paths into "elements" by special characters as delimiters;
3. Flag the "elements" as "RANDOM," if they are randomly generated or encoded;
4. Calculate the number of key-value pairs in the URI query;
5. Concatenate HTTP method, "derandomized" URI path, and the number of the URI query as an event.
6. If an event has never seen in the training set or has occurred less than T times, convert the event into a "RARE" event.

2.2 Context-Based Modeling

We propose context-based web request modeling, which takes a sequence of contextual events as input and outputs a sequence of corresponding events. We can mask the event of interest in the input sequence and train a model to predict it for the given sequence. Recurrent Neural Networks (RNNs), as well as their variants such as Long Short-Term Memory (LSTM) [11], have been proposed for security analytics in the sequential analysis due to their outstanding performance. Recently, self-attention neural networks [5] have been shown to be much more effective to capture long-term dependencies in a sequence compared to RNNs. Specifically, RNN passes the hidden states through the previous state while self-attention neural networks construct direct links between events within the context, which brings great merit in learning from the long-distance context.

Self-supervised Learning. To compensate for the lack of labeled data, we design a self-supervised learning task for event forecasting. Most existing supervised models are limited to the high-quality labeled data. In this paper, we leverage the existing event requests as the labels without any manual annotations. In practice, we randomly mask 25% events in the input sequence and replace these masked events with "mask" labels in the input sequence. We train the neural networks to predict "mask" events. In this way, the neural network learns the relationship of events and their dependency in the sequences. We use this neural network as a pretrained model for further event forecasting and anomaly detection. Our experimental results show that self-supervised pre-training significantly improves the prediction performance.

2.3 Anomaly Detection

We propose a way to calculate the anomaly score to quantitatively measure the likelihood of a new web request being anomalous. Given the current context, we predict a set of web requests that are likely to appear with associated probabilities. For a received web request, we rank it with the predicted set of web requests based on their associated probabilities calculated by the trained neural network. We calculate the anomaly score for the incoming web request as follows:

$$s = 1 - \frac{1}{\tau + 1}, \tag{1}$$

where τ denotes the rank of the newly received request based on its likelihood to appear (*i.e.*, the probability calculated by the context-based model), and s is in the range of $(0, 1)$. Higher anomaly scores indicate higher confidence level in classifying the event as an anomaly.

The anomaly score indicates the degree of deviation of the incoming web request from the expected normal requests. In Sect. 4.3, we show that the proposed anomaly score is able to differentiate anomalous web requests (*e.g.*, produced by various real-world web based attacks) from normal requests.

3   Methodology of Context-Based Modeling

In this section, we describe the detailed approach for context-based modeling (Sect. 2.2) and explain how we adapt three different types of neural networks to predict web requests. We compare the performance of the three neural networks in Sect. 4.4.

3.1   Self-attention Based Modeling

The design of self-attention based modeling is shown in Fig. 2. We first embed input events using the embedding layer, then use a self-attention neural network to encode the sequence and learn the dependency between events. In the output layer, we apply a Softmax function to squash the neural network and predict future events with associated probabilities.

We introduce two critical components of our adaptation: 1) event embedding and sequence embedding; and 2) a self-attention neural network.

Event Embedding and Sequence Embedding. Word embedding is widely used to represent the semantic meaning of tokens in NLP tasks. We adopt the basic idea of word embedding by extracting semantic representation of web events and generate event embedding. Sequential information represents the relative positions of events in the sequence. However, self-attention neural networks do not contain sequential information of events, because the distances of events are the same. Therefore, we add sequential information into the neural networks using a sequence embedding layer. Specifically, our embedding layer maps the web event and its position in the sequence into two 128-dimension vectors: $\{EE_1, EE_2, \ldots, EE_n\}$ and $\{SE_1, SE_2, \ldots, SE_n\}$. After generating the embedding on events and their positions, we sum up these two sequences as an embedded sequence $\{em_1, em_2, \ldots, em_n\}$, and feed it to the encoding layers of the self-attention network.

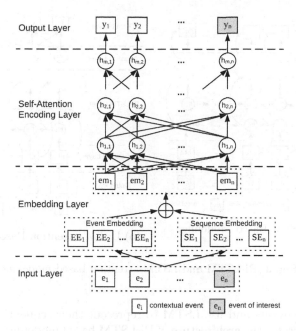

Fig. 2. Self-attention based modeling.

Self-attention Neural Network. We use a new type of neural networks, self-attention neural network [39], to solve sequential prediction problem. Specifically, we adapt BERT [5], a self-attention based neural network. BERT has been shown to outperform RNNs in almost all NLP tasks, and achieve state-of-the-art performance [5]. The success of BERT mainly comes from a scaled dot-product attention neural network:

$$\text{Attention}(Q, K, V) = \text{Softmax}(\frac{QK^T}{\sqrt{d_k}})V, \tag{2}$$

where Q, K, V are the query, key, and value of dimension d_k. In the self-attention neural network of DEEPEVENT, Q, K, V come from the same sequence of embedded events. The network learns to pay attention to the specific events in the sequence and captures the dependencies between events in the sequence. We use a model called Transformer, including a multi-head attention neural network (stacking several self-attention neural networks), a normalization layer, and a Softmax function. For the details of self-attention mechanism and Transformer, we refer the reader to [39].

3.2 Bi-LSTM Based Modeling

In addition to self-attention neural network, we implement a bidirectional LSTM neural network, called Bi-LSTM, which is widely used in sequential analysis. Similarly to Self-Attention Neural Network, we apply the event embedding

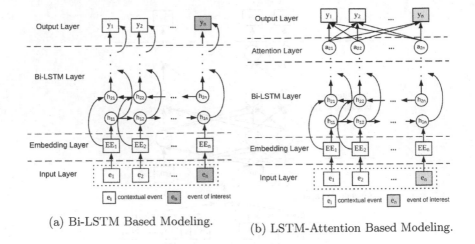

(a) Bi-LSTM Based Modeling.

(b) LSTM-Attention Based Modeling.

Fig. 3. Bi-LSTM and LSTM-attention based modeling.

here to encode events and use LSTM to represent their sequential relationship. Figure 3a illustrates the architecture of Bi-LSTM based modeling. Bi-LSTM uses an embedding layer to convert an input event into a 128-dimensional vector, then deploys multiple bidirectional LSTM layers to extract semantic information from the events. We test 1, 2, 3 layers of LSTM for each direction in the experiment. A fully connected layer with a Softmax function is stacked on top of LSTM layers to output the final prediction related to the event of interest.

3.3 LSTM-Attention Based Modeling

Attention mechanism is recently proposed to surpass recurrent neural networks by remembering longer sequences. The attention mechanism aims to pinpoint key events from a long sequence. We adapt an LSTM-Attention neural network using an additive attention mechanism. Figure 3b illustrates the architecture of LSTM-Attention based modeling. The additive attention mechanism sums up the outputs of LSTM with their weights and outputs the weighted sum as the prediction. The LSTM-Attention neural network consists of an embedding layer, bidirectional LSTM layers, an additive attention layer, and a fully connected layer with Softmax. The embedding layer and LSTM layers follow the setting in Bi-LSTM neural network. The attention layer learns the weight of each event and applies them to the final output. Note that the neural network in [37] detects anomaly based on the content of a single request. However, we use LSTM-Attention to predict an event in a sequence. We set the hidden number of the embedding layer in Bi-LSTM and LSTM-Attention to 128 and apply a drop-out mechanism with 20% dropout in LSTM layers to avoid overfitting.

Table 1. Dataset description.

Application	# of Events			# of Unique Events
	Train	Valid	Test	
Workqueue	146,489	18,026	19,004	101
DataRepo1	98,798	11,500	13,596	258
DevOpsApp	134,230	23,652	35,517	1,787
DataAnalyzer1	757,626	106,836	64,681	1,442
DataAnalyzer2	363,787	59,285	65,222	329
DataRepo2	63,862	7,235	8,307	37

4 Evaluation

In this section, we describe the experiments to evaluate DEEPEVENT on real-world web applications. We introduce our experimental settings in Sect. 4.1. We designed experiments to answer the following questions:

1. What is DEEPEVENT's performance in web event forecast compared with existing methods (Sect. 4.2)?
2. How effective is DEEPEVENT in evaluating real-world threats (Sect. 4.3)?
3. How do different neural networks perform in DEEPEVENT (Sect. 4.4)?
4. How do different model settings (*e.g.*, pre-training, window size) affect prediction performance (Sect. 4.5)?

4.1 Experimental Setup

Dataset. We evaluate DEEPEVENT on six real-world enterprise web applications described: 1) Workqueue: work queue of data collections and analysis; 2) DataRepo1: meta data repository; 3) DevOpsApp: continuous integration application for DevOps; 4) DataAnalyzer1: data reporting and visualization; 5) DataAnalyzer2: data analysis and visualization; 5) DataRepo2: graph and meta data repository. We collected 84 days of HTTP requests from the above applications in a real-world enterprise network. Figure 4 shows the number of HTTP requests for each web application in the dataset. We separate the dataset based on the date and use the first 64 days of data for training, 10 days for validation, and the last 10 days for testing. We assume all the HTTP requests are legitimate. Note that we only use the HTTP requests produced by normal users, and we exclude HTTP requests that are automatically generated by machines (*e.g.*, heartbeat requests). Table 1 summarizes the statistics of training/validation/test data of those six applications. We report the number of web events used in training/validation/test data and the number of unique events observed in the training data. The number of unique events indicates how many different events after event extraction occur in the datasets.

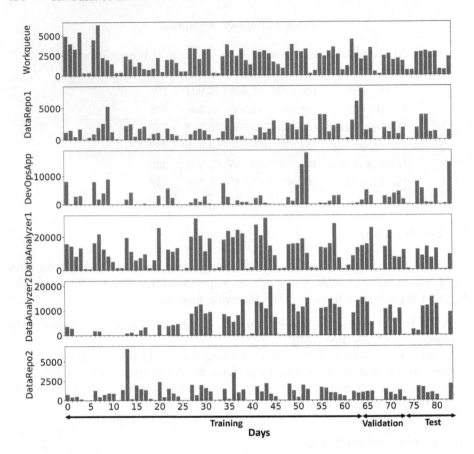

Fig. 4. Number of HTTP requests of six web applications in the dataset. We annotate the days used in the training/validation/test data. The number of HTTP requests on weekdays is higher than that on weekends, indicating the activity pattern of an enterprise network.

Evaluation Metrics. In the experiments, we evaluate the performance of DEEPEVENT using Top-N Accuracy and Anomaly Score. **Top-N Accuracy** measures the event prediction performance. *Top-N Accuracy* calculates the percentage of the correct event occurs among the top N events predicted by the model. In the experiments, we report Top-1 and Top-10 accuracy. **Anomaly Score**, as defined in Eq. 1, evaluates the capability in terms of differentiating anomalous requests from normal requests.

Modeling Settings. We use self-attention based modeling in DEEPEVENT in the experiments in Sect. 4.2 and Sect. 4.3 as it performs better in general compared to Bi-LSTM, and LSTM-attention based modeling for the six enterprise web applications. We show and discuss the comparison among the three for all six web applications in Sect. 4.4.

We set the threshold of "rare events" to 2 ($T = 2$). We set the number of hidden layers of DEEPEVENT to 8, the number of attention heads in each layer to 8, the number of hidden neurons in each head to 128, the batch size to 128. We use Cross-Entropy as our loss function. We optimize the loss function using Adam [17] with L2 weight decay. We set the learning rate to 0.001 in pre-training and reduce the learning rate by 10 in training. We train the models for 100 epochs. To accelerate the training process, we adopt an early-stop strategy, which ceases training if the cross-entropy loss of the validation data does not decrease in the past 10 epochs.

4.2 Evaluation of DeepEvent on Web Event Forecast

In this section, we evaluate DEEPEVENT on the web event forecast. We compare DEEPEVENT with two baseline models: a Markov model and an N-gram model.

The **Markov model** predicts the upcoming event depending on the current event. It assumes the upcoming event does not depend on the previous event. It learns transition probability from the training data. In this paper, we use a first-order Markov model [16].

The **N-gram model** aims to provide maximum likelihood estimates for the last event e_N given previous $N - 1$ contextual events $\{e_1, e_2, \ldots, e_{N-1}\}$ [36]:

$$\arg \max Pr\{e_N | e_1, e_2, \ldots, e_{N-1}\}, \tag{3}$$

where N denotes the number of events considered for prediction. Following the same setting in [33], we use a 3-gram model to predict the upcoming events.

In our experiments, we observe that DEEPEVENT performs better than the Markov and the 3-gram models. We report Top-1 and Top-10 accuracy of the three methods in Table 2. We highlight all the best results among the three methods. For all six applications, DEEPEVENT increases 11.2% Top-1 accuracy and 3.48% Top-10 accuracy on average compared with the best results of the Markov model and 3-gram Model.

The 3-gram model performs better than the Markov model, and DEEPEVENT outperforms both of them. This is because the long-distance context is lost in Markov model and 3-gram model. In contrast, DEEPEVENT has longer-term memory compared with the other two models so it can capture the sequential relationships of events that are not adjacent to each other, which is especially important for web applications because task-critical web requests may be separated by "not so relevant" requests. For example, browsing a web page can produce a sequence of web requests, where one web request is made for the HTML of the web page itself, and subsequent requests are made for each image, plug-in, audio clip, and other content referenced in the HTML. The web requests for each piece of content increase the length of the sequence. These make task-critical requests located far from each other. In general Top-10 accuracy is better than Top-1 accuracy because it is more likely to provide a correct prediction with more candidate events.

Table 2. Model comparison. We compare the performance of Markov model, 3-gram model, and our proposed DEEPEVENT model.

Application	Method	Top-1 Accuracy (%)	Top-10 Accuracy (%)
Workqueue	Markov Model	56.30	91.24
	3 Gram Model	61.90	94.17
	DeepEvent	**75.21**	**99.27**
DataRepo1	Markov Model	62.59	95.73
	3 Gram Model	74.17	96.76
	DeepEvent	**79.53**	**97.82**
DevOpsApp	Markov Model	44.84	80.42
	3 Gram Model	48.01	82.34
	DeepEvent	**56.73**	**89.51**
DataAnalyzer1	Markov Model	55.10	86.53
	3 Gram Model	63.07	90.90
	DeepEvent	**70.10**	**95.44**
DataAnalyzer2	Markov Model	70.21	95.96
	3 Gram Model	73.21	97.10
	DeepEvent	**78.45**	**97.72**
DataRepo2	Markov Model	95.05	99.74
	3 Gram Model	95.56	99.79
	DeepEvent	**97.47**	**99.87**

4.3   Evaluation of DeepEvent on Anomaly Detection

In this section, we evaluate DEEPEVENT's capability in distinguishing normal web requests from different types of anomalous requests such as real-world exploits, popular web attacks, and randomly injected HTTP requests. We compare their anomaly scores evaluated by DEEPEVENT with normal requests.

Real-World Exploits: We investigate five real-world exploits on DevOpsApp, which is built on top of Jenkins (jenkins.io/): CVE-2016-9299, CVE-2016-0792, CVE-2018-1999001, CVE-2018-1999002, CVE-2019-1003000. We mix the requests generated by the exploits with normal ones and test how DEEPEVENT evaluates the exploits.

Web Attacks: We investigate five widely-used attacks against web applications: SQL Injection [27], Cross-site Scripting (XSS) [25], Buffer Overflow [23], CRLF Injection [24], Server-Side Includes (SSI) Injection [26]. We mix the requests produced by those attacks with normal ones in the same way as real-world exploits and test how DEEPEVENT evaluates such requests. We use OWASP Zed Attack Proxy (ZAP) [28], to actively scan and attack web applications. ZAP is

Table 3. Anomaly score evaluation for DevOpsApp.

Request type	Average Anomaly score
Normal requests	0.316
CVE-2019-1003000	0.996
CVE-2016-9299	0.996
CVE-2016-0792	0.996
CVE-2018-1999001	0.787
CVE-2018-1999002	0.996
SQL Injection	0.976
Cross-site Scripting	0.975
Buffer Overflow	0.964
CRLF	0.964
SSI Injection	0.964
Random Injection	0.995

Table 4. Average anomaly score comparison between normal requests and randomly injected requests.

Application	Normal Request	Random Injection
Workqueue	0.151	0.948
DataRepo1	0.132	0.978
DevOpsApp	0.316	0.995
DataAnalyzer1	0.197	0.995
DataAnalyzer2	0.140	0.980
DataRepo2	0.014	0.887

one of the most popular open-source tools for web security and vulnerability assessment. ZAP accesses the web application using a normal user's credentials. It first crawls all the URIs of the web application and then crafts malicious web requests to exploit the vulnerabilities. We collect all the malicious requests and categorize them by the type of attacks. Then we randomly inject them into normal web requests to evaluate DEEPEVENT.

Random Injection: We conduct experiments to test how DEEPEVENT evaluate requests produced by abnormal behaviors, such as requests are generated by normal users but at abnormal occurrences. We simulate arbitrary web requests based on normal requests and inject them into a sequence of normal requests.

Table 3 shows the performance of anomaly detection for DevOpsApp. All real exploits achieve high anomaly scores, compared to normal requests (0.316). CVE-2018-1999001 gains the lowest anomaly score (0.787). Yet, it still has a large distance from normal requests. Four real exploits (CVE-2016-9299, CVE-2016-0792, CVE-2018-1999002, CVE-2019-1003000) were identified as "RARE" events. "RARE" events gain a high anomaly score (0.996), which suggests EventExtractor performs well in extracting web events from HTTP requests.

In our experiments, anomaly scores calculated by DEEPEVENT perform well at distinguishing the requests generated by web attacks from normal requests. In general, our proposed solution can distinguish anomalous requests from the normal request. For instance, the malicious requests and normal requests can be distinguished with a threshold value of 0.9 - most malicious requests have an anomaly score higher than 0.9 while most normal requests have a score lower than 0.9. We observe a few false positives for normal requests due to the low

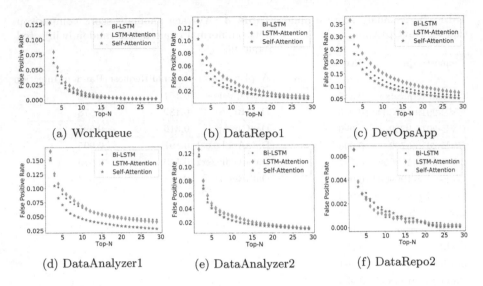

Fig. 5. False Positive Rate (FPR) comparison: we report FPR of Bi-LSTM, and LSTM-attention with different alarm thresholds (Top-N).

frequency of these normal events, which might be further improved with more training data to recognize unexpected normal requests. Some web attacks may gain a slightly high false negative rate (being classified as normal requests) than others. For example, Buffer Overflow has 2.37% false positive rate, because Buffer Overflow usually targets URI parameters as well as payload, which is not covered in this paper.

Table 4 shows the average anomaly score of normal requests and randomly injected requests for six web applications. Normal requests get low anomaly scores (0.158 on average) while randomly injected ones could raise the alarm with an extremely high anomaly score (0.964 on average). The large performance gap indicates that we can set a threshold to differentiate normal requests from randomly injected requests.

4.4   Neural Network Comparison

We compare three different neural networks proposed in context-based modeling in DEEPEVENT: Bi-LSTM, LSTM-attention, and Self-attention. To make a fair and comprehensive comparison, we use the same settings for three neural networks. We evaluate Bi-LSTM and LSTM-attention networks with three different numbers of LSTM layers: 1, 2, 3, and evaluate all three neural networks with five different window sizes: 8, 16, 32, 64, 128 and report the best results.

In Table 5, we report the best results of three neural networks with different settings (window size, number of LSTM layers, with/without pre-training). From the experimental results, we observe that Self-Attention usually achieves the highest accuracy (Top-1, Top-10). In most cases, Bi-LSTM performs second best.

Table 5. Comparison between three neural networks.

Application	Neural network	Top-1 accuracy (%)	Top-10 accuracy (%)
Workqueue	Bi-LSTM	74.69	99.00
	LSTM-Attention	73.55	98.66
	Self-Attention	**75.21**	**99.27**
DataRepo1	Bi-LSTM	78.20	97.36
	LSTM-Attention	78.61	96.39
	Self-Attention	**79.53**	**97.82**
DevOpsApp	Bi-LSTM	53.06	87.52
	LSTM-Attention	51.58	84.63
	Self-Attention	**56.73**	**89.51**
DataAnalyzer1	Bi-LSTM	70.84	93.47
	LSTM-Attention	**71.51**	93.15
	Self-Attention	70.10	**95.44**
DataAnalyzer2	Bi-LSTM	78.23	97.21
	LSTM-Attention	77.75	97.05
	Self-Attention	**78.45**	**97.72**
DataRepo2	Bi-LSTM	97.21	**99.91**
	LSTM-Attention	97.45	99.90
	Self-Attention	**97.47**	99.87

Bi-LSTM and LSTM-attention networks need to pass the hidden states through a long path to learn from the long-distance context. The context might be lost in a long path because of gradient vanishing [10]. This may not be suitable for web applications that have task-critical requests located far from each other. On the other hand, the self-attention neural network constructs direct links between requests within the context, which brings great merit in learning from the long-distance context.

To evaluate false positive and false negative rates of the three neural networks, we flag an event as an abnormal event if it is not among the top K candidate events predicted by the neural network. Correct predictions are considered as true positives. We select the best setting of the three neural networks (Bi-LSTM, LSTM-Attention, and Self-Attention) and calculate their false positive rates based on different alarm thresholds using Top-N, *i.e.*, threshold 10 means if the event is not in Top-10 prediction, it will be labeled as an alarm. As illustrated in Fig. 5, false positive rate decreases when we use a large threshold K. For the same threshold, Self-Attention based model achieves lower false positive rates than the other two models for all web applications except for DataRepo2. For DataRepo2, all three neural networks achieve extremely low false positive rates, less than 1%.

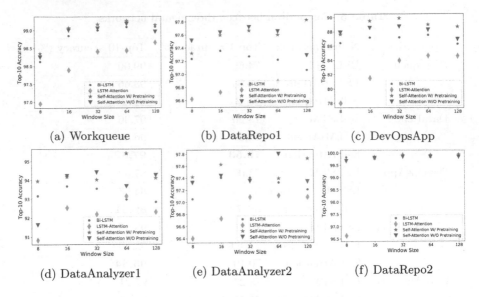

Fig. 6. Model comparison with different settings (window size and pre-training).

4.5 Evaluation of Different Model Settings

In this section, we evaluate the impact of different model settings on prediction performance.

Impact of Window Size. To evaluate the impact of window sizes, we test five different window sizes of contextual events: 8, 16, 32, 64, 128. As illustrated in Fig. 6, self-attention based model performs better than Bi-LSTM and LSTM-attention based models for longer sequences (*i.e.*, 128). The performance of Bi-LSTM and LSTM-attention based models degrade when the window size becomes 128. Bi-LSTM and LSTM-attention based models have decreasing weights on long-distance events as opposed to short-distance events, which may lead to vanishing gradients for longer-distance context.

Effectiveness of Pre-training. Pre-training helps to learn not only the last-event prediction but also the semantic information and relationship of all events among the sequence. We compare the performance of DEEPEVENT with and without pre-training. As shown in Fig. 6, the performance is improved with the proposed pre-training technique for all six applications in general. On average, self-attention with pre-training increases Top-10 prediction accuracy compared to self-attention without pre-training.

Especially, web applications with a large number of unique events may raise more uncertainty and lower accuracy in prediction. Pre-training largely improves the accuracy of prediction for these applications. For instance, the Top-10 accuracy of the three applications with the largest number of unique events (*i.e.*,

Table 6. Performance of predicting centered events.

Application	Model	Top-1 accuracy (%)	Top-10 accuracy (%)
Workqueue	Bi-LSTM	97.07	99.79
	LSTM-Attention	97.27	99.81
	Self-Attention	**98.33**	**99.91**
DataRepo1	Bi-LSTM	89.35	98.44
	LSTM-Attention	89.78	98.06
	Self-Attention	**90.33**	**99.16**
DevOpsApp	Bi-LSTM	74.00	91.72
	LSTM-Attention	71.85	89.41
	Self-Attention	**81.25**	**94.67**
DataAnalyzer1	Bi-LSTM	84.31	96.00
	LSTM-Attention	81.70	**96.78**
	Self-Attention	**85.01**	96.61
DataAnalyzer2	Bi-LSTM	86.87	97.93
	LSTM-Attention	86.83	97.71
	Self-Attention	**87.79**	**98.57**
DataRepo2	Bi-LSTM	96.87	99.87
	LSTM-Attention	97.23	99.90
	Self-Attention	**97.96**	**99.96**

DevOpsApp, DataAnalyzer1, and DataAnalyzer2) is greatly increased by applying pre-training models on the self-attention based models.

Evaluation of Predicting Centered Events. In the previous experiments, we predicted the last event in a sequence. For many web applications, requests are generated concurrently by a single action. The concurrent requests make it possible for us to leverage contextual events following the event of interest. We study the case where the event of interest to be predicted is centered by contextual events.

Table 6 shows the performance of DEEPEVENT predicting centered events. Comparing Table 5 and 6, we observe that the prediction performance of centered events is improved for all three models in general. For example, for Workqueue, the Top-1 accuracy achieved by self-attention based model increases from 75.21% to 98.33%. Self-attention based model achieves more improvement than Bi-LSTM and LSTM-attention based models when the event of interest is centered by contextual ones. The performance of prediction improves significantly when we predict the centered event instead of the last one. When predicting centered event, events located after the event of interest provide important information. In this way, the model incorporates context from both directions (i.e., left and right). On average of six applications, DEEPEVENT reduces Top-1 error rate by 52.56% and Top-5 error rate by 57.84% for predicting centered events.

5   Related Work

5.1   Web Event Forecasting

Web event forecast has been investigated for many years. Su *et al.* extracted access path from server logs and used n-gram models to predict web events for web caching and prefetching [35]. Awad *et al.* analyzed various supervised machine learning approaches for forecasting web events, such as Support Vector Machine, Markov Model and its variant, All-Kth Markov Model [1,2]. Da *et al.* summarized several clustering and Markov-based approaches for predicting web page access [4]. In this work, we target the enterprise web applications and demonstrates superior performance in forecasting web events compared to the existing approaches.

5.2   Web Anomaly Detection

Many statistical models have been used to detect anomaly for web applications [9,18,31]. Kruegel *et al.* [18,19] leveraged statistical models for characterizing HTTP query attributes such as query attribute length, attribute character distribution, and etc. Statistical models output probability values of a query and its individual attributes. The probability values reflect the likelihood of the occurrence with respect to an established profile. Juan *et al.* conducted Kruskal-Wallis and Kolmogorov-Smirnov test on payload length and payload histogram and modeled payload of normal web requests using Markov Chain [9]. Sakib and Huang detected HTTP-based Botnet C&C traffic based on features from web request URLs and DNS responses. Three anomaly detection methods were used in the detection system: Chebyshev's Inequality, One-class SVM, and Nearest Neighbor based Local Outlier Factor. Many supervised machine learning provides have been used to detect anomaly for web applications by providing a binary prediction of normal or abnormal web requests learning from the historical data. Pham *et al.* surveyed different machine learning algorithms such as random forest, logistic regression, decision tree, AdaBoost, and SGD that are used to build Web intrusion detection systems [29]. Oprea *et al.* detected malware in enterprises based on malicious HTTP traffic [22]. They leveraged 89 features extracted from enterprise networks and applied several supervised machine learning algorithms (*e.g.*, logistic regression, decision trees, random forest, and SVM) to learn from these features. Clustering and dimension-reduction are common techniques used in unsupervised learning based solutions [14,15,34]. These solutions first extracted features from HTTP GET parameters and URLs, and then used Random Projection (RP), Principal Component Analysis (PCA), and Diffusion Map (DM) to reduce the dimensionality of the data. Clustering algorithms (*e.g.*, K-means) have been applied to identify abnormal behavior.

Zolotukhin *et al.* [38] used several unsupervised learning algorithms such as PCA, K-means, Density-Based Spatial Clustering (DBSCAN) to model URL and User-Agent in HTTP headers and detect anomalies in web requests.

Recently deep learning approaches, in particular RNNs, have been established as state-of-the-art approaches in anomaly detection tasks. Liang *et al.* considered URLs as natural language sequences and applied LSTM and GRU to classify URLs as normal or abnormal requests [20]. Yu *et al.* proposed a neural network consisting of Bidirectional LSTMs and an attention model to extract critical components from URI path and body [37]. Liu *et al.* proposed an attention-based deep neural network, which located the malicious regions from HTTP requests and posts, and classified the malicious HTTP requests [21]. These approaches focus on analyzing the contents in a single web request. We focus on a sequence of web requests, which involves connections among requests and represents users' normal patterns and web application flow characteristics.

5.3 Deep Neural Networks for Log Data Analysis

Deep neural networks have been used to analyze log data. Du *et al.* proposed to model a sequence of system logs using LSTM and identified abnormal logs from normal execution [7]. An abnormal event is flagged if such an event is not within top-K probabilities to appear next. Shen *et al.* leveraged RNNs to predict future events based on previous observations using security logs collected from an intrusion prevention system [33]. The work focuses on the prediction of the upcoming security event given a sequence of events. Recently, Recurrent Neural Networks (RNNs) and its variants, Long Short-Term Memory (LSTM) and gated recurrent neural networks [3], have been established as compelling techniques in security analytics research. The RNN based methods analyze the behavior of security event logs or system logs in a session. However, applying these models to web anomaly detection is non-trivial. Logs generated by machines (*e.g.*, heartbeat) are much easier to be detected and predicted compared to web events generated by humans due to human's unpredictable behaviors. To analyze web events, we adapt a self-attention mechanism to learn from the contextual events. With the proposed event and sequence embedding techniques, the adapted self-attention mechanism captures the dependency of long-distance events from human behaviors.

6 Conclusion

In this work, we proposed a self-supervised neural network based approach, DEEPEVENT for web event forecasting and anomaly detection. We evaluated DEEPEVENT on web requests collected from real-world enterprise web applications. By connecting web event forecasting with anomaly detection, DEEPEVENT outperformed baseline methods and improved the performance of web event forecasting for complicated web events, while detected anomalies by identifying the most unlikely events in the sequence. We also demonstrated DEEPEVENT's capability in distinguishing normal web events from different types of anomalous events and measuring their anomaly scores.

References

1. Awad, M., Khan, L., Thuraisingham, B.: Predicting www surfing using multiple evidence combination. VLDB J. **17**(3), 401–417 (2008)
2. Awad, M.A., Khalil, I.: Prediction of user's web-browsing behavior: application of Markov model. IEEE Trans. Syst. Man Cybern. Part B (Cybern.) **42**(4), 1131–1142 (2012)
3. Chung, J., Gulcehre, C., Cho, K., Bengio, Y.: Empirical evaluation of gated recurrent neural networks on sequence modeling. In: NIPS Deep Learning and Representation Learning Workshop (2014)
4. Da, N.T., Hanh, T., Duy, P.H.: A survey of webpage access prediction. In: 2018 International Conference on Advanced Technologies for Communications (ATC), pp. 315–320. IEEE (2018)
5. Devlin, J., Chang, M.W., Lee, K., Toutanova, K.: BERT: pre-training of deep bidirectional transformers for language understanding. In: Proceedings of the 2019 Conference of the North American Chapter of the Association for Computational Linguistics: Human Language Technologies, Volume 1 (Long and Short Papers), pp. 4171–4186 (2019)
6. Dong, Y., Zhang, Y.: Adaptively detecting malicious queries in web attacks. arXiv preprint arXiv:1701.07774 (2017)
7. Du, M., Li, F., Zheng, G., Srikumar, V.: DeepLog: anomaly detection and diagnosis from system logs through deep learning. In: Proceedings of the 2017 ACM SIGSAC Conference on Computer and Communications Security (CCS) (2017). https://doi.org/10.1145/3133956.3134015
8. El-Sayed, M., Ruiz, C., Rundensteiner, E.A.: Fs-Miner: efficient and incremental mining of frequent sequence patterns in web logs. In: Proceedings of the 6th Annual ACM International Workshop on Web Information and Data Management, pp. 128–135 (2004)
9. Estevez-Tapiador, J.M., Garcia-Teodoro, P., Diaz-Verdejo, J.: Measuring normality in http traffic for anomaly-based intrusion detection. Comput. Netw. **45**, 175–193 (2004)
10. Hochreiter, S., Bengio, Y., Frasconi, P., Schmidhuber, J., et al.: Gradient flow in recurrent nets: the difficulty of learning long-term dependencies (2001)
11. Hochreiter, S., Schmidhuber, J.: Long short-term memory. Neural Comput. **9**(8), 1735–1780 (1997)
12. Japkowicz, N., Stephen, S.: The class imbalance problem: a systematic study. Intell. Data Anal. **6**, 429–449 (2002)
13. Jing, L., Tian, Y.: Self-supervised visual feature learning with deep neural networks: a survey. IEEE Trans. Pattern Anal. Mach. Intell. (2020). https://ieeexplore.ieee.org/abstract/document/9086055
14. Juvonen, A., Sipola, T.: Adaptive framework for network traffic classification using dimensionality reduction and clustering. In: 2012 IV International Congress on Ultra Modern Telecommunications and Control Systems, pp. 274–279. IEEE (2012)
15. Juvonen, A., Sipola, T., Häämäläinen, T.: Online anomaly detection using dimensionality reduction techniques for HTTP log analysis. Comput. Netw. **91**, 46–56 (2015)

16. Kemeny, J.G., Snell, J.L.: Markov Chains. Springer, New York (1976)
17. Kingma, D.P., Ba, J.: Adam: a method for stochastic optimization. In: International Conference for Learning Representations (2015)
18. Kruegel, C., Vigna, G.: Anomaly detection of web-based attacks. In: Proceedings of the 10th ACM Conference on Computer and Communications Security, pp. 251–261. ACM (2003)
19. Kruegel, C., Vigna, G., Robertson, W.: A multi-model approach to the detection of web-based attacks. Comput. Netw. **48**(5), 717–738 (2005)
20. Liang, J., Zhao, W., Ye, W.: Anomaly-based web attack detection: a deep learning approach. In: Proceedings of the 2017 VI International Conference on Network, Communication and Computing, pp. 80–85. ACM (2017)
21. Liu, T., Qi, Y., Shi, L., Yan, J.: Locate-then-detect: real-time web attack detection via attention-based deep neural networks. In: Proceedings of the 28th International Joint Conference on Artificial Intelligence, pp. 4725–4731. AAAI Press (2019)
22. Oprea, A., Li, Z., Norris, R., Bowers, K.: MADE: security analytics for enterprise threat detection. In: Proceedings of the 34th Annual Computer Security Applications Conference, pp. 124–136. ACM (2018)
23. OWASP: Buffer overflow. https://www.owasp.org/index.php/Buffer_Overflow
24. OWASP: Crlf injection. https://www.owasp.org/index.php/CRLF_Injection
25. OWASP: Cross-site scripting (xss). https://www.owasp.org/index.php/Cross-site_Scripting_(XSS)
26. OWASP: Server-side includes (ssi) injection. https://www.owasp.org/index.php/Server-Side_Includes_(SSI)_Injection
27. OWASP: Sql injection. https://www.owasp.org/index.php/SQL_Injection
28. OWASP: Zed attack proxy project. https://www.owasp.org/index.php/OWASP_Zed_Attack_Proxy_Project
29. Pham, T.S., Hoang, T.H., Vu, V.C.: Machine learning techniques for web intrusion detection - a comparison. In: Proceedings of the 8th International Conference on Knowledge and Systems Engineering, pp. 291–297. IEEE (2016)
30. Raina, R., Battle, A., Lee, H., Packer, B., Ng, A.Y.: Self-taught learning: transfer learning from unlabeled data. In: Proceedings of the 24th International Conference on Machine Learning, pp. 759–766. ACM (2007)
31. Robertson, W., Vigna, G., Kruegel, C., Kemmerer, R.A., et al.: Using generalization and characterization techniques in the anomaly-based detection of web attacks. In: NDSS (2006)
32. Sharif, M., Urakawa, J., Christin, N., Kubota, A., Yamada, A.: Predicting impending exposure to malicious content from user behavior. In: Proceedings of the 2018 ACM SIGSAC Conference on Computer and Communications Security, pp. 1487–1501. ACM (2018)
33. Shen, Y., Mariconti, E., Vervier, P.A., Stringhini, G.: Tiresias: predicting security events through deep learning. In: Proceedings of the 2018 ACM SIGSAC Conference on Computer and Communications Security (CCS) (2018). https://doi.org/10.1145/3243734.3243811
34. Sipola, T., Juvonen, A., Lehtonen, J.: Anomaly detection from network logs using diffusion maps. In: Iliadis, L., Jayne, C. (eds.) AIAI/EANN -2011. IAICT, vol. 363, pp. 172–181. Springer, Heidelberg (2011). https://doi.org/10.1007/978-3-642-23957-1_20
35. Su, Z., Yang, Q., Lu, Y., Zhang, H.: WhatNext: a prediction system for web requests using n-gram sequence models. In: Proceedings of the First International Conference on Web Information Systems Engineering, vol. 1, pp. 214–221. IEEE (2000)

36. Yang, Q., Zhang, H.H., Li, T.: Mining web logs for prediction models in www caching and prefetching. In: Proceedings of the Seventh ACM SIGKDD International Conference on Knowledge Discovery and Data Mining, pp. 473–478 (2001)
37. Yu, Y., Yan, H., Guan, H., Zhou, H.: DeepHTTP: semantics-structure model with attention for anomalous HTTP traffic detection and pattern mining. arXiv preprint arXiv:1810.12751 (2018)
38. Zolotukhin, M., Hämäläinen, T., Kokkonen, T., Siltanen, J.: Analysis of http requests for anomaly detection of web attacks. In: Proceedings of the 12th International Conference on Dependable, Autonomic and Secure Computing. IEEE (2014)
39. Vaswani, A., et al.: Attention is all you need. In: Advances in Neural Information Processing Systems, pp. 5998–6008 (2017)

Performance Analysis of Elliptic Curves for VoIP Audio Encryption Using a Softphone

Nilanjan Sen[1]([✉]), Ram Dantu[2], and Mark Thompson[2]

[1] Western Illinois University, Macomb, IL 61455, USA
N-Sen@wiu.edu
[2] University of North Texas, Denton, TX 76207, USA
{ram.dantu,mark.thompson2}@unt.edu

Abstract. The usage of online media streaming has become an essential part of our daily lives due to COVID-19 pandemic. The security issues have gained in importance as well with the proliferative use of real-time media. Usually, symmetric key encryption schemes are used for encrypting real-time media, which are transmitted as Real-time Transport Protocol (RTP) payload. RTP uses the Secure RTP (SRTP) to secure its payload. Several issues exist in the existing SRTP media protection scheme that can be solved by applying lightweight asymmetric key cryptography such as Elliptic Key Cryptography (ECC). We have proposed some suitable Elliptic Curves for real-time audio encryption, which do not compromise the quality of the audio calls.

Keywords: Real-time audio · SRTP · Elliptic curve · ECC · Security · VoIP

1 Introduction

Real-time media streaming is a popular mode of entertainment and is used for professional and academic purposes. The present COVID-19 situation has increased the importance of real-time media services even more. VoIP audio calls are the integral part of real-time media. However, the proliferative use of real-time media streaming is simultaneously increasing the security threat, such as eavesdropping, copyright infringement, sensitive data revelation, and more. Real-time media is transmitted through the Real-Time Transport Protocol (RTP) with the help of Voice over IP (VoIP). The Secure Real-time Transport Protocol (SRTP) works over RTP and transmits encrypted RTP payload. SRTP uses a symmetric key encryption scheme. The existing SRTP encryption scheme may be vulnerable to the eavesdroppers due to some problems discussed in Sect. 2. These problems can be rectified using an asymmetric key encryption scheme. Since audio/ video quality is an essential issue in real-time media streaming, we

N. Park et al. (Eds.): SecureComm 2020, LNICST 335, pp. 503–508, 2020.
https://doi.org/10.1007/978-3-030-63086-7_28

should use a lightweight asymmetric key encryption scheme, such as Elliptic Key Cryptography (ECC). Its key size is smaller, and the computation time is lesser than other asymmetric key encryption schemes such as RSA.

ECC is based on Elliptic curves (EC). To maintain real-time media quality, we need to choose suitable elliptic curves, which result in less network latency and jitter. In this paper, we have discussed our work to find suitable ECs to secure real-time audio calls a.k.a. VoIP calls. We have also developed a new short-Weierstrass elliptic curve, EW_{256357} at the 128-bit security level, which is more secure than a widely used NIST-recommended P-256 curve, and suitable for real-time audio encryption.

2   Motivation

We have noticed following issues in existing SRTP system:

- Session Initiation Protocol (SIP) is used for real-time audio call establishment [9] and is also used to exchange key information. The SIP messages are not encrypted, so the eavesdroppers can intercept those to get the key information. Security expert Anthony Critelli discussed one such attack in [3].
- Gupta and Shmatikov showed that the sender might unknowingly transmit old key information during the key exchanging phase of a new audio call session. Consequently, the attacker may decrypt the payloads by exploiting that old key information [11].
- The plaintext and ciphertext sizes are the same in the AES-CTR encryption scheme. If the Variable Bit Rate encoder is used during the audio call, the attacker may guess some phrases and words by comparing the bit-rate patterns of the captured packets with the known encrypted data [4–6].

These problems can be rectified using a light-weight asymmetric key encryption protocol such as ECC. Different types of elliptic curves are commercially used, such as X9.62 curves, NIST-recommended curves and Brainpool curves. NIST P-256 curve is an efficient elliptic curve. However, this curve has some security issues, such as lack of transparency in the curve generation process. NIST P-256 curve is weakly twist secure [8], hence vulnerable to specific attacks, such as Invalid-curve attack [7]. So, we developed a new elliptic curve suitable for VoIP audio encryption.

3   Methodology

All experiments were performed on 64-bit Ubuntu 16.04 platform. We used C and OpenSSL crypto library for the audio encryption experiments. A softphone, named Linphone, was used in this experiment. The Elliptic Curve Integrated Encryption Scheme was used as an ECC encryption scheme. We implemented

Fig. 1. Block diagram of experimental setup.

the newly proposed elliptic curve in Java and Bouncy Castle crypto library to test its real-time audio encryption performance.

For the audio encryption experiment, we used one SIP server and two clients where the server and one client were connected to the institutional network through WiFi. The second client was connected to the Internet. All clients had a pair of an EC-based public and private keys, known as their original keys which are publicly available, and certified by some Certificate Authority. During the call initiation phase, one of the clients (or caller) generated an ephemeral pair of EC-based pubic and private keys, known as session keys. The caller sent its encrypted ephemeral public key to the other client (the callee). The caller's ephemeral public key was encrypted by callee's original public key. The callee decrypted the caller's ephemeral public key by its original private key, generated its ephemeral pair of EC-based session keys, and followed the same steps to send its encrypted ephemeral public key to the caller. In this way, the caller and callee exchanged the EC based session key during the call setup. This method protected the real-time transmission system from the Man-in-the-middle attacks. The two pairs of session keys were used for real-time media encryption. For every session, the caller and callee generated a new pair of EC based session keys. The key exchange operation is described in detail in the next section. Figure 1 depicts the block diagram of our experimental setup.

3.1   Key Exchange Phase of Real-Time Audio Encryption

The SIP protocol is used for initiating a real-time media transmission session. SIP packets contain call setup and key exchange information. The later is available in plain text within the Session Description Protocol (SDP) portion of the SIP INVITE and 200 OK packets. SIP packets are generally un-encrypted, so the key information is visible.

We have used the ECC-based encryption technique where the clients' encrypted public keys are exchanged through SIP messages. Since the clients' private keys are not shared, if the attacker can somehow know the clients' public keys from intercepted SIP messages, she/ he cannot decrypt the SRTP payload. In our experiment, the caller had sent its ephemeral public key through SIP INVITE message, and the callee had sent its ephemeral public key through SIP 200 OK messages. The screenshot of such a SIP INVITE message is shown in Fig. 2.

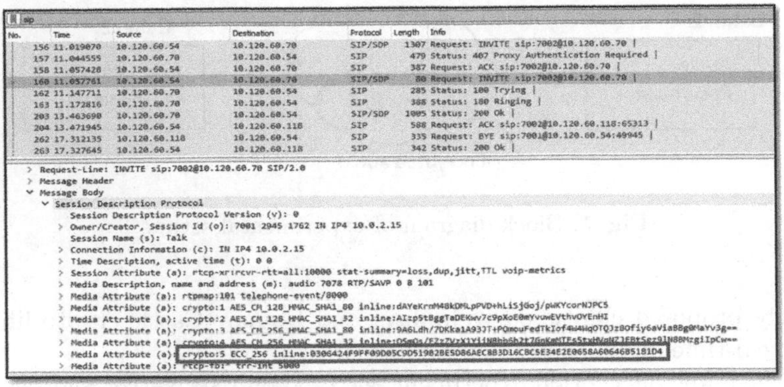

Fig. 2. SIP INVITE message with sender's 256-bit Elliptic curve public key.

The figure also shows the presence of AES session key information in SIP INVITE message. Since the AES key information is in plaintext, it becomes vulnerable to attacks.

3.2 Replacement of SRTP's Existing AES Scheme by ECC

Due to the security issues discussed in Sect. 2, we have replaced the existing AES scheme of SRTP by ECC. Usually, asymmetric key encryption schemes are not used for payload encryption, but we saw that real-time audio quality was not affected by ECC encryption. The network latency and network jitter are two essential parameters to measure the performance of real-time media transmission. In our experiments, the latency of chosen ECs are within 12 ms, and jitter values are within 9 ms for real-time audio. These values are far below the maximum values recommended by ITU-T G.114 [2] and Cisco [1]. So, we can rectify the problems of the existing SRTP system by ECC implementation for better security. In our proposed scheme, the existing AES-based SRTP system is replaced by an ECC-based encryption system. The proposed SRTP real-time media encryption system is depicted in Fig. 3.

4   Results of the Experiments

We experimented with four types of elliptic curves, viz. X9.62 prime and binary curves, SECG prime curve, NIST prime, and binary curves, and Brainpool prime curves. 15 elliptic curves were tested for real-time audio encryption.

4.1   Suitable Elliptic Curves for Real-Time Media Encryption

After analyzing the performance of 15 elliptic curves with respect to network latency and jitter, we concluded that X9.62 256-bit prime curve, SECG 256-bit

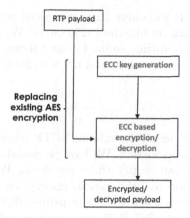

Fig. 3. Proposed SRTP media encryption system architecture.

prime curve, and Brainpool 256-bit random and twisted prime curves could be suitable for real-time audio encryption. We have also noticed that the prime curves' performance was better than that of binary elliptic curves on audio encryption.

4.2   New Secure Elliptic Curve for Real-Time Media Encryption

Based on all requirements of a secure elliptic curve, we have developed a 256-bit twist secure short-Weierstrass elliptic curve (a prime curve) at 128-bit security level [10]. The equation of our proposed curve EW_{256357} is

$$E : y^2 = x^3 - 3x + 5029 \tag{1}$$

Our newly proposed curve contains all traits that are essential for a secure curve. Our curve is compatible with the NIST P-256 curve, which means it can fit all applications that use the NIST P-256 curve. At the same time, our curve

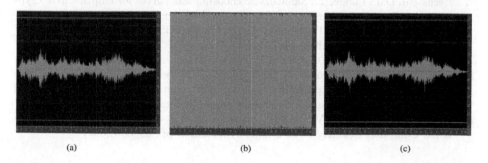

(a)   (b)   (c)

Fig. 4. (a) Original waveform of the audio before encryption (b) waveform of the encrypted audio (c) waveform of the decrypted audio.

is more secure than the P-256 curve since it is twist secure, and its generation process is fully transparent, unlike the P-256 curve. We have successfully tested our curves by encrypting real-time audio. Figure 4 shows the original audio waveform, the waveform after encryption, and the waveform after decryption.

5 Conclusion

In this paper, we have discussed the existing SRTP scheme's problems regarding secure real-time media transmission. We have proposed an ECC based alternate encryption scheme that can rectify those problems. We have suggested some suitable elliptic curves for real-time audio encryption to protect VoIP audio calls. We have also developed a new 256-bit prime elliptic curve, which is more secure than the widely-used NIST P-256 prime curve and is suitable for real-time audio encryption.

References

1. CISCO - Quality of Service for Voice over IP. https://www.cisco.com/c/en/us/td/docs/ios/solutions_docs/qos_solutions/QoSVoIP/QoSVoIP.pdf
2. ITU-T, Series G: Transmission Systems and Media, Digital Systems and Networks. https://www.itu.int/rec/T-REC-G.114-200305-I
3. Critelli, A.: Hacking VoIP: Decrypting SDES Protected SRTP Phone Calls. https://www.acritelli.com/blog/hacking-voip-decryptingsdes-protected-srtp-phonecalls
4. White, A.M., Matthews, A.R., Snow, K.Z., Monrose, F.: Phonotactic reconstruction of encrypted VoIP conversations: hookt on fon-iks. In: IEEE Symposium on Security and Privacy (2011)
5. Wright, C.V., Ballard, L., Monrose, F., Masson, G.M.: Language identification of encrypted VoIP traffic: alejandra y roberto or alice and bob. In: 16th Usenix Security Symposium, pp. 43–54 (2007)
6. Wright, C.V., Ballard, L., Monrose, F., Masson, G.M.: Spot me if you can: uncovering spoken phrases in encrypted VoIP conversations. In: IEEE Symposiumon Security and Privacy **28** (2008)
7. Bernstein, D.J., Lange, T.: SafeCurves: choosing safe curves for elliptic-curve cryptography. https://safecurves.cr.yp.to. Accessed 09 August 2020
8. Bernstein, D.J., Lange, T.: Security dangers of the NIST curves. https://cr.yp.to/talks/2013.05.31/slides-dan+tanja-20130531-4x3.pdf
9. Rosenberg, J., et al.: RFC 3261: SIP: Session Initiation Protocol
10. Sen, N., Dantu, R., Morozov, K.: EW_{256357}: a new secure NIST P-256 compatible elliptic curve for VoIP applications' security. In: Accepted in 16th EAI International Conference on Security and Privacy in Communication Networks (2020)
11. Gupta, P., Shmatikov, V.: Security analysis of voice-over-IP protocols. In: 20th IEEE Computer Security Foundations Symposium, pp. 49–63 (2007)

TCNN: Two-Way Convolutional Neural Network for Image Steganalysis

Zhili Chen(✉), Baohua Yang, Fuhu Wu, Shuai Ren, and Hong Zhong

School of Computer Science and Technology, Anhui University, Hefei, China
zlchen@ahu.edu.cn, 779541664@qq.com, 12088@ahu.edu.cn, 154209401@qq.com,
zhongh@mail.ustc.edu.cn

Abstract. Recently, convolutional neural network (CNN) based methods have achieved significantly better performance compared to conventional methods based on hand-crafted features for image steganalysis. However, as far as we know, existing CNN based methods extract features either with constrained (even fixed), or random (i.e., randomly initialized) convolutional kernels, and this leads to limitations as follows. First, it is unlikely to obtain optimal results for exclusive use of constrained kernels due to the constraints. Second, it becomes difficult to get optimal when using merely random kernels because of the large parameter space to learn. In this paper, to overcome these limitations, we propose a two-way convolutional neural network (TCNN) for image steganalysis, by combining both constrained and random convolutional kernels, and designing respective sub-networks. Intuitively, by complementing one another, the combination of these two kinds of kernels can enrich features extracted, ease network convergence, and thus provide better results. Experimental results show that the proposed TCNN steganalyzer is superior to the state-of-the-art CNN-based and hand-crafted features-based methods, at different payloads.

Keywords: Steganalysis · Two-way · Convolutional neural network

1 Introduction

Steganalysis is a kind of reverse analysis technology against steganography. Its purpose is to judge whether there is hidden information according to the extracted features of the image, and then distinguish the cover and stego.

Recently, deep convolutional neural network (CNN) has been increasingly applied to image steganalysis, and achieved better performance compared to conventional methods based on hand-crafted features. For instance, Xu et al. [12] proposed XuNet based on CNN, adding the absolute value (ABS) layer to narrow the range of feature map. In addition, TanH activation [4] was used in the front part of the network to improve the learning ability of features. Ye et al. [13] proposed a CNN which marks a significant breakthrough in the field of steganalysis. They initialized the first layer with the high-pass filter set in SRM,

N. Park et al. (Eds.): SecureComm 2020, LNICST 335, pp. 509–514, 2020.
https://doi.org/10.1007/978-3-030-63086-7_29

adopted a new activation function called truncated linear unit (TLU) and introduced the information of selection channel. This scheme greatly improved the detection performance and had obvious advantages over the traditional methods. Boroumand *et al.* [1] proposed a deep residual network called SRNet, which has made the latest achievements in image steganalysis.

As far as we know, existing CNN based steganalyzers extract features through either constrained convolutional kernels [11–13] or random ones [1]. In other words, they use one-way networks of either constrained or random convolutional kernels. The resulted limitations are as follows. First, if constrained convolutional kernels are used, it is unlikely that the optimal result is learnt due to the constraints enforced artificially. Second, if random convolutional kernels are applied, the parameter space to learn will become very large, and it is difficult to learn the optimal result without falling into sub-optimal ones.

In [8], the authors proposed a dual CNN for image steganalysis that consists of two parallel, identical sub-CNNs. Each sub-CNN applies Xu and Wu's design [12]. Two different forms of inputs are fed into the two sub-CNNs, respectively. The authors showed that different forms of inputs would improve the steganalysis performance. However, it is shown that the improvement is quite limited.

Different from the work [8], in this paper, to further improve the performance, we build a two-way network structure, each subnetwork of which is designed differently but complementarily. Specifically, we combine both constrained and random convolutional kernels into a two-way convolutional neural network (TCNN) for image steganalysis, expecting to extract more comprehensive features, and globally optimize the detection in a uniform network. We input images into two sub-networks for feature extraction, respectively. The first sub-network are initialized with all the 30 basic filters (convolutional kernels) used in the computation of residual maps in SRM [3], while the second sub-network are initialized with random filters with the same sizes. The two kinds of initialization are supposed to extract stego noise residual with both empirical convolutional kernels and learnt ones. Both sub-networks are then processed similarly, except with their respective appropriate pooling operations. Finally, the features extracted from both sub-networks are fused together, input to the classifier module, and the whole network is globally optimized. The proposed network combines the very best of constrained and random convolutional kernels, and its depth is shown to be shallow when getting a good result.

The rest of the paper is organized as follows. Section 2 describes the proposed network. Section 3 shows the experimental results and analysis. Finally, the concluding remarks of this paper and future works are given in Sect. 4.

2   The Proposed TCNN

2.1   Motivation

To illustrate the necessity of the two-way idea, we design 2 two-way networks, and investigate their performances as follows. The first network combines two sub-networks, each of which are initialized by the high-pass filters mentioned in SRM

Table 1. Performance comparison among one-way network, HPF+HPF and HPF+RND two-way networks in terms of detection error (P_E).

Model	S-UNIWARD		WOW		HILL	
	0.2	0.4	0.2	0.4	0.2	0.4
One-way	0.1670	0.0910	0.1368	0.0764	0.1918	0.1329
HPF+HPF Two-way	0.1985	0.0983	0.1271	0.0655	0.1805	0.1151
HPF+RND Two-way	0.1583	0.0805	0.1173	0.0585	0.1725	0.0959

[3]. The second one consists a sub-network initialized with the same high-pass filters, and the other sub-network initialized with random filters. Moreover, for each two-way network, the average pooling and maximum pooling algorithms are used in the two sub-networks, respectively. For convenience, we call the first two-way network as HPF+HPF two-way network, and the second one as HPF+RND two-way network.

Table 1 shows the performance comparison among HPF+HPF and HPF+RND two-way networks, and one way network, which is initialized with the SRM high-pass filters and applies average pooling operations, for steganography methods S-UNIWARD, WOW and HILL at payloads 0.2 and 0.4 bpp. From the first two rows, we can see that the performance of HPF+HPF two-way network is slightly better than that of one-way network for WOW and HILL, while slightly worse for S-UNIWARD, especially at low payloads. This indicates that the HPF+HPF two-way network perform comparatively with the one-way network, since many extended features in the HPF+HPF two-way network are repetitive or useless. Table 1 also demonstrates that the performance HPF+RND two-way network is obviously better than both one-way and HPF+HPF two-way networks. This shows that, by combining both constrained and random filters (convolutional kernels), the features extracted become more comprehensive, and the detection results are significantly improved.

2.2 TCNN Architecture

From the motivation above, our design takes the HPF | RND two-way structure. As shown in Fig. 1, the proposed TCNN network consists of two sub-networks (A/B), each of which is composed of pre-processing module and feature extraction module. The sub-network A is initialized with constrained convolutional kernels, while the sub-network B is initialized with random ones. Both sub-networks take as images as input, and share the same classification module. The structures of the two sub-networks are similar, but there are some differences detailed as follows.

In sub-network A, the first layer, also known as a pre-processing module, consists of 30 high-pass filters used in SRM [3] and an Absolute Value (ABS) layer. The ReLU function [9] serves as the activation function of the entire sub-network A. The feature extraction module consists of six layers, in which batch

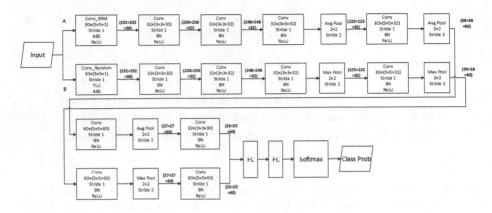

Fig. 1. The proposed TCNN architecture.

normalization [7] is added. And the pooling operations from 1st to 3rd layers are suppressed, the average pooling is set from the fourth layer. Unlike sub-network A, the weights of the first layer in sub-network B are initialized at random. Except that the activation function of the first layer is TLU [13], all other layers use the ReLU function. Moreover, we apply the maximum pooling algorithm in sub-network B. In particular, The ABS layer is following the TLU activation function in the pre-processing module. Finally, the outputs of the last layers of the feature extraction module in sub-network A and B are fused, and the fused features are transferred into the classification module. Two fully-connected layers and a softmax function map the vector to classification probability.

3   Experiments

3.1   Experiment Setup

We perform experiments using our TCNN to detect three spatial domain content-adaptive steganographic algorithms: S-UNIWARD [6], WOW [5] and HILL [10], with embedding rates from 0.1 bpp to 0.5 bpp. The dataset comes from BOSS-base v1.01, which contains 10000 original grayscale images of size 512×512. Constrained by our available GPU computing platform, all involved images are resized to the ones of size 256×256. To alleviate overfitting, data augmentation methods including random mirroring and 90 degrees rotation are used. For a given steganography and a payload, we have totally 20, 000 cover-stego image pairs. The training set includes 16,000 image pairs, which are randomly selected. The validation set includes 2000 image pairs. The test set includes the remaining 2000 image pairs.

3.2   Comparison with Other State-of-the-Art Methods

In this subsection, we compare the performance of the proposed TCNN model with three state-of-the-art steganalyzers in spatial domain, i.e., maxSRMd2 [2],

Table 2. Performance comparison of the steganalyzers in terms of detection error (P_E).

Algorithm	Payload (bpp)	maxSRMd2	SCA-YeNet	SCA-SRNet	The Proposed TCNN
S-UNIWARD	0.1	0.3806	0.3220	0.2969	**0.2613**
	0.2	0.2999	0.2224	0.1918	**0.1583**
	0.3	0.2542	0.1502	0.1309	**0.1098**
	0.4	0.2136	0.1281	0.0935	**0.0805**
	0.5	0.1732	0.1000	0.0667	**0.0630**
WOW	0.1	0.3163	0.2442	0.2197	**0.2139**
	0.2	0.2325	0.1691	0.1401	**0.1173**
	0.3	0.1918	0.1229	0.0980	**0.0812**
	0.4	0.1536	0.0959	0.0769	**0.0585**
	0.5	0.1331	0.0906	0.0578	**0.0514**
HILL	0.1	0.3894	0.3380	0.3014	**0.2716**
	0.2	0.3226	0.2538	0.2159	**0.1725**
	0.3	0.2804	0.1949	0.1664	**0.1160**
	0.4	0.2410	0.1708	0.1290	**0.0959**
	0.5	0.2115	0.1305	0.1026	**0.0645**

SCA-YeNet [13] and SCA-SRNet [1]. Table 2 shows the performance comparison in terms of detection error (P_E) for all the tested schemes. We observe that TCNN model has obvious advantages over other steganalyzers for the involved embedding schemes and tested payloads. And in contrast to SCA-SRNet, the performance gap becomes most pronounced for HILL at 0.3bpp, where the detection error is decreased by 5%. The proposed model also has a better improvement at low payload. For instance, the detection errors of the proposed model for S-UNIWARD and WOW at 0.2 bpp are decreased by 3.3% and 2.3%, respectively. Moreover, the proposed TCNN has higher detection accuracy than other steganalysis methods at high payloads. For example, when the payload is 0.5 bpp, the detection accuracy for WOW has been improved to 94.8%. It is worth noting that the proposed TCNN is the most effective for HILL, in contrast to SCA-SRNet, the detection errors are reduced by more than 3%. The experimental results above demonstrate that the two-way network design combining both constrained and random convolutional kernels together with their respective subnetwork structures contributes to the detection performance improvement over other state-of-the-art steganalysis methods.

4   Conclusion

In this paper, we further improve the detection performance of the CNN based steganalysis methods by proposing a two-way convolutional network (TCNN) architecture. The TCNN is the first two-way CNN, which combines both man-made constrained convolutional kernels and freely learnt random ones to extract

514   Z. Chen et al.

stego noise residual signals to learn more complementary, comprehensive features. Furthermore, for different residual signals, different sub-network structures are designed to enhance the performance. Experimental results have shown that the proposed TCNN steganalyzer is superior to the state-of-the-art CNN-based and hand-crafted features-based methods, against steganography algorithms in spatial domain like S-UNIWARD, WOW and HILL. In future, the proposed network may be extended to multi-way networks or combined with selection-channel-aware methods to further improve performance.

Acknowledge. This work is supposed by the Special Fund for Key Program of Science and Technology of Anhui Province, China (Grant No. 18030901027).

References

1. Boroumand, M., Chen, M., Fridrich, J.: Deep residual network for steganalysis of digital images. IEEE Trans. Inf. Forensics Secur. **14**(5), 1181–1193 (2018)
2. Denemark, T., Sedighi, V., Holub, V., Cogranne, R., Fridrich, J.: Selection-channel-aware rich model for steganalysis of digital images. In: 2014 IEEE International Workshop on Information Forensics and Security (WIFS), pp. 48–53. IEEE (2014)
3. Fridrich, J., Kodovsky, J.: Rich models for steganalysis of digital images. IEEE Trans. Inf. Forensics Secur. **7**(3), 868–882 (2012)
4. Glorot, X., Bengio, Y.: Understanding the difficulty of training deep feedforward neural networks. In: Proceedings of the Thirteenth International Conference on Artificial Intelligence and Statistics, pp. 249–256 (2010)
5. Holub, V., Fridrich, J.: Designing steganographic distortion using directional filters. In: 2012 IEEE International Workshop on Information Forensics and Security (WIFS), pp. 234–239. IEEE (2012)
6. Holub, V., Fridrich, J., Denemark, T.: Universal distortion function for steganography in an arbitrary domain. EURASIP J. Inf. Secur. **2014**(1), 1–13 (2014). https://doi.org/10.1186/1687-417X-2014-1
7. Ioffe, S., Szegedy, C.: Batch normalization: accelerating deep network training by reducing internal covariate shift. arXiv preprint arXiv:1502.03167 (2015)
8. Kim, J., Kang, S., Park, H., Park, J.I.: Dual convolutional neural network for image steganalysis. In: 2019 IEEE International Symposium on Broadband Multimedia Systems and Broadcasting (BMSB), pp. 1–4. IEEE (2019)
9. Nair, V., Hinton, G.E.: Rectified linear units improve restricted Boltzmann machines. In: Proceedings of the 27th International Conference on Machine Learning (ICML 2010), pp. 807–814 (2010)
10. Pevný, T., Filler, T., Bas, P.: Using high-dimensional image models to perform highly undetectable steganography. In: Böhme, R., Fong, P.W.L., Safavi-Naini, R. (eds.) IH 2010. LNCS, vol. 6387, pp. 161–177. Springer, Heidelberg (2010). https://doi.org/10.1007/978-3-642-16435-4_13
11. Qian, Y., Dong, J., Wang, W., Tan, T.: Deep learning for steganalysis via convolutional neural networks. In: Media Watermarking, Security, and Forensics 2015, vol. 9409, p. 94090J. International Society for Optics and Photonics (2015)
12. Xu, G., Wu, H.Z., Shi, Y.Q.: Structural design of convolutional neural networks for steganalysis. IEEE Signal Process. Lett. **23**(5), 708–712 (2016)
13. Ye, J., Ni, J., Yi, Y.: Deep learning hierarchical representations for image steganalysis. IEEE Trans. Inf. Forensics Secur. **12**(11), 2545–2557 (2017)

PrivyTRAC – Privacy and Security Preserving Contact Tracing System

Ssu-Hsin Yu[✉]

Scientific Systems Company, Inc., 500 W. Cummings Park, #3000, Woburn, MA 01801, USA
syu@ssci.com

Abstract. Smartphone location-based methods have been proposed and implemented as an effective alternative to traditional labor intensive contact tracing methods. However, there are serious privacy and security concerns that may impede wide-spread adoption in many societies. Furthermore, these methods rely solely on proximity to patients, based on Bluetooth or GPS signal, ignoring lingering effects of virus, including COVID-19, present in the environment. This results in inaccurate risk assessment and incomplete contact tracing. A new system concept called PrivyTRAC preserves user privacy, increases security and improves accuracy of smartphone contact tracing. PrivyTRAC enhances users' and patients' privacy by letting users conduct self-evaluation based on the risk maps download to their smartphones. No user information is transmitted to external locations or devices, and no personally identifiable patient information is embedded in the risk maps as they are processed anonymized and aggregated locations of confirmed patients. The risk maps consider both spatial proximity and temporal effects to improve the accuracy of the infection risk estimation. Experiments conducted in the paper illustrate improvement of PrivyTRAC over proximity-based methods in terms of true and false positives. An approach to further improve infection risk estimation by incorporating both positive and negative local test results from contacts of confirmed cases is also described.

Keywords: Contact tracing · Privacy preserving · Smartphone locations · Risk estimation · Spatio-temporal effects · COVID-19

1 Introduction

As severe travel restrictions due to COVID-19 are being gradually relaxed in order to minimize further damage to the economy, it is expected that there will be continued cases of infection and pockets of community transmission until vaccines become widely available. To prevent sporadic cases from becoming sources of another outbreak, rigorous contact tracing is essential. Compared to the traditional approach of interviewing patients, the smartphone location-based approach has proven to be an effective alternative to accomplish comprehensive contact tracing with much less labor demands. However, there are serious privacy and security concerns associated with the smartphone-based

N. Park et al. (Eds.): SecureComm 2020, LNICST 335, pp. 515–525, 2020.
https://doi.org/10.1007/978-3-030-63086-7_30

methods that may impede adoption and wide-spread use in the many societies [1]. Effectiveness of the smartphone contact tracing approach can be significantly improved with active cooperation from the public by alleviating the security and privacy concerns.

We propose a privacy-preserving, secure and accurate COVID-19 contact tracing systems called PrivyTRAC: Privacy and Security Preserving Contact Tracing System. PrivyTRAC

1. is a smartphone location-based contact tracing system with security and privacy inherent in the tracing mechanism that protects the privacy of both the patients and the public, and
2. infers from confirmed cases COVID-19 infection risk at given places and time that allows individuals to self-assess exposure risk from their movement histories.

The proposed system, illustrated in Fig. 1, is built on two innovations (see Sect. 3 for details). One is the innovative mechanism that utilizes the infection risk maps (Step 1 in Fig. 1), which are processed from anonymized, aggregated patient locations information, that individual users can download to a smartphone App (Step 2). The users can then evaluate locally their own risks of contracting COVID-19 due to contacts (Step 3). This mechanism does not require users to upload their personally identifiable information (PII) to an external platform, nor do the users need to broadcast their PII to other smartphones in vicinity.

The second innovation is the estimation of the spatio-temporal infection risk maps that allow users to self-assess their own risks. The risk maps consider not only the spatial proximity to COVID-19 patients, as in most contact tracing approaches, but also the temporal effect of how long the virus can stay virulent in the environment. We have learned that the novel coronavirus can remain contagious on surface for an extended period of time [2, 3, 15] and virus-containing droplets can travel significant distances [4, 5]. The risk-based approach that considers not only instantaneous proximity to the patients but also the lagging effects after a patient has left thus offers a more accurate

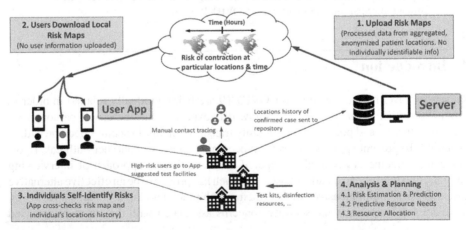

Fig. 1. PrivyTRAC contract tracing process and information flow

risk assessment of contracting the virus. Furthermore, as researchers continue to learn the factors that influence the virus spread, new findings can be quickly incorporated into our risk estimation model to refine the risk maps.

2   Current Smartphone Location-Based Contact Tracing Methods

Many smartphone location-based contact tracing approaches have been proposed or implemented recently [2, 5–11, 13, 14]. They generally fall into two categories. One is to aggregate all smartphone movements of a population, whether a person is ill or not, in a centralized repository to identify encounters with the confirmed COVID-19 cases. The other category of methods is to use a phone's Bluetooth radio to record encounters of all other phones in proximity [3] and later alert the user when the unique cell phone ID of a confirmed case matches an ID in the user's phone.

These two approaches suffer two main drawbacks – the first is privacy and security, and the second is accuracy. Their mechanisms require exposing individuals' locations and unique IDs, either in a centralized, externally maintained repository or to all other phones in vicinity. Privacy concerns may cause people to be less willing to adopt the tools, and hence render the tools less effective. Moreover, whether individuals' movement data and their encounters with other people are stored centrally or locally, there is always inherent risk that sophisticated and determined hackers can exploit software weaknesses to acquire personally identifiable information (PII) of individuals and their encounters, similar to the actions taken by some data brokers and aggregators for advertising purposes. In fact, Cybersecurity and Infrastructure Security Agency (CISA) has issued warning of Advanced Persistent Threat (APT) actors exploiting the COVID-19 pandemic to collect bulk personal information [4].

Besides privacy and security concerns, those contact-tracing tools offer an incomplete measure for determining the infection risk. As we have learned, novel coronavirus can survive on surface for an extended period of time and its droplets can travel for extended distances, depending on the surface materials and other environmental factors. A person does not need to be in the immediate vicinity of a patient to be exposed to the virus through indirect contacts. Hence, determining a person's risk of contracting the virus based solely on direct proximity to the infected does not provide an accurate risk assessment.

3   PrivyTRAC Approach

3.1   System Architecture

Our contact-tracing approach PrivyTRAC is illustrated in Fig. 1. The system consists of two main components – one residing on individual users' smartphones and the other on the server. On the user side, the smartphone App regularly (or as requested by the users) downloads up-to-date spatio-temporal exposure risk maps from the server. The risk maps quantify the likelihoods of infection at particular locations and time. Based on the maps, the App would then cross-check with the user's smartphone locations data. Using the risk maps and the locations data, the App computes the aggregated risk of contracting the virus. If the person's risk exceeds a certain threshold, the App would notify the person and suggest follow-on actions, such as the testing sites for confirmation.

Under this process, a user's private locations history and PII never leave his/her own phone nor are they being recorded by other phones. Patients' privacy is preserved as well, since the patients remain anonymous and the downloaded risk maps contain only processed and aggregated locations information from many patients, making it extremely challenging to extract PII. Furthermore, the ability for users to maintain control of their private data and decide when the service is activated will significantly encourage adoption by the public.

On the server side, the spatio-temporal risk maps are computed and continually updated as new cases are reported. The movement histories of confirmed cases are collected by public health agencies. The sever software computes the infection risks at particular locations and time, based on the aggregated locations of the patients from the public health agencies and factors affecting the virus' persistent virulence. Those factors include distance from an infected person, durations of the virus' survival on various surface materials, length of exposure, and environmental conditions such as temperature and sunlight. By incorporating the disease vector and environment's effects on virulence rather than merely considering direct encounters based on smartphone proximity, the resulting infection risk estimation is more comprehensive and accurate.

3.2 Infection Risk Map Computation

To evaluate the risk of contracting the disease from an infected person, we assume that the probability of infection decreases exponentially with distance and time. For the risk analysis, we consider a spatio-temporal grid consists of 1 m by 1 m by 1 s cells. (Note that other grid sizes can be chosen with corresponding changes in the values of the parameters in the model.) If a person with the disease stays in a 1 m by 1 m area centered at location (x_p, y_p) for 1 s around time t_p, a person in an area of the same size around location (x, y) for 1 s around time t is assumed to have the probability of contracting the disease $(C = 1)$ as follows:

$$P(C = 1 | x, y, t, x_p, y_p, t_p) = \begin{cases} p_0 \exp\left(-\frac{(x-x_p)^2}{\sigma_x^2} - \frac{(y-y_p)^2}{\sigma_y^2} - \frac{(t-t_p)^2}{\sigma_t^2}\right) & \text{if } t \geq t_p \\ 0 & \text{otherwise} \end{cases}$$

(1)

If there are a total of N such spatio-temporal cells $\left(x_p^i, y_p^i, t_p^i\right)$ with a patient present, regardless of whether they are occupied by the same patient or not, a person in the 1 m. by 1 m. by 1 s. cell (x, y, t) has the probability of being infected as follows:

$$P\left(C = 1 | x, y, t, x_p^i, y_p^i, t_p^i, i = 1, \dots, N\right) =$$
$$1 - \prod_{i=1}^{N} \left(1 - P\left(C = 1 | x, y, t, x_p^i, y_p^i, t_p^i\right)\right)$$

(2)

Note that the cells $\left(x_p^i, y_p^i, t_p^i\right)$ are not necessarily due to the same patient. Hence, we can easily aggregate multiple patients in the same risk map.

If a person is in the area for a certain duration, we consider each contact within one second as an independent event. Hence, the person's overall probability of contracting the disease is

$$P(C = 1|s) = 1 - \prod_{j=1}^{M} \prod_{i=1}^{N} \left(1 - P\left(C = 1|x^j, y^j, t^j, x_p^i, y_p^i, t_p^i\right)\right) \qquad (3)$$

where s represents a sequence of M such 1 m by 1 m by 1 s spatial-temporal cells $\left(x^j, y^j, t^j\right)$ that the person of interest occupies in the vicinity of infected people.

Based on the above analysis, an area risk map can be created from Eq. (2). By using aggregated locations and time of people with the disease $\left(x_p^i, y_p^i, t_p^i\right)$, the risk of contracting the disease $P\left(C = 1|x, y, t, x_p^i, y_p^i, t_p^i, i = 1, \ldots, N\right)$ at any location and time (x, y, t) can be computed. When a user downloads the spatio-temporal risk map into their smartphone App, their own individual risk $P(C = 1|s)$ can be computed by the App according to the location history s on the smartphone using Eq. (3). The App can apply a risk-based metric, for example, to advise whether a person should seek further medical help based on their probability of contracting COVID-19 due to the contacts.

To illustrate the varying risk of contracting the disease depending on the distance from an infected person and the elapsed time since the person's presence, we plot in Fig. 2 the log-probability of infection. For this example, it is assumed that a patient is present at time 0 at location $x_p = 0$ and $y_p = 50$ for 1 s. We also assign $p_0 = 0.01/\sqrt{2\pi}$, $\sigma_x = \sigma_y = 1$ and $\sigma_t = 100$ in Eq. (1). The resultant log-probabilities $P\left(C = 1|x = 0, y, t, x_p = 0, y_p = 50, t_p = 0\right)$ of infection risk for different y locations (vertical axis) at different time (horizontal axis) after the 1-second presence of the patient at time 0 are shown in Fig. 2. The figure shows that despite the patient not being present (or in proximity) after the initial 1 s, the risk of contracting the disease is still present, albeit small as elapsed time increases. Hence, to fully account for the risk of contracting the disease for contact tracing purposes, it's essential not only to consider the immediate proximity to the patient but also the lingering effects of the virus in time.

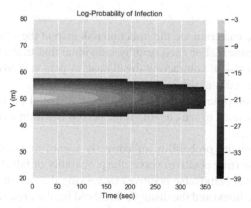

Fig. 2. Log-probability of infection risk when a patient is at location $y = 50$ for 1 s

4 Simulation Experiment Results

To illustrate the difference between the risk-based and the proximity-based contact tracing approaches, we conducted simulated experiments of the two methods. In the experiments, we consider an area of 100 m by 100 m (Fig. 3) in a 350-second span. At the beginning of this time span $t = 0$, a patient enters the square area from the middle of a side and travels across the area parallel to another side at the constant speed of 1 m/sec, as shown in red in Fig. 3. In the time span, a person enters the same area at random time, location and speed. The time was chosen with a uniform distribution between time 0 and 200 s; the location was chosen with a uniform distribution from the middle halves of the 4 sides enclosing the area; the speed remains constant as the person traverses the area and was chosen with a uniform distribution between 0.75 m/s and 1.25 m/s. Under the above simulation conditions, the experiments were repeated 20,000 times. Figure 3 shows the trajectory of the patient in red in (a) spatial and (b) spatial and temporal coordinates, as well as sample trajectories of 5 healthy individuals in blue.

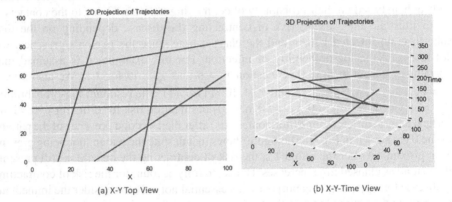

Fig. 3. Trajectory of a patient (red) and 5 sample trajectories of healthy individuals (blue) (Color figure online)

Using Eq. (2), we can compute the infection risk map in the square area induced by the presence of the patient. For each healthy individual that traverses the area, Eq. (3) provides the person's risk of contracting the disease. A person is advised to seek further testing if their risk exceeds a certain threshold.

For comparison purposes, we also implemented a spatial proximity-based metric. That is, a person is advised to seek testing if the person is within a certain distance from the patient at any time.

We plot in Fig. 4 the probability of correctly identifying a person that actually contracted the disease (true positive) versus the probability of falsely advising a healthy person to seek medical help (false positive) by varying the risk threshold for the risk-based approach (blue lines) and the distance threshold for the proximity-based approach (red lines). An ideal system would have true positive probably 1 at 0 false positive probability, i.e. the upper left corner in the plots. The 4 plots in Fig. 4 from left to right show the different choices in Eq. (1) for $\sigma_t = 10, 50, 100, 150$ s respectively. If the ability for the virus to infect diminishes quickly over time (e.g. $\sigma_t = 10$ s), the difference between risk-based and proximity-based contact tracing is small Fig. 4(a). On the other hand, as the decay time increases ($\sigma_t = 50, 100$ s), the risk-based approach performs significantly better than the proximity-based approach Fig. 4(b)(c). It becomes apparent in the cases where the virus' ability to infect diminishes slowly that the proximity-based approach cannot fully identify the infected people without incurring unacceptable false positives.

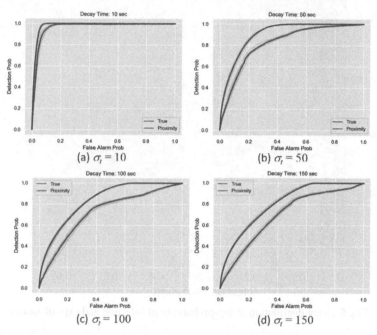

Fig. 4. True positive vs. false positive for different σ_t decay rates; lighter-colored lines are from results using 1/10 of the simulated trajectories. (Color figure online)

The reason the risk-based and the proximity-based measures differ can be seen in Fig. 5. In the figure, we plot the probability of contracting the disease on the x axis and, on the y axis, the 1 over the exponential of minimum distance from the infected person (i.e. $e^{-\text{min distance}}$), for $\sigma_t = 50$ in Eq. (1). $e^{-\text{min distance}}$ is chosen such that a higher number means a person is closer to the patient at some point in time and hence subjects to a higher probability of being infected. Each point on the scatter plot represents a case in the experiment. The marginal distributions (histograms) of the cases are also plotted on the top and on the right for the risk-based and the proximity-based measures respectively. If the proximity- and risk-based measures are similar, we would expect to see positive correlation on the plot. Even though most cases that are in proximity to the patient tend to have higher probabilities of infection, there are significant number of cases that are far enough from the patient spatially but are still subjected to high infection probabilities. It is mainly due to the delayed effect when the patient has left a location but the virus in the environment still has the ability to infect.

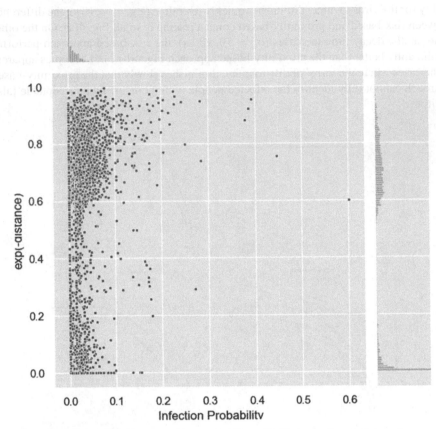

Fig. 5. Joint distribution of log-probability of infection and exp(-distance)

5   Model Refinement

The experiments conducted in this paper utilize the probabilistic infection risk model in Eq. (1) that assumes exponential decay of infection risk in space and time. Since various environmental factors can impact how far virus-containing droplets can reach and how long the virus can remain contagious in air and on surface, the models can be extended to improve its accuracy by incorporating those factors if they are available. For example, the variances σ_x^2 and σ_y^2 in Eq. (1) can be replaced by a 2-dimensional covariance matrix to capture the effects of prevailing wind speed and direction on the spread of the droplets. The temporal variance σ_t^2 can be a function of the local temperature and humidity. In a confined environment, where infection by way of indirect contacts is possible, we can incorporate surface properties as part of the model.

Another direction to refine the infection risk estimation is to consider reported cases of infection as observations. Consider the scenario where several people that came into contacts with a patient in a particular area have been tested for infection. Some of them were tested positive while others negative. The test results and their movement histories in the area are observations of the underlying risk model. The initial risk model is constructed mainly based on the knowledge of average reach and decay time of the virus. The new test results, positive or negative, provide additional information to adjust the model parameters so as to better align with local conditions. A Bayesian probabilistic model is well suited for this purpose:

$$\tau \sim \text{Gamma}(\alpha, \beta), \tau_t \sim \text{Gamma}(\alpha_t, \beta_t) \tag{4}$$

$$P\left(C = 1 | x, y, t, x_p^i, y_p^i, t_p^i\right) =$$
$$\begin{cases} p_0 \exp\left(-\tau\left(x - x_p^i\right)^2 - \tau\left(y - y_p^i\right)^2 - \tau_t\left(t - t_p^i\right)^2\right), & \text{if } t \geq t_p^i \\ 0 & \text{otherwise} \end{cases} \tag{5}$$

$$P(C = 1|s) = 1 - \prod_{j=1}^{M} \prod_{i=1}^{N} \left(1 - P\left(C = 1 | x^j, y^j, t^j, x_p^i, y_p^i, t_p^i\right)\right) \tag{6}$$

$$T \sim \text{Bernoulli}(P(C = 1|s)) \tag{7}$$

Equation (5) is similar to Eq. (1) except that the variances are re-defined as precisions for the convenience of specifying their prior distributions in Eq. (4). The prior distributions of τ and τ_t are Gamma distributions of hyper-parameters (α, β) and (α_t, β_t) respectively, where the symbol tilde (~) denotes "distributed as." Eq (6) is the same as Eq. (3). Recall that s represents a sequence of M such 1 m by 1 m by 1 s spatial-temporal cells (x^j, y^j, t^j) that a person of interest occupies in the vicinity of the patients, and $P(C = 1|s)$ is the probability of the person contracting the disease. The result of the test, positive ($T = 1$) or negative ($T = 0$), is modeled as the outcome of a Bernoulli trial as in Eq. (7) where the parameter of the Bernoulli distribution is the infection probability $P(C = 1|s)$.

Based on the above Bayesian probabilistic model, we can refine the model parameters τ and τ_t by computing their posterior distributions:

$$P(\tau, \tau_t | T_1, T_2, \dots, T_L) \tag{8}$$

where $T_1, T_2, \dots, T_L$ are L individuals' test outcomes, which are either positive $T_i = 1$ or negative $T_i = 0$. Computational methods such as Markov chain Monte Carlo (MCMC) [12] can be applied to compute the posterior distribution.

The refined model parameters τ and τ_t and the resultant spatio-temporal infection risk probability in Eq. (5) then provide a more precise local risk map. By using the improved risk map, we can further reduce the chance of missing positive cases and optimize the use of resources by avoiding unnecessary testing.

6 Conclusions

The impacts of severe travel restrictions are enormous and their cost has been felt throughout the economy. Effective contact tracing is a key step in relaxing those measures while keeping the infection under control. Traditional contact tracing measures based on interviews with patients are labor intensive and error-prone. Contact tracing through personal electronic devices such as smartphones has been proposed as an effective measure to overcome these challenges. Although smartphone-based contact tracing has been successfully implemented in some countries, the privacy implication and security concerns can impede broad adoption of similar measures in other societies. Without wide-spread adoption, the effectiveness of electronic contact tracing can be severely limited.

The proposed electronic contact-tracing approach PrivyTRAC respects privacy of individuals and increases security of the system through a de-centralized mechanism. By preserving privacy and enhancing security, it will significantly promote cooperation from the public and facilitate adoption by public health agencies. Additionally, PrivyTRAC improves the accuracy of infection risk estimation and consequently contact tracing effectiveness. As public health agencies are struggling to meet the expected demands of qualified personnel for traditional contact tracing measures, PrivyTRAC can be an effective tool to fill the resource gap.

The proposed capability also provides valuable actionable information for authorities to better allocate resources and plan follow-on actions. First, based on the estimated infection risks and visitors/foot traffics, authorities can identify and prioritize areas that require disinfection. Second, decision makers can pre-position test kits and allocate other health resources according to locations, populations and severity of the virus exposure. Similarly, when a person is potentially exposed to the virus, the user App can suggest local test locations that best balance test site workloads and convenience.

The system concept is applicable for COVID-19 as well as for other contagious diseases. By adjusting the disease vector, risk model and environmental effects, the system can be tailored to other infectious diseases in the future. The system architecture remains the same. The risk maps are tailored to different diseases in the same App environment.

References

1. How Digital Contact Tracing Slowed Covid-19 in East Asia, Harvard Business Review, April 2020. https://hbr.org/2020/04/how-digital-contact-tracing-slowed-covid-19-in-east-asia?utm_medium=email&utm_source=newsletter_daily&utm_campaign=dailyalert_not_activesubs&referral=00563&deliveryName=DM76785
2. Tang, J.W.: The effect of environmental parameters on the survival of airborne infectious agents. J. R. Soc. Interface **6**, S737–S746 (2009). https://doi.org/10.1098/rsif.2009.0227.focus
3. Bhardwaj, R., Agrawal, A.: Likelihood of survival of coronavirus in a respiratory droplet deposited on a solid surface. Phys. Fluids **32**, 061704 (2020)
4. Lewis, T.: How coronavirus spreads through the air: what we know so far. Sci. Am. (2020)
5. Bourouiba, L.: Turbulent gas clouds and respiratory pathogen emissions. JAMA **323**(18), 1837–1838 (2020)
6. Servick, K.: COVID-19 contact tracing apps are coming to a phone near you. How will we know whether they work?. Science (2020) https://www.sciencemag.org/news/2020/05/countries-around-world-are-rolling-out-contact-tracing-apps-contain-coronavirus-how
7. Privacy-Preserving Contact Tracing https://www.apple.com/covid19/contacttracing
8. CISA Alert (AA20-126A) https://www.us-cert.gov/ncas/alerts/AA20126A

9. Zastrow, S.: Coronavirus contact-tracing apps: can they slow the spread of COVID-19? Nature (2020). https://www.nature.com/articles/d41586-020-01514-2
10. TraceTogether. https://www.tracetogether.gov.sg/
11. Rivest, R.L., Weitzner, D.J., Ivers, L.C., Soibelman, I., Zissman, M.A.: PACT: private automated contact tracing. https://pact.mit.edu/wp-content/uploads/2020/05/PACT-Mission-and-Approach-2020-05-19-.pdf
12. Decentralized Privacy-Preserving Proximity Tracing (DP-3T). https://github.com/DP-3T/documents
13. Exposure Notifications: Using technology to help public health authorities fight COVID-19. https://www.google.com/covid19/exposurenotifications/
14. Abeler, J., Bäcker, M., Buermeyer, U., Zillessen, H.: COVID-19 Contact Tracing and Data Protection Can Go Together. JMIR Mhealth Uhealth **8**(4) (2020)
15. CDC: How COVID-19 spreads. https://www.cdc.gov/coronavirus/2019-ncov/prevent-getting-sick/how-covid-spreads.html

Author Index

Printed in the United States
By Bookmasters